Streams and Coast Lines as they appear on
Contemporary Maps

PRINCIPAL POST ROADS
CANALS
RAILROADS

HOUSTON'S RETREAT >>>>>

Scale of Miles
10   50   100   200

ANDREW JACKSON

Portrait of a President

ANDREW JACKSON
President of the United States 1829-1837
From a portrait made at the White House in 1835 by Ashel B. Durand,
now owned by the New York Historical Society.

ANDREW JACKSON

Portrait of a President

BY

MARQUIS JAMES

Author of

Andrew Jackson: The Border Captain

The Raven, a Biography of Sam Houston

ILLUSTRATED

THE BOBBS-MERRILL COMPANY

Indianapolis   *Publishers*   New York

To the Memory of My Father

HOUSTIN JAMES

CONTENTS

CONTENTS — *Continued*

ILLUSTRATIONS

ILLUSTRATIONS— *Continued*

ANDREW JACKSON
Portrait of a President

BOOK ONE

A Reluctant Candidate

"If I was to travel to Boston where I
have been invited that would insure my
election.—But I would feel degraded the
balance of my life."

ANDREW JACKSON to one of
his campaign managers.

ANDREW JACKSON

CHAPTER I

THE NASHVILLE JUNTO

I

THE gray weariness of winter was taking leave of the Cumberland Valley in March of 1822. Impertinent little redbud trees and graceful dogwood brightened the small-growth of the copse which screened the Hermitage from the highroad a quarter of a mile away. Northern rains had fallen and northern snows melted to swell the brown bosoms of southern rivers. The warehouses of General Jackson's two plantations were empty. His Hermitage cotton and his Melton's Bluff cotton from Alabama had begun the long journey to the sun-washed wharves of New Orleans[1] to be sold directly to forwarders, thus eliminating the takings of local middlemen which cut so deeply into the profits of planters too poor or too unenterprising to provide their own transportation.

Still, the best price this cotton could hope to command would not exceed eleven cents a pound. The dead weight of a depression in trade, which three springs before had laid in monotonous ruin the bright edifice of a fictitious prosperity, continued to press cruelly upon the West and the South. Dismal columns of sheriffs' sales, marshals' sales and notices of foreclosure and of execution darkened the pages of Nashville's newspapers; of lands and goods and slaves offered at sacrifices. Friends of General Jackson who a few years before had been reckoned as affluent in their circumstances were not exempt. The Nashville Inn was bankrupt, and former Congressman Felix Grundy advertised to sell his plantation on Mill Creek, with "a good orchard, several excellent springs and a distillery."[2] The Nashville Bank, in which General Jackson was a small shareholder, kept open its doors and paid a dividend of four per cent; but none was paid to stockholders in debt to the bank, and sixty thousand dollars in profits were sequestered to meet "probable losses by the late disastrous change in business."[3]

Similarly prudent management characterized Andrew Jackson's administration of his private affairs. Owing to his long absences from home on public business, the retired soldier's expenses had been heavy that winter, yet he was able to meet obligations with agreeable promptitude, to pay his taxes, to take advantage of a hard-times bargain now and then and, while other places were running down, to build and better about both his Tennessee and his Alabama properties. He and Rachel continued their unostentatious charities, and there were even a few luxuries for the Hermitage. His cotton shipped, Jackson placed an order with Thomas Barron & Company, wine merchants and fancy grocers of New Orleans: "4 demij mad.ª wine 64, 1 cask best claret 65, 21 Boxes Johnsons wine 22, 1 Box sp candles 13.28, 1 do Best Raisens 4.50, 1 Keg almonds 7." The General was fond of almonds, though they had no place in the diet of a man trying to rid himself of dysentery.[4]

An important aspect of life at the Hermitage was changed, however. The stalls of the great racing stable were empty. The defeat of Western Light and the DeWett mare by Jesse Haynie's Maria in 1815 had convinced General Jackson that the itinerant nature of official duties made it impossible to attend properly to the minutiae of his racers' training—and Jackson's horses ran best when prepared for their contests under the eye of the master. So gradually the stable had been sold, all excepting Truxton. Who could have sold Truxton? Jackson gave him to one of the Butlers who carried the big stallion away to Mississippi. So it was that, although the Hermitage remained as well provided with horseflesh as any plantation on the Cumberland, the animals were no longer bred or trained for the track.

But other details were much the same. Newspapers remained the General's favorite reading, and the twenty to which he subscribed protected the red carpet on the floor of his study. Despite the repeated and abrupt assertions that his retirement from public life this time was to be permanent, the name of Andrew Jackson figured in these journals almost as prominently as that of any other American. The press had not exhausted the abundant controversial possibilities of the General's tenure of the governorship of Florida; and occasionally there were even more interesting personal mentions. In January the Philadelphia *Aurora* contained an item that went the editorial rounds. This writer "understood" that there were seven candidates for the presidency. "If a choice of Clinton or Jackson could be made, then our country would prosper."[5]

To these insinuations Jackson had said nothing publicly, but his private answer was no and no and no.

Nevertheless, one Nashville and one Knoxville newspaper[6] insisted upon an answer to the question: Why this preponderance of presidential talk centering about Mr. Monroe's three Cabinet officers, Adams, Crawford and Calhoun? "The name of Andrew Jackson to a document would command more respect than the signatures of all the secretaries in the nation." Therefore, an observer might have been more than casually interested to learn that during the second week of March, 1822, Old Hickory had put his signature to the first public communication since his departure from Florida five months before. The notice was addressed to the editor of the Nashville *Whig:*

"YOUNG TRUXTON
"(One of the best sons of the celebrated running horse Truxton, by Diomed.)
"SIXTEEN hands and one inch high, a beautiful dark bay, of fine bone and sinew, and great in action, will stand one half of his time at my stable, where I now live, the other half of his time at the stable of Mrs. Donelson, widow of Col. Wm. Donelson, deceased ... at the moderate price of three hundred pounds of good merchantable seed Cotton ... or eight dollars cash. .... His colts are finely formed, large and strong, fit for saddle or geer, or any other use ..."

"ANDREW JACKSON."[7]

2

Rachel also glanced at the newspapers occasionally, and in her tall east chamber she, too, was engaged with a pen for she owed her niece, Mary Donelson, a letter.

"I do hope they will now leave Mr. Jackson alone." Mister, again, not General. "He is not a well man and never will be unless they allow him to rest. He has done his share for the country. . . . In the thirty years of our wedded life . . . he has not spent one-fourth of his days under his own roof. The rest of the time away, travelling, holding court, or at the capital of his country, or in camp, or fighting its battles, or treating with the Indians; mercy knows what not. . . .

"Through all such trials I have not said aye, yes or no. It was his work to do, he seemed called to it and I watched, waited and prayed most of the time alone. Now I hope this is at an end. They talk of his being President. Major Eaton, General Carroll, Mr. Campbell, the Doctor and even the Parson . . . come here to talk, talk everlastingly about his being President. In this as all else I can say only, the Lord's will be done. But I hope he may not be called again to the strife and empty honors of public place."[8]

3

Visitors continued to come and to breathe life into the topic which above all others threatened the peace of mind of Rachel Jackson. Even now a traveler was turning from the Lebanon Pike into the level lane which traversed the copse of hickory and oak and sycamore and made its way between the brick gateposts to join the driveway that led to the house.

General Jackson's caller was a friend whose fealty had withstood the changing fortunes of a quarter of a century. Moreover George Washington Campbell's name, like his present errand, bore the stamp of patriotic initiative. He was born in Scotland plain George Campbell, and while attending the College of New Jersey at Princeton he had interpolated the "Washington." Then coming to Tennessee to practice law, he presently found himself in Congress largely through the instrumentality of Judge Andrew Jackson. Those were the days when Judge Jackson, of the nabob wing of the Republican Party, was disputing for control of the state with the leathershirt wing captained by John Sevier. Through all that followed, G. W. Campbell had served the cause of his patron, and served it well, rising to become Secretary of the Treasury. Able, conciliatory, persuasive in debate and in negotiation, he yielded one point only to gain two in the end.

After General Jackson's military raid into Florida, President Monroe had looked about for a post that would get his peppery commander out of the way until the storm subsided. The embassy at St. Petersburg fell vacant. Its remoteness particularly appealed to the President. He consulted his venerated preceptor, Thomas Jefferson who, with incidental profanity, assured the Executive that if Andrew Jackson went to St. Petersburg we should have a quarrel with Russia in a month. So General Jackson was wheedled into accepting the governorship of Florida, where there was a quarrel in less than a month, but helpless Spain was not the empire of the Romanovs.

Thus it was that tactful George Washington Campbell, rather than the forthright frontier soldier, had journeyed to the banks of the Neva, there for three winters to endure the cold green fogs and the interminable state dinners, and to see three of his children die in one week of typhus. After this Campbell had fled to Tennessee, arriving in the autumn of 1821 when General Jackson was on his way home from Pensacola.

Before a cheerful fire the two friends lighted their pipes and found a great deal to say. Old Hickory was as firm as ever in his decision to be done with public life. He spoke of his health which was bad when he left Florida and had mended slowly. A distressing cough and inflammation of the lungs had added themselves to the dysentery contracted in the Creek campaign.

"I am no longer a young man. I can't stand the fatigues and

privations I used to. George, do you realize we are getting old? I'm fifty-five!"

The returned diplomat ventured that the General was merely tired. The mission to Florida had been too much. But a few months' relaxation would restore him. Adroitly Campbell built up the concept of his friend again in the throbbing prime of his powers with new vistas of glory unfolding before him. A fact. Did not Jackson comprehend that he was "by no means safe from the presidency in 1824—"

With an arresting sweep the fingers of Old Hickory plowed his unruly gray hair. The lines of the long, appreciative face were taut. The intense blue eyes kindled.

"I really hope you don't think, George, that I'm damned fool enough to believe that!"

Then, relaxing his severity a little: "No, sir; I may be pretty well satisfied with myself in some things, but I'm not vain enough for that."[9]

The words had an air of finality, the preparations to enjoy the Hermitage a look of permanence. Knowing well that Andrew Jackson's self-made rules of life were never so likely to set other regulations at naught as when too abruptly opposed, the listening diplomat permitted the conversation to seek its own level.

4

There was much else to speak of. Captain Alpha Kingsley had taken over the insolvent Nashville Inn, and was making a brave effort to restore the fortunes of the pleasant house of entertainment which was General Jackson's favorite place of resort when in town. . . . Sam Houston, the handsome and rather baroquely attired young lawyer, was getting on despite hard times and convivial habits. A card in the *Whig* announcing a relocation of his office assured the public that he "can be found at all times where he ought to be." Nevertheless, those who knew Sam best would continue to expect him at the sociable bar of the Nashville Inn at any time after three in the afternoon. . . . On Court House Square over J. Decker's confectionery, Rachel's

JACKSON IN FLORIDA

A pencil sketch, owned and copyrighted by Emil Edward Hurja of
New York City. The artist is unknown.

protégé, Ralph E. W. Earl, the artist, had opened a "Museum of Natural and Artificial Curiosities." Among the latter were several portraits of General Jackson. . . . Despite the low state of public finances, work continued on the great bridge across the Cumberland, buoyantly voted in more prosperous times. . . . Thomas Yeatman offered cash for cotton, tobacco and "a few likely *Young Negroes*."[10] . . . But better bargains in negroes were said to be available in Kentucky, and the General had asked Andrew Jackson Donelson, still pursuing his legal studies at Transylvania University, to be on the lookout for a good buy.

In Kentucky bargains of every character awaited the purchaser so fortunate as to possess real money. The collapse in 1819 of the wildcat bank and paper currency craze had intensified the financial depression in the Ohio River Valley and the Southwest. This proved a lesson to most states, but not to Kentucky where debtors had taken charge of the Legislature. A replevin law was enacted, a new state bank erected on the ruins of the old, and its paper styled "legal tender." This money immediately fell to fifty cents on the dollar and, when a justice of the Supreme Court declared the replevin law unconstitutional, he was hauled before the Legislature for removal, which was the beginning of a long course of judge-breaking in Kentucky.

Nearly every instinct and interest of Andrew Jackson's long life set him in opposition to this undisciplined rising of the masses. As a former judge, a sound money man and a creditor rather than a debtor, the shrewd old frontier aristocrat was anxious that his namesake at Transylvania should view matters correctly. To young Mr. Donelson went another of a long series of letters of counsel: "The conduct of Kentucky . . . augurs the destruction of our republican government—for let me tell you that all the rights secured to the citizens under the constitution are worth nothing . . . except guaranteed to them by a virtuous and independent Judiciary. . . . I hope Kentucky will . . . preserve the . . . Judiciary unimpaired by faction or the designing demagogues of the day— ? which side of this does Mr. Clay take."[11]

Perhaps it discomfited the General a little to learn that Mr. Clay had taken the sound-money side.

Though Tennessee escaped some of the tribulations of economic reconstruction that beset her sister commonwealth to the north, the lines were drawn between the Haves and the Have Nots. Jackson stood with the Haves. After the crash of 1819 he had opposed the popular stampede which, taking control of the Assembly, enacted a law "staying" the collection of debts and set up loan bureaus for the relief of private debtors from public funds. The next round of the battle was fought out in the election of 1821, with the governorship as stake. Andrew Jackson's neighbor and one-time racing-stable partner, Edward Ward, bore the conservative standard against William Carroll, who espoused the cause of "the people." Viewing the contest from Florida, Old Hickory was bitter at the defection of the man he had raised from obscurity to be second in command at New Orleans; and, indeed, there was something peculiar in the sudden revelation of elegant Billy Carroll as a crusader for the poor.

Ward was pictured as a slave-holding land baron, and his college education enumerated among the reasons why an awakened electorate should reject him. As champion of the *sans culottes,* Carroll had numbers on his side, yet few anticipated the devastating nature of the triumph that awaited: Ward carried only two counties in the State.

Once Carroll was in office the dire prophecies of the conservatives remained unfulfilled, however. Instead of a revolutionist, William Carroll was proving a sagacious and practical liberal leader, deftly controlling his radical followers and, without alienating their support, averting the destructive extremes which might have swept Tennessee into the sea of troubles that engulfed Kentucky. But the shining testimonial to the Governor's skill was his reappearance at the Hermitage on what seemed to be the old basis of intimacy, and his participation in the persistent conversations that so disturbed the heart of Rachel.

5

Yet there seemed to be little tangible cause for her uneasiness. March stretched into sunny April, April into May and a month of rain. But it was warm and Mr. Decker, the confectioner, advertised *"ICE CREAMS AND ICE PUNCH* every day."[12] A journeyman dentist established himself in a room next to Sam Houston's law office. "Those who desire his services had better avail themselves of the present opportunity," ran his card in the *Whig,* "for unless business will justify him in making a permanent residence in Nashville he will leave the Western country in the ensuing fall."[13]

On one of his frequent visits, Houston brought to the Hermitage a rare tale of a duel between General John Cocke and a Mr. Darden. General Jackson's relations with the Cocke family had been singularly disappointing. Twenty-five years before he had challenged John Cocke's father, but friends intervened and prevented a meeting. Houston's story was that in this latest affair of honor Cocke had worn a bullet-proof "shield," afterwards found in a hollow tree. Sam promised to recover the shield and place "it in Mr. Earl's museum for the inspection of the curious."[14]

"Houston," declared Old Hickory, "is a truly noble-minded fellow" who deserves a seat in Congress "at our next election."[15]

This, however, was no evidence that Jackson's interest in public affairs went deeper than a desire to be of service to his friends; in particular to young men who like Sam Houston had marched in his battle-sore little armies.

To another such soldier, Captain Richard K. Call, he found occasion to express his creed of public service. Call, who had settled where Jackson left him in Florida, wrote to ask his former chief's advice about running for Congress. His election would strengthen Jackson's hand in Florida as well as in Congress, a circumstance no current candidate for the presidency could have overlooked.

The General responded that Captain Call should consider carefully before embarking on a public career. He would not thereby establish himself financially, and would lose the law practice he had created. "On the other hand society has claims on every individual who compose it, and if your country calls on you to represent her . . . you are bound to obey that call; the services of every man belongs to his country when that country requires it, and with this principle I have commenced and will end my life."[16]

Jackson's health had much improved when a cold contracted at church in Nashville,[17] brought an alarming relapse. Colonel James Gadsden, another of Jackson's subalterns now farming in Florida, wished to compile a history of the Jackson campaigns, and wrote to remind his old commander that he had promised his military files for that purpose. Old Hickory replied that he would have them collated and sent. "I resign to you my papers with great pleasure; with the request that they be . . . returned to my adopted son. . . . I have been oppressed with a violent cough and have been recently vissited with my old bowell complaint, which has weakened me very much, having . . . in the last twelve hours upwards of Twenty passages. . . . In short Sir I must take a rest or my stay on Erth cannot be long."[18]

The hand of the sick man trembled as he signed his name, but the day's writing was not done. Andrew Jackson Donelson again stood in need of advice. "Whatever may be thought of the pretentions of Mr. Clay to the presidency by the Kentuckians he has not the prospect of being elected. Virginia . . . will not support him— But my young friend keep yourself from the political vortex . . . until your age & experience will justify your country in calling you. . . . Let this be a stimulant to your application to your studies. . . . Prepare yourself for the bar and . . . be able to meet . . . even Mr. Clay in Forensic debate."[19]

Still in school were four other youngsters whom the childless couple at the Hermitage regarded as their own. Andrew, junior, the adopted son aged twelve, and his cousin, Andrew Jackson Hutchings, attended the elementary classes of Cumberland College in Nashville. Their holidays were a source of joy to Rachel and General Jackson. Lincoyer, the Creek Indian refugee, went to a country school near the Hermitage. Daniel Donelson was at West Point and on the honor roll of his class. Andrew, junior, was too immature for one to judge of his capacities, but of all the young ones—eleven or more—whom the General and Mrs. Jackson had reared and educated, "Jack" Donelson, at Transylvania University, showed the greatest promise. Each week from one to four long letters were exchanged by Old Hickory and his nephew.

"My wish is that you complete your education fully. . . . Your talents if life lasts will lead you to fill the highest stations in our Government. . . . That you may fill them with benefit to your Government and honour to yourself I have drew your attention to the Models of patriotism such as Wallace [the Scottish chieftain] and Washington."[20]

And more specifically:

"I look forward . . . to the time when you will be selected to preside over the destinies of america."[21]

6

The homecoming of United States Senator John Henry Eaton with the latest under-cover gossip from Washington gave fresh impetus to the purpose of Andrew Jackson's friends. The little group that shared his confidences was an interesting one. In all the country, boiling as it was with political intrigue in behalf of avowed candidates, it is doubtful whether one could have found the counterpart of the singular company which gathered in remote Nashville to attempt to introduce, against his will, another aspirant into the race.

There was John Overton, Old Hickory's oldest friend in Tennessee, who knew, for instance, the private secrets of Rachel's and Andrew Jackson's courtship as no other man knew them now that Lewis Robards was dead. With scarcely a ripple to mark his progress, the unobstrusive stripling lawyer who once shared a bed in a blockhouse with Prosecutor Jackson had become one of the wealthiest, wisest and quietest men in the West. Deliberately this self-effacing figure has sought to elude the vigilance of History. On his death-bed he all but obliterated the traces of his masterful hand in the campaign of 1824 by directing his son-in-law to burn before his eyes his papers, including Jackson's letters which pertained to political subjects.[22] There was also Eaton of histrionic air, who might plume himself on having "made" Andrew Jackson Governor of Florida. Although he fell short of genius, the Senator was sufficiently adept at the political arts to keep his local colleagues *au courant* with the complicated and capricious pattern of the national situation. There was William Berkeley Lewis whose plantation lay near the Hermitage. In this drama Lewis was an actor whose motives and true rôle puzzled even his contemporaries. Better than six feet tall, with shoulders as broad as a door, he was an imposing figure. His intellectual attainments were of less heroic mold; yet there is no denying an unaccountably effective quality to the man and his works. For several years Lewis had enjoyed a small reputation as one of Andrew Jackson's confidants. In this he found a satisfaction which observed the limitations of good taste. He held no public offices and was unknown outside Davidson County. In the War of 1812 he had not gained or apparently aspired to a rank above that of commissary major.

Such was the inner circle. On the fringe were Felix Grundy, a scheming man of flexible convictions, G. W. Campbell, Sam Houston, George Wilson, editor of the Nashville *Gazette* and three or four others, not including William Carroll. With this intimate coterie the Governor was still on probation, his visits to the Hermitage and conciliatory overtures notwithstanding.

By April of 1822 the members of this junto had pretty well mapped out General Jackson's destiny. Their plan was apt because so agreeable to the temper of the hour. It was audacious because almost diametrically opposed to the position Andrew Jackson had previously maintained in politics. They meant to sweep aside precedent, ignore party machinery which they knew they could not control, and plant the flag of their man amid the restless masses groping for leadership.

Hitherto national tickets had been selected by congressional caucuses of the different parties. This system and the method of choosing electors in the various states, combined virtually to exclude the people from participation in the selection of a president. It made for party solidarity, and no other method yet devised has brought forward as nominees men of larger calibre.

The caucus belonged to a day when the country was governed by leaders who imposed their will, rather than by popular men who must propitiate to preserve their prestige. Thus it was undemocratic and out of step with the times. Moreover, the disappearance of the Federalist Party made a caucus less necessary because of the lack of opposition. Meantime the lean years had made men think, made them eager to grasp the reins of government and contend against abuses by which they saw themselves ground down and their last cow taken. All this reacted against the caucus.

And the junto perceived another salient circumstance. Secretary of the Treasury William H. Crawford was the "regular" Republican candidate because he controlled most of the party machinery. In a caucus he might have more votes than the combined votes of all other aspirants. But Crawford must pay for this advantage. He must confront the mounting popular resentment against the caucus system, meanwhile bearing the responsibility for necessarily painful items of the nation's fiscal policy during a period of diminished revenues and increased taxes. He must contend also against the personal ill-will of Andrew Jackson who abided by his declaration to "support the Devil" before he would support William H. Crawford.[23]

The junto's next problem was to start the ball rolling. After much discussion, the decision was reached amid elaborate secrecy that the Tennessee Legislature would be the best agency to present Jackson's name to the nation. This would afford a sponsorship to suit the most popular palate. The present Assembly was a thoroughgoing creation of the people—so much so that two years before it had rejected as "disrespectful" a communication from General Jackson inveighing against the enactment of the stay law and loan bureau bill.

This being agreed upon, William B. Lewis said he was going to North Carolina to pay his wife's family a social visit. Mrs. Lewis's father was United States Senator Montfort Stokes of Wilkesboro who had known Andrew Jackson as a rollicking law student. Colonel John Stokes, who prepared Andy for his bar examination after another tutor had disclaimed further responsibility for the future of so wild a youth, was the Senator's brother. Major Lewis's conversations with his father-in-law turned to political topics. "I . . . found him a warm, personal friend and admirer of General Jackson," recorded the Major, "but he gave not the slightest intimation that he preferred him for the presidency. This occasioned me some uneasiness."

Lewis believed Monfort Stokes's support essential to the success of the Jackson cause in North Carolina and, when his visit was drawing to a close, nothing remained but to lay the case before the Senator "without reserve." He spoke of the quiet activities of the General's Nashville friends. Stokes was surprised. He asked if the little group really expected to place Jackson in the race.

"Unquestionably," replied Lewis, and to prove it he revealed the covert scheme for nomination by the Legislature.

The old politician was interested, but not swept off his feet by the novel proposal.

"What support," he inquired, "do his friends expect him to get, if nominated?"

"They expect him to be supported by the *whole* country," Lewis replied.

"Then," said the Senator dryly, "he will certainly be elected."

But the son-in-law had made an impression. Assuming a more serious tone, Montfort Stokes spoke of his long acquaintance with Andrew Jackson. He admired "no living man" more, but, in the forthcoming campaign he said his support was already pledged to Secretary of War John C. Calhoun.[24]

"This was very unwelcome news to me," wrote Lewis—doubly so because Lewis knew that Jackson himself, though at present for John Quincy Adams, probably would transfer his allegiance to Calhoun should the South Carolinian's name be formally brought forward.[25] The unwelcome news, however, made it plain that the junto had no time to lose. It must get the name of its man in the lists before he committed himself to Calhoun, as Stokes had done.

"Suppose," ruminated Lewis, "Mr. Calhoun should not be a candidate. Can you support the General as your next choice?"

Senator Stokes replied promptly, "Yes, with great pleasure."[26]

This conversation terminated the sojourn of Major Lewis with his wife's relations. Hurrying across the mountains he arrived in Nashville about June 1, 1822.

7

The returned emissary received pleasing news. General Jackson was in better health, and for Old Hickory health always meant activity. Even now he was absent from home, having ridden to Alabama to inspect his Melton's Bluff Plantation, and incidentally to adjust one of those difficulties which more and more had begun to disturb the tranquillity of a southern planter's days.

"50 DOLLARS REWARD

"RAN AWAY from the plantation of Gen. Andrew Jackson ... in Franklin County (Ala) ... Gilbert, a negro man, about 35 or 40 years of age, very black and fleshy, with a full round face, has a scar on one of his cheeks, but not recollected which. . . .

"JOHN COFFEE"[27]

The euphemisms and amenities of the black code were in the making. The word "slave" seldom met the eye or ear. One spoke of "servants," "the hands" or "the force"; and "slavery" was translated as the South's "peculiar domestic institution." Something of the oblique character of dueling correspondence came to feature the announcement of a runaway. A gentleman might lend his own name to a public offer of the services of his stud horse, but in the case of a fugitive negro his overseer or a friend usually undertook that obligation to society.

"Ran away from Col. E. Wards, a negro man named CHARLES. . . .

"CHAMBERLAYNE JONES."[28]

Notices of escaping slaves were eagerly read and discussed. The prospect of a man-hunt arouses a deep-seated instinct. Nor

were the cash rewards to be overlooked. But underneath all
this lay the consciousness of a threat to the economic order upon
which, for better or for worse, the cotton states staked their future.
The social position of the owners was sufficient to insure attention to the losses of General Jackson and Edward Ward, but
features inherent in the escape itself might elevate to temporary
distinction a citizen otherwise obscure.

"250 REWARD

"A man by the name of George W. Harvy, after loitering in
few days about the plantation of Maj. Thos. B. Scott . . . did on
Friday last steal a remarkable likely bright mullato woman, named
POLLY, about twenty years old, light hair, inclined to curl a
little. . . . They will no doubt travel as man and wife as she
. . . would . . . pass as a white woman. . . . They will undoubtedly
try to reach the free states . . . or some Spanish Territories. . . .
"JOHN SCOTT."[29]

Harvy, a young Georgian, had been Scott's overseer. He had
fallen in love with the blonde mulatto who could pass for white
and they were to have a child. Scott discharged him and other
employment in the neighborhood was hard to find. Harvy
bought two horses and a suit of man's clothing for the girl.
Waiting until the master was absent in Nashville, they made
their perilous bid for happiness, apparently finding it in a new
land, under a new name and, for Polly, a new race—for Major
Scott's reward was never claimed.

General Jackson was an ideal slave-owner. He called the force
at the Hermitage, numbering about a hundred, "the family";
and relations between the bond and the free were marked with
instances of genuine and reciprocal attachment. Over the sixty
slaves at Melton's Bluff, on the Tennessee River near Florence
in northern Alabama, Jackson was endeavoring to establish a
similarly patriarchal relationship. This proceeded slowly for the
planter must deal with them through an overseer and good overseers were hard to find. Moreover the negroes themselves were
suspicious. Jackson had acquired them, along with Melton's

Bluff, from a former river pirate who had ruled his hands with a horsewhip.[30]

Upon learning of the flight of Gilbert, Jackson cautioned his Alabama overseer, Egbert Harris: "I have only to say, you know my disposition, and as far as lenity can be extended to these unfortunate creatures, I wish you to do so; subordination must be obtained first, and then good treatment."[31] The overseer lacked his employer's ability to handle men, and when Jackson reached Melton's Bluff three other negroes were missing. Old Hickory took command and all were recaptured; "and although I hate chains, I was compelled to place two of them in irons."[32] Meantime the stand of corn had suffered from inattention, buildings were out of repair and, in all, General Jackson was a fortnight putting matters to rights.

With that friend of friends, John Coffee, who now made his home on a neighboring plantation in Alabama, Old Hickory journeyed northward, arriving at the Hermitage on June 22 to plunge into the newspapers that had accumulated during his absence. He fumed at a political attack on John Quincy Adams, rejoicing at Adams's vigorous answer, which offered a theme for another letter of advice to Jack Donelson. "This exposure by Mr. Adams . . . has increased . . . his popularity in the west and south."[33]

8

General Jackson's absence had afforded the junto a splendid opportunity to further its aims.

The presentation of another ceremonial sword was arranged for July 4, after which Old Hickory contemplated a trial of the curative waters at Harrodsburgh Spring, Kentucky. On June 27 Felix Grundy sent a note saying that his inability to leave home obliged him to deliver in writing a message which, he intimated, he would have preferred to communicate orally. "The subject . . . is this, Your friends wish to know, whether there is any cause; unknown to them, which would render it improper . . . to exercise their own discretion . . . in bringing forward your name . . . for the office of Chief Magistrate of the United States. The General Assembly will meet next month. Then is the time to take a decisive step."[34]

General Jackson had received letters from every quarter of the Union asking the same question in one form or another. He had answered none of them. He did not answer Mr. Grundy's communication and, indeed, apparently laid it aside without a careful reading.[35]

General Jackson received his sword from the hands of Governor Carroll. This was followed by an enormous barbecue at McNairy's Spring on the purlieus of the town. Festivities closed with a ball at the Nashville Inn. Nowhere in the oratory or long round of toasts was breathed an allusion to the topic in every mind—the presidential election.

The departure for Harrodsburgh was delayed. After these ceremonies guests lingered at the Hermitage, obliging Jackson to cancel the trip to Harrodsburgh. Meantime the Legislature convened at Murfreesborough,[36] the capital, and, amid the commotion caused by the burning of the courthouse where the lawmakers held their sessions, the apparently casual arrival of Sam Houston escaped comment. Felix Grundy also was there and in his place as a member of the Lower House which took refuge in the Presbyterian Church.

The Hermitage, too, was the scene of activity. The General started to write Jack Donelson a long letter on the evils of Kentucky's banking policy, but he was unequal to more than a short note. "My cough sticks by me, and the pain in my side and shoulder [from Jesse Benton's bullet] continues." He thought that a rest and change of scene might bring relief. "I have agreed to travel with Genl Coffee next week to the Assembly and spend a few days— perhaps this may be beneficial."[37]

If Andrew Jackson had read Felix Grundy's letter, he was not dealing candidly with Rachel's nephew—a circumstance out of character with Jackson.

On the following day, July 17, the General wrinkled his brows over an item in the Nashville *Whig*.

"GREAT RACING! ! ! . . . The prize to be run for is the

Presidential Chair. . . . There have already four states sent their nags in. . . . Why not Tennessee put in her stud? and if so, let it be called *Old Hickory.* . . ."

Before another sun had set the Nashville *Clarion* put the case rather less breezily. "A new candidate for the Presidency, being number fifteen," would presently be brought forward by "the friends of the nation." This entrance of Andrew Jackson into the lists would serve the useful purpose of saving the other fourteen candidates from any amount of bootless exertion. For, "having done more than any man now living," continued the *Clarion* in a matter-of-fact way, General Jackson was unquestionably the choice of "the people, in justice to themselves."[38]

After reading the above, Old Hickory concluded a long letter to his former aide and military physician, James C. Bronaugh, in which the presidential question was disposed of briefly. "You will see from the papers that my name has been brought forward. To every application to me, I give the same answer—that I have never been a candidate for any office. I never will. . . . But when the people call, the Citizen is bound to render the service required. I think Crawford is lost sight of. . . . I am told Mr. Adams is at present the strongest in this state."[39]

The proposed visit to the capital was abandoned, the General explaining to Jack Donelson that he had received a "hint" of what was in the wind.[40] It appears that Old Hickory had got around to reading Grundy's letter.

Meanwhile, at Murfreesborough, the junto's plan went forward. On July 20, 1822, Representative Pleasant M. Miller of Knoxville, a son-in-law of William Blount, Andrew Jackson's first political mentor across the mountains, placed the following before the Lower House of the Legislature:

"The members of the general assembly of . . . Tennessee, taking into view the great importance of the selection of a suitable person to fill the presidential chair . . . have turned their eyes to *Andrew Jackson,* late major-general in the armies of the United States. In him they behold the soldier, the statesman, and the honest man;

... calm in deliberation, cautious in decision, efficient in action. ..."
Therefore, *"Resolved* ... that the name of major-general Andrew
Jackson be submitted to the consideration of the people of the
United States . . ."[41]

The ayes were unanimous.

Old Hickory received the news with little show of interest. He
made no public acknowledgment, writing privately to Bronaugh:
"I have never been an applicant for office. I never will. . . . I have
no desire, nor do I expect ever to be called to fill the Presidential
chair, but should this be the case . . . it shall be without exertion
on my part."[42]

Affairs at Murfreesborough, however, were not unfolding according to the design of the junto. The Lower House had behaved handsomely, but the obstinacy of the Senate presented
difficulties to which day after day of silence gave embarrassing
emphasis. The pride that Tennesseans, irrespective of caste, had
in their first citizen was insufficient to overcome, at once, the
resentment of some of these legislators over Jackson's unparlia-
mentary characterization of their hard-times emergency laws.

Not until August 3 did the senators appear well enough in
hand for the manipulators to chance a vote. Then the resolution
was adopted unanimously, though rather than vote aye and
lacking courage to vote nay, "some one or two gentlemen quit
the house."[43] Glowering down from his six-feet-six, the ordinarily
urbane and always stylishly waist-coated Sam Houston eyed the
recalcitrants darkly. "They will repent this!" he said.[44]

CHAPTER II

A Grass Hat

I

The New York *Evening Post* observed that if the country were under martial law General Jackson by all means would be the best man for President.[1] This not being the case, the *Post* continued its cordial allusions to Secretary of the Navy Smith Thompson, one of a treeful of early birds.

In general, however, editors remained on the fence, waiting for time to diminish their problem by narrowing down the field of aspirants. "Not one in fifty," complained the Knoxville *Register,* "have *come out.*"[2] The *Columbian Observer* of Philadelphia presented three-quarters of a column of florid encomium of Jackson's career as a soldier though, alack, no syllable on the topic so dear to the hearts of the Nashville Warwicks.[3]

Nearer home several issues of Salisbury's *Western Carolinian* passed over in silence the action of the Tennessee Legislature, while continuing to criticize Crawford's administration of the Treasury, assail the caucus, and give other indications of an impulse to take up the battle of the common man. Eventually the coup at Murfreesborough was noticed with a commendation of General Jackson's military services. As to the presidency, however, this influential newspaper "could point to several men who are greatly preferable." Old Hickory might be a dependable pilot in a storm, but "in times of tranquility and with brisk and favorable gales we should greatly fear he would carry too much sail."[4] All of which bore the threatening aspect of preparing the way for a declaration in favor of John C. Calhoun, whom Nashville's schemers saw as their most dangerous competitor in North Carolina.

35

Except in Tennessee, the opening gesture of the junto had not achieved a "good press."

2

The gray-haired soldier seemed sincerely unconcerned. "Believe me my Dr Andrew," he assured Rachel's nephew. General Jackson never addressed his namesake as Jack. "Believe me my Dr Andrew I never had a wish to be elevated . . . to the executive chair. . . . My sole ambition is to pass to my grave in retirement. But as the Legislature of my state has thought proper to bring my name forward without consulting me, I mean to be silent—and let the people do as seemeth good unto them."[5]

Silence, of course, was not refusal. It merely conformed to Jackson's rule of conduct not to seek a public office or to shun a public responsibility. Yet, beneath a calm exterior the quick blood of the old warrior stirred a little. The man who had never, in season or out declined a challenge, took a quiet satisfaction in construing the action of the Legislature as a fling at Crawford and the congressional caucus.[6]

Jack Donelson did not share his uncle's indifference to the Legislature's nomination. Anxious to be in the thick of things, he wrote of abandoning his studies and returning to the Hermitage. Although Jackson needed the services of a secretary, he suggested that young Donelson keep to his books. "The Presidential election will not give me either trouble or pain."[7] The General asked for details of the law course at Transylvania. "It is sheer Legal knowledge, abstracted from Politicks, that I wish you to learn—not the absurd doctrine that the Legislature is the people."[8]

The Legislature not the people! Had the statesmen at Murfreesborough suspected such heresy more than one or two of them would have braved Sam Houston's scowl. For Jackson had expressed the conservative and not the popular thought of the country. What a morsel that would have been for the Messrs. Crawford, Adams, Calhoun and Clay, as each, mindful of the awakening of the masses, strove to clothe himself in the garments of the people's true and original friend.

3

Notwithstanding the timidity of editors, some political entre-
preneurs did not fail to perceive that a national hero, the common
man's toast on all occasions, might cut a wide swath in a campaign in which the substratum seemed determined to play a leading rôle. Mr. Clay was especially anxious about the western vote,
but before he could decide what to do James Monroe had undertaken to maneuver Old Hickory gracefully out of the race. The
President availed himself of a method employed once before,
when he found the Florida governorship a handy means of reliev-
ing himself of Andrew Jackson's overshadowing presence—a
stratagem rendered the more innocent in appearance by the collaboration of John Henry Eaton. The first week in January,
1823, the Senator from Tennessee again was summoned to the
Executive Residence. This time the President flattered him with
an exposition of our relations with Mexico.

The Mexican question was a stepchild of the Florida problem,
so expeditiously solved by Jackson's military raid and the hardly
less robust diplomacy of John Quincy Adams. To smooth the
ruffled feathers of Spain, and to accommodate our own expansionists who wanted Florida in a big hurry, Adams had incorporated
in the treaty of annexation a clause recognizing the Sabine River as
the boundary between the United States and Mexico, thus relinquishing a shadowy claim to the Rio Grande. At the moment,
Jackson had consented to this,[9] only to regret it when the West set
up a howl, for the eyes of our pioneers were on the fertile savannas
of Texas. Our desire for Texas prompted Mr. Monroe to suggest
to Senator Eaton the advisability of the preliminary of sending a
minister to Mexico City; and for this post who was better qualified by experience than Andrew Jackson? No one was better
qualified, yet the case presented certain perplexing difficulties.
"He has been nominated for President," blandly continued the
Executive, "and you know he has my good wishes." But, pursued
Mr. Monroe, "I'm afraid it may be thought & said if nominated
for the Mexican mission that it is done . . . to get him out of
the way."

To this entirely true statement, Eaton replied that while "some might say so the genl would impute nothing of the sort."[10] The Senator asked for time in which to consult Jackson's friends, and a few days later returned to give his acquiescence to the appointment. At the same time Eaton gave Jackson his first intimation of what had happened. "If you accept, well and good; if not, no disservice will be produced."[11]

The Senator understated the case. A refusal would be tantamount to an announcement of Jackson's readiness to stand for the presidency. But Eaton was careful to leave with Monroe the impression that the General would accept.

The nomination of Andrew Jackson to be Envoy Extraordinary and Minister Plenipotentiary to Mexico was confirmed by the Senate and the formal commission dispatched to the Hermitage with a personal letter from the President. "I have intended this as a new proof of my confidence in your integrity and patriotism and of your ability to execute a very high and important trust. Should you accept it, you will be put aboard a public vessel with your family." Mr. Monroe explained that Senator Eaton had been consulted "on the propriety of making . . . the nomination in respect to yourself at this interesting moment" and that he favored it "decidely."[12]

4

These exercises in statecraft coincided with the marketing of the Hermitage cotton crop which, in the early spring of 1823, seemed to absorb General Jackson to the exclusion of all other matters. The quiet life of the Hermitage was restoring the planter's health. He would have avoided the local celebration of the anniversary of the Battle of New Orleans had he been able to do so politely. "You know I am opposed to pomp & parade but," he added honestly, "the sincere approbation of the community must be acknowledged to be gratifying. . . . I see in the last Intellegencer that Mr J. Q. Adams has given Mr Clay a severe dressing. . . . You will see in the quill of Mr Adams a happy nack at satire."[13]

The severe dressing had failed, however, to diminish the energy with which Henry Clay pursued the presidency. The Kentuckian had joined Crawford and Calhoun in rendering obsolescent the code established by General Washington when the office sought the man. With little concealment these aspirants personally directed their campaigns. Mr. Monroe's proposal to send Jackson to Mexico sharpened the efforts of Mr. Clay to obtain the western vote without division. The Kentucky Legislature answered the Assembly of Tennessee with a resolution endorsing its favorite, and missionary work to the same end was begun in Ohio, Missouri, Alabama and Louisiana. Jackson's perfect silence, his failure to give his closest friends a sign which the freemasonry of politics might identify as conveying tacit approval of their labors, strengthened the cause of Mr. Clay and cheered his adherents.

Cautiously Clay scouts infiltrated through Tennessee. When the Legislature of Ohio nominated Mr. Clay, Governor William Carroll of Tennessee sent the Kentuckian a letter of felicitation, expressing regret that the Alabama Legislature should have adjourned without taking similar action. "If General Jackson should cease to be a competitor," continued the Governor, "you may rely with the utmost confidence on the support of Tennessee. . . . In a conversation with Mr. Grundy a few days ago he assured me that if the prospects of General Jackson became hopeless he would be for you and that he would endeavor to have you nominated at the next meeting of our Legislature."[14] Felix Grundy was never the most constant of men, and just now he and General Jackson found themselves on opposite sides of a land controversy.

So far so good, but the eastern post brought from Congressman Henry Shaw of Massachusetts, working in the Clay interest there, a picture of the situation drawn on a larger canvas. This placed the Jackson candidacy in a different light. One hundred and thirty-two electoral votes were necessary for a choice, and at present Crawford appeared to have one hundred and fourteen. Adams was a distant second with forty-eight; next Clay, forty-one—Kentucky, Missouri, Illinois, Indiana and Ohio; next Calhoun, thirty-nine—South Carolina and Pennsylvania; and lastly

Jackson, nineteen—Tennessee, Mississippi, Alabama and Louisiana. The question of the withdrawal of either Jackson or Calhoun was a delicate one at present, however. Mr. Shaw quoted Daniel Webster as saying that "at heart" Massachusetts preferred Calhoun to Adams, who would be the only beneficiary of the withdrawal of Calhoun at this time. The withdrawal of Jackson, continued Shaw, would present Crawford with six votes from Tennessee and two or three from Mississippi, bringing the votes of the Secretary of the Treasury to the dangerous aggregate of one hundred and twenty-three or twenty-four.[15] Thus the need for caution in any attempt to disperse the Jackson following or to remove the General from the race.

Old Hickory a stalking horse for Henry Clay: a piquant speculation to say the least. Yet the suggestion of Congressman Shaw contained a good deal of common sense, and in the political arena stranger things have come to pass.

A similarly complacent attitude toward the Jackson movement was imputed to Adams and Calhoun,[16] who preferred to see a body of western votes temporarily in the hands of a man who showed no sign of going through with the canvass than to see them pledged to an aggressive rival like Crawford. The Florida campaign furnished the basis of the hope each of these gentlemen entertained of becoming the ultimate beneficiary of the Jackson activity in the West. Adams's support of Jackson in Florida had been courageous and real. To no other man in the Government was Old Hickory so deeply indebted. Mr. Calhoun's support existed largely in the domain of expedient afterthought. In the secrecy of those warm Cabinet discussions of the summer of 1818, the Secretary of War had been outspoken against Jackson's imperial behavior. But, as the popular tide swung in the soldier's favor, Mr. Calhoun swung with it and began an umbrageous courtship of the commander of the Southern Division. Beguiled into the belief that all along Calhoun had stood with him on the Florida issue, Jackson viewed with favor the progress of Calhoun's prospects in the West.[17] Punctually the Secretary of War had accepted at face value Jackson's coolness to the Murfreesborough resolutions, explicitly writing the General, "It will be manifest in six months that I am the only man from slave holding states that can be elected."[18]

This situation enhanced interest in the proffered mission to Mexico. Should Jackson accept, it would be necessary for Clay, Adams and Calhoun to revise their plans of campaign in the West. And the Nashville junto's exhilarating vision would dissolve entirely.

5

John Henry Eaton continued to cruise about Washington, interviewing Jackson's friends as to the advisability of accepting the Mexican appointment. Mr. Adams unselfishly favored it. So apparently did the others to whom Eaton spoke, excepting only Mr. Calhoun who thought the General could better serve his country by remaining at home.[19] As the Secretary of War imagined, this might better serve his own cause, too.

Old Hickory himself considered the subject with care, soliciting the opinions of Joel R. Poinsett, our soundest authority on Latin-American affairs, and of Mrs. Jackson. Reasoning from different premises, each offered the same advice.

"I have the pleasure," General Jackson scrawled to the President with more than his usual haste, "to acknowledge recpt. of your letter. . . . I cannot accept. . . . Under the present revolutionary state of Mexico, caused by the despotic acts of Iturbide [who had overthrown the republic and proclaimed himself emperor] . . . the app of a minister from the United States . . . might help Tyrant Iturbide in rivitting . . . Despotism upon his country. . . . Added to this Mrs Jackson could not be prevailed on to go."[20]

The Nashville junto took a deep breath, congratulated their chief upon his decision,[21] and sedulously spread the impression that the refusal of the diplomatic appointment made Jackson a receptive candidate. The General himself could not have been blind to this. During the progress of the Mexican negotiations Eaton himself had said as much, writing letters such as no man would address to Old Hickory without knowledge that the General's early aversion to presidential politics was undergoing a change. One of these communications revealed how well the scheming Senator understood the temperamental weaknesses of his patron.

"It is incumbent on you therefore to act with the caution that belongs to you. . . . Commit not your opinions; nor let the malevolence whatever insinuating shape it may assume, drag you into any *news paper* controversy. Already are Mr. Crawfords folks seeking to convey the idea that you have not consented to be placed before the nation. . . . The enquiry has several times been made of me & I have generally replied that . . . you would not decline any call of your country. . . . Should any man of standing and character address you on the subject I suggest . . . a reply . . . in sentiment & language like this. 'That you had at no period of your life sought . . . after office . . . and . . . altho . . . retired . . . from public service . . . yet if your country should think it in your power to . . . promote her happiness it would be a departure from the uniform course of your life to refuse.' "[22]

6

Governor Billy Carroll had a clear right to support Mr. Clay or anyone else he might prefer, but to make that support effective while still professing friendship for General Jackson called for strict heed to the rules of discretion. Difficult as it was for Andrew Jackson's intent nature to see good in those who opposed him, nevertheless there were occasions when he respected an open adversary. But duplicity he could never condone. Therefore, when Carroll elected to write letters in Henry Clay's behalf, he should have selected his confidants with care. He did not do this, for the substance of his letters was at once relayed to the Hermitage. Old Hickory took fire, exhibiting an interest in the campaign which the overtures of all his friends had been unable to elicit.

"Carroll has been writing . . . that Clay will get the unanimous vote of Tennessee. I mean at first oportunity to shew the Governor this letter. . . . His friends shall also see it, and I suppose the individuals of Tennessee will inquire by what right he attempted to give lye to the expression of the Legislature of the state."[23]

A kind word for the Murfreesborough resolutions! The quotation is from a letter to John Coffee in Alabama, which continued: "Should the people take up the subject of my nomination in the south, and west, as they have in Pennsylvania they will soon undeceive Mr. Clay's friends. if the people of Alabama, Mississippi, and Louisiana, follow the example of Pennsylvania, they will place Clay and Crawford . . . *Dehors the political combat.*"[24]

John Coffee had been in Nashville when the Murfreesborough plan was hatched. If, with the Nashville junto, he had suffered on account of Jackson's want of enthusiasm for that work of art, now he had an oil for his wounds. Clay and Crawford must be defeated. To this end Jackson was ready to go to the extremity of permitting the use of his name as a candidate. Moreover he had made a specific recommendation: "Follow the example of Pennsylvania."

7

Had the foremost political seers of the generation sat at Andrew Jackson's elbow as he wrote they could have imparted no better advice than to follow the example of Pennsylvania. The fact that Old Hickory should have discerned this is tribute to his intuition and evidence of the fact that, from the quiet of his study, he had followed the vagrant currents and source-springs of the campaign with more penetration than his ambitious friends had dared to hope.

Pennsylvania favored a protective tariff, internal improvements at the expense of the Federal Treasury, and sound banking. Calhoun and Clay were both high-tariff, internal-improvements and sound-banking men; and Mr. Clay had dramatized these issues more effectively than any other American in public life. Further to enhance his attractions in the eyes of Pittsburgh especially, Harry Clay was a Westerner, at home in the vernacular of trans-Appalachia and reflecting its social outlook with his fast horses, his game cocks and his devotion to the pleasures of the taproom. These virtues would appear to have given him an advantage over Mr. Calhoun who lacked them, but such had not proved to be the case. One reason was the bringing forward, by Tennessee, of the name of Andrew Jackson, known friend of Calhoun and known foe of Clay.

Unlike Nashville, Pittsburgh supporters of General Jackson were not embarrassed by the propinquity of the General him-self, throwing cold water on their efforts. Andrew Jackson was known to Pittsburgh as early as 1795 when he transshipped there, from wagons to flatboats, merchandise destined for the trading post at Hunter's Hill. When the war brought Jackson fame, Pittsburgh recalled and embroidered these half-forgotten visits. James Riddle, Jackson's old bootmaker, whose native wisdom had elevated him to the bench of the court of common pleas, had many a tale to tell. Robert J. Walker, a twenty-one-year-old lawyer, David Lynch, a tobacco forwarder, and Robert Steele, a storekeeper, listened to these stories and formed a "Jackson Committee" in Pittsburgh. Their advertising agent was Edward Patchell, a coal miner and nomadic preacher without parish, who ranged the countrysides expounding the glory of Jehovah and of Andrew Jackson.

The response, as one of Mr. Patchell's associates admitted, was limited to "the lower and middle classes of society"[25]—small farmers, miners, river men and artisans. Jackson committees multiplied and began to call mass meetings. Such a gathering in Pittsburgh formally considered the question of the presidency. "Wm. H. Crawford received one vote, H Clay five, J. Q. Adams two, J. C. Calhoun four and Gen Andw Jackson upward of 1000."[26] A meeting at Harrisburg made the choice of Jackson unanimous, and H. W. Peterson, a barkeeper, wrote to ascertain if the General approved of his name "being used at this time as a candidate."[27]

Andrew Jackson had received similar communications almost without number, many of them from persons well situated in life. He had replied to none. Yet he answered Mr. Peterson, apparently without knowing anything more about him than his name. The nature of this response suggests that the political advice of Senator John Henry Eaton had not fallen on barren soil. Another significant fact is that the copy of the letter found in Jackson's files after his death is in the handwriting of Major William Berkeley Lewis, charter member of the Nashville junto.

The letter bears the date of February 23, 1823, which was four days after the Mexican mission had been declined. The General began by reiterating that he had been "richly repaid" for his services to his country, and longed only to perpetuate his retirement and "be a spectator merely of passing events." Yet— "my undeviating rule of conduct through life . . . has been neither to seek or decline public invitations to office. . . . As the office of Chief Magistrate of the Union . . . should not be sought, . . . so it cannot, with propriety, be declined. . . . It was with these impressions, I presume, . . . that the Members of the Legislature of Tennessee . . . thought it proper to present my name. . . . My political creed prompts me to leave the affair uninfluenced by any expression on my part . . . to the free will of those who have alone the right to decide.

"Your obedient, &c
"H. W. Peterson   ANDREW JACKSON"[28]

When this momentous communication reached Harrisburg John M. Farland, an unemployed newspaperman, got his hands on it long enough to strike out the name of Mr. Peterson and substitute "Dauphin County Committee." In this form the letter reached the Harrisburg *Commonwealth* from whose columns it was quickly reproduced by the press of the whole country.[29]

Hitherto John Farland has been overlooked in the scramble to discover those responsible for General Jackson's political career. He has his place. The democratic genesis of the Jackson movement in Pennsylvania had been established beyond the necessity of addressing the candidate's formal announcement to the proprietor of a river-front grogshop.

8

Though his ardor to crush Crawford and Clay seemed to transcend any expectation of winning himself, Andrew Jackson had lifted his eyes to the hills. His acquiescence in the rôle of candidate gave the campaign the external form it was to exhibit to the country until election time. The contest of 1824 beheld the meeting and parting of two political generations. It witnessed the opening of the schisms that were to wreck the Republican Party and remold it, Andrew Jackson's violent moderation superseding the mild radicalism of Thomas Jefferson as the swelling, dividing, diverging stream of American life swept toward the climactic cataracts of the 'Thirties. Superficially the contest wore the aspect of a clash of personalties rather than of issues. Nevertheless, early in 1823, it was possible to distinguish differences of principle as well as of personality in four of the five aspirants among whom it was now apparent that the country must choose a president.

The first candidate invariably considered was Secretary of the Treasury William H. Crawford who, though the field was united against him as against no other man, entered the spring of 1823 the leading contender.

The greatest strength of Crawford lay in the tactical position into which he had maneuvered his cause. He asserted himself to be the "regular" candidate of the party, the only "true Jeffersonian." The claim to regularity was vindicated by control of the machinery of the party and insistence on the traditional caucus method of nomination which he, alone of the candidates, could dominate. The claim to authenticity as a Jeffersonian was vouched for by the support of the sage of Monticello himself; and the adhesion of venerable James Madison made Crawford veritably the candidate of the fading Virginia Dynasty which, through a working agreement with New York, had controlled the presidency for twenty-four years. The political dictator of New York, Martin Van Buren, respected that ancient understanding, and, setting his face against strong popular pressure, prepared to deliver the State's vote to Crawford by virtue of his whip hand over the Legislature.

So much for Crawford's political strength. His popular strength was not coextensive, being limited in the main to the southern aristocracy which honored the Secretary as a state-rights advocate, opposed to a tariff and internal improvements. Actually his utterances on these issues were evasive so as not to make the burden of his northern supporters, particularly Van Buren, any heavier.

Crawford was a southern man, born in an impoverished but genteel family in Virginia, and reared in Georgia where he won his way back among the people of his own class, the final victory being a marriage into the manor-house nobility. Boyhood had been a struggle: to obtain a classical education; to support a widowed mother and a cluster of sisters and brothers; to restore his family to its place in the social scale. In every case he had triumphed. The battle had left no scars, but on the other hand had imparted understanding and a hearty approach to men in every walk of life. Crawford was a giant in size, in muscular strength and mental vitality. A mellow sense of humor and a booming laugh took the sharpness out of an otherwise too persistent ambition which on occasions did not hesitate at intrigue to promote its ends. Lacking the statesmanlike breadth of John Quincy Adams or of Calhoun, Crawford was as intently self-seeking as the latter, though the easy camaraderie of his manner helped to disguise it.

During a time of trial William H. Crawford had been a satisfactory Secretary of the Treasury, but in hard times that post is ill-calculated to engender popular enthusiasm. Mr. Crawford's commitment to a caucus was a source of weakness as well as strength and placed attractive cards in the hands of his adversaries. The appeal of his principles was limited to the wealthy class of the South. His support in other quarters, though impressive, was in the hands of politicians against whom the tide was rising.[30]

9

The aspirant second to Crawford in 1823 was John Quincy Adams.

With DeWitt Clinton eliminated in his own state by the dexterity of Martin Van Buren, Adams was the only northern candidate in the race. This was a source of much prestige and placed him first among the voters of New England and New York as well, though Mr. Van Buren had no intention of giving New York's voters a voice in the selection of presidential electors. Mr. Adams's friendly attitude toward the tariff and internal improvements helped him in the Middle States and in the West. He despised slavery and all its works but, abiding by the Missouri Compromise, confined his acidulous observations to the privacy of his diary.

No candidate possessed higher proved qualifications or was as generally respected by his adversaries; and in all but the final stages of the contest no candidate adhered more faithfully to the vanishing school of political ethics which precluded a display of personal interest in his fortunes. John Quincy Adams belonged to the generation of the founding fathers, having served every president since Washington. He made admirers but not friends. Looking at himself as objectively as he would look at a problem of government he discerned the reason. "I am a man of reserve," reads the diary, "cold, austere and forbidding manners. My political adversaries say a gloomy misanthrope; and my personal enemies an unsocial savage. With a knowledge of the actual defects in my character, I have not the pliability to reform it."

In this campaign, as always, he stood much alone. "An undercurrent of calumny has been flowing in every direction adapting its movements to the feelings and the prejudices of the different parts of the country. It has a story for Pittsburg and a story for Portland, a misrepresentation for Milledgeville and a lie for Lexington. . . . I have no countermining at work. . . . I make no bargains. I listen to no overtures for coalition. I give no money. I push no appointments of canvassing partisans to office."[31]

Thus did Mr. Adams put the case for himself, and put it rather too well. J. Q. Adams wanted the presidency more than he had wanted anything in his starved and singular life—but he was slow to make up his mind to adopt the most effective means of getting it. Yet, like Crawford and Calhoun he had his newspaper in Washington, the aggressive *National Journal*. Like his rivals, he found loans for his editors and public printing for their columns. And eventually Mr. Adams was to go much farther than that.

10

With Crawford carrying the frayed banner of old-line Republicanism and Adams steering a middle course, Secretary of War John Caldwell Calhoun strode forth a frank champion of the "new" school of Jeffersonians developed by the war. Of late years hard times and the consequent drift back to sectionalism had tended to outmode the "new" school; but the Hamiltonian sweep of Calhoun's nationalism and the challenging vigor of his advocacy served to recapture, for the moment, something of the one-for-all-and-all-for-one spirit of 1811.

Even South Carolina, by logic the property of Crawford, was carried away. The Palmetto State might rebel at the moderate tariff and public improvements views of J. Q. Adams; but sentimental pride in the brilliance of a native son prevailed over the extreme position of Calhoun on those same issues. In North Carolina, too, the Secretary of War promised to give his colleague of the Treasury the battle of his life. In New England Calhoun was the only candidate with a chance against Adams, being particularly strong with former Federalists angered by the "desertion" of the statesman from Braintree on the war question. "He is conceded," declared one enthusiastic supporter, "*almost* a northern man."[32] A newspaper in New York City came out for Calhoun, increasing the concern of Mr. Van Buren. His high tariff and improvement policies had early captured the party organization in Pennsylvania, where the spontaneous Jackson manifestations were looked upon as helpful backfire against the encroachments of Clay. As to the West, Calhoun had Jackson's word for it that he stood first in the hearts of the frontiersmen.

As 1823 opened Crawford, though leading, had ceased to gain. Adams gained slowly. But Calhoun's fortunes appeared to be distinctly on the rise. An untoward accident to the Adams cause or to that of Mr. Clay and the presidency seemed within the grasp of the eager South Carolinian. He pursued his ambition a little less openly than Clay. He was not yet forty-one, a grave, restless being, of whom a friend said, "I have never heard him utter a jest."

II

Next, Henry Clay, Speaker of the House of Representatives, a "Kentucky gamester in politics"; tall, angular, careless of attire and rather unfavored of countenance yet, withal, the most personable of the candidates.

He was born in Virginia during the Revolution, the son of a hand-to-mouth rural clergyman who also gave dancing lessons. Fatherless at four, orphaned at seventeen, Harry Clay had made his way in a world ever responsive to the charms of an engaging temperament and the sheen of a mind so quick and so apt as to find little need for exercises in depth. As a barrister, an hour's preparation sometimes would suffice to dazzle a jury and rout a less agile adversary who had spent weeks methodically formulating a case. So natural was his behavior that Mr. Clay was said to be the only man who, while arguing before the United States Supreme Court, could walk to the bench and take a pinch of snuff from one of the boxes reserved for the use of the justices.

In 1811 the War Hawks had huzzaed him into the speakership of the House which, under his flashing leadership, plumped a country picturesquely unready into war. He represented that spirit now but only in the West was he able to make headway against Calhoun who stood for the same things. From the first his candidacy was almost purely local, and never able to rise above it. His friends early saw that the best chance for victory lay in throwing the choice into the House where the influence of the Speaker remained paramount. To achieve this he must neatly divide the vote of the West with General Jackson and, in any event, strive to keep a single western vote from his other rivals.

12

These were the four leading contenders when his letter to

Harrisburg definitely added the name of General Jackson to the roll.

All his life Andrew Jackson had been something of a law unto himself, stripping of their usual authority the conventions that govern the commonality of mankind. It was so with Jackson the candidate. Other aspirants might be northern men or southern men or western men, but not Jackson. Policies and principles might bait and bedevil *them,* but not Jackson. Where did he stand on the tariff? He did not say and no one else attempted to say. Internal improvements? The same. Caucus? Against it, of course. Currency and banking? Jackson was a sound money man identified with the economic group supporting the Bank of the United States: not a very flattering recommendation for a candidate of the western proletariat. Did it make any difference with Jackson? Not appreciably. Did his silence on tariff or improvements make any difference? None. As "the nation's hero" he was above such things. In good time no doubt the General would consent to tell the people all they needed to know.

Thus far he had said that he did not wish the office and would do nothing to obtain it, but if elected, he would serve from a sense of duty. He said no more and this Roman reticence became more formidable than all the words of his fretting rivals. What call for words from one whose deeds shaped so large? Did not the world know Andrew Jackson to be infallible in decision and instantaneous in action; that victory was his habit and the republic's glory his diadem? Mr. Adams had drawn the mantle of an aloof dignity about him, but as yet Adams stood almost alone whereas a corps of the ablest politicians of the day was silently surrounding Jackson. They caught the possibilities of their man's unique deportment. While others offered controversial issues, they offered an axiom: Old Hickory, the Nation's Hero and the People's Friend.

13

The pulse of the campaign beat faster. First to feel the changed tempo was Calhoun, still addressing affable letters to the Hermitage while his eyes turned toward Pennsylvania, the keystone of his hopes. A friend penned a cheerful report. "Pennsylvania unquestionably will support Calhoun. . . . The movements for Jackson have been made by the grog shop politicians & the rabble. . . . A republican convention will be called, which will secure a fair expression of the popular voice, & . . . nominate Calhoun."[33]

Supporters of Mr. Clay, too, found the Jackson candidacy exhibiting more life than they had bargained for. In Pennsylvania "Gen. Jackson has so possessed the public mind that your friends have been unable to make much headway. . . . He is supported by exactly that school . . . who would otherwise have been for you."[34] In Alabama a veritable "contagion" for Jackson was "spreading largely through the influence of Gen Coffee. . . . Your friends have at present a difficult part to play. Believing that Gen Jackson will not finally be a candidate we have deemed it bad policy to give the slightest offense."[35]

On the whole, though, Clay remained hopeful of sufficient western votes to enable him to fight the final round of his battle on the familiar floor of the House. Thomas Hart Benton was in Tennessee again. That State had seen little of Benton since 1813 when he changed his residence to Missouri as a consequence of a tavern brawl in which Andrew Jackson's arm was broken by a bullet. In St. Louis he had improved as a marksman, killing his man in a duel and eventually winning a seat in the United States Senate. Mr. Benton now toured the West in the quiet interest of Mr. Clay. "Jackson out of the way . . . Tennessee will go for you,"[36] he wrote.

In Baltimore William H. Crawford also strove to trade upon the popularity of the soldier. A pro-Calhoun observer on the Chesapeake sized up the situation in this way: "I am pretty confident that unholy bargains have been made for votes. . . . Friends of Mr. Crawford here will get up a ticket for Jackson to divide" the opposition.[37] The South Carolinian professed to be undisturbed. "An effort is making for Jackson in the City of Washington," he wrote. "This will do no harm. . . . The in-

"THE NATION'S HERO AND THE PEOPLE'S FRIEND"

A bas-relief by the distinguished American sculptor, William Henry Rinehart. The artist grew up during Old Hickory's heyday and began work shortly before his death. This is one of his early pieces. It is owned by Emil Edward Hurja of New York City.

terest both of Mr C--d & Mr Clay is greatly distressed. . . . The rise of Genl Jackson will be fatal to the latter."[38]

When he penned these brave lines, Mr. Calhoun was in greater distress than either Crawford or Clay. A serious and unexpected blow had fallen in Pennsylvania where the state convention, held March 4, 1823, and upon which the immediate prospects of the entire Calhoun campaign depended, had declined to endorse the Secretary of War. Up to the moment the delegates took their places, Mr. Calhoun had hoped for a nomination there. His workers in other states had been assured of it. The voice of Pennsylvania was to sweep hesitant North Carolina and New Jersey into the Calhoun fold. It was to inaugurate a drive upon Maryland, New York and New England. George M. Dallas had journeyed from Philadelphia to Harrisburg to transmit to the country the pleasing intelligence that would set this machinery in motion.

He transmitted news of a stunning reverse, for the convention passed over the presidential question in silence, limiting its labors to the selection of a State ticket.[39] Though Calhounites assuaged their disappointment as best they could, it was difficult to conceal the fact that the South Carolinian's keystone had cracked.

14

Aunt Rachel's favorite sister Jane Hays, whose hospitable blockhouse beside the Cumberland once sheltered the unhappy wife of Lewis Robards, had left the valley that was her home for forty years to share the rigors of a new frontier in western Tennessee with her married son Samuel. When the longing for familiar scenes and faces became too acute she would write a letter.

"How does my dear sister Jackson do. I cannot take up my bonnet and meet you at sister Betsys or sister Marys, . . . smoke our pipes, laugh and talk over occurrences of former days, each one taking the words out of the others mouth. . . . It was a pleasant neighborhood. . . . You will regret leaving it sister

Jackson and your fine farm and comfortable house, for the city of Washington when the General is elected President, for there is no doubt of his election from the present popular opinion. I hear you are about to build a church in the neighborhood, this will add to its pleasantness, but you will miss our good Mr. Hodge. O, how often I think of him hovering over the sick bed of my dear departed husband. . . . You may get more flowery speakers, but none that will disseminate the truths of the Gospel with more faithfulness.

"I hope you wont give out your intention of visiting us. I have right comfortable cabins, plenty of chickens, flow in milk and butter, the barrens abound with strawberrys— hurtleberrys abundant in the swamps, sloes, service berrys and grapes— do come and see us. You shall be met by the Hickory Guards, styled in honor of your General. . . . The uniform is very handsome, a hickory leaf wrought on the skirts of the coat."[40]

Yes, Rachel would have enjoyed a visit with her Sister Hays— all except the Hickory Guards. She envied Jane's seclusion and gratefully would have exchanged the Hermitage for a cabin in the woods, there to enjoy the society of her husband free of the intrusions of a tale-bearing world.

True, the Hermitage neighborhood was to have its church house. Though not a church member, General Jackson had made the largest contribution to the erection of this edifice, where Rachel could kneel in pious supplication that Andrew might never leave her side again to become President or for any other reason. Thus continued the unceasing struggle against the claims of fame in which Rachel had won her little victories, but in the end the world that was in arms against her always had its way. The world fought unfairly and under false colors, like an Indian creeping up inside a deer skin. Always some unsuspected device. Even now, alongside the letter of Sister Hays, a courteous communication from a gentleman of Philadelphia lay on Rachel's table.

"Mrs. General Jackson:
". . . I have been favoured with an opportunity to forward to

you an *American Grass Hat or Bonnet* . . . made by Miss Pike and Miss Andrews, both under the age of twelve.
"I am, Madam . . ."[41]

Bless the children! Rachel would wear the hat.

"Colonel Robert Patterson:
". . . I accept the bonnet, sir, as a just emblem of the sphere in which my sex should move, and be useful to our country. . . .
"Your obedient, humble servant . . ."[42]

As innocent a thing as this grass hat made by two little girls served as an instrument for Pennsylvania protectionists to sound out the General on the tariff:

"General A. Jackson;
"Sir: I have this day forwarded a Grass Bonnet or Hat, made by *American* hands, and of *American* materials, which I request your lady to accept . . . as a token of gratitude for . . . your distinguished services . . . especially during our late contest with Great Britain. The offering is small, sir: but it is hoped it will be . . . worn as an encouragement to *domestic manufacturers*.
"I have the honor to be . . .
"ROBERT PATTERSON."[43]

Small, indeed, the offering, but mighty the response it drew forth:

"Hermitage, near Nashville, May 17, 1823
"Sir—A few days since, I had the pleasure to receive the Grass Hat. . . . Mrs. Jackson will wear with pride a hat made by American hands, and made of American materials: its workmanship . . . will be regarded as an evidence of the perfection which our domestic manufactures may hereafter acquire, if properly fostered and protected. Upon the success of our manufactures, as the handmaiden of agriculture and commerce, depends in a great measure, the independence of our country. . . .
"Accept, sir . . .
"ANDREW JACKSON."[44]

The Grass Hat Letters placed Old Hickory in the race, not to confound the ambitions of Crawford or Clay or to assist those of Adams or Calhoun, but to win for himself. Eighteen months of subtle graduations had sufficed to complete the metamorphosis from explosive refusal[45] to open consent to his own candidacy. Like a train of ignited powder these communications, including Rachel's, ran the rounds of the press.

CHAPTER III

The Canvass

I

FAIRFIELD, the residential seat of William Berkeley Lewis, lay on the Lebanon Pike some twelve miles west of the Hermitage. The easy financial circumstances of the retired commissary officer had absolved him from anxiety over the low price of cotton during the most pessimistic period of the current depression in trade. With commerce showing signs of revival and cotton quotations plodding upward on the New Orleans exchange, Major Lewis found less distraction than ever from his labors to advance the cause of his neighbor toward the fragrant gardens of political preferment. For a time in the spring of 1823, he had acted as amanuensis to the General, this term of service coinciding with the production of the epochal Dauphin County Committee and Grass Hat Letters. Andrew Jackson Donelson, having completed his legal studies and taken up his abode at the Hermitage, released the Major for employment in other fields.

He found one under his own roof when William Polk of Raleigh paid a visit to Tennessee. General Polk, a Revolutionary soldier and one of North Carolina's famous men, came from the Waxhaws where he had known Andrew Jackson as a child. Formerly a Federalist but now a man without a party, General Polk's personal influence at home remained unimpaired. As the conversation wore around to the campaign, Lewis heard his guest brand Adams as "a *damned Traitor*," and Jackson as an old and valued friend, but nothing was said as to his preference for President.

After bidding his guest good night, Major Lewis retrieved from his store of papers a copy of a letter that General Jackson had written James Monroe, then President-elect, under date of November 12, 1816. At that time Mr. Monroe was wrestling with the problem of Cabinet selections and Jackson had suggested Colonel William Drayton, a South Carolina Federalist, as Secretary of War. "Party feelings ought to be laid out of view," he wrote, "by selecting those the most honest, possessing capacity and firmness."[1]

Next morning finding General Polk taking the air in the garden, Major Lewis handed him Jackson's letter.

The old Federalist was surprised. "Did General Jackson really write this?"

"Certainly," said Lewis.

"Then he is my man," the North Carolinian replied.[2]

2

With the tactics of a determined and skillful fighter, John Caldwell Calhoun met his unexpected rebuff in Pennsylvania with slashing blows. On other fronts he sought to consolidate his positions before the poison from Harrisburg should have a chance to spread or the enemy to exploit his advantage. Skirmishes were won and hopes ascended. In Washington Congressman George McDuffie, of South Carolina, convalescing from a dueling wound inflicted by a Crawford retainer, condensed for wider dissemination buoyant reports streaming in from the scenes of action. "Mr. Calhoun is rising rapidly in all quarters. . . . New Jersey will give . . . [him] an undivided vote."[3] "Calhoun taking like wild fire in the western part of New York."[4] "The strongest indications are given that New England, believing that Mr. Adams cannot be elected, will . . . support Mr. Calhoun."[5] (The Secretary himself was striving to win over the singularly inert Daniel Webster.)[6] "In the western states Calhoun . . . [is] clearly next to Jackson & Clay in their respective strongholds."[7]

One competent observer, John Pendleton Kennedy of Baltimore, viewed these broad claims with an active distrust. To the director of Calhoun's Maryland campaign, Colonel Virgil Maxcy of Tulip Hill Plantation, near Annapolis, he wrote a long letter.

"What do you think of the *people*"—that new and unpredictable element in a presidential contest—"of Baltimore being all alive for Jackson?" They were two to one for him. This reflected merely the vagaries of the populace, of course, and not the wholesome judgment of the politicians. Nevertheless, rather than court defeat or even victory by a small majority, Mr. Kennedy asked if it would not be wiser for Calhoun, who was so young, to withdraw in favor of the New Englander and rest content to be Adams's *premier . . .* for the next 8 years."[8]

The embattled minister of war repelled the thought, however, and threw his reserves into the fight for North Carolina where, true to his word, William Polk had come out for Jackson. There had been a time when Mr. Calhoun was glad to see the development of Jackson strength in this State, as once he had looked upon it as an ally in Pennsylvania. Now, unless something were done, the enthusiasm for Old Hickory might prove another case of the tail wagging the dog. "Our cause with the people," a Calhoun lieutenant wrote from Raleigh, "would . . . succeed if"— and it was a big if—"the friends of Jackson, who seem to be *intoxicated with military glory,* do not start a ticket for him."[9]

3

Crawford, too, was losing ground. To the structural defects already discernible in the Georgian's political edifice was added another, as he failed to develop that secondary strength deemed so important in a crowded contest where last-minute horse trades might tell the tale. Granted the Secretary of the Treasury was first in Georgia, North Carolina, Virginia, Delaware and New York. These states could not elect him, and in what states was he the runner-up? While grappling for a solution of this difficulty, Crawford's campaign organization was staggered by the most overwhelming personal calamity which has assailed a pilgrim toiling the steep slope toward the presidency.

In August or early September, 1823, Mr. Crawford left Washington, his jovial mood unruffled by the clouds upon the horizon of his fortunes, his enormous frame apparently bearing with ease the burden of fifty-one years. A fortnight later a form under a sheet was carried into a house in the Virginia hills. The Secretary of the Treasury was paralyzed in every limb, speechless, nearly blind and nearly deaf. Friends, whom it was indispensably necessary to inform of the tragedy, waited anxiously to ascertain whether his mind, too, were gone.

So closely was William H. Crawford guarded during the next year and a half, so many were the tricks to dissemble his true condition, so few, and they so close-mouthed, knew the facts, that even now it seems impossible to reconstruct what had happened. The most probable story is that a paralytic stroke had been induced by an overdose of lobelia prescribed by a country physician treating an attack of erysipelas.[10]

The stricken man rallied and the bedside watchers learned that his mind was unimpaired. Nor was this all. The blow that had prostrated the flesh could not prevail against the spirit of William Harris Crawford and, as soon as his thick tongue could mumble a word, it was for his friends to carry on the fight because he would get well. Then the world received its first news of the affliction that had befallen the candidate. A paragraph in the Crawford press announced that the Georgian was convalescing from the painful illness.

General Jackson was the first to feel the effects of the suffering man's refusal to ask for quarter. Crawford had a strong ally in Tennessee, United States Senator John Williams, who had made trouble for Andrew Jackson before and was prepared to do it now. The Senator was up for re-election by the Legislature and, so carefully had he prepared his lines, victory seemed a foregone conclusion. Colonel Williams had long filled Washington with tales of Jackson's weakness in his home state, and rather late in the day the General's presidential monitors realized that the defeat of Congressman John Rhea, Jackson's preference for Senator, would endow this assumption with an unpleasant amount of credibility.

John Henry Eaton and Major Lewis hastened to Murfreesborough to save the day for Rhea. The Williams managers, already on the ground, had combed Tennessee for men who had felt the hard hand and harsh temper of old Jackson—not an in-

considerable company when a prospect of retaliation seemed sufficiently bright to bring them into the open.

Eaton and Lewis toiled as men possessed, but every effort
splintered against the pledged and unbreakable Williams majority. The best combination they could contrive for Rhea lacked
three votes of victory.[11] "It became necessary," related Lewis, "now
to play a bold game."[12] Unless Jackson were to lose what had
developed into an important battle, he himself must enter the
lists against Williams. Eaton and Lewis put his name forward
and dispatched a messenger to the Hermitage, imploring the
General to come to Murfreesborough and inspire the waverers
with his presence. Old Hickory refused, refused even to sanction
the use of his name; but an admission was drawn from him that
if elected he would serve. A second, a third envoy posted to the
Hermitage, the last one on the night of September 30, and the
Assembly was to vote on the morrow. Old Hickory held his
ground.[13]

When the Legislature convened at seven o'clock in the morning on October 1, 1823, the Jackson forces made a desperate
attempt to obtain a postponement for two days. Davy Crockett
led a successful fight against delay[14] and preparations for the
roll call went forward amid signs of soul-searching anguish among
legislators, confronted with the choice of repudiating their
pledges to John Williams, a power in eastern Tennessee, or flying
in the face of the gray-haired Hero. Seven men switched their
allegiance and the vote was Jackson, thirty-five; Williams, twenty-
five. Thus was an astonishing triumph clutched from the shadow
of defeat when a reverse, as Lewis believed, "might possibly have
destroyed . . . his prospects for the presidency."[15]

"I have been elected senator," the victor wrote wearily to John
Coffee, "a circumstance which I regret more than any other in
my life.[16] . . . To leave . . . Mrs. Jackson . . . fills me, as well as
her, with much regret."[17]

4

Want of promptitude was never a failing of Andrew Jackson.

Although utterly unprepared to leave home, the Senator-elect departed for Washington during cotton ginning time, a planter's busiest season when expenses were greatest and debts heaviest. To defray the cost of his journey, it was necessary to accept a personal loan from John Overton and, to meet outlays at home, to dispatch Jack Donelson to Alabama for the collection of fifteen hundred dollars owing him there.

Jackson began the eight-hundred-and-sixty-mile journey on horseback attended only by John Henry Eaton and a colored body servant. Except on one day when a mail coach afforded refuge from the rain, he remained in the saddle all the way to Staunton, Virginia. At Fredericksburg the party boarded a steamboat which arrived in Washington a little after daylight on December 3. Anxious letters sped back to Rachel.

"Staunton Novbr. 28th 1823.

"My Love

"I have been greeted by the people wherever I have halted, to avoid much of which was one reason why I took the stage, & even then in many places . . . were collections who hailed & stopped the stage, This through Virginia [a Crawford stronghold] I did not calculate on. . . . Were you only with me I could be satisfied— But should providence once more permit us to meet, I am solemnly resolved, with the permission of heaven, never to separate, or be separated from you in this world."[18]

"Newburn Virginia Novbr.—

"My Love

"The separation, so unlooked for, from you . . . has oppressed my mind very much, still I hope that your mind is become calm. . . . I hope you will not permit yourself to want for anything."[19]

"City of Washington
"Decbr. 3d. 1823

"My Love

"I have not heard from you . . . [and] am anxious to receive a letter. . . . I have been treated with marked attention. . . . Altho this is gratifying . . . my heart is with you & fixed on Domestic

Life. . . . Without you this will be a Tedious and unpleasant winter present me to the Andrews [the adopted son and Andrew Jackson Hutchings], . . . write me often and believe me to be your affectionate husband."[20]

Modestly lodged at Major William O'Neale's boarding house, General Jackson immediately became the most conspicuous personage in Washington. In vain did he seek the seclusion of his rooms where he had expected to dine privately with Eaton and Richard K. Call, the Delegate from Florida Territory. "There is nothing done here but *vissiting* and *carding*," he complained to Rachel. "You know how much I was disgusted with Those scenes when you and I were here [in 1815]."[21] Eaton helped with his patron's mountainous correspondence, even writing to Mrs. Jackson. "The general is in very fine health, and just as good sperits. . . . He is constantly in motion to some Dinner party or other, and tonight stands engaged at a large Dancing party at Genl Browns."[22]

The anticipated tedium of these obligations was not altogether realized. Jackson, who always liked people about, enjoyed himself. For evening wear he ordered a "pr of Sup fine Blk mill'd cassimere Pantaloons," and had his dress coat spruced up with new silk-covered buttons. Nor was he oblivious to the fact that the hospitable attentions coming his way did no harm to the cause of a candidate. As his mind dwelled anew on the demonstrations that had attended his progress through Virginia, the vexatious features of that journey, as recounted to Mrs. Jackson, began to disappear. The General found time to give Jack Donelson a considerable account of a reception at Fredericksburg, to which was added this significant instruction: "Nothing from my pen is to appear in print, whatever may be used under other names—or as coming from a friend in Virginia. . . . Take care of Mrs. Jackson and attend to the little Andrews— Write me often and make known to me the amount of my cotton crop."[23]

As usual, Jackson's cotton brought satisfactory prices, the state of the market considered, twenty-seven bales being selected for export to France at a cent and a quarter a pound in excess of the highest New Orleans quotations.[24] Also, as usual, there were extraordinary demands on this income. From New Haven arrived a letter saying that the General's troublesome ward, Anthony Wayne Butler, a student at Yale, had neglected to honor a draft for one hundred and fifty dollars. Jackson forwarded one hundred dollars, reminding Anthony's creditors that this was all he had authorized them to advance the young man, but promising to see that the balance was paid.[25] From New Orleans came further light on the financial affairs of the widely distributed Butler family which Jackson had so long befriended. A draft of Robert Butler and Dr. William E. Butler for three thousand dollars was protested, and Jackson called upon as endorser to pay. He immediately directed the Nashville Bank to place one thousand and eight dollars to W. E. Butler's account, and advised his New Orleans brokers to advance another one thousand and eight dollars out of the proceeds of the cotton revenue.[26] Apparently the Butlers themselves scraped up the remaining nine hundred and eighty-four dollars.

5

General Jackson's appearance in the capital outmoded one form of electioneering hitherto used with considerable effect by partizans of Old Hickory. No longer could their broadsides proclaim:

"With the exception of this great man
The Hero of Orleans
ANDREW JACKSON
all the candidates have toiled through the winter at Washington seeking . . . to press themselves into favour. Why is not
JACKSON *there?*
"Because he has a soul that towers above intrigue. . . ."[27]

But now that the Hero was, indeed, "there," the only embarrassment fell upon his rivals who had cherished lingering hopes that something might occur to dissuade the Tennessean from making a finish fight of it. Senator Eaton, Sam Houston—a member of Congress—and others of the old Nashville junto were correspondingly elated, though they knew their work to be far from complete.

On the frontier Andrew Jackson had made his fame by methods that were uncompromising and direct. Now Old Hickory found himself on a stage which called for a modification of the border technique.

Major General Winfield Scott was in the city when Jackson arrived. General Scott's refusal to meet his military associate in a duel in 1817 had not ministered to that soldier's prestige in Army circles. When gossips ran to Scott with the tale that Jackson meant to challenge him again, Scott decided to do nothing to avoid a collision. On December 5, when Jackson presented his credentials to the presiding officer of the Senate, General Scott ranged the corridors of the Capitol in the hope that Jackson would see him.

For six days Scott frequented the Senate wing of the Capitol without encountering Jackson—a circumstance that suggests adroit management by friends of both parties. Then General Scott sent the Senator a note of restrained politeness soliciting a meeting on any terms that Jackson might elect. Old Hickory responded the same day suggesting that the meeting be "on friendly terms."[28] And so it was.

Meantime another little tableau had been unfolding in the Senate Chamber. Jackson took a seat on the floor, only to notice that the adjoining chair was occupied by Thomas Hart Benton. This was the nearest these gentlemen had been to each other since 1813, when Tom Benton's brother had fired into Andrew Jackson's body two bullets that nearly cost his life. Perceiving the situation, several senators offered to exchange places with Benton, but he declined. Jackson also refused the proffer of another seat—all this taking place without a sign of recognition passing between the old acquaintances.

A few days thereafter the junior Senator from Tennessee was appointed chairman of the Committee on Military Affairs and Senator Benton made a member of the same body. Without rising Jackson turned to him. "Colonel, we are on the same

committee; I will give you notice when it is necessary to attend."
"General," replied Benton, "make the time to suit yourself." As
a meeting of the committee broke up, Senator Benton exchanged
civilities with the chairman and asked about Mrs. Jackson's health.
In the old days Tom Benton had been a favorite of Aunt Rachel.
One afternoon the two senators found themselves face to face
in the drawing room of the Executive Mansion. Benton bowed
and Jackson held out his hand.[29]

From these signs Henry Clay concluded that Jackson had "resolved upon a general amnesty"—the benefits of which presently
were, indeed, offered to the Speaker himself. A number of
Tennessee congressmen, who maintained a "mess" at Mrs. Clax-
ton's boarding house on Capitol Hill, waited on the Kentuckian
with an invitation to a dinner at which Jackson had consented
to be present. Clay was not a man to harbor personal resent-
ments. He attended the dinner after which Jackson and Eaton
took him to his lodgings in their carriage. Later the General
gave a rather large dinner at which three competitors for the
presidency—Clay, Adams and Calhoun—honored his board.[30]

These events damaged the authority of the widely propagated
stories of Old Hickory's implacable hatreds and original ideas of
etiquette. "It will afford you great pleasure to know," John Henry
Eaton informed Rachel, "that all his old quarrels have been
settled. . . . The General . . . is in harmony and good understanding with everybody."[31]

6

Nor was Old Hickory blind to the effects of his reformed deportment. Of the reconciliation with Scott he wrote to a Tennessee
friend, "This has destroyed the stronghold . . . of those whose
minds were prepared to see me with a Tomahawk in one hand
and a scalping knife in the other."[32]

It was somewhat true. Representative Daniel Webster, supporting Adams without enthusiasm because really more attracted
to Calhoun, wrote his brother: "General Jackson's manners are
more presidential than those of any of the candidates. He is

grave, mild and reserved. My wife is decidedly for him."[33] Senator Elijah Hunt Mills of Massachusetts who had violently opposed Jackson on the Florida question, considering "him little advanced in civilization over the Indians with whom he made war," confessed to Mrs. Mills that "these opinions [were] unfounded. . . . He is exactly the man with whom *you* would be delighted."[34]

"I get on pretty well amidst the intrigue for the next presidency," Old Hickory himself admitted, "as I touch not, handle not of that unclean procedure[35] . . . I intermix with . . . [no] president makers . . . and should the choice of the people fall upon another it will give me no pain . . . [unless] the choice fell upon Wm H. C. . . . [which] would be a great curse to the nation."[36] Declining a social invitation from a Virginia friend the Senator wrote: "Your request to vissit Richmond cannot be complied with . . . [because] it . . . would be attributed to any thing than the real cause. . . . My course is to . . . take no step which may have imputed to it a disposition to recommend myself to anyone."[37]

Sam Houston complained that the General kept too close to his lodgings. "He has not yet been to the Rep's Hall,"[38] a chamber much in the eyes of the other aspirants, owing to the ultimate probability that the election would be decided by the Lower House. Nevertheless, for one so explicit in his professions of disinterestedness and so ostensibly withdrawn from the practical affairs of the campaign, General Jackson was able to sprinkle his private letters with some remarkably apt political comments. "Mr. Vanburen can not *manage* New York."[39] "A gentleman of N. Carolina of the first respectability . . . says if Pennsylvania declares for me N Carolina is certain."[40] "South Carolina, alab, Mississippi, Louisiana, Tennessee, Kentucky, ohio and Maryland will all come out in my favour."[41]

The effect was not lost on observant James Buchanan, a representative from Pennsylvania. "He is a real & not a nominal candidate."[42]

While the General's cultivation of the elect in Washington was repelling stories of his coarse manners, no effort was made in the country at large to diminish the Hero's appeal to the less exalted strata of society. In North Carolina General Polk was receiving reports from every county. One informant brought to light the advantage accruing to Jackson from the fact that so many voters could not read. "[Therefore] they are illy acquainted with the character and qualifications of the [other] candidates," scholarship not being a requisite to an appreciation of "the glorious exploits which have crowned the military career of Jackson."[43] Wrote another: "Printers may puff, office men may dogmatize, politicians may calculate, . . . but rely on it, the effectual voice of the people, now . . . scarcely recognized amidst the clamor will be uttered in favor of Andrew Jackson."[44]

Meantime the great and the near-great of the capital continued their courtship. Calhoun, Clay and Adams returned the Tennessean's hospitality, the Secretary of State pre-empting the most fitting of days—January 8—for a reception which was one of the winter's shining events. For a week Mrs. Adams had been preparing decorations of tissue paper and evergreens. Chalked on the floor were eagles, flags and a motto, "Welcome to the Hero of New Orleans." A thousand guests viewed the sight. "The ladies climbed on chairs and benches to see General Jackson," one who was present informed Dolly Madison. "Mrs. Adams very gracefully took his arm and walked through the apartments."[45]

After this the General assured Rachel that a forthcoming levee at the President's would terminate his social activities for the season.

7

Yet Jackson did not want for pleasurable company to lighten his few leisure hours. "The kind attention of my friend Eaton has been great, and to him I feel truly indebted for the comfortable quarters we occupy. . . . Mr Oneale's amiable wife and two daughters take every pains. . . . This family has been wealthy but by misfortune has been reduced to keeping a boarding house. . . . In the evening Mrs. Timberlake the maryed daughter whose

THE GENTLEMAN FROM TENNESSEE

This is probably the best of Ralph E. W. Earl's many portraits of General Jackson. The original, painted in 1835, is owned by Charles W. Frear of Troy, New York.

husband belongs to our Navy plays the piano delightfully, and every Sunday evening entertains her pious mother with sacred music. . . . Every Sunday we spend at church. on last Sunday I went to the Presbyterians, today a Baptist. . . . Mrs Timberlake has requested me to present you with her respects. . . . Accept of my prayers for your happiness and believe me your affectionate Husband."[46]

John Eaton was in truth a kindly man, to which Major O'Neale as well as General Jackson could testify because it was to Eaton that the Major owed the roof above his head. For more than twenty years William O'Neale had prospered as proprietor of the Franklin House, strategically situated midway between Washington and Georgetown. Sunning himself in the reflected renown of his patrons the host expanded into something of a personage about the capital. In this tavern house the O'Neales' six children were born. Friendly guests obtained West Point nominations for two of the boys, and the three girls were excessively pampered, children being a rarity in Washington in a day when few statesmen subjected their families to the discomforts of the unfinished city.

The eldest of these daughters was Margaret: a small, apple-cheeked brunette, vibrant, clever and strangely alluring. Before she was fifteen the trail of romances in her wake gave Peggy O'Neale a certain distinction. On her account the nephew of an Acting Secretary of the Navy had killed himself; two young army officers had passed a challenge to a duel; an elderly general was in a state of distraction; an elopement with a major had been forestalled only because, in climbing from a window, Peg overturned a flower-pot which awakened her father. This miscarriage of plans had afflicted Margaret with a broken heart from which she did not recover for a week. Next Peg was immured in a boarding school in New York City where a captain in our armed forces attracted the new pupil's favorable notice. A runaway marriage was agreed upon but, when the Captain made an awkward speech in returning a handkerchief his fiancée had dropped, the young lady decided that he was not the man of her choice.

One Sunday afternoon the following summer a tall, blond

Adonis from Virginia, named John B. Timberlake, caught sight of Miss O'Neale through a window of the Franklin House and announced to a chum his intention of making her acquaintance by six o'clock in the evening. He allowed himself more time than was necessary and by eleven had received Margaret's promise to marry him.[47] Peggy had frequently declared a brisk elopement to be, in her opinion, the most zestful approach to the delights of matrimony. But so enduring was her ardor for Mr. Timberlake, that she consented to wait for a month. The ceremony was performed in the tavern parlor by a Presbyterian minister of Georgetown, on July 18, 1816. The bride was sixteen. Though none of the bridegroom's family came, Major O'Neale was able to make quite an event of the wedding.

John Timberlake was a purser in the Navy, at the moment on furlough because of a discrepancy in his accounts. O'Neale set his son-in-law up as a merchant, an experience which cost the old gentleman fifteen thousand dollars. About this time Senator John Henry Eaton of Tennessee had appeared at the Franklin House—twenty-eight years old, wealthy and a widower. He opened his pocketbook to the hard-pressed landlord, pulled wires to send Timberlake to sea again, and by his amiable attentions sought to compensate Peggy for the loss of her husband's society. In this he succeeded so well that Mrs. Monroe sent a note desiring her not to attend the presidential receptions to which, as a naval officer's wife, she was eligible. "Mrs. Timberlake," a member of Congress from Virginia recorded, "was considered as a lady who would . . . dispense her favors wherever she took a fancy. . . . Eaton's connection with . . . [her] was notorious."[48]

When O'Neale failed in business Eaton took over the Franklin House, sold it to the Baltimore hotel owner, John Gadsby, and provided the O'Neales with a smaller property in which to begin anew. Meantime Timberlake had returned, again in bad odor with the Navy Department, for his bookkeeping had not improved. With these accounts still unsettled, Eaton posted a bond of ten thousand dollars and obtained a fresh berth for the purser on the frigate *Constitution* which weighed anchor for a cruise that was expected to last four years. The sailor departed on this voyage shortly after General Jackson, Senator Eaton and Congressman Richard K. Call established their abode at O'Neale's.

The three gentlemen took their meals in a private room and Peggy formed the habit of joining them to pour the coffee. Her talent for table talk charmed the General almost as much as the piety of her demeanor on Sundays. Another admirer was Call who associated more freely with his colleagues on Capitol Hill than did General Jackson and, in the barroom beneath the legislative chambers, heard Mrs. Timberlake's name used without reserve. This appeared to increase the emotional confusion which beset Captain Call, owing to the fact that a girl in Nashville whom he loved was under parental injunction not to correspond with her suitor. In any event one afternoon Call returned home in advance of his messmates and took Peg in his arms. It was necessary to emphasize her remonstrances with a fire-shovel before the puzzled young man left the room.

Tearfully Mrs. Timberlake complained to Jackson that she had been "grossly insulted." She could hardly have come to a more sympathetic person. Eaton's infatuation was too patent for disguise, but had not Jackson himself courted a woman mismated to another? Moreover Old Hickory knew from experience what gossip could make of such a state of affairs. Call admitted to Jackson the truth of Peg's accusation, offering as his excuse that "she was a woman of easy virtue and familiar with others," whom he named. Old Hickory was unconvinced. "I gave him a *severe lecture* for taking up such ideas of *female virtue* unless on some positive evidence of his own."[49]

The incident clouded the pleasant family intercourse Jackson had come to enjoy, for Peg did not again appear at the gentlemen's table.

8

The campaign's increasing complexity offered a diversion. William H. Crawford did not participate in the polite exchanges which marked the relations of the other four candidates. He had been removed from Virginia to his home in Washington where, despite the assurance of partizans, the Secretary of the Treasury remained a very sick man, shut up in a dark room and seen by almost no one. This was not, however, the only reason for Mr. Crawford's isolation. "Calhoun, Clay, Jackson & Adams have a perfect understanding," noted Congressman McDuffie. "[They are out] to give the Caucus a death blow. The explosion will blow up Mr. Crawford . . . & end his hopes forever."[50]

But should the coalition fail to give the caucus a mortal wound, the effects of the explosion would be more detrimental to the allies than to Mr. Crawford. Although his cause had declined since the middle of 1823, Crawford remained the strongest single candidate, since only the candidacy of Jackson, starting from scratch, had made measurable gains in that time. Moreover, the anti-caucus candidates were bolder in speech than in action. For all their impassioned war-cries—"Shall Congress or the People elect our President?"—the caucus was an old and respected institution. The record fails to confirm the implication that had Jackson, Adams, Clay or Calhoun been able to raise up the support in Congress enjoyed by Mr. Crawford, there would not have been so much high-minded indignation against the caucus.

At length the Jackson people made the first move. Glowing with the victory which had sent the General to the Senate, Jacksonians in the Tennessee Legislature adopted a resolution against the caucus mode of nomination in which they asked the assemblies of the other states to concur.

Georgia, Virginia and New York declined, as was expected of Crawford states. But elsewhere the result was disappointing. Ohio and North Carolina refused to act. South Carolina could not agree on a report. In Pennsylvania consideration was postponed indefinitely. Rhode Island laid the resolution on the table and Maine approved the caucus. Only Maryland and Alabama stood with Tennessee.

The Crawford managers had not been in better mood since their candidate's illness. Their contention—in the words of Eaton—that "he who was strongest before congress would assuredly be strongest before the nation"[51] seemed to possess an uncomfortable amount of logic. Mr. Crawford's competitors redoubled their efforts and their imprecations. The caucus was "undemocratic"; it was "unconstitutional"; it encouraged "bargain" and "intrigue"; it deprived the "sovereign people" of an "unalienable right" to something more than spear-bearing rôles in the selection of a president.

Four-fifths of the politicians and four-fifths of the newspapers of the United States thundering against the caucus made an impression. The practical object was to render that mode of nomination so unpopular that Crawford would drop it and take his chances before the country. But the sick man was not intimidated. He could not afford to be. He knew the caucus to be the best shot in his locker, his strength among congressmen being greater than his strength with the voters. On January 21, 1823, Andrew Jackson wrote: "A *caucus* is the last hope of the friends of Mr Crawford, and I have no doubt it will be attempted—with what success time will determine. But it appears to me that such is the feelings of the nation that . . . a congressional caucus would politically Damn any name put forth by it."[52]

The last sentence expressed a hope rather than a conviction, for Jackson men still toiled to avert the convocation of a caucus. They failed. A caucus was ordered, whereupon the opposition decided to boycott it. On the evening of February 14, 1824, lamps in the colonnaded Hall of Representatives were lighted. Anti-caucus members and their friends crowded the galleries, making a noisy show. The floor was reserved for caucus members who were slow to arrive. "Adjourn, adjourn," came the mocking cry from the gallery. An alarmed caucusite suggested a postponement, only to be opposed by Van Buren who knew it was now or never. When sixty-six gentlemen had put in an appearance, they went through the form of nominating Crawford for president and Albert Gallatin for vice president.[53]

Crawford had polled the votes of more than a fourth of the Republican membership of Congress, a figure no rival could have attained. But the Fabian tactics of the opposition made it a blow struck in the air. "The caucus," dispassionately observed Webster, "has hurt nobody but its friends. . . . Mr. Adams and General Jackson are likely to be the real competitors at last."[54]

9

These words of Webster seemed prophetic when four days after the caucus the battle-flag of John C. Calhoun fell in the dust.

This dénouement came with heart-breaking suddenness. Since the preliminary reverse in pivotal Pennsylvania, the energy Calhoun threw into the fight to hold his lines had served as an autohypnotic, restoring a measure of confidence to the Secretary and his followers. And not without reason. From Maine to Louisiana Calhoun was, in all but a few states, still second choice at least. No other aspirant could exhibit popularity so widely spread.

Pennsylvania was to hold a state convention on March 4. The state was aboil with town and county mass meetings shouting advice to the delegates. Almost without exception these gatherings favored Jackson. Calhoun pinned his faith on populous Philadelphia and on the management there of his capable friend George Mifflin Dallas.[55] On the evening of February 18 Mr. Dallas addressed a meeting of the ward leaders of the city. His partiality to Mr. Calhoun, he said, was well known, but the hour had come when "predelictions must be sacrificed: the cause of the nation . . . [is] at stake." The speaker introduced a resolution urging "all sound Democrats" to unite in favor of "a single illustrious individual . . . ANDREW JACKSON."[56]

This turned Washington upside down. "The movement at Philadelphia," wrote Mr. Calhoun, "was as unexpected to me as . . . to any of my friends. . . . Had Pen[a] decided favorably the prospect would have been most fair. Taking the U. S. together I never had a fairer prospect than on the day we lost the State." Though bitterly disappointed, the practical South Carolinian wasted no more ink on lamentations. The remainder of a six page letter dealt with proposals for clinching the vice presidency.[57]

Nominating Jackson with one dissenting vote, the Pennsylvania convention changed the complexion of the swiftly paced campaign. In North and South Carolina, in Maryland and New Jersey, the Calhoun organizations went over to Jackson virtually lock and stock, receiving in exchange second place for their man on the ticket. With Old Hickory thus clearly in the van, his lieutenants renewed their threats to Clay in Kentucky, Ohio, Illinois and Missouri, and licked their chops over Van Buren's discomfiture occasioned by a bill to transfer the selection of New York's electors from the Legislature to the people. New England felt the stir for Jackson. "I have no doubt," Old Hickory wrote William Berkeley Lewis, "if I was to travel to Boston where I have been invited that would insure my election— But this I cannot do— I would feel degraded the balance of my life."[58]

10

The persistent anxiety as to how Rachel would react to triumphs which her husband knew she did not desire wore on the conscience of the prospering candidate. His long letters to her contained little of politics. "My love, remember that you have promised me that you would bear up in my absence— recollect that your health much depend upon your keeping your mind calm & at ease." He tried to see that she was never alone. "I am grateful to your nieces for staying with you, present me affectionately to them."[59] While awaiting the decisive word from Pennsylvania, he "rejoiced" to learn from Jack Donelson that she "keeps up" her "spirits." "I have always wished my name had not been brought before the nation. . . . I am tired of this place and will leave it as soon as I can." Before the letter went into the post the news came from Harrisburg. In a post-script the impulses of a candidate superseded those of a solicitous husband. "This will carry the South and West." Would Donelson relay the tidings to the Nashville editors "without giving my name?"[60]

The Pennsylvania victory and consequent demotion of Mr. Calhoun's ambitions assumed the nature of birthday gifts to Andrew Jackson, who on March 15 entered his fifty-eighth year. "I had," he wrote to Rachel, "a few friends to dine"—about twenty, as appears, including Messrs. Adams, Clay and Calhoun.

On the morrow these gentlemen met again, with a great many others, to honor General Jackson on the occasion of the last public ceremonial that was to draw him from O'Neale's during his sojourn in Washington. "This morning at 11 I was requested to attend Mr Monroe to receive the medle voted me by Congress on the 27th Fbry 1815." The delay of this presentation had been occasioned in part by the General's tardiness in furnishing a portrait to guide the artist who fashioned the token. "You are aware how disagreeable to me these shows, and I performed it not without a tremor which always seises me on such occasions."

Yet the old soldier was deeply moved. "Tell my son how anxious I am that . . . he may become the [worthy] possessor of those things that a grateful country has bestowed upon his papa— Tell him . . . [to] read & learn his Book . . . [because] his happiness thro life depends upon his procuring an education now; & . . . on all occasions to adhere to truth. . . . Never to make a promise unless on due consideration, and when made to be sure to comply with it. . . . Having experienced so much inconvenience from the want of a perfect education myself makes me so solicitious. . . . I would to god I could now leave the city. . . . Present me to all friends & neighbors & believe me to be your affectionate Husband."[61]

II

To gain votes, others might consume hours with fancy disquisitions on Jeffersonism, the tariff and internal improvements, or wear themselves thin contriving political combinations while, as John Quincy Adams observed, about all the Jackson people had to do was to shout "8th of January and battle of New Orleans." The New Englander had foreseen something like this. At a time when no other rival pretended to consider the General seriously, Adams surprised a friend by saying that he regarded Jackson as a formidable candidate and a deserving one. If elected, he said the General would govern honestly and ably, which was more than could be expected of Crawford, Calhoun or Clay, though of the three he preferred Clay. Calhoun's "underhand course" was the object of especial resentment.[63]

Mr. Adams's distrust of Calhoun became more rankling when the Secretary of War hitched his vice-presidential ambitions to the Adams candidacy in New England. In the East Adams did not need the alert South Carolinian's help, and in the West, where he did need it, Calhoun was running under the Jackson colors. Presumably Adams knew that Jackson's high regard for Calhoun arose from the belief that he had supported the Florida invasion. The Secretary of State's idea of honor saved his colleague from exposure, but this was as far as he intended his aid and comfort should go. Adams told his lieutenants that another man must be found for the vice-presidency on his ticket.

But what man? Andrew Jackson, blandly replied the Secretary of State. Old Hickory's character would lend a desirable lustre to the vice-presidential office and "afford an easy and dignified retirement for his old age."[64] No one seems to have raised the point that Jackson was the New Englander's senior by one hundred and eighteen days. Moreover, drolly continued the Secretary of State, "the Vice-Presidency . . . [is] a station in which the General could hang no one."[65]

Under this proposed arrangement, a question of some moment was whether Jackson would accept the lesser honor; but the Secretary seemed at ease.[66] So a slogan was coined:

"John Quincy Adams
Who can write,
Andrew Jackson
Who can fight."[67]

12

During all this while Congress was transacting business, though not a great deal of it. No senator, however, was more dutiful in his attendance than Andrew Jackson, and none stood less in the way of his fellow statesmen seeking to distinguish themselves in debate. In six months General Jackson took the floor only four times and altogether spoke less than twenty minutes: once to recommend a New Orleans veteran for a pension; twice to urge the construction of roads of military value; once to support a bill for the purchase of armament for fortifications. He voted, however, on every important division, consistently supporting internal-improvement legislation. Though unpopular with his supporters in the deep South, the only explanation Senator Jackson vouchsafed concerned the necessity of the projects for national defense.

The great issue was the tariff. Since January the lawmakers had been considering a bill which on March 31, 1824, Henry Clay espoused in the greatest protectionist speech in American history. The bill sought to erect a high-duty system in imitation of that of Great Britain, but this did not prevent Clay from christening it "the American System" and branding almost anything to the contrary a "foreign policy." Much that was native to Mr. Clay's character adorned that address: a warm and brilliant imagination, fervid felicity of phrase, shallow but showy research, half-knowledge dexterously disguised. Yet the effort constitutes a model for protectionist orators to this day.[68]

Daniel Webster answered the speaker. Here, too, was an indolent man, given to late hours and gay tavern company. But methodically he disclosed the historical and economic unsoundness of Mr. Clay's contentions.

Yet the American System carried the day in the House by five votes and came up to the Senate.

At this moment the Jacksonians were striving to complete their conquest of Calhoun's following in North Carolina. The situation prompted Dr. Littleton H. Coleman of Warrenton to suggest that a dig at the tariff from Jackson would assist his cause. The same post conveyed a similar expression from Colonel Arthur P. Hayne, now a planter in Alabama. "Manufacturing establishments I look upon as a *curse* to the country."[69]

To Coleman, Jackson replied:

"So far as the Tariff before us embraces the design of fostering, protecting, and preserving within ourselves the means of national defense . . . I support it. . . . Providence has filled our mountains and our plains with . . . lead, iron and copper, and given us a climate and soil for growing hemp and wool. These being the grand materials of our national defense, they ought to have extended to them . . . protection, that our manufacturers and laborers may . . . produce within our own borders a supply . . . essential to war. . . .

"This . . . judicious . . . Tariff . . . possesses more fanciful than real dangers. . . . Where has the American farmer a market for his surplus products? Except for cotton he has neither a foreign nor a home market. Does this not clearly prove . . . that there is too much labor employed in agriculture? common sense points . . . the remedy. Draw from agriculture the superabundant labor, employ it in . . . manufacturers, thereby creating a home market for your breadstuffs. . . .

"Believing . . . my opinions . . . correct . . . I would not barter them for any office that could be given me."[70]

The publication of this challenging declaration caused a stir. Friends of the legislation seized so ardently upon the words "judicious tariff" that Henry Clay felt a twinge of jealousy. "Well, by ——, I am in favor of an *in*judicious tariff!"[71]

Jackson having declared himself on the tariff in the Grass Hat Letters eighteen months before, the really significant passage in the Coleman letter occurred in an aside which seemed to escape notice. "I am one of those who do not believe a national debt is a national blessing . . . as it is calculated to raise around the administration a moneyed aristocracy dangerous to the liberties of the country." This was a break from the past. The man of property, ever identified with the moneyed aristocracy in the West, had been raised on the shoulders of a resentful and impoverished populace to an eminence which overlooked exhilarating vistas. Something within Andrew Jackson responded to this allegiance— something not assignable to opportunism or to egocentric ambition. By degrees he was drifting into an acceptance of the protestations of these lowly supporters who claimed Old Hickory for their own. A member of the Tennessee Legislature had explained Jackson's election as senator in these words: "The commonality . . . thought him the only man . . . [to] revise what they thought a corrupt system of government, Meaning the caucus—the treasury and Bank influences."[72]

This appears to be the earliest mention of the Bank of the United States as one of the dragons Andrew Jackson was expected to slay.

13

The interminable tariff discussion wearied the junior Senator from Tennessee.

"My Dear wife, . . my heart bleeds when I read of the pain that our separation has cost you.[73] . . . I always believed I never was designed for a Legislator— I am sure I was not in the days like these whilst others are endeavoring by Log rolling . . . to defeat the Tariff Bill. . . . I shall leave here as soon as this Bill is acted on; before I cannot."[74]

"I have recd many letters on this subject . . . but I cannot be intimidated from doing that which my . . . conscience tells me is right. . . . I will vote for the Bill."[75]

It passed the Senate and a wave of angry protest welled up from the South infusing new life into the languishing campaign of the Secretary of the Treasury. "The best judges believe," a visitor from Nashville warned John Overton, "that the stand taken by the Genl . . . will give S. C. to Crawford."[76] The Georgian risked his life to take advantage of the first favorable turn of his political fortunes in more than a year. Summoning a carriage he quit his darkened room and, propped against pillows, showed himself in the streets of the capital. He attended cabinet meetings and visited the corridors of the all-important House of Representatives, led like a blind man.[77]

Another circumstance gave Mr. Crawford an unexpected lift at Jackson's expense. The Tennessean had endeavored to obtain the ministry to Mexico for the friend and protector of his boyhood, Colonel John Stokes of Salisbury, but the post went to a Calhoun worker, Ninian Edwards of Illinois. En route to assume his diplomatic duties, Edwards published charges accusing Crawford of official corruption, and forthwith was shuttled back to Washington to prove them. Edwards later declared that friends of Jackson had promised to support him. The glee with which certain Jacksonians received the new thrust at Crawford lends color to the assumption. But Jackson himself had nothing to do with this. "If an impeachment should be preferred against Mr Crawford I would not sit upon his trial and will object to it."[78] A committee of the House dominated by anti-Crawford men delved into Edwards's accusations and submitted a report vindicating the Secretary.

Crawford scored again with the publication of the Jackson-Monroe correspondence of 1816. It will be remembered that William B. Lewis had won over the ex-Federalist Polk of North Carolina, with one of those letters, in which Jackson had urged Monroe to place a Federalist in his Cabinet. Polk, or someone, talked too much about the General's advice to Monroe, and all winter long the Crawford press had printed innuendoes assailing Jackson's record as a Republican. With the recrudescence of Crawford's drooping hopes in the spring, the editors grew bolder, and to clear the record Eaton was forced to publish the correspondence. This caused quite a commotion. Many good Republicans were dumbfounded that the Hero could have soiled paper with a considerate word for a Federalist. Nor were Federalists pleased to read that had the Hartford Convention been held within General Jackson's military jurisdiction he would have hanged the leaders.[79]

In May, 1824, a Cumberland planter visiting in Washington sent John Overton a disturbing account of Jackson's prospects. "I think his strength is [giving] out. . . . Crd is undoubtedly the strongest man."[80] Daniel Webster surveyed the field with satisfaction. "Jackson's interest is evidently on the *wane*."[81]

With storms from every quarter swirling about his head, Old Hickory retracted nothing. To a criticism of his tariff vote, he flung back that he would not change it to place himself "in the Presidential chair."[82] The old warrior seemed content for the first time since he had become a senator. Another battle was behind him, and General Jackson did not tarry to witness the polysyllabic demise of Congress. The last week in May, 1824, saw him off through the young Virginia summer toward home and Rachel in too great haste for wayside hospitality. "I hope in god we will never be separated again until death parts us. . . . May Jehovah Take you in his holy keeping is the prayer of your affectionate Husband."[83]

CHAPTER IV

The Election

I

Senator John Henry Eaton, who had scarcely permitted Jackson out of his sight since leaving Tennessee six months before, made his preparations to bear the General company on his return to Nashville. Eaton hoped to dissuade the candidate from his impractical resolution to decline invitations enroute. A little electioneering in Ohio, where a well-articulated Clay campaign was being pressed with vigor,[1] would be especially useful. It seemed that the thing could be arranged with a degree of naïveté sufficient to overcome the General's scruples. Merely for Old Hickory to show himself at a militia muster or a veterans' barbecue might spell the difference between winning the state or losing it. And Ohio would cast sixteen electoral votes.

These were the concerns uppermost in the mind of the senior Senator from Tennessee when, during one of the concluding sessions in the Upper Chamber, a pink envelope addressed in the flowing script of Margaret Timberlake was laid on Major Eaton's desk. The Senator scanned its contents and left the hall. At O'Neale's that evening Jackson found Peggy's eyes red from weeping and Eaton also visibly disturbed. As to the cause Eaton offered no explanation but later told his friend that he would be detained in Washington until after the adjournment.[2] So Jackson departed for the West attended by Congressman Richard K. Call. There were few stop-overs on the way for, like his patron, Captain Call felt a powerful attraction drawing him toward the graceful curves of the Cumberland.

Nashville first had known Dick Call at the close of the New Orleans campaign as a presentable aide-de-camp to General Jackson. He fell in love with Mary Kirkman. Though conceding her daughter's admirer to be "a splendid man, morally and physically," Mrs. Kirkman forbade the suit through a sense of loyalty to the memory of her late husband, Call being a protégé of Jackson and Thomas Kirkman having quarreled with Jackson over a speculation in Indian lands.[3] Old Hickory advised the young couple to elope or forget each other at once, adding that in case they wished to elope the Hermitage was at their disposal.[4] They did not elope and four years of separation failed to bring forgetfulness—if the episode with Mrs. Timberlake can be classified as a momentary aberration.

In mid-June, 1824, the travelers reached Nashville. When General Jackson failed to obtain Mrs. Kirkman's blessing upon the proposed match, his own sufficed and the marriage was performed by Dr. A. D. Campbell of Hermitage Church.[5] This little brick edifice, dedicated to the Presbyterian faith, had been completed during Jackson's absence. Mrs. Kirkman vowed to cut off her daughter without a penny and, bundling up copies of the letters that had passed between her and General Jackson when he was trying to win her consent to the marriage, she placed a ten dollar note on top of the pile and dispatched the whole to the editor of the *National Gazette,* Mr. Crawford's organ in Washington.[6]

The threat of disinheritance moved Jackson to another effort to soften the old lady's heart. Ellen Kirkman was perhaps the wealthiest woman in Tennessee. Her business interests extended from Philadelphia to New Orleans. Yet she lived upstairs over the hardware store at the corner of Cedar Street and the Square which her husband had founded upon their arrival in the West from Ireland.

Old Hickory climbed the steps to this abode.

"General Jackson, what are you doing in my house?" Mrs. Kirkman asked.

"I came to see you about Mrs. Call's property," replied the visitor in a pleasant tone.

"General Jackson, get out of my house," said Mrs. Kirkman. She spoke with a clipped Old Country accent.

"Not until I have had my say," parried Jackson.

From a drawer Mrs. Kirkman produced a large pistol, which she cocked and leveled at her caller.

"General Jackson, get out of my house."

For a moment Pakenham's conqueror looked her in the eyes. They were as blue and as steady as his.

"As you are a woman I will go," he said. "But if you were a man I would not."[7]

2

The *National Gazette* failed to publish Mrs. Kirkman's contribution in support of the hypothesis that a successful matchmaker might not necessarily embody the qualities required of a successful Chief Magistrate. The editor of this Crawford journal viewed with more favor, however, a literary production of Jesse Benton, and admitted it to his columns. Jesse Benton still resided in Tennessee. When his brother, the Senator from Missouri, took the hand of Andrew Jackson in friendship, a sense of humiliation moved Jesse to write thirty-four pages describing the General as bloodthirsty, dishonest and incompetent; a "mediocre politician," a cock-fighter, horse-racer, gambler, brawler and participant in shady land deals; a military chieftain whose renown rested on the deeds of subordinates.[8]

The appearance of this feuilleton sent the quills of John Henry Eaton and Andrew Jackson Donelson driving to establish that, detail for detail, the exact antithesis of Mr. Benton's portrait should be accepted as the true likeness.

This conscious effort to bring the campaign to an ideological plane, accessible to citizens who might fail to grasp the subtleties of opposed schools of thought on the tariff, worked no injury to General Jackson. Every slur on the name of the Hero seemed to raise up new defenders. An item of political sharp practice on the part of the General's adversaries was a sin against public morality and a poisoned spear pointed at popular rights. Similar practice on the part of the General's friends was a blow struck in the interest of virtue imperiled, or at worst an example of the end excusing the means.

The enforced consolidation of the Calhoun and Jackson interests had Crawford definitely on the defensive in North Carolina. In vain did the Secretary of the Treasury's supporters cry out that the "People's Ticket," the Jacksonian vehicle in that state, was a misnomer made up in an irregular way by a secret committee whose attachment to the shouting populace was of recent origin and questionable sincerity. "It is very difficult," one confessed, "to electioneer successfully against Genl Jackson— his character and his services are of the kind which *alone* the people can appreciate and feel— one cup of *generous whiskey* produces more military ardor than can be allayed in a month of reflection and sober reason."[9]

No vagary of a hurried pen should be blamed for the fact that this tribute from an adversary included Andrew Jackson's "character" among the rocks against which the opposition blunted its lances.

Whatever the flaws in the character of Jackson, vacillation, untrustworthiness and disloyalty were not among them. He deserved the reputation he bore for standing by those who stood by him. Only the public welfare, as he saw it, took precedence over the needs of a friend, and Jackson's normal impulse was to consider the two as coextensive. In matters upon which much depended, a sense of differentiation usually came to the rescue, however—the recent tariff controversy in Congress being a conspicuous example.

Less conspicuous, but not less notable, was the conduct of Senator Jackson on the subject of pensions. "Old soldiers in arms, hearing I have turned politician," he wrote during the late session, flooded his mail with "their long standing & almost obsolete claims."[10] Jackson answered each letter and examined each claim, only one of which did he present to the Senate. It is difficult to see how his attitude toward this tempting subject could have exhibited a higher degree of integrity.

Yet, where many another man would have been ruined, Jackson's prestige suffered little. A phenomenon was rising with which

American politicians were to wrestle for fifteen years to come, exclaiming in an apostrophe of impotent despair:

"General Jackson's popularity can stand anything!"[11]

Already a legend was in the making as the masses displayed their unruly determination to accept the infallibilty of the Hero. Primitive courage and a gift of leadership which animated followers to deeds beyond their strength, in truth, made it, in the words of the vexed North Carolinian, "difficult to electioneer successfully against Genl Jackson."

3

The recrudescence of Crawford hopes stimulated by early reactions to Jackson's tariff and internal improvement votes was transitory. The strain of personal leadership proved too much for the vitiated strength of the convalescent standard-bearer and, seven weeks after his resolute sally from the sick-room, Mr. Crawford collapsed again.

Hidden away in Virginia[12] where the most important of his political lieutenants failed to obtain dependable information of his condition, the afflicted candidate once more was the vortex of a hundred rumors. Those emanating from opposing political camps were ominous. "Mr. Crawford is *sick—very sick*," Webster wrote his brother. "In event of Mr. C's death (which I anticipate), Mr. Adams will be chosen by the *People* & by a great vote."[13] One Jackson supporter cheered another with these tidings: "A proposition to withdraw his name . . . would, I understand, have been made to Mr C——d by his friends before this—but for the *peculiar* and *unfortunate situation of his mind!!*"[14]

Martin Van Buren, bearing now the heaviest burden of the Crawford campaign, did not, could not, yield to the counsels of despair. His personal prestige and the complicated political organism in New York by which he maintained himself in public life were at stake. Needing a presidential candidate who would be an asset in his struggle to overcome the revolt against his dictatorship at home, the eminently practical sachem from the banks

of the Hudson found himself saddled with a liability. But there
was no turning back now. Anxiously he wrote to his confidential
friends Messrs. Gales and Seaton, publishers of the *National Intelligencer,* for an account of the "real state of Mr Crawfords
health." The reply was not reassuring. "Every function of his
body was impaired unless perhaps his hearing."[15]

Van Buren was able to circumvent the popular demand to
deprive the Legislature of its antiquated right to choose presidential electors only to behold unmistakable signs among the
personnel of that body, soon up for re-election, of a drift from
Crawford, who in a general plebiscite probably would have stood
last among the presidential aspirants. Turning their eyes upon
this scene of Mr. Van Buren's discomfiture, Mr. Clay and especially Mr. Adams felt a renewal of their hopes. In other quarters,
however, these gentlemen perceived little for which to congratulate themselves.

Mr. Adams's extraordinary formula for effacing Jackson as
Jackson had effaced Calhoun with an offer of the vice-presidency
came to naught. The cases were dissimilar. In the West and the
South Mr. Calhoun had accepted second place on the Jackson
ticket because his defeat in Pennsylvania made higher aspirations hopeless. Not even the wave of criticism following his
refusal to compromise on the issues before the Senate reduced
Jackson's campaign to that extremity, and the General's clever
managers turned the Adams proposal into an endorsement of
their chief in New England. Certainly, they told Mr. Adams,
General Jackson would accept with pleasure the vice-presidential
designation at the hands of Adams's eastern friends. But a withdrawal from the presidential lists elsewhere was a manifest impossibility. Jackson himself dropped his reserve to assure an
eastern supporter that "the friends of Mr. Adams when they
assert that I have 'abandoned the field in his favour' . . . are
guilty of the grossest misrepresentation."[16]

Adams was politician enough to know who would reap the
advantage of having Jackson a vice-presidential candidate in New
England and a presidential candidate in the rest of the country.
Consequently nothing more was done to disturb John C. Cal-

houn in the enjoyment of his reward as a virtually unopposed
nominee for the second office.

In the mind of the ambitious South Carolinian this was a paltry
prize, and the enjoyment thereof correspondingly meager. A
friend described him as encompassed by gloom.[17] Indeed, the
only speculation left to a driving intellect never to know the
restorative powers of relaxation was whether the Calhoun star
would fare better hitched to the wagon of Andrew Jackson or
to that of John Quincy Adams. A Crawford journal in Washington surmised that he preferred Adams because a South Carolinian would stand a better chance of succeeding a northern man.[18]
Another potential source of embarrassment in event of Jackson's
election lay in the danger of disclosure of Calhoun's equivocal
conduct in the Florida "war." When Mr. Calhoun's political
situation rendered superfluous the expense of a personal organ
in the national capital, his Washington *Republican* merged with
Adams's *National Journal* which thereafter spoke in the interest
of both candidates. With a foot in each camp the unhappy suitor
for the vice presidency appeared circumspectly neutral, though a
letter to his mother-in-law, a strong minded personage who spent
much time under the Calhoun roof, referred to General Jackson
without enthusiasm as "your candidate."[19]

4

Thus the campaign thundered into its final phase with every
principal, excepting Jackson, beset by fresh anxieties. The flurry
of disapproval over Jackson's tariff and internal improvement
votes had amounted to nothing. In parts of the country where
his stand ministered to local popularity, it was served up as campaign fodder. Elsewhere pyrotechnics in honor of a military conqueror diverted the spirit of objective inquiry. "[He] has slain
the Indians & flogged the British & . . . therefore is the . . .
wisest & greatest man in the nation."[20] How could a tariff orator
expect to hold an audience against a rival who simply started
the bung in a barrel of whisky and invited his auditors to step

up and toast "Old Hickory, last of the Revolutionary patriots" whose "history is ... the record of his country's glory?"[21] The cordiality of some of the responses indicates the effect of this mode of appeal to the judgment of the electorate: "May the SKINS of the enemies of Jackson be converted into a CARPET-ING for his friends to dance on."[22]

What other aspirant could display his qualifications as succinctly as this:

"Under Washington our independence was achieved; under Jackson our independence has been preserved ...
"WASHINGTON, LAFAYETTE, and JACKSON,
"Brandywine, Yorktown and New Orleans."[23]

An epidemic of "straw" voting spread among mass meetings, militia musters and even grand juries. "He is a favorite of the people; he belongs to them; he has been raised with them; he has served them both in peace and war; they feel grateful."[24] This from a resolution by a North Carolina grand jury is notable only for the chaste tone of its language.

A sentiment often heard in the United States found its way across the ocean to the dinner table of an English baronet where someone remarked that Jackson's imperious temper would imperil Anglo-American relations. After Washington Irving had undertaken a defense of his countryman, Colonel William Thornton, late of His Majesty's Eighty-Fifth Regiment, asked permission to say a word. "Had ... Jackson not used the power confided to him in the high handed way alluded to, New Orleans would infallibly have been captured. As to the charge of implacable hostility, . . Genl. Jackson . . . [was] peculiarly courteous and humane."[25]

Alarm at the momentum of the sweep for Andrew Jackson betrayed opposing politicians into other incautious expressions. Said a Louisville newspaper reporting a militia muster in Ohio at which Jackson bested Clay in a test vote: "The Rowdies, ... the very dregs of the community" won the day. "Can anything be more vexingly provoking?"[26] A commentary from North Caro-

lina, across the mountains: "In almost every Captain's company
the drums were beating and fifes whistling for the hero of New
Orleans. The officers would treat the men, . . . and then raise the
war whoop for General Jackson. Then the poor, staggering . . .
creatures would sally forth to vote. The result was always in
favor of Jackson."[27]

While the amount of liquor they could stow away at a muster
should have made American militiamen heroes by Lord Nelson's
definition, this was not in itself conclusive evidence that they
sprang from the dregs of society. To assert as much fell short
of an approach sufficiently tactful to woo their allegiance from
Old Hickory.

5

Autumn saw Jackson leading the field and gaining. Flushed
with confidence his supporters proclaimed that no other candidate had a chance for a victory at the polls, thus obviating a
"run-off" election by the House of Representatives. Publicly the
rival managers disputed this heartily, exhibiting columns of figures
to support their contentions; privately most of them seemed reconciled to a House election as the best they could hope for. The
vital concern of every politician was that his man should stand
among the first three candidates and so be eligible to go on the
ballot. This had been Clay's strategy almost from the first.

The Crawford-Van Buren cause was desperate. In mid-Sep-
tember the Secretary of the Treasury was carried back across the
Potomac, his "recovery" proclaimed and the candidate himself
placed on public exhibition to establish that he could, indeed,
walk across a room, converse understandably and laboriously
write his name on official papers. A less shrewd man than Martin
Van Buren would have known that without an alliance the game
was lost.

But to whom to turn? Before adversity waylaid his fortunes,
William H. Crawford had carried on with hand so high as to
excommunicate himself politically. Obviously no rapprochement
with the exultant Jackson following was possible. Adams's sprout-

ing hope of taking New York from Crawford barred the road to compromise with the New Englander. Clay, then, it must be; and Clay it was. Senator Van Buren threw all the persuasiveness of his subtle nature into a communication which, taken first and last, may be unique in the body of literature concerning contests for the presidency.

When revised and recopied, this letter filled seven pages and was dispatched to Benjamin Ruggles, a Clay lieutenant of St. Clairsville, Ohio.

Mr. Van Buren proposed a coalition of "men who ought never to have been separated & whose union is natural." With the Jackson victory in Pennsylvania, all chance of Mr. Clay's getting his name before the House was gone. But with Ohio and Kentucky Crawford could be elected "by the people." So argued Mr. Van Buren. If Clay were ever to support Mr. Crawford let him do it now. In exchange for this service would not the vice presidency appeal to the Speaker as a convenient stepping stone? The Kentuckian's friends should consider his future. The triumph of either Adams or Jackson would be injurious. But the union of Crawford and Clay "would constitute" a great new national party, "like . . . the old Republican Party, . . & such an one as I would be willing to stand or fall with." Let the minds of Mr. Clay's friends dwell on the choice of prospects that confronted them: their man eclipsed by the victory of Adams or Jackson, or their man serene in the vice presidency, leading "a powerful party" capable of crushing opposition to his advancement. And in conclusion the broadest hint of all: would not Henry Clay in the second office "relieve them [the Speaker's friends] from much of their apprehension on the score of Mr Crawfords health?"[28]

Not the least important facet of the situation which this letter ignored was the circumstance that Mr. Crawford already had a vice-presidential running mate, duly nominated by the caucus. But Albert Gallatin's distinguished services to his country belonged to a generation swiftly being shouldered into the shadows. His name had not brought the strength to the Crawford ticket that had been anticipated. Mr. Gallatin simplified matters by withdrawing, at the same time privately advising Van

Buren against "negotiation with Mr Clay for the office of V. President. . . . It would only increase that gentleman's hope of success for the first office."[29]

Crawford himself failed to warm to the suggested bargain, and feebly expressed the hope that Clay would decline.[30] Yet Van Buren held to his course and was momentarily cheered by the significant support of Thomas Hart Benton. What poor, prostrated Crawford might hope counted for little now. The question was, Will Clay take the bait? Benton dangled this before him in its most enticing light: a certain door to the presidency. But the sick man had his wish. For Clay declined.[31]

After this, all that remained to Van Buren was the tenuous hope that should Crawford's name go to the House at all, he might slip in through a deadlock of the forces of Jackson and Adams.

To the end of the canvass, however, the shattered Crawford following continued its courtship of Clay, while its shrill attacks on the other candidates approached hysteria. An example of Mr. Adams's unfitness was construed from the allegation that he had endorsed the note of Mrs. Moulton, a milliner of Washington, and upon her default sought to avoid payment.[32] The Raleigh *Register's* concluding summary of General Jackson's career had the merit of brevity. "A disgusting detail of squabbling and quarreling—of pistolings dirkings & brickbattings and other actions reconciliable neither to regulations nor morals."[33]

Seven days before North Carolina voted, the same spirited journal lashed out again, and on this occasion established a dark and fruitful precedent. Clandestine whispers there had been, but, as far as can be discovered, this was the first time the innuendo that laid John Dickinson in his grave found its tortuous way to the printed page.

"I make a solemn appeal to the reflecting part of the community, and beg of them to think and ponder well before they place their tickets in the box, how they can justify it to themselves and posterity to place such a woman as Mrs. Jackson! at the head of the female society of the U. States."[34]

6

During the last weeks before the balloting began, General Jackson visited Melton's Bluff to make arrangements for the marketing of his Alabama cotton—an important detail, as the winter in Washington had been costly and the absentee planter was pressed for funds. Yet he found time to bestow on the trying task of managing the property of his ward, Andrew Jackson Hutchings, and to supervise the boy's schooling, along with that of Andrew, junior, and Lincoyer, the young Indian. He also found some time for politics, though remaining to the end the least active of the candidates, not excepting the crippled Crawford.

He seemed to believe, however, that he would win, this being a fixed attribute of the Jacksonian character. Men (or horses) might fail *him*. The failure of means to an end on which he had set his heart was likewise possible. But a concept of failure as something indigenous to himself did not belong to the psychology of Old Hickory. *He* could do what he willed to do.

Yet, this fierce will had not wholly claimed the presidency as its perquisite. Moments of frank elation over a local victory were succeeded by moments of regret that he had allowed himself to be drawn into the contest at all. In Alabama, Jackson smoked his pipe on the porch with John Coffee to whom he could open his heart as to few men. Of the peace of that domestic scene the troubled traveler carried away a touching remembrance. "How much your situation are to be envied and how prudent you have been to keep yourself free of political life, surrounded as you are by your lovely children, and amiable wife, you ought not to abandon it for anything on earth— The man in office greeted with smiles and apparent friendship, his confidence often sought to be betrayed; surrounded thus, where a man must be always guarded, happiness cannot exist."[35]

7

By an act of Congress the twenty-four states had from October 27 until December 1 to select presidential electors. Ohio and

Pennsylvania, where the choice was made by general election, acted first on October 29. Leisurely Louisiana and South Carolina, whose legislatures performed this duty, concluded the procession on November 22. As ballots were counted post riders, river steamers, coastwise vessels, indeed every traveler, bore the news piecemeal, to and fro. Not until mid-December, however, was the final result known in Washington.

Yet, from the moment of the receipt of the first fragmentary returns from Ohio and Pennsylvania, Jackson led the race and dominated every speculation concerning it. In Ohio Clay had waged a strenuous campaign, for victory there was indispensable to his hopes. The early news of the result placed Jackson so far ahead that many neutral and some opposition newspapers conceded the State to him. From Pennsylvania came word that Old Hickory was smothering his rivals under a majority of three to one.

Tennessee voted early in November and, with the slow count showing Old Hickory ahead by thirty to one, Senator Jackson, Rachel, Jack Donelson and his young wife Emily took their places in the morocco-lined carriage of Florida remembrance and, drawn by four horses, were on the long red road to Washington. The sight of this costly equipage moved a few unfriendly editors to comment on the insincerity of the candidate's democratic pretentions.[36] The fact is that the carriage was taken for the comfort of Mrs. Jackson whom the General, twelve months before, had determined to bring to Washington for companionship should he be obliged to make the pilgrimage again.[37]

Kentucky received the travelers warmly, staunch supporters of Henry Clay crowding around to shake Jackson's hand and to assure him of their allegiance in event the Speaker should be eliminated from the expected contest in the House. "Stick to Old Hickory— Give us a Western President."[38] Mr. Clay's elimination seemed more than likely. Kentucky's ballot boxes being opened as Jackson passed through, the result in Louisville (Clay, three hundred and eighty-seven; Jackson, seven hundred and forty-three) provided a surprise which sent expresses drumming the autumn highways in every direction. In the country at large the

Louisville vote gave rise to an assumption that the Speaker might lose his own state.[39]

Then came tidings that Missouri, which Benton had counted in advance for Clay, was safe for Jackson.[40] With Missouri and Ohio in the Jackson column, the Speaker would be out of it, regardless of Kentucky.

His bags packed for Washington, Mr. Clay rode from his beautiful country seat to nearby Lexington and, unruffled by disappointment, begged his friends not to distress themselves whatever the issue of the election might be. He spoke well of General Jackson and was understood to say that he had written to solicit his company on the journey to Washington, but, having received no reply, had "given him out."[41] Yet, when state Senator Thomas Carneal announced that should Mr. Clay be excluded from consideration by the House he would introduce in the Legislature a resolution instructing the Kentucky delegation to vote for Jackson, Mr. Clay asked him not to do so. He said it would be best if the members remained uncommitted. Mr. Carneal promised not to put forward such a resolution, but, if introduced by another, he said he would vote for it because next to Clay Jackson was clearly Kentucky's choice.[42]

A few days after the Speaker had set out for the national capital, General Jackson arrived in Lexington and a respectable company of Mr. Clay's neighbors organized a ball in his honor.

John Quincy Adams's election news, though more encouraging than Mr. Clay's, also left much to be desired. The Secretary of State had New England's fifty-two votes as a matter of course, and he stood a good chance of getting the lion's share of the thirty-six from New York where Van Buren fought with his back to the wall. But Jackson won New Jersey and was leading in Maryland. On top of this the reports of his alarming pluralities in the West led at least two New England newspapers to admit the possibility of the Tennessean's election by the people.[43] Other eastern journals, such as the New York *Evening Post,* began to recall agreeable sides of the General's character which they had overlooked during the distractions of the campaign.

Next came the upheaval in New York, burying Van Buren's

state ticket and electing Jackson's friend, DeWitt Clinton, governor. Before the echo of this overturn died away the Legislature met to consider the presidential question. One of Van Buren's advisors, Jacob Barker, hastened to Albany. A banker and lawyer not given to panic in a crisis, Mr. Barker surveyed the scene of chaos and contrived a formula calculated to salvage something from the wreck. "I pray you at once throw your whole influence into the scale for Jackson & do it promptly & openly & boldly— do not stop to count consequences. . . . No matter how hopeless the game may appear it will succeed . . . altho the probability is that it will make Jackson President without allowing the Question to go to the House."[44]

Mr. Van Buren failed to act on this suggestion and the Legislature he had so long exploited deserted the beaten politician, giving Adams twenty-six of New York's thirty-six votes.

This intelligence met Jackson in Virginia, and, coming on the heels of fresh tidings from the West, established that, after all, the finish of the race would be in the vaulted chamber of the House. For the reports of a Jackson victory in Ohio had proved to be premature, Clay carrying the state by seven hundred and ninety-eight votes out of fifty-nine thousand, nine hundred and ninety-two cast. Moreover the Speaker had carried Kentucky and Missouri, events which, combined with the collapse of Van Buren in New York, revived the Kentuckian's hope of nosing out Crawford and entering the House contest as the third man. But the first man would be Jackson with about one hundred electoral votes, and the second Adams with eighty votes or a little better.

This was the posture of affairs on December 7, 1824, when, on the twenty-eighth day of its journey, the carriage from Tennessee rumbled across the bridge into Washington. A strong current of opinion, by no means confined to the protagonists of General Jackson, favored the conclusion that the next President of the United States had attained the scene of his labors.

8

It went without saying that in the contest ensuing many who

had opposed Andrew Jackson would stand their ground to the end. But when the editor of the Alexandria *Herald,* not a Jackson organ, forecast "a high game against gen. Jackson," involving "intrigue, . . . formidable opposition, . . . gross dissimulation,"[45] he was chided,[46] and properly it seemed, for seeing things under the bed.

Certainly this newspaper's surmise that Old Hickory would strike out against fancied machinations was wanting in confirmation; for lest one should mistake that, with the prize so nearly in his grasp, the Tennessean was prepared to liberalize his code of campaigning, Jackson promptly reiterated it.

"In no one instance have I sought either by promise or management to draw to myself the good opinion of a single individual in society. . . . That so many should have preferred me to take charge and to administer the affairs of our great and growing country, is to me a matter of the highest consolation, let the result now be what it may. . . . If any favourable result could be secured, through any intrigue, management or promises . . . I would at once unhesitatingly and without reserve spurn [it]. . . . The choice of a President is a matter for the people; to be installed against their wishes . . . I would feel myself [a] degraded man."[47]

This was a political letter written for dissemination, and apparently hurried off without benefit of the attentions that Eaton or Lewis sometimes bestowed upon their chief's correspondence. Otherwise, perhaps it would not have been directed to Samuel Swartwout, a colleague of Aaron Burr in his unfortunate western adventure of more than twenty years before. Some of the General's friends felt that a disclaimer of intrigue could have been more suitably addressed than to this protégé of a man still remembered for his equivocal part in a previous House election.[48]

Yet a charge of insincerity would be difficult to sustain against Jackson who wrote in the same vein to John Coffee, adding: "I am wearied with a public life, and if I could with propriety would retire, but my lott is cast, and fall as it may I must be content. should it be that I can retire next March to my home I will be

A Portrait by Thomas Sully

From the original, owned by Mrs. Breckenridge Long of Laurel, Maryland. A conventionaliza-
tion of this likeness of Jackson survives on the current twenty-dollar bill.

happy. If confined here I must exercise my best exertions for the public weal until the four years runs around. . . . We are at Mr. Gadsbys tavern, well lodged, but *I pay for it*. How my funds may hold out I cannot say."[49]

They did not hold out very well and the General was obliged to ask his old friend for five hundred dollars.

"[This] will clear me of the city if I am permitted to leave it the 4th of March next. . . . How often does my thoughts lead me back to the Hermitage. there surrounded by a few friends would be a paradise . . . and . . . it would take a writ of habeas corpus to remove me into public life again."[50]

CHAPTER V

THE BARGAIN

I

ON DECEMBER 16, 1824, the result of the vote in Louisiana reached Washington, calming somewhat the mounting fever of the politicians as Henry Clay's last hope of placing his name before the House of Representatives went glimmering. Louisiana had chosen three electors for Jackson and two for Adams, giving the General ninety-nine votes in the electoral college and Adams eighty-four. Mr. Crawford retained third place with forty-one. Clay was fourth with thirty-seven.

Weary of politics citizens turned to the eye-filling spectacle of Lafayette's triumphal pilgrimage, most of them apparently satisfied to dismiss the election with a perfunctory concession of Old Hickory's victory, and no hard feelings.[1] The New York *Statesman,* a journal not unfriendly to Mr. Adams, pointed out that Jackson, having carried eleven states to the New Englander's seven, needed only two more to prevail in the House. It predicted that he would get three on the first ballot—Ohio, Kentucky and Missouri.[2] In these states the Jackson vote had been more than double that of Adams.

Indeed, the histrionics of the long campaign seem to have bored the public even before the autumn elections. The rising of the masses, alternately courted and feared by political leaders, had not taken place. Though larger than in any previous presidential contest, the vote fell measurably below that in recent local elections. With a population of one million Pennsylvania had sent only forty-seven thousand men to the polls; Virginia, with a white population of six hundred and twenty-five thousand, sent fifteen thousand. Massachusetts cast thirty-seven thousand votes in con-

trast with sixty-six thousand for governor a year before; Ohio
fifty-nine thousand, in contrast with seventy-six thousand for governor a month before. The weakness of opposition to Adams in
New England and to Jackson in Tennessee and Pennsylvania
was said to explain the light vote in those quarters; but this did
not account for the apathy of closely-contested North Carolina,
New Jersey and Ohio. Aside from the general overdoing of the
campaign and the swing toward better times, the probable reason
was a feeling that the plethora of candidates would throw the
decision into the hands of the politicians anyhow.

When it transpired that this had come to pass, an occasional
squib on current developments sufficed even partizan presses,
which yielded entire pages to the phenomena of the marquis with
the indestructible smile, bouncing over six thousand miles of
half-made roads to be fêted from morning until night for eleven
solid months, and gaining twelve pounds and a fortune meantime.

2

Nevertheless, the people had left an expression of their preference which congressmen, taking over the tavern houses of Washington, seemed inclined to respect. On the surface the removal of
resourceful Mr. Clay as a contender seemed to facilitate this, for
poor Crawford's cause was hopeless. Mr. Van Buren had slipped
into town looking "like a wilted cabbage."[3]

Clay's most distinguished supporter in the West, Thomas Hart
Benton, who had private reasons to oppose Jackson if any man
had, promptly announced that as Missouri preferred Jackson to
Adams he was for Jackson.[4] Senator Benton would not have
the casting of Missouri's vote, however. That would be the duty
of the state's sole representative, John Scott, whose one ballot
would have as much bearing on the result as Pennsylvania's twenty-
six or New York's thirty-four. When Scott declared that nothing
could induce him to vote for Adams,[5] hasty observers, of whom
there were many, counted the twelfth state for Jackson.

Under this view of things only one more would be required.
It seemed within easy reach.

All the word from Kentucky indicated that its delegation would receive formal direction from the Legislature to support Old Hickory. Richard K. Call gleefully exhibited a letter from former United States Senator John J. Crittenden, intimate of Clay and a power in the Blue Grass: "I hope you will be able to make the General beat the Yankee."[6] On the streets of Frankfort, a Kentuckian quoted Crittenden as saying, "Mr. Clay & the rest of the delegation" would support Jackson.[7] Representative Francis Johnson, a colleague of Mr. Clay, told a caller from home he had a sheaf of letters from constituents urging him to vote for Old Hickory.[8] "Kentucky," said he, "will come out strong for Jackson."[9] Clay, too, received such letters. "Sentiment in favour of Genl. Jackson grows . . . too powerful to be resisted," counselled William T. Barry, Secretary of State of Kentucky.[10]

Ohio was expected to follow Kentucky.

Georgia's Legislature instructed its delegation to regard Jackson as the choice after Crawford. This was taken to mean a complimentary vote for the doomed man and then a switch to Old Hickory should there be more than one ballot.

Even New York was not beyond hoping for. Henry Randolph Storrs, a Clay man from Utica, exclaimed that the only way Adams could get New York was through the support of the Crawford people. "And let them do it if they dare."[11]

These quick and uncritical calculations rested on the assumption that Jackson would hold the eleven states he had won in the electoral college. From the outset it was apparent that four of these states would bear watching: (1) Maryland, where Adams had received a small plurality of the popular vote, despite Jackson's capture of a majority of the electors; (2) North Carolina, a majority of whose representatives favored Crawford and seemed determined to give him a complimentary first-ballot vote, at least; (3) Illinois and (4) Louisiana, which had given Adams good second-place positions. Illinois's lone representative, Daniel P. Cook, was personally an Adams man. However, on his arrival in Washington, Mr. Cook said he would vote for Jackson in obedience to the will of the majority of his constituents.[12] When sounded out by the active R. K. Call, Brent of Louisiana sententiously observed, "Vox populi, vox Dei."[13] Call interpreted this to mean that Brent would vote for Jackson, rendering Louisiana secure as the state had only two other members, one of whom was Jackson's war-time friend, Edward Livingston.

These four potential sources of trouble notwithstanding, a judge of such matters so competent as Martin Van Buren considered Jackson's chances best by a considerable margin.[14] Able Willie P. Mangum of North Carolina picked the Tennessean to win, though he did not intend to vote for him.[15] After putting the best possible face on Mr. Adams's prospects, A. H. Everett of Massachusetts wrote, "I am not very sanguine."[16]

3

Not in two decades had an opening of Congress filled up Washington so promptly. Amid throngs that peopled inns, taprooms, Capitol corridors, theatres and made for a self-perpetuating series of balls and banquets, Jackson men were distinguishable by the buoyancy of their bearing. To place their chieftain's triumph beyond the pale of speculation, only one more voice was needed in his behalf—that of the Speaker of the House. "It is in fact very much in Mr. Clay's power to make the President," nervously declared an Adams adherent on the day the Louisiana vote came in.[17]

The thought did not alarm the Jacksonians. Benton's declaration, Crittenden's stand, the active sentiment of the Kentucky electorate, the friendly attitude of some of the Kentucky representatives, even the demeanor of the Speaker himself, were remarked as encouraging signs.[18]

Circumstances excused the Speaker from making an immediate public announcement of his choice. Not until mid-December did Mr. Clay know, beyond doubt, whether he, himself, was still a candidate. After that a decent interval seemed meet for the obsequies of his own aspirations. Meantime, the gayeties incident to Lafayette's arrival in town were not to be overlooked. During the thirty years of his residence in Washington, few men were more successful as hosts, or more sought for as guests, than the pleasure-loving statesman from Kentucky who seldom carried politics into a drawing-room. This attribute also served to explain his reticence on the topic that preoccupied every other tongue.

On December 8 General Jackson, Senator Eaton and Congressman Call were traversing the rotunda of the Capitol when Clay hailed them.

"General, I have a *quarrel* with you: why did you not let me know you were coming through Lexington? I certainly should have waited for your arrival. We should have travelled together."[19]

This cordial meeting and an exchange of ceremonial calls concluded the intercourse between the two men, however. As the social affairs of the town partook more and more of the flavor of political forums, the General withdrew from them and rarely appeared in public except at church with his wife.

Mr. Clay's relation to the presidential issue served to make him the center of engaging attentions. "I am enjoying while alive," he wrote to a friend, "the posthumous honors which are usually accorded the venerated dead. . . .[20] I am sometimes touched gently on the shoulder by a friend (for example) of Gen[l] Jackson, . . . 'My dear Sir, all our dependence is on you. . . . We want a western President—['] Immediately afterward a friend of M[r] Crawford will accost me 'The hopes of the Republican party are concentrated on you'. . . . Next a friend of Mr. Adams, . . . 'Sir Mr Adams has always had the greatest . . . admiration of your talents'. . . . I sometimes wish it was in my power to accommodate each of them."[21]

Mr. Clay seems to have done something of this sort. John Floyd of Virginia quoted him as follows: "When I take up the pretentions of Mr. Adams and weigh them, . . . then take up the pretentions of General Jackson . . . I never was so puzzled in all my life as I am to decide between them."[22] Representative Thomas P. Moore of Kentucky was ill in his lodgings at Brown's Indian Queen Hotel when the Speaker called, and in the course of a conversation remarked: "We could vote for either of the three candidates and justify ourselves to our constituents."[23]

In this manner observers were favored with a picture, con-

trived from Mr. Clay's own words and those of men who knew
him well, representing the Speaker in a nicely balanced attitude of indecision, hesitating among the three candidates.

Then came Congressman William Plumer, junior, of New
Hampshire to add another shade to the portrait. Lafayette paid
a visit of ceremony to the House of Representatives. When the
affair was over Plumer congratulated Mr. Clay on the felicity of
his address of welcome in which, it seemed to the New Englander,
the Speaker had especially emphasized the *"civil* virtues" of the
distinguished visitor.

"You will not find me, Mr. Plumer," said Clay, in acknowledgment of the complimentary remarks, "disposed by *any act of
mine,* unnecessarily to increase the *military fever* which has already produced some *strange effects* upon us."

Thus on December 10, Mr. Clay appeared to be leaning from
Jackson and Mr. Plumer went away happy.[24]

In view of other evidence which time was to bring to light,
the wonder is that Clay said so little to Plumer. For it appears
that prior to his departure from Kentucky, where the Speaker's
friendly references to General Jackson created much comment,
he had, at the same time, told a few friends he would never
vote for the Tennessean for President;[25] that en route to the
capital he had told a travelling companion that in a contest between Jackson and Adams he would support the latter;[26] and
that, after his arrival in Washington, at a conference with Thomas
Hart Benton, Mr. Clay had declined to follow his lieutenant
into the Jackson camp and affirmed to him his intention to vote
for Adams.[27]

In the light of these facts, later offered to show that Clay's determination to support Adams was of long standing and definitely settled by the time he reached the capital, why, then, did
the Speaker send away Plumer, a member of Adams's inner
circle, with no more than a shadowy hint of his supposed intentions? Nor is this the only feature of Mr. Clay's behavior, or of
the general situation, that confounds ready explanation. Political
secrets are so notoriously difficult to keep that one may almost
set down the expression as a contradiction in terms. With all

Washington clamoring for the least indication of Henry Clay's intentions, the gentlemen to whom he had confided this priceless information kept their tongues so well as almost to impose a strain upon credulity. Not only was a prying public left in the dark, but the whole Adams crew as well as many of Clay's most trusted friends both at home and in the capital; and also other politicians not often so badly misled.

4

So little did one Clay follower, Representative Thomas Moore of Kentucky, suspect that his chief could have committed himself to Adams that, when the Speaker merely expressed a doubt as to how the Kentucky delegation should vote, Moore was surprised. Or so he said in a later account of the interview which took place in his bedroom at Brown's Hotel, the implication being that until then he had expected the Speaker to support Andrew Jackson. At any rate, when Mr. Clay had departed, Moore lost no time sending for Representative Robert P. Henry and United States Senator "Tecumseh" Johnson of Kentucky, to whom he repeated Clay's words. Henry said that Clay had made the same statement to him. Whereupon Moore and Henry, concluding that something was in the wind they did not fully understand, agreed forthwith to announce for Jackson.[28]

The public inferences, drawn from the avowal of two members from Kentucky, could not have been very comforting to those Jackson people who were counting on a majority of Kentucky's delegation of twelve. The question that intruded was, "What of the other ten?" Already afloat were vague stories that Clay was maneuvering in the direction of Adams. Assuredly something was happening to disturb the optimism of the Jacksonians. Van Buren reported them not in such high feather as before, but offered no speculation as to the cause.[29] Others did not hesitate to lay the Jacksonians' discomfiture at the door of Mr. Clay. "Late events," Mangum of North Carolina wrote on Christmas day, "leave Jackson's prospects more doubtful. . . . All depends on Kentucky. . . . Ohio and Missouri will go with her."[30] Still, neither he nor Van Buren saw reason to change their prediction that Jackson would win.

A feeling that more was going on than met the eye began to communicate itself to the country. "We *cannot* get a [dependable] whisper from Washington," complained a member of the Virginia State government at Richmond. "Now and then a faint rumour reaches us that *Adams* will be President." The Virginian was unprepared to accept such a contradiction of the portents, however. "Jacksons want of information [education] and his temperament are the only obstacles in his way. I think he will probably be the *man*. It is not however so certain now . . . as *it appeared* to be."[31]

From an unexpected source came a ray of light on the Virginian's reference to Jackson's "temperament." Of a sudden Daniel Webster had shaken off the lethargy he had exhibited throughout the presidential contest, and, returning from an excursion beyond the Potomac, he repeated the substance of an interview with Thomas Jefferson. "I feel much alarmed," the philosopher of Monticello had said, "at the prospect of seeing General Jackson President. He is one of the most unfit men I know of for such a place. . . . His passions are terrible."[32] No sooner was this story in circulation than Thomas Hart Benton muddied the water a little more with a correction. Senator Benton had been to the Blue Ridge where he, too, climbed the bad road to the ill-kept mansion on the mountain which the sage inhabited by the indulgence of creditors, receiving callers in a stained dressing-gown and shabby slippers. "I told it [the report that Clay would support Adams] as my *belief*, . . . that Mr. Adams would, from the necessity of the case, . . . make up a mixed cabinet, . . . and asked Mr. Jefferson . . . how it would do? He answered: 'Not at all— would never succeed— would ruin all engaged in it.' "[33]

Mr. Benton's inexplicit allusion to the possibility of a "mixed" Cabinet was putting it delicately, for by this time a tale was abroad specifying the Secretaryship of State as the price of the Kentuckian's support of Adams. R. K. Call had this brought home to him in direct fashion, according to his own version. A man approached the member from Florida to ask Jackson's intention about filling the State Department. The visitor mentioned the superior qualifications of Mr. Clay. Call replied that he did not know the answer to the gentleman's question, which concerned a subject he could not mention to General Jackson.

"Then I venture to say," crisply observed Call's visitor, "that General Jackson will not be elected."[34]

5

It remained, however, for James Buchanan to carry to Andrew Jackson a statement of the alleged aspirations of Mr. Clay. This tall young man of good appearance and address, just elected to his third term from Pennsylvania, had been a good deal in the company of Clay's intimate set that winter. He was not anxious to undertake the rôle of courier between the headquarters of Clay and of Jackson, and had gone first to Major Eaton, then to Representative George Kremer from his own state, asking each of them to convey the substance of a message to Jackson. Learning what the message was they declined.[35]

So Buchanan presented himself at Gadsby's Hotel, outstayed the rest of the company, and accepted the General's invitation to take a walk. The Pennsylvanian's opening speech gave him some trouble. He said he had come as a friend, and, whatever the General's reply to the communication he was about to make, he hoped that it would not alter their personal relationship. Jackson helped his caller over the difficulty by saying that his reputation was assurance of the purity of his motives. Whereupon Mr. Buchanan continued:

Friends of Mr. Clay had informed him that friends of Mr. Adams had approached them with the information that, if Mr. Clay would aid in Mr. Adams's election, he should be Secretary of State; that to induce the friends of Mr. Clay to accede to their proposal, Mr. Adams's friends said that, if Jackson were elected, he would continue Adams as head of the State Department. The friends of Mr. Clay were distressed to hear this. They had assured Mr. Buchanan that "the West did not wish to separate from the West"; if Jackson would permit a confidential associate to say that if he were elected Mr. Adams should not be Secretary of State, "a complete union of Mr. Clay and his friends would put an end to the presidential contest in one hour."

The General had his answer ready.

"Say to Mr. Clay and his friends that before I would reach the presidential chair by such means . . . I would see the earth open and swallow both Mr. Clay and his friends and myself with them. If they had not the confidence . . . that I would call to . . . the cabinet men of the first virtue, talent and integrity, [tell them] not to vote for me."[36]

A disappointed young politician took his leave of General Jackson. To Kremer he argued the old soldier's ignorance of the seriousness of the situation and the necessity of meeting the opposition "with their own wepons."[37] Mr. Buchanan's motive seems not to have been more reprehensible than an effort to help Jackson despite himself, and to spare Clay the possible consequences of a dangerous game.[38] Concerning the nature of the Speaker's activities others had the same thought. Jefferson's opinion had been expressed to Benton. By this time Van Buren also had discovered the basis of the anxiety pervading the Jackson camp. When light-hearted Francis Johnson of Kentucky appealed to him to concert his influence with Clay's the New Yorker, who had reduced the science of politics to a settled system of diagnosis and pathology, declared that to elect Mr. Adams by the means proposed would be "Mr. Clay's political death warrant."[39]

In this situation James Buchanan himself determined to run a few risks. The message he set out to convey to Mr. Clay was not the message entrusted to him by General Jackson. Finding the Speaker in the lodgings of a messmate, Robert P. Letcher of Kentucky, Buchanan guided the conversation to the subject of cabinets, venturing that Jackson would bring forth the most notable ministry in the country's history. Letcher asked where he would find the equal of Jefferson's Cabinet in which were Madison and Gallatin.

Buchanan looked at Henry Clay. "He would not go outside of this room for a Secretary of State."

The Kentuckian laughed. The only Cabinet timber he saw in the room was the gentleman from Pennsylvania.[40]

How to construe the jest of this attractive, enigmatical man who seemed to take nothing over-seriously? Would he accept as a bona fide assurance from Jackson the daring bid of James Buchanan? Or had he more dependable information of Old Hickory's attitude? Or, again, was it now too late to turn him from Adams? Nearly a week of January had slipped by. Time was getting short.

6

Adams men, too, eyed the calendar. The time was as short for them as for the Jacksonians and much remained to do. But whereas the apprehensions of Hickoryites tended to increase, those of the Adams following subsided in almost direct proportion. In a little better than a month they had gained much.

In the beginning loyal Adams retainers had had enough to depress them as they pondered the possibility of drawing Henry Clay to their side. But ponder it they must, for the bristling antipathy of the Crawford group left no alternative. Moreover, none but Clay had the slightest chance of diverting from Jackson the western states Adams must have to succeed. These calculations could not have overlooked a consideration of the *raison d'être* Mr. Clay must advance for the desertion of the western candidate. Under this head were three distinct possibilities, one excellent and one plausible enough to serve.

Mr. Clay could support Mr. Adams on the high and well-nigh unassailable ground of his superior fitness.

He could support him on the ground that his tariff and internal-improvement views were more to Clay's liking than the views of Jackson on those issues.

He could support him on the negative ground of personal and political estrangement from Old Hickory, the core of which was the "military chieftain" charge.

This on one hand. On the other stood the unmistakable preference of the West, to which Clay owed his career, for General Jackson; the fact that in times past Adams and Clay had fought each other as bitterly as ever Jackson and Clay had fought, Adams branding the Kentuckian as a "half-educated" man of "loose public and private morals";[41] and the disconcerting indications of a happy adjustment of the differences that once had separated Jackson, Clay and their respective friends.

Such had been the unpromising outlook from the Adams watch-towers at the opening of December. Then, the slow but sure change. Presently the Adams people detected in the air signs that Clay was inclining toward their man. In this Mr. Clay's actual, not his ostensible, motive seemed to concern none of the reasons enumerated above. What the Speaker wished to know was how an alliance with Adams would affect the immediate political future of Henry Clay.

In any event so reasoned one of Mr. Adams's alert friends who lost no time in apprising his chief of the lay of the land. On the fifteenth day of December Edward Wyer called on Adams to say that the Speaker's support was available if, by that means, Clay "could be useful to himself."[42] Wyer was a political journalist close to Adams. He knew and Adams knew, if they knew anything, that without Clay's help Adams was lost. Benevolent neutrality would not do; it must be active help. Adams's reply to Wyer's feeler is not of record, but there was no rebuff such as Jackson was to give Buchanan. Next day the arrival of the Louisiana returns sent Wyer back to repeat his story.

From then on things moved apace. The day after Wyer's second trip Clay's friend Robert P. Letcher called on a pretext of State Department business. After an expansive exposition of the intricacies of Kentucky politics he asked Mr. Adams point-blank what he thought of Mr. Clay. The Secretary responded that he "harbored no animosity." Letcher said the Speaker's sentiments were similar. Before his visitor had departed Mr. Adams concluded that Wyer had given a true picture. "Clay would willingly support me if he could serve thereby himself. . . . [He wishes] a prominent share in the administration."[43]

Should he care for Mr. Clay's support on those terms, it was for Adams to convey such assurances as the Kentuckian would understand and would accept.

This was a difficult thing for one of John Quincy Adams's political training to do. For five days Clay waited, and heard nothing. On December 23, Letcher returned with definite and thinly veiled proposals, holding up to Adams the importance of carrying Kentucky, Ohio, Indiana, Illinois, Missouri and Louisiana on the first ballot, states which everyone believed without Clay's intervention, would go to Jackson. To this lucid demonstration of the obvious, the Secretary of State appears to have said little. John Quincy Adams was a master of euphemism. As a diplomat he could intrigue with the best, clothing a doubtful cause in language that made it shine forth as a thing above reproach. These talents he had used to the advantage of his country, but never to that of himself. With his political ideals undergoing the test of a lifetime Adams hesitated, sending Letcher away with an answer apparently not wholly satisfactory. That night a restless conscience relieved itself with a closing line in the Adams diary. "I consider Letcher as moving for Clay. . . . Incedo super ignes. [I walk over fires.]"[44]

On the next day William Plumer, jr., fully cognizant of the Kentucky game—"Clay's friends would have the merit of making Adams President, & have it to themselves"—found the Secretary in "better spirits" over his prospects than at any time before.[45]

Back went Letcher to say that Mr. Adams should meet the Speaker for a conference. To this the Secretary agreed "very readily." That evening—January 1—the two men found themselves seated together at a dinner to Lafayette. Clay requested "a confidential conversation" and Adams said to fix the time.[46]

Now it was Mr. Adams's turn to wait. In the meantime, Buchanan made his spirited sally, after which he, too, waited, and in vain, for a response from Henry Clay. The Speaker went his unruffled way. Privately he told Senator Bouligny of Louisiana,[47] and in reply to an audacious question he told Lafayette, that his intention was to vote for Adams.[48] Yet, in view of all the available evidence, it is difficult to confirm the claim later made that these and earlier conversations constituted commitments, and furnished proof that the Speaker had come to Washington imbued with a determination to support Mr. Adams from which he had never receded. With equal plausibility they could be placed in the category of tentative expressions which politicians less adroit than Henry Clay repudiate with impunity. Up to mid-January, or later, the accepted view was that Mr. Clay had not made up his mind. "It is not known," observed Nathaniel Macon, "for whom the friends of Mr. Clay will vote."[49] On January 10 Markley of Pennsylvania conversed with the Speaker without ascertaining whom he would support.[50] Cobb of Georgia saw the Clay crowd conscious of their possession of the balance of power, but apparently undetermined on a candidate. "Their conduct is extremely mysterious and doubtful."[51]

The anxiety in the Adams camp was plain to see.[52] In fact on January 8, when Mr. Adams had been a week without word from the Speaker, Clay was sure enough of his man to burn his bridges and take the decisive step. His first act was to notify a confidential lieutenant, Francis P. Blair of Kentucky, in a letter which does not appear to be the reflection of a man for weeks confirmed in his resolution to support John Quincy Adams.

"We are beginning to think seriously of the choice that must be made [between Adams and Jackson]. To both of these Gentlemen there are strong personal objections. . . . In the election of Mr Adams [however] we shall not . . . inflict any wound upon the character of our institutions. . . . I should much fear hereafter if not during the present generation that the election of General Jackson would give to the Military spirit a stimulus . . . that might lead to most pernicious results." This from a War Hawk of 1811. "[As] a choice of evils . . . I shall, with great regret, . . . support Mr Adams. . . . My friends entertain the belief that their kind wishes toward me will . . . be more likely to be accomplished" by following suit. Therefore, would Mr. Blair write to his representative (the wavering David White) to vote for Adams? "Be pleased to shew this letter to Crittenden alone."[53]

With this missive, calculated to put in motion an important

part of the machinery of the coalition, on its way, Mr. Clay asked permission to call at the Adams residence. The following evening, January 9, 1825, the "Kentucky gamester" and the Puritan met, talked long and parted allies to stand or fall together.[54]

7

Two days later the first shadow crossed the path of the new coalition: resolutions of the Kentucky Legislature directing Henry Clay and colleagues to vote for Andrew Jackson. This brought two other members of the delegation to the sides of Thomas Moore and R. P. Henry who had previously come out for the General. With Adams's cohorts in a state of "excessive alarm,"[55] Clay stemmed the revolt, holding the remaining Kentuckians in line for the New Englander.

Something now depended on how well Blair and Crittenden should do their work of setting backfires against the pronouncement of the Legislature.[56] They did as well as could be expected, considering that neither had his heart in it.

The letter of the ordinarily masterful Crittenden to the least distinguished of Kentucky congressmen was a shame-faced thing throughout, summarizing the business under review as "trashy politics." Jackson for President and Clay for Secretary of State would be the ideal slate, he said. This unattainable, "the common good is more concerned with Clay's being Secretary than it is . . . [with] whether Jackson or Adams shall be president."[57] Blair performed better, setting forth that, had it been known Adams intended Clay for the Cabinet, the Legislature "scarcely" would have hesitated to ask the Kentucky delegation to vote for him.[58] Then Mr. Blair sped to the Assembly chambers to importune members for letters in support of that interesting hypothesis.[59]

This and similarly inspired activity worked a temporary alteration in the complexion of congressional mail from Kentucky. Mr. Clay chanced to be present when the recalcitrant Moore broke the seal of a letter urging him, as he said, "to vote for whoever would make Mr. Clay Secretary of State, and intimating

that Mr. Adams would do it." Clay genially asked the news
from Kentucky. Moore observed that the missive was from a
close friend of the Speaker.

"And what does he say?" pursued Mr. Clay.

"You know very well," replied Moore.

Mr. Clay smiled and moved away.[60]

8

Thus was the presidential question reopened, precipitating an
unconcealed scramble for votes. The drama set Washington by
the ears. "Society is now divided into separate battalions. . . .
Mrs. Adams collected a large party [for the theatre], . . . Mrs.
Calhoun another, so it was thought that Mrs. Crawford, . . . too
[should] . . . show our strength."[61] Nerves were so jumpy that
Lafayette imagined himself in danger of becoming involved.
Living at the same hotel, he and General Jackson had been seen
exchanging reminiscences of the Revolution. To repel suspicion
of a deflection from his course of meticulous neutrality, the marquis abandoned his uniform, even when inspecting troops.

Deftly Mr. Clay moved against the Jackson lines, West and
East. The switch of Cook of Illinois added the first new state
to Mr. Adams's list. Storrs of New York promptly followed his
Kentucky leader in the new alliance, and Brent of Louisiana
seemed ill at ease in the presence of his old comrade, R. K. Call.
Scott of Missouri was approached with less success. "[Though]
one of Clay's best friends," Kremer of Pennsylvania related of
the Missourian, "he [said he] would be damned if he would be
sold like sheep."[62]

The ethical factor in the Adams-Clay understanding began to
receive more attention. So open a confederation of men and
forces, previously uncongenial, marked still another departure
from the standards hitherto prevailing with reference to the
presidency. It flew in the face of the swelling demand for a recognition of the will of the populace, noted on all sides as one
of the distinguishing features of the campaign of 1824.

Out in the country, people were manifesting a revival of interest in the presidential question, and beginning to coin their own names for the phenomena narrated by the Washington dispatches. The names coined by John Campbell, an intelligent young Virginian, not at this time a partizan of Jackson, were uncomplimentary. From his family correspondence, composed with no eye to public effect: "Letters from Washington inform us that Adams is certainly to be the President. Clay & him have compromised. . . . *Bargain* & *sales* are going on . . . as infamous *as you* can imagine. This office & that are held out provided you *vote this way and that &c &c* What is this but bribery and corruption."[63] Regarding the effect on the fortunes of Henry Clay, Mr. Campbell voiced sentiments already expressed by Jefferson, Van Buren and Buchanan. "His conduct is beyond my comprehension. . . . What will the western people say?"[64]

If a more or less disinterested spectator could feel so strongly, the effect on the Jacksonian politicians may be imagined. "The monstrous union between Clay & Adams," exclaimed Senator Robert Y. Hayne of South Carolina, "[renders] the results doubtful. . . . We are in great danger."[65]

Old Hickory's followers did more than wring their hands, however. They took practical counter-measures. The strides of the coalition gave them something akin to a common cause with the friends of Crawford, however personally distasteful to all the gentlemen concerned that circumstance might be. One heard strange rumors. Aaron Burr's friend, Samuel Swartwout, was no head-in-the-clouds idealist, and his free access to the distinguished lodger at Gadsby's vexed some of the Jackson men who were jealous of their chief's reputation. Burr was close to Crawford leaders in New York. "Jackson's friends," wrote a New Yorker who was for Adams, "are pushing their intrigues to as desperate an extreme as Burr's did in 1801."[66] In proof whereof, the Representative made the astounding assertion that the General had called in person on William H. Crawford.

The news spread like quick-silver. Someone flew with it to Adams, now meeting his lieutenants daily to review the progress of their efforts. The reaction was a mixture of alarm, lest the Jackson and Crawford forces actually unite, and of relief over the fact that the pot could no longer call the kettle black. "Jackson last winter made up with all his other enemies—Clay, Benton, Cocke, Scott &c [but] kept aloof from Crawford," Plumer of New Hampshire, fresh from the Adams presence, reminded his father. "Now it is said that he has been to see Mr. Crawford & made very humble submissions and profered him any terms which he might ask as the price of his cooperation."[67]

"Intrigue," "terms," "price": with something of relish Adams men rolled on their tongues syllables that were becoming too common for comfort in the threatening speech of the hard-pressed Jacksonians. The hubbub over the Crawford interview story was short-lived, though. Even before the letter to his parent was finished, Plumer learned that no such meeting had occurred.[68] Nevertheless, he insisted that friends of General Jackson and friends of Mr. Crawford were getting together.

Though no specific instance has been disclosed to the present writer, the general evidence supports this contention. Andrew Stevenson of Virginia, an influential man in the House, heard from his sister that Crawford partizans in Richmond were "universally denouncing Clay and Adams. . . . They would like Jackson now. . . . Quite a fashionable subject of conversation [is] 'who is to be bought and sold.' "[69]

Nor had the Jacksonians entirely abandoned their efforts to divert Clay men from the standard of the New Englander. The Ohio members seem to have been the object of a frontal attack by Jacksonians who "often repeated in a menacing manner that . . . [we] *durst not* vote for any other than General Jackson."[70] The approach of Sam Houston, however, gave less offense and suggests collaboration with James Buchanan. "Aid in electing General Jackson," John Sloane of Ohio, years later quoted Houston as having said, "and your man can have anything he pleases. What a splendid administration, . . . with Old Hickory as President and Mr. Clay as Secretary of State."[71] One flaw in these overtures was that Buchanan and Houston acted without the consent of their principal.

Adams-Clay men prosecuted their missions armed with that consent. This was verified by continuous contact with the Adams residence. Useful Robert Letcher brought in Scott with two things on his mind: first, the West's desire that Clay be in the administration; second, the plight of Scott's brother, a Federal judge who, having slain a dissenting member of the bench in a duel, imagined his robe in danger. Mr. Adams left Scott with the idea that Clay would be taken care of and the powder-stained jurist undisturbed. But, under the watchful care of Benton, Scott announced no change of allegiance.[72] Clay himself helped to pave the way for the visit of Daniel Webster who also had his boon to crave. Webster wished to be minister to England. Clay needed Webster's influence with the Federalist members from Maryland and Delaware. Webster left Mr. Adams's large brick house in F Street feeling the London appointment was to be his and straightway went to work on the Federalist congressmen.[73] In contrast to these gentlemen stood Cook of Illinois. Always an Adams man by personal preference, he had been one of the first accessions to the New Englander's camp. At this the Jacksonites had risen in their wrath and were making it uncomfortable for Cook when Mr. Adams asked him to dinner. Promises being unnecessary, for Cook had sought nothing in exchange for his vote, the object of the invitation seems to have been merely to bolster the Congressman's resistance. When the evening was over, Mr. Adams doubted whether he had done an effective job.[74]

Thus did the campaign etiquette of J. Q. Adams yield to the importunities of the times, giving away under the attrition of the stream of politicians, from Wyer to Webster, crowding across the New Englander's threshold, until the partnership with Clay manifested itself in a candid quest for votes by the time-honored means of promises, patronage and protection.

9

Exposed to identical importunities, Andrew Jackson yielded nothing. Though his rooms were usually filled, politics was a forbidden topic. His personal correspondence indicates that he closed his ears even privately to tales with which Eaton, Call, Houston, et al. were only too familiar.

While gossip of the Adams-Clay rapprochement filled Washington, he wrote to John Coffee: "There are various rumours . . . but whether any of them is founded in fact I do not know, as I do not . . . join in any conversation on the subject of the presidential election. . . . Altho Mrs J and myself goes to no parties . . . [tonight] the young [members of the Jackson entourage] are at parties and Mrs J and myself at home smoking our pipe and send love to you Polly and the children."[75]

After sending Congressman Buchanan about his business the General confided to the same trusted friend: "Information of today gives some reasons to believe that a coalition is about to be formed . . . [of] the interest of Crawford, Clay and Adams combined for the purpose of defeating my election. be this as it may, I shall continue my course, . . . and I assure you I shall not envy the man who places himself in the chair of state by intrigue of his friends."[76]

When at length Mr. Clay admitted what nearly everyone already knew, and formally announced his alignment with Adams, Jackson referred to it in a letter to W. B. Lewis as "such an unexpected course."[77]

Once only did Old Hickory unbridle a flash of the spirit for which he was famous. Rumors that were thirty years old had preceded the arrival in Washington of Mrs. Jackson. "A dilemma was presented, and a grand debate ensued as to whether the ladies would visit her."[78]

They came, though Aunt Rachel would not have minded had they stayed away. "Oh, my dear friend," she wrote home to a neighbor, "how shall I get through this bustle, . . . from fifty to one hundred persons calling in a day." Lafayette delighted her. "He wears a wig and is a little inclined to corpulency. He is very healthy, eats hearty, goes to every party, and that is every night. . . . The General and myself . . . [go only to] church. Mr. Baker the pastor . . . is a fine, plain preacher. . . . The play actors . . . [requested] my countenance to them. No. A ticket to balls and parties. No, not one. Two dinings; several times to drink tea. Indeed, Mr. Jackson encourages me in my course."[79]

One gentleman was on the *qui vive* for a sight of the lady concerning whom he had heard "industriously circulated . . . a thousand slanders . . . of her awkwardness, ignorance and indecorum." Upon acquaintance he added: "I . . . find her striking characteristics to be an unaffected simplicity of manners, with great goodness of heart."[80]

It was a friend in Virginia who informed the General of "papers" imputing to Rachel shortcomings apparently more racy than unfamiliarity with the forms of polished society would evoke. These documents had been mysteriously left in the hands of "an individual in Alex.ª," who appeared so disturbed over their nature that "he is afraid to communicate or even speak about them." Yet Jackson was warned to be on his guard.[81]

To which Rachel's husband replied with a pen that fairly stabbed the paper:

"I can assure you that whenever my enemies think it worth while to investigate . . . the character of Mʳˢ. J I fear not . . . as I know how to defend . . . her."[82]

The pistol that killed Dickinson was behind in Tennessee; but still in order.

10

Mr. Clay's formal declaration for Adams came a fortnight before the question was to go before the House.[83] The Speaker had been too long in public life not to have expected a measure of recoil; but seasoned politician and man of courage though he was, Henry Clay was taken aback by the fury of the tempest that smote him. "The friends of —— [Jackson] have turned upon me. . . . I am a deserter from democracy; a giant at intrigue; have sold the West— have sold myself."[84]

"For God's sake be on your guard," warned Crittenden from Kentucky. "A thousand desperadoes . . . would think it a most honorable service . . . to shoot you."[85]

The *Columbian Observer* of Philadelphia, whose editor was a friend of John Henry Eaton, printed a statement purporting to be from a Pennsylvania representative:

"For some time past the friends of Clay have hinted that they, like the Swiss, would fight for those who pay best. Overtures were said to have been made by the friends of Adams . . . offering . . . [Clay] the appointment of Secretary of State. . . . The friends of Clay gave the information to the friends of Jackson and hinted that if the friends of Jackson would offer the same price they would close with them. . . . The friends of Jackson . . . [refused]."[86]

After which a Richmond editor asked whether Clay had "gone over to . . . Mr. Adams with a view to constitute a part of his cabinet?"

Boldly Clay met the assault. "Do you believe it?" he countered in reply to the query of the Virginia journalist. "Then you ought not to respect me. Do you wish me to deny it? Then you cannot respect me. What do you desire?—That I should vote for Mr. Crawford? I cannot. For General Jackson? I will not."[87]

Yet, on the same day in another communication, Mr. Clay did deny it. "My dear Sir, I want no office."[88] And the implications of this letter differed from those of a missive penned twenty-four hours before the storm broke, in which the Speaker wrote with evident satisfaction: "I believe I can enter [Mr. Adams's Cabinet] in *any* situation I choose."[89] If Mr. Clay meant his statement that he wished no office, many of the Speaker's followers were supporting Adams under a misapprehension of the facts. Simple-minded Congressman White of Kentucky had put the case too bluntly for comfort, when he said he was not going "to vote for Mr. Adams but for Mr. Clay."[90]

The *Observer's* correspondent had sought to indict Mr. Adams jointly with Mr. Clay, yet only Clay felt that he must defend his name. In a published "card" the excited Kentuckian called upon the author to "unveil himself" and accept a challenge to the field of honor. Adams people were aghast at this display of western manners so long urged as a valid reason for rejecting the pretensions of Andrew Jackson.

However, the brave scene dissolved in quiet laughter when Mr. Clay's accuser briskly unveiled. He was George Kremer, a quaint little rustic from a "Pennsylvania Dutch" district, in private life

a cross-roads storekeeper and in his official capacity hitherto conspicuous only because of the leopard-skin coat he wore on the
floor of the House. "Mr. Kremer is a man," Webster informed
his brother, "with whom one would think of having a shot about
as soon as with your neighbor, Mr. Simeon Atkinson, whom he
somewhat resembles."[91]

The dueling threat out of the way, Mr. Clay demanded an investigation by the House. Mr. Kremer rose in his place to say
that he would appear before any properly constituted body and
prove his charge. Thus Kremer in public, the flaming champion
of political virtue, a rôle which, alas, Kremer in private seemed
unable to sustain for, when taken off guard by irate friends of the
Speaker, he bewilderingly denied any intention "to charge Mr.
Clay with corruption."[92] After some delay a committee was
chosen before which Mr. Kremer refused, on constitutional
grounds, to appear. Although ultimately a good deal was made
of Kremer's unseemly back-down, the Clay faction remained
curiously silent at the time, it being tacitly understood by Clay,
Adams and Jackson people alike that no good would come from
pressing this inquiry too hard in face of the fact that every side
had its secrets to guard. Mr. Clay believed the *Columbian Observer* letter to have been written by Eaton, and that may have
been the way of it.[93]

The investigating committee receded from view, eventually
to compose a milk-and-water report and lay it unnoticed before
the House on February 9, 1825, a day which found that body
engrossed in other concerns. Lafayette had returned to town
to wedge his way into the gallery, for once a spectator, and not
a spectacle. On the floor before him the representatives had come
together to elect a President of the United States.

II

The domed, ill-ventilated chamber, outlined by a semi-circle
of pillars of Potomac marble, breathed forth a sweet odor of wet
wool and leather as the used-up air melted the snow which people
tracked in. Before the canopied dais of the Speaker, the desks

of members stood in concentric curves. On each desk was a
snuff box, provided at public expense, and beside each desk a
spittoon environed by a dark aura of stains—evidence that the
astonished accounts of European observers concerning one particular of American marksmanship erred on the side of flattery.
The interstices between pillars were filled by sofas and behind
these were the galleries, raised only a foot or so above the common level. The sofas were grimly held down by excessively
privileged characters while the less fortunate trod on their toes.
A few representatives lounged in their seats. Others conversed
in small groups or worked off their nervous vitality by visiting,
from floor to foyer to gallery, as the hands of the marble-faced
clock on the wall, chaperoned by a comely representation of History, measured the minutes. The special nature of the occasion
was indicated by the fact that the members were not wearing
their hats.

Galleries and politicians expected a long fight in which time
would be the ally of General Jackson. Washington throbbed at
the prospect, for the Clay-Adams coalition had reanimated the
interest of the country. The Speaker's belated acknowledgment
of that alliance was lashing the West into a lather beside which
the local storm seemed as nothing. Missouri and Kentucky sent
up cries of rage and Pennsylvania militiamen talked of laying siege
to Washington if Jackson were not chosen.[94] With this wrathful
wave of protest rolling eastward, Mr. Clay was in no position
to prolong the contest. To win for Adams he must win quickly.

The snowy morning when the Speaker left his lodgings for the
Capitol he did not have the thirteen states necessary to give Mr.
Adams a majority on the first ballot. Lot Clark of New York, a
Van Buren lieutenant and a clear-sighted observer, placed Adams's
strength at ten states[95]—an estimate which must have been shared
by many others. Actually Mr. Clay had been able to do better
than that. In the face of a blistering denunciation from Benton,
Scott of Missouri had announced for Adams[96] at the last moment,
and Webster's drive on Maryland had won that state, for the first
ballot only, by the margin of a single vote. Louisiana also was
Adams's by one vote in the hands of a timid, unsteady man.

Nevertheless, the New Englander had the pledges of twelve states for the first ballot, or only one short of a majority. But on the second ballot it was said that he would lose Maryland where one member had promised to switch to Jackson.[97] In that event Adams would be two votes shy, and in no good position to regain the ground lost. On the other hand Jackson would be only beginning to show his second-line strength.

One effect of the Clay-Adams coalition had been to drive Crawford people into Jackson's arms where they found a hospitable welcome. On the eve of the balloting, such conspicuous Crawford adherents as John Randolph of Virginia, Cobb and Cuthbert of Georgia, and McLane of Delaware, equaled the Jacksonians in their hostility to Adams. Van Buren was more cautious in his expressions of preference, though it is significant that Cuthbert and McLane, supposed to look to the New York Senator for political guidance, shared with him a house in the capital.[98] The fourth resident of this congenial bachelor's hall was General Stephen Van Rensselaer, the Albany patroon and largest landowner in the eastern states.

On the first ballot Jackson was expected to poll the votes of seven states. After that Georgia, North Carolina and perhaps Virginia, having observed the amenities toward Crawford, seemed to be his. This assumption would give Jackson at least nine states to Adams's ten with the Jackson bloc probably in the better position to stand the hammering of a long contest.

Such were the prognostications on the morning of February 9. The hands on the marble clock-face moved toward the hour of noon. The tension in the crowded chamber increased. In the galleries were men who remembered the threats of armed intervention to bring an end to the seven-day battle between Jefferson and Burr. The son-in-law of Lafayette recalled the temper of the Pennsylvania militiamen he had seen. At ten minutes before twelve, a North Carolina member, "with countenance discovering deep concern," besought a colleague from Maryland. "I hope to God you may be able to terminate the election on the first ballot."[99]

But where was Mr. Clay? He had not appeared, as he often

did, to mingle and jest with the members before taking up the gavel. The fact is that in the brief time that remained the Speaker was engaged elsewhere, in the effort of his life to win the one state needed to terminate the election on the first ballot. And unerringly he had picked the weakest link in the encircling chain of his adversaries.

12

The New York delegation was tied, seventeen votes for Adams and seventeen[100] in the hands of Van Buren which meant that, until the deadlock should be broken, the vote of the State would be counted for none of the candidates. Such was the utmost the Adams managers had been able to accomplish after weeks of effort, effort in which a promise of the ministership to England was said to have been whispered to DeWitt Clinton.[101] This story would have interested Daniel Webster whose zeal for Adams dated from the interview in which he had understood Mr. Adams to say that the London post should be his.

One of Van Buren's embattled band was General Van Rensselaer whose family exercised a sort of proprietary right to the congressional seat for the Albany district, the present incumbent being the fourth of his name to hold it. The old gentleman was immensely rich and sincerely pious; but in his veins the imperious blood of the line had run thin, so that the General often found himself in agreement with the views of the last person to speak to him, and especially his strong-minded wife. A dinner-party story had it that someone asked the General if he had read the Baron von Humboldt's latest work. He pondered and glanced at his wife. "Have I read Humboldt's work, my dear?" Margaret Schuyler frowned. "Certainly you have read it."[102]

In this situation Mr. Van Buren had made a personal concern of the political welfare of his aged protégé. Clay had been after him, had convoyed him to the Adams fireside along with the rest of the benighted he was struggling to show the light, but watchful Van Buren was able to counteract these ministrations. The old land baron clung to his determination to vote either for Jackson or for Crawford. The last preference he had expressed was for Jackson.

At breakfast on the ninth, Stephen Van Rensselaer had reassured his messmates. The four rode to the Capitol where Mr. Clay guided the patroon into the Speaker's private room. There they found Webster. These vigorous masters of persuasion plied Van Rensselaer with every word, every argument, every artifice at their command. They said the question of whether the House would or would not be able to select a President depended upon him. The two advocates agonized the old man with a dark picture of national chaos "that would in all probability result from the disorganization of the Government," the stake the Van Rensselaers with their vast estates had in the preservation of order, and so on.[103]

Though weak and shaken Van Rensselaer would not retract his promise to Van Buren. Leaving Clay and Webster he encountered McLane who was shocked by his colleague's distraught appearance.

"The election turns on my vote," stammered the old man. *"One* vote will give Adams the majority— This is a responsibility I cannot bear. What shall I do?"

"Do!" exclaimed McLane. "Do what honor, what principles direct. General, you are an old man. . . . You want nothing, you have no motive but duty to sway you. Look at me. . . . *My vote,* like yours, would turn the scale. [McLane was the sole representative from Delaware.] But, General, the greater the responsibility the greater the honor. . . . Let us march boldly in and do our duty."

This speech seemed what the old waverer needed. "I am resolved," he said. "Here is my hand on it."[104]

Feeling that the emergency called for a word from Van Buren, McLane sent for him. By the time Van Buren arrived Van Rensselaer had shuffled down the aisle toward his seat. Cuthbert of Georgia told the Senator that it would be unnecessary to trouble the old man with further questions as Van Rensselaer had just assured him that he would not vote for Adams. After reaching his desk the patroon made the same statement to J. J. Morgan, a Jackson member of the New York delegation.[105]

On the stroke of noon the forty-eight senators filed into the hall, two and two, led by their president *pro tempore,* the aged and wrinkled Gaillard of South Carolina. The senators took seats on the right of the dais. Mr. Gaillard occupied the Speaker's chair and Henry Clay that of the Clerk.

The first order of business was the formality of counting the electoral votes. This done, Gaillard announced the election of John C. Calhoun as Vice President, but that no candidate had received a majority of the votes for President.

The elder statesmen's participation in the tableau at an end, they solemnly filed out. Poised and pleasant-looking, Mr. Clay stepped behind his accustomed desk and, with the informal dignity that helped to make him the most popular moderator the House ever had, assumed the gavel.

State delegations were directed to poll their members. As the New Yorkers' box was passed General Van Rensselaer dropped his head on the edge of his desk in a silent appeal to his Maker. Removing his hand from his eyes he saw at his feet a discarded Adams ballot. Accepting this as an answer to his prayer, the old man picked up the ticket and dropped it in the box.[106] This act gave Mr. Adams a majority of one in the New York delegation, and the vote of that state.

Each delegation having balloted, the name of the candidate of its choice was written on two pieces of paper which were placed in separate boxes to be counted by the tellers, Webster and Randolph. The votes in the two boxes tallied. First Webster, then Randolph announced the result.

Adams had received the votes of thirteen states, Jackson of seven, Crawford four.

The Speaker arose. "John Quincy Adams, having a majority of the votes of these United States is duly elected President of the same."[107] Surely none had a better right than Henry Clay to give that message to the world.

A spattering of handclapping came from the astonished galleries; then a few hisses.

A Jackson firebrand from South Carolina leaped to his feet and demanded that the galleries be cleared. The applause, apparently, had angered him. Mr. Clay so ordered and the embarrassed sergeant-at-arms gestured toward the exits. In a few moments the benches were bare.

A motion to adjourn was carried and the members trooped out on the heels of their expelled guests.

Randolph of Roanoke's sallow face was hard. "It was impossible to win the game, gentlemen. The cards were packed." Cobb of Georgia stumped about the foyer muttering imprecations. "Treachery, treachery! Damnable falsehood!" Van Rensselaer was the target of his wrath. "The poor, miserable wretch!"[108]

13

Silently the crowd dispersed into snow-filled thoroughfares swept by a stinging wind. Only the alleys inhabited by free negroes resounded with rejoicing. No bonfires blazed for the victor, and the state of the weather discouraged a proposal by partizans of the vanquished to burn an effigy of Mr. Adams.[109]

A committee of the House repaired to the residence in F Street to perform the rite of notifying Mr. Adams. The President-elect presented an unforgettable spectacle. "Sweat rolled down his face. He shook from head to foot and was so agitated he could hardly stand or speak." One member of the committee thought he was going to decline the honor. With effort Mr. Adams begged leave to avail himself of the precedent set by Mr. Jefferson and reply in writing.[110]

Asbury Dickins, faithful chief clerk of the Treasury, bore the tidings to Crawford. "Is it possible!" exclaimed the invalid. "I thought it would . . . [be] Jackson."[111]

That night the President held his regular Wednesday levee. The crowd was immense and a pickpocket took General Scott's wallet. Old Nathaniel Macon, the Nestor of Congress who had seen Andrew Jackson, a stripling from the wilderness, sworn in at Philadelphia in 1796, surveyed the scene. "Mr. Adams was there, but less an object of attention than General Jackson."[112] A lady of fashion observed "*Clay* walking about with . . . a smiling face . . . [and] a fashionable *belle* on each arm. . . . And Van

Rensselaer, too, tho' . . . he looked more in want of support himself. . . . Poor man his messmates wouldn't speak to him. . . . More than one, pointing to A. said, there is our *Clay President.*"[113] The rivals in the day's balloting found themselves face to face. "Mr. Adams was by himself; Gen. Jackson had a large, handsome lady on his arm. . . . Gen. Jackson reaching out his long arm said—'How do you do, Mr. Adams? I give you my left hand, for my right as you see is devoted to the fair; I hope you are very well, sir.' All this was gallantly and heartily done. Mr. Adams took the General's hand and said, . . . 'Very well, sir; I hope Gen. Jackson is well.' "[114]

14

Jackson accepted defeat in better part than many of his followers. While members of the House were assembling to cast their votes he had remained in his hotel suite conversing with friends. Editor Hezekiah Niles of the *Register,* who had seen the General often during the winter, heard him mention the election for the first time. "He had no doubt but that a great portion of the citizens would be satisfied with the choice, . . . and he seemed to think it most probable that it would devolve upon Mr. Adams. . . . He observed that many . . . were unpleasantly situated, seeing that they were compelled to act either against Mr. Adams or himself. . . . And he further remarked that it was a matter of small moment to the people who was their president, provided he administered the government rightfully."[115] The day after the election the General quashed an impulsive move for a testimonial dinner because it "might be viewed as conveying . . . a feeling of complaint which I sincerely hope belong not to any of my friends."[116] The week following Jackson treated twenty-two men who had stood by him to a supper with champagne.[117]

This sportsmanlike attitude of a man beaten fairly, and the refusal to countenance tales to the contrary, had a practical side as well. Jackson could afford to wait; for, if the price of Mr. Clay's support were the Secretaryship of State, the fact could not be long concealed.

The disclosure came in five days when "Tecumseh" Johnson burst upon Jackson in hot blood with the story that Clay had been offered the first place in the Cabinet and probably would accept. The Jovian ire blazed forth, mayhap the fiercer for its long repression, though if Jackson had entertained prior suspicions of Clay his most intimate correspondence was not allowed to betray them. Nevertheless, the tone of the first brief explosion does not appear to be one of surprise. "So you see the *Judas* of the West has closed the contract and will receive the thirty pieces of silver. his end will be the same. Was there ever witnessed such bare faced corruption?"[118]

Though they made good use of it, neither Andrew Jackson nor his Washington entourage invented the "corrupt bargain" cry, a wealth of political folk-lore to the contrary notwithstanding. When Jackson wrote the foregoing, the sound and the fury of that cry already was sweeping upon the capital. It came from the country—West, South and to a slight extent East.

This had been an evolutionary process. The first faint accents of disapproval coincided with the obscure beginnings of the Adams-Clay understanding, and the stubborn impression that it embodied something that would not bear the light of day. As the objects of the alliance grew more distinct hostile murmurs increased. Mr. Clay's formal announcement, by chance or design timed so that western reactions could not reach Washington until after the eventful February 9, swelled these murmurs to a strident chorus. With the achievement of Mr. Adams's election and the punctual proffer of reward to Mr. Clay, the savage cry burst from savage throats.

An item from General Jackson's mail-bag:

"Pittsburgh March 4th a black fourth for
the American nation—a black 1825
"Your conduct and your behavior upon the late trying occasion both surpassed even the utmost stretch of thought. . . . Thy Throan shall be in Heaven"—the writer was Edward Patchell, the General's preacher friend—"at the right hand of Jehovah linked in the arm of the Immortal Washing [ton]," whereas "the corrupt

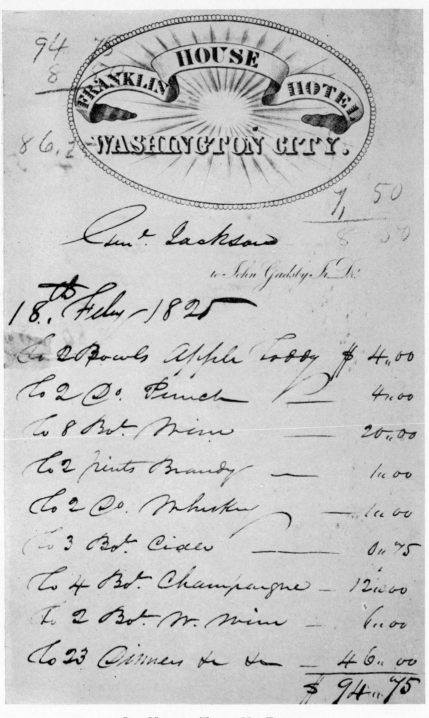

OLD HICKORY TOASTS HIS FRIENDS

Bill for a dinner to twenty-two supporters given by General Jackson after his defeat in the House election for President in 1825. The host received a refund of eight dollars and fifty cents for a pint of whisky, one of brandy and three bottles of wine which were not consumed. From the Jackson Papers, Library of Congress.

Adams & Clay" would sizzle in hell "unless they be born again."
As a starter Clay had been burned in effigy. "I . . . proposed sending a Barrel of whiskey to Grants hill to treat the fellows."[119]

Another:

"I have not the language to express the sorrow and Mortification that I feel. . . . The *West* surely will not protect those men . .
nor let them go unpunished. . . .

"Louisianians!—Degraded!—Ungrateful men!! to vote against
you! you!! who under God they are indebted to for the . . . Chas-
tity of their wives and daughters ! ! . .

"The Pride of Kentucky like Lucifer has fallen! . . .

"Your dignified conduct during the late Contest . . . and your
subsequent Magnanimity has exacted praise even from those
who . . . sacrificed you."[120]

Gems from the western press:

"HENRY CLAY, . . . morally and politically a gambler, a
blackleg and a traitor."[121]

"We for one, should not be sorry to see [Henry Clay] *tarred
and feathered,* nor shall we shrink from the responsibility of the
expression."[122]

To such music did John Quincy Adams, after two sleepless
nights, ride down the Avenue to take the oath.

"He will stand worse in four years than his father did," predicted a Crawford man from New York who witnessed the pageant. "Clay is ruined."[123] A Kentucky colleague shared these
misgivings. "I fear we have done too much for our friend."[124]

A number of western congressmen made the dust fly in their
rush for cover. Admitting that nineteen-twentieths of the people
of Missouri were opposed to Adams, unhappy John Scott again
and again justified himself on the ground that he had voted for
Clay, not Adams. Virtuously he announced that he would accept
no appointment under the administration.[125] Metcalfe of Ken-

tucky was quoted as explaining his vote as an effort to prevent a deadlock which, if extended until March 4, would have made Calhoun President by default.[126] Another Kentuckian, David Trimble, hurried home to defend himself from the stump. The orator's success was not all that could be wished for. "If I had [carried] a gun," remarked one of his auditors, "I would have shot him."[127]

Representative Henry of Kentucky who had voted for Jackson asserted that Old Hickory could have had the vote of his state had he "authorized or permitted his friends to give . . . an assurance that Mr. Clay should . . . be made Secretary of State."[128]

Clay knew what he had done. On his desk lay a letter from Amos Kendall of Frankfort. This gifted man had been a member of the household at Ashland, a tutor to the Clay children. He had participated in the letter-writing calculated to stiffen the resolution of Kentucky congressmen to follow their chief for Adams. He edited the *Argus of Western America,* which had long fought the battles of Henry Clay. It could not fight them now. "Passion is taking the place of reason and you have little conception of the ferocious feelings." Kendall advised his patron to attempt no explanations, to emulate the *Argus* and keep still. "Even your voice would have little influence . . . [and] you might do yourself . . . much harm."[129]

Thus the spontaneous and national origin of the accusative cry roaring in from the land to claim its place in the argot of politics.

15

Seven days elapsed between the proffer of the State Department and its acceptance by Mr. Clay. They were days of doubt, divided counsels and indecision; days that have changed the face of much history. Though making light of it to Adams, Clay was troubled by the violence and volume of criticism. Adams men, once willing to offer almost anything for Clay's support, recoiled. They appealed to the warm-hearted Kentuckian to make a free gift of his great service to their cause, and, by declining the stipulated reward, bid the new Administration bon voyage on a tranquil sea. Clay's personal followers thought this hardly sporting. They pressed the Speaker to accept. Any other course would be an admission of wrong-doing, leaving them without an excuse for their votes. Had not Mr. Clay the right to support, and Mr. Adams to appoint, whom he chose?

They had that right. Mr. Clay could have supported Adams on lofty grounds, but he did not. His reason for his vote had alleged not the fitness of Mr. Adams, but the unfitness of General Jackson on the theatrical premise that he was a "military chieftain."[130] At best this was an oversimplification of the issue between Henry Clay and Andrew Jackson, thin and unconvincing. The man-on-horseback bogey derived from the Florida campaign which Adams had supported to the hilt. So people looked elsewhere for the real motive of Mr. Clay. They fancied they found it in what Mr. Adams had discerned after his first interview with Robert Letcher: Clay's ambition to advance himself. Adams had small talent for party leadership. Clay, then, could control the political machinery of the Administration, and apply it to prepare himself for the succession, not blinking the fact that it would be easier to succeed a New Englander than a fellow Westerner. Men who had followed Mr. Clay into his present interesting position accepted this line of reasoning.

Thus the Kentuckian's glove fell at the feet of Andrew Jackson, the last man to ignore so direct a challenge. He thought himself cheated, and Old Hickory bore affronts badly. His arresting countenance like a thundercloud, the General marched into the Senate chamber and, when Mr. Clay's name was presented for confirmation, he voted No. Thirteen other senators, an unprecedented number to oppose a Cabinet nomination, voted with him. He placed his seal of adoption on the bargain and corruption cry which impassioned liegemen were to make their *Marseillaise,* to damn Henry Clay with bell, book and candle, and harry him through the rest of his days.

Was the cry true? Jackson believed that it was. "What is this barter of votes for office but bribery?" [131] Thomas Hart Benton believed it. "No man, in his right senses, at the public scene of

action as I was, could believe otherwise."[132] This is notable testimony. Benton and Clay were related by marriage. The Missourian
viewed the course of his friend with regret rather than reproach,
and strove to avoid too personal an application of the bargain
charge. The private association of the two men long remained undisturbed. Their political separation constitutes a significant event
in the march of American democracy as Benton turned to follow
his constituents, Clay his star.

CHAPTER VI

A PREOCCUPIED CINCINNATUS

I

BUNLAND'S TAVERN at Washington, Pennsylvania, was thronged with Westerners homeward bound from Mr. Adams's inaugural. Word that General Jackson was passing through had brought out a good share of the townfolk as well. Andrew Wylie, president of Washington College and destined to be a man of mark among the educators of his day, introduced himself to the distinguished wayfarer.

"You return, General, from a boisterous campaign."

"Yes, sir," Old Hickory replied.

"A campaign in which you were not quite so successful as in some former ones," pursued Mr. Wylie.

"My success in those to which you allude was owing to the firmness of the brave men whom I had the honor to command."

Wylie was a Jackson man. "It is more honorable," said he, "to lose than to win if, indeed, things were managed as has been reported."

"Who can doubt it?" agreed Jackson.

The educator replied that many found it impossible to believe "that such men as Adams and Clay would, in the face of the nation, engage in such a transaction."

"Let any man in his senses," cut in Old Hickory, "take a view of the circumstances. Let him compare the prediction of honest George Kremer with its accomplishment."

Mr. Wylie repeated the argument that the "talents and local situation" of Mr. Clay sufficed to justify the appointment. "There is, however," he added, "another circumstance which, if true, will settle that point."

135

Jackson asked what it was.

"The proposition that is said to have been made to *you?* Is that a *fact?*"

The General's tone had been inaudible to those not standing very near him. At Wylie's last question he raised his voice. "Yes, sir, such a proposition *was* made. I said to the bearer, 'Go tell Mr. Clay, tell Mr. Adams, that if I go to that chair I go with clean hands.' "[1]

The words were welcome to the ears of western Jacksonians. They corroborated the continued accusations of their partizan editors. "Expired at Washington," one had written, "on the ninth day of February, of poison administered by the assassin hand of Henry Clay, the virtue, liberty and independence of the United States." "Five Western States," exclaimed another, "bought and transferred to the usurper like so many live cattle or a drove of negroes."[2] Yet, during the long journey over the National Road toward Wheeling, Jackson had sent ahead canceling acceptance of invitations made before his departure from the capital, and requesting that other demonstrations in his favor be omitted. Mrs. Jackson's health was the excuse. Nevertheless, crowds assembled. The General could not have been altogether displeased. His dander was up and the remarks to Mr. Wylie were characteristic rather than exceptional.

The further west Jackson went, the greater the enthusiasm of the people. Two newly-made fathers—Richard K. Call and Editor Stephen Simpson, whose *Columbian Observer* had been first to disclose the prediction of "honest George Kremer"—deplored the fact that their wives had presented them with daughters. A Kentuckian in like situation was more resourceful. "We shall call her Rachel Andrew Jackson Hitt."[3] Leaving the steamboat at Louisville, Old Hickory broke his resolution and attended a banquet.

2

As usual the General had brought some things for the Hermitage—on this occasion a lemon tree and a box of plants for Rachel's garden. Yet, the homecoming of April, 1825, differed from any other. Many times this far-faring man had turned his steps toward the comely Cumberland, sincerely determined to be done with offices and titles and to end his days on his own placid acres by the side of an adoring wife who, above all things, feared and distrusted renown's searching light. Always some emergency of war or peace or politics had drawn him forth again. In the ceaseless conflict Andrew Jackson had passed from a young man to an old man, Rachel from a radiant beauty to a dumpy little woman of fifty-eight, ill in body and in spirit. Now, for the first time, Jackson approached the Hermitage not as a permanent refuge from the cares of the world, but as winter quarters, wherein to rest, recruit and then sally forth to smash Henry Clay. Alas, for Rachel's peace of mind, this would mean another campaign for the presidency in 1828.

Before leaving the capital Old Hickory had served notice in an ostensibly private letter, already trickling through the press. "I became a soldier for the good of my country: difficulties met me at every step; I thank god it was my duty to surmount them. . . . If this makes me so, I am a 'Military Chieftain.' . . . To him [Henry Clay] I am no wise responsible. There is a purer tribunal to which in preference I would refer myself—to the Judgment of an enlightened patriotic and uncorrupted electorate."[4]

The document elicited from Mr. Clay a reply in which, contrary to advice, the Secretary not only defended his course in electing John Quincy Adams, but altered the provocative position he had assumed with reference to General Jackson. Greatly modifying the military chieftain charge, Clay praised Old Hickory's soldierly qualities, asserting that only Adams's superior statesmanship had drawn him to the side of the New Englander. To Kentucky constituents Mr. Clay offered ingenuous reasons for disregarding the instructions of the Legislature and the wishes of a majority of the voters.[5]

A copy of this production reached Jackson a few days after his arrival at the Hermitage. "How little common sense this man displays," the General wrote to John Coffee, " 'O that my enemy would write a book.' . . . Silence would have been to him wisdom.[6] . . . Mr. Clay left himself so open to a severe scourging that

it has been with difficulty I could withhold my pen." But, profit-
ing by his rival's example, "for the present I have determined to
be silent."[7]

3

There was scarcely more than time for a quick survey of his
three plantations, including the one the General operated for his
ward, Andrew Jackson Hutchings, when the Marquis de Lafayette arrived in Nashville. After five hundred receptions, a thousand speeches and the cheers of five million Americans, this remarkable traveler was still as fresh as the day he stepped from the
ship. Formalities out of way, the party adjourned to the Hermitage. "The first thing that struck me," noted the visitor's son-
in-law, "was the simplicity of his house. Still somewhat influ-
enced by my European habits, I asked myself if this could really
be the dwelling of the most popular man in the United States."
Jackson's crops were flourishing. "We might have believed ourselves on the property of one of the richest and most skillful German farmers if, at every step, our eyes were not afflicted by the
sad spectacle of slavery."

Someone begged Jackson to display his arsenal of ceremonial
weapons. Lafayette recognized a pair of pistols he had given
George Washington and expressed his delight at finding them
still in worthy hands. The compliment was well turned and Old
Hickory's eyes sparkled. The Marquis sought his host's counsel
upon what he described as the "delicate But Very interesting
Subject"[8] engrossing the energies of a young woman the Frenchman called his "daughter." She was Frances Wright, a tall, titian-
haired Scottish lass of large means and larger ideals.

Having emancipated herself from the conventions that customarily surround unmarried females, Fanny Wright had con-
ceived the idea of emancipating American negroes from slavery.
Dropping in at the Lafayette country seat near Paris to discuss the
matter she had remained there, off and on, for three years. When
the Marquis came to the United States, Fanny would have been a
member of the party except for an adverse ruling by the family,

which held that Fanny's demonstrations of filial affection for her "venerable father" might be misunderstood in America. So the friend of freedom sailed under the chaperonage of his son, George Washington Lafayette, and his daughter's husband, Lavasseur. Fanny followed on another ship. On the day of the election in the chamber of the House, she sat beside the General, whose lusty appearance and gallant attentions did not allay gossip touching the "venerable" tourist and his beautiful protégée.

A few weeks after the Marquis's departure, Miss Wright appeared at the Hermitage in the company of George Fowler, one of her pupils in the manumission scheme. Jackson suggested the acquisition of a tract below Memphis. At Nashville the Scottish heiress purchased a coffle of negroes and marched them off toward the promised land[9] to establish what became rather too sweepingly known as "Fanny Wright's free love colony."

4

Expenses in Washington had been heavy beyond calculation, and the General had been obliged to borrow money to settle his hotel account and to defray the cost of the journey home where a fresh crop of bills awaited. The three boys—Andrew, junior, his cousin, Andrew Jackson Hutchings, and Lincoyer, the Indian— were in school where Andy II lived like a young lord. He had his own horse and a body servant to care for a wardrobe which included such newly purchased items as a suit, seventy-six dollars and eighty-seven cents; a hat, ten dollars; silk hose, a dollar fifty a pair, and imported kerchiefs. In six and one half months, the young man incurred indebtedness of three hundred and nine dollars to the establishment of Josiah Nichol who could outfit Nashville's *beau monde* from saddle blankets to hair oil.[10] The sum would have kept the average Tennessee family for a year.

And there were other claims on the time and purse of the planter. The overseer on the Hutchings boy's Alabama place died during cotton picking throwing the work into confusion. Jackson's first thought was for the care of the man's widow and children.[11] Colonel Robert Butler, husband of Rachel's favorite niece, Jane Hays, sent their son, Samuel, from Florida for Jackson to educate.[12] Thus were befriended by the master and mistress of the Hermitage three generations of Butlers, beginning with young Samuel's Revolutionary grandfather.

Fortunately, the long spell of hard times seemed at an end, with southern planters coming into their own again. Cotton prices were soaring. The first of the General's 1824 crop had brought thirteen and a half cents at New Orleans, the last thirty cents. "My [1825] crop is more promising than any I have ever seen." Jackson attributed the turn of the tide in large measure to a boom in domestic manufacturing which he hailed as vindication of his tariff vote, so roundly condemned by the planting class a year before.[13]

Politics also were booming. Four thousand vociferous Kentuckians got up a barbecue for their four congressmen who had voted for Jackson. Old Hickory resisted strong and subtle pressure calculated to inveigle him into attending. When Mr. Clay came home for the summer, invitations were sent forth to a dinner designed along more dignified and exclusive lines, which the Governor of the State and other notables, by their refusal to accept, rendered more exclusive than had been contemplated by the friends of the Secretary. Thus the breach in Kentucky widened as old Clay followers deserted and the organization of a permanent Jackson party got into its stride. Before Old Hickory's trunks were unpacked, invitations from a variety of states began to descend upon the Hermitage. A favorite approach was to bid the General to include this or that town in his itinerary to Washington next autumn.

This raised the first question Jackson must decide: whether to resign or to retain his seat in the Senate. Never happy as a legislator, the General's impulse was to resign. This was fortified by excellent reasons of policy. Congress would be a cock-pit of the Administration and anti-Administration forces. Would not the Hero present a fairer spectacle in pursuit of the occupation of a planter while others toiled amid the slippery gore of party conflict? A candid correspondent pointed out to the General that "opposition to the administration, and to the mode of the late election are very distinct and should be kept so." For General Jackson to express disapprobation of the "bargain" was proper, but as a disinterested patriot he should "support Mr Adams . . . so far as . . . the good of the country requires." At the end of four years the people "will select you whether at the *Hermitage* or in the *Senate* and I am not certain your remaining in the latter station will . . . give strength to the great cause."[14]

So the Hermitage it was. A graceful exit from the Senate was not difficult to contrive. Punctually the Tennessee Legislature renominated Andrew Jackson for the presidency. And how different the reception from that of the nomination of 1822. Without losing a day the General posted to Murfreesborough. In perhaps the longest political speech of his career, lasting fifteen minutes, Old Hickory told the assemblymen their step made it improper for him to continue in the Senate where events might place him under the imputation of shaping his official behavior to further his fortunes as a candidate.[15]

The General continued to comport himself with greater seemliness than the run of his followers. When Henry Lee, an unsteady son of Light Horse Harry, accepted the assistant postmaster-generalship under Adams, the Nashville *Republican,* owned by a personal friend of Old Hickory, attempted to drum Lee out of the Jackson camp. "I much regret the attack," Jackson assured the Virginian. "Sir, I am too charitable to believe that the acceptance of an Office under Mr Adams is either evidence of a change of principle or of corruption."

The Adams-Clay transaction stood on different legs, however.

"I had esteemed [Mr. Adams] as a virtuous, able and honest man; and when rumour was stamping the sudden union of his and the friends of Mr Clay with intrigue, barter and bargain I did not, nay, I could not believe that Mr. Adams participated. . . . When the election was terminated, I manifested publicly . . . my disbelief of his having had knowledge of the pledges which many men of high standing boldly asserted to be the price of his election. But when . . . Mr Clay was made Secretary of State . . . I could not doubt the facts. . . . I do not think the human mind can resist the conviction that . . . Mr Adams by the redemption of the pledge stood before the American people as a participant in the disgraceful traffic of Congressional votes for executive office.

"From that moment I withdrew all intercourse with him, not however to oppose his administration when I think it useful to the Country. . . . Mr. Adams is the Constitutional President and as such I would be the last man . . . to oppose him on any other ground than principle."[16]

5

The appearance before the Tennessee Legislature was a little masterpiece. Jackson's resignation from the Senate, his few words and those so restrained, answered every purpose. The opposition had its leader: Andrew Jackson; its cry: the "bargain"; its cause: popular sovereignty.

In December, 1825, the nation's glance turned again to Washington for the convocation of the first Congress of the régime of Mr. Adams. There the opening guns of the new campaign would be touched off. Surely Mr. Clay must move in force to recapture the initiative, so boldly seized and so dexterously held during the House battle, but swept from his hands immediately thereafter by the surprising fury of the bargain charge. His first move as political impresario of the Administration had been defensive, a retreat from the defiant stand heretofore taken against Jackson. It had not been very successful.

The next skirmish centered about the President's message. This document was eagerly awaited. From a man of J. Q. Adams's training in the practical affairs of government, it proved to be an interesting production. Vainly had Mr. Clay contended for its modification. Since the decline of war-time nationalism, the trend had been toward Jefferson's dictum that the best government governed least. Against this the new President set his face with splendid idealism. Not only would he have the Federal authority construct roads, canals, harbors and light-houses, concerning which there was an active division of opinion in Congress; he would have it embark upon a great academic program embracing a national university, an astronomical observatory and geographical and exploring expeditions. The firmest believer in these projects could not have offered them at this time as an ideal foundation for a political party. The closing sentence was calamitous. "Are we to slumber in indolence . . . and proclaim to the world that we are palsied by the hands of our constituents?"

General Jackson privately observed that the President "gave evidence of a want of discretion,"[17] which was putting it more temperately than some of Mr. Adams's own people. Retaining the initiative Mr. Clay had sought to seize, Jacksonians deluged Congress with bills, resolutions and constitutional amendments aimed at the Administration. Ritchie's Richmond *Enquirer,* the most influential newspaper in the slave-holding states, the Albany *Argus,* whose editorial pen was guided by Van Buren, and Isaac Hill's blatant but effective *New Hampshire Patriot* joined the critics. Their swift metabolism into Jackson organs had begun.

Then Mr. Clay played a good card. Americans had watched with approval the collapse of Spanish power in the New World as colony after colony established itself as an independent state. No foreigner, except Lafayette, exceeded Bolivar in our esteem, and no other American statesman had championed the Latin-Americans with the eloquence and the fire of Henry Clay. Now he plumped before Congress a proposal that we join a council of the Latin nations called to meet, like that of the Greek republics, at the isthmus. This was the Panama Congress.

Here was something the "Friends of Jackson," as the opposition styled itself, could not so readily render ridiculous. But they did their best, pecking away, misrepresenting, and overlooking no opening to drag all discussions back to the bitter refrain of "bargain." A Tennessee member gleefully depicted for Jackson a scene in the House.

"Vance said he was peculiarly situated; that he had come from the lowest order of society; that at the Age of 22 years he could not connect the letters of the Alphabet; that promoted as he was by the People of Ohio when an Imputation of Corruption was cast on them he would sustain their character at the hazard of his life. Mr. Trimble of Kentucky made a Talk somewhat in the same way. . . .

"McDuffie [of South Carolina] in reply said Genl Vance . . . had not changed his . . . grade of society . . . [when he chose to follow] the great political Juggler, Poltroon and Puppy, the Secretary of State Clay. If Mr. Vance or Trimble thought themselves aggrieved he would for once forget they were not Gentlemen and would attend to their Calls. The House was a perfect scene of confusion for half an hour, . . . the Chairman crying out Order, Order, Order, hurly burly, helter skelter, negro states and Yankies."[18]

It remained for John Randolph, a senator now, to bring the debate to its climax. Never has our national legislature seen the counterpart of that imperious cynic, half mad, half genius. After twenty years in Congress, he would saunter down an aisle followed by a young negro and, flicking his riding boots with a whip, observe, "I have not the honor to know, even by name, a large portion of the members of this House."[19] Usually Randolph spoke without notes or other aid to memory than a flagon of porter which the colored boy periodically replenished from a jug. His speeches were long. Often they had nothing to do with the subject at hand. However, one interested in sprightly diction, salted impartially with classical allusions and the argot of the racing stable, was sometimes repaid for listening.

Senator Randolph's random remarks on the Panama Congress wore around to the bargain issue which he characterized as "the coalition of Blifil and Black George, . . . the Puritan and the Blackleg."[20]

This was more than Clay could stand. In what Thomas Hart Benton described as the last "high-toned duel" he was privileged to witness, Randolph, one of the best shots in Virginia, threw away his fire and took Mr. Clay's bullet through the coat-tail. Not to be outdone in magnanimity, the Secretary of State sent his adversary a new coat. But this did not save the Panama Congress or impede John Randolph's epigram which rang through the country.

6

Every few days Jackson received from John Henry Eaton an account of the progress of affairs at Washington.

"All that is necessary for you is to be still and quiet," he read after the duel. The General's friends promised to do the rest. "This administration, wretched & rotten, is already crumbling. . . . Hal [Clay] walks alone, crest fallen, dejected and almost without associates." He likened the sweep for Jackson to the current of the Mississippi.[21]

The figure was not amiss. Van Buren had thrown in with the Friends of Jackson. From New Hampshire to Georgia other leaders of the defunct Crawford organization were following suit. Deprived of a populace-rousing issue by the return of prosperity, the hard times party in Kentucky and Alabama, champion of paper money and state banks, overlooked the fact that Andrew Jackson had been largely responsible for the exclusion of similar economic experiments from Tennessee and clutched at the tail of Old Hickory's rising kite. Nor was this the only quarter in which General Jackson reaped where he had not sown. The "outs" of varying complexions began to drift to him. The task of accelerating the movement and regimenting disparate elements into an effective party was assumed by a group in Washington including Calhoun, Van Buren, Benton, Randolph, Sam Houston, McDuffie of South Carolina, Livingston of Louisiana and Duff Green of the United States' Telegraph. Intimacy with Jackson made Eaton their chief in name if not in fact.

This body formed central committees of correspondence in each state, and under them local committees which were furnished with materials for dissemination. It won over old newspapers and started new ones. Mass meetings, militia musters, barbecues and fish frys were provided with orators primed on the imperfections of the Administration, the iniquities of the bargain, and the virtues of General Jackson. In Congress the hostile drum-fire was unceasing. Nothing escaped. When an inventory of the belongings in the Executive Residence included a billiard table and chess men, a Georgia patriot let loose about squandering public money for "gaming tables and gambling furniture." In vain did Mr. Adams disclose that the articles had been purchased with his private funds: the original account was too good to be marred by a correction.

Well for Major Eaton and colleagues that General Jackson was not in Washington that winter. Never had any man or set of men acted with such authority in the concerns of the Old Chief. They told him what they thought he should hear and kept him satisfied. When John Overton's nephew protested that Randolph and some of the others were hurting his cause, Jackson did not answer the letter.[22] When Duff Green, a political adventurer from St. Louis, was selected to establish the *Telegraph*, Eaton went through the form of taking him to the Hermitage to discuss the policy of the periodical with Jackson. The General bade his caller godspeed with the admonition: "Truth is mighty and shall prevail."[23] On money raised by Eaton the paper appeared in March, 1826. Green proved an able partizan editor and organizer. Within a few months his aspersive columns were the pattern for fifty Jackson journals.

Eaton's reiterated injunctions to "say nothing and plant cotton" enabled the Friends of Jackson to point to a somewhat ink-stained Cincinnatus, tilling his farm, plying the quill over a mountainous if often trivial correspondence and, on the whole, discharging very well the campaign's lighter amenities.

"I beg you sir to accept my sincere thanks for this repeated assurance of your desire to see me in Massachusetts, and particularly on so interesting occasion as that of our national jubilee [July 4]." The invitation was declined, but with a reciprocal "proffer of such accomodations as the Hermitage affords to yourself and any of your friends should you ever be inclined to visit this section of the Union."[24]

He begged off from addressing a Bible society on the ground that "having lost many of my teeth it is with difficulty I can articulate.... [Moreover] I might be charged...with...[electioneering] hypocritically under the sacred garb of religion."[25]

A set of teeth made by a Nashville dentist removed Old Hickory's difficulty in speaking, but not his aversion to public appearances. When the restoration of Mrs. Jackson's health canceled a proposed excursion to a healing spring in Kentucky, a friend of the General protested: "We hope that she may experience a slight relapse . . . and . . . wou^d beg to recommend . . . the Greenville,

Blue-Lick & Bath Waters. . . . The people of Kentucky want to see Gen¹. Jackson. . . . The Public Interest requires that they shouᵈ see him. . . . He will be taken to some three or four barbecues. . . . Solicit Mrs Jacksons pardon for the freedom with which I have usᵈ her Name."[26]

The approach of the local elections of 1826, providing the first practical test of the new Jackson machine, found the Friends in jubilant spirits. "Don't forget my bets," reminded Van Buren. "This election . . . should make up for past losses." The Senator was willing to risk ten thousand dollars and, if that sum could not be placed, any smaller amount, "or even a suit of clothes."[27] Whatever the extent of the wagers, Mr. Van Buren could hardly have lost. Jackson candidates held all ground gained in 1824 with flattering accessions in New York, Ohio, Virginia and the old Crawford territory southward. Scott of Missouri and Cook of Illinois were beaten on the bargain issue. Of the eight Kentuckians who had supported Adams four were not candidates. One was defeated and three re-elected.

Sam Houston pictured to his patron the "consternation" of the Administration. "Desperation is their only hope!!"[28]

7

The Cumberland cotton grower was prepared to believe it. Before him lay a report of a dinner-table colloquy imputing to Secretary of Navy Southard the opinion that James Monroe deserved the laurels for New Orleans, Jackson having abandoned his army and taken the road home when Monroe's peremptory order sent him back to the threatened city.

Off to Sam Houston went a letter with instructions to deliver it to Mr. Southard.[29]

Houston was an energetic lieutenant. Only a month before he had left for dead on the field of honor a supporter of Mr. Clay who had offered to arbitrate with firearms an issue growing out of the campaign. In the present instance the Congressman acted with equal boldness. Instead of delivering the letter to Southard, he showed it to Eaton and other party managers. In their judgment, too, the tone was too severe for a Tennessee planter whose pacific temperament was a recurring theme of the Washington junto. So Houston prepared in his own name a courteous request that Mr. Southard state whether he had been correctly quoted and asked Jackson's permission to deliver it. If this would not do, Houston begged the General to recast his note in softer terms. "I trust that you will not for one moment suppose that my course has been dictated by an eye to your political advancement."[30]

Jackson answered that any communication to Southard must come from him. The Secretary might put Houston off. *"He must reply."*[31] Another note to Mr. Southard, much milder than the first, however, was enclosed.[32] By this time the story was in the newspapers. Monroe put in his oar, smugly taking credit to himself in a manner that made Jackson boil. In a letter to a United States Senator, Old Hickory declared the War Department's support of the Louisiana army had been so tardy and ineffective that, had New Orleans fallen, either Monroe or his ordnance officer should have been shot for "criminal neglect."[33]

Here was the making of a Jacksonian imbroglio of the first magnitude. Before things got any worse, Houston delivered the letter to Southard as the quickest way of ending the matter. The Secretary responded with a long and argumentative communication in which, however, he said, "My object was to vindicate Mr. Monroe and not . . . to depreciate your military exploits. They form a part of our national glory." Jackson's acknowledgment contained the crisp recommendation that at his "wine drinkings hereafter" Mr. Southard should be more careful of his tongue.[34]

There the matter rested, but the peace of mind of the gentlemen who hoped to keep General Jackson tending cotton was never the same again.

8

The next alarm came from North Carolina where the Fayetteville *Observer* printed an unsigned communication, reporting a social conversation at the Hermitage in which the General was quoted as saying that, in 1825, Clay would have dealt with Jackson had he said the word. Party managers were distressed not only because they preferred a candidate eloquently mum on the subject of his wrongs, but also because of a disturbing letter Duff Green had received from James Buchanan. "I had no authority from Mr. Clay or his friends. . . . I am clearly of the opinion that whoever shall attempt to prove by direct evidence any corrupt bargain between Mr. C—— and Mr. A—— will fail."[35] This was giving the celebrated visit a different face from what had been plain enough to Jackson, Eaton and Kremer at the time.

When the *Observer* item began to go the rounds of the papers, Henry Clay came out with a denial in which he expressed doubt that Jackson had made the remarks attributed to him. Coming on the heels of Buchanan's strange letter, the Secretary's assurance gave the General's campaign strategists a new cause for concern. Were the two events connected? Green speculated with the thought that the Pennsylvanian had been subtly reached by Mr. Clay. He advised Jackson to "leave the subject where it now is" and trust in his friends.[36] As soon as Congress adjourned Eaton deprived himself of the companionship of Margaret Timberlake and headed for Tennessee.

Jackson chose to act for himself. In response to questioning, Eaton gave his chief a memorandum stating that Buchanan had approached him with an offer of negotiation from the friends of Clay, and only after Eaton had refused to convey this to Jackson had Buchanan done so. George Kremer sent a statement along the same line.[37] Sure of his ground concerning Buchanan, Jackson then took up a letter signed Carter Beverley in which that gentleman, a recent house-guest at the Hermitage, admitted the authorship of the *Observer* letter and asked the General to confirm the quotations imputed to him. Jackson complied in detail with an account of the Buchanan interview in which he identified his caller as "a member of Congress of high respectability."[38] Beverley sent the letter to the *Telegraph* and Green, falling in with the master's plan, published it.

This pleased Clay, who fancied himself in possession of the

initiative.[39] In a "direct, unqualified and indignant denial," he called upon General Jackson for proof. The American public, he said, should be the jury.[40]

Jackson came back with a lengthy broadside going over the whole story again. "This disclosure was made to me by Mr. James Buchanan."[41]

The challenge and the reply thundered through the press, partizans of each champion claiming the advantage. "Your letter . . . is a Death Stroke," boomed Captain Maunsel White, late of the Battalion of Uniformed Companies, now General Jackson's cotton broker in New Orleans. "But, they say, suppose Mr Buchanan denies it. That is impossible. Mr Eaton is a living witness."[42]

Surrounded by advisers who were in Nashville during the summer recess of Congress, General Jackson himself had pondered the possibility of Buchanan's failure to sustain him, and had taken steps to forestall it. Ahead of the newspapers which carried the General's statement eastward went a carefully composed, friendly but explicit letter to the Pennsylvania member. "I have no doubt . . . you will come forth and affirm the statement [you] made to Major Eaton, then to Mr. Kremer and then to me, and give the names of the friends of Mr. Clay who made it to you."[43]

It had been permitted to few men to refuse, with impunity, such a request from Old Hickory. The *Telegraph* exulted. "When Mr. Buchanan replies . . . we shall have more light to guide our way."[44] Fearing the worst, the Administration's *Journal* sought to impeach Buchanan's testimony in advance.[45]

Mr. Buchanan's reply came within a few days. This effort, also, showed scrupulous attention to composition; and it was tediously long. Up to the critical point the writer corroborated Jackson. Then, instead of giving the names the General called for, Mr. Buchanan declared that he had acted "solely on my individual responsibility and not at the agent of Mr. Clay or any other person."[46] In the light of this statement, Buchanan might have had some difficulty in explaining why he should have gone to Mr. Clay with a message impossible to justify, either on the basis of his or of General Jackson's version of their conversation. The Pennsylvanian avoided this embarrassment by omitting to mention the visit to Clay. When Clay himself offered to supply this detail, Buchanan begged him to be silent and Clay consented.[47]

Clay people threw their hats in the air and the *National Journal* repented its pre-judgment of Buchanan. A recent convert to the Jackson cause made a wry face. "This novel triangular controversy between Jackson, Clay & Buckhaun . . . has afforded a most singular triumph indeed to Henry Clay. Why does Genl. Jackson make such a *dam'd old fool* as Carter Beverley one of his confidential friends. . . . Who are the Generals advisers? Eaton, Sam Houston, Wm. B. Lewis & Tom Claiborne. I am apprehensive."[48]

Among the letters which poured upon the Hermitage was one from Frankfort, Kentucky, inscribed in an unfamiliar, delicate hand, fair enough for a lady's album.

"Although I have never had the pleasure of a personal acquaintance with you there are some circumstances of a peculiar nature which now induce me to address you. I am one of those who were told by one of his [Clay's] friends, as I think about the 20th day of January 1825, that if Mr. Adams should be elected he would make Mr. Clay his Secretary of State and I was three times solicited to write to Mr. White, our representative, to vote for Mr. Adams on that account. Thus urged I did write."[49]

Below stood the legible signature of Amos Kendall, editor of the *Argus of Western America*. A second communication in the same small script:

"Buchanan's statement has been received here by the Adams men with much exultation but their joy has very much abated. 'Sweet in the mouth,' they find this document, 'but bitter in the belly.' "[50]

General Jackson replied at once to his new correspondent. "We live in days of wonder. It would be now only necessary for me to publish Major Eatons statement and Mr. Kreamers, contrast them with his [Buchanan's] and it would show that his recollection had materially failed him. . . . However, I shall deliberate fully before I act."[51] The deliberation was assisted by some direct advice, of which Martin Van Buren's is representative. "Our people do not like to see publications from candidates. . . . Although our friend Buchanan was evidently frightened and therefore softened and obscured the matter still the fact of your entire aversion to any and all intrigue or arrangement is clearly established, and nothing could be of more value."[52]

The General lapsed into silence. Kendall and Van Buren were more than a little right about the effect of the Buchanan letter, once the impact of unexpected disappointment passed. Cursing under his breath, Duff Green grimly set to work to make the most of the material at hand and the Jackson press throughout the land performed to perfection. Never did the bargain issue seem more alive and damning than during the afterclap of Mr. Buchanan's refusal to sustain it. The tides of fortune that had seemed in the eventful weeks of December '24 and January '25 persistently to favor the coalition which elevated J. Q. Adams to the presidency had run contrary for thirty months. Introspective and heartsick, Mr. Adams began to prepare his mind to accept defeat.

Not so the Secretary of State. "Clay is a man of hazards," remarked an observer whose vision remained comparatively unclouded by prejudice.[53] In the spring the Kentuckian had rushed west with the expectation of turning the tables on his rival. He failed, and midsummer brought no truce to the defensive battle. In the August election loss of the Kentucky Legislature was averted by a narrow squeak. With Adams useless as an ally, with hope abandoned for the strength-giving repose he had expected to find at Ashland, the man of hazards fought on—wan, ill, and, according to unfriendly report, lashing up with whisky his reserves of energy. Neither weapons nor tactics were scrutinized as closely as they might have been, until Mr. Clay's name was involved in a blow at General Jackson beside which the worst implications of the bargain charge seem an innocent party stratagem.

9

This touched the Sacred Name.

"There was at Frankfort," a correspondent in Kentucky, too

circumspect to identify himself, wrote to John Overton, "an old ill looking Englishman named Day. His apparel was threadbare rusty and dirty, his professed employment was a collector of debts for the Baltimore and Philadelphia merchants. . . . He rendered himself conspicuous with the partisans of the coalition and . . . travelled at leisure to get such testimony as he might picked up [concerning General Jackson's marriage]. In this vindictive and diabolical occupation Day . . . passed through that part [of Kentucky] where Mrs. Jackson formerly resided; he then went to Nashville in Tennessee and then to Natchez."

Kentucky to Nashville to Natchez: the trail of romance blazed nearly forty years before by a headlong wilderness Lochinvar and the mismated wife of Lewis Robards.

"After an absence of some time he returned to Frankfort having obtained as he said what [enabled? Manuscript illegible.] him to demonstrate that General Jackson and his lady had never been married. he brought with him copys of some records from Mercer County Stating that Mr. and Mrs. Robards had been devorced . . . on the testimony of one Hugh McGary; this record and some other papers he showed in Frankfort to the partisans of the coallition; . . . after a while they were . . . left at Lexington, it has been said, with Mr. Henry Clay, who delivered them to Charles Hammond."[54]

When the shadow of Andrew Jackson's courtship threatened the campaign of 1824 Jackson had said, "I know how to defend *her.*" He used that tone now. "I have lately got an intimation of some of his [Clay's] secrete movements which if I can reach with possitive and responsible proof I will wield to his political and perhaps his actual destruction. he is certainly the bases[t], meanest scoundrel that ever disgraced the image of his god. . . . Even the aged and virtuous female is not free from his . . . slander—but *anough, you know me.*"[55]

Sam Houston, to whom this communication was addressed, did, indeed, know his patron, having trained for his recent duel on the Hermitage grounds under Jackson's experienced eye. He felt, however, that in the present canvass pistols had done all that could reasonably be expected of them. Yet, this might be serious: the Mercer County court records, Hugh McGary's testimony, in the hands of a man like Charles Hammond, editor of the Cincinnati *Gazette*. John Henry Eaton went straight to the Secretary of State. Mr. Clay admitted having seen Hammond during his recent stay in the West, but so emphatically did he deny knowledge of or agency in a contemplated attack on the character of Mrs. Jackson that Eaton wrote Jackson he believed the Secretary to be telling the truth.[56]

However, the General's friends did not place their sole reliance in Mr. Clay's veracity or in any endeavors that he might make to curb Hammond. Eaton in Washington and Lewis and Overton in Tennessee began collecting statements from old Cumberland residents giving their versions of Rachel's troubles with her first husband, her marriage to Jackson, her irreproachable character, and so on. A fortnight after the interview with Clay, Eaton felt this activity prudently undertaken. By that time he had begun to doubt the sincerity of the Secretary's protestations, and so told Jackson. Before him was an uninvited disclaimer from Hammond insisting that Clay had nothing to do with the affair. Eaton felt this inspired by the Secretary. Hammond confirmed the report that he had profited by the researches of Day. "What use I shall make of these documents depends upon future events."[57]

As he wrote, Hammond was already making use of Day's gleanings, stealthily by word of mouth. From the Mississippi to the Atlantic spread underground tales of the annihilating revelations in Hammond's power to make. Jackson got wind of this and[58] the veteran's friends trembled lest he be goaded to some rash act. His threats grew bolder. "A day of retribution . . . [for] Mr Clay and his tool Col° Hammond must arrive should I be spared."[59] Eaton begged his chief to understand that this would be playing into the hands of the whisperers. "I know them all, & well, & everything I have to say is, be cautious— be still— be quiet. . . . Weigh & bale your cotton & sell it; and if you see any thing about yourself just throw the paper into the fire . . . & go on to *weigh the cotton*."[60]

By the time, or shortly after, Eaton's letter was in Jackson's hands, the slander had attained the tangibility of print—and this from an unexpected source. Thomas D. Arnold, an East Tennessee candidate for Congress, published a hand-bill proclaiming that Andrew Jackson had "spent the prime of his life in gambling, in cock-fighting, in horse-racing . . . and to cap all tore from a husband the wife of his bosom." A vote for him would be a vote to sanction the code whereby if a man should fancy his neighbor's "pretty wife . . . he has nothing to do but to take a pistol in one hand and a horse whip in another and . . . possess . . . her."[61]

After this Hammond opened his *Gazette* to the story in more detail. "Gen. Jackson prevailed upon the wife of Lewis Roberts [*sic*] to desert her husband and live with himself." Then followed an account of the divorce on McGary's testimony of adultery, ignoring the three years the Jacksons had supposed themselves to be legally married.[62]

Arnold was an obscure country politician, Hammond an editorial light of shifty character. The collaboration of the *National Journal,* Adams's mouthpiece and mentor of the Administration press, made them personages of note overnight. When this newspaper reprinted Arnold's screed, the assault on Rachel Jackson was before the country in a guise that could not fail of attention.

The General left off weighing cotton long enough to consent to a forthright counter-move. William B. Lewis signed a call for a mass meeting at the Davidson County court house at which, after "animated and eloquent" oratory, a committee was named to "detect and arrest falsehood and calumny." A preponderance of the wealth and prestige of the Nashville district was embodied in the eighteen men—not all unwavering admirers of Old Hickory—who served thereon.[63]

The committee produced a document notable for its judicial calm and accuracy. By the statements of the surviving witnesses in Virginia, Kentucky and Tennessee was traced the thorny path of Rachel Donelson's married life with Robards; her meeting with Jackson; the flight to Natchez; the supposed divorce; the marriage ceremony on Spanish soil; the actual divorce by ex-parte proceedings. Though the skillful work of advocates, little of importance in this recital can be overthrown by evidence we know today.[64] It shines by contrast with the reckless productions of the opposition. Plus flourishes by Duff Green, this was published in the *Telegraph,* filling ten columns, and in the Jackson press nationally.[65]

Arnold returned to the attack.

"Gen. Jackson has admitted that he boarded at the house of old Mrs. Donelson, and that Roberts became jealous of him, but he omits the cause of that jealousy . . . [namely] that one day Roberts surprised General Jackson and his wife exchanging most delicious kisses. . . . In this case Roberts acted a cowardly part" in that he failed to shoot "Jackson dead in his tracks." Concerning Mrs. Robards's voyage to Natchez in the company of Jackson and Colonel Stark, "the Gen. omitted to tell that . . . they slept under the same blanket."[66]

Hammond followed with a pamphlet said to have been distributed under the franks of Administration congressmen: "Ought a convicted adulteress and her paramour husband to be placed in the highest offices of this free and christian land?"[67]

Old Hickory fought for self-command. "How hard it is to keep the cowhide from these villains. I have made many sacrifices for my country—but being . . . unable to punish those slanders of Mrs. J. is a sacrifice too great to be well endured." Firm John Coffee counseled patience a little longer. "Controul your feelings. Let nothing draw you out."[68]

But the harried man could endure no more. He seized a pen.

"I could not [at first] believe that even you, sir, . . . could descend so low. . . . It did not seem possible to me that the Secretary of State, the second officer in the government of our Republic, . . . would travel through the country for the cowardly purpose of slandering a virtuous female—one who has passed from infancy to old age in the confidence and friendship of the good and pious citizens of every society in which she has lived and who [has] received the mark[ed] and I may say honored attentions of Mrs. Clay and yourself. . . . Were all these professions base hypocrisy? . . . Sir, assassination of character in all its horrid forms and colorings is not as bad as such conduct as this. . . ."

The object of this letter? Certainly not to split the hairs of social usage. That was never Jackson's way. He had started to draw up what looked like a summons to an interview at twenty paces, the form and language of which he knew by heart. Old Hickory took a fresh grip on the quill.

"Sir, One would have looked for something less degrading from a champion of the Pistol Gag Law. . . ."

Again the pen faltered sliding off into irrelevancies. Evil day, evil day when Andrew Jackson permitted himself to be caught up in the fatal web which had rendered him impotent to strike a blow for the woman he loved as he loved no other creature of earth. But the thing was done and Coffee was right: an aspirant to the presidency could not fight a duel.

Yet the pen ran on, tracing out sentences as futile as anything Andrew Jackson had uttered in twenty years.

". . . I have only to add that Mrs. J and myself hurl at you our defiance. A virtuous and well spent life has assured her a skirt which such men as you and your worthy associate Charles Hammond cannot sully."

There the baffled writer stopped. It is not known whether this letter ever was actually sent to Henry Clay.[69]

The free style of campaigning put Duff Green at no disadvantage. After an unheeded warning to Peter Force, publisher of the *Journal*, that further affronts would bring retaliation, Green smote his lyre and forth came a fabrication attributing to Mr. and Mrs. Adams premarital relations similar to those alleged against the Jacksons.[70] "Let Mrs. Jackson rejoice," the editor of the *Telegraph* reported to the Hermitage, "her vindication is complete."[71]

Old Hickory's rebuke was swift and final. "Female character should never be introduced or touched unless a continuation of attack should be made against Mrs. Jackson, and then only by way of *Just retaliation* on the known GUILTY. . . . I *never war against females* and it is only the base and cowardly that do."[72]

This terminated the retaliation though, to Jackson's mind, the known guilty were John Quincy Adams and Henry Clay. The General believed that a word from Adams to Peter Force, such as Jackson gave to Green, would have halted the *Journal's* encouragement of Hammond's and of Arnold's filthy pens. The case of the Secretary of State is less negative. Disregarding questionable tales that reached Jackson's ears, such as that of a midnight meeting between Clay and Hammond,[73] it seems clear that Clay, an experienced politician and practiced manager of editors, was close enough to Hammond to have suppressed him had he wished to do so. More than that, Eaton's intuition had served him well when it attributed Hammond's effort to absolve Clay to the inspiration of Clay himself. The fact is that immediately after Eaton's visit the Secretary informed Hammond of the Senator's call. "I have now no recollection that the case of Mrs. Jackson formed any topic of conversation between us when you were at Lexington."[74] This was not the language Henry Clay had used to Major Eaton; nor was the effect of it the same. "Suppose you had furnished me the documents," brazenly replied Hammond, "what right had Gen. Jackson to complain? He keeps no terms with you."[75] Despite his virtuous disclaimer, Mr. Clay knew what his man Hammond was about, and gave silent consent to his depredations.

So much touching briefly on the question of responsibility for the episode which, above all others of his political life, Jackson never forgot or forgave. It appears to have gained the Administration no advantage with the voters; such assaults seldom do. The salient accomplishment was to lay waste to the joy of life, desolating an aged and pious woman whose fortune had been in youth to be beautiful, to marry a bounder and, existence with him becoming intolerable, to win the heart of Andrew Jackson.

10

Jackson people, too, are accountable for the depths to which the campaign declined. The trend dates from the contest of

THE COFFIN HANDBILL

A campaign poster of 1828, published by John Binns of Philadelphia.

Reproduced from an original in the museum of the North Carolina State Historical Commission, Raleigh.

Jacob Webb *David Morrow* *John Harris* *Henry Lewis* *David Hunt* *Edward Lindsay*

A brief account of the Execution of the Six Militia Men.

As we may soon expect to have the official documents in relation to the Six Militia Men, arrested, tried, and put to death, under the orders of General Andrew Jackson, this may not be an improper time to give to the public some of the particulars of their execution, as we have them from "AN EYE WITNESS," who appeals to Col. Russell, for the truth of every word he relates.

Harris was a Baptist preacher, with a large family. He had hired as a substitute for three months. This was the case with most of them. They were ignorant men, but obstinate in what they believed right, and what they had been told by their officers was right.—They were all sure they could not be kept beyond three months, and they gave up their musquets, and had provisions dealt out to them, from the public stores, before they left the camp.—This confirmed their convictions that they were right and doing what was lawful.

Col. Russel commanded at the execution. The Militia men were brought to the place in a large wagon. The military dispositions being made, Col. Russel rode up to the wagon and ordered the men to descend. Harris was

the only one who betrayed feminine weakness. The awfulness of the occasion; his wife and nine children; the fear of a parting with his son; and the fear of a quickly approaching ignominious death! quite overcome him, and he sunk in unmanly grief. No feeling of manly pride could brace him up.

Col. Russel, doubtless, felt as a man, but he felt also for the pride of the army, and desired to animate the men with fortitude. "You are about to die, "said he, by the sentence of a Court "Martial—die like men; *like soldiers.* "You have been brave in the field— "you have fought well—do no disfredit- "it to your country, or dishonour to the "army, or yourselves, by any unmanly "fears. Meet your fate with courage."

Harris attempted to make some apology for his confusion, but while he spoke, he wept bitterly. The fear of death, the idea that he should never again behold his wife and little ones, and his son weeping near him, had taken such entire possession of his mind that it was impossible he should rally.

Lewis, the gallant Lewis, said in a clear and manly tone, "Colonel, I have "served my country well. I love it "dearly, and would, if I could, serve "it longer and better. I have fought "bravely—*you know* I have, and HERE "I have a right to say so MYSELF. I

give his very words; here his voice fail.... here he passed the back of his right hand over his eyes —"I did not expect it: But, I am now "as firm as I have been in battle, and "you shall see that I will die as he- "comes a brave man," you know I am a "brave man," "Yes, Lewis, said the Colonel, you have always behaved like a brave man." Other sentences were uttered, other declarations were made, and words of comfort spoken, but they were lost on me: my attention, say's an Eye Witness, being chiefly directed to Lewis.

Six coffins were ranged as directed, and on each of them knelt one of our condemned American Militia Men.— Such a sight was never seen before! I trust to God it never will be seen again! Six soldiers were detailed and drawn up to fire at each man. What an awful duty! Their white caps were drawn over the faces of the unhappy men.— Harris evidently trembled, and I could almost persuade myself that the heart of Lewis was enlarged, and that his bosom rose with manly courage to meet death. The fatal word was given and they all fell.

As we approached the scene of blood and carnage, Lewis gave signs of life: the rest were all dead—he crawled upon his coffin. After the lapse of a few

minutes he said—I give his very words; here his voice fail.... ... he passed —"Colonel, ... the Colonel, was close to him—"Colonel, I am not killed; but I am sadly cut and mangled." His body was now examined and it was found that but four balls had wounded him. "Co-lonel," said he, "did I behave well." "Yes, Lewis," said the Colonel in the kindest tone of voice—"like a man." "Well sir," said he, "have I not atoned for this offence? Shall I not fire?" The Colonel was much agitated, and gave orders that the Surgeon should, if possible, preserve his life. They did all that skill and humanity could do— it was all of no avail. Poor Lewis expressed a great desire to live—"not," said he at one time, "that I fear death, "but I would repent me of some sins, "and I desire to live yet a little long- "er in the world." He suffered inconceivable agony, from his wounds, and died on the fourth day.

Many a soldier has wept over his grave. He was a brave man and much beloved. He suffered twenty deaths. I have seen the big drops chase each other down his forehead with pain and anguish. There was much sensibility and sympathy throughout the camp.— I would not have, unjustly and unnecessarily, signed this death warrant for all the wealth of all the Indies. The soldiers detailed to shoot Lewis had

from strong feelings of sympathy, or mistaken humanity failed to shoot him —but four balls had entered his body.

"An Eye Witness" appeals to Col. Russell, who he thinks now lives in Alabama, for the perfect truth of this sketch. He does not fear but the Colonel will keenly recollect and faithfully depict the horrors of the day on which six Americans were shot to death under his command—but not by his orders.

The order bears date the very day after General Jackson returned in triumph to New Orleans, and the day before he joyfully went, under triumphal arches, to the Temple of the living God; where, says the historian, "they crowned their adored General with laurels." The order for the execution of these six unhappy men bears date January 22, 1815. His crown of laurels had not yet withered, when blood, the life's blood of his countrymen, of his fellow soldiers, flowed plentifully by his order. May that order and its consequences, sink deep into the hearts of the American people and steel them against him who had no flesh in his obdurate heart; who did not feel for Man; in the midst of Joy and Revelry, almost in the more immediate presence of his Creator, who issued the fatal order to put his fellow creatures to death, and to make their

Do not be startled, gentle reader at the picture before you. It is all true and every body ought to know it. Gen. Jackson having made an assault upon Samuel Jackson, in the streets of Nashville, & the latter not being disposed to stand still and be beaten, stooped down for a stone to defend himself. While in the act of doing so, Gen. Jackson drew a sword cane from his cane, and through Samuel Jackson's body, the sword entering his back and coming out of his breast. For this officer an indictment was found against Genl Jackson, by a grand jury, upon which he was subsequently arraigned and tried. But finding means to persuade the petit jury that he committed the act in self-defence, he was acquitted. Gentle reader, I leave you to run it through the body of any one who you may presume to stand in his way, as a fit person to be our President.

Farewell to life and love!
See six black coffins rang'd along—
Six graves before them made;
Webb, Lindsey, Harris, Lewis, Hunt,
And Morrow kneeled and prayed.

The dreadful deed is done!
All six militia men were shot,
And O! it seems to me
A dreadful deed—a bloody act
Of needless cruelty.

In such a case, O noble Lady,
"Let mercy's voice be heard."
'Twas all in vain, John Harris' par'y,
"I'm past the soul's belief!"
Hark! as the flint was Jackson's heart,
He would not grant relief.

proved by Major General Jackson, and by his order the whole six shot.

O! DID you hear that plaintive cry
Borne on the southern breeze?
Say, was it your or right to go—
"For mercy, on his knees?"

"Fly! for my county's cause is lost,"
"And next, great Chief, for you."
"We thought our time of service out—"
"Thought it our right to go!"
"We meant to violate no law,
"Nor wish'd to shun the foe."

"At home an aged mother waits
"To clasp her only son;
"A wife, and little children—this arm
"Alone depend upon."

A short time before the execution of the militia-men, seven regular soldiers were shot near Nashville, by a band of regulars scarcely sufficient to guard the prisoners. They were confined in a house, and taken out and executed one at a time, there being scarcely enough men each month before the one had expired. General Jackson doomed an eighth soldier was to have been executed at the same time. He was a young man who had served faithfully. He was saved by a writ... General Jackson's displeasure for smuggling this one victim from his doom. Capital punishments in an blood-stained land... as well as for penalty; but in this case it was a transaction of horror to peaceful citizens; no army was there to witness the bloody tragedy.

POOR JOHN WOODS was a generous hearted, noble fellow as ever lively, who had volunteered in the service of his country. He was on guard one day at Fort Strother—the officer of the guard permitted him to go to his tent, and make a hasty breakfast, whilst disposing of his scanty meal, seated on the ground, the officer chanced to pass, and ordered him to mount guard again. Woods' equal at home, undertook to pick up and carry off some bones that lay scattered about the place—Woods refused, and the little officer attempted to compel him. At this instant, Gen. Jackson, having heard the dispute, came out of his tent, and without knowing any thing of the merits of the case, repeatedly vociferated, "Shoot him! Shoot the damn'd rascal!" Before his trial, Gen. Jackson used this language, though he did afterwards provide the... took the life of man!

On the 27th day of March, 1814, General Jackson found at an Indian village, at the called themselves under the banks of the river, bend of the Tallapoosa, about 1000 Indians with their squaws and children, running about among their huts. The following is BEEN CONCEALED. We ask you to pause and reflect that the... an account of the sanguinary massacre which therefore made the first attempt to escape by water when we killed sixteen which had began "MORNING WE KILLED 16 WHICH HAD upon his conscience, as he has upon his hands—he, forsooth, is to be hailed the took place—it is Gen. Jackson's own. WE intend to DESTROY among of them who had concealed—and warrior, like of Washington, the empty

MINING AND EXTERMINATE them, I de- Jackson.

FRANKLIN, Tenn. September 10, 1828.

THOMAS HART BENTON. Lieut. Col. 39th Infantry.
And now a resident of the State of the United States.

1824 in which the General was an unwilling candidate, his personal conduct the most proper of all the aspirants. Yet lieutenants were allowed to introduce militia muster and fish fry methods, long sanctioned in frontier elections but hitherto absent from presidential campaigns. The other candidates protested, perhaps the more passionately after each had attempted, without success, the western technique.[76] Jackson's border upbringing condoned the conduct of his aides who succeeded where rivals failed, Old Hickory being the only true borderer in the race.

The campaign of 1824, however, seems respectable by contrast with its successor in which the art of character assassination attained a perfection as yet unsurpassed. In this the Adams people were by a good margin the busiest practitioners. The ghosts of Dickinson, of poor John Woods, of six Tennessee militiamen executed in Alabama,[77] of Arbuthnot and Ambrister were caused to walk. Years later the tale was related of a New England Sunday school teacher who asked the name of the slayer of Abel. "General Jackson," a pupil replied.[78]

The case of the six militiamen was presented in the Coffin Handbill, perhaps the most easily remembered political broadside in our history, and in a pamphlet entitled *Official Record from the War Department* which deserves to be better known. This assumed the style of a government document and bore the legend, "Ordered to be Printed by the Congress." Distributed under the franks of Adams congressmen, it could be mistaken for an authentic transcript of the proceedings of the court-martial which sentenced the men. Actually it was a part of that record, so garbled as to constitute a forgery. The Burr conspiracy was revived with éclat until the discovery that Henry Clay had appeared as an attorney for the accused. The *National Journal* published a *Sketch of the Life &c of General Jackson* convicting Old Hickory of the Florida "crimes" of which Mr. Adams had acquitted him at the time. Charles Hammond's *Gazette* had the last word, calling Jackson's mother a prostitute and his father a mulatto who had sold an older offspring of that union into slavery.[79]

In the light of this record, the comparatively minor allegations that Andrew Jackson drank, gambled and occasionally shot or sword-caned an acquaintance might have served to endow him with a few plausible failings. But the Hero's friends would not allow it. "Gen. Jackson *does not at any time play cards,*" adjured Duff Green. "Neither does General Jackson swear."[80]

John Henry Eaton contributed to his reputation as an observer when he wrote his patron: "Nothing now to be said of you can . . . [work] the least injury. The Press has overthrown its own power through repeated falsehoods."[81]

Although the Hermitage was overrun with visitors, Jackson continued almost as removed from the purely political aspects of the campaign as he had been four years before. Then the attitude was genuine for, except when smarting under some hostile thrust, he had no deep-seated wish to be elected. Now he intended to triumph, and to that end permitted a dash of the conscious Cincinnatus to tincture the picture of masterly in-action. The General's cotton seemed to have suffered from in-attention, however, the 1827 crop being no better than average in quality. A plague decimated the stables leaving Jackson with-out a team to take him to Alabama to straighten out an over-seer tangle. Convinced that one plantation was enough for a man about to be called to other responsibilities, the General sold Melton's Bluff. Lincoyer, the Indian boy, died of tuberculosis and was buried as a member of the family. Andrew Jackson Hutchings was expelled from Cumberland College. "Tell him," his guardian wrote, "how much I have regretted the want of education and how much I wish him to possess one."[82] Henry Lee, having resigned his appointment under Adams, found him-self homeless because of a sentimental affair with his wife's sis-ter. Jackson took him in. "Black Horse Harry" fell to, help-ing Donelson write letters and even began a biography of his protector.

Old Hickory was persuaded to accept an invitation to go to New Orleans for the thirteenth anniversary of his greatest feat of arms. Attended by a mixed company of politicians and war veterans, the General and Mrs. Jackson boarded the steamer *Poca-hontas* for the only electioneering tour he was ever to make in his own interest. One of the last persons to be included in the party was James Alexander Hamilton of New York, who had reached Nashville somewhat breathlessly on the eve of the sailing.

Colonel Hamilton, a son of the first Secretary of the Treasury, was of the cosmopolitan group engaged in promoting the advancement of Martin Van Buren. The New York statesman had come so far since his leadership of Crawford's doomed cause that only John C. Calhoun seemed to stand between him and the ultimate goal of a public man's ambition. Jackson's declaration not to seek re-election rendered the early settlement on an heir apparent a matter of first importance. Drifting down the Mississippi, Hamilton, W. B. Lewis, Sam Houston and other anti-Calhoun spirits were soon in congenial conversation. Several months previously Houston had endeavored to get in a lick at the South Carolinian by showing his chief an old letter, written by Monroe to Calhoun, throwing light on the subject which above everything Mr. Calhoun wished to conceal from Andrew Jackson: the truth of the Cabinet's secret deliberations concerning the Florida campaign. "My hair stood on end for an hour," exclaimed Jackson after reading the missive.[33] Conciliators had got busy, however. Old Hickory's gray locks came to rest and Sam's industry seemed wasted—until the apparently providential appearance of James Alexander Hamilton.

At New Orleans the celebration lasted longer than the battle and made almost as much noise. One relatively small act tended to make General Jackson's path in Louisiana smoother than it had been in 1814: he slept at the home of Bernard de Marigny de Mandeville.

Colonel Hamilton was not a member of the returning Jackson party. He was on his way to Georgia to try to get from William H. Crawford a statement on those old Cabinet confidences which Houston and Lewis fondly hoped would blow Calhoun sky high. Back in Nashville, Houston sought to prepare the way by stirring up things on the basis of the Monroe letter which had aroused Jackson momentarily the year before. This time Mr. Calhoun himself bore into the breach with wordy explanations. Then it transpired that Hamilton had performed his mission badly, failing to see Crawford and obtaining only a letter from Governor Forsyth giving a second-hand version of Calhoun's criticism of Jackson in 1818. Lewis felt the production too weak to present to the General. Calhoun's explanations succeeded. The campaign moved on with the ambitious South Carolinian still ascendant over his ambitious rival from New York.[84]

II

The sulphurous clouds of personal abuse all but obscured the only issues of policy before the country—the tariff and internal improvements—as well as the fact that on these heads there was not a great deal to choose between the candidates. Early in the campaign Jackson's advisers had pressed him to be discreet so as not to make difficulties for sectional leaders of the party. The object was to insinuate the General on the East as a friend of protection, on the West as a Federal road and canal advocate, on the South as a very mild tariff and improvements man. Old Hickory bristled. "I have nothing in my political creed to keep secrete."[85] He said he had voted for certain internal improvements and for Clay's American System, and still held the views those votes expressed. The managers persisted. "A laconic, very laconic note referring to your [tariff] votes would be ample."[86] Jackson did not retreat from the tariff position which had brought so much southern criticism in 1824. Though clear, his statements were brief enough to satisfy the strategists, however.[87] The "bargain" and slander farragoes made livelier reading, and what the General said about duties was not widely circulated. Consequently the practical idea of running him as chameleon on the issues succeeded to some extent.

Yet, all these things gave way before the ruling consideration of personality: Old Hickory or John of Braintree? From the first a majority of people had seemed to prefer Jackson, which simplified the problems of his lieutenants. The campaign was almost an uninterrupted extension of that of 1824 which had opened with a populace in arms against hard times, determined to achieve a more equal distribution of wealth and of burdens.

The defeat of their champion by the enterprise of Henry Clay afforded the most effective cry for 1828. Hard times passed. The place of the spur of want to drive the people on was supplied by a whipped-up frenzy of politicians mindful of their own needs and greeds—with the reticent figure of the outraged Hero etched upon their banners. Against this concatenation of circumstances, Adams began the race with less than an even chance. Soon the situation was desperate, which desperate measures failed to repair.

By midsummer, 1828, Jacksonites ceased to worry over the outcome. A party worker sent Lewis predictions on the vote in Kentucky, Indiana and Ohio merely to "enable our friends to make betts somewhat advisedly."[88] On election day a traveler in Illinois described a typical western polling place. "Platform some thirty feet high in front of the court house. . . . Thirty gallon barrel of whisky with the name of 'ANDREW JACKSON' written on it; and in a short time another barrel with the name of 'JOHN QUINCY ADAMS.' " The story was told of a stranger in a Tennessee town who saw no men on the streets. A hotel proprietor explained that they were looking for a couple of rascals. Asked what the rascals had done, the tavern-keeper said they had voted for Adams.[89]

In some New England precincts the situation was almost reversed. Heavy eastern majorities gave Mr. Adams a total popular vote within twelve per cent of that of his rival—508,064 to 647,276; but so much more widely diffused was Jackson's support that the triumph in the electoral college was overwhelming—one hundred and seventy-eight to eighty-three.

"I am filled with gratitude," he wrote simply to John Coffee. "Still, my mind is depressed."[90]

His heart ached for Rachel.

CHAPTER VII

END OF FLIGHT

I

AFTER handsome John Dickinson had futilely emptied a pistol into Andrew Jackson's breast and then folded his arms to receive the consequences of a hasty use of Rachel Jackson's name—in fact during all the early episodes that enliven Jackson's defense of his wife's reputation—precautions were taken to veil from Rachel the true nature of events. This was to small purpose. She always seems to have known more than she was supposed to know. Within her the conviction deepened that the only hope for peace lay in obscurity; and this proved a vain hope. When partizans of Mr. Adams branded Rachel Jackson an adulteress so publicly that pretense of concealment from her was useless, she faced the issue with the determined composure of one confronting an ordeal long expected.

Her own remonstrances were mildly put. "the enemys of the Genls have dipt their arrows in wormwood and gall and sped them at me. . . . they have Disquieted one that thaey had no rite to do." The afflicted woman prayed for her tormentors. "my judg will know how many prayers have I oferd up."[1]

There was also a reward for one of her champions, Moses Dawson, editor of *The* [Cincinnati] *Friend of Reform or Corruption's Adversary*—a suit of clothes woven and made up at the Hermitage, in part by Rachel's own hands. Such recognition all but deprived Mr. Dawson of the power of coherent speech.

"Madam

"With feelings which no language can discribe no eloquence express I received your very flattering letter and highly worthy

estimable present by the hands of your respected Worthy friend
Judge Isaacs. . . .

"To Advocate the cause of truth and to defend exemplary virtue and exalted worth against the pointless shafts of falsehood
and malvolence is a task not only easy of performance, but, to
a generous mind, is full and sufficient reward." Mr. Dawson
promised that Rachel's gift "for the residue of my life [shall]
be my only Holliday dress, and then left as an Heir loom in my
family.

"Permit me at this time Madam to congratulate you on the
event which. . . ." Then followed three lines of untrammeled
prose, fortunately attended by a translation: "I mean the election
that has called your illustrious Consort to the chief Magistracy
of this great nation."[2]

William B. Lewis delivered this letter to the mistress of the
Hermitage. It may be assumed that she made a proper—and
properly spelled, thanks to Nephew Donelson—acknowledgment
as she did to other messages in similar strain when the news of
victory roused the Cumberland. But to Lewis she did not dissemble.

"For Mr. Jackson's sake I am glad. For my own part I never
wished it."[3]

2

Friends noted a relinquishment of courage, a lapse into melancholy. "She supported herself under it [the slander] until the
excitement produced by the late contest was over. From that
moment her energy subsided, her spirits drooped, and her health
declined— She has been heard to speak but seldom since."[4]
Youthful Henry R. Wise, who had come to Nashville to practice law and had married the daughter of a clergyman dear to
Rachel, called at the Hermitage with his bride and some members
of the wedding party. Never was he to forget the marks of time
and sorrow on the countenance of his hostess. "Mrs. Jackson
was once a form of rotund and rubiscund beauty, but [is] now

very plethoric and obese. . . . [She] talked low but quick, with a short and wheezing breath." Yet he found her "the very personification of affable kindness and of a welcome as sincere and truthful as it was simple and tender."[5]

The bridal couple accepted an invitation to pass their honeymoon under the roof that had sheltered so many newlyweds. "The house was full of guests, . . . visitors from all parts of the United States, numbering from twenty to fifty per day, constantly coming and going, all made welcome and all well attended to. The cost . . . [of this hospitality] was very great and burdensome; but the general showed no sign of impatience, and was alive and active in his attentions to all comers and goers. He affected no style, and put on no airs, but was plainly and simply . . . polite to all." Andrew Jackson Donelson, Stockley Donelson and Henry Lee assisted with the honors.

"General Jackson bade us feel at home but gave us distinctly to understand that he took no trouble to look after any but his lady guests; as for the gentlemen, there was the parlor, the diningroom, the library, the side-board and its refreshments; there were the servants, and all that was necessary was to ring. He was as good as his word. He did not sit at the head of the table, but mingled with his guests, and always preferred a seat between two ladies, seeking a chair between different ones at various times. He was quick to perceive every point of word or manner, was gracious in approval, but did not hesitate to dissent with courtesy when he differed. He obviously had a hidden vein of humor, loved aphorism, and could politely convey a sense of smart travesty. If put upon his mettle he was very positive, but gravely respectful. He conversed freely, and seemed absorbed in what the ladies were saying; but if a word of note was uttered at any distance from him audibly, he caught it by quick and pertinent comment, without leaving the subject about which he was talking to another person."[6]

On a soft October evening while facile Henry Lee entertained the company in the drawing room, young Wise was bidden to join a smaller and less fashionable group, though more difficult of access. He found Rachel in her first floor bedroom, seated be-

side an open window overlooking the garden. Her circle con-
sisted of the General; old Judge Overton, bald, beak-nosed and
toothless; the Reverend Obadiah Jennings, father-in-law of Mr.
Wise; Mary Eastin, a pretty niece whom Rachel intended to take
to Washington; and Henry Baldwin, son of a Jackson leader
in Pennsylvania and a groomsman at the recent wedding. On
hearing that Henry Wise was from Accomac County in Virginia,
the home of her maternal ancestors, Mrs. Jackson had sent for
him. As it turned out, the visitor was familiar with the hip-
roofed mansion in which Rachel's mother was born, with Assawaman Church which she attended as a girl—in fact, the whole
countryside of which Rachel had heard at her mother's knee.
She asked the young man many questions.

There were other such evenings, as more and more the wife
of the President-elect avoided the kaleidoscope of company, keeping to her chamber to sit with her Bible, or a few old friends,
partaking of the additional consolation of a pipe of tobacco. Once
she spoke of having "lived with Mr. Jackson for nearly forty
years . . . [without] an unkind word passing between them, and
the only subject on which they had ever differed . . . was his
acceptance of appointments, . . . she being always unwilling for
him to enter public life."[7]

On the eighth day of November, 1828, young Dr. Henry Lee
Heiskell who made one or two trips a week to the Hermitage
attending the negroes, examined Mrs. Jackson. He bled her, after
which Rachel apparently felt better for a while. Yet the cause
for concern was not removed. Forty years of selfless generosity
had won Rachel Jackson an army of friends, but the thing went
deeper than that as speculation arose as to the effect her brooding might have on the General.

Martin Van Buren was alert for news. John C. Calhoun still
stood athwart the path of the New Yorker. With the South
Carolinian already Vice President-elect, this was no time to permit Old Hickory's health to fail. Therefore, the news Mr. Van
Buren received from Tennessee was not good news. "J[n] appears
to be well but (enter nous) he is wearing away rapidly. . . . Already J[n's] successor is as much spoken of as J[n's] late success."[8]

3

Something had been said of permitting Rachel to remain in Tennessee until the inaugural should be over and the General's administration under way. Eaton had agreed to this.

"That opinion is now changed since I have arrived here and heard the reasoning of your friends," wrote the Senator, again at the helm in Washington. "The storm was abated— the angry tempest has ceased to howl. . . . You cannot but look back on the past as an idle fading vision . . . that should produce to you [not] one moments feeling, one moments pain. . . . The attentions to be meeted out to the general, and to you, are such as . . . [befits his triumph.] The Ladies from . . . remote parts of the Union will be here . . . to manifest to you their feelings and high regard. . . . If you shall be absent how great will be the disappointment. Your persecutors may then chuckle and say that they have driven you from the field. . . . Such is my confidence that you will be along with the general that I shall no longer speak of it as doubtful."[9]

No respite. Arrangements for departure added to the scene of bustle at the Hermitage. The place was like a camp. A journey that would be so slow and tedious required an early start. State legislatures, municipal bodies, military organizations, political clubs feverishly planned what would amount to a continuous ovation along the route. A North Carolinian volunteered to drive the General and his lady all the way in a coach with six white horses. In Columbus, Ohio, sympathetic females chewed their quills over "an *Address* of Congratulation to Mrs. Jackson . . . as evidence of their contempt for those unprincipled slanderers."[10]

Nashville would take its leave on December 23, the anniversary of the Night Battle. A week beforehand old soldiers and politicos, new friends and hungry hangers-on began to put in an appearance from as far away as the Gulf until the little city, surprised from its accustomed leisure, was crowded to bursting. The

General was expected down from the Hermitage in the morning "to receive the congratulations of his friends & partake with them a parting glass,"[11] the fête day closing with a banquet and ball at the Nashville Inn.

The overwhelming preparations engulfed Rachel, who desired no coach and six white horses, no address of congratulation, no ball and banquet at the Nashville Inn. The storm Major Eaton spoke of had not abated in her breast. "I assure you I had rather be a doorkeeper in the house of God than to live in that palace at Washington."[12] But as her immediate destination was taken to be the palace, a party of women friends assumed the task of making her ready for the journey. As usual Mrs. Jackson's wardrobe was in a state of neglect. The poor woman submitted to be borne off to Nashville to begin the process of measuring and fitting her unstylish form to attire deemed suitable for the first lady of the land.

Concerning one such expedition a story has been told in the Cumberland country so long that it is traditional. According to one version Aunt Rachel, who had retired to the parlor of the Nashville Inn to rest off the fatigue of a session with the seamstresses, overheard a feminine conversation lamenting the impossibility of rendering presentable to official society this illiterate country-woman. Another account has it that in the office of a newspaper editor she chanced to pick up a pamphlet issued by the friends of the General, revealing that the foulest part of the slander had been kept from her after all. When her companions returned they found her "crouching in a corner," terror-stricken and hysterical. Rachel demanded her carriage. On the way home she stopped at a creek to bathe her tear-swollen eyes so that her husband might not know the depth of her grief.[13]

A few days later, on December 17, a horseman riding recklessly into Nashville's Square summoned young Doctor Heiskell and Dr. Samuel Hogg, the regular physician to the Hermitage household. Heiskell reached the plantation first, finding Mrs. Jackson's face contorted with pain from a "spasmodic affection of the muscles of the chest and left shoulder, attended with an irregular action of the heart." A physician Jackson had called in from the countryside bent over the patient. He had bled her without abatement of the distress. Heiskell bled her again. Toward evening Doctor Hogg repeated the operation. This "produced great relief," noted Heiskell, "and an entire subsidence of all alarming symptoms." In her high French bed Rachel was soon asleep. The physicians, but not Jackson, retired to a room adjoining. The vigil was rewarded. In the morning when he saw his wife open her eyes, the cruel marks of pain were gone from her countenance and she had gained strength.

For three days Rachel mended. She sat in a chair before the fire, received a few friends and seemed to be cheerful. Andrew was ever at her side. Perhaps not in a year had she enjoyed so much of her husband's company in so short a time. On Sunday evening, December 22, she sat too long and was put to bed with a cold and slight symptoms of pleurisy. The physicians brewed drinks, brought on a profuse sweat and, announcing that the incident was not serious, reminded General Jackson that he would be on the way to Nashville early in the morning. In the interest of his own health, they begged that he take himself to bed in another room. When Rachel seconded the suggestion he consented to go. It was one of the few times he had left her since the beginning of the illness. Presently the attending physicians retired.

They could bring repose to the body but not to the mind of their patient. Twice she had her maid Hannah help her to the chair by the fire and fill a pipe with tobacco. Sitting there in her night-dress shortly before ten o'clock, Aunt Rachel made a remark she had been heard to make before. "I had rather be a door-keeper in the house of God than to live in that palace."

Twenty minutes later she cried out, "I am fainting!" and collapsed in Hannah's arms.

The servant's screams roused the house. Jackson burst into the room in time to help lift Rachel to her bed. In her form he felt a convulsive muscular movement. Life? Andrew Jackson saw the doctors bend down and listen for the heart-beat. He saw them straighten and he read in their glance that life had gone. Rachel Jackson's long flight from fame was over.[14]

RACHEL JACKSON

This portrait, by Earl, hung in General Jackson's bed chamber at the Hermitage and at the White House. It was made about 1825. From the original, owned by the Ladies' Hermitage Association, Nashville.

4

"How shall I describe the agony," wrote Doctor Heiskell, "the heart-rending agony of the venerable partner of her bosom!"

The old chieftain's breast seemed to swell as if the heart within were about to burst.

"Bleed her!" he cried.

No blood flowed from her arm.

"Try the temple, Doctor."

Two drops, but no more, stained her cap.

Servants filled the house with piercing supplications to Heaven. They could not believe their mistress dead. "She's only fainting." Something of this blind negation entered the numbed mind of Jackson. He refused to leave his wife's side. When a table was brought in to lay her out he said:

"Spread four blankets upon it. If she does come to she will lay hard on that table."

By midnight relatives and neighbors and friends began to fill the house and fill the yard. Lewis came at dawn. In Hannah's simple language, he found Jackson "grieving"—alone with his loved one and with the paralyzing realization that a world can end. His head in his hands, his eyes dry, his long fingers thrust through his gray hair, the stricken husband was almost speechless. Thought seemed to have left him. A shaking hand stroked the cold brow as a child would to assure itself of the reality of an object by the sense of touch.

"John, can you realize that she is dead. I certainly can't."[15] This to John Coffee.

Throughout the day, except when she was being dressed in white for burial, Andrew Jackson remained by the side of the woman he had made his own thirty-seven years before and from that hour to this had defended against all things and all men. Physicians hovered watchfully, fearing even Andrew Jackson's resources unequal to the commands he placed upon them. Toward evening the General was induced to swallow a little coffee.[16]

At one o'clock in the afternoon of the next day—December

24—Rachel was buried in her garden one hundred and fifty paces from the east door of the house. Tennessee has never seen such a funeral. Ten thousand persons, or twice as many as lived in Nashville, filled the garden, the great lawn, and overflowed into the level pasture. The news of death had reached town after midnight. By daybreak on the twenty-third, handbills were spreading it through the streets and the countryside. Before posting to subscribers his issue of that date, the editor of the *Republican* had only time to scrawl on the margins, *"Mrs. Jackson has just Expired!"* The message surprised early-rising residents attiring themselves for a gala day. It intercepted conveyances on the roads from farms and plantations.

On the morning of the twenty-fourth the conveyances were on the roads again. Every buggy and carriage and coach in Davidson County was on the roads, and places in them could not be bought for money. Every manner of farm wagon and rig, every saddle horse and hundreds of work horses were on the road. Two or three thousand persons trudged on foot, taking short-cuts across fields, for every thoroughfare converging upon the Hermitage was choked as rich and poor, high and low, white and black, made their way as if impelled by instinct to the grave prepared for Rachel Jackson. Some there may have been who made the journey as a mark of respect to the memory of the wife of the President-elect, but they would have been strangers to the Cumberland country. Davidson County mourned Aunt Rachel for reasons with which her husband's fame and station had little to do.

Under a bleak sky, Sam Houston led the pallbearers along the curved garden walk to where the earth had been opened. Behind the casket walked Jackson as a man would walk in a trance, his arms linked with those of ever-dependable John Coffee and of Henry M. Rutledge; then a great train of Donelson relations; then the household servants, moaning and chanting. When Hannah flung herself beside the grave someone asked her to control her grief. Jackson shook his head, and Hannah lay there sobbing.

The Reverend William Hume spoke for twenty minutes. Seldom it is that words uttered on such an occasion are so free from exaggeration.

" 'The righteous shall be in everlasting remembrance.' These words might be applied to that venerable matron, with much propriety, as she gave every reasonable evidence that she was among the righteous. . . . Her character was so well known . . . that the following remarks will readily be acknowledged as true: . . .

"Her seat was seldom empty in the house of God. The tears of genuine penitence were often shed by her in the temple of the Lord. She had a tender and a feeling heart, and sometimes I have seen the tears bedewing her cheeks while she was speaking of . . . those around her, who seemed to be entirely careless about a future state.

"While she rejoiced in the honor of a nation, yet no unbecoming elation of mind, no haughtiness, no overbearing conduct, could ever be seen, even by an inimical eye, in this amiable lady. She was adorned with the ornament of a meek and quiet spirit. . . . By her kindness and affability, her husband was [rendered] more happy in his own family than in the midst of his triumphs.

"The tears and lamentations of the servants are proofs of her excellence as mistress of her household. . . . The widow and the orphan will long lament the death of Mrs. Jackson. . . . Blest with affluence, she had a heart to feel and a hand to relieve the poor and the needy. She viewed the bounties of Providence . . . as designed by her Benefactor to flow in channels leading to the doors of those who were perishing of thirst, that they, also, might quaff and be satisfied.

"Some, indeed, during the presidential struggle, with unfeeling hearts and unjustifiable motives, exerted all their powers to throw her numerous virtues into the shade. . . . Under this cruel treatment, Mrs. Jackson displayed the temper of a disciple of Him who was meek and lowly of heart. . . . She felt the injustice of the warfare. Her compassionate heart was wrung with sorrow. Her tears flowed, but there was no malevolence in her bosom. She could have received no pleasure in giving pain to her detractors. . . .

"While we cordially sympathize with the President of the United States in the irreparable loss he has sustained in the death of his amiable lady, whom he deemed so worthy, as he said, of our tears; we cannot doubt but that she now dwells in the mansions of glory in company with the ransomed of the Lord."[17]

For the first time since the tragedy tears coursed the white and taut cheeks of Jackson. "But one wish pervaded the assembly," wrote one who stood near. "That the individuals who had hastened this scene by their relentless attacks on an unoffending woman could be brought to witness the saddest spectacle that any present has ever beheld." When Doctor Hume ceased speaking Jackson, "by a muscular and almost superhuman effort, endeavored to check the current of his grief. 'I know 'tis unmanly,' said he, 'but these tears are due her virtues. She has shed many for me.' "[18]

The old soldier raised his voice a little, speaking slowly, in a tone that seemed to come from another world.

"In the presence of this dear saint I can and do forgive all my enemies. But those vile wretches who have slandered her must look to God for mercy."[19]

5

Pale was glory's coronet. With all that bound him to life returned to earth, the unconquered spirit of Andrew Jackson seemed on the brink of surrender. Some feared he might decline to make the effort to journey to Washington and take the oath. At best, it was felt that he could not long survive.

Old Captain Will Alexander, Cumberland pioneer and Revolutionary veteran, addressed Jackson by a title used, at this late day, perhaps by no other man.

"My dear Son,

"I have heard it remarked by your Sincere but I thought weak friends That the loss of your wife would impede the march of your Administration— your Bosome companion and my dear friend . . . is gone on a grand party of pleasure I hope—and I think I am not deceived— Religion in my opinion is a comprehensive term—it takes in every duty we owe to our God or our fellow creatures, even to our animals— Our departed friend . . . possessed that very kind of religion. . . . For my part I . . . [believe] you certainly have philosophy enough to Submit to a dispensation from the Great first cause of things. . . . Be temperate my Son in every thing you do."[20]

The sorrowing husband permitted no affair of state to intrude until all was done that he could do for his beloved. The grave was covered with a wooden shelter to shield it from the rain until a permanent tomb in the form of a Greek cupola could be erected. Corners of the burial plot were marked with cuttings from a willow tree planted by James Robertson, founder of Nashville and associate of Rachel's adventurous father. With all the directness of his feudal soul, Andrew Jackson had defended his wife in life. His breath on a stone would defend her memory. The legend for a long and moving epitaph contained these words: "A being so gentle, so virtuous, slander might wound but could not dishonor."

Impotent grief began to yield to a mood of sinewy hatred. "May God Almighty forgive her murderers as I know she forgave them. I never can."[21] To Washington, then, to ride down Adams and Clay, and to hunt their hirelings from the temple. It was easier to say than to do. On the eighteenth day of January, at the little landing where he loaded his cotton, the President-elect stepped on board a steamboat. "My heart is nearly broke. I try to summon up my usual fortitude but in vain."[22]

BOOK TWO

THE "REIGN"

"Though we live under the form of a
republic we are in fact under the absolute
rule of a single man."

JUSTICE JOSEPH STORY,
United States Supreme Court,
in a letter to a friend.

CHAPTER VIII

THE HAGGARD HERO

I

"Mr Clay's furniture is to be sold this week," noted Margaret Bayard Smith, distinguished for her knack of discerning the pertinent minutiae of Washington's fashionable world. Notwithstanding prospects for an advantageous disposal of his household things—the sprawling city being crowded already with Jacksonians reckoning on a four-year stay—the spirits of the Secretary of State were overborne by gloom. Mrs. Smith was "shocked at the alteration of his looks. . . . His eyes [are] sunk in his head." At that, she found Mr. Clay in better case than his colleagues— the Secretary of the Treasury being "alarmingly ill," the Secretary of the Navy not out of his room for three weeks, the head of the War Office "almost blind from inflammation of the eyes," the Attorney General afflicted with vertigo and "loss of the sense of motion." Though least understanding the debâcle that had struck down his régime, Mr. Adams bore it the best of all. But even the President's legs had given out, obliging him to abandon his daily walks.

"Never before," continued Mrs. Smith who had seen every Executive except the first one come and go, "did the city seem to me to be so gloomy— so many changes in society— so many families broken up, and those of the first distinction. . . . Drawing rooms in which I have so often mixed with gay crowds, distinguished by rank, fashion, beauty, talent, . . . now empty, silent, dark, dismantled. Oh! 'tis melancholy!"[1]

A dirge for the days that were done. As for the days to come, Daniel Webster's guess seemed as good as any:

179

"General Jackson will be here abt. 15. of Feb.——

"Nobody knows what he will do.

"Many letters are sent to him; he answers none of them.

"His friends here pretend to be very knowing; but. . . .

"Great efforts are being made to put him up to a general sweep as to all offices; springing from great doubts whether he is disposed to do it.

"Nobody is authorized to say whether he intends to retire after one term. . . .

"Who will form the cabinet is as well known at Boston as at Washington. . . .

"My opinion is

"That when he comes he will bring a breeze with him.

"Which way it will blow I cannot tell."[2]

General Jackson's health was a universal topic. A rumor of his death gripped the nervous city for a day. "I hope it is not true," said a friend of Clay, "for I would rather trust him than Calhoun."[3] No better informed than Webster, the Vice President-elect was nevertheless a busy man. A grand plan was formulated to meet the General's party with a cavalcade at Pittsburgh and escort him to the city under the Calhoun aegis. Though this was abandoned the journey from Tennessee was ordeal enough. Frances Trollope saw Jackson disembark at Cincinnati and walk, uncovered, through exulting throngs to a hotel. "He was in deep mourning. . . . He wore his gray hair carelessly but not ungracefully arranged, and in spite of his harsh, gaunt features looked like a gentleman and a soldier." This English woman had not found occasion to describe many Americans as gentlemen. On the Pittsburgh-bound packet sensitive travelers were "disgusted by the brutal familiarity to which they saw him exposed at every place they stopped. . . . There was not a hulking boy from a keel-boat who was not introduced. . . . A greasy fellow accosted him thus:—

" 'General Jackson, I guess.'

"The General bowed assent.

" 'Why they told me you was dead.'

" 'No. Providence has hitherto preserved my life.'

" 'And is your wife alive too?' "

Jackson shook his head sadly.

" 'Aye, I thought it was one or the t'other of ye.' "[4]

On February 12, 1829, while jabbering partizans planned a "formal" entry into the city, John Henry Eaton quietly sent his carriage into Maryland, and had the General safely in an apartment at Gadsby's four hours before the cannon supposed to signal his approach let loose.

2

The throng that was taking possession of Washington in the assured manner of an army of occupation laid siege to the hotel. Donelson, Lewis and Lee performed sentry duty, but the General's assumption that he had been elected by "the people" rather than by a party set much of their effort at naught. Democratic episodes of the journey from Tennessee were re-enacted at "the Wigwam," as scandalized representatives of the old order dubbed the Jackson ménage at Gadsby's. Night and day applicants for an audience filled lobby, stairways, corridors, pressing and jostling until nervous persons feared for the safety of the building.

During a change of administrations Washington was accustomed to a few days of stimulating confusion, but to no such horde as descended upon the embryonic city to see Jackson reap and allot the rewards of six years of championship of the common man. "It was like the inundation of northern barbarians into Rome. . . . Strange faces filled every public place, and every face seemed to bear defiance on its brow."[5] Tennessee backwoodsmen and pioneers from the Northwest mingled with Irish immigrants from the seaboard cities, old soldiers, politicians of high and low degree, editors, adventurers, schemers. "I never saw anything like it before," said Webster. "They really seem to think the country is [to be] rescued from some dreadful danger."[6] They roamed the streets, surging in and out of taprooms until the spectre of a whisky famine contributed to an outlook already unsettled. They overflowed Washington into Georgetown and Alexandria, sleeping five in a bed or on billiard tables, or on floors, or apparently not at all. They patronized barbers who advertised "haircutting in the Jackson style," and a haberdasher sold "Jackson stocks" copied from the old-fashioned neckwear the General had worn since the day when frankly one of the Cumberland uppercrust. Other defects in the proletarian composition of the scene met the eye. The sight of an Archer, a Hayne, a Van Ness, a Livingston, a Hamilton quitting his carriage at Gadsby's was evidence that not every scion of the Virginia tradition, the Cotton Kingdom, or the commercial East regarded himself an outcast on the morn of the people's triumph.

Against this encroachment it would be an error to assume that the lower orders stood as a band of brothers. The victory was won but the spoil undivided—some eleven thousand offices directly or indirectly within the gift of the President. Certain editors and politicians called for a "clean sweep," and the hosts liked the full-throated cry. Because it was mathematically obvious that even the cleanest sweep must fail to provide for every aspirant, or even those who had already come or sent in their petitions to Washington, rivalries began to cleave the democratic ranks. Little of this seems to have been lost on the sombre-faced old man in the Wigwam who listened to so many words and uttered so few. "It appeared," he wrote two years later, "that instead of love of principle it was love of office that had induced [many of] them to support the good cause as they pleased to term it, . . . that self-exertion was about to be abandoned and dependence for a livelihood placed upon the government."[7]

Such was the atmosphere in which General Jackson toiled over the first problem of appointments to confront a President: the selection of his Cabinet.

Long before, he had determined in event of election to bring into his official family one man who, in addition to the weight his counsel might contribute to the scale of public affairs, could be trusted as a steadfast and confidential friend. In this connection Tennessee's senators, John Henry Eaton and Hugh Lawson White, occurred to him. Judge White was the abler of the two, Eaton the closer friend. The choice fell upon White, to whom

Jackson wrote before leaving Tennessee. Knowing White to be low in mind because of illness and death in his family, Jackson requested that, if for any reason the Senator could not accept, would he pass the letter on to Eaton who should construe it as an invitation to the Cabinet.

On Jackson's first night in the city White called to say that domestic afflictions unfitted him to participate in the Government. Jackson usually meant what he said, and there is every reason to believe that White was actually the first, and Eaton the second, choice for a Cabinet portfolio. Nevertheless, it appears that the undiplomatic effort to kill two birds with one stone, which made acceptance by White a virtual act of exclusion against Eaton, had some bearing on White's answer. On the next day Eaton also refused the office. Although he did not say so, domestic considerations were probably a factor in his declination, for the *haut monde* was still gasping over the Senator's recent marriage to Margaret Timberlake. "Public opinion," noted Mrs. Smith, "will not allow Genl. Eaton . . . [to] bring *his wife* into society."[8]

This was not the kind of talk to turn Andrew Jackson from a friend. The more Eaton demurred, the stronger grew Old Hickory's insistence that he join the Cabinet. "Surely . . . [you] and Judge White both would not desert me." After ten days of this sort of thing Eaton "very reluctantly," as Jackson said, consented to accept the War Office.[9] The whole episode suggests something of a game on Eaton's part, for it seems that he had desired the post all along.[10] And certainly his wife desired it for him.

By this time the other selections had been virtually decided. The State Department was for Van Buren, the Treasury for Samuel D. Ingham, Pennsylvania paper manufacturer and dull though successful business man with fourteen inconspicuous years in the House. Brilliant, caustic, vain John MacPherson Berrien of Georgia, an excellent lawyer and showy orator, was the choice for Attorney General. John Branch, Navy, represented the best social traditions of the slave-holding aristocracy. He had been an enlightened governor of North Carolina and a senator. John McLean of Ohio was to remain in charge of the mails,

Jackson announcing his intention to raise the postmaster general-ship to Cabinet rank. Though McLean had favored Jackson dur-ing the campaign, Adams had declined to replace for political considerations the ablest director of the postal service since Ben-jamin Franklin.

Publication of the list gave Jackson's adversaries their first cause for congratulation in many a day. It dismayed many of his friends. "The Millennium of the Minnows!"[11] exclaimed one who evidently thought himself a pretty big fish. "A miserable cabinet," intoned another. "Gen. Jackson came down to the city full of grief and out of health. . . . The eleventh-hour men flocked around and they forced upon the President men like themselves by every artifice."[12] The success of these eleventh-hour men was a fruitful cause of resentment, one old follower who now re-pented his politeness having written on the day after the General's arrival: "In consequence of the crowd of *new Converts* it be-hooves his old Troops to stand back."[13] Recalling Jackson's com-mitment against the appointment of congressman, Louis McLane of Delaware pointed out that three of his selections were from Congress and "of the least capacity in the country!"[14] James A. Hamilton, looking after Van Buren's interests, wrote his chief uneasy letters. The New Yorker had but one friend in the Cabinet—Eaton—while Calhoun had three. And so cleverly was the business managed that Eaton had been persuaded to go to Jackson with puffs for the eleventh-hour men, Berrien and Branch.[15]

Critics fairly pounced upon the War Office nomination. Vari-ous reasons for a change were urged, but what everyone had in mind was the Senator's matrimonial adventure. The Tennessee delegation in Congress screwed up enough courage to ask the General to drop their colleague. Another idea was to give him the Post Office and refrain from raising it to Cabinet rank. A foreign berth was also suggested—France, for example, or, in a less helpful spirit, Haiti, "that being the most proper Court for *her*." A spark of the old-time fire lighted the blue eyes of Old Hickory as he penned a stern answer to the respectfully worded protest of the Tennessee congressmen. Jackson forsake a friend!

That kind of opposition almost made him forget his troubles, he said. John Henry Eaton would be the Secretary of War.[16]

Considered on the basis of its individual members, the Cabinet was not below average, every man on the list being competent to administer with credit the department assigned to him. Except in the case of Eaton, the dissatisfaction sprang from the fact that the selections represented the unequal results of a contest between the partizans of two candidates for the succession to the presidency.

3

Our diplomatic relations with Portugal reveal nothing calculated to attain so long or so honorable a survival as the *mot* of an emissary of Mr. Monroe's time who called Washington the "city of magnificent distances." In 1829 the most presentable thoroughfare was unpaved Pennsylvania Avenue, connecting the Capitol and the White House, at the four corners of whose newly-planted grounds stood the brick buildings, simple but in good taste, of the State, Treasury, War, and Navy Departments. To the north and south of this street houses were scattered over a prodigious area as if sown by a careless farmer. To reach a neighbor one picked his way through swamps, across ditches and over hillocks clad in scraggly pine, extemporized roads and paths mocking the geometrical exactitude of L'Enfant's theoretical avenues. On a fair day a carriage was more than a convenience, in wet weather the only thing to save a wayfarer's clothing from ruin. In this paradise for hackney coachmen, the fastidious paid more for transportation than for bed and board.

Only a small proportion of the admirers of General Jackson who flocked to Washington could afford to be fastidious, and as the day of days—March 4—drew nigh, their weather-beaten exteriors lent verisimilitude to the dark forebodings of revolution. John Quincy Adams had signified his intention not to be present at the east front of the Capitol to see his authority pass to his successor. This suited Jackson, who gave promise of making good his word to show no mercy to those whom he regarded as slanderers of his wife. On his arrival he had vowed not to "go

near" Mr. Adams, and consequently omitted the traditional courtesy call.[17] Deeply hurt, Adams sought to re-establish the amenities by sending a messenger to say that the Executive Residence
would be ready for occupancy on March 4. Orally General Jackson replied that he hoped Mr. Adams would not subject his household to the inconvenience of a hasty removal. On the afternoon
of the third, the Adams family departed for the suburban residence of a friend. The President of the United States followed
on foot, alone, unrecognized, tortured by bitter reflections.

Next morning the cannons boomed. Pennsylvania Avenue and
the sloping west lawn of the Capitol were dense with humanity.
The ground was spotted by thin patches of snow, fortunately firm.
The sun shone. As the erect, gray-haired figure emerged from
Gadsby's a mighty cheer rolled up the Avenue toward Capitol
Hill. Having vetoed a plan for a military pageant, the General
and a small party made their way along the sidewalk. Tories
who had come to scoff felt the exhilaration of the scene. "It is
true greatness which needs not the aid of ornament and pomp,"
exclaimed Mrs. Smith. "I think I shall like him vastly when I
know him." Francis Scott Key said, "Sublime!"[18]

Skirting the multitude on the east terrace, the President-elect
scaled a wall and entered the Capitol by the basement. Reappear-
ing on the roped-off portico, he stood for a moment bowing
acknowledgment to the ovation "with a grace and composed
dignity" which a doubting free trader from South Carolina confessed, "I never saw surpassed."[19] The crowd fell silent. Though
it did not catch a word of the inaugural address, those who
were nearest saw the pages tremble as the Hero turned them.
To miss the speech was no great deprivation, most of it being
too conservative to thrill a populace. But office-seekers would
have applauded this line: "The task of *reform* . . . inscribes
itself on the list of executive duties"—"reform" being a brief
way of saying, "Turn the rascals out."

One of the least distinguished-looking persons on the portico,
Chief Justice Marshall, administered the oath, thereby endanger-
ing, as he imagined, the work of a lifetime on the bench. Jackson raised a Bible to his lips; Marshall held out his hand; an

active little man scrambled over the barricade and up the steps. The second person to congratulate the President was "honest" George Kremer, the People's Friend. That touch repaid the crowd for having missed the inaugural address.[20]

Down the Avenue the President rode on horseback with a mob at his heels which brought to one onlooker's mind descriptions of the march on Versailles. The destination was the White House where a reception had been announced. In the stately East Room long tables were spread with cakes and ice-cream and orange punch for the officially and socially eligible as defined by precedent. Precedent? The mob in the horseman's wake swept through the Mansion gates and through the portals, leaving the "eligible" to shift for themselves. Representative and Mrs. George Gilmer of Georgia got in by clutching the coat-tails of Representative and Mrs. John Floyd whose "two stout sons" cleaved a path. They remained long enough to see clothing torn, women faint, glasses and china broken. "One hundred-and-fifty-dollar official chairs [were] profaned by the feet of clod-hoppers" anxious for a glimpse of their President. "A regular Saturnalia," a South Carolinian informed Mr. Van Buren, happily detained at Albany. "It would have done Mr. Wilberforce's heart good to have seen a stout black wench eating a jelley with a gold spoon on the President's House."[21] Mr. Wilberforce was an English abolitionist.

But the rarest sight was Andrew Jackson, helpless, "sinking into a listless state of exhaustion." The Georgians left through a window, "in doing which," Mr. Gilmer related, "I had to sustain with a weak leg from a fracture scarcely healed the weight of Mrs. Floyd equalling three hundred pounds." Locking arms, men threw a cordon about the President enabling him to escape by the back way. As Old Hickory retreated to Gadsby's and to bed, the departure of the White House guests was facilitated by placing tubs of punch on the lawn.[22]

The eventful day closed with a ball at which Mrs. Andrew Jackson Donelson, Mrs. Calhoun, Mrs. Ingham and Mrs. Edward Livingston seemed unaware of the presence of Margaret Timberlake Eaton.

4

A solitary lamp shed its feeble beams in the vestibule of the White House. A single candle illuminated the study where the President sat with Major Lewis. In office three weeks, General Jackson looked grief-stricken and weary.

Emily Donelson had not taken wholly in good part the fatherly talk he had felt duty bound to administer after the neglect of the wife of the Secretary of War at the inaugural ball; and in this Emily's husband seemed to sustain her. True, she and Jack had returned a call of Major and Mrs. Eaton, but it was done as an act of obedience to their uncle, the President, and with no cordiality. This hurt the old man for he loved these young people. Emily, born a Donelson, was Rachel's niece by blood as well as marriage, and before her death Rachel had expressed the wish that Emily should go with her to Washington to manage the official entertaining. In making her the feminine head of his household, Jackson felt that he carried out the desire of the saint who slept in the Hermitage garden. Yet Emily must understand that John Henry Eaton was her uncle's friend, and that his wife must be accorded the courtesies due the wife of a friend as well as a Cabinet minister.

Old Hickory attributed the Eaton gossip to "Clay and his minions."[23] But no such convenient explanation would suffice for the criticism of the Cabinet and of other appointments, much of which came from the General's own followers. Jackson realized that his régime had not caught the airs of success. Deliberately he sought to stir his ebbing forces to greater effort. "You know when I am excited all my energies come forth. . . . If my constitution will bear me up for one year, . . have no fear."[24]

So the President sat chatting with Lewis when the Secretary of State was announced. Ah, Mr. Van Buren was punctual.

The smallish figure that paused in the doorway presented "a rather exquisite appearance. His complexion was a bright blond, and he dressed accordingly"—favoring for day-time wear snuff-colored coats, white trousers, lace-tipped cravats, yellow gloves and morocco shoes.[25] As the visitor's quick and perceptive glance rested on the haggard old man in the shadowy room, Martin Van Buren better understood some of the things he had heard on his journey to Washington, finished a little more than an hour ago.

Strong effort had been made to prevent Mr. Van Buren from undertaking that journey. He had been urged to sidestep the proffered Cabinet appointment on the ground that General Jackson's Administration was foredoomed to failure. Having accepted, he had been urged to withdraw his name because failure was at hand. On the way to Washington, this advice had been reiterated by a particular friend, Louis McLane, on the ground that failure was too far along for one man to arrest. Mr. McLane mentioned the mediocrity of the Cabinet and the widespread belief that, taking his appointments as a whole, Jackson seemed under the domination of "evil counsellors." Mr. Van Buren could understand his friend's poor opinion of the Cabinet since he, McLane, was not in it as he had expected to be. This factor, however, did not operate on the judgment of Edward Livingston whom the New Yorker had encountered in Philadelphia. Livingston had obtained a tender of the office he wanted—the ministry to France. Yet the Livingstons were doleful, very doleful. The egalitarian spirit of the first White House "reception," the Eaton situation—in short, the social aspect of matters, by which they saw our country's prestige degraded in foreign capitals, troubled the aspiring diplomat and his beautiful lady.

Descending at his hotel in Washington, Mr. Van Buren had confronted another aspect of the problem to which he had given much sober thought. A pack of patronage-seekers trailed the New Yorker to his room. Stretched on a sofa, Van Buren listened to them for an hour. Then he closed the interview saying, in his invariably pleasant way, that he disapproved of applicants appearing at the seat of government and suggested that they return to their homes. A few minutes later Martin Van Buren presented himself at the Executive Residence for his first meeting, as a political friend, with Andrew Jackson.

The native courtliness of the President's greeting struck the caller at once. Old Hickory seemed to lay aside his weariness as one would shed a dingy cloak. When business was mentioned it was Mr. Van Buren who must guard against over-taxing his strength. General Jackson could not think of burdening a man fatigued by travel, and appointed an hour of the next day. Van Buren took his leave in better heart than he had come. Something in "that noble old man" had moved him.[26]

5

If the rebuked patronage-hunters followed the advice of Mr. Van Buren their departure did not noticeably diminish the army that remained in town, parading their Jackson stocks, their Jackson hair-cuts, and their insistent claims. Forces that were stronger than the admonition of the tardily-arriving Secretary of State operated to keep them there.

After an unsuccessful campaign effort to commit Jackson to "rotation in office,"[27] editorial leaders of the spoilsmen had bided their time until after the election when they laid down a bombardment that seemed to take much for granted. *"Punish the* DECEIVERS, *but reclaim* the DECEIVED!" was the title of a masterful effort by Isaac Hill. "Shall we . . . appoint to office and continue in office the men who have . . . libel[ed] the purest patriots in the country? . . . Forbid it, Heaven!"[28] Old Hickory's failure to acknowledge himself a celestial agent did not arrest the pen of Duff Green. *"Jackson and Reform. . . .* Cleanse the Augean Stable."[29] Even Ritchie's respectable Richmond *Enquirer* chimed in. On Jackson's arrival in Washington the "reform" journalists increased their din. The *National Journal* denounced the coming Administration in advance while placeholders shook in their shoes. Duff Green was on the spot. Isaac Hill, Amos Kendall of the *Western Argus,* Mordecai Noah of the New York *Courier and Enquirer,* and half a dozen others lost no time getting there. In Lewis, in Henry Lee, and in Eaton, they found friendly spirits. Such was the coterie—the "evil counsellors," and the "eleventh-hour men," of whom critics spoke —that encircled Jackson at the time of his induction into office.

DRAWN FROM LIFE, SEPTEMBER 23, 1829

The artist was James Barton Longacre. Reproduced from an old wet plate photograph of the original by Mathew B. Brady, owned by the L. C. Handy Studios, Washington.

The first voice raised against their schemes came from the Cabinet in the person of Postmaster General McLean, who had at his disposal more patronage than the rest of officialdom combined. This able and abrupt Westerner told the President that, if he must remove postmasters who had taken part in the election, he would dismiss those who had worked for Jackson as well as those who had worked for Adams. Old Hickory took a turn of the room, puffing his pipe. "Mr. McLean, will you accept a seat on the bench of the Supreme Court?"[30] McLean was willing, and after four days as a Jackson minister he gave way to William T. Barry of Kentucky.

As nothing in Mr. Barry's brief catalog of distinctions suggested the McLean type of backbone, the reformers lifted high their hickory brooms—for the doctrinaires of the "clean sweep" had their visible symbol. Yet, bold as had been the propaganda and terrific the pressure, Jackson moved slowly. The first seventy-six names, including Cabinet nominations, sent to the Senate for confirmation were to supply existing vacancies. On March 17, however, the Senate adjourned, not to reconvene until December. Immediately the President announced a batch of "recess" appointments. All the "counsellors" received handsome rewards—and so the Kitchen Cabinet was born. The impatient champions of rotation had their taste of blood and, though only a taste, they made the most of it. *"The Barnacles Shall be Scraped Clean from the Ship of State,"* shouted Isaac Hill's newspaper. Every "traitor" (*i. e.,* Adams man) must go.

Fear smote the hearts of thousands of placemen as the tranquil world in which they had their being was threatened with a Judgment Day. Though the heat of the late campaign had moved many of his kind to political activity, the average Federal appointee was not a party worker. Accepting changes of Administration as matters of course, he served each with equal fidelity, to which sometimes was added a touch of condescension. Removed from competitive employments, he was apt to be soft and leisurely. Mingling with the distinguished, he was apt to feel himself above the mass. Assured of an easy income, he was apt to be improvident. The civil servant's Elysium was not a diffi-

cult place in which to sow panic. Sensational journalism on both
sides fanned the flames. Day after day Administration organs en
couraged their followers with exaggerated accounts of the extent of the "purge." Crying "proscription," opposition sheets accepted their adversaries' fancy figures and presented exceptional
cases—a lighthouse keeper's family penniless, a War Department
clerk driven to suicide—as typical of "the terror."

David Campbell, one day to become an anti-Jackson Governor
of Virginia, viewed things more sanely. Though his brother had
obtained the important post of Treasurer of the United States,
Mr. Campbell was no spoilsman.

"On Monday last," he wrote his wife, "John entered upon the
duties of his office. The opposition prints . . . stated that Gen'l
Clarks first notice of his removal was Johns walking into the
Treasury office with his commission in his pocket. So far from
this being the case Gen'l Clark some days before he went out of
office called on John & myself and invited John to the office &
sat nearly all day shewing John how the business was done. On
Tuesday when he was about to leave the City he called . . . [and]
wished . . . [John] good success. . . . I mention these circumstances
to shew you how little credit ought to be given to the statements
in the *National Intelligencer*. . . .

"The President has removed several . . . who have held their
places for a long period and have been considered, perhaps more
from that circumstance than any other, very faithful officers. But
as it respects most of them it is not so. Old Mr. Nourse the
Register of the Treasury had been in the employ of the government from the revolution. . . . Yet this old man is now a defaulter
for about ten thousand dollars. . . . The conversation between
him and the President was very interesting. . . . [Admitting] he
was a defaulter . . . [Nourse] urged that he be retained. . . . The
President endeavored to induce him to resign but he would not."
Whereupon Jackson dismissed him saying, " 'I would turn out
my own father under the same circumstances.' The truth is that
a considerable number of the officers who have been long in office
are old men and drunkards. Harrison the first auditor . . . I
have not yet seen sober."[31]

To regulate the business of reform, General Jackson wrote

with his own hand an "Outline of Principles." "Every Head of Depar^t [will conduct] a strict examination into the state of his Dep^t and report to the President . . . what . . . retrenchments can be made, .. what offices dispensed with, and what improvements made in the economy and dispatch of public business." More- over, chiefs would consider the "moral habits" of their subordi- nates, dismissing those found lax in "private or public relations." These clauses—no honest interpretation of which would impair the public service—were not the whole of the President's decree, however. "It becomes his duty to dismiss all officers who were appointed against the manifest will of the people or whose official station, by a subserviency to selfish electioneering purposes, was made to operate against the freedom of elections."[32] How the eyes of the hickory broom-bearers must have sparkled over that.

To the moral aspects of the situation the President gave his first attention. The dusty recesses of Government bureaus were aired as they had not been since Jefferson's day, bringing to light some curious circumstances. Amos Kendall, the Kentucky editor, taking the post of Fourth Auditor of the Treasury, found himself blessed with subscriptions to twenty-odd newspapers for which his predecessor had paid from the public funds. He discontinued them, as well as the favor of forwarding the letters of friends under his frank—a form of politeness long sanctioned by usage and almost universal in official circles, though against the law. But when Kendall declined to frank his wife's letters, fellow Jacksonians felt that to be holding the torch of reform too high. Then there was a matter of strange-looking charges for cord- wood for Marine officers, and for subsistence on shore for mid- shipmen, as well as disbursements for the hire of extra clerks who seemed to have had no corporeal existence. Digging deeper, Kendall and colleagues brought forth other interesting particu- lars. A large number of civil servants were habitually delinquent in their private obligations, some having taken the bankrupt's oath twelve times within a few months. Eighty-seven had jail records. In one Department, the Treasury, at least ten employees besides Mr. Nourse were short in their accounts with the Gov- ernment.[33]

A defaulter in the amount of seven thousand dollars was found
to be Tobias Watkins, Kendall's predecessor as Fourth Auditor.
Watkins was a personal friend of Adams and Clay. During the
campaign his political activity had given the Jackson managers
considerable trouble. This ideal victim behaved admirably for
the purposes of the stable cleansers. He fled, was caught, convicted,
and sentenced, while the Jackson press and privately, Jackson
himself, glowed with a consciousness of worthy accomplishment.[34]

While this *cause célèbre* did something to disarm criticism of
the reform policy, the reform leaders were far from pleased. For
all their talk and spilling of printer's ink, few heads had fallen.
Even Barry, the mild-mannered, courteous new Postmaster General, in whom the clean sweepers had reposed implicit confidence,
was writing "No cause for removal" opposite name after name
on the lists the proscriptionists laid before him. Blunt, red-faced
Duff Green, who even in repose wore the look of a man sitting
for a portrait, called to see what was the matter. Failing to
obtain the dismissal of the postmaster of Washington, Green
stormed from Mr. Barry's office. *"I will pursue my course &
leave you to yours,"* a trembling subordinate heard the editor
roar as he strode from the building and directed his steps toward
the White House.[35]

6

Martin Van Buren deplored this state of affairs. Schooled from
young manhood in the ways of New York where politicians maintained an interesting form of communal life, the object of which
was survival by rewarding the faithful, the Secretary of State
regarded all this clatter attending Federal removals as the clumsy
work of amateurs. In New York thrice as many public servants
as Jackson had sent on their way might vanish into the void
without awakening so much as an echo. Moreover, small as the
number of Federal replacements had been, too many offices had
fallen to friends of John C. Calhoun. That was Duff Green's
doing. Mr. Van Buren addressed himself to the task of reform-
ing the reformation.

A few days after their first conversation, the President received from his Secretary of State a communication on the subject of patronage. It was brief, merely asking "liberal and respectful consideration" of a letter from Thomas Ritchie, the Richmond editor, who saw the "bright prospect" of Jackson's Administration "somewhat clouded over within the short space of thirty days." "The Cabinet," continued Ritchie, "has disappointed many of the sincerest of the President's friends." But the greatest danger arose from the nature of removals and of appointments. In the latter category were too many "personal friends," too many editors and congressmen—precisely the type of appointments for which Jackson had denounced Adams. "The enemies of the Administration are . . . availing themselves of all our errors."[36]

In a spirited rejoinder Old Hickory assured Mr. Van Buren that Ritchie was altogether wrong and the Administration altogether right. "The people expect reform—they shall not be disappointed; but it must be *Judiciously* done, and upon *principle.*"[37] Noting the qualifying clause, the Secretary failed to press his point. Having declined a Supreme bench seat from Monroe, Mr. Van Buren did not wish one now.

Yet it well may be that Ritchie's letter, and others in similar vein, were not without effect on Jackson. In any event, the President's attitude continued to disappoint the spoilsmen. Anxious underofficials began to look hopefully to the Secretary of State to produce a split in the Administration ranks. "Parties have avowed [themselves]," one wrote. "Van B. refuses to assent to proscription. . . . Green greatly dissatisfied. . . . Messrs Eaton, Ingham, Hill [checked in their designs]."[38] Amos Kendall, ablest and, after Andrew Jackson Donelson, the least predatory of the Kitchen Cabinet, came to perceive a difference between the theory and the practice of rotation. "I turned out six clerks on Saturday, . . . the most painful thing I ever did."[39] To one the Fourth Auditor gave fifty dollars and started a fund to move his family back to Ohio. Dismay began to penetrate the ranks of job-seekers, watching their tavern bills climb.

Jackson himself showed growing impatience over their incessant importunities for "a tit . . . to suck the Treasury pap."[40] In all likelihood, more instances of distress could have been found among applicants who had blown themselves to bootless trips to the capital than among displaced appointees. "would you believe it," the President wrote a Tennessee neighbor, "that a lady who had once rolled in wealth, ... and is an applicant for office, and well recommended, . . . with tears in her eyes . . . [assured] me that her children were starving, and to buy a morsel of bread she had to sell her thimble the day before. an office I had not to give, and my cash was nearly out, but I could not withhold from her half the pittance I had with me." These episodes were wearing. "Late in the night I retire to my chamber . . . deprived of all hope of happiness this side of the grave and often wish myself at the Hermitage there to spend the remnant of my days & drop a daily tear on the tomb of my beloved wife."[41]

After a White House reception an elderly man asked for a personal word with the Executive. He was the postmaster at Albany, New York. "The politicians want to take my office from me and I have nothing else to live on."

When Old Hickory did not reply, the caller began to peel off his coat. "I am going to show you my wounds." The postmaster had fought under George Washington.

"Put on your coat at once, sir!" exclaimed Jackson.

The next day Congressman Silas Wright presented a list of officials recommended for dismissal. The venerable postmaster was on it. Wright began to argue that he had supported John Quincy Adams. Old Hickory leaped to his feet and, in his excitement, threw his pipe in the fire. "By the Eternal! I will not remove the old man. Do you know that he carries a pound of British lead in his body?"[42]

A young man named David Buell bore an introduction from Van Buren's old New York associate, William L. Marcy, who illuminated contemporary history with the phrase, "To the victors belong the spoils." Considering this sponsorship, Buell's was a curious mission.

"Mr. President——"

Jackson interrupted to inquire if Marcy were correct in introducing his friend as an ex-soldier.

"Yes, sir."

"Then call me 'General.' "

The visitor spoke in behalf of another veteran, who had left a leg on a battlefield and needed to retain a small postmastership to support his large family. "But I must tell you that he voted against you."

"If he lost a leg fighting for his country," said Jackson, "that is vote enough for me."[43]

A clergyman was an insistent applicant for a place.

"Are you not a Christian minister?" inquired the President.

"I am."

"Well, if you discharge the duties of that office, which is better than any I can confer, you will have no time for any other."[44]

After things had simmered for awhile Martin Van Buren himself brought up the office of collector of customs at New York. Samuel Swartwout was in town pulling wires. So unfavorably did the claims of this candidate impress the Secretary of State, that he refused to treat with him even by correspondence. But the letter he wrote to the President recommending another was a model of good temper. Nevertheless, Swartwout became collector, taking the most remunerative office in the gift of the Administration—that is to say, the office Mr. Swartwout was able to make the most remunerative. So agreeably did Van Buren accept the reverse that Jackson gave him the unexpected privilege of naming the district attorney for Nashville—an unequal exchange, but a significant gesture.[45] After weeks of close quarters with Eatons and Lewises and Greens, the President had begun to sense the contrasting mental stature of his Secretary of State.

Smoothly Van Buren moved on to another topic, which he prefaced with a series of confidential and intelligent talks on American problems before the foreign courts. These discourses included some incidental allusion to the qualifications desirable in the ministers who must act as the Secretary's agents in the business under review. Impulsively Jackson apologized for having named the envoys to England and France without consulting Van Buren. This was all the Secretary needed to know. Off went letters to Littleton W. Tazewell and to Edward Livingston, directing attention to the formidable state of affairs at their respective stations, and politely asking them to depart with the least delay. The effect was so discouraging to the diplomatic ambitions of these gentlemen that each relinquished his appointment. Where- upon, at Mr. Van Buren's suggestion, the President sent William C. Rives to London and Louis McLane to Paris,[46] thus obtaining two able foreign representatives and binding to the Administra- tion a corps of valuable friends who were on the verge of estrange- ment. Thereafter, the quiet word of Martin Van Buren was supreme in his own department.

As the season advanced, the President sought occasional relaxa- tion on horseback. Yielding to an urge dormant for years, Mr. Van Buren abandoned his carriage for a saddle. Sometimes the two rode together. Perhaps rather than advert to his companion's horsemanship, the courteous old gentleman jockey drifted into the habit of discussing with the New Yorker things that per- tained to the domains of the other Cabinet officers.

7

The glories of the springtime on the Potomac brought scant satisfaction to the army of occupation. Less blatant, less convinc- ing, was the rodomontade about a clean sweep. To be sure, the turnover in offices continued, but quietly—perhaps one might say "*Judiciously*" and "upon *principle.*" In any case, machinations of the unblushing pack that swarms about thrones to live by bend- ing great men to small uses were less easily discernible than before. A man at home seemed to stand as much chance of finding himself the happy possessor of a warrant as postmaster or deputy marshal or Indian agent, as a competitor resting his uneasy head on an expensive Capitol Hill boarding-house pillow. Private exchequers ran low, and the word was out that Jackson required strict explana- tions of those behind in their bills. Washington heard of the boarding-house mistress who had gone to the President with an unpaid account. Jackson bade her return with the delinquent's note for the amount due. Old Hickory wrote his name on the back as endorser. "I think he will pay it now."[47]

The host which had dominated the inaugural was disintegrat-
ing, its remnants inspiring sly ridicule where once they had inspired awe. To a bartender at Gadsby's was attributed an anecdote
which genially grew with the years. It seems that an important-
looking party worker, honoring the President with a call of congratulation, expanded on the warm nature of the contest in his
district. "What I did, I did for my country—and I thought, sir,
that I might be of further use to you in some official capacity."
The Cabinet being filled, perhaps a post abroad would suit his
particular gifts. Jackson replied that no diplomatic vacancies
existed. A chief clerkship, then? Those places were filled by the
respective heads of departments, the President said. Postmastership of Washington? Filled. A clerk's berth in that post office? It
would be necessary to speak to the postmaster about that. "Well,
then, General, haven't you an old black coat?"[48]

Mr. Van Buren had been right again. The cost of the siege was
disproportionate to the gains. The army dwindled, dissolved. As
crestfallen crusaders for preferment picked their ways homeward,
richer only in experience, General Jackson, for the one time in his
life, looked with complacency on the retreat of a force that had
advanced under his banners. "Not one in five hundred," he remarked with some exaggeration, "had obtained office."[49] Angry
subalterns among the spoilsmen sought to check the rout with sub-
terranean threats of rebellion. "If the president pursues this course
the party is Ruined and the sooner We begin to build up a new
one the better."[50] The threats achieved nothing, the murmurs
which arose with the dust of the retiring platoons moving not at
all the man who had dealt with disaffection under sterner circumstances than this. "If I had a *tit* for every one of these *pigs* to
suck at they would still be my friends."[51]

This observation was to John C. McLemore of Tennessee, who
had brightened an hour in the busy life of the Executive with
proof of exalted friendship. McLemore was married to one of
Aunt Rachel's innumerable nieces. Plunged into debt by the
failure of a man whose notes he had endorsed, he was striving
desperately to save his plantation from seizure when Jack Donelson prevailed on Secretary of the Navy Branch to offer him the

lucrative post of naval agent at Gibraltar. Though acceptance might mean the difference between solvency and ruin, McLemore had replied: "I cannot place myself in any situation likely to do Genl Jackson an injury. . . . It would at once be said that the Genl was bringing into Office his relations when others could be found better qualified."[52]

With the patronage situation leveling off, General Jackson heard his premier speak again of overseas affairs. Mr. Van Buren was considering a problem which had been on his mind since that talk with Livingston in Philadelphia. Few persons in the capital had been more apprehensive of the coming of the frontier President than the corps of foreign representatives. His actual arrival had not tended to subdue their alarms. In Europe and in Latin-America the appearance at a seat of government of a victorious soldier and his hardy partizans entailed consequences too often predictable.

Would it not be an excellent thing (Mr. Van Buren was saying) for the President to establish a personal acquaintance with the foreign representatives residing in Washington? Jackson, who liked nothing better than to form his opinions of men face to face, fell in with the idea. The Secretary suggested a private reception to the diplomatic corps at which the President, while "avoiding anything like a set speech," might diffuse certain sentiments useful to our concerns abroad. These sentiments Mr. Van Buren experimentally tabulated, with credit to Jackson's inaugural address. From this circumstance a careless observer might be led to doubt the diligence of the Secretary's scrutiny of that paper. The suggestions went farther than the address.

Many persons, some of them skeptical, have left their impressions of a first meeting with Andrew Jackson as President of the United States. In no instance which this writer recalls was the effect unfavorable to him. Instinctively one felt the presence of a superior being—a chieftain and a gentleman. Such was the impression of the ministers. The remarks suggested by the Secretary of State were spoken in a "happy and expressive manner." Guests began to request manuscript copies to forward to their governments. A dinner was served at which the "old-school manners of the host," and the "exceptional quality" of meat and drink completed the conquest[53]—justifying the "judicious" removal policy in one particular: General Jackson had retained Vivart, Mr. Adams's French cook.

The clouds at which Editor Ritchie had shaken his head seemed to be clearing from the skies over Washington.

CHAPTER IX

Emergence of a Quiet Statesman

I

Originating with the "light airs" which, on April 2, 1828, had coursed the remote Mediterranean, another spell of squally weather was on its way to the Potomac. On that day and on that sea John B. Timberlake departed this life aboard the frigate *Constitution,* thus relinquishing the employment Senator Eaton had obtained for him by posting a bond in the sum of ten thousand dollars to insure an improvement in the purser's accounting. The ship's record gave the cause of death as "pulmonary disease," the ship's gossip as drink. Presently the tale was abroad in Washington that the naval officer had cut his throat because he believed his wife to be living in sin with John Henry Eaton.[1] Timberlake dead proved even more of a problem than Timberlake living. On the rising of Congress the Senator returned to Tennessee, by his own admission, "anxious and distressed" in mind.

The election over, he laid the case before Jackson. "The hand of Providence . . . [has put it] in my power to snatch . . . [Mrs. Timberlake] from the injustice done . . . by a gossiping world. . . . All considerations of honor and of justice point to the course for me to pursue. . . . Under such circumstances it is not possible to hesitate [over] what is right and proper." Yet, if not hesitating, the Senator was able to refrain from unseemly precipitation. "At a *proper time"*—the words appeared to come with effort—"I will tender her the offer to share my life and prospects."[2]

"Major," Jackson replied, "if you love Margaret Timberlake go and marry her at once and shut their mouths."[3]

The Major had spoken of honor and justice, not love.

On his return to Washington the "proper time" was vaguely

allocated to the future, "after the adjournment." Then Andrew Jackson would be President, and Eaton too, so he hoped, in a higher sphere of public usefulness. But before this cautious arrangement could be reported to Jackson, the Senator received, by private messenger, a pointed communication from the Hermitage. There should be no delay, Old Hickory said. Eaton should marry Peg "forthwith" or leave the O'Neale boarding house.[4]

In a long and labored letter Senator Eaton returned "sincere thanks . . . for the kind suggestions made in reference to . . . [this] delicate subject. Your admonition shall be regarded. . . . In the first week of January (the 6th) an honorable discharge of duty to myself and to her will be met and . . . I rendered a happy and contented man. Judge! General, you who have known me long and well, if I could do such an act as this apart from the belief that she has a soul above everything of crime and design. . . . If I could entertain any wish more ardent than another it would be that you might honor us with your presence at the time, but the considerations you suggest are of a character so important as to induce us to forego this pleasure and close the business earlier than you can be here."[5]

Congressman Cambreleng apprized Martin Van Buren of the spirit in which Washington received the news of the betrothal. "Poor Eaton is to be married tonight to Mrs. T——! There is a vulgar saying of some vulgar man, I believe Swift, on such unions —about using a certain household —[sic] and then putting it on one's head."[6]

Five days sooner than Eaton had promised, that is to say on January 1, 1829, the vows were exchanged in the presence of the chaplain of the Senate. This could not have displeased the old chieftain, who laid so much store on the virtue of punctuality in the performance of his "admonitions." Yet the wedding failed to realize either the hopeful prediction of the troubled bridegroom or the emphatic one of its distinguished sponsor. "The General's friends are much disturbed. His enemies laugh and divert themselves." Ignorant of Jackson's compelling rôle, Margaret Bayard Smith overcredited the hand of the bride in the matter. "She is irresistible and carries whatever point she sets her mind on."[7]

2

Washington society said, "We shall see about that." The *haut monde,* from which Margaret Timberlake had been dropped by Mrs. Monroe, raised its barriers against Margaret Eaton. The ladies declined to call on her. Very well, Margaret would call on them—and, perhaps, as the fourth of March drew nigh, women with the welfare of their husbands at heart might read in the political skies portents that would suggest a reciprocation of those civilities. A card was left at the residence of Mrs. Daniel T. Patterson, wife of the Master Commandant of the Navy and as precise in her social relations as her spouse had been in the aim of his cannon at New Orleans. Mrs. Patterson did not return the call. One day, when Senator and Mrs. Eaton casually encountered the Commandant, Margaret remarked that she had called on Mrs. Patterson. Had Mrs. Patterson noticed the card? The surprised sea hero bowed. He presumed that the card had been received. "I had supposed," said Margaret, "that as she has not returned my visit, the card had not been received. Will you please tell her that I left it for her?" The Commandant bowed again and resumed his promenade.

"This anecdote," related David Campbell, "is perfectly characteristic of the lady."

Mr. Campbell's letters to his wife form an almost continuous narrative of the passing show in Washington. The Virginian had come to town prepared to judge Mrs. Eaton sympathetically. "I am under the impression that the stories I hear are not true." Campbell made his call. The bride of General Jackson's friend was twenty-nine years old. Her small, active form, well-rounded and voluptuous, trailed an odor of toilet water, which men were more apt to admire than women. Her apple complexion was still perfect; her large dark eyes, never still, could communicate much. Full lips were ready to part in a smile and, then with a tom-boyish toss of her head, the generous mouth would yield to immoderate laughter exhibiting the prettiest teeth in Washington. Deportment brought out the imperfections in the portrait. "She rose and saluted me very handsomely," Mr. Campbell continued, "and seemed to be very much at her ease." Eaton, on the contrary, appeared uncomfortable, although his wife went "out of the road to make us believe she was extremely fond of her husband. . . . Entering into conversation she talked *away* about anything and every thing—jumbling great and small subjects together. . . . She loves admiration and bedaubs every one almost with flattery who notices her. The gentlemen who call on Eaton [for political purposes], knowing this, pay her considerable attentions."

The polite Virginian's visit brought an invitation to dinner, after which Mr. Campbell made a prophesy. "Eaton can never get along [in public life] with such a woman."[8]

The fourth of March drew nigh with Old Hickory at the Wigwam and the town aswarm. The Eatons had taken a large house across the street from the British Legation. Their wines and food were good. They were blessed with numerous visitors from out of town. Cabinet-making time came on and the reluctance which Jackson saw in Eaton's attitude toward a portfolio was discernible to few others who were in the know. Margaret watched every move. When old and tried friends of the General suggested that the Senator be shifted to a foreign capital, Peggy put her foot down. She told her husband she would remain in Washington "in the presence of my enemies," and conquer there.[9] More cards fluttered into her basket. The patrician Branch, his eye on the Navy Department, the fastidious Berrien, candidate of the Calhoun wing for Attorney General, were all smiles. When Jackson put it to him cold turkey "M^r. B[ranch] . . . disavowed any knowledge of any thing disreputable to M^{rs}. Eaton, or any belief of the rumors about her." Delighted with the behavior of his newly-found friends, Eaton went to Jackson with encomiums which Old Hickory later called the deciding factor in the appointments of Branch and of Berrien to the Cabinet.[10]

After these successes the snubbing that Margaret received at the inaugural ceremonies came as a shock. And this was not the end. The Cabinet sworn in, neither Mrs. Branch nor Mrs. Ingham nor the daughters of Mr. Berrien, who was a widower, visited the home of the recently popular Eaton. Mr. Calhoun left his own card but not that of his wife. Emily Donelson wrote to her sister, Mrs. John Coffee: "[Mrs. Eaton] is held in too much abhorrence ever to be noticed. The ladies here have determined not to visit her. To please Uncle we returned her first call. She talked of her intimacy with our family . . . [which] so disgusted . . . [me] that I shall not visit her again. I fear this is to be a source of great mortification to our dear old Uncle, . . . [but] if Major Eaton had felt any disinterested friendship he would have never accepted the [Cabinet] appointment."[11]

Emily had been listening to Mesdames Branch and Ingham, and one or two other ladies who were prepared to dispute Peg's claim to irresistibility. On the evening of April 9 two messages for Mrs. Donelson were delivered at the Executive Residence. Though signed by Eaton they could hardly have been written without the help of Margaret. "You are young and uninformed of the ways . . . of the world and therefore I speak to you. . . . I have understood that a certain family have gratuitously stepped forward to become councellors, to tell you what to do and what not to do; and in secret to whisper slanders respecting . . . me and my wife. . . . You yourself may become a victim of those meddling gossips. Your excellent aunt. . . ."[12]

Visitors meeting for the first time the person to whom Major Eaton's communications were addressed, were wont to describe her as "amiable," though something in the set of a well-shaped mouth and the candid glance of her hazel eyes suggested a mind of her own. Emily Donelson was good-looking and, in the opinion of Martin Van Buren, "unaffected and graceful" in demeanor. Her figure was slight and youthful, her countenance alert and of aristocratic cast, her most arresting feature a wealth of fine auburn hair. As Eaton said, Emily was young. Married at seventeen, she was now under twenty-one. Absent from her native West for the second time in her life, she had, indeed, much to learn, and the situation in which she found herself would have tried a more experienced woman. Yet, accustomed to the responsibilities of a large plantation homestead, she had energetically laid hold of the management of the Executive Residence with its eighteen serv-ants, finding time to continue the lessons of her three-year-old

EMILY DONELSON

Niece of Rachel Jackson, wife (and cousin) of Andrew Jackson Donelson. She was mistress
of the White House during General Jackson's administrations saving for a year of exile during
the ascendency of Margaret Eaton whose calls Mrs. Donelson would not return. From a
portrait by Earl, owned by Mrs. Donelson's great-granddaughter, Mrs. Pauline Wilcox Burke
of Washington.

son, Andrew Jackson, as well. A second baby was expected at the end of the summer.

The other feminine member of the President's household was Mary Eastin, a young cousin of Mrs. Donelson and a great pet of the General. This Cumberland Cinderella liked her new life. "I have a room fit for a Princess, with silk curtains, mahogany furniture, a carpet such as you Tennesseans have in your parlour, and a piano." She had a beau for every day in the week and Emily predicted a White House wedding before long. The attentions of Abraham Van Buren, a son of the Secretary of State, were such as to further this speculation. And the Secretary himself had been in town scarcely a week when this perspicacious young thing confided, "He has fine manners, . . . and bids fair to be our President one of these days."[13]

If Emily Donelson seemed qualified to discharge her duties with a fair amount of credit, General Jackson was even better served in the important matter of a private secretary. Jack Donelson had grown with the responsibilities of recent years. It is probable that no more intelligent or more useful man, excepting Van Buren, now stood closer to the President; and surely none was so selfless or so inconspicuous in his devotion. The once-modest Lewis, who also lived at the White House, had responded differently to developments. He seemed to swell rather than to grow. His jealousy of his prerogatives as the General's man Friday became noticeable to others.[14] This began to annoy Donelson. The fact that Lewis was a constant visitor at the Eatons, and an advocate of Margaret's cause with the President, failed to diminish the breach. Lewis and Eaton were brothers-in-law by Eaton's first marriage, but, this notwithstanding, Donelson remembered the time when the Major had induced Branch to remove his daughter from the O'Neale boarding house on the ground that her associates should be above suspicion.[15]

Eaton's unusual letters did not set well with Donelson and his wife. Particularly were they unable to appreciate the propriety of the Secretary of War's intimation that the mistress of the White House had placed herself under the guardianship of slanderers, or that an analogy existed between the history of Margaret Eaton and of the departed Aunt Rachel.[16]. The missive, bearing Mrs. Donelson's name, which Secretary Eaton received in return for his pains was one that Talleyrand need not have disclaimed. Emily's husband was doubtless the actual co-author, however.

"It was with some surprise that I recd. your letters . . . and was not much relieved by a perusal of their contents. With regard to those who are understood to have 'stepped forward to be my councellors and advisors and to direct me what to do and what not to do' I must say I am totally unacquainted with such. . . .

"Having drawn my attention to slanders got up for political purposes to tarnish the reputation of my lamented Aunt you will suffer me to say that the most conclusive proof of her innocence was the respect in which she was universally held by her neighbours. . . . As to the probability of my becoming a victim to the slanders of this or any other place I feel it due to myself to say that altho I am conscious of possessing many faults . . . I hope I shall maintain my reputation as it has heretofore been, . . not only pure but unsuspected. . . .

"As you say I am young and unacquainted with the world, and therefore I will trouble myself as little as possible with things that do not concern me. . . . I do not wish to decide upon any persons character nor controul in any way the etiquette of this place; and that so far from arrogating to myself any honour or privilege from the circumstance of my being in the Gen^{ls} family I shall act as if I was not a member of it nor expect to be considered in any light than the proper one as a private person. . . .

"very Respect.

"EMILY DONELSON."[17]

For the General's sake Donelson himself made a show of seeking to soften his wife's letter a little, writing one over his own signature in which, with more tact than truth, he assured Eaton that Emily placed no credence in the gossip she had heard.[18]

Then the President and his nephew, but not Emily, honored Mrs. Eaton with a call.

"The cloud is blowing over," the General wrote to one of Emily's connections in Tennessee. "Satelites of Clay are falling in the pitts [they] dug for Eaton."[19]

These amicable gestures fell short of what Margaret desired, however, and boldly she prepared to play for higher stakes. If Emily Donelson would not meet her, was it beyond the pale of possibility that a more amenable First Lady might find herself in the White House? William B. Lewis was Margaret's ally— and Lewis had a daughter, conveniently near, in Philadelphia. The Major had come to Washington with the expectation of remaining only long enough to see the General comfortably settled. Margaret, for one, and Jackson for another, begged him to prolong his stay—a suggestion that could not have been repugnant to the Major's own ideas of his enlarging importance. Mrs. Eaton was credited with helping to pull the strings whereby the Second Auditor of the Treasury was sacked and Lewis given the post.[20] Margaret also sought to bring Amos Kendall within the sphere of her influence, and succeeded to the point of establishing social relations with his family. The account of a politically influential stage-coach firm, which had a contract for carrying mail, came to the desk of Mr. Kendall. He thought the account padded. According to a tale later related by Kendall's son-in-law, Mrs. Eaton informed Mrs. Kendall that a new carriage should be hers in event her husband passed the account. But this proved too much to ask of the officer who had declined to frank his wife's correspondence.[21]

Meanwhile Mrs. Eaton and Mrs. Donelson had met face to face for the first time since the notable exchange of letters. The occasion was a presidential excursion by water to Norfolk. Margaret offered Emily the use of her cologne bottle, which Mrs. Donelson refused in such a manner as to "shew a disposition not to be intimate with her." A little later Donelson noticed Mrs. Eaton's emotional confusion. Unaware of the cause, he proffered his arm. Whereupon Margaret poured forth an indignant account of the cologne bottle incident, adding that if Mrs. Donelson chose to persist in such behavior she might as well prepare to return to Tennessee. The President, she said, had given his word to pack Emily off unless she made amends.[22]

Thus the declaration of war. David Campbell gave his wife a candid impression of the contenders. Mrs. Donelson was "a very amiable little woman," though untrained "for court life." "Her ladyship [Mrs. Eaton] is *decidedly* the greatest fool I ever saw in a genteel situation."[23]

3

Emily neither made amends nor departed for Tennessee. The approaching accouchement excused her from formal society in which the Cabinet women avoided Mrs. Eaton more pointedly than ever. Yet, in the face of this formidable array, Margaret scored a series of triumphs. Martin Van Buren called on her. And so for the first time a Cabinet officer's card fell in Mrs. Eaton's basket and for the first time a Cabinet officer graced her dinner table, though alack, no Cabinet officer's lady, the Secretary of State being—and how fortunately, the envious said—a widower without daughters. The want was soon supplied. Postmaster General Barry and his wife arrived from Kentucky. The Eaton carriage bore them off to the Eaton house, and Peggy had her Cabinet lady.

To this add the open protagonism of the President of the United States, which was assuming the dimensions of an Administration policy. The Reverend Ezra Stiles Ely of Philadelphia, an old friend of Jackson who had previously spoken well of Eaton, wrote Old Hickory a letter saying, among many other things, that Mrs. Eaton had borne a bad reputation from girlhood; that before their marriage she and Eaton had traveled together; that a gentleman breakfasting at Gadsby's had remarked that "Mrs. Eaton brushed by him last night . . . having apparently forgotten the time when she slept with him."[24]

General Jackson responded in a communication longer than his inaugural address. "The high standing of Mr. Eaton as a man of moral worth and a Mason [Timberlake also was a Mason] gives the lie direct" to the charges involving his name. As to the accusations involving other men, Jackson said he would entertain no "rumors or suspicions." But if Ely had "facts and proofs sustained by reputable witnesses in the light of day" let him bring them forth—a large order for Doctor Ely, or for anyone, to fill.[25]

The clergyman retreated before the slashing counter-attack, merely expressing the hope that Margaret's repentance would justify the President's faith in her. *"Repentance,"* Jackson shot back, "presupposes the existence of *crime.* . . . Where is the witness who has thus far come forth in substantiation of these slanderous charges?"[26] Doctor Ely could produce no witness. However, a gray-haired gallant in the person of Colonel Nathan Towson, the Paymaster General of the Army, came forward unasked. Jackson blasted him off his feet. "How fallen the military character whose boast is that they are the protectors of Female character."[27] Young R. K. Call came forward. Jackson taunted the former Congressman upon the admitted ill-success of his own effort at seduction. "My Dear Call *you* have a right to believe that Mrs. T. was *not* a woman of easy virtue."[28] The Reverend Mr. Ely returned to the lists, repeating to Jackson a story to the effect that Mrs. Timberlake had had a miscarriage at a time when her husband's absence at sea precluded him from responsibility in the matter.[29]

Major Lewis was collecting contrary evidence in the form of testimonials as to the spotless nature of Margaret's reputation. In a city filled with politicians aspiring to office and office-holders aspiring to keep their places, the inescapable inference that to be on Mrs. Eaton's side was to be on Jackson's side did not obstruct the performance of the task. Statements to the effect that her character was as white as snow poured upon the President. This scramble for evidence, pro and con, made boudoir tales a topic of the day. True to prediction, no woman's reputation seemed safe. Duff Green heard a young buck holding forth at Gadsby's bar on the feasibility of carrying his campaign of conquest across the threshold of the White House where, he declared, "the female part of the family . . . were of easy virtue."[30] There is no proof that Green passed this particular morsel on to the male contingent in the Executive Mansion, and a world of presumption that he did not.

Mr. Van Buren increased the emphasis on his friendly attention to the Eatons. He intervened in their behalf with Mrs. Donelson and with Mary Eastin, but to no avail. On the other hand, John C. Calhoun and his followers remained conspicuously un-co-operative with Old Hickory's effort to induce society to accept the marriage he had pushed his friend into. Some of Van Buren's admirers thought this the wiser course. "God knows," insisted one, "we did not make him [Jackson] president to work the miracle of Making M^rs E—— an honest woman."[31] The Secretary of State declined to be diverted, however. Mr. Calhoun and his friends rejoiced. In their belief the position of Eaton and his empress of confusion was untenable. Were they to carry Martin Van Buren with them into obscurity that would be the simplest imaginable solution of the problem of the presidential succession.

In August, 1829, the President sailed down the Potomac for a short vacation on the Rip Raps, a breeze-swept islet in Hampton Roads, off Norfolk, returning September 1 somewhat invigorated by the rest and the sea bathing. That evening the Reverend John N. Campbell, pastor of the Presbyterian Church which Jackson attended in Washington, asked to speak to the President privately. They mounted to the study where Mr. Campbell revealed himself as the source of Doctor Ely's account of the alleged miscarriage. Campbell said he had the story from a physician named Craven, then dead, who had had professional knowledge of the case. He fixed the date as in 1821.

Thirty-six hours later, in the presence of Jack Donelson and Colonel Towson, General Jackson confronted the clergyman with documentary proof that Timberlake had been in Washington in 1821. Whereupon Mr. Campbell changed the date to 1822 when, it appears, Timberlake was at sea. Jackson read his pastor an explosive lecture on Christian charity. There was more to the interview, however. Campbell told of a call that he and Colonel Towson had made only a few hours before on Mrs. Craven, the physician's widow. This lady had described a previous visit to her residence by Major Eaton and his wife who, she said, had endeavored to frighten her with allusions to duels and law-suits into denying any knowledge of the miscarriage story. The widow, in truth, knew nothing of the reported miscarriage, but she said she had unhesitatingly told the Eatons that Timberlake had made a sort of father confessor of the old doctor and had left him with "impressions not favourable to the character of Mrs. T."[32]

ANDREW JACKSON ("JACK") DONELSON

Nephew of Rachel Jackson and husband of Emily Donelson, reared at the Hermitage from the age of four, educated at West Point and at Transylvania University. Private secretary to General Jackson and later chargé d'affaires to the Texas Republic. He was the most disinterested and one of the ablest of Old Hickory's intimate counselors. From a portrait by Earl, owned by Mrs. Betty Donelson of Nashville.

Each of Mr. Campbell's three auditors drew from the recital what it pleased him to hear. Without presuming to pass on the truth or falsity of specific charges, Towson recalled a prophecy of his that the appointment of Eaton to the Cabinet would prove "most unfortunate." Donelson stressed the visit to the doctor's widow. To these things Jackson refused to listen. Like a shaft of lightning he fixed on the clergyman's change of dates, and declared that Campbell had told a wholly incredible tale.[33] Applied strictly to the miscarriage story this was hardly an exaggeration.

Swiftly Jackson moved to expand this victory into an acquittal of Mrs. Eaton of all the charges and rumors that overhung her name. Members of the Cabinet were summoned to a meeting unique in the history of that body, the explicit purpose being to examine evidence bearing on the private lives of the Secretary of War and his wife. Campbell and Ely accepted invitations to attend. Every Cabinet officer was present excepting Eaton, in whose place Lewis sat. Calhoun and Donelson were also there.

Before these statesmen Jackson laid the voluminous testimony Lewis had gathered as to Mrs. Eaton's impeccable character. Then he called on Ely, who admitted he had nothing of a tangible nature to convict Major Eaton of misconduct.

"Nor Mrs. Eaton either," broke in the President.

"On that point," said the pastor, "I would rather not give an opinion."

"She is chaste as a virgin!" exclaimed the President.

The Reverend Mr. Campbell started to offer his testimony. When he digressed to explain a point, Jackson interrupted to say that the clergyman had been summoned to "*give* evidence, not discuss it." Campbell declined to accept the ruling. Gathering up his papers, he bowed and withdrew declaring himself prepared to prove his case in a court of law. Whereupon the President adjourned the meeting with the air of one who had given Margaret Eaton's vindication the finished aspect of a *fait accompli.*[34]

4

The day florid-faced Duff Green ended a patronage dispute with

Postmaster General Barry by stamping out of his office and making tracks toward the White House, he had carried his point. The postmaster of Washington was removed in favor of a partizan of John C. Calhoun. Such a thing was not to happen often again, however. The editor's great influence with the program of "reform" was on the wane. Not without result had Martin Van Buren purchased a saddle horse and adopted the President's form of recreation. Not without consequences had been the fact that the Postmaster General was the only fellow-Cabinet officer the Secretary of State found in Margaret Eaton's drawing room. Years before the New Yorker had urged that, "instead of spending our time on small matters," steps should be taken to utilize the vast Postoffice Department as material for a political machine.[35] Monroe had interfered that time. Now the situation was different.

When Mr. Van Buren arrived in Washington, he was understood to be a foe of removals. Office-holders had rejoiced and looked to him to halt the proscription. In helping to rid the city of the army of job-hunters, that silent statesman had performed a service much appreciated by the President; and he had eliminated from the political landscape the most open and inconvenient advertizement of the work that was going on. But this was accomplished without checking the progress of "reform," for "slowly but surely," as one apprehensive postal official pointed out, the removals continued.[36] Before long a light began to dawn upon Government employees who had welcomed the Secretary of State as their protector. "Van Buren not Calhoun I believe is the head of the proscription party."[37] It was true. "The Post offices are swept clean in Newyork and eastward." Barry had resisted the brusque demands of Duff Green, representing the ambitions of Mr. Calhoun, to succumb to the suave suggestions of the Secretary of State, representing the ambitions of himself. Though the remark about a clean sweep of eastern postoffices was much exaggerated, the ascendency which Martin Van Buren had attained by almost imperceptible degrees was presently so well established that Duff Green confessed the defeat of his pro-Calhoun candidates in distant Illinois.[38]

The actual number of removals was the subject of much speculation and wide differences of opinion, however. After Congress convened in December, 1829, precise figures became available on the appointments which the President was obliged to submit to the Senate for confirmation. These included the famous recess appointments. The lists contained three hundred and nineteen names, of which one hundred and twenty-one were to supply the places of officials who had been removed by Jackson. In sixty-two instances incumbents were reappointed.[39] Considering the hulla- baloo of both the Jackson press and the opposition press, as well as the prevailing opinion of more than a century, the noteworthy thing is not that actual removals had been so numerous, but so few.

Some of the appointments were subjected to severe criticism in the Senate, ten being rejected. Henry Lee, who had received the consulship at Algiers, was turned down by unanimous vote— Benton, Livingston and Hugh Lawson White joining the opposi- tion. The senators also rejected Isaac Hill, and lived to regret it. Born in squalor, kicked and cuffed as a printer's ragged and oft- hungry apprentice, this frail, embittered cripple early in life had launched upon a career of revenge, opposing nearly everything the New England Brahmins held sacred. He refused to accept defeat now. Jackson stood by him and within a year the little lame Marat with a zealot's gleaming eyes returned to Washington, a senator from New Hampshire and a peer of those who had pronounced him unfit for a subordinate office in the Treasury. The vote on Amos Kendall was a tie, which the Vice President broke in favor of the Kentuckian. Of the ten men rejected, four were later con- firmed on renomination so that finally Old Hickory's will was overridden only in six of three hundred and nineteen instances. These figures indicate the need for revision of a good deal that has been written about the extent of the Senate's disciplinary action against the spoils proclivities of General Jackson.[40]

Over the bulk of Federal offices, numbering in the neighbor- hood of eleven thousand lesser posts, the Senate had no authority. Through this vast domain the "terror" was supposed to stalk unre- strained. In April, 1830, Holmes of Maine attacked proscription on the Senate floor, declaring that one thousand nine hundred and eighty-one persons had been thrown out of office in twelve months. The percentage of removals in Washington during the first year seemed to confirm these figures. In the Navy Department two out of nine clerks had been dropped; in the War Department eight out of forty; in the Treasury twenty-six out of one hundred and and forty-five; in the Postoffice Department fifteen out of forty-three, and in the Department of State, where Van Buren controlled in person, eighteen out of twenty-six.[41] The total was sixty-nine removals out of two hundred and sixty-three opportunities, or a little better than one in four.

Something like definite measures to halt the President seemed in the making. It was said that Justice McLean spoke privately of the feasibility of impeaching the man who had lately elevated him to the Supreme bench.[42] Daniel Webster, revolving similar thoughts in his mind, went so far as to consult unofficially McLean's colleague, the learned Justice Kent, on the constitutionality of certain removals. To this remarkable inquiry Kent regretfully replied that Jackson had acted within his rights. "That the President grossly abuses the power of removal is manifest," the gloomy jurist continued, "but it is the Genius of Democracy to be the sport of faction. ... All theories of Government that suppose the mass of people virtuous and able to act virtuously are purely Utopian."[43] Practical rather than Utopian motives directed much of the opposition to removals, however. One of the things that irked McLean was the disruption, attempted by Calhoun and achieved by Van Buren, of the nucleus of an organization the former Postmaster General had created in that department to feather his own political nest.[44] Webster also revealed something of the spirit that actuated the senators in the discharge of their duties. "Were it not for the outdoor popularity of the President ... [we] would have negatived more than half of his nominations."[45] And in view of what was said then and has since been widely repeated touching Mr. Adams's freedom from partizanship, it is interesting to note that in the closing days of his Administration he sent seventy-eight nominations to the Senate.[46]

Duff Green answered Senator Holmes and other critics, claiming only nine hundred and nineteen removals in eighteen months, or about one in eleven, taking the civil list all in all. These figures seem to be nearly correct.[47] Moreover, by the time Green's figures appeared Jackson had greatly tempered the execution of his "reform" policy. Thenceforth comparatively few removals were made and one heard no more about a clean sweep—a term so offensive to the ears of soft-footed Mr. Van Buren. According to the best estimate available, Jackson replaced, during the eight years of his presidency, about one government employee in six, leaving more than nine thousand out of eleven thousand undisturbed.[48] The proportion of Jefferson's removals was almost as large.[49]

Some good flowed from all this shaking-up. Smuggling along the southern coasts was cut down and the customs revenues rose. A notorious ring of grafters in the Indian service was smashed. The internal administration of departments and bureaus was simplified and, in the main, improved, an exception being the Post Office until Kendall succeeded the incapable Barry. Many unworthy and unfit and some dishonest officials were replaced by better ones. But to enumerate these things—and the list could be extended—is to make out a better case for rotation than General Jackson deserves. The aggregate of the defalcations so showily exposed by him comprises less than a fourth part of the million and a quarter dollars Old Hickory's friend Samuel Swartwout stole as Collector of the Port of New York. Though the President exercised commendable restraint in acting upon applications from his late wife's almost countless western connections, no objection came from him when the father and a brother-in-law of Mrs. Eaton appeared on the War Department payroll. The grand object of curtailing political activity among employees and rendering the public service free of partizan obligation failed utterly. In this respect Jackson was to leave the service a great deal worse than he found it, about the only political activity in which it was unsafe for an officer of the Government to engage being activity against the interests of General Jackson. Though succeeding presidents were to go further and to do much more than Andrew Jackson toward turning the civil service into a political tool, the fact remains that he had opened the door.

5

Up to December, 1829, when his first message to Congress was due, the most conspicuous issues to engross the energies of General Jackson had been the private life of Margaret Eaton and rotation in office. Friends of the Administration were under the impression that the country would appreciate a sight of Old Hickory in action in other fields. The message, an able and vigorous document, presented several possibilities.

Item, Foreign Affairs: For twenty years France had dodged and delayed negotiations for a settlement of our claims for damages arising from the Napoleonic wars; British West Indian ports had been closed to our commerce since the foundation of the Republic; the Maine boundary was in dispute; the South and the West desired to annex Texas. In these matters Jackson adopted a firm tone proposing "to ask for nothing that is not clearly right and to submit to nothing that is wrong."

Item, the Tariff: South Carolina, in revolt against the Act of 1828, threatened openly to "nullify" the law and refuse to pay the duties. This Act, a piece of political jugglery designed to promote the Jackson campaign alike in pro- and anti-tariff territory, had been framed with the expectation that New England votes would defeat it. But it became a law and now Jackson faced the consequences. He proposed conciliation and compromise.

Item, Indian Removal: True to the spirit of the West, Jackson would push the red people further back, exchanging new promises for promises broken. Reversing the policy of Adams, he sided with Georgia in its violent measures to expel the peaceable Creeks and Cherokees from lands guaranteed to them by Federal treaty.

Item, the National Debt: It should be paid and Jackson meant to pay it, thereafter distributing surplus revenue among the states.

Item, Internal Improvements: Small consolation for western appropriation-grabbers here. Jackson was for "constitutional" improvements, but his remarks on the debt and the surplus indicated his real intentions as to the disposition of Federal funds.

Item, the Bank of the United States: Its charter would expire in

1836, when the stockholders would apply for a renewal. The President suggested that Congress "and the people"—mark the phrase—begin to consider whether another agency might not be devised to replace the bank since it had "failed in the great end of establishing a uniform and sound currency."[50]

So much for the message. Before its delivery the tariff had been by long odds the pressing thing. Nor did the President's balanced treatment of that topic placate South Carolina where influential men spoke more openly than ever in favor of declaring the Act of 1828 to be null and void and Charleston to be a free port. One as capable as Jackson of smelling a fight from afar could not have been unaware of the significance of this. With the issue of nullification and the shadow of disunion at his gate what, then, was the object of that surprising paragraph on the Bank of the United States, whose charter had six years and more to run? If he held to his announced determination of refusing a second term, Jackson would be out of office by that time. Nicholas Biddle, president of the bank, stared with amazement at his newspaper. In November Biddle had had a long, cordial conversation with Lewis and a pleasant chat with the President. Moreover, there was Jackson's record in the West as a sound money man when it required courage to be one. At this moment the President's personal account was with the bank's Washington branch. And even if these things were not true what, in the name of veracity, did Andrew Jackson mean when he said the bank had failed to provide the country with a stable currency?

Mr. Biddle received no satisfactory answer to the enigma which, for the time being, slid into eclipse behind a façade of more timely concerns. Jackson seemed content that this should be. He seemed content to let the tariff pot boil a little longer. He had, however, selected an issue and determined upon the tactics by which he intended to see it boldly through. By a surprise move he meant to strike down the growing demands upon the Treasury for funds to build roads, canals and other internal improvements purely local in their benefits.

The plan originated in a series of talks casually begun by Martin Van Buren some months before. Throughout his public career, the Secretary of State had been an undeviating opponent of internal improvements as a Federal policy. This had set him apart from Clay, from Adams and—what was at this time of more importance—from John C. Calhoun. It had also set him apart from Jackson during the winter of 1823-24 when the General was in the Senate. Fresh from his frontier campaigns, Jackson had been dragged back into public life impressed with the military virtues of roads. On that ground he had voted for a comprehensive survey bill and for some minor roads. These votes he had continued to defend. From the mounting enthusiasm for public spending stemmed an evil difficult for the average congressman to resist. Having obtained appropriations for measures of national significance, members courted favor by proposing all sorts of local schemes to be paid for with public funds. Log-rolling alliances were beginning to be the talk of Capitol Hill. Would Representative A support Representative B's measure for a canal in return for B's promise to support A's bill for a highway connecting the county seats in his district? Van Buren believed that nothing short of prompt and drastic action would avert "a torrent of reckless legislation." Otherwise, he foresaw the improvement mania knit in with the reviving spirit of speculation in western lands, involving calls and renewed calls upon the Treasury. Another thing he could not have overlooked was the prospect of Mr. Calhoun riding the crest of the improvements wave.

Jackson agreed that the tendency should be stopped short, telling Van Buren to watch Congress and bring to the White House the first vulnerable bill to meet his eye. Few leaders, reflected the Secretary, would have behaved with equal resolution, for the "improvement" virus was at work in the veins of Jackson's western supporters. At the end of April, 1830, in the course of a horseback ride, Mr. Van Buren said he thought he had his bill—a measure to build a turnpike from Maysville to Lexington, Kentucky, through the heart of the strongest Jackson district in the State. It had passed the House and would pass the Senate. Returning to his study the President roughed out a veto message.[51]

Though the whole matter was supposed to be a secret between Jackson and the Secretary of State, a disturbing rumor brought

Representative "Tecumseh" Johnson of Kentucky to the White House so agitated that he could hardly sit in a chair.

Nor was the Congressman's devotion to the cause of improvements the only thing to mark him as a faithful exemplar of border ideals. He wore no cravat. His nickname came from the War of 1812 in which he had reputedly slain Tecumseh in personal combat. To prove it some of his men came home with razor strops which they said had been cut from the Indian's hide.

Advancing toward the President with his left hand extended and his right fist clenched above his head, Johnson exclaimed: "General, if this hand were an anvil on which the sledge hammer of a smith were descending and a fly were to light upon it that fly would not be more surely crushed than you will crush your friends in Kentucky if you veto that bill."

Jackson sprang to his feet. "Sir, have you looked at the condition of the Treasury—at the amount of money it contains—at the appropriations already made by Congress—at the amount of other claims upon it?"

"Tecumseh" confessed that he had not.

"Well," said Old Hickory, "I have. There is no money to be expended as my friends desire. I stand committed before the Country to pay off the National Debt. This pledge I am determined to redeem."

The blustery Kentuckian returned to the Capitol a much, troubled man. "Nothing less than a voice from Heaven," he told fellow-Westerners who crowded around, "will prevent the old man from vetoing the Bill." And on second thought Johnson doubted the efficacy of a voice. Pennsylvania, linked to the West by strong ties of commerce, joined in the protest. On the morning the veto was due, Mr. Van Buren called at the White House. Eaton, Barry, Lewis, and Felix Grundy, who had succeeded to Eaton's Senate seat, were at breakfast with the President. Their "desponding" countenances told Van Buren what he had come to make sure of. Eaton was the president of a western canal company. The veteran at the head of the table tapped a bulging breast pocket. "The thing is here and shall go up as soon as Congress convenes."

This veto message was a work of art, to which Van Buren had given a final form that exhibited little more than a nodding acquaintance with Jackson's original outline. The document relied on Old Hickory's power over the imagination of the masses, and his uncanny ability to make his measures their measures—a phenomenon of statesmanship the country was to see much more of in the seven tumultuous years to come. Speaking over the heads of politicians and of politically-intrenched contractors, the President addressed the people, predicating his case on the welfare of the common man. Jeffersonian precedents were dexterously handled to the point, in one instance, of doubtful interpretation. An appeal to patriotism was supplemented by an appeal to self-interest. The payment of the national debt would diminish taxes, the pursuit of an unrestrained improvement policy increase them.

The performance was successful, one Pennsylvania member confessing astonishment at the way his constituents accepted the dictum of the Hero.[52] Out west Henry Clay let off steam in a speech against the veto, but, to their dismay, Clay men perceived the victory Jackson had wrought in holding "the allegiance of the south & Virginia with as little offense as possible to the North & West."[53] More than this, he had done the nation a service that was to endure for many years.

6

The most fortunate individual beneficiary was Van Buren, who had achieved much more than merely sealing up another source-spring of Mr. Calhoun's declining prestige. In the summer of 1829, when Jackson and his Secretary of State had first begun to discuss the subject, the President was so ill and vexed that he wrote a brother of Aunt Rachel:

"My time cannot be long upon earth. . . . My earthly house [is] in order and [I am] prepare[d] for another & I hope a better world." But if die he must it would be on the field of duty, however acute the longing to "withdraw from the scenes that surround me to the private walks of the Hermitage, . . . there to spend my

[last] days ... at the tomb of my Dr wife, ... in peace from the toils & strife of this world with which I have long been surfeited. But this is denied me— I cannot retire with propriety."[54]

After the delivery of the message to Congress Jackson fell ill again. His legs swelled and Lewis, in alarm, feared a fatal attack of dropsy. Old Hickory frankly discussed his condition with the household. Lewis suggested that his old friend's political as well as his spiritual house should be in order and urged the claims of Van Buren against those of Calhoun as heir to the Jackson mantle. In the six months past, Old Hickory had leaned upon the New Yorker as never upon another man. Their collaboration on the message to Congress was just finished, the scheme to check internal improvements rounded into shape. Lewis suggested that Jackson leave, in effect, a political will to be used in case of his death. He did so in a letter to John Overton, of which Lewis retained a duplicate.

"Permit me to say here of Mr. Van Buren that I have found him everything that I could desire him to be, and believe him not only deserving of *my* confidence but the *confidence* of the *Nation*. Instead of his being selfish and intriguing, as has been represented by some of his opponents, I have found him frank, open, candid, and manly. As a Counsellor he is *able* and *prudent*, ... and one of the most pleasant men to do business with I ever saw. He, my dear friend, is well qualified ... to fill the highest office in the gift of the people. ... I wish I could say as much for Mr. Calhoun. You know the confidence I once had in that gentleman. However, of him I desire not now to speak."[55]

Jackson usually knew when he had said enough.

CHAPTER X

THROB OF A DISTANT DRUM

I

IN DEFERENCE to orators who, with an eye on posterity, wished to revise their efforts after delivery the Washington newspapers sometimes lagged a fortnight behind in printing important speeches made before Congress. Jackson circumvented this delay by stationing Donelson or Lewis in the galleries to apprize him immediately on adjournment of a session's doings. On one of the coldest days of the winter, January 27, 1830, Major Lewis returned from such a tour of duty.

"Well, and how is Webster getting on?" inquired the President.

"Delivering a most powerful speech," replied Lewis. "I am afraid he's demolishing our friend Hayne."

"I expected it," said Old Hickory.[1]

Reluctant as Andrew Jackson was to say a good word for Daniel Webster, there was no blinking the fact that the New Englander had unmasked Hayne as too sympathetic with the South Carolina "nullifiers" to please the hero of New Orleans. And not only Hayne, but John C. Calhoun as well.

In the beginning, the President had been prepared to take a different view of the debate which Thomas Hart Benton had precipitated with an orthodox Jacksonian arraignment of eastern capitalists whom he charged with hindering western emigration to safeguard New England's cheap labor supply. There Robert Y. Hayne took up the thread. The Cotton Kingdom could not have wished for a more presentable advocate. Schooled in the best southern traditions of public service, the blond, mercurial Hayne at thirty-eight was one of the able men of the Senate, and in his social relationships one of the most popular. Branching out from

Benton's rugged and rather sententious presentation, he gracefully invited the West to unite with the South against encroachments inimical to both sections. It was a skillful bid for an alliance in dealing with the frowning tariff and state rights questions.

As the South Carolinian began to speak, a thick-set, swarthy man in a blue coat with brass buttons tucked a bundle of papers under his arm and lounged against a pillar on the edge of the chamber. The lazy, card-playing Webster had been more than usually derelict that session in his attendance upon the deliberations of the Senate. He had just ascended the marble stairs from the quarters of the Supreme Court, where a rich practice occupied the greater part of the time he was willing to surrender to laborious concerns. Wholly ignorant of the nature of the issue before the Senate, he imagined himself too engrossed to pause for more than a moment. But as Hayne progressed, he took a seat and honored his southern colleague with strict attention.

On the next day Webster answered him. After an eloquent defense of the loyalty of New England, not altogether in agreement with the facts, the Senator from Massachusetts touched provocatively the weak spots in the Charlestonian's armor. Seizing on Hayne's declaration that "no evil was more to be deprecated than the consolidation of this government," Webster demanded proof. What was consolidation but the strengthening of the Union? He regretted a disposition—which he trusted Hayne did not share—of some in the South to "speak of the Union in terms of indifference, or even disparagement."

Hayne took the bait. In a bitter and brilliant reply, the South Carolinian attacked not only New England's long record of doubtful devotion to the Union, but Webster personally. With an array of historical precedent, he defended his State's contention for the right to set aside oppressive Federal legislation. This was nullification.

The speech, which many thought unanswerable and which Mr. Calhoun from his place on the dais had punctuated with smiles of approval, gave Webster the opportunity he had sought. He assailed Hayne's proposals as impossible of practical application, as ruinous to the welfare of all, and as unconstitutional. "The Constitution is not the creature of the State government. The very chief end, the main design, for which the whole Constitution was framed and adopted was to establish a government that should not . . . depend on State opinion and State discretion."

Webster was not a superficially dramatic type of orator. Using few gestures, he would speak for half an hour at a time in a tone only a little more formal than ordinary conversation. Yet the rich and deep voice, the sonorous rhythm of his sentences, and the glance of the great luminous dark eyes exercised something akin to an hypnotic sway. At the same time, listeners were left under the flattering impression that the appeal was to the intellect rather than to the emotions; for Webster dealt chiefly with arguments, not exhortations. The calmness, the good nature, the pervading sense of mastery and of subdued power clothed exaggeration in the confident garments of understatement. With Senate and galleries in his grip for two days, he delivered the most telling plea for the perpetuation of the Union that one man has ever made. In sentences that were to invite comparison with Demosthenes's *Oration on the Crown,* Mr. Webster concluded by urging the "folly" of the doctrine of "liberty first and Union afterwards." "Liberty *and* Union, now and forever, one and inseparable."

When John C. Calhoun's gavel and petulant cry of "Order, order!" broke the spell, others than Major Lewis were of the opinion that the man from Massachusetts had demolished Hayne.

A few hours later the contending giants met again at a White House levee.

"How are you this evening, Colonel Hayne?" asked Webster.

"None the better for you, sir," said the Southerner with a smile.[2]

As to the truth of that polite answer much, very much, would depend on the venerable host of the evening. After the last orator had spoken, Andrew Jackson must *act* on the issue which already had sensitive ears straining to catch the throb of a distant drum.

2

As somber shadows deepened, the incongruous note of travesty supplied by Mrs. Eaton continued its work of attrition on the inner harmony and the outward dignity of the Administration. General Jackson's extraordinary Cabinet meeting had failed of its purpose to open the portals of society for the lady of the Secretary of War, Branch making a particular display of his audacity. When Jackson withdrew from the church of the Reverend J. N. Campbell, an accuser of Mrs. Eaton, the Secretary of the Navy invited the clergyman to one of his dinners.[3] Whereupon the President discontinued Cabinet meetings, assuming without complaint the added burden of work this threw on his shoulders. Andrew Jackson bore a heavy personal responsibility for the unpleasant situation in which his Secretary of War found himself. Weak in body but strong in loyalty, he did not shirk it. *"Eaton is the last man on earth I ought or would abandon. . . . I would sooner abandon life."*[4] The strain of this lashing defiance was great. The veteran's hair turned from gray to white. "[The Eaton trouble]," said Jack Donelson, "has done more to paralize his energies than 4 years of the regular and simple operations of the Gov^t."[5]

The President's private secretary, well-balanced in his outlook on most things, felt that General Jackson's course did more credit to his heart than to his head. Donelson saw nothing added to his revered uncle's renown by a struggle that drained the energy needed for important public affairs. This view took for granted that the President's championship of Mrs. Eaton represented a purely personal determination to force upon society one whom a considerable proportion of that body did not think eligible to its privileges. In the affair's early stages, this narrow conception was widely accepted. Any political significance that might attach to the slighting of Mrs. Eaton was hastily shovelled onto the doorstep of Henry Clay. As time went on, however, the Clay theory ceased to hold water. The nature of the alignment for and against the Secretary of War's consort was becoming too plain for disguise. Against her were the friends and political followers of John C. Calhoun; for her, the friends and followers of Martin Van Buren. At the beginning of the Administration, Calhoun had had by far the larger and more distinguished retinue of the two. In eight months Van Buren had made important gains, no considerable part of which was attributable to the dapper little man's politeness to the wife of the President's friend.

So through the thick haze of his partizanship Andrew Jackson came to see Van Buren as the gallant champion of an innocent and injured female; Calhoun as the confidant of her traducers. Thus, in the President's mind, the whole thing began to take on a new and larger growth, with the good name of Mrs. Eaton the ostensible stake in a game involving the prosperity of the Jackson Administration. Loyalty to Eaton and nothing more, probably would have induced Old Hickory to persist in this fierce strife, especially when one considers the secret which even Donelson (judging by his actions) appears not to have known: the fact that Jackson had prodded Eaton into a marriage he would have gladly postponed. But, all this aside, by autumn of 1829 the President had begun to feel that, in his fight for Margaret Eaton, he was defending a position upon which the ultimate prestige of his presidency might well depend.[6]

The events of the forthcoming social season were to throw this aspect of the situation into sharper relief.

Cabinet dinners formed the axis about which a Washington "season" revolved. The procedure was for the President first to entertain his official family, after which the Cabinet members, beginning with the Secretary of State, dined their colleagues in turn. Early in November, 1829, the President and Mr. Van Buren were taking a horseback ride—by this time an almost daily occurrence—when Jackson mentioned that thus far he had postponed his dinner to the Cabinet because of the situation prevailing. He doubted, however, whether he should delay much longer and thought "the sooner it was entered upon the better." So the invitations went out.

Not even the wit and spirit of the Secretary of State could raise the dinner that followed above the level of "a formal and hollow ceremony." When Mrs. Donelson rose to lead the ladies from the table, the President and the other gentlemen also filed out. After a halting attempt at drawing-room conversation the guests departed, leaving Old Hickory mortified and resentful.

Mr. Van Buren's dinner came next. Mr. Branch, Mr. Berrien and Mr. Ingham accepted for themselves but not for their wives or daughters, Branch offering the gratituous excuse of "circumstances unnecessary to detail." Eaton and Barry, too, came without their wives. Mr. Van Buren, a notable judge of wine, later implied that the men made quite a night of it. No other Cabinet dinner was attempted, leaving society in a state of fluttering disorganization. When Mr. Van Buren distributed cards for a large but unofficial party, the *National Journal* proclaimed it an effort of the Secretary of State and his friend, the British Minister, to force into society an unwelcome figure. In a sprightlier contribution to the *belles-lettres* of the day, Mrs. Eaton became "Bellona, the Goddess of War," a name quickly taken up by the town. Nevertheless, Mr. Van Buren's affair was well-attended and it surpassed expectations when Bellona collided with the wife of a general while dancing, precipitating a scene which sent one nervous guest in quest of his host to act as peacemaker.

The Russian Minister, Baron Krudener, was also a friend of Mr. Van Buren's and, like his British colleague, unmarried. He good-naturedly gave a ball at which he took Mrs. Eaton to supper, assigning the Secretary of War to Madame Huygens, the wife of the Minister from Holland. The Dutch diplomat's spouse failed to conceal her displeasure at the arrangement. A published report, doubtless exaggerated, said she left the table. In any event the story was soon abroad that Madame Huygens, Mrs. Ingham, Mrs. Branch and the daughters of Attorney General Berrien would give a series of dinners at which the danger of such contretemps would be obviated by the expedient of not inviting the Eatons.[7]

The Cabinet ladies gave their dinners. Eaton's friends retaliated with parties of their own, which the energies of Mr. Van Buren and of the bachelor diplomats rendered smarter in appearance than otherwise would have been the case. The political complexion of this division became more discernible every day. "Calhoun leads the moral party," noted an exceptionally detached spectator, John Quincy Adams of Massachusetts, "Van Buren that of the frail sisterhood."[8] Hostilities spread beyond the glass walls of the drawing rooms. "Branch and Eaton don't speak," recounted

John Campbell of the Treasury. "How Old Hickory (who always becomes greater by difficulties) is to get out of the Scrape I cannot say." A Cabinet rupture was openly spoken of. In that case who should go? "The President . . . BELIEVES Eaton & his wife are innocent & would no longer be Andrew Jackson if any earthly consideration of popularity could induce him to give way and surrender them up." On the other hand "Branch & Ingham have many friends & to dismiss them . . . would shake the *old fellows* popularity confoundedly. So it is an *uggly affair* . . . [upon which] hangs a great deal more than you would suppose." Yet the blind faith of followers in his prowess remained, as ever, one of the General's greatest sources of strength. "Old Jackson," concluded Campbell, "will get thro' somehow."[9]

One morning before breakfast, Mr. Van Buren received a summons to come at once to the White House. Old Hickory's eyes were bloodshot, his face drawn from lack of sleep, his manner ominously calm. He had, he said, decided upon a course of action. If the reputed pact between Madame Huygens and the Cabinet ladies were true, he said he would dismiss Ingham, Berrien and Branch and hand Chevalier Huygens his passports. Jackson had sent for the Cabinet officers. Would Mr. Van Buren interview Madame Huygens?[10]

Though other items of our foreign policy were in delicate balance at the moment, the Secretary of State departed on his errand.

3

With the three distinguished gentlemen seated before him General Jackson held on his knee a single sheet of paper and began to read:

"I do not claim the right to interfere in the domestic relations or personal intercourse of any member of my Cabinet. . . . But from information and from my own observation I am fully impressed with the belief that you and your families have, in addition to the exercise of your and their undoubted rights, taken

No.

The PRESIDENT,

Requests the honor of

Mr. Kendall's

Company at dinner

Monday the 18th inst at 4 o'clock

The favor of an Answer is desired

SOUVENIR OF AN UNPLEASANT EVENING FOR MRS. EATON

Amos Kendall's card of invitation to the President's dinner to the Cabinet, at which the wife of the Secretary of War was snubbed by the ladies of the President's household. From the original, owned by Mrs. Arthur Chester of Rye, New York, a great-granddaughter of Mr. Kendall.

measures to induce others to avoid mrs Eaton and thereby to exclude her from society and degrade him. . . . If her character is
such as to justify measures on the part of my cabinet, . . . it is I
who am responsible for this alleged indignity to public morales.
. . . I will not part with major Eaton and those of my cabinet who
cannot harmonize with him had better withdraw, for harmony I
must and will have."

Old Hickory removed his spectacles. What had the gentlemen
to say?

The gentlemen had considerable to say. They were the last
persons in the world to do an injustice to Major Eaton or his
family. Their wives' parties had had no such purpose in view.
Naturally, they could not undertake to regulate each small detail
of the social activities of their families, but— To these magnificent liars General Jackson responded with sentiments that did
him credit. He was bound to accept, he said, the word of his
Cabinet officers. But let them mark this, and mark it well: "An
indignity to Major Eaton is an indignity to me." Let the gentlemen reflect. If they were not prepared to work in harmony with
Eaton they should resign.[11]

The renewed invitation was not accepted and presently Martin
Van Buren returned with Madame Huygens's assurance that
she had been outrageously misquoted.

"The petticoat war has ended, no lives lost," chronicled Jack
Donelson. "The General in the goodness of his heart thinks
M^rs. E has attained a triumph."[12] And so thought a dazzled
citizen of Ohio, attending his first White House levee, when he
beheld Margaret sweep in, gloriously gowned in calico as an
encouragement to American manufactures. "The Secretary's
lady, whose form is symmetry itself, needed no ruffle or single
ornament on her person. No sooner had she taken her place near
the President's family than all the beauty and fashion in the room
gathered around to do her honor."[13] Our western visitor barely
mentioned that Emily Donelson and Miss Mary Eastin also wore
calico. Had his preoccupation with the wife of the Secretary of
War been less intent, he might have observed in the averted coun-

tenances of those ladies something to cause him to question the permanence of Bellona's ascendency.

4

Its interest whetted by fragmentary reports and alarms, the country fell hungrily upon the speeches which, after painstaking rectifications of phrase, Webster and Hayne at length gave to an impatient press.[14] By the tens of thousands the copies were snatched up; nullification was the topic of the hour at every cross-roads. After the speeches had been read the question was, "Does Jackson stand with Webster or with Hayne?" A word, a nod from him would decide the course of a host of people. Mayhap it would decide the issue.

Report had it that after Hayne had made his first speech the President sent him a note of congratulation.[15] This, however, was before the South Carolinian had been led into an open advocacy of the right of a state to sit in judgment upon an act of Congress. Certainly, since Webster's famous Second Reply, Old Hickory had kept his counsel, and neither principal to the great debate knew to what extent he had succeeded or failed to influence the views of an Executive who gave annoying evidence of a disposition to direct, rather than to obey, the masses that had elevated him to the chief magistracy. Webster, of course, had little chance to feel out the sentiment pervading the White House, which he visited only on formal occasions. On the other hand Hayne was a frequent social caller, familiar with the intimate atmosphere of the pipe-scented study on the second floor. In fact the President was contemplating the offer of a choice appointment to the Senator's brother who had fought at New Orleans. Mrs. Donelson and Miss Eastin were planning a trip to New York in company with the Senator's family.[16] More than this, Benton, Felix Grundy and other Administration senators, not of the distinctly southern branch of the party, felt that for the benefit of his pro-tariff constituents Mr. Webster had over-stressed the perils of the situation. On the floor Benton came to Hayne's defense, accusing the New Englander of going too far in his characterization of the South Carolina movement as a step toward disunion and civil war.[17]

Nevertheless, the continued silence of the President filled the Calhoun camp with vague misgivings. Writing under the eye of the Vice President, Duff Green began an increasingly warm series of editorial attacks on Webster's speech. "The doctrine contended for by General HAYNE is too well understood and too firmly established . . . to be shaken."[18] Webster had joined Clay "in an unholy crusade against the administration."[19] A praiseful column on Benton's rejoinder was made occasion for contrasting New England's attitude during the War of 1812 with that of the West in which Jackson's exploits were given significant attention.[20] As the *Telegraph* was supposed to reflect the views of the White House, Mr. Webster was moved publicly to dispute Green's interpretation of a passage from his speech.[21] Whereupon Green dug up and reprinted a scurrilous campaign attack upon Jackson, which he said had appeared in a New England newspaper with "Mr. WEBSTER'S public sanction."[22]

After a month of this, and no sign from the White House, a subtler plan was formed to draw Old Hickory closer to the side of the South Carolina group. A grand subscription dinner in ostensible tribute to the memory of Thomas Jefferson was announced for April 13, 1830, the anniversary of his birth. The affair was to be at once distinguished and democratic. A subscription list left on the bar of Brown's Indian Queen Hotel enabled the humblest disciple of the great promulgator of liberal political thought, now four years under Monticello's sod, to sign his name, pay his fee and get a ticket entitling him to sit and to sup with the famous. Less openly was the evening's program of speeches and toasts contrived, beginning on a broad note of appreciation of the Jeffersonian ideals, then narrowing to the Virginia Resolutions of 1798 adopted in opposition to the Alien and Sedition Laws, and then, as an analogous case, moving on to implied approval of South Carolina's resistance of the tariff. The President accepted an invitation to attend. This meant that, the prearranged speaking over, Andrew Jackson would offer the first volunteer toast of the evening.

As the date drew near, Old Hickory began to give thought to what he should say on that occasion. From the moment Webster had revealed the extent to which the nullification doctrine possessed the minds of the South Carolinians, Jackson had leaned toward the views of the Northerner, though this secret was so closely guarded that apparently only Lewis, Donelson and Van Buren knew it. Studiously these three observed the preparations for the banquet and reported to their chief. Van Buren's confidential man, C. C. Cambreleng of New York, and Benton and H. L. White, were on committees in charge of the dinner. The result was information leading Jackson to the conclusion that, if carried off as its promoters hoped, the affair "might menace the stability of the Union."[23] His direct mind swept aside the fulminations of Duff Green, the fine-spun arguments of Hayne, the criticisms of Benton. He saw, as Webster had seen, one central fact: the Union endangered. Jackson's political creed and social culture had been molded by the South. But his ideas of state sovereignty stopped short of any intention of allowing South Carolina to say what Federal statutes it would obey. Any tariff that was the law of the land Andrew Jackson would enforce. This line of reasoning placed him squarely beside Webster.

Taking up a pen Old Hickory fell to drafting a toast. Several sheets of paper went into the fire before a sentiment evolved that he regarded sufficiently compact and expressive. On the evening of the dinner he set out with Van Buren, as animated, the Secretary later said, as if he were preparing to defend the Union on a field of battle.[24]

At the Indian Queen they encountered a scene of excitement and suspense. A printed list of the regular toasts lay beside each plate. Members of the Pennsylvania delegation had read them and marched from the room. A few others also left. The banquet under way, Hayne started the oratory with a flowery address. Then came the regular toasts, twenty-four in number, building, bit by bit, support for the South Carolina point of view. Jackson sat impassive. The volunteer toasts were next in order. Toastmaster Roane introduced the President of the United States. Old Hickory stood, waiting for the cheers to subside. So many diners were on their feet that the diminutive Van Buren, whose place was at the foot of the second table, climbed on his chair in order to see the President.

Old Hickory fixed his glance upon John C. Calhoun.

"Our Union: It must be preserved."

Utter silence. "A proclamation of martial law in South Carolina," remarked Isaac Hill, "and an order to arrest Calhoun where he sat could not have come with more blinding, staggering force." The white-haired soldier raised his glass, a signal that the toast was to be drunk standing. Calhoun rose with the rest, his hand trembling so that a little of the yellow wine trickled down the side of the tumbler.[25] A moment more the chieftain stood there, as much the master as on the day he faced down a mutinous army at Fort Strother. Then, crossing to the far side of the room, he spoke to Benton. By this time the Senator from Missouri had altered his ideas concerning the impropriety of Webster's "Liberty *and* Union, now and forever," destined, with Jackson's strikingly similar phrase, to become a rallying cry in the long fight begun that night to strangle secession.

Hayne rushed up. Would the President consent to the insertion of one word in his toast before the text was given to the newspapers? What was the word? asked Jackson. It was "Federal," making the toast read, "Our Federal Union—" Mistakenly the Southerner imagined this might give the sentiment a state rights flavor, diluting a little the pungency of the rebuke. Jackson agreed and, like many another historic epigram, the toast went forth amended to the world. Curiously Hayne's suggestion gave the President's utterance the exact form he had intended it should have. In speaking he had left the written slip in his pocket, and so omitted one word unintentionally.[26]

When the gentlemen had resumed their places and the buzz of conversation ceased, the chairman called upon Mr. Calhoun for the second volunteer toast. The Vice-President arose slowly.

"The Union," he said, "next to our liberty, most dear."

After a moment's hesitation, and in a way that left hearers in doubt as to whether he was continuing the toast or beginning a speech, he added: "May we all remember that it can only be preserved by respecting the rights of the States and by distributing equally the benefits and burdens of the Union."[27]

Never to learn the art of brevity, the Vice-President had left the honors with Jackson. A little later when the President withdrew, two-thirds of the company followed within five minutes, leaving not more than thirty diners to bring Mr. Calhoun's banquet to a formal close.

Though Duff Green's eleven-column report covered the President's participation with only two lines of type,[28] the cat was out of the bag. A wave of nationalistic ardor swept the country, heartening the small Union Party in South Carolina which opposed the extremists' program.

The "reign" of Andrew Jackson had begun.[29]

5

John C. Calhoun sagged under the strain. Once more Martin Van Buren had scored over his rival in the contest to ride Old Hickory's popularity into the presidency. A visitor to the Senate gallery found the South Carolinian "more wrinkled and careworn than I had expected from his reputed age." The Vice-President was forty-eight. "His voice is shrill and to my ear disagreeable. . . . His manners have in them an uneasiness, a hurried, incoherent air."[30] Mr. Calhoun was, in truth, uneasy. "The times are perilous beyond any that I have ever witnessed," he wrote following the banquet at Brown's Indian Queen.[31] The day after this sentiment was committed to the mails the Vice-President opened a communication which did nothing to allay his apprehensions.

"Sir . . . The Enclosed copy of a letter from William H. Crawford, Esq. . . . was placed in my hands on yesterday. . . . The statements and facts it presents being so different from what I had heretofore understood to be correct requires that it should be brought to your consideration. . . . My object in making this communication is to announce to you the great surprise which is felt, and to learn whether it is possible that the information given is correct. . . .

"I am, sir, very respectfully

"Your humble servant

"ANDREW JACKSON."[32]

The Florida campaign secrets again. Twice had Calhoun repelled the charge that he had stood for sacrificing Jackson on the altar of international comity when the conquest, undertaken with James Monroe's unwritten assent, brought a growl from the British lion. Could he do so again? The intervention of William H. Crawford, a party to the Cabinet meetings in question, was a new and difficult obstacle.

The Vice President acknowledged at once the receipt of his superior's letter, saying he would reply at length as soon as he had the leisure. Though usually impatient of delays, Jackson did not complain. "Time to explain . . . is due him. . . . *He shall have it,* but I am afraid he is in a dilemma."[33] In this state of mind, Jackson could afford to wait—1832 being a long way off as yet.

More than the Florida business stood against Calhoun on the black books this time. Clearly the part of the Vice President's followers in the Eaton affair encompassed something that struck deeper than a fastidious objection to a female of spicy background. Jackson's inclination to regard it as an effort to render his Administration ridiculous agreed with recent reports showing Ingham's hand at work to promote Calhoun's interests in Pennsylvania at Jackson's expense.[34] Added to this was the Webster-Hayne debate and the nullification banquet. Nor should one forget that nearly three months before throwing his oral hand grenade into the Vice President's dinner party, Old Hickory had privately placed with John Overton the codicil of political disinheritance. Now he sought only an excuse for a definite break, which an opportune and deliberate revival of the Florida issue seemed about to provide.

This was the clever work of Lewis, taking up where Sam Houston had left off two years before. In November, 1829, when feeling between the Eaton and the Calhoun cliques was acute, Jackson had entertained ex-President Monroe. After the company, with the exception of Eaton and Lewis, had retired, Jackson was having a meditative smoke while the others talked. A remark about the Florida campaign brought the General from his reverie. He asked Lewis to repeat it. Lewis said a guest had claimed that Mr. Monroe's entire Cabinet had opposed Jackson's course. The President said the man must be mistaken. Lewis said he was not sure of that.

"Why are you not?" demanded Jackson.

"Because I have seen a letter in which Mr. Crawford is represented as saying that it was not he but Mr. Calhoun who was in favor of your being arrested." Thus Lewis described the letter James Alexander Hamilton had obtained from Governor Forsyth of Georgia in 1828, which Lewis at that time had deemed too weak to show to Jackson.

"You saw such a letter as *that?*"

"Yes," repeated Lewis, adding that the letter was now in New York.

"I want to see it, and you must go to New York tomorrow."

Lewis returned with the story that Hamilton objected to turning over the letter without the consent of Forsyth, who was on his way to Washington to take a seat in the Senate. Forsyth also balked, saying he would have to consult Crawford[35]—as well he might, considering the supposed inviolability of Cabinet secrets. Not until after the nullification dinner did Forsyth write the former Secretary of Treasury, now partly recovered in health and charitably provided with a judgeship in Georgia. Back came a vindictive and astonishing epistle in which Crawford sought to cover up his former notorious hatred of Jackson and to throw the blame on Calhoun.[36] "A poor tale this," reported wise old John Overton to whom the President had passed the letter for comment, "scarcely fit to deceive a sensible school boy." He placed Crawford beneath the level of Calhoun who, though evading responsibility for an act, had not sought to fasten it on another. Yet Overton said he believed the part about Calhoun's participation in the criticism of Jackson.[37]

Such was the letter the President had sent to Mr. Calhoun. Overton thought his friend had blundered.

If so, Calhoun blundered more seriously. Pascal once apologized for the length of a letter, saying he had no time to write a short one. The Vice President took two weeks to cover fifty-two pages with his nervous scrawl. To an impartial judge he refuted Crawford's thin claim to Jackson's regard, and showed the whole to be a political intrigue.[38] What he did not show was the grace to admit his original position in 1818. Nor was any explanation offered as to why he had allowed Jackson to be deceived in that particular for all these years.

Eagerly Old Hickory made the most of this weakness. "In all your [previous] letters to me [you have] professed to approve. . . *entirely* my conduct in relation to the Seminole campaign. . . . Your letter now before me is the first intimation that *you* ever entertained any other opinion. . . . Understanding you now, no further communication with you on this subject is necessary."[39]

John C. Calhoun pondered the melancholy fact that when two ride the same horse one must ride behind.

6

Small was the personal satisfaction these events afforded the President. "My hope of hapiness had fled. . . . The only consolation this side of the grave is when I look forward to the time when I can again retire to the Hermitage, . . . there to spend my latter days beside the tomb of the only solace of my life, . . . and lay my bones beside her." Being President was only "dignified slavery,"[40] and times came when all the sense of duty that Jackson possessed was required to stimulate more than a serf's interest in his tasks.

During fifteen months of ceaseless toil, made the more burdensome by grief, by illness, and by disappointment in men he had given the hand of friendship, the hope of seeing the Hermitage once more remained before him like a mirage of cool springs beckoning a desert wanderer. From the brief reports of Graves Steele, the overseer, and of neighbors, he sought to give reality to the image of this nirvana. How fared the flowering shrubs and the willow slips by Rachel's grave? How fared the negroes, the stock of blooded horses, the work horses and mules, the work steers, the beef steers, the milch cows, the sheep? What of births and deaths—negro babies, colts, and calves? What the amount and the quality of cotton baled, of corn cribbed, of fodder stacked, of oats, of rye? The quantity and quality of meat in the smoke house? How went the work of clearing the "new ground," sending the large timber to the sawmill, making charcoal of the rest? How the work at the brick kiln?[41]

In the answers to these questions, rather than in councils of state, the old planter sought his personal solution of the riddle of life. No public career for his adopted son, Andrew, junior, now in his twentieth year. Let him stick to the Hermitage and learn the run of its affairs. "I have just . . . recd a letter advising me of the death of my negroman Jim," he wrote the boy. "I pray you examine minutely into this matter and advise with Col Love. . . . My negroes shall be treated humanely. . . . Since I left home I have lost three of my family. Old Ned I expected to die, but I am fearful of the cause of the death of Jack and Jim. . . . Your Uncle John Donelson writes that *Steel has ruled with a rod of iron.* . . . Unless he changes his conduct dismiss him."[42] Fortunately for Steele, Uncle John was mistaken.

Some understanding of the instincts of a horseman is necessary to comprehend the fact that General Jackson should have chosen this preoccupied time to re-establish his racing stable, with the hope of producing a champion from the Truxton strain. His principal partner was the Reverend Hardy M. Cryer of Gallatin, whose interests were evenly balanced between the Methodist pulpit and the turf. As Jackson's agent Cryer sold, on credit, the gray colt Tariff to two aspiring Kentucky sportsmen named Moore and Shaw. After winning several races, they staked their accumulated capital on a single contest. Parson Cryer admitted that it looked like a good stroke of business, Colonel George Elliott, one of Nashville's shrewdest connoisseurs of fast horseflesh, laying bets at two to one on the gray. Just before the race there was a rain and a freeze. Tariff lost, and a permanent injury to his wind was feared.

The plight of the young Kentuckians also excited Cryer's com-

ANDREW JACKSON, JUNIOR

Nephew of Rachel Jackson, born December 22, 1809, and four days later legally adopted by General and Mrs. Jackson. From a portrait by Earl, owned by the Ladies' Hermitage Association, Nashville.

passion. Although Moore was "a strong Clay and Adams *Politician*," the sportsmanlike preacher consented to take Tariff off their hands and asked Jackson to approve the arrangement. He did so, requesting that the horse be rechristened Bolivar and turned over to Colonel Elliott. If fit for the track, Elliott was to enter him in the spring meets "for the benefit of my son." If windbroken, Bolivar was to be put to thoroughbred mares and several colts acquired. The tired pulse of the one-time proprietor of the Clover Bottom race course revived a little at the thought of the Hermitage colors carried to victory by a horse of the Truxton blood.[43]

Another restorative was the companionship of young folk, a hundred of whom the General could call by name. "Present me to Betsey and the children, to my good old friend Mrs Hays, [to] Narcissa, to Saml J. Hays and his sweet little wife and kiss my namesake, and [convey my remembrances] to the Doctor and Patsy and son, to Stockley and Lydia Jane and little Hickory and believe me your friend. . . ."[44] When correspondents neglected to include word of their broods Jackson would remind them of it. Childish shouts rang through the White House halls; little feet clattered on the stairs. The President did not complain. A conference was delayed when Mr. Van Buren entered the Executive study to find Emily Donelson's baby, Mary Rachel, asleep in the General's arms. The Secretary of State's prerogative of riding horseback with the President was usurped by ten-year-olds. "They are the only friends I have who never pester me with their advice."[45]

Andrew, junior, arrived for a visit bringing his cousins, Andrew Jackson Hutchings and Samuel Jackson Hays. Daniel Donelson, a brother of the President's secretary, came a little later. Young Hutchings had been expelled from another college. The President placed him in a Catholic institution at Georgetown, hoping the strict discipline would be a good thing. Young Hays ran up a haberdasher's bill of two hundred and eighty-three dollars, which the President paid. Andrew, junior, was recovering from the effects of unrequited love. The General had watched the progress of this romance. "You are very young, but having placed your affections upon Miss Flora I have no desire to interfere. . . . Early attachments are the most durable, and having been raised together in the same neighborhood I have only to recommend to you to say to her at once the object of your visit and receive her answer. . . . Should Miss Flora not favour your wishes, then my son I have one request to make of you. That is that you will give up all idea of Marriage for the present."[46]

Flora did not favor his wishes.

"I expected the result you name. . . . Flora is a fine little girl, . . . but as I told you she has give[n] herself up to coquetry. . . . I assure you I am happy at the result, as I seldom saw a coquett make a good wife, and I wish you to marry a lady who will make you a good wife and I a good daughter, as my happiness depends much upon the prudence of your choice. . . . I have councilled you through life to make no promises, or engagements, but what you punctually perform. . . . You are now free from all engagements and I trust you will keep so untill you advise with your father on this interesting subject."[47]

The four Tennessee blades, newly garnished by a Pennsylvania Avenue tailor, found the White House gay with girls—Cora Livingston, Margaret and Rebecca Branch, Rebecca McLane, and a Mary Smith of Abingdon, Virginia—who flocked about Mary Eastin and flirted becomingly. Donelson and Hays were soon in their toils. Mary Smith was able to expel from Andy II's mind the poignant memories of Flora. The young man brightened. "His countenance," observed a lady of experience (Mrs. Anne Royall, Washington's only newspaperwoman), "is sweetness and innocence itself, his eyes as soft as the dew-drop."[48] Pursuing Mary Smith to Virginia the innocent swain lost sight not only of his father's advice, but also of an important item in the etiquette of courtship. Reminding the President's son of this omission, the self-possessed young lady sent him jogging back to Washington.

General Jackson was deeply embarrassed. "Maj. Francis Smith,

ANDREW JACKSON HUTCHINGS

Great-nephew of Rachel Jackson and ward of General Jackson, reared at the Hermitage. From a portrait by Earl, owned by Edward Asbury O'Neal III, of Florence, Alabama.

Dear Sir, This will be handed to you by my son. . . . He has erred in attempting to address your daughter without first making known to you and your lady his honorable intentions and obtaining your approbation. Admonished of this impropriety, he now awaits upon you to confess it. I find his affections are fixed upon her, and if they are reciprocated, with your approbation, he looks upon the step which would follow as the greatest assurance of his happiness. Mine, since the loss of my dear wife, has almost vanished except that which flows from his prosperity. He is the only hope for the continuation of my name; and has a fortune ample enough with prudence and economy. . . . With these prospects he presents himself again to your daughter." The suit was reinforced by the efforts of a friend of the President who wrote his brother in Abingdon. "Go with him to Smith's. He is after Mary & you must throw all facilities in his way." It was of no use. Having left Tennessee to forget one girl, Andy started back with the job to do over.[49] Mrs. Royall asked how he would like to be President. "Not at all, Madam," said Old Hickory's heir.[50]

The President missed this gullible though good-natured boy, for the agitating silhouette of Margaret Eaton again lay across the threshold of the Mansion. The Cabinet officers' glib pledges had amounted to nothing. In a black mood Old Hickory muttered renewed threats of dismissal and of public exposure of their infidelity to a promise. "The people shall judge."[51]

Choosing this auspicious moment to pour oil on the flames of her champion's ire, Mrs. Eaton declined, in writing, to dine at the Executive Residence. "It would only be another feast . . . [for a] part of your family . . . to make me the object of their censures and reproaches."[52]

General Jackson gave his niece and nephew the choice of receiving Mrs. Eaton or of banishment to Tennessee. Rather than "bow to her commands" they chose Tennessee. "[I shall part]," wrote Donelson, "[from one] to whom I have stood from my infancy in the relation of son to Father. . . . The wretched expedients . . . [of those who would] gratify the vain desire of being understood to possess the controul of his confidence . . . have served their turn."[53] With Mary Ann Lewis, daughter of Bellona's ally, "snugly recoiled in the White House,"—the irritated phrase is Donelson's—the Secretary of War and wife soared away to New York where Administration satraps burst their buttons to honor the lady whose ensign floated over Old Hickory's own tent.[54]

7

It would have been inconsistent with a record of forty years' indulgence toward members of the Donelson clan had General Jackson not abated a little his severity toward Emily and her husband. The concession took the unexpected form of an announcement that the President would accompany the trangressors to their seat of exile in Tennessee. A hundred ties and longings contributed to this decision, for which a petition of the Choctaw chiefs to meet the White Father in council furnished an official excuse. On June 17, 1830, they began the journey,[55] leaving Mary Ann Lewis mistress *ad interim* of the White House and her important-looking father in a situation that any man in the country might have envied. "I pray you," the President wrote en route, "to keep your eyes wide awake, and advise me of every occurrence"—with especial reference to John C. Calhoun, Duff Green, the Nullifiers and congressional partizans of the Bank of the United States. "Advise me whether Mary Ann got her pairsol we happened to bring on and sent back from Clarksburgh. Say to Mr. Van Buren I will be glad to hear from him often. . . . Affectionate regards to you and your amiable daughter and believe me yr. friend ANDREW JACKSON."[56]

This was, perhaps, the only time that a President of the United States has journeyed to an Indian council ground for the purpose of making a treaty. Although public attention was not directed to the exceptional nature of the General's hasty decision, circumstances justified his action. With his mind made up to oppose South Carolina in any effort to nullify Federal authority in the matter of the tariff, the President wished to get rid of another form of nullification which he had no intention of opposing. For forty years Indian treaties had been made only to be broken whenever frontiersmen should become sufficiently numerous or intrepid to do so. To this fast and loose policy of nullification of Federal instruments Andrew Jackson, in the successive rôles of border lawyer, land-speculator, frontier soldier and member of Congress, had frequently been a party.

His campaign of 1813 and '14 had broken forever the military power of the southern Indians. On the lands left to them after that disaster, the Cherokees and the Creeks in Georgia, the Choctaws and Chickasaws in Mississippi and Alabama, had kept their word to bury the tomahawk. They trod the white path, cultivating the civilized arts of peace in which the progress of the Cherokees was astonishing. Discarding tribal forms for those of a republic functioning under a written constitution modeled after our own, the Cherokees lived in houses, planted fields and orchards and established beef herds. They manufactured cloth, built roads, operated fair taverns and dependable ferries. A code of simple and apparently sensible laws was administered by native courts and peace officers. The duties of these functionaries were not burdensome, crimes of violence being rare in the Cherokee republic and disputes of the nature that usually clutter courts less numerous than among Caucasians.

This development, noteworthy in the whole history of primitive races, had begun to attract national notice and much encouragement in parts of the country sufficiently long-settled for the whites to cease to regard Indian problems from a frontier perspective. The other tribes were behind the Cherokees but making headway; and they gave their white neighbors no trouble.

The same cannot be said for the whites who, alarmed at the success of the Indians' cultural experiments, saw the red men on the road to permanent possession of their soil. To be sure, permanent possession had been guaranteed by the United States, in one case in a treaty to which Andrew Jackson, as commissioner, had affixed his signature;[57] but on a frontier the violation of an Indian treaty was regarded as a prerogative of the superior race. Georgia began a truculent course calculated to induce Cherokees and Creeks "voluntarily" to remove to wild lands in what is now Oklahoma. The dignified courtesy of the Indian refusal made strange reading beside the chaotic utterances of white statesmen ranting about "savages." Whereupon, shortly before General Jackson took office, Georgia tore up Federal treaties and annexed the territory of the Cherokee and Creek nations. Mississippi and Alabama did likewise in the cases of the Choctaws and Chicka- saws. In his message to Congress, Jackson upheld the states though he spoke solicitously of the welfare of the Indians which, he said, would be promoted by their "voluntary" removal to the western wilderness to live free of white interference. Similar promises the Indians had heard made and had seen broken since George Washington's day. The answer of the intelligent Chero- kees was to engage William Wirt of Baltimore, former Attor- ney General and an eminent constitutional lawyer, to take their case into court on the issue denying a state's right to annul a Federal contract. As no state possessed this right, the outcome of any such suit, once it should reach the Supreme Court, seemed a foregone conclusion.

General Jackson traveled westward to cut the ground from under the courts by persuading as many Indians as possible to agree to emigrate before any suit should come up for adjudication. Of the Choctaws and Chickasaws he had strong hope; and his emissaries were among the Creeks and Cherokees, reinforcing their arguments with those time-honored aids to Indian diplomacy, silver and whisky. Success would mean not only the accomplish- ment of a great stroke of western policy, but relief from the ticklish possibility of having to support nullification in three states while opposing it in another.[58]

The first reports General Jackson received at the Hermitage were dismaying. The Cherokees stood firm, and with them the Creeks. The behavior of the latter particularly incensed the old Indian fighter. "We have answered," he wrote Lewis, "that we leave them . . . to the protection of their friend Mr. Wirt. . . . The course of *Wirt* had been truly wicked. It will lead to the destruc- tion of the Indians. I have used all the persuasive means in my power, . . . and now leave the poor deluded Creeks and Cherokees to their . . . wicked advisers." Jackson expressed the more en- lightened frontier point of view in that his remarks included some concern for the fate of the Indians. His characterization of Wirt was more normally western, this lawyer's villainy arising merely from an assurance to the Indians that, in his opinion, the United States must protect their treaty rights or flout the authority of its own Supreme Court—a dilemma which General Jackson wished to avoid. "I am sure," continued Jackson, "the stand taken by the Executive was not anticipated. . . . It was expected that the more the Indians would hold out, . . . the greater would be the offers [of indemnity]. . . . The offer sent has blasted these hopes and if I mistake not the Indians will now think for themselves and send to the City [of Washington] a delegation prepared to cede their country and move X the M [across the Mississippi.]"[59]

Even the Choctaws, who had invited the President to their council, delayed assembling, and when he reached the meeting place only the Chickasaws had appeared. The President moved among chiefs and sub-chiefs, mingoes and headmen, greeting each one with grave respect. Old Indians were there who had long known General Jackson, and called him Sharp Knife. Indians were there who had fought at New Orleans. After the ceremonial pipe was passed, Sharp Knife addressed them, an interpreter translating.

"Friends and Brothers: . . You have long dwelt on the soil you occupy, and in early times before the white man kindled his fires too near to yours . . . you were a happy people. Now your white brothers are around you. . . . Your great father . . . asks if you are prepared and ready to submit to the laws of Mississippi, and make a surrender of your ancient laws. . . .

"Brothers, listen— To these laws, where you are, you must submit—there is no alternative. Your great father cannot, nor can Congress, prevent it. . . . Old men! Lead your children to a land of promise and of peace before the Great Spirit shall call you to die. Young chiefs! Preserve your people and nation. . . .

"Brothers, listen— Reject the opportunity which is now offered to obtain comfortable homes, and it may not [come] again. . . . If you are disposed to remove, say so, and state the terms you may consider just."[60]

The Indian dignitaries retired for consultation. General Jackson stepped into his carriage and drove away, leaving John Henry Eaton and General John Coffee to complete the negotiation. At the Hermitage he received word of the Chickasaws' capitulation. They would cross the Mississippi in 1832. Meantime the Choctaws had agreed to treat. Directing Eaton and Coffee to meet them, the President set out for Washington the first week in September.

8

Andrew Jackson Donelson accompanied his uncle, a circumstance representing the fruit of negotiations almost as complicated as those surrounding our Indian relations.

General Jackson had found his numerous family connections, and for that matter a large part of Tennessee, divided over the propriety of his defense of Mrs. Eaton. Bellona was an issue of the congressional campaign in the blue-blooded Gallatin district northeast of Nashville. Congressman Robert Desha, declining to run again, took the stump for ex-Governor William Hall and denounced the Secretary's lady as an "abandoned" woman. A supporter of Hall's opponent, running on a pro-Margaret platform, invited Desha to a fist fight. Desha won the fight and Hall the election.[61] This was somewhat offset by a gala dinner at the Hermitage for the Secretary and Mrs. Eaton. The combined pressure of the President, and of John Coffee, next in rank among the Donelson kith, brought a respectable family representation to the table.[62]

The banishment of Jack and Emily Donelson had failed, however, to strengthen Eaton's position in Tennessee, and Old Hickory sought a compromise. Consulting with Coffee and John Overton, he asked Donelson to return to Washington, leaving Emily in Tennessee, with the understanding that Eaton also should leave his wife behind. To this arrangement both the Donelsons and the Eatons consented. Margaret's consent, to be sure, was not heartily given. What woman could easily yield up the dream of a winter in Washington with the boon of White House favors hers to dispense? But Jackson was in earnest and went ahead with his plan to keep bachelor's hall. "A. J. Donelson, my son and Mr. Earle [the artist] will constitute my family." This word to Lewis tactfully foretold the end of Mary Ann's brief regency.[63]

The four men were hardly settled in the Mansion when General Jackson heard of the success of the Choctaw negotiation. Together with the Chickasaw treaty this provided for the cession of sixteen million acres in Mississippi, doubling the tillable area of that state, and of a million acres in Alabama. On the heels of this came an Executive proclamation of equal interest to the maritime and commercial people of the Atlantic littoral: a decree opening the British West Indian ports to American trade. Since our independence this rich market had been virtually closed. With the effective support of the President, Martin Van Buren had broken the deadlock in nineteen months. This conspicuous stroke in the field of foreign policy increased, in one year, the value of our commerce with those islands from one hundred and one thousand to more than two and a quarter million dollars annually.[64]

With these laurels to his credit, General Jackson turned to the knotty questions surrounding the Bank of the United States— a disturbing decision for those Administration statesmen who preferred to let sleeping dogs lie.

CHAPTER XI

A GREEK TEMPLE IN CHESTNUT STREET

I

A TALL and still room in a replica of a Greek temple facing Chestnut Street, Philadelphia, sheltered another man who pondered the affairs of the Bank of the United States—tireless, elegant Nicholas Biddle, his imaginative mind emboldened by success. After eight years as the presiding officer of that institution, Nicholas Biddle could contemplate a record of singular achievement. Through its twenty-seven branches and agencies, the Bank of the United States ruled the commerce, the industry, the husbandry of a nation; and Biddle ruled the bank. His control of the circulating medium was nearly absolute. By expanding or contracting credits he could make money plentiful or scarce, business brisk or dull in any locality in the land saving, to a certain extent, New England whose independent banks were strong and well-managed. Nothing short of a declaration of war could effect the everyday concerns of Americans as profoundly as this man, who looked more like a poet than a financier, could affect them by a stroke of the pen—with which he had, indeed, struck off some passable pentameters.

Though the son of a Philadelphia banker, Biddle had broken his own path to power in the realm of money. Completing at thirteen the prescribed studies at the University of Pennsylvania, Nicholas was refused a diploma because of his youth. At fifteen he was valedictorian of the class of 1801 at the College of New Jersey at Princeton. At eighteen, as secretary to the American Minister to France, a family friend, he handled important financial details of the Louisiana Purchase. Wandering the face of Europe, he discoursed with savants on the distinctions between classical and modern Greek. Art, architecture, history and languages also engrossed the handsome boy. Home again, upon finishing a law course, he turned to the editorship of a literary magazine of such elevated taste that few could appreciate its virtues. A more substantial work was a history of the Lewis and Clark expedition, a more delightful one the *Ode to Bogle,* immortalizing a versatile Philadelphia negro who had attained distinction as a fancy cook and as an undertaker. Biddle dedicated the book "with a mint stick" to his little daughter.

From these occupations Secretary of War James Monroe, who had known him in London, drew the rich young man into his country's service during the dire and splendid hours that followed the sacking of Washington by Admiral Cockburn. The Treasury empty and the Government paralyzed, hope of national survival seemed to rest on the issue of a collision impending somewhere near New Orleans between the mightiest military expedition Europe had ever sent to the New World, and a picked-up army led by a gaunt Indian fighter who had hardly seen the face of a civilized foe. With inspired energy Biddle fell upon tangled Treasury records, obtaining loans to turn the wheels of government. Although his father, foreseeing the profits of his own bank trenched upon, opposed it, Biddle, junior, fought to re-establish the Bank of the United States as a means of lifting the country from financial chaos. The war over and the bank re-established, Biddle declined an invitation to become a director for the majority stockholders and prepared to return to the reposeful life of a literary dilletante. But when Mr. Monroe asked him to accept one of the five Government directorships he did so from a sense of duty.

Biddle became the best-informed man on the board. In 1823, at thirty-seven, he was elected president. A period of brilliant expansion followed, carrying the bank to the zenith of its power and usefulness.

The terms of this institution's charter favored a revival of the Hamiltonian ideal of concentrating control of the financial affairs of the people of the United States in the hands of a few men. The capital was thirty-five million dollars of which the Government subscribed seven million. Control resided in a board of twenty-five directors, five of whom were appointed by the President of the United States, the remainder by the outside stockholders. The bank was designated the depository for all Government funds, though the Secretary of the Treasury might deposit such funds elsewhere provided he informed Congress of the reason. On these deposits the bank paid no interest, but it was required to pay a bonus of a million and a half dollars, to transfer public money without charge, and to perform other services. The bank might issue currency, providing each note was signed by the president of the institution and redeemed in specie on demand. Such currency was receivable for Government dues, a privilege extended to the notes of only such state-chartered banks as redeemed in specie.

Biddle made the most of these monopolistic concessions. By refusing to recognize the notes of state institutions which did not redeem in specie, the great bank did much to end the fantastic era of American banking born of the post-war boom and subsequent depression. Government patronage kept the great bank's notes at par. The great bank made state banks toe the mark by calling on them, at the first sign of undue expansion, to redeem in coin. The result, in a few years, was the most satisfactory currency the country had yet known.

Broad as was its charter, Biddle enlarged the domination of his bank beyond anything intended by the compact. While the charter specified no limit to the currency of the bank, the provision that each note must be signed by the bank's president was calculated to keep down this circulation. Biddle got around the restriction by devising "branch drafts." In appearance these drafts looked so much like notes of the present bank in Philadelphia that Mr. Biddle said not one person in a thousand knew the difference. Actually they were checks on the parent bank drawn by the cashiers of branches and endorsed "to bearer." The Government received branch drafts in payment for public obligations and they circulated as money. In theory the drafts were redeemable in specie, though in practice the bank made this difficult, thus stretching its charter again. Redemption at par was possible only at the branch of origin. The bank would place these drafts in circulation remote from their places of origin, western drafts being released in the East and *vice versa,* so that a holder wishing coin was put to the expense of transporting across the country both the actual notes and the specie received in return. As a result he usually cashed them locally, at a discount. Thus the great bank was able to expand its paper issues beyond anything permitted to a state bank.[1]

Among men of business these were usually accounted small defects, however, and the advantages derived from the bank's operations proclaimed to outweigh the drawbacks. Conservative and very able management tended to minimize fear of an inflation of its own issues, as the branch draft adventure easily made possible. The bank had rehabilitated the currency and reformed banking practices. Its system of swift and cheap exchanges moved crops and facilitated commerce. It simplified the operations of the Treasury. The bank's stock was a good investment for the public and for the Government. The bank avoided politics, setting another good example for state banks. During the presidential campaign of 1828, which saw many things lugged in that had no business there, the Bank of the United States was not mentioned.

2

Yet, it would seem, Nicholas Biddle had been quietly preparing for Jackson's election. In 1827 he had sent his confidential man, Thomas Cadwalader, to Nashville to supervise the establishment of a branch of the bank. This skillful agent went out of the way to make himself agreeable at the Hermitage. He appointed W. B. Lewis and George Washington Campbell as directors of the branch. The presidency was conferred on Josiah Nichol, the wealthy merchant whom General Jackson customarily left in charge of his financial affairs when absent from Tennessee. After Cadwalader's departure friendly letters from him reached the Hermitage, congratulating Jackson on the triumph of his party in a Philadelphia city election. The bank's agent solicited

Old Hickory's opinion of the officers of the Nashville tributary, intimating that changes were contemplated. Jackson sidestepped the diaphanous invitation. "Never having been connected with Banks, and having very little to do with this one here, I feel unable to give you any satisfaction."[2]

The deliberate immersion of the Nashville branch in influences friendly to the political aspirations of General Jackson represented a departure from Biddle's usual political code.[3] It wore the aspect of a conscious design to propitiate Old Hickory who, for some time past, had been falling away from his old position of cordiality, if not to the bank, at least to the friends of the bank. Mr. Biddle's task was rendered the more delicate by the fact that, taken as a whole, the General's attitude toward the Bank of the United States had followed a rather mixed pattern.

So early as 1815, or perhaps earlier, Jackson had bought a few shares of stock in the Nashville Bank, the pioneer institution of its kind in Tennessee. The ownership of these securities gave Jackson "banking connections," but only in the sense that every wealthy man had such connections. In 1817 Jackson had opposed, though not conspicuously, the admission of branches of the Bank of the United States to Tennessee, approving of a state law which imposed a prohibitive tax of fifty thousand dollars a year on such subsidiaries. In this he showed independence, as most of the wealthy class were in favor of a branch at Nashville.[4] In 1821, however, while Governor of Florida, he had forwarded a petition for a branch at Pensacola—not because, as he was later to explain, he then favored the bank, but because the commercial sentiment of the town favored it.[5] Considering the extent to which personal opinions flavored Jackson's official acts in Florida, the suspicion arises that, had the General's antipathy to the bank been very strong at the time, he would have mentioned it when he dispatched the petition.

Reviewing the situation after his retirement from the presidency, Jackson said his early opposition rested on "grounds of expediency as well as of constitutionality."[6] The constitutional objection is not hard to understand, for Jackson was bred in the Jeffersonian state-rights school. The objection as to the expediency of the bank, however, seems difficult to reconcile with the General's known views on banking matters at the time. From 1818 until about 1824, the bank issue had been bound up with the Relief Party strife throughout the West. Jackson also was bound up in that strife, inveighing against popular but economically unsound hard-times legislation, and against equally popular and equally unsound printing-press banks[7] whose efforts to relieve the depression in reality had prolonged it. This attitude definitely placed the General on the side of the Bank of the United States, which was the particular obsession of the masses.

Such was Jackson's position when his name went before the country in 1822. Almost immediately he had found support among the very people whose economic legislation and banking philosophy he opposed—a fact explicable only on the ground of Jackson's military popularity. By 1826 when his second campaign for the presidency was getting under way, the depression was wearing out, and the Relief politicians needed a new cause. In Kentucky and in Alabama, they went over to Jackson almost in a body, taking with them their hatred of the bank. That same year the friends of the bank in Tennessee, who had been Jackson's political consorts during the hard-times upheavals, had moved to repeal the prohibitory tax. But Jackson opposed this, and only over his protest was the tax repealed.[8]

This brought the diplomatic Cadwalader to town to superintend the opening of the Nashville branch. Although the Philadelphian was courteously received at the Hermitage, other pilgrims returning from the General's home during the winter of 1827-28 quoted Old Hickory as speaking out against the bank.[9] So it came about that he had returned to his position in 1817. Jackson's inconsistency amounted to this: in normal times he had decried the bank's monopoly of our financial concerns but, in the abnormal depression period, he had deemed it a lesser evil than proletarian finance.

3

After the election had passed off, however, friends of the bank among the General's intimates were able to assert themselves strongly enough to exclude from the inaugural address a contemplated criticism of the institution.[10]

But the subject refused to stay down. During Jackson's first summer in the White House, John Catron, a Nashville lawyer close to Jackson and anxious to rise in the political scale, published in the Nashville *Banner & Whig* a series of attacks on the bank in which he declared the question of recharter to be the most important public issue of the day. Addressing himself to "the cultivators of the soil and the laboring people in Tennessee," Catron suggested a democratic substitute for Mr. Biddle's monopoly: all directors to be appointed by the President and Congress; branches to be set up only on petition of state legislatures; branch directors to be appointed by the legislatures. Catron disclaimed acting on impulse. "Some of us, gentlemen, have for years been pledged to stand together boldly and firmly, when the day should arrive for the execution of a policy new in these States."[11]

The articles kindled a local debate, one anonymous dissenter from Mr. Catron's views asking the *Banner's* readers to "call to mind that General Jackson is very hostile to the Bank of the United States, and has expressed sentiments very similar to those" embodied in Catron's substitute plan.[12] This dissenter turned out to be better informed than most people suspected at the time.

In the autumn of 1829 the President reviewed with Felix Grundy, Amos Kendall and James Alexander Hamilton his objections to the bank, which he called unconstitutional[13] and "dangerous to liberty." The latter criticism, inspired by the great power of the privately-chosen majority of the directorate, dealt with what the bank might do rather than with what it had done. No charge was made that Mr. Biddle and colleagues had misused their authority, the President restricting himself to the contention that such imperial power in the hands of a few persons, not responsible to the electorate, was inadvisable.[14] After this review the President asked Grundy, Kendall and Hamilton to transmit their observations on his remarks for consideration in connection with the Executive's first message to Congress.

The memoranda tendered by the President's confidants reveal the unmistakable affinity between Jackson's notion of an alterna-

tive to the Bank of the United States and the crude skeleton of
Catron. Jackson wanted an institution in which the Federal and
state governments should own all the capital stock and appoint all
the officials. With a simple bank of deposit, or a bank of deposit
and exchange, this might conceivably work. At that point perplexities began to embarrass the President's friends. The limited
services such a bank could offer the commercial body of society
would by no means compensate for the advantages withdrawn
by the suppression of Mr. Biddle's helpful system. Yet to expand
a "people's institution" into a bank of issue and discount, empowered to loan out depositors' money and do a general commercial
banking business brought one face to face with complications
inseparable from public ownership. Would people entrust their
private funds to a bank run by office-holders in preference to one
run by financiers disciplined by the profit motive? If the public
would not entrust its funds to such a bank should the Government
do so? Destroy confidence in a bank and what is left of it? To
indicate potential, yea actual, evils of Mr. Biddle's bank was one
thing. To devise, even on paper, a better bank was something
else—particularly for four persons no better equipped by training
for the task than Old Hickory and his present coadjutors.[15]

Even the loosest thinker among them, Felix Grundy, drew
back. "A great difficulty [is] how are the Directors of Branches to
be appointed?" he said. "To authorize the Directors of the principal bank to appoint them would give them an alarming power.
To say that the Congress should do it would destroy anything
like accountability. . . . To say that the State Legislatures should
do it would be a very unstatesmanlike Idea."[16] Amos Kendall, an
old Relief Party man, had, from the security of his editorial chair
in Kentucky, slashed at the bank like Mamaluke cavalry. In the
privacy of the President's council chamber, he displayed greater
discretion. "I am not prepared to say that . . . [your plan] is
the best that can be devised. . . . I could wish that . . . [it] might
not *as yet* be thrown before the public."[17]

Last of the triumvirate to report was Hamilton, a successful
New York attorney whose career is a discouragement to enterprise in the field of political augury. On that July morning twenty-

five years before when they rowed Alexander Hamilton home from Weehawken, who would have been willing to foretell a day when the dying man's son should be leagued with Aaron Burr in politics? Yet, such was another manifestation of Martin Van Buren's conciliatory magic. Again, who would have had the temerity to predict such a son at work to overturn the monetary system which the first Secretary of the Treasury regarded as his most enduring monument?

Hamilton's effort to knit Jackson's views into a workable scheme showed a firmer grasp of the realities and more constructive thought than the attempts of Grundy and of Kendall. An appreciation of the difficulties of successfully supplanting individual initiative with Government regulation troubled the New Yorker. A Government-owned bank denied the privilege of making loans must inevitably prove unsatisfactory, he informed the President. But for such a bank to make loans would be to run "the risk of far greater evils."[18]

So much, briefly, for the travail of three staunch critics of the bank unexpectedly summoned to scrutinize both sides of the question.

4

Nicholas Biddle's first counter-move uncovered a friend at court in the person of Major Lewis. In response to a reference to the appointment of new directors at Nashville, Lewis, himself no longer a member of the subsidiary board, warmly commended the selections. "If your Directory is composed of men . . . in whom the people have *confidence,* it will have a tendency to prevent opposition."[19] Placation was too menial an artifice for the proud Biddle to sustain for long, however. When Secretary of the Treasury Ingham, Senator Woodbury of New Hampshire and Isaac Hill framed a provocative protest alleging discrimination by the Portsmouth branch against Jackson men the financier saw red. "[Are we] to suffer ourselves to be tramped down by the merest rabble?"[20] he snorted in private, while striking back at the complainants as he had been accustomed to strike in his early battles to create and to preserve the great prestige of his bank. The branch, said he, had enforced the rules of prudent banking upon borrowers without regard to person or political affiliation. The bank would continue to operate on those lines regarding it "better to encounter hostility than appease it by unworthy sacrifices of duty." This was followed by a communication in which Mr. Biddle's racing pen got away from him entirely. Distorting the remarks of the Secretary into an assertion of the Treasury's right to interfere with the election of bank officials and to plunge them in politics, the banker read Mr. Ingham a lecture on the evils involved.

Actually the shoe was on the other foot, Biddle having been the one to introduce questions of political expediency into the hallowed rite of selecting the bank's personnel. Mr. Ingham replied with dry assurance. "In the arena of party conflict which you almost tempt me to believe unavoidable, the hostility to the bank, as a political engine, would be preferable to its amity." Washington friends of the bank were alarmed and Biddle saw that he had gone too far. In a good-tempered rejoinder to the Secretary, the banker retraced his steps without ruffling a feather and began to lay himself out to captivate the Administration.[21] But for all that, a new and subtly disquieting atmosphere pervaded the classic corridors of the Greek temple in Chestnut Street. Nicholas Biddle felt insecure. His change of front was too abrupt, his technique a trifle obvious.

Postmaster General Barry received an extension of a long-due loan.[22] To Asbury Dickins, the chief clerk of the Treasury, whose confidential asides on Ingham's firm state of mind had had something to do with Mr. Biddle's altered attitude, the bank expressed its gratitude in even more substantial terms, permitting Dickins to settle a loan for fifty cents on the dollar.[23] The friendly correspondence with Lewis was resumed. The testimony of a Jackson partizan was adduced to contradict a story circulated by Amos Kendall that bank money had been used against Jackson in Kentucky. The cashier of the New Orleans branch journeyed to the White House to refute a like report from his jurisdiction, and the President professed himself satisfied.[24] A batch of Jackson politicians were named branch directors from one end of the country to the other[25] and, when Lewis signaled that the time was ripe,[26] Biddle displayed his ace.

This was a request for a recharter of the bank four years ahead of time, coupled with a proposal for achieving the darling ambition of Andrew Jackson to extinguish the national debt, the final payment to be made January 8, 1833, the anniversary of another feat of his. We owed forty-eight million five hundred and twenty-two thousand dollars. Biddle's brilliant scheme was sound, simple in its essentials, and advantageous to the Government—though, on a second reading, as one became more inured to the fascination of millions marching into the limbo, the advantages to the Treasury appeared to be rather less and those to the bank rather more than the face of the figures revealed. Still, it was a fair offer.[27]

Mr. Biddle, himself, called on the President. The meeting of these strong men was pleasant, the conversation apparently casual, though Biddle strove to store away in memory every word spoken. General Jackson said he was grateful for the plan for paying the debt, which he would unhesitatingly recommend to Congress except for the recharter feature. "I think it right to be frank with you. I do not think that the power of Congress extends to charter a Bank out of the ten-mile square." The President went on to express appreciation of previous services of the bank in the liquidation of the debt, and said he would refer to them in his message. Ingham's name came into the interview. "He and you got into a difficulty thro' foolishness," the President observed good-naturedly. "Oh, that has all passed now," said the banker, and the awkward subject was dropped. Immensely pleased with the tenor of the interview the financier coupled to his adieux a happy little speech anticipating the pride with which he would read the promised allusion to the bank's help with the debt. "Sir," said Old Hickory, "it would only be an act of justice to mention it."[28]

5

But, despite Amos Kendall's tactful remonstrance the President persisted in the determination to illuminate his message with another mention of the bank as well.

Obstacles intruded at every step. Called upon for an opinion as to the constitutionality of the bank, Attorney General Berrien suggested that the question be deferred. "In the meantime I am bound to state respectfully to the President my opinion that it is not expedient . . . to make the proposed communication to Congress."[29] The Secretary of the Treasury, though still smarting from his brush with Biddle, dealt even less gently with his superior's proposal to present a tangible substitute for Biddle's bank. With deep concern Mr. Ingham cited "serious objections" to the idea. Before embarking on "a new and untried system," he suggested "mature reflection" as to whether the existing bank could not "be so modified as to evils it is liable to and secure the benefits desired." Nine days remained in which to complete the message. "I do apprehend Sir that we have not time to enter safely upon this complicated question."[30]

Jackson met his advisers half way. Following congratulatory remarks on its services in the matter of the debt, he declared that, in view of the doubtful constitutional status of the bank and in view of its failure "in the great end of establishing a sound and uniform currency," it might be wise to study the practicability of a substitute "founded upon the credit of the Government and its revenue."[31]

As soon as he could recover from his surprise, Biddle began to provide fodder for the efforts of editors and of the more articulate body of the public who disagreed with the President. Though impressive, the showing did not disturb Jackson. "I was aware the bank question would be disapproved by all the sordid and interested. . . . Although I disliked to act contrary to the opinion of so great a majority of my cabinet, I could not shrink from a duty so imperious. . . . I have brought it before the people, and I have confidence that they will do their duty."[32] Old Hickory's conception of the people's doing their duty was that they should sustain him in the issue he had raised in their behalf. This he did not doubt would be the case for Andrew Jackson understood the mind of the inarticulate mass well enough to know that he had spoken for a vast multitude seldom heard in the columns of the press or in the forums of statesmen. As one correspondent assured him:

"The open mouthed million already Scorn and revile the institution. . . . It is our business to wrench from its gripe . . . a monopoly of the circulating medium, . . . calculated to make the few richer, the many and the poor still poorer."[33]

Standing committees of the Senate and of the House took notice of the references in the message. Both reported in favor of the bank and recommended its recharter. Commenting on the President's charge that the bank had failed to establish a uniform currency, the House report, with some exaggeration, declared that it had *"furnished a circulating medium more uniform than specie."* The constitutional objection was dismissed with reference to Supreme Court decisions, and Jackson's idea of a bank founded on Government revenues condemned as a dangerous experiment in patronage.[34] Duff Green published the committees' findings without rising to the defense of the Executive's program.[35]

To dispute Jackson was seldom to convince him. A reading of the congressional reports merely entrenched him in the opinion that the bank was a "hydra of corruption, dangerous to our liberties everywhere."[36] Had the General known the secret history of those documents he might have employed less temperate language. Nicholas Biddle had supplied the House committee with much of the data upon which its conclusions were based; and he had written the Senate report nearly word for word.[37]

Fresh objections to the hydra occurred to the President. Was not Government patronage the mainspring of its great wealth and power? The average monthly balance of public funds in the bank's keeping was seven million dollars and it drew no interest. The profits from this and from all other operations of the bank enriched a comparatively small number of stockholders. Jackson thought the profits of such an institution should "onure to the whole people, instead of a *few monied capitalists* who are trading on our revenue."[38] But the problem of attaining this goal still defied solution. Lewis cheered Biddle with the assurance that in the end the President would be satisfied with a few modifications of the existing institution.[39] Since Biddle had Lewis's word for it, Jackson must have seriously considered this possibility. But it was not what he wanted. He wanted a new bank, owned by the

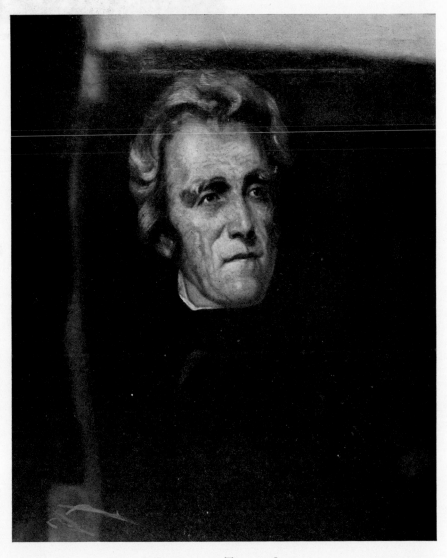

A PORTRAIT BY THOMAS SULLY

Owned by the United States, it hangs in the Capitol at Washington. Sully painted several portraits of Jackson, one of which is reproduced in the first volume of this biography with comment by the writer which a few artists have taken as a disparagement of Mr. Sully's talent. Aware that nothing I can say will, or should, diminish Sully's reputation as a painter, I remain of the opinion that his delicately relaxed lines do not shadow forth Andrew Jackson as he seems to me to be.

people and answerable to them. To serve the needs of trade, however, this must be a bank of discount as well as of deposit. Hamilton was sent back to his desk to devise a satisfactory pattern. At the end of five months he reported no success. A bank of discount in the exclusive hands of Government functionaries would fail of public confidence, said Hamilton. Depositors would be afraid of political loans. "The untiring watchfulness of individual interest is always a better manager of pecuniary concerns than Governments."[40]

While General Jackson was in Tennessee in the summer of 1830 his friend and counselor of forty years, John Overton, accepted a place on the board of the Nashville branch. Josiah Nichol, president of the branch and steward of the Hermitage finances, entertained Old Hickory at his home. Primed by Biddle, the host regaled his guest with the excellences of the bank, forthwith reporting to his chief: "I am well convinced that he will not interfere with Congress on the subject of renewing the Charter. Altho on this subject he keeps his opinion to himself he speaks of You in the most exalted terms and says No Gentleman would manage the Bank better."[41]

Encircled by pressure and persuasion Jackson did not give up. Guarding his tongue, he clung to the conviction that there must be a way of reshaping the financial structure so as to diminish the unwholesome power wielded over the masses by an isolated coterie of almost unreachable and almost unteachable men. In the familiar Cumberland Valley the impress of that power met the eye of the President. After years of close management of its money in the West, the bank had launched an era of free credit, the Nashville branch loaning out two million dollars. Family connections of Old Hickory were borrowing. This rush to mortgage the accumulations of thriftier seasons artificially accelerated business. "Those who borrow are encouraged in their extravagant modes of dressing and living which are greater than their means will justify," Alfred Balch, a prosperous planter of the Hermitage neighborhood, informed the President. "Many are building little palaces, furnishing them in very expensive style, and . . . [dress their] children as though they were the sons and daughters of

Princes."[42] Andrew Jackson knew well the old, old story of such economic cycles, ever enticing in their beginnings. He himself had one time succumbed to the blandishments of easy credit, emerging within jail bounds for debt. From that day forth an abhorrence of debt, public as well as private, had been a guiding principle of Jackson's life.

Undeterred by the barren nature of Hamilton's researches, by the misgivings of Ingham, and the elbow-plucking of Lewis, the old pioneer pressed on impelled by an untranslatable instinct which Andrew Jackson would follow when he would not follow reason. Throwing off all importunities that his second message to Congress should restrict mention of the bank to a commendation of its continued usefulness in the matter of the debt, the President wrote into that document that his views on the bank "as at present organized" were unchanged.

Thus until the opening of 1831 the Executive's fight for the reformation of the monetary system was waged without the visible support of another figure of national calibre. Actively arrayed on the opposite side were all the organized wealth and a good share of the choice statesmanship of the United States. Though sympathetic, the masses who had carried Jackson on their shoulders into the White House were not stirred to the fighting pitch; the sting of necessity, as in 1820, was wanting to stir them. Surveying these circumstances, Thomas Hart Benton felt that a turning point was at hand. "The current was all setting one way," he later said. "I foresaw that if this course . . . [should continue] the Bank would triumph." After many attempts to dissuade him, the Senator from Missouri obtained the floor in February, 1831. In a long speech he arraigned the bank as a kingly autocracy with perilous power over the welfare of the people and the servants of their republic. Designed for popular consumption, the speech was somewhat demagogic, which quality was rather out of character for Benton. For the grand problem perplexing the President, he proposed a simple solution. "I am willing to see the charter expire without providing any substitute for the present bank. I am willing to see the currency of the federal government left to the hard money mentioned and intended in the constitution."[43]

"The President aims at the destruction of the Bank," cried Biddle.[44] With the masses poring over Benton's production, the financier prepared to set presses whirring in his own endeavor to carry the fight to the people. A friendly senator, better grounded in the subject of proletarian prejudices and impulses, advised him to hold off.

At this juncture the dissimilar careers of Margaret Eaton and of John C. Calhoun, their fates curiously joined, imparted a fresh aspect to the seemingly unrelated affairs of Nicholas Biddle.

CHAPTER XII

MARTIN VAN BUREN'S MASTERPIECE

I

BEFORE his departure for Tennessee in the summer of 1830, the President reminded Duff Green of the growing lack of warmth for Administration measures displayed by the *Telegraph*. To this the editor stiffly replied that, before he could advocate the measures of the Administration, he must know what they were.[1] The implications of the remark were true only in part. Although much less of a fixture in the presidential study than during the hectic pin-feather period of the Jackson régime, Green knew where Old Hickory stood on all the issues. Yet the platonic nature of his ardor had been a source of increasing irritation at the White House. Plainly Green and his influential newspaper preferred the orbit of Mr. Calhoun. The situation caused less positive men to hesitate, but not Jackson. "We must get another organ," he instructed Lewis.[2]

Upon the President's return at the end of September, the Kitchen Cabinet had agreed upon a candidate for the editorship of a new paper. Passing over all the established journalists who had won their spurs in Jackson's service, the choice had fallen upon a comparative unknown, Francis P. Blair of Kentucky. This was the work of Amos Kendall. Blair had begun his public career as a leader of the Relief Party whose ideas of public finance had virtually bankrupted Kentucky, and had quite bankrupted Blair. In 1825 Blair had supported Clay, to the point of some useful connivance in the "bargain" arrangements, though that issue later separated them. As a contributor to Kendall's *Argus,* he had done good work for Jackson since 1827. His style was terse, trenchant, direct. He opposed the Bank of the United States, internal improvements and nullification. Mr. Blair's position on the bank could be described either as a brave adherence to principle or an example of ingratitude. Owing that institution twenty thousand two hundred and forty-four dollars, the Kentuckian had been allowed to settle for ten cents on the dollar.[3]

Jackson confirming the nomination, Blair's arrival was eagerly awaited, only Kendall and Barry of the White House coterie having so much as seen the paragon from the Blue Grass picked to overthrow Duff Green and his mighty *Telegraph*. Interest was not diminished by the fact that some of the President's friends thought he had acted hastily, arguing that a safer policy would be to bring Green into line and to heal, if possible, the breach with Calhoun. With Henry Clay rallying the forces of opposition in the West it was felt that this was a time to avoid rather than to invite family discord.

On a November afternoon W. B. Lewis, prepared by Kendall's testimonials to confront a personage somewhat larger than life, descended the White House stairs to greet the recruit. The towering Major beheld an underfed-looking individual with one side of his bony head done up in court plaster, the result of a stage upset en route. From the travel-stained appearance of his frock coat, Lewis surmised that the visitor had no other coat. Mr. Blair was thirty-nine years old, five feet ten inches tall and weighed a little over a hundred pounds. He shook hands shyly and spoke in a low, modest voice. But his blue eyes returned a glance unwaveringly[4]—a thing Jackson liked. The President put the newcomer at his ease and within a few minutes they were deep in talk. Though usually more apparent than real, Old Hickory's lack of reserve often shocked Mr. Van Buren. This time Lewis seems to have been uneasy as Jackson unburdened himself on nullification, the bank, Henry Clay and the Eatons. "And there's my nephew, Donelson. I raised him. Let him do what he will, I love him. Treat him kindly but if he wants to write for your paper you must look out for him." The visit concluded with an invitation to dinner.

In formal black the President stepped into the East Room to greet the guests of the evening. A group of ambassadors and other

personages, superbly costumed, made their bows. Beside a wall
stood an abashed figure in a seedy frock coat and bandages. Mr.
Blair had accepted the President's offer of hospitality thinking the
dinner would be as casual as the invitation. General Jackson drew
him into the center of the company, and at the table placed him on
his right hand.[5] Frank Blair knew the formulas of polite society.
He was well-born, well-educated and had been married in the
governor's mansion in Kentucky. In the fluency and range of his
social conversation was little to suggest the slashing manner of a
partizan editor.

Nor was this manner apparent in the first issues of *The Washington Globe* which began their appearance on December 7, 1830,
the day after Congress convened. Jackson himself solicited subscriptions. "I expect you all to patronize the Globe."[6] Names
rolled in and a modest amount of Government printing was shifted
from the columns of the *Telegraph*. Yet the care with which the
new journal avoided offense to the Calhoun wing escaped no one.
The latch-string on the door of reconciliation was out. Studiously
did the Vice President, too, consider his every act, feeling the
crisis of a political epoch at hand. Without importuning he, too,
left unobstructed the way to harmony in case Jackson should make
the first move. Unctuous Felix Grundy and forthright "Tecumseh" Johnson of Kentucky actively spread the sentiment in Jackson circles that, by dragging in Crawford, Lewis had gone too far
with his conspiracy to advance Van Buren at Calhoun's expense.
Bluff, ingratiating Sam Swartwout came down from New York to
lounge in the White House study and descant oracularly on the
virtue of peace in the camps of friends. With pardonable satisfaction the Vice President wrote: "Those who commenced this affair
are heartily sick of it."[7]

One day Martin Van Buren was conversing with his chief while
Ralph E. W. Earl plied the brushes on one of his countless portraits of General Jackson. A servant announced Colonel Swartwout. Excusing himself, the President returned after a while to
say that "the whole affair was settled." The unfriendly correspondence that had passed between the President and the Vice President was to be destroyed, Calhoun was to dine at the White House,

and the estrangement to be ended signally. Perhaps no American in public life has equaled Martin Van Buren's control of tongue, pen and countenance in the face of adversity. The Secretary of State offered his congratulations on the restoration of amity in the executive councils.[8]

In the light of his traditional stubbornness, Andrew Jackson's announcement to Mr. Van Buren is extraordinary. Willingly had the President lent himself to Lewis's underhand machinations about Florida, virtually convicting Calhoun of Crawford's charges without a hearing. Now all that was to be sponged out for considerations of party harmony. Was it possible that the President also was looking to Mr. Calhoun for help with the nullification snarl in South Carolina?

With the reconciliation publicly spoken of as an accomplished fact, Mr. Calhoun was impatient to complete the demolition of his rival. The Florida lapse notwithstanding, the South Carolinian could exhibit a longer record of support of Andrew Jackson than Van Buren. In two years' time he had seen the prestige of that record dimmed almost to the vanishing point, while the clever New Yorker had installed himself at the President's right hand. Now Calhoun decided to strike back.

Why destroy the Jackson-Calhoun letters if they could be made to destroy Van Buren? With Duff Green the Vice President prepared the manuscript for a fat pamphlet embodying the correspondence and the statements of several other persons disputing the charges of Crawford. The object was to expose Van Buren as a plotter of party dissension. Grundy and Johnson asked Blair to publish this production in the *Globe*. What a stroke that would have been! It failed because the newcomer refused to fish in any such troubled waters. Then Grundy got Eaton in a hotel room and read him the manuscript, requesting that he indicate any changes necessary to make it acceptable to the President. Eaton offered several suggestions. The men parted with the understanding that Grundy was to submit the alterations to Calhoun and Eaton to lay the whole matter before the President. Nothing to which the General might object was to be published. The following day Grundy sent Eaton a note saying that Calhoun accepted the changes. To this Eaton made no reply and Grundy took the Secretary's silence as an indication of the President's approval. In the belief that he was acting with the knowledge and consent of Jackson, Calhoun ordered the publication of the pamphlet, which appeared on February 15, 1831, accompanied by a suitable review in the *Telegraph*.[9]

Whereupon the thunderbolt that flashed from the White House fairly stunned the unfortunate authors. "They have cut their own throats,"[10] flared Old Hickory.

Blair's moment had come. He reached for his broadax. "A firebrand [has been] wantonly thrown into the Republican party. . . . Mr. Calhoun will be held responsible for all the mischief which may follow."[11] Fifty Administration presses echoed the *Globe's* cry. John C. Calhoun's long and precariously sustained attempt to ride the Jacksonian tide into the presidency was over.

So soon as they could assemble their wits, Calhoun and Green learned the simple cause of their downfall. John Henry Eaton had not so much as mentioned the existence of the manuscript to Andrew Jackson: a humiliated husband's revenge.[12]

2

The Secretary of War stood in need of the morale-lifting stimulus this achievement afforded, for his domestic difficulties had broken out anew.

The recurrence had its inception in the unexpected return from Tennessee of Bellona, bent on claiming the place in the sun she fancied the President's championship assured her. In this she was disappointed. "M^rs. Ingham gave a splendid party last night and left out M^rs. Eaton. Barry & wife did not go. Lewis was not there. Donelson & Earl were there."[13] Matters were further complicated when the Secretary of the Navy and Mrs. Branch announced the marriage of their daughter Margaret to Daniel Donelson, a brother of the President's secretary. After the honeymoon, the old General took the couple in for a visit, temporarily altering the bachelor aspect of the White House ménage in a manner distasteful in the last degree to Mrs. Eaton.

With the Secretary's lady in town Jack Donelson saw no reason why he, too, should not enjoy the society of his wife. In a moving letter, the President asked Mary Eastin to prevail upon Emily to return. "The House appears lonesome.... [I miss] you and Emily and the sweet little ones. . . . First and last [the separation] has almost destroyed me."[14] But if she came Emily must change her attitude toward Margaret Eaton. This controversy was no longer a personal affair involving only the fate of the Secretary of War and Mrs. Eaton. It was a political affair by which John C. Calhoun hoped to "weaken me . . . and open the way to his preferment on my ruin."[15] And aside from that Emily must remember Eaton as "the able defender of your dear aunt."[16] Mrs. Ingham and Miss Rebecca Branch also were importuning Emily to return, but for less pacific reasons.[17]

Donelson suggested a middle course to his uncle. Within the four walls of the White House, but not elsewhere, Emily would accord Mrs. Eaton the civilities due her husband's station. Sadly Old Hickory said this would not do. The vein of iron in the amiable young man's composition refused to yield further. Though they continued to eat at the same table, virtually all but official intercourse ceased between the President and his private secretary. In a final endeavor to reach an agreement on the overshadowing issue, they resumed communication with each other by note. On one day five missives passed between them.[18] Useless. At the end of a week, they were further apart than ever.

Then followed a tense interview with his secretary in which the General announced that ministers whose families felt themselves the social superiors of Eaton would be dismissed.

Donelson said the step would be "fatal." "It is that which your enemies are looking for."

Let them do their worst, Old Hickory blazed back. "I will show the world that Jackson is still the head of the government."[19]

Donelson submitted his resignation to take effect at the President's pleasure.[20] With a breaking heart the old man wrote out his acceptance.

"My D'r Andrew, . . . if you should not think it too great a sacrifice, for which I ask of none, I will be glad that you remain until after the meeting of congress. . . . For upwards of a year you [have] appeared to be estranged from me, . . . which under my bereavements made my tears to flow often. . . . When you leave, whatever cause I have to regret or complain you will carry my friendship with you, and my prayers for your happiness and that of your amiable family I can never cease to love. . . . Very affectionately your uncle and sincere friend. . . ."[21]

So shaken did this rupture leave the old Spartan that friends took alarm. Fresh efforts were made to induce him to promote Eaton into the effacing mists of the diplomatic service. Of these maneuvers Donelson was informed and he was asked to be patient. "I implore you by all that is sacred *not to desert our dear old friend*."[22] Even Emily was unable to hold out against her uncle's desperate display of loyalty, tragically mistaken though she thought it to be. In a touching letter she told her husband that, despite everything, she loved the old man as she had loved him in her childhood. She said she would rather support her loneliness than have Andrew leave his side. More than that, if it would help matters, she offered to swallow her pride, return to Washington, and "to please our dear old Uncle . . . visit Mrs E. sometimes officially."[23]

On the scene in Washington was a nephew of John Overton reporting to that sound advisor of the Executive. "Public opinion does not sustain him in relation to Mrs. E. . . . This is a game too insignificant for a President."[24]

The renewed pressure to send Eaton abroad coincided with the effort to bring Jackson and Calhoun together again. Anxious days, these, for Martin Van Buren and for his handy man Lewis. Young Overton met a Tennessee friend, Samuel Bradford, on Pennsylvania Avenue.

"Bradford," said he, "there must be a change in the Cabinet."

"Change! What change, sir, do you mean?"

"Eaton must be removed," said Overton, adding that otherwise one hundred congressmen would go home dissatisfied.

Bradford relayed the conversation to Jackson. The fire of battle brightened Old Hickory's eyes. "Let them come— let the whole hundred come on— I would resign the Presidency sooner than desert my friend Eaton."[25]

What might have happened remains in the realm of conjecture, for the Calhoun pamphlet and attending earthquake gave the hundred congressmen something else to think about. By the time they were ready to reconsider the affairs of Margaret Eaton, the protection of that lady's social position had miraculously ceased to be a policy of the Jackson régime.

3

Mr. Calhoun's luckless pamphlet having removed all public doubt as to General Jackson's choice of a successor, Martin Van Buren found leisure to form the conclusion that he had done his full duty to the Eatons. The Secretary of State was able to see what hitherto he had professed not to see, namely, that Eaton was a liability to the party and a drag on the Administration. Should he resign, it would not only relieve Jackson of a vast burden but afford an excuse for a complete Cabinet house-cleaning, whereby the retirement of Messrs. Ingham, Branch and Berrien would remove the last trace of Calhoun influence from the President's official circle.

But how to face Andrew Jackson with a scheme, however artfully disguised, that included the unseating of John Henry Eaton as Secretary of War? The problem proved too much, on the spur of the moment, even for Martin Van Buren's ingenuity. At length, he decided to set the train of events in motion during a horseback ride. However, Van Buren returned from the canter to confess to his son, his only confidant, that he had lacked the heart for it. Twice, thrice, four times the same thing occurred, and Abraham Van Buren began to rally his illustrious sire.

Emily's generous offer of accommodation had availed nothing. Andrew Jackson Donelson joined his family in Tennessee, leaving the President much alone, indeed. Again the New Yorker and his chief rode out. The General spoke with feeling on the situation in his household, making a brave effort to look on the bright side.

"No, General," said the Secretary of State, "there is but one thing can give you peace."

"What is that, sir?" Jackson asked quickly.

"My resignation."

To the last year of his life, Martin Van Buren could recall the look on the General's face as he replied: "Never, sir! Even you know little of Andrew Jackson if you suppose him capable of consenting to such a humiliation of his friend by his enemies."

For four hours Van Buren argued that his withdrawal would smooth the way to a solution of many vexations, and the engrossed equestrians reached Washington very late for dinner. Jackson asked the Secretary to call in the morning.

The President's greeting was cool. "Mr. Van Buren, I have made it a rule thro' life never to throw obstacles in the way of any man who desires to leave me."

This was the turn the New Yorker had most feared the thing might take in Jackson's mind. Again the Secretary put forth his powers of persuasion, reassuring the President that the offer to resign proceeded wholly from a sense of loyalty to the Administration. Old Hickory took his friend by the hand. "Forgive me. I have been too hasty." The President asked permission to consult with Postmaster General Barry. Van Buren consented—adding that the advice of Eaton and Lewis might also be useful.

The following night the resignation of the Secretary of State was agreed upon. As Eaton, Barry, Lewis and Van Buren emerged from the White House, the thoughtful New Yorker said that he had ordered a supper spread at his home. On the walk thither Eaton suddenly stopped. "Gentleman, this is all wrong! I am the one who ought to resign."

Had Martin Van Buren written the Secretary's lines, he could not have improved on that speech.

Eaton's companions said nothing. Silently the four men entered the house. At the table the Secretary of War seemed depressed. Again he said that he should resign, and this time Martin Van Buren spoke.

"What would Mrs. Eaton say to this?"

The Tennessean said that his wife would agree.

But Mr. Van Buren said he must be sure. He could not entertain the Secretary's suggestion until the views of his wife had been ascertained.

On the next evening the four again sat down at Mr. Van Buren's well-stocked board. The Secretary of War announced that his wife "highly approved" of his decision to retire.[26] The President, however, did not intend to part entirely from his favorites. Van Buren was to become minister to Great Britain, Eaton to carry on as a senator from Tennessee as soon as Jackson could bring about a vacancy.

On April 20, 1831, the two resignations and the President's notes of acceptance were published in the *Globe*. "Many a cigar [was] thrown aside ere half consumed," remarked a visitor to the city, "that the disinterested politician might give breath to his cogitations. . . . But not all the eloquence of the smokers, nor even the ultra-diplomatic expositions from the seceding secretaries themselves could throw any light on the mysterious business."[27]

Before Van Buren left Washington he and the President called on Mrs. Eaton. "Our reception," recorded the ex-Secretary, "was to the last degree formal and cold." Leaving the house Old Hickory shrugged his shoulders. "It is strange." As careful a student of human nature as Martin Van Buren could hardly have said as much.[28]

4

The President requested and received the resignations of Messrs. Ingham, Berrien and Branch, thus realizing the ultimate object of Martin Van Buren's masterpiece. Deprived of the public printing, Duff Green obtained a loan from Nicholas Biddle's bank. Thrust into the ranks of the opposition, he began to enliven the *Telegraph* with allusions to Mrs. Eaton. Other anti-Jackson prints joined the game. "Has the Administration been ruled by a *Madame Pompadour* or a *Duchess duBarry?*"[29] From the seclusion of the North Carolina hills, John Branch issued a communication to the press, upon which Eaton challenged him to a duel, using the columns of the *Globe* for that purpose. The former head of the Navy Department replied in the *Telegraph* loftily declining to accommodate.[30] Then Eaton challenged Ingham who couched his refusal in terms of insult. For a day or so the ex-Secretary of War ranged the town with a pistol seeking to interview his late Cabinet colleague. When Ingham's sudden departure for Baltimore seemed to render a meeting unlikely, Eaton challenged Berrien.[31] Again the result was disappointing.

The refusal of these gentlemen to submit their convictions to the test of powder and ball confirmed Old Hickory in his estimate of them. Tramping the floor, he sputtered about the "treachery" of Branch and "the *disgraceful flight of Ingham. The Wicked Flee* when no man pursueth." Berrien's behavior was the last straw. *"What a wretch!* This *southern hotspur* will not fight— My Creed is true— there never was a base man a brave one."[32] These philosophical lines were addressed to a philosophical man, Mr. Martin Van Buren. Alone of the retiring Cabinet functionaries, the ex-Secretary of State had taken his departure from Washington without a firearm by his side, to pack his trunks for London and the Court of St. James's.

With his enemies quiet or out of pistol shot Eaton lingered in the capital blustering, brooding and drinking. Disillusionment descended like a shroud upon the deserted pair sitting alone in the massive residence opposite the British Legation. The few who, like Postmaster General Barry, remained loyal suffered agonies of embarrassment. The Major's recent demonstrations of his fitness to resume official life as a member of the Senate had only the spice of novelty to recommend them. The President was deluged with letters urging him to send the Eatons away. "But it is a subject," Lewis confessed to Van Buren, "upon which *I* cannot venture to speak to him."[33] At length, in September, 1831, while Margaret scornfully kept to her dismantled house, John Henry Eaton called at the Executive Mansion. With a warm handclasp, Andrew Jackson took leave of the man his hot friendship had done so much to ruin.

Harmony in his Cabinet, tranquillity in his home: the President seemed a new person. "Old Hickory is as full of energy as he was at New Orleans."[34] Although leaving Washington only for a brief sojourn at the Rip Raps, he approved and started work on a plan for remodeling the Hermitage. The changes projected were so sweeping as to alter the entire appearance of the house. The east and west wings were enlarged and extended, the east wing housing the library and a study, the west wing a dining room that would seat a hundred persons. Across the south front was flung a two-story portico supported by ten slender Doric columns, the line of which was broken by ornately figured balustrades, upstairs and down. The whole effect was one of elaborate ornamentation in contrast with the unostentatious lines of the original house.[35]

Jack Donelson, Emily and their children returned to the capital in September, bringing Mary Eastin and another Tennessee cousin, Mary McLemore, whom Justice Joseph Story, seldom inclined to flattery where the White House ménage was concerned, found a "pleasant and well-bred" dinner companion.[36] Andrew, junior, and his crony, Andrew Jackson Hutchings, also returned. Though Hutchings's college career had again been interrupted at the request of the faculty, the young man was on his good behavior just now, trying for the favor of Mary McLemore. The President encouraged the suit, reminding Hutchings that a bright girl such as Mary would have none but a "scholar." Mary Eastin's man of the moment was a Navy captain. Susceptible Andy, junior, wrote ardent letters to a little Quakeress in Philadelphia.

Into this melting atmosphere came a traveler from the Waxhaws with news of the neighborhood where Andrew Jackson was born. He spoke of Mary Crawford Dunlap, a widow with grown children. Memory swept the old cavalier back to the autumn forty-seven years before when he had courted Mary Crawford on the bank of the tumbling Catawba. After the caller had gone, the President wrote a short note to Mrs. Dunlap asking her to honor A. Jackson by accepting a snuff box in exchange "for the endearing recollection of the pleasure he enjoyed in his boyhood in the agreeable society of herself."[37]

5

Once Van Buren had opened the way, the statesmanlike manner in which Jackson had gone about the reconstruction of his Cabinet presented a refreshing contrast to the fumblings of the grief-ridden sexagenarian who had two years before suffered a Cabinet virtually to be imposed upon him through the zeal of second-rate wire-pullers.

The War Office was again tendered to Senator Hugh Lawson White, the President urging "the claims of private friendship" as well as those of public welfare. White was invited to bring his son and daughter and take quarters in the Executive Mansion. By this appointment, Jackson expected to draw into the Cabinet an excellent man whom he had always wanted there, and to provide a senatorial toga to cover the abrasions of John H. Eaton's dignity. Therefore, when White surprisingly refused the warmly proffered berth, Old Hickory's aspirations were doubly disappointed. So the war portfolio fell to Lewis Cass, a ponderous, solemn-faced man with a large bald head. But he had lived a life that Jackson could understand. Crossing the Alleghenies on foot, riding the rounds of backwoods courts as a border lawyer, this New England-born frontiersman had achieved the governorship of the wilderness called Michigan when the title was a risky distinction. For eighteen years General Cass held that office, leaving a record not surpassed in the annals of our territories.

Mr. Van Buren's place went to the awkward-looking but accomplished Senator Edward Livingston of Louisiana. The new Secretary of State wrote a letter to his charming wife. "Here I am in the very cell where the great magician, they say, brewed his spells."[38] Capable Louis McLane, who two years before had urged Van Buren to desert Jackson's standard, was called from London to be Secretary of the Treasury. Smug Levi Woodbury of New Hampshire, a former senator of above average ability, took the Navy Department. Isaac Hill said the only thing against him was his aristocratic background. The appointment that ex-

THE THIRD HERMITAGE

Completed 1831, destroyed by fire 1834. This structure represents an extensive remodeling of the second Hermitage which was built in 1818. On the right is Rachel Jackson's tomb. This likeness, reproduced from an engraving in the gallery of the Tennessee Historical Society, Nashville, appeared in early editions of the first volume of this work as the second Hermitage, erected in 1818. The Society and the writer have discovered their error and a proper likeness of the 1818 house has been substituted in Volume One.

cited the most surprise was that of a Marylander named Roger B. Taney as Attorney General. Seemingly Nature had not modeled Mr. Taney—pronounced Tawney—for greatness. His form was spare, excessively stooped and carelessly clothed. Near-sighted eyes gave a perpetual squint to a narrow countenance, revealing uneven, tobacco-stained teeth. His flat voice was not designed for oratory. At fifty-one Taney was so little known outside of the state of his birth that apparently he preferred the uncomplicated life of a lawyer and a country squire. The insignificant, gentlemanly Barry remained as Postmaster General.

The selections were well-received, except by the dwindling party of Mr. Calhoun which was sure Van Buren controlled the Government.[39] It was true that all the new officials favored the former Secretary of State as Jackson's successor; but Jackson would have appointed none who did not. On the other hand, Van Buren's departure tended to quell the impression that the New Yorker had had more to do with shaping Jackson's policies than was healthy for the Administration. Some minor changes following in the wake of major ones were of consequence. With the return of the Donelsons, William B. Lewis found a residence of his own.[40] His importance diminished, that of Kendall and Blair grew.

"I was fortunate enough," wrote Harriet Martineau, "to catch a glimpse of the invincible Amos Kendall. . . . He is supposed to be the moving spring of the Administration; the thinker, the planner, the doer; but it is all in the dark. Documents are issued the excellence of which prevents them from being attributed to the persons that take the responsibility; a correspondence is kept up all over the country; work is done with goblin speed which makes men look about them with superstitious wonder. President Jackson's letters to his Cabinet are said to be Kendall's; the report on Sunday mails is attributed to Kendall; the letters sent from Washington to remote country newspapers, whence they are collected and published in the 'Globe' as demonstrations of public opinion, are pronounced to be written by Kendall. . . . The moment I went in [to the drawing room] intimations reached me from all quarters, 'Kendall is here.' 'There he is.'

I saw at once that his plea for seclusion (bad health) is not a false one. The extreme sallowness of his complexion, the hair of such perfect whiteness is rarely seen in a man of middle age. . . . A member of congress told me he had watched through five sessions for a sight of Kendall and had never obtained one until now. . . . In a moment he was gone."[41]

An attractive rendering of an attractive legend which Kendall's recluse-like habits did much to sustain. It would be more than discourteous to censure an English woman for putting too much faith in it; most Americans did the same. But Francis P. Blair spoke from a point closer to the throne. "Old Hickory . . . is to his cabinet here what he was to his aids [in the army]."[42]

6

The Indian removal program, by which Jackson hoped to limit the issue of nullification to South Carolina, had struck a snag. Though the Chickasaw treaty was ratified by the United States Senate and declared operative, the Choctaws had rebelled against the removal agreement which some of their chiefs had made under the compelling spell of Old Hickory's presence. Jackson did not press them, but tactfully reopened negotiations looking toward a new arrangement acceptable to the rank and file of the tribe. This fortified the Cherokees and Creeks in their attitude of refusal to discuss removal on any terms, relying upon the Supreme Court to protect their land rights.

The matter came before that tribunal unexpectedly when a Cherokee named Corn Tassel killed another Indian within the limits of the Cherokee Nation. A court of the State of Georgia, which in violation of the Federal treaties had extended its jurisdiction to the Cherokee territory, sentenced Corn Tassel to be hanged. On behalf of the condemned Indian, application was made to the United States Supreme Court for a writ of error on the ground that Georgia's action was unconstitutional. The writ was granted and Georgia requested to show cause for its infringement on Cherokee sovereignty. The Georgia Legislature instructed local officers to ignore the mandate of the Supreme

Court. To give this defiance reality, the involuntary author of the crisis, Corn Tassel, was hastily restrained from further participation, by means of a rope.

Opposition presses which had applauded, albeit grudgingly, the President's "Federal Union" toast uttered grave warnings. "The Union is in danger. Gen. Jackson must sustain the Court." Friendly journals remained silent or offered lame excuses. South Carolina Nullifiers welcomed Georgia as an ally, jubilantly proclaiming the "usurpations" of Federal power "bravely met" by a sister state.[43] When anxious members of the Union Party in South Carolina planned a demonstration of strength in Charleston on July 4, the Nullifiers started to get up a counter demonstration. Jackson received an invitation from the Unionists. He sent a letter expressing the hope that the "declarations inconsistent with an attachment for the Union" reflected nothing more serious than "momentary excitement." But should the case prove otherwise, he promised to sustain the Union "at all hazards."[44]

Vexing their brains for an answering stroke, the Nullifiers turned to John C. Calhoun. The Vice President was summering in his native State, his mind a maelstrom of doubt and indecision. In a "feverish" conversation with a friend, "he spoke of the three great interests of the Nation, The North, the South and the West. . . . He thought the period was approaching that was to determine whether they could be reconciled or not so as to perpetuate the Union."[45] For three years the views of the South Carolinian had been in a state of transition. Covertly he had guided the Nullifiers without repudiating the support of his nationalist friends. The time was at hand when he must march under the one banner or the other.

South as well as north, nationalists implored the Vice President not to desert them. With no view to affording "pleasure to friends of Gen'l Jackson," a distinguished Georgian warned Mr. Calhoun that Georgia would oppose South Carolina's brand of nullification. "I could not desire my enemy a worse employment than to appear before the people on this subject." The Georgian followed exactly the reasoning of Jackson's Fourth of July letter. "Nullification . . . destroys not the [tariff] law but the government. And for what? For evils a thousand fold magnified, ... Civil War."[46] Duff Green had rushed off to New York in an effort to beat up manifestations of friendly northern sentiment calculated to divert the Vice President from an open espousal of the state sovereignty cause. Green wrote to the Governor of South Carolina that at one swoop the Nullifiers were placing the strongest possible cards in Jackson's hands and snuffing out the career of their first citizen as a national statesman. "[He asks]," related the Governor, giving a digest of the letter, "if we were all crazy, ... if we intended to start open rebellion and insure the empire of the whore of Washington (Mrs E. I suppose)." The Governor was unmoved. "to these civil things my Reply was . . . that whether we decreed perpetual empire to the W—— of Washington or not, or started into rebellion, we would abate not one jot our zeal . . . for Nullification."[47]

The fire-eaters prevailed. Three weeks after Jackson's message was read in Charleston, John C. Calhoun published a lengthy *Address,* taking the leadership of the nullification movement. In this way the challenging nationalist of 1824 at last stepped down from his pedestal to marshal the forces of sectionalism, though not without an eye to some combination of elements in the unpredictable panorama by which he might reascend to power. Emboldened by this adhesion, the nullificationist majority in the Legislature surpassed that of Georgia by singling out Jackson for attack. "Is this . . . [body] to legislate under the sword of the Commander-in-Chief?"[48] Secession was declared a right of any state, and it was defended as being neither treason nor insurrection.

But unlike Georgia, South Carolina did not suit action to the word. Andrew Jackson smoked his pipe and waited. Despite an almost irretrievable reputation for acting on impulse, Old Hickory could be very good at waiting. Strange it is how comparatively few persons observed that as he grew older much that passed for impulsiveness had been thought out ahead. Before the Legislature at Columbia had finished its brimstoning, the President privately assured a northern friend: "The *Union will be preserved.*"[49]

CHAPTER XIII

MR. BIDDLE'S DILEMMA

I

On a sparkling September day in 1831 the four dappled grays, which all Washington and the countryside had learned to recognize, whirled a carriage over Maryland roads to the princely estate of Charles Carroll of Carrollton. Deferentially the President of the United States stood before the only man living who had signed the Declaration of Independence. Memory carried the visitor back to the August day in 1776 when he had read the stirring words of that paper to the people gathered in his Uncle Robert Crawford's yard. Andy Jackson, "public reader" of the Waxhaws, was then nine years old. The present occasion was Charles Carroll's ninety-fourth birthday.

On the ride to this meeting the President had remarked to Secretary of the Treasury Louis McLane that he did not intend to pull down Mr. Biddle's bank merely to set up a similar one—an allusion, no doubt, to the ambitions of certain New York and Boston capitalists suddenly conspicuous for their affable interest in Jackson's monetary program. The Executive went further. He abandoned his objection to the bank based on the fact that much of its stock was owned abroad.[1] Foreign-owned shares had no voting power.

These sentiments were pleasing to Mr. McLane, who recently had confided to a senatorial friend of the bank: "If the old Chief would consent to recharter what a glorious operation I could make for him!"[2] At Carrollton the bank became the subject of a general conversation during which Old Hickory was reported to have declared himself willing to risk re-election "upon the principle of putting the bank down. . . . No bank and Jackson—

or bank and no Jackson."[3] The outburst probably bothered the assembled Carrolls with their heavy investments in bank stock more than it did the Secretary of the Treasury who was beginning to understand the Executive's state of mind.

General Jackson was still at sea as to the best means of achieving his contemplated financial reforms—whether to hew out a new instrument to that end or to remodel the present one. Perhaps for the personal satisfaction it would give him because of some hastily-considered remarks made early in the contest, Jackson would have preferred to displace the bank; but, in the light of Hamilton's failures and advice from other quarters, caution deterred him. The flare-up at Carroll's indicated nothing conclusive, for Jackson leaned now this way, now that. It may well be that he was smarting under the effect of a recent election in Kentucky where friends of the bank had made the institution an issue, winning the contest by frightening the mercantile and debtor class with predictions of the bank's extinction under Jackson.[4] Such a challenge to Old Hickory could hardly be expected to pass without notice.

If vacillation and uncertainty were states difficult for Andrew Jackson to support with composure, they were doubly so for Nicholas Biddle. At least the initiative was Jackson's. He led, as he was accustomed to do, but Biddle must follow, must accommodate, must suit his mood and actions to conform to the shifting course of the President—a poor tonic for the nerves of a man used to ruling what he surveyed. Occasionally Biddle rebelled, only to draw back and truckle.

In the business under review, General Jackson had kept a tight rein on his headstrong streak. He listened to Amos Kendall, Blair, Benton and Isaac Hill, it is true. But in his new Cabinet he had placed three men friendly to the Bank of the United States, one who opposed it and one who turned out a straddler with the idea of backing the winning horse. Jackson listened to those who favored the bank, and they were men of weight—McLane, Livingston and Cass. Nicholas Biddle tried to see to it that his supporters in the Cabinet should be well informed. He primed his agent in the Treasury, Chief Clerk Asbury Dickins, with arguments to insinuate upon the attention of his chief. Particularly was Mr. Dickins to direct notice to the precedent that a secretary of the treasury could take the lead in a recommendation for recharter.[5]

Messrs. McLane and Livingston trod up and down the White House stairs. Usually Donelson was on hand, and sympathetic with their work. Smoking a long-stemmed pipe, Old Hickory would sit nodding, correcting, interpolating, as his lieutenants bent over an untidy desk developing modifications of the bank's structure and sweeping powers, which were calculated to remove the Executive's misgivings as to constitutionality. The Government's stock was to be sold to the public, although five Government directors would remain on the board; the bank was to carry out its part of the national debt payment program according to the Biddle plan of 1829; branch drafts were to be abolished in favor of currency of the mother bank which designated officers should sign; the bank was to be denied the privilege of loaning money on merchandise, branches limited to two in a state, the corporation made suable in and taxable by states, and its real estate holdings limited.[6]

These were steps, and long steps, toward the ideal Jackson had in mind. Mr. Biddle's assent was a guaranty of their practicability. Still, the modifications did not insure all that the President wished to accomplish. He withheld from the hovering secretaries the vital promise to sign a bill for recharter on the terms outlined. But McLane encouraged Biddle to be patient, that this would come in time.[7]

2

The President had cause for hesitation. In the beginning, his skepticism concerning the bank had included no reflection on the abilities or prudence of Mr. Biddle as a banker. On those scores Jackson had praised him. But in 1830 the President had noted in the liberalization of western credit a movement that more than once had desolated the West, its borrowers and bankers alike. Was history to repeat itself? Some were beginning to fear so. The 1831 crop was short. Instead of paying, borrowers were forced to increase their loans. From the consequences of his first serious banking error, Nicholas Biddle struggled to extricate himself. Balances with state banks were drawn upon, foreign balances likewise. They were not enough. The East felt the shock as its funds began to flow west to meet mounting demands. Biddle notified the Barings in London that he must draw to the limit of his standing credit of one million dollars. Then he asked for an additional million. The position of the Bank of the United States was fraught with peril.[8]

Although a banking error, the new western loan policy strengthened Biddle's hands politically. As in the case of Asbury Dickins, a debtor was more likely than not to do the bank's bidding. Thousands of Westerners who were at its mercy had no desire to see the bank legislated out of existence and their loans called. The Kentucky election had established that. Indeed, it seems probable that this was one of the things Nicholas Biddle had in mind when in 1830 he suddenly made credit easy in the section where the bank was politically weakest.

Mr. Dickins performed his work well.[9] McLane came to the President with a proposal to recommend in his annual report a renewal of the bank's charter with modifications. Jackson heard the Secretary out and offered no objection. "With a view to show the Pres^t the full extent to which his report might lead," McLane pointed out that the pro-bank House Committee on Ways and Means might use it as an excuse to report a bill for recharter. The Secretary said that he could not oppose such a course. "I should be sorry," observed the President, "if the question were forced upon me in that way." But Mr. McLane was in good form that day. Before taking his departure, he obtained the President's acquiescence not to mention the bank in his forthcoming message to Congress.

Off to Philadelphia posted the Secretary of the Treasury to lay the whole case before Biddle. He proposed so to link, in his annual report, the recommendation for recharter with the tariff and the public lands issues "that even Mr Benton would not attack it." However, he advised the banker not to petition for the charter's renewal until after the presidential election of 1832, lest Old Hickory take it as a campaign "dare" to veto the bill. In that event he would probably veto it, the Secretary said. After a triumphant re-election the situation would be different. "What I see of Genl Jackson I think he would be more disposed to yield when he is strong than when he is in danger."[10]

Nicholas Biddle accepted this sage advice, and Louis McLane returned to Washington believing the bank question solved.

3

A fortnight thereafter, in November, 1831, Henry Clay arrived to take a seat in the Senate. Social and political admirers flocked about the likable statesman. Margaret Bayard Smith, wife of the president of the Washington branch of the Bank of the United States, perceived little to remind her of their last meeting at the wake over Mr. Adams's régime. Two years and eight months at Ashland had restored the Kentuckian remarkably. His countenance was "animated," his spirit borne up by imperishable ambition[11] and a rare fund of good nature. The acknowledged leader of the opposition, whose nomination for the presidency on the anti-Jackson ticket was conceded, Mr. Clay seemed the picture of confidence. In this, appearances obscured reality, for the Kentuckian did not feel confident. "Something, however, may turn up," he wrote to a friend, "to give a brighter aspect to our affairs."[12]

Mr. Clay had canvassed the field: tariff and nullification, internal improvements, Indians, public lands, foreign relations. By skillful and effective handling of these questions General Jackson had, on the whole, strengthened his Administration in every part of the Union, save South Carolina; and Henry Clay was unprepared to champion nullification. The manipulation of patronage, plus a discipline reminiscent of Jackson's armies, had transformed into an energetic and obedient party the loose confederation of discrepant elements which had carried Old Hickory into power.

There remained, then, the bank. On this question alone, General Jackson's course had lacked the precision and clarity essential to the consolidation of political strength. His opposition to the bank "as organized" had been insufficiently defined or exploited to rouse up the anti-bank strength of the country. Mr. Clay was inclined to doubt its potentialities for popular exploitation. He had seen the bank issue used to defeat a Jackson slate in Louisville. He believed it afforded the most promising material available for a contest in the nation at large. A less nimble logician might have been embarrassed by the fact that Mr. Clay, at various times a member of the bank's corps of paid counsel, had hitherto advised Mr. Biddle to withhold an application for recharter until after the election. Brushing this aside, the Kentuckian came out for immediate action on the question. Adroitly he concerted pressure on Biddle to repudiate his tacit arrangement with Jackson and throw the bank into the campaign. This was what Henry Clay had in mind when he expressed the hope that something would turn up to brighten his prospects. And it was *his* prospects that concerned Candidate Clay foremost.

4

Early in December the Cabinet assembled to hear the first draft of the annual message. Donelson read it, pausing for discussion and to note suggested amendments. At length he reached the subject of the bank, which the President had finally decided to mention—in his own way. Actually, this had come about through the over-zealousness of Mr. Biddle. When McLane had reported the President's earlier promise to pass over the bank in silence, Biddle had suggested that judicious mention would be preferable to silence. Then the banker undertook to dictate that part of the message. The President, he said, should avoid a repetition of his previous criticisms and merely say that "having on former occasions brought the question before the Congress it was now left with the representatives of the people."[13] But McLane had been unable to bring this off. The President had written into the message that his opinion of the bank "as at present organized" was unchanged—after which he was willing to leave the matter to "an enlightened people and their representatives."

The silence that followed the reading of this passage seemed to denote unanimous approval until Attorney General Roger B. Taney remarked that the language proposed might suggest that the President had gone over to the side of the bank. McLane and Livingston disputed this. It was Taney's first Cabinet controversy, but after a mild beginning the countrified-looking Maryland lawyer warmed up. McLane warmly opposed him. Taney stood alone, not even Barry, the old Kentucky Relief Party man, uttering a word. After some indications of impatience, the President interrupted to say that he did not mean to imply that he would sign any bill that Congress might pass; nor did he mean that he would veto any bill. Donelson picked up the manuscript and read on, a sign that the bank paragraph was to remain intact. Taney left the meeting feeling that the Chestnut Street influence had been too much for him.[14]

The almost simultaneous appearance of the message and of McLane's report, recommending recharter, threw the anti-bank people into a spasm. Frank Blair leaped on the report with such vigor that McLane threatened to resign. The result was the softening of a further word of censure which the editor had ready for the type-setters.[15] "Mr. McLane and myself understand each other," the President reminded James Alexander Hamilton, another anxious member of the anti-bank group "and have not the slightest disagreement about the principles which will be a sine qua non to my assent to a bill rechartering the bank."[16] The nervous New Yorker thought of taking a fast vessel for England to consult Van Buren.

Mr. Clay also was disturbed, for he had committed himself and his party to a campaign predicated on Jackson's hostility to the bank. Six days after the President's message had gone to Congress the Clay party, under the new title of National Republican, had made its nominations, condemning Jackson as a foe of the bank. Mr. Clay's running mate was John Sergeant of Philadelphia, chief of the bank's legal staff. Should Jackson and Mr.

Biddle come to terms, as it seemed that they were about to do, this fine work would be for nothing. Railing against Jackson's "deep game" to coast through the campaign without committing himself on the bank question, the Kentuckian intensified the effort to destroy the possibility of an accord between Mr. Biddle and the Administration, and to this Daniel Webster lent his practised hand. Friends of the bank with no ax to grind begged Biddle to stand fast.

Pulled this way and that, the banker sent Thomas Cadwalader to study the situation on the spot. For seven days and nights, without resting on Christmas, the indefatigable agent button-holed senators, congressmen, party managers and Washington nondescripts, covering page after page with cryptic tabulations indicating the expressed, probable or supposed sentiments of each of the two hundred and sixty-two members of Congress. At the outset McLane warned Cadwalader that Jackson would return a bill with his veto, which the Senate would sustain. The bank must wait until after the election. Then the Clay people began their work, which was finished to their satisfaction when Peter Livingston, a brother of the Secretary of State, but a supporter of Clay, whispered that Edward Livingston, McLane and Cass would prevent a veto. Cadwalader wound up the reports to his chief with a recommendation for the immediate submission of the question.[17]

One of Mr. Biddle's recurrent moods of boldness was setting in. Chafing under the necessity of bending his will to that of General Jackson, the banker grew captious. So small a thing as the President's insistence on his own rather than Biddle's formula for the message was made a subject for complaint.[18] No sooner did Cadwalader's last memorandum reach Philadelphia than, with a flaring gesture of independence, the financier plumped for recharter. "The bank cares not whether . . . [Jackson] is benefitted or injured," he proclaimed. "It takes its own time & its own way."[19]

Henry Clay's scheme had succeeded. Mr. Biddle had delivered the destiny of his bank into the keeping of a desperate candidate panting for an issue.

5

The eve of the battles, whose littered fields were to exhibit President Jackson's greatest contributions to the American saga, saw Old Hickory in the finest fighting trim since he had taken the oath three years before. His step was springier, his eye brighter. Something of the old banter reanimated his social conversation, making it, indeed, difficult to remember the heart-crushed old man of 1829, hauled about by second-rate politicians.

Yet the striking levels of success to which he had raised his Administration were not the sole causes of the new spirit which infused the veteran. For years the bullet which Thomas Hart Benton's brother had fired into Jackson's left arm in 1813, had periodically troubled him, at times rendering the arm almost useless. Physicians who concluded that the ball was poisoning Jackson's system hesitated to operate for fear of the shock to the heart against which lay another bullet which could never be disturbed—Charles Dickinson's. In January, 1832, when a visiting surgeon from Philadelphia expressed the opinion that the Benton bullet could be safely removed, Jackson asked him to take it out at once. The work was done in army field hospital style. Baring his arm to the shoulder, Old Hickory took a firm grip on his walking stick. In a few minutes the operation was over, and the President appeared at a small dinner party that evening.[20] His general health improved at once.

A story went around that Frank Blair had got hold of the bullet and offered it to Senator Benton. The Missourian declined the token, saying that Jackson had "acquired clear title to it in common law by twenty years' peaceable possession."

"Only nineteen years," corrected Blair.

"Oh, well," retorted Benton, "in consideration of the extra care he has taken of it—keeping it constantly about his person, and so on—I'll waive the odd year."[21]

Another measure to the General's cup of happiness was the continued felicity of his domestic circle, to which had been added a daughter-in-law.

Her arrival was a surprise. Early the preceding autumn, the fact that the vulnerable heart of Andrew, junior, had been touched by a girl in Philadelphia seems to have been occasion for little family comment. Nor was much attention paid to the matter when, late in October, the young man departed on a trip to the Pennsylvania city. Then came a letter to which General Jackson dispatched a reply that cost some effort.

"My son, . . . the sooner this engagement is consummated the better." Jackson was never a believer in long engagements. "You say that Sarah possesses every quality necessary to make you happy. . . . You will please communicate to her that you have my full and free consent that you be united in the holy bonds of matrimony; that I shall receive her as a daughter, and cherish her as my child. . . . Present me affectionately to Sarah for, although unknown to me, your attachment has created in my bosom a parental regard for her. That, I have no doubt, will increase on our acquaintance. I am

"Your affectionate father. . . ."[22]

It increased profoundly. An orphan of Quaker heritage, Sarah Yorke was small, of dark complexion, gentle voice and gentle manner. Except as the wife of the President's son, she would have been inconspicuous in the gay company that centered about Emily Donelson and Mary Eastin. She conquered the old General's heart as she had conquered young Andrew's. A large portrait of Mrs. Jackson by Earl hung in the General's bedroom. But the likeness he prized most was a miniature, painted by Anna C. Peale in 1815, which he wore about his neck suspended by a black cord under his garments.[23] At night after the General's mulatto body-servant, George, had assisted his master into a long white nightgown, Jackson would remove the picture and prop it up on a bedside table so that it might be the first thing to meet his eyes on awakening. In bed the General would open the worn Bible which had belonged to Rachel, and read a chapter before George snuffed the candle and stretched out to take his own sleep on a pallet on the floor beside the bed of his master. Sarah had not been in the house a month until she was permitted to hold

SARAH YORKE JACKSON

Wife of Andrew Jackson, junior. Married in Philadelphia, November 24, 1831. "She has been more than a daughter to me," General Jackson wrote of her in his will. From a portrait by Earl, owned by the Ladies' Hermitage Association, Nashville.

the doubly sacred Book in her own hands and read the chapter to her "father," as she ever called him.[24]

The General's stories of Tennessee life thrilled Sarah. With a view to introducing to the ways of slavery this little Northerner who must one day be mistress of the Hermitage, Jackson gave her as a personal maid a bright young negress named Gracie. Within a few weeks, so great was his confidence in Sarah, Jackson acceded to the wish of the young couple to depart that spring to take formal charge of the plantation. "I mean to throw the care of the farm on . . . [Andrew], never more [to] pester myself with this worlds wealth— My only ambition is to get to the Hermitage so soon as the interest of my country . . . will permit me, and there to put my [spiritual] house in order and go to sleep along side my dear departed wife."[25]

The old soldier was ready to lay down his arms.

6

And he would lay them down in triumph—at the very hour when Henry Clay once would have had America believe that the "military chieftain," drunk with power, would only be ready to begin his real work of destruction in the field of popular liberty. Is it any wonder that, after three years of Jackson as President, the Kentuckian was obliged to bring forth a new issue for 1832?

Yet one may well ask: If General Jackson were sincere in his protestations about retirement why had he consented to stand as a candidate for re-election?

The answer to this question was known at the time to only two men—Andrew Jackson and Martin Van Buren.

Jackson had consented to run again to vindicate the record of his tenure of office. The New Yorker was to be the second man on the ticket. At the end of the first, or, at most, the second year of his new term, Jackson said that he intended to resign, by that means elevating Martin Van Buren to the chief magistracy. The magnanimous proposal, which stands alone in the history of American politics, was made in the fall of 1830 during a horseback ride over the Georgetown hills with the then Secretary of State. Almost overcome by the generosity of his superior, Mr. Van Buren, nevertheless, saw in the proposition "nothing but danger" to himself. Admitting the White House to be within the scope of his ambition, the Secretary said that he preferred to take his chances at the polls. Otherwise "enemies . . . would stigmatize the proceeding as a selfish intrigue designed to smuggle me into the Presidency and to gratify his [Jackson's] own resentment against" Calhoun. So tenaciously did the Secretary urge his point that, at length, the General admitted the possibility of having insufficiently considered the matter from Mr. Van Buren's point of view.[26]

Yet Jackson did not give up the idea. A year later he wrote about it to Van Buren in England. Three months thereafter, with delegates assembling at Baltimore to nominate Henry Clay, he wrote again, employing stronger terms.[27] In 1830 Jackson's proposal might have been susceptible of the interpretation of proceeding from weakness, for the current crisis of the Eaton affair had the old man in a wretched state of mind and health. But the end of 1831 saw the prestige of the Administration vastly improved, the President's family troubles solved, his health better. The bank issue seemed on the way to settlement. Of major matters pending only nullification remained, with which Old Hickory did not mistrust his ability to cope should South Carolina attempt to execute her threats. No possibility of misinterpreting the renewed proposal existed; it came from a consciousness of strength.

7

With these thoughts in his head, it was natural that General Jackson should have observed closely the performance of his Minister to the Court of St. James's. It was satisfactory, Martin Van Buren being in every way a credit to his country. Opposition eyes also ranged across the Atlantic. His opponents did not guess all that was in Jackson's mind with reference to the New Yorker, but this much they did know and it was enough to excite their ire: Van Buren would be the candidate for Vice President, and in 1836 he would be Jackson's choice for the succession. Clay, Calhoun and Webster joined in a plan to diminish the popularity of that too-fortunate politician.

Mr. Van Buren's had been a recess appointment. The three allies proposed that the Senate refuse to confirm the nomination, thus obliging the President to recall his minister with a stain on his political shield that would render him ineligible, as they imagined, to the second place on the Jackson ticket.

In January, 1832, a fastidious young idler from Philadelphia named Henry Wikoff visited the Senate gallery. He saw Mr. Clay "with his tall stately form, his urbane demeanor and courageous eye, indulging ever and anon in a pinch of snuff while listening to a member of the Opposition; Webster with his broad expanse of brow which looked like the very dome of thought, his tranquil mien and stolid figure; Calhoun, erect, slim, stern . . . and resolute; . . . the polished Hayne; . . . the stalwart Benton." He did not see so very much of them, however, because the galleries were cleared and the Senate went into executive session to consider, as all Washington knew, the nomination of Martin Van Buren.

On the evening of January 25, Mr. Wikoff called at the White House with a letter of introduction to the President. As General Jackson was presiding at a dinner party, his visitor was asked to wait in the Red Room—"a lofty, well-proportioned apartment," as Mr. Wikoff observed, "richly furnished in damask of the colour which designated it. . . . It was not long before the doors were thrown open and General Jackson entered at the head of his company, talking and laughing with much animation. . . . Seating himself near the fire, his friends formed a group about him. I was absorbed for some minutes scanning the face and mien of this remarkable man. In person he was tall, slim and straight. . . . His head was long, but narrow, and covered with thick grey hair that stood erect, as though impregnated with his defiant spirit; his brow was deeply furrowed, and his eye, even in his present mood, was one 'to threaten and command.' His nose was prominent and indicated force. His mouth displayed firmness. His whole being conveyed an impression of energy and daring." A

touch on the elbow roused the young man from his contempla-
tion. A friend offered to present him to the President. Before
they could reach the Executive, however, another man entered
the room hurriedly and gained his ear. Jackson sprang from his
chair.

"By the Eternal! I'll smash them!"

The startled guests demanded to know what had happened.
They learned that the Senate had rejected the nomination of
Martin Van Buren.[28]

Benton brought intimate particulars of the secret sessions. A
tie had been purposely contrived to give Mr. Calhoun the distinction of casting the deciding vote. Descending from his dais
the Vice President had pronounced Martin Van Buren's obsequies.
"It will kill him dead, sir, kill him dead. He will never kick,
sir, never kick." All along Benton had been of a different opinion.
When the vote was announced the Missourian turned to Gabriel
Moore of Alabama. "You have broken a minister and elected a
Vice President." "Good God!" exclaimed Moore, as the light
began to dawn. "Why didn't you tell me that before I voted?"[29]

Billy Carroll of Tennessee furnished tidings from the West,
where Van Buren had never been strong: "Two men know him
now to one that knew him sixty days ago."[30]

8

"You wish to know, you say, precisely how the old Genl stands
the wars," wrote John Campbell of the Treasury Department
to his brother David in Virginia.

"The evening before last I spent with him. When I went in
there were some 20 or 30 ladies & gentlemen seated and standing
He was in the midst of the ladies in as fine a humour as I ever saw
him He took me by the arm in his usual gallant style and introduced me to all the Ladies with whom I was not acquainted. . . .
He then handed a young lady to the piano and stood by her while
she play'd several airs. . . . He paid her some pretty compliments
and then handed her back to her seat again. . . .

"At eight o'clock the whole party went off to a ball except [the President], Genl Gibson of the Army and My self. . . . We drew our chairs around the fire. . . . I asked [the President] if he was entirely relieved of pain since the ball was extracted [from his arm]. He reply'd that the strength of his arm had been completely restored so that he could manage a horse [with it]. . . . The old hero gave a very minute account of the manner in which his arm was broken *all to pieces* in his conflict with Benton [and] of its dreadful situation when he took command of the army to go into the Creek country— It remain'd in a sling for Six Months In a violent effort to draw his sword to cut [the retreating Colonel] Stump's head off in the battle of Enichopco [Enotachopco] . . . he tore the broken bones of the arm to pieces again."[31]

In April, 1832, the White House lost its bright-eyed ingénue when Mary Eastin, throwing over her navy captain after a wedding date had been set, was married to Lucius J. Polk, a boy from home, and set out for Tennessee to live.[32] Jackson missed her, but not so greatly as he missed Andrew, junior, and Sarah when they departed. The alterations at the Hermitage were finished and Jackson made a heavy purchase of furniture in Philadelphia to fit it out in style for Sarah. Andrew carried with him a compact manual on plantation administration, written in the General's own hand and concluding: "You will have to begin to learn the wants of a family & supply it— this will require oeconomy & care which you will have to attend to if you expect to get through life well by always knowing your means & living within them. . . . Write me fully as to the situation of all things— the health & condition of the negroes, the appearance of my stock, . . . the colts in particular, their form size and which promises best."[33]

And he wrote to Sarah: "I hope this night you are reposing under the peaceful roof of the Hermitage . . . and that you have found . . . [it] a pleasing home. . . . I wish I was there. I have spent a lonely time since you left me. . . . Do write me my Dr Sarah. . . . When alone in my room your letters will be company for me."[34]

The old man's thoughts were much on Tennessee. He said

he envied Eaton his retirement.[35] The General might have spared himself. Margaret Eaton was not a social success in Tennessee, and many of the attentions she received bore the forced aspect of obedience to the wishes of husbands who desired to retain the good opinion of Andrew Jackson. Time hung heavily on the hands of the former Secretary of War whose distant view of the alignment of forces for the coming campaign filled him with wistful longing. Only four short years ago— Ah, but he could still do something.

The General had persevered in his ambition to build up a string of race horses from the Truxton strain. For the past year he had kept a number of colts in the White House stable. They were entered at the National City and other nearby tracks under the name of A. J. Donelson, but it was no secret to whom they actually belonged. Though none of them won an important race, the supervision of their care and training proved a wholesome relaxation for the President. In April, 1832, Major Eaton and his wife, stopping at the Hermitage, learned that on the day before, Steele, the overseer, had started on the road to Washington three horses and three colored jockeys. Behaving with the promptness that had once characterized his actions in larger concerns, the Major directed Steele to call back the horses. Then he wrote to Jackson. With a campaign coming on, further display of the President's sporting proclivities would be inadvisable; and to run the horses under Donelson's name would deceive no one.[36]

Old Hickory did not criticize the well-intentioned action of his friend. But he ordered the colts and jockeys sent on to Washington.[37]

Andrew Jackson Hutchings also put in an appearance at the Executive Residence, with his fourth notice of dismissal from a seat of learning—this time the University of Virginia. Old Hickory was discouraged in his effort to educate his ward. Giving the boy two hundred dollars, Jackson sent him to Tennessee to learn plantation management under the eye of John Coffee.[38] Other callers were W. H. Sparks and his bride of Natchez. Mrs. Sparks was the youngest daughter of Abner Green in whose home near Natchez Rachel Robards had found refuge at the end of the

A WHITE HOUSE BRIDE

Mary Eastin, a grand-niece of Rachel Jackson, whom the General brought to Washington in 1829. She kept the hearts of various young men aflutter until 1832 when she married Lucius Polk, a relative of James K. Polk. This likeness, which shows Mrs. Polk with her son William, is from a portrait owned by Mrs. Sarah Polk Burch of Nashville.

famous flight from Nashville. At the sight of her, memories
more than forty years old engulfed Andrew Jackson.

"He did not speak, but held her hand . . . gazing intently into
her face. His feelings overcame him and clasping her to his
bosom he said, 'I must kiss you my child for your sainted mother's
sake'; then holding her from him, . . . 'Oh! how like your mother
you are— She was the friend of my poor Rachel when she so
needed a friend.'"[39]

9

On January 9, 1832, three days before the Benton bullet was
cut from Jackson's arm, Nicholas Biddle surprised the Administration and some of his own friends by memorializing Congress
for the recharter of the Bank of the United States. The votes
seemed at hand to pass a bill in both houses. The Clay forces felt
that should Jackson veto the measure he would lose Pennsylvania
in the coming election, and should he fail to veto it he would lose
in the South and the West. The immediate effect, however, was
to offend McLane and other pro-bank men in the Administration,
and to restore to life all Jackson's personal antipathy to the "monster." "I will prove to them I will not flinch."[40]

It was Biddle who flinched, making overtures to McLane and
Livingston. The bank, said Mr. Biddle, would go nine-tenths of
the way to meet the President. "Let him write the whole charter
with his own hands."[41] Bank men and Livingston put their heads
together on the subject of modifications of the charter and, unaware that the President had begun to lose confidence in his Secretary of State,[42] Biddle's mercurial spirits rose. He had begun to
perceive the difference between an alliance with Henry Clay and
an alliance with Andrew Jackson.

But he was too late. Though the Livingston negotiations probably would have fizzled out in any event, Thomas Hart Benton
made certain of this by proposing, through Representative Au-
gustin S. Clayton, a new member from Georgia, an investigation
of the bank by a committee of the House. Speaking from notes he
endeavored to conceal because they were in Benton's handwriting,

Clayton enumerated seven thumping violations of the bank's charter and fifteen "abuses" of the same.[43] The bank party was caught off guard. To accede to an investigation would be to surrender the initiative and go into the campaign fighting a defensive battle; to oppose an inquiry would be tantamount to an admission of guilt. There was nothing to do but yield. Whereupon antibank forces scored another victory, obtaining four places on the committee to the bank party's three.

This body was allowed the inadequate space of six weeks in which to conduct its researches. The result was three reports, one by the four majority members, one by two minority members and one by ex-President John Quincy Adams who had begun his long and singular career in the House. If the findings of the majority are to be believed fully—and they cannot be—virtually every charge when Benton had beguiled the inexperienced Clayton into laying before the House, was sustained. Yet these members, overwhelmed by a mass of abstract data thrown upon them by the bank in what appears to have been an attempt to confuse, did establish the dangerous, extra-legal nature of the branch draft system and other questionable points in the bank's conduct, such as leniency in the matter of loans to congressmen. Moreover, they reached behind the scenes and uncovered an interesting corollary to the abrupt switch of the New York *Courier and Enquirer,* the leading Jackson journal in the East, from an anti-bank to a pro-bank policy. A loan of fifteen thousand dollars, made in an irregular way for purposes of concealment, had immediately preceded this change of heart. And once in the bank ranks these useful journalists were quickly advanced thirty-five thousand dollars more.[44]

Where the majority report sought to prove everything, the minority reports sought to refute everything—another impossible task. In this the minority members enjoyed the warm co-operation of the bank officials, including Mr. Biddle, whom later events were to reveal as a too-accomplished explainer, if not a deliberately untruthful witness.[45]

With the bank issue in the campaign, Jackson placed his imprimatur on the report that favored his cause.

10

The investigation over, Biddle assumed personal command of
the bank's Washington lobby and prepared to drive a bill for
recharter through Congress. But unusual moderation tempered
this act of defiance. Several amendments to the existing charter
were incorporated—all in keeping with Jackson's ideas, though
stopping short of the changes to which Biddle had consented
the previous autumn. They included, however, a rectification of
the important branch draft evil. This conciliatory policy won a
few waverers to the bank's side, and even inspired some hope
that Jackson might approve the bill. Without sharing this optimistic expectation, Mr. Biddle drew encouragement from the fact that
McLane, Livingston and Cass had begun to urge upon the President that a veto should be mild, opening the way to further negotiation once the election were over and the issue out of politics.

An interested spectator of these negotiations was Attorney General Roger B. Taney who, since his reverse in December at the
hands of the pro-bank members of the Cabinet, had not mentioned the subject to the President. The events of the seven months
intervening had turned Mr. Taney more than ever against the
bank. En route to court one morning, the Attorney General
shared a hack with a member of the House who was supposed to
be one of the President's personal friends. The member said he
was going to make a speech against the bank bill, and asked Taney
for pointers. When the bill came to a vote, Mr. Taney was surprised to see that the Representative in question had voted for it.
Inquiry elicited the information that he had obtained a loan of
twenty thousand dollars from the bank.

With the final passage of the bill only a matter of days, Mr.
Taney visited the Executive Residence. He told the President that
in his opinion the bill should be met with a positive veto which
would close the door to any expectation that, at some future time,
Jackson would agree to a continuation of the bank. Because he
would be in court at Annapolis when the matter should come to
the Executive for consideration, the Attorney General had put his

reasons in writing. Jackson accepted the paper and said he would be glad to read it, but gave no indication as to his own attitude.

On July 3, 1832, the bill passed the House and Mr. Biddle's friends gave him a banquet. General Jackson summoned his Cabinet, with the exception of Taney who was in Annapolis. He had decided, he said, to return the bill with an uncompromising veto. Not a member of the official family sustained his chief. Importunities were renewed for a veto that would leave Jackson free to approve a modified bill in the future. Offers were made to help in framing such a message. Declining this assistance, the President dismissed the council and set Amos Kendall to work on a message of flat rejection. Kendall turned in a document which Jackson passed on to Donelson for revision. When this proved beyond his nephew's depth Old Hickory sent for Taney.

The Attorney General began his labors in seclusion at the White House, few being aware of his return to the city. On the second day Secretary of the Navy Woodbury, the fence-straddler, came to offer his services. On the third day the message was finished— the work of Taney, Jackson, Kendall and Donelson. On July 10, Jackson sent it to the Capitol.[46] At this juncture Martin Van Buren arrived from London. The President had overtaxed his strength and taken to bed. Holding the deposed diplomat's hand in one of his own and passing the other through his white locks Old Hickory said, "The bank, Mr. Van Buren, is trying to kill me, *but I will kill it.*"[47]

Such was the purpose of the message, destined to become the most widely read and discussed presidential veto in our annals. Since it was, in an important sense, a campaign document designed to cope with Henry Clay's stratagem in bringing the bank into the political vortex, the production contained unbalanced statements and weak though popular arguments. But it also contained sound and cohesive arguments—against the constitutionality of the bank and against the expediency of concentrating so much power in the hands of so few persons irresponsible to the electorate. Nor was this all. With deep and moving conviction, the message gave expression to a social philosophy calculated to achieve a better way of life for the common man.

"Distinctions in society will always exist under every just Government. Equality of talents, of education, or of wealth, can not be produced by human institutions. In the full enjoyment of the gifts of heaven and the fruits of superior industry, economy, and virtue, every man is equally entitled to protection by law. But when the laws undertake to add to these natural and just advantages, artificial distinctions, . . . to make the rich richer and the potent more powerful, the humble members of society, the farmers, mechanics, and laborers, who have neither the time nor the means of securing like favors to themselves, have a right to complain of the injustice of their government. Its evils exist only in its abuses. If it would confine itself to equal protection, and, as heaven does its rains, shower its favors alike on the high and the low, the rich and the poor, it would be an unqualified blessing. In the act before me, there seems to be a wide and unnecessary departure from these just principles."

Thus spoke not the frontier land lawyer and land baron, but the Andrew Jackson who in his canvasses for the presidency had accepted the support of the masses groping for leadership. And characteristically he meant to lead, not to follow, his flock.

That this philosophy and this form of leadership should fail to appeal to Nicholas Biddle is not surprising. "A manifesto of anarchy," he called the message.[48] So convinced of this was Mr. Biddle that he had printed, at the bank's expense, thirty thousand copies of the "manifesto," thinking its circulation would benefit Mr. Clay's campaign. This was not his major effort, however. Although it was at once obvious that Congress would uphold the veto, Mr. Biddle did not intend to let pass an opportunity to get something into the record. The brunt of this duty fell to Daniel Webster, of the bank's standing counsel. On July 11, the Senator from Massachusetts delivered his attack upon the message. Already in the bank's debt twenty-two thousand dollars, the following week he received an additional accommodation in the amount of ten thousand dollars, after which Mr. Biddle distributed one hundred and forty thousand five hundred copies of the address.[49] On July 13 the veto was sustained.

CHAPTER XIV

A Sword Against Disunion

I

WHILE Andrew Jackson was winning in Congress the fight into which Nicholas Biddle and Henry Clay had incautiously plunged the Bank of the United States, the twin-headed question of nullification thrust itself forward.

Elated by the triumph over the United States Supreme Court in the case of Corn Tassel, made possible by the benevolent neutrality of the Executive, Georgia had dealt the Indians another blow. White persons residing in the Cherokee country were ordered to take an oath of allegiance to the State. The New England missionaries, Samuel A. Worcester and Elizur Butler, refused and were imprisoned. The Supreme Court of the United States issued a writ of error which a Federal marshal served on the Governor of Georgia. The Governor denied the court's authority, and again the Georgia Legislature instructed local officers to decline to obey its orders.

In February, 1832, the missionaries' case was argued before a full bench in Washington. No counsel appeared for Georgia. The Chief Justice delivered the opinion of the court, holding that the Federal Government had exclusive jurisdiction over Indian lands and that Georgia was without authority to extend its laws over them. The judgment of the Georgia court was reversed, and a mandate issued calling for the release of Worcester and Butler. This mandate Georgia refused to obey, and again Jackson supported the State's defiance.

"John Marshall has made his decision, now let him enforce it." Years later a Whig congressman from Massachusetts attributed this remark to the President.[1] Jackson may have said it, for he wrote to John Coffee: "The decision of the supreme court has fell still born, and they find it cannot coerce Georgia to yield. . . . If a colision was to take place between them [the Indians] and the Georgians, the arm of the government is not sufficiently strong to preserve them from destruction."[2] This poor plea deceived no one. As much as any man living, Andrew Jackson could give strength to the arm of the government when he chose to do so. "The prerogatives of nullifying laws and political decisions by denying their conformity to the court," observed the *National Journal,* "makes . . . [the President] supreme—the final arbiter—the very Celestial Majesty."[3]

While yielding to the greed of the whites, Jackson endeavored to obtain a measure of practical justice for the Indians. Liberal terms were held out to them to remove peaceably beyond the Mississippi. The Creeks gave in and signed a treaty of evacuation. The Chickasaws signed a second treaty, so that by the end of 1832 only the Cherokees persisted in the struggle to retain the soil of their fathers.

These happenings bolstered the blustery confidence of the South Carolina Nullifiers, led now by the Vice President of the United States. In February a convention adopted menacing resolutions. "The State looks to her sons to defend her in whatever form she may proclaim her purpose to *Resist.*"[4] South Carolina Unionists pinned their hope of averting a crisis to an effort to modify the tariff. Despite the preoccupation of Congress with the bank and presidential politics, an act was passed which Jackson signed the day after the bank veto was sustained. Though far short of what the radicals demanded, the new schedules certainly afforded a basis for amicable parley. But the Nullifiers rode boldly on. At the close of the eventful session in mid-July, 1832, Robert Y. Hayne and a majority of the South Carolina delegation issued an *Address,* calling upon their constituents as the "sovereign power" of the commonwealth to determine whether their liberties should be "tamely surrendered without a struggle or transmitted undiminished to posterity."

Jackson took notice of the declaration in his parting words to a South Carolina congressman who was setting out for home.

"Tell . . . [the Nullifiers] from me that they can talk and write resolutions and print threats to their hearts' content. But if one drop of blood be shed there in defiance of the laws of the United States I will hang the first man of them I can get my hands on to the first tree I can find." In Benton's hearing, South Carolina's senior Senator expressed a doubt as to whether the President would go that far. "I tell you, Hayne," the Missourian replied, "when Jackson begins to talk about hanging, they can begin to look for the ropes."[5]

2

By this time the campaign was in its stride. A carefully timed entrance had returned Mr. Van Buren to his native shore, not in the rôle of repudiated public servant, but a party hero duly designated by a convention in Baltimore as Jackson's running mate. In 1824 Andrew Jackson had suffered the sort of defeat that solidifies a party. In 1828 he had won the kind of victory that tends to divide it, coalitions being impermanent by nature. But again the country was treated to the spectacle of common rules being without effect where Old Hickory was concerned. After some more or less deliberate pruning, such as the elimination of Mr. Calhoun, the President had knit the patch-work of 'Twenty-eight into a political machine of which he was the master. In the Eaton affair and in other matters, Mr. Van Buren had attained some distinction as a "magician." At the Baltimore convention, Jackson returned these favors in kind by making the New Yorker virtually the unanimous choice of the delegates for Vice President. A suggestion of the iron fist in the velvet glove was responsible for that appearance of unity, the Magician being far from the actual preference of Jackson men in many sections of the West and the South.

While uniting his own adherents, General Jackson divided those of the opposition. Henry Clay and his National Republican Party had won over Webster on the bank issue and most of the Calhoun group because they believed Clay the only man with a chance against Jackson. But the Kentuckian was unable to bring into his camp a curious political sect known as the Anti-Masons. This group had its beginning in western New York in 1826 when William Morgan, a wandering stone-setter, was kidnapped for attempted exposure of the secrets of Freemasonry and never seen again. By 1832 the Anti-Masons were fairly well organized in several states. Jackson's militant pride in his record as a Mason precluded union with Old Hickory's followers. The Anti-Masons, therefore, nominated for the presidency, William Wirt, Attorney General under Mr. Adams and more recently counsel for the Cherokee Indians in their actions against Georgia.

Frank Blair shortened the name National Republicans to "Nationals." Duff Green's *Telegraph,* wearing the livery of Mr. Clay, flung back "Democrats" at the Democratic Republicans, as the Jackson people called themselves.[6] The great issue was "Czar Nicholas" and his "hydra of corruption" which Blair accused of bribing statesmen and buying editors, charges the defenders of the institution were unable entirely to refute. Liberty-loving commoners were pictured at grips with the moneyed aristocrats. Senator Isaac Hill's *New Hampshire Patriot* struck a less impersonal note: "Twenty-one Reasons Why Henry Clay Should Not Be Elected President," reason number twenty being, "Because . . . he spends his days at the gaming table and his nights in a brothel."[7] Even scholarly William Cullen Bryant, editor of the decorous New York *Evening Post,* fell so far under the spell of the Hero as to cane a Clay supporter on Broadway.

The well-furnished purses of the opposition insured an equally spirited contest against "King Andrew I." The social status of Mrs. Eaton was engagingly discussed, point being lent to the case by her husband's effort to recapture, with General Jackson's blessing, the seat of Felix Grundy in the Senate. The spoils system and the incongruity of Martin Van Buren as a champion of the proletariat came in for lusty whacks. But mainly the Nationals stuck to the economic issue and a campaign of fear. The bank tried to frighten borrowers, with the exception of a few preferred editors and statesmen. Borrowers endeavored to pass on the shock. A Cincinnati wholesaler offered two dollars and fifty cents a hundred for pork in event Mr. Clay should win, a dollar fifty in event he lost. A Pennsylvania manufacturer laid off his hands until after election. A Clay newspaper in Pittsburgh announced a suspension of steamboat building along the Ohio.

In August Jackson went to Tennessee, making part of the journey on horseback. Wayside bills were paid in gold, which the bank in the effort to retrieve itself from the follies of over-expansion had almost driven from circulation. "No more paper money you see, fellow citizens, if I can only put down this Nicholas Biddle and his monster bank."[8] Long letters from the President to Jack Donelson reported Sarah's pregnancy and the state of roads, crops, stock and negroes. Politics was mentioned incidentally. "The veto works well. . . . Instead of crushing me it will crush the Bank."[9] To Hill he observed, "Isaac, it'll be a walk." The remark moved Benton to increase his election bets.[10]

Nor was the President especially aroused by the warning that "Nullification continues to rumble like distant thunder in the south."[11] "Calhoun is prostrate," Jackson replied. "I heard one of his best former friends say . . . he ought to be hung." Moreover, this "friend" had offered to march with ten thousand volunteers against the Nullifiers. "These," observed Old Hickory, "are and must be the sentiments of all honest men."[12]

3

That they were not the prevailing sentiments in Charleston General Jackson was soon to learn. He acted instantly. "To the Secretary of the Navy, *Confidential.* . . . *Efforts have been made, and perhaps not without success* . . . to disaffect the Officer of the Navy in command at charlston. . . . The idea is . . . to prevent a blockade. *This must be guarded against.*" The squadron at Norfolk was ordered ready for sea.[13] In September the Nullifiers swept the State elections in South Carolina. On the heels of this, word reached the Hermitage that officers in command of the Regular troops at Charleston were prepared to surrender the harbor forts.

Ordering the garrisons replaced by detachments of unquestioned loyalty, Jackson left post haste for Washington. "My dear Sarah," he wrote en route, "yesterday and today [I] traveled 70 miles

"KING ANDREW I"

A cartoon of the campaign of 1832. From the Library of Congress collection.

thro a broken country. . . . Until I hear of your confinement and safe delivery I shall have great anxiety."[14] And again: "My Dr. Sarah I regretted most of all being prevented from . . . visiting with you & Andrew alone [at] the tomb of my Dr departed wife. . . . When you visit me in the winter I trust we will be more to ourselves. I am happy to learn that all the necessary precautions have been taken to prepare you for your confinement. . . . Dr. Sarah your affectionate father ANDREW JACKSON."[15]

Ominous tidings awaited the President at the capital: South Carolina hopelessly in the hands of the extremists; the staffs of the customs houses corrupted; a call out for a convention to proclaim nullification of the revenue laws; demands for troops to "defend" the State against Federal "aggression." But the Navy was ready, the Charleston garrisons had been changed, and Major General Winfield Scott hurried south to command them. "The Secretary of War," further directed the President, "will cause secrete orders to be Issued to the officers commanding the Forts in the harbour of charleston So Carolina . . . to prevent a surprise in the night or by day. . . . *The attempt will be* made . . . by the militia, and must be . . . repelled with prompt and exemplary punishment."[16]

Frank Blair interrupted to present some campaign reports. "Thank you, sir," said the President, and putting down the papers he launched into a denunciation of the Nullifiers. The editor noted that the lines of the President's face "were hard drawn, his tones full of wrath and resentment."[17] Early in November, while the first returns from the polling places were coming in, Jackson received word of a plot to assassinate him,[18] and Jack Donelson heard from a neighbor that Sarah had been in labor for two or three days and was doing poorly. Ignoring the threatened assassination, Old Hickory rebuked Sarah's husband. "Why do you not write me— her fate must be sealed ere this."[19]

National Republicans and Anti-Masons had united on the same electoral slate in New York. National victories in a few state elections in August and September gave Mr. Clay's party further last-minute encouragement. But Andrew Jackson was not running on those state tickets. The earliest news from the presidential contest indicated a triumph for Old Hickory so overpowering that one opposition editor confessed he had "no heart to publish election returns."[20] But for this delicacy of feeling readers of the *Vermont Journal* might have learned sooner than they did that the popular vote for Jackson was six hundred and sixty-one thousand; for Clay, three hundred thousand; for the Clay-Wirt ticket in New York, one hundred and fifty-four thousand; for Wirt, one hundred thousand. The electoral vote was Jackson, two hundred seventeen; Clay, forty-nine; Wirt, seven.[21]

Some of the more enthusiastic Jackson newspapers nominated the General for a third term. "My opinion," observed ex-Candidate Wirt, "is that he may be President for life if he chooses."[22]

The victor cherished other desires. "What would I not give to be free . . . and in retirement at the Hermitage.[23] . . . The best thing about this [huge plurality], gentlemen, is that it strengthens my hands in this [nullification] trouble."[24]

Strong hands were needed. On the Executive's desk lay a dispatch from Joel R. Poinsett, the Unionist leader in South Carolina. "Grenades and small rockets are excellent weapons in a street fight." Mr. Poinsett had learned that in Mexico. "I would like to have some of them."[25]

The weapons sent,[26] the white-haired soldier bided the future more tranquil in mind than at any time since he had left Tennessee. For General Jackson was a grandfather; and Sarah was well; and they had named the baby Rachel. "I feel deeply indebted to you and my dear Sarah," he wrote to Andrew, junior. "Shall I be spared it will be a great pleasure to watch over and rear up the sweet little Rachel, and make her a fair emblem of her for whom she is called."[27]

4

Sergeant Sam Dale, a hero of the Creek and the Louisiana campaigns, had risen to become a general of Mississippi militia. After the election Dale appeared in Washington but was too modest to join the press of visitors that besieged his old commander. Whereupon Jackson sent Senator King of Alabama to bring in the veteran. The Mississippian found the President in the upstairs study discussing nullification with Benton and five or six others. Jackson put the visitor at ease by addressing his remarks to him. "General Dale, if this thing goes on our country will be like a bag of meal with both ends open. Pick it up and it will run out."

When the company took its leave, the President placed a decanter of whisky beside his friend. Jackson himself, never a heavy drinker, had abandoned the use of hard liquor almost entirely though he bought it by the barrel for his guests. At meal-time he would take a glass or two of wine and, though the White House table was famous, he dined sparingly, favoring the old army diet of rice.

They talked until late. "Sam, you have been true to your country, but you have made one mistake in life. You are now old and solitary, without a family to comfort you." Jackson started to speak of his wife but his eyes filled and he took a few turns of the room. "Dale," he said, at length, "they are trying me here; you will witness it; but, by the God in Heaven, I will uphold the laws."

General Dale expressed the hope that things would go right.

"They SHALL go right, sir!" exclaimed Old Hickory, bringing his hand down on a table so hard that he broke one of his pipes.

The President had a great collection of pipes. Admirers sent them from all parts of the world. "These will do to look at," he said, showing Dale the fancy specimens. "[But] I still smoke my corn cob, Sam. It is the sweetest and best pipe."[28]

South Carolina moved swiftly to precipitate a crisis before Congress should assemble. On November 24, 1832, the tariff acts were proclaimed void and not "binding upon this State or its citizens," after February 1, 1833. The truculent State declared that the use of force in an attempt to collect the duties after that date would be met by secession. Jackson jotted down a memorandum for his own eye. "South Carolina has passed her ordinance. . . . As soon as it can be had in authentic form, meet it with a proclamation. Nullification has taken deep root in Virginia, it must be arrested . . . by a full appeal . . . to the good sense of the people."[29]

In the case of South Carolina, the President continued his preparations to supplement this projected mode of persuasion. Seven revenue cutters and a ship of war were sent to Charleston. They anchored off the Battery, their guns commanding the fashionable waterfront lined with the homes and brick-walled gardens of the city's elect. General Scott strengthened harbor defenses against attack from the land side. With the Charleston post office in the hands of Nullifiers, a courier service was established to keep Jackson in constant touch with Joel Poinsett. "No state or states," the President wrote the leader of the Unionists, "has a right to secede. . . . Nullification therefore means insurrection and war; and other states have a right to put it down.[30] . . . [In this position] I am assured by all the members with whom I have conversed that I will be sustained by congress. If so, I will meet it at the threshold, and have the leaders arrested and arraigned for treason. . . . In forty days I can have within the limits of So. Carolina fifty thousand men, and in forty days more another fifty thousand."[31]

Elsewhere than in South Carolina anxious eyes turned toward Andrew Jackson. "Those who but yesterday," said Senator George M. Dallas of Pennsylvania, "opposed your re-election with ferocity now loudly profess their reliance on your saving the Union."[32]

Congress convened amid great excitement, which the President's message did little to allay. This document seemed poor company for the martial alarms and even more threatening private assertions of General Jackson. Its tone was conciliatory. Further tariff reductions were recommended and nothing said of resisting nullification by force. "The message," remarked John Quincy Adams, "goes to dissolve the Union . . . and is a complete surrender to the nullifiers."[33] Others asked if the intention were to permit South Carolina to emulate Georgia's successful defiance of the Federal Government. Nullifiers took heart. That scarred knight of the state sovereignty cause, Randolph of Roanoke, proffered the service of his lance to South Carolina and insinuatingly wrote the President: "You are now in a situation to recede with d[ignity]."[34]

There was no recession. On the day the message was read to Congress, Edward Livingston was engaged on Jackson's answer to the country's question, with Old Hickory peering over the Secretary's shoulder as he worked. "I submit the above as the conclusion of the proclamation," prompted the President. "Let it receive your best flight of eloquence. . . . The Union must be preserved, without blood if this be possible, but it must be preserved at all hazards and at any price."[35]

The Proclamation on Nullification was given to the world on December 10, 1832. The words are Livingston's, the initiative, the thought and the spirit Jackson's, comprising in all the greatest state paper of the spacious Jacksonian Epoch and one of the greatest to bear the name of an American president.

By skillful blending of argument, entreaty and warning the Executive addressed himself to the intelligence, the pride, the interests and the fears of the citizens of South Carolina; and he sought to unite the rest of the nation against the recalcitrant State.

Nullification was branded an "impractical absurdity." "If this doctrine had been established at an earlier day the Union would have been dissolved in its infancy. . . . Admit this doctrine and . . . every law . . . for raising revenue . . . may be annulled. . . . I consider, then, the power to annul a law of the United States, assumed by one State, incompatible with the existence of the Union, contradicted expressly by the letter of the Constitution, unauthorized by its spirit, inconsistent with every principle on which it was founded, and destructive of the great object for which it was formed."

The right of secession was categorically denied. "The Constitution . . . forms a *government* not a league. . . . To say that any State may at pleasure secede from the Union is to say that the United States is not a nation." Relief from burdens of which South Carolina complained was foreshadowed by the "approaching payment of the public debt." But meanwhile the laws would be enforced.

"Fellow-citizens of my native State, let me admonish you. . . . I have no discretionary power on the subject. . . . Those who told you that you might peaceably prevent . . . [the execution of the laws] deceived you. . . . Their object is disunion. . . . Disunion by armed force is treason. Are you really ready to incur its guilt? If you are, on the heads of the instigators of the act be dreadful consequences. . . . [Your] first magistrate cannot, if he would, avoid the performance of his duty. . . .

"ANDREW JACKSON

"By the President:
"EDW. LIVINGSTON, *Secretary of State.*"[36]

Bonfires blazed, bells rang, men paraded. Military volunteers offered themselves, state legislatures denounced nullification. John Quincy Adams and Daniel Webster joined the President promptly and cordially. Embittered Henry Clay's tongue fell silent. In Illinois a village lawyer and captain of volunteers, lately returned from participation in a detail of Indian swindling which history obscures behind the respectable name of the Black Hawk War, pored over the proclamation. In 1861 Abraham Lincoln was to read it again before composing his inaugural address.

5

The story in South Carolina was different. "Gen Jackson's extraordinary proclamation has just reached me," wrote James H. Hammond, an editor of Columbia, to Robert Y. Hayne, who had resigned his Senate seat for the governorship of the embattled State. "Upon the timid and ignorant of our party I fear it will have great influence."[37] So did Hayne, who splashed his signature upon a counter-proclamation in which the Governor promised to maintain the sovereignty of South Carolina or perish "beneath its ruins." Proffers of military service poured upon the state Executive; calls for commissions, for pistols, sabers, powder and ball; for Hoyt's *Tactics* and an " 'Abstract for the Manoeuvres of Infantry' adopted by the last Legislature." Hayne concentrated on the organization of *"Mounted Minute Men"* to enable him to throw "2,500 of the *elite* of the whole state upon a given point in three or four days. . . . The uniform of my staff will be the same as my Predecessors except *under boots* and a *short yellow crane* Plume.

Palmetto Buttons of a beautiful pattern may be had at Roche's, Charleston."[38]

Union men refused to be overawed. "God and Old Hickory are with us."[39] Either would have sufficed Poinsett who continued to arm his men and to drill them at night.

John C. Calhoun quit these tense scenes to start north with the intention of resigning the vice presidency and taking the place in the Senate vacated by Hayne. The journey required courage. Friends of years' standing turned their backs. The curious gathered at every stage stop to start at the man who, rumor said, would enter Washington a prisoner under charge of treason; and it seems more than probable that only the absence of an armed clash between the opposing forces in South Carolina averted this. Pale but determined, the South Carolinian walked into the Senate chamber on January 4, 1833, and swore to uphold and defend the Constitution of the United States.

Jackson charted a direct course. "I am now waiting," he apprized Van Buren, "for the [official] information from the assembly of So. Carolina of their having passed their laws for raising an army to resist the execution of the laws, which will be a levying of war, and I will make a communication to Congress . . . ask[ing] power to call upon volunteers to serve as a posse commitatus of the civil authority. . . . If the Assembly authorises twelve thousand men to resist the law, I will order thirty thousand to execute [it]".[40] Leaders of nullification would be seized wherever found "regardless of the force that surrounds them, [and] deliver[ed] into the hands of the judicial authority of the United States" to be tried for treason.[41] The President was already scrutinizing an inventory of infantry, cavalry and artillery weapons in the custody of the War Department. "Tenders of service is coming to me daily and from Newyork we can send to the bay of charleston with steamers such number of troops as we may be pleased to order, in four days."[42]

On to this lively stage stepped comely Fanny Kemble, the English actress. She charmed Henry Clay and made John Marshall weep. Webster paid for his visit to the theatre with a cold. Aware that history was unfolding before her eyes, the visitor faithfully recorded impressions. Washington struck her as a "rambling red-brick image of futurity where nothing *is* but all things *are to be*. At night the scattered lights of the town looked like a capricious congregation of Jack-o'-lanterns, some high, some low, some here, some there, showing more distinctly by the dark spaces between them the enormous share that emptiness has in this congressional city." The envied Representative who escorted Miss Kemble through the Capitol said he had just left the President in a stern frame of mind. "They say the old General is longing for a fight," Fanny confided to her journal.

The Donelsons and Miss Mary Coffee, visiting from Alabama, attended the theatre, after which came the prized opportunity to call on the President. "Very tall and thin, but erect and dignified in his carriage," noted Miss Kemble, who used superlatives sparingly, "a good specimen of fine old well-battered soldier. . . . His manners are perfectly simple and quiet, therefore very good; so are those of his niece, Mrs. —— [Donelson], who is a very pretty person. . . . Of his measures I know nothing, but firmness, determination, decision, I respect above all things; and if the old General is, as they say, very obstinate, why obstinacy is so far more estimable than weakness, *especially* in a ruler, that I think he sins on the right side of the question."[43]

6

Martin Van Buren would have preferred Fanny Kemble's acting to her opinion of General Jackson's attitude toward South Carolina. Remaining circumspectly aloof in Albany, the Vice President-elect moved subtly to modify the chieftain's Draconian impulses. "You will say I am on my old track—caution—caution—caution: but my Dr Sir I have always thought that considering our respective temperaments there was no way perhaps in which I could better render you service."[44] The New Yorker politely disagreed with Jackson's contention that the mere raising of troops by South Carolina constituted actual treason.[45] Constructive treason it might be, but constructive treason was a vague accusation so abused in Europe that it was bound to be unpopular with Ameri-

"A Fine Old Well-Battered Soldier"

The characterization of Fanny Kemble, the English actress, who saw Jackson during the nullification crisis in 1833. The portrait, by Earl, is owned by the Ladies' Hermitage Association, Nashville.

cans. The President's adviser went so far as to "regret" the inclusion in the famous proclamation of certain "doctrinal points,"
meaning, at bottom, Jackson's flat denial of the right of a state to
secede. He said this was borrowing trouble. It had offended Virginia. Besides, "South Carolina has not and will not secede."
Even if she did, would not the question of bringing her back by
force be better decided by Congress than by the Executive? The
letter closed with an intimation that a gesture toward tariff reduc-
tion might pave the way to a happy solution of everything.[46]

Mr. Van Buren's anxieties arose chiefly from the fact that, like
many others, he regarded the crisis through the spectacles of
partizan politics. This northern statesman had threaded his way
to national eminence in candid alliance with southern state-rights
leaders, notably those of Virginia. He feared the political aftermath of a break with them now. On the other hand Jackson had
thrown such considerations to the winds, placing himself mili-
tantly at the head of the union sentiment of the nation, irrespective of person or party.[47]

Yet the man of caution had raised two points which the man of
action could not ignore:

The first concerned the definition of actual treason and the
constitutional right of the Executive to intervene in a state's
affairs. Legally he could intervene only (1) at the request of the
Governor to suppress insurrection, or (2) on his own initiative,
to enforce the laws of Congress. In the latter case no clear procedure existed. In the past it had been contemplated that a Federal
officer might summon a *posse comitatus* to aid in this duty. But,
when Jackson notified Poinsett that in event of emergency his
newly formed unionist military companies would be called to act
as a *posse,* they objected. The word did not have the right ring.
They preferred to be a part of the United States Army, which
would give them the status of prisoners of war if captured.[48] The
President promised to take the subject before Congress.

The second restraining consideration centered upon the necessity of keeping state-rightists in other commonwealths from making common cause with South Carolina. To South Carolina's
surprise and discomfiture the high-hearted words of the proclama-

tion had stunned most of that crowd into silence. Then came the parade of resolutions from state legislatures which, under pressure from Administration sources where necessary, soon were to isolate South Carolina from the declared support of a single state.

These circumstances constituted a salutary triumph for Jackson's leadership, a triumph which made things look better for him than they really were. The President was able to cheer Poinsett with the assurance that "the national voice from Main to Louisiana . . . declares . . . nullification and secession consigned to contempt and infamy."[49] But to a confidential friend he wrote: "There are more nullifiers here than dare avow it,"[50] and it was true. Virginia incurred Jackson's wrath by coupling to her resolution a proposal to mediate between South Carolina and the general government, and authorizing an agent to proceed to Columbia. New York legislators sat on their hands until a stiff letter from Jackson moved them to act. Then the resolution Mr. Van Buren wrote for them was so sleek and mild that the President filed it away without a word of comment.[51] Only the President's beneficent Indian policy averted difficulty in Georgia, Mississippi and Alabama. General John Coffee, wintering with his old comrade in the White House, wrote a relative in Memphis, "Nullification will be put down, but it has taken deeper root in the Southern States than any one could have supposed."[52]

While moving to cut off South Carolina from outside sympathy and succor, the President permitted an extension of the olive branch. In the last days of December Representative Verplanck of New York laid before the House a hastily drawn bill calling for heavy reductions of the tariff duties. This was no fresh or enforced concession. The principle was in keeping with a promise implied in the proclamation.

Such was the only offer of accommodation to the Nullifiers countenanced by Andrew Jackson.

7

The offer made, Old Hickory plowed grimly on rebuking the sly Van Buren, encouraging staunch Poinsett.

"No, my friend," reiterated the Executive to the Vice President-elect, . . . "[your policy] would destroy all confidence in our government both at home and abroad. . . . I expect soon to hear that a civil war has commenced. . . . [If] the leaders . . . are surrounded with 12,000 bayonets our marshall shall be aided by 24,000 and arrest them in the midst thereof."[53]

Silas Wright, whom Mr. Van Buren had just made a senator from New York, forwarded further disturbing details of the presidential state of mind. "He does not expect that . . . [any thing can] prevent an open rupture." Before a room filled with company, Wright had heard Jackson tell of a steamer sailing from Charleston with the stars and stripes upside down. "'Sir,' said the old Gentleman, 'for this indignity to the flag she ought to have been instantly sunk, no matter who owned or commanded her.'"[54]

In the same crowded drawing room, the President spoke of the advisability of "disciplining" Calhoun and Hayne[55] as an object lesson to others. General Jackson could be something of an artist at dropping apparently unguarded expressions. Flying from tongue to tongue in the nervous capital, such threats grew with repetition. In the fullness of time, Congressman Letcher of Kentucky, so one story goes, called at the White House to learn the President's true intentions. Old Hickory said that "if one more step was taken he would try Calhoun for treason and, if convicted, hang him as high as Haman." In the middle of the night the South Carolina Senator is said to have been called from his bed to hear this not improbable tale. "There sat Calhoun," related a contemporary apt to improve a story in the telling, "drinking in eagerly every word, . . . pale as death and . . . [trembling] like an aspen leaf."[56]

Beyond doubt Jackson had them scared—Nullifiers and near-Nullifiers alike, along with political tight-rope performers of the Van Buren stamp. And not in Washington alone did knees shake behind façades of bravado. In December the President had said he would suspend positive action awaiting officially certified copies of the acts of the South Carolina Legislature giving effect to the ordinance of nullification. When these failed to arrive

Jackson shot off a courier to fetch them. Ten days passed without word from the courier. It was January 16, 1833. Fifteen days remained until February 1 when the ordinance and supporting decrees were to go into force. Jackson waited no longer. Acting without the official copies, he asked Congress for authority to use military force to collect the customs. This would mitigate legalistic scruples about employing troops.

But what if Congress, in that short time, should fail to convey the power requested? Andrew Jackson was ready for the contingency. He would take unto himself the power, stretching the Constitution to suit the needs of the case. "The preservation of the Union is the supreme law."[57] On January 24 seven days remained in which to act before the first of February. The inability of Congress to agree on a bill seemed imminent. A hurried scrawl to Poinsett left Washington by night.

"Should congress fail to act, . . . [and should] So. Carolina oppose the execution of the revenue laws . . . [with] an armed force . . . I stand prepared to issue my proclamation warning them to disperse. should they fail to comply I will . . . in ten or fifteen days at farthest have in charleston ten to fifteen thousand well organized troops well equipped for the field, and twenty thousand, or thirty, more in their [sic] interior. I have a tender of volunteers from every state in the union. I can if need be, which god forbid, march two hundred thousand men in forty days to quell any and every insurrection that might arise." Should the Governor of Virginia attempt to prevent the passage of regiments bound for South Carolina, "I would arrest him at the head of his troops. . . .

"I repeat to the union men, fear not, *the union will be preserved.* . . . It is very late and my eyes grow dim. Keep me well advised, and constantly. . . . I keep no copy nor have I time to correct this letter. In haste. . . . ANDREW JACKSON."[58]

On the next day the President's proclamation was ready.[59] So were preparations to call on the governors of New York—Martin Van Buren, please note—Pennsylvania, Virginia—local Nullifiers ditto—North Carolina, Ohio, Tennessee, Alabama, Georgia and

South Carolina for thirty-five thousand men "ready to march at a moment's warning."[60]

Martin Van Buren later said that Andrew Jackson yearned to lead this force in person.[61] Who can doubt it for an instant?

But the proclamation was never issued; the requisitions on the governors never sent. The courier who bore the President's letter of January 24 to Poinsett passed a messenger hurrying northward with news that South Carolina had yielded. Jackson's awesome mobilization had been too much for the Nullifiers' nerves. On January 21 they had suspended their belligerent ordinance pending the outcome of the tariff debate.[62] Moving in an almost straight line, Old Hickory had outmaneuvered his foemen at every point and, sword in hand, faced them down.

8

The sword having had its vital hour, the time had come for the pen, and for many tongues. The major responsibility shifted to the halls of Congress, where the removal of the time limit encouraged loquacity. Although it was still known as an Administration measure, General Jackson had lost much of his early interest in Verplanck's tariff bill which, weighed down with amendments, made little headway. But the President insisted on the enactment, without one barb blunted, of the "Force Bill," or "Bloody Bill," as opponents variously called the measure authorizing the use of the military to collect the Government revenue. The demand unleashed an oratorical onslaught which John Tyler carried to a climax.

The Senator from Virginia called Charleston a "beleagured city." Suppose, he said, this bill were to pass and "the proud spirit of South Carolina" should decline to submit. Would we then "make war upon her, hang her Governor, . . . and reduce her to the condition of a conquered province?" Mr. Tyler saw South Carolina's towns leveled, her daughters in mourning, her men driven "into the morasses where Marion found refuge." But he did not see them conquered. Rome had her Curtis, Sparta her Leonidas—and South Carolina had John C. Calhoun.

Mr. Calhoun did not repudiate the heroic part. "I proclaim it," said he, "that should this bill pass . . . it will be resisted at every hazard—even that of death."

Daniel Webster followed the South Carolinian. When he finished, the lamps in the Senate chamber had been lighted. Major Lewis hurried to the White House with an evaluation of the scene which the President passed on to Poinsett. "Mr. Webster replied to Mr. Calhoun yesterday . . . handled him like a child. . . . Keep me constantly advised of all movements in South Carolina."[63]

Oblivious to threat and to political entreaty, Jackson refused to give an inch. He insisted on the passage of the Force Bill. The last ten days of February were at hand, and on March 2 Congress must adjourn. Jackson could be angered by delay, but he could not be beaten. The votes to pass the Force Bill were pledged. Only something akin to a miracle could relieve John C. Calhoun of the unpleasant option of capitulating or of validating his menacing words.

The situation afforded Henry Clay, a practiced dispenser of parliamentary miracles, the opportunity that he sought. On the Force Bill the Kentucky Senator had been silent; he could not uphold nullification, and he would not uphold Jackson. The tariff, however, was Clay's specialty, and in this field he saw a number of serviceable possibilities: reconciliation between South Carolina and the general government; Calhoun rescued from his perilous position; something of the protective system saved from the devastations of the Verplanck Bill; Henry Clay in the rôle of pacifier instead of Martin Van Buren as would be the case should Verplanck's measure go through. The outcome was a bewildering maneuver which Clay counted on Calhoun's desperation to crown with success. As an independent "compromise," he introduced a bill which in ten years would lower tariffs by twenty per cent. The Verplanck Bill would cut them that much in two years or less. Yet Calhoun, sweating blood, was dragooned into supporting Clay's measure on the strange ground that it was promulgated as a compromise to which South Carolina could accede with dignity, notwithstanding the fact that the Administration bill embodied the more liberal terms.

This metaphysical proposition agreed to, the Force Bill was called up for a vote in the Senate. Mr. Calhoun and all his supporters except one left the chamber. Irate John Tyler of Virginia stayed and cast the only negative vote. Jackson ordered his congressional captains to drive the bill on through the House ahead of Clay's tariff.[64] Skillfully the Kentuckian spread the meshes of delay, and Jackson's captains failed. On the last day but one of the session, the two measures—Jackson's Force Bill and Clay's tariff—finished their legislative journeys together and at the same hour came to the President's desk. Old Hickory winced as he signed the tariff bill. South Carolina would make the most of the opportunity to accept peace from the hands of Mr. Clay rather than from those of General Jackson. But veto the bill he could not; that would be pushing Calhoun too far.

9

On Old Hickory's sixty-sixth birthday, March 15, 1833, South Carolina rescinded her ordinance of nullification. Snatched from the brink of civil war, the nation gave way to rejoicing that lifted Andrew Jackson's popularity to a pinnacle not before attained by a President of the United States. Daniel Webster extolled the Executive in a public address and Washington heard that, in event of the retirement of the aged John Marshall, the Senator from Massachusetts would be Chief Justice.

General Jackson regarded the demonstrations with sober mien. Twenty years as a popular idol had rendered him somewhat immune to the dangers of an excess of acclaim. His sensitive intuitions perceived too well the ever-tangling skein of our national life to accept the recent events as a cause for unqualified congratulation. With the plaudits of millions ringing in his ears, Jackson's private estimate of his accomplishment was modest. "Nullification and secession are for the present, I think, effectively, and I hope forever put down. But the coalition between Clay and Calhoun, combined . . . with a few nullifiers in Virginia and Poindexter [of Mississippi] and his coadjuters in the south and southwest portends no good, but much evil."[65] But the late crisis had ended more tamely than Jackson had reckoned on. "I thought I w^d. have to hang some of them & [I] wd. have done it."[66]

Charleston gave a "victory ball" for volunteers who had taken up arms against "the invader." It was easy to smile at the face-saving device; too easy. The President observed and reflected deeply. He knew the real issue to be slavery—as yet untouched and almost unavowed. From the shadow of the gallows John C. Calhoun emerged with a new and sinister prestige. In Virginia John Tyler responded to the toast, "Nullification the rightful and, as it proved, the efficient remedy." Andrew Jackson saw that the viper he had set out to kill was only scotched. "The nullifiers in the south intend to blow up a storm on the slave question. . . . This ought to be met, for be assured these men would do any act to destroy this union and form a southern confederacy bounded, north, by the Potomac river."[67]

As time furnished a clearer perspective on these scenes, many who had been in the thick of them came to believe that, had the resolute old man had his way with South Carolina in 1833, our national annals would have borne fewer blood stains in the end. Among these was Henry Clay who lived to regret the day he had stayed the upraised arm of Andrew Jackson.[68]

CHAPTER XV

"A KNIGHTLY PERSONAGE"

I

ON THE last official day of his first term of office, the President was about to sit down to dinner when word came that the House of Representatives had adopted the following:

"Resolved, that Government deposits may, in the opinion of the House, be safely continued in the Bank of the United States."

The parting slap was delivered with the combined strength of Henry Clay, John C. Calhoun and the pro-bank men of Jackson's own party. This performance took place twenty-four hours after the House, at Mr. Clay's bidding, had finished its equivocal part in the drama of nullification.

Old Hickory did not enjoy his dinner. With fire in his eyes, he drove to the Capitol, as precedent had established for these last hours, to sit in the little-used President's Room until Congress should adjourn *sine die.* John Coffee went with him—a fortunate choice of companion, for the nerves of Old Hickory were fraying. Few men have known the blessings of a deeper or more satisfactory friendship than John Coffee gave Andrew Jackson. The big, even-keeled, slow-spoken man who had commanded the left wing of the line of battle at New Orleans was a natural sedative to the other's temper. Though often invited, this was his first visit to Washington during his friend's presidency, and the last. He had kept Jackson company throughout the critical winter.

The presidential vigil did little to shorten the deliberations of the law-makers. As the night wore on bottles appeared on the desks. Half a dozen tipsy members of the House were on their feet at once. Rulings of the Chair were howled down. In shadowy ante-rooms, members of the bank's well-staffed lobby rubbed their hands with satisfaction. One such functionary, previously distinguished as the go-between in Mr. Biddle's purchase of the New York *Enquirer's* support, felt the historical impact of the scene. Snatching a moment he indited a message to his chief: "We have met the enemy and they are ours."[1] Two or three congressmen found time to use their pens. "I hope you will all feel satisfied with what has been done," reported the pliant tool, John Watmough of Pennsylvania, with the bland recommendation that Mr. Biddle open his purse to certain other members of the House.[2]

Hour after hour Jackson sat with John Coffee reading, writing, chatting of family things and bygone times. Although no other hostile resolutions received parliamentary recognition, Administration floor leaders, including the ordinarily efficacious James K. Polk, seemed powerless to stem the pointless talk—a situation upon which one student of causes and effects, Sam Houston, may have shed some light when he pronounced Polk a victim of the use of water as a beverage. Dawn of Sunday, March 3, 1833, was sketching in the profile of the low hills on the far side of the Anacostia when a delegation waited on the President to say that, if he had no further communications, their colleagues were prepared to adjourn. The Executive had no further communications. Whereupon the Twenty-second Congress of the United States reeled into history and its personnel into bed. President Jackson's first four years were behind him.

2

On the following day he began his second term with an inaugural as simple as Jefferson's. Snow covered the ground and thermometers stood at eleven degrees above zero. Outdoor arrangements were given up. Its floor cleared of broken glass, the House chamber served as the scene for administering the oath. No reception was held at the Executive Residence. Before dinnertime the President said goodnight and withdrew to his bedroom, leaving Jack and Emily Donelson, Andrew, junior, and Sarah,

General Coffee and his daughter Mary, Lucius Polk and his wife Mary Eastin, Mary McLemore and R. E. W. Earl to represent the White House at the two inaugural balls.

As the General lay in bed turning the pages of Rachel's Bible, he hoped this quiet day might be prophetic. But would it? The incomplete nature of the victory over nullification, the prospect of the preservation of an harassing alliance between Clay and Calhoun, the stirring up of the bank issue even before the ghost of disunion was laid: these were vexing things. Though Andrew Jackson could look ahead from a height of personal popularity not scaled by another President, the burdens of the winter had sapped his strength. Now that a lull in the battle had come, suddenly he felt very old again and so tired and homesick that for almost the first time in his life Andrew Jackson admitted the need for rest and restoration. As ever, he looked longingly toward the Hermitage and the prospects of a visit there.

Yet the White House was a pleasanter abode and Washington a more sightly city than in 1829. A strip forty-five feet wide in the middle of expansive Pennsylvania Avenue had been paved. The grounds of the Executive Residence had been regraded, graveled walks laid and trees planted. The Mansion's pillared portico facing Pennsylvania Avenue was completed, giving the northern exterior the appearance it exhibits today. A show-place carriage house and stable, with stalls for ten horses, had supplanted the barn and sheds of wartime construction. Two friendly pumps were gone from the east and west yards, and the house was provided with running water, including hot and cold shower baths.

Life within doors retained the agreeable pattern re-established after the departure of Bellona. The young folk of courting age and the children remained the General's abiding joys. Emily's eldest, Andrew Jackson who was six, had his own pony and rode with his great uncle. Mary Rachel (Martin Van Buren her godfather) was three. Another baby was to arrive in May. When measles took them down in a row, the President fretted as much as their mother. He could hear a cry in the nursery as quickly as she. To encounter the General in the middle of the night making his way along the dim corridor to see that all was right with his "pets" was no rare occurrence. A new tooth, a first step, were attainments apt to take precedence in his family letters over the concerns of statecraft. When absent he worried constantly lest the little ones forget him. The crowning domestic event of the winter, of course, had been the arrival of Andrew, junior, and Sarah, with the pet of pets, the four-months-old granddaughter, Rachel.

No President before Jackson had so many house guests or spent so much on their entertainment. Young connections of the fabulous Donelson clan were especially favored. Sometimes their thoughtless antics vexed Uncle Andrew, but when the house was clear of them he would complain of loneliness. So on and on they came, to move through the enchantments of Washington like creatures in a fairy tale. The hour before dinner was a popular time. Wine and relishes waited on the tables of the Red Room. Youthful ornaments of the Army and the Navy clicked their heels; diplomatic underlings with well-turned compliments and continental bows and junior officials from the departments and from Capitol Hill came without specific invitation—three or four of them squiring each current White House belle. If he could possibly get away, the General would descend from his study to have a glass and a few jests with them.

In this way it was that Alphonse Pageot, of the French Legation, met Mary Lewis, the Major's daughter, whom he married, and Thomas P. Barton, a prospective light of our own foreign staff, began a swift conquest of the heart of alluring Cora Livingston, who had her mother's dark, communicative eyes. Wedding gifts became a standing item in the President's personal budget. However, Abraham Van Buren, an alumnus of West Point, and his brother, "Prince" John, spruced up in English clothes and evincing inherited talents for evasion, adroitly defended the bastions of bachelorhood against protracted sieges. Eliza Blair was a favorite of everyone, the General foremost. With her father, the editor, Jackson had developed the most enduring personal friendship of his presidential years. Frank Blair had more than one coat to his name now. He was preparing to buy a fine house and to provide it with running water. He kept cows and, learn-

Two White House Young Ladies

Mary Eastin (left), grand-niece of Rachel Jackson, and Mary Ann Lewis, daughter of William Berkeley Lewis. These girls were on opposite sides in the Margaret Eaton "war" and, when Mrs. Eaton's temporary triumph resulted in the banishment of Miss Eastin and Emily Donelson, it appeared as if Miss Lewis might become mistress of the White House. From a portrait owned by Mrs. Sarah Polk Burch, of Nashville, a descendent of Mary Eastin.

ing that an increase of milk had been prescribed for the General's diet, at seven the next morning brought a foaming pailful to the White House door. Every morning thereafter a bucket from the Blair dairy was on hand, often carried by the journalist himself.

3

In April, 1833, Andrew Jackson Hutchings attained his majority. The President put the young man in possession of his estate, terminating a guardianship undertaken in 1818, in compliance with a death-bed request of Hutchings's father. "One word as to matrimony," was the General's parting advice.

"Seek a wife who will aid you in making a competency and will take care of it when made, for you will find it easier to spend two thousand dollars than to make five hundred. Look at the economy of the mother and you will find it in the daughter. recollect the industry of your dear aunt, and with what economy she watched over what I made, and how we waded thro the vast expence of the mass of company we had. nothing but her care and industry could have saved me from ruin. . . . Think of this before you attempt to select a wife. . . . I would bring to your view Genl Coffee and [his wife] Polly. take Coffee for your guide, receive his admonitions and pursue them. live within your means, never be in debt, and become no mans surety. If your friend is in distress aid him if you have the means to spare. if he fails to be able to return it, it is only so much lost. your property is not sold by the sheriff to raise it."[3]

The President's own money matters were on his mind at the time. For a year, or since paying for Mary Eastin's and Andrew, junior's weddings, Jackson had been short of funds. The ruin of a new carriage in a runaway had cost a thousand dollars, and two thousand had been spent to make the Hermitage more attractive for Sarah. During the visit to Tennessee in 1832, Jackson had changed plantation overseers. Though the new man, Burnard Holtzclaw, seemed energetic and capable, the Hermitage books showed an operating loss for the year. "So much for my absence," observed Jackson, with warm words of approval of young Hutchings's plan to keep the management of his place in his own hands.[4] "Settle all your debts the first of every year and you will know your means and can keep within it." To settle his own debts, Jackson had been forced to the distasteful expedient of asking friends to return personal loans. Yet not a tithe of what he had generously handed out came back.

Putting away adolescent foolishness, the young planter profited by this counsel, and seven months later he married Mary Coffee. Amid grave affairs the President paused to write a long letter. "To me it is joyfull. . . . I view her as a treasure."[5]

Treasure though Mary Coffee was in truth, when neither she nor her cousin Mary McLemore sent General Jackson a scratch of a pen during the homeward journey from the inaugural, he scolded both young ladies for "lasy toads."[6] Tennessee news from other sources was cheering, however. Holtzclaw was taking hold of things at the Hermitage—a circumstance rendered the more desirable by the fact that, for all the General's coaching, Andrew, junior, seemed slow to get his bearings as a landed proprietor. Though the place still suffered from the slack stewardship of Steele, the new overseer had two hundred acres in cotton, three hundred in corn and a hundred and twenty in oats. Only the hay fields were in bad order. Stock was much improved, fences and gates repaired. The spinning jenny, the wheels and two looms were going. The negroes were well-clothed, including the children, whose numbers had increased to fifty-eight. On his latest visit General Jackson had gently expressed to Aunt Hannah, an aged negress who for nearly a generation had ruled the fowl yard, his "mortification" at finding no poultry fit for the table of the "big house." Through Major Lewis, Hannah reported that despite a visitation of "the gaps," carrying off many young turkeys and chickens, plenty of fowl would be on hand for the master's next homecoming.[7]

Though immensely gratified by these reports from home, General Jackson said that the excellent showing must not be permitted to prejudice the health of "the family." "Treat my

A White House Belle

Mary Coffee, daughter of General John Coffee and grand-niece of Rachel Jackson. She spent the winter of 1833-34 at the White House and shortly after was married to General Jackson's ward, Andrew Jackson Hutchings. From a portrait by Earl, owned by Edward Asbury O'Neal III of Florence, Alabama, a descendant of General Coffee.

negroes with kindness." Holtzclaw was further instructed to prevent Betty, the colored cook, from "abusing the little negroes that are under her about the kitchen. A small switch ought only to be used." The white folk's physician, Doctor Hogg, was directed to prescribe for the injured hip of a young victim of Betty's corrective measures. "I would be sorry [were] she [to] become a cripple."[8]

Then came news hard to bear. Dr. William Hume, Rachel's beloved pastor, wrote to say that John Overton was no more— John Overton, with whom the fiery young public prosecutor for the Mero District had shared a bed in the Widow Donelson's blockhouse in 1788. . . . His last words were of Andrew Jackson whom, like John Coffee, he had visited at the White House only once. "Altho," replied the President, "I could lament in the language and feelings of David for Absolom I am constrained to say, *peace to his manes,* let us weep for the living and not for the dead."[9] A succeeding post brought the tidings that Parson Hume himself had passed to his reward. The world was emptying of familiar faces. The third blow in three months, taking off John Coffee, proved more than the old man's stoicism could parry. "[It was] so unexpected, . . . such a sudden shock upon us that . . . our philosophy fled & we were unmanned and I waited for composure of mind before I could acknowledge your letter."[10]

Andrew Jackson offered to stand in the place of a father to the children of his friend. At the request of one of them, he composed the epitaph which in an Alabama graveyard perpetuates "the memory of General John Coffee. . . . As a husband, parent and friend he was affectionate, tender and sincere. He was a brave, prompt and skillful general, a disinterested and sagacious patriot, an unpretending, just and honest man."[11]

4

Tranquillity seemed to elude the public as well as the private concerns of General Jackson. After the nullification crisis, he had indulged himself in the hope that the country "would be permitted to enjoy at least some repose." Before the second term was three weeks old, this aspiration seemed endangered by "a new combination between Clay and calhoun" actuated by "the corrupting influence of the Bank of the U. S. . . . These men are bound, I have no doubt, to have it rechartered." Were not "the late proceedings of Congress," declaring "the government deposits safe . . . evidence of the power of this institution over the government so strong as naturally to excite reflections on the subject?"[12]

Weary as the old man was, his meditations ranged a bold course. Jackson pondered a dramatic seizure of the initiative, striking the bank a disabling blow before it should strike him. The blow contemplated nothing less than the withdrawal of Government deposits, in defiance of the House resolution.[13]

This subject had been first mentioned officially at a Cabinet meeting in the November preceding—1832—when the conduct of the bank in the matter of the retirement of a series of three per cent Government bonds came under review.

The episode of the three per cents was something that not even the bank's warmest friends in Congress could defend. In the spring of 1832, the Treasury had told Biddle to be prepared to advance six million dollars of Government deposits on July 1, to take up these securities. Biddle obtained a postponement on the representation that the disbursement would derange commerce. The true reason was that Biddle's politically-minded liberality in the matter of loans had stripped the institution of the necessary funds. The bank's versatile journeyman, Cadwalader, hastening to London, arranged with the Barings to buy up several millions' worth of certificates and withhold them from the Government. This was a breach of faith and a violation of the charter. The Baring arrangement was to be secret, however, and might have succeeded but for a disclosure by the New York *Evening Post*.

Incensed, Jackson told the Cabinet he believed the bank unsafe and asked which would be the better course, to seek the revocation of its charter or to remove the Government deposits. The question reopened the squabble between Secretary of the Treasury McLane and Attorney General Taney, whereupon Jackson adjourned the meeting and turned to face nullification.[14]

Three months later, when the storm over South Carolina began to relent, the bank situation stood thus: in response to a suggestion in the President's annual message that Congress conduct a "serious investigation" to see whether the Government deposits were safe, two reports were submitted to the House by its Committee on Ways and Means. The majority report, offered by the committee chairman (Van Buren's friend Verplanck, author of the tariff measure which Mr. Clay put to sleep) in five printed pages, pronounced Mr. Biddle's bank sounder than the state banks taken as a whole. It recommended the retention of the deposits. The minority report, submitted by James K. Polk, comprised one hundred and eighty-four pages. Though partizan in tone, it bore evidence of an inquiry worthy of respect. This document indicated that the majority had waived aside much in order to give the bank a clean bill. In addition to other delinquencies, Polk exposed the critical, if not insolvent, condition of several western branches owing to Biddle's loan policy. It showed how "race horse bills" kept the weak branches afloat. That is to say Lexington would boost its assets by writing out a draft on Nashville, which Nashville would cover by drawing for like amount on Natchez, whose cashier would draw on his colleague in New Orleans, who would draw on Louisville, and so on again around the circle. The circulation of monetary fiction in this fugitive form ran into millions of dollars.[15]

Verplanck's report and the first forty-two pages of Polk's reached the House on March 1. The remainder of the Polk report was delivered on March 2, the last day of the session. Its forbidding length, the impending adjournment and the convivial state of many of the members, helped Mr. Clay's men to whoop through a resolution based on the conveniently brief findings of the majority.

5

General Jackson was correct in the assumption that this performance revealed a compact between Clay and Calhoun for the purpose of rechartering the bank. The Kentuckian was in a happy frame of mind. As soon as he had slept off the effects of that all-night tour of legislative duty, a letter went forward to Nicholas Biddle: "I do believe if we had two weeks more to go we could have renewed the charter in spite of all Vetoes."[16] Without waiting to go to bed, a North Carolina Congressman had assured the banker that, after the House vote, Jackson would not dare to remove the deposits.[17]

Nor was Old Hickory on the wrong scent when he spoke of "the corrupting influence of the Bank" in this regard.

Representative John Watmough had asked Biddle to show Congressman Verplanck "some attentions" during his passage through Philadelphia on his way home in New York; "to re-instate old Gilmore [a Representative from Pennsylvania] on his feet"; and to advance Representative Clayton of Georgia three thousand dollars "as the only means of preventing the terrible mischiefs which such men have it in their power to perpetuate."[18] Clayton, previously active against the bank, had grown cool toward the Administration during the nullification fight. After this Mr. Watmough spoke for himself. "I write you in the greatest possible state of distress." Mr. Biddle provided twelve hundred dollars to relieve it.[19] These and other generosities seem to have endowed the banker with an underground notoriety as a "soft touch." An editor wrote for two hundred dollars; a pamphleteer for five hundred; a wayfarer stranded in Philadelphia as a result of his own "imprudence" for twenty—each on the plea that he had been "useful" to the bank.[20] Duff Green rated his services higher; and General Jackson heard that the editor of the *Telegraph* had been allowed to overdraw his account ten thousand dollars.[21]

The turn of affairs fortified Jackson's conviction that the bank should go—and by the shortest practicable route. "I tell you, sir," the Executive was quoted as saying, "she's broke. Mr. Biddle is a proud man and he never would have . . . ask[ed] me for a post-ponement [of the three per cents] if the bank had had the money."

This, however, sounds more like something dressed up by Blair or Kendall for word-of-mouth dissemination than an accurate expression of the presidential mind.[22] True, the bank had not on hand the money for the three per cents, but, when the Baring trick failed, Biddle had been able to raise it; and in all his bank seems to have been as well off as the run of state institutions. On their own, some of the western branches[23] would have failed ere this, but as components of a national system few really doubted that eastern strength would pull them through. Jackson himself appreciated this, or he would not have continued to keep every dollar he owned in the Washington and Nashville branches.

On the other hand the events of the year past had, and with reason, tended to confirm Old Hickory's basic objections to the bank as a consolidation of power prejudicial to the purity of government and indifferent to the welfare of the plain people. Current embarrassments which Mr. Biddle sought to tide over by shady devices—race horse bills, the Baring deal—simply exposed a breach in the wall that could be attacked with advantage.

6

The President did not delay. Spurred by the offensive House resolution, he turned on the bank and turned furiously.

On March 19, the wheels were put in motion with a memorandum to the Cabinet asking: (1) Whether anything had occurred since December to lessen concern for the safety of deposits? (2) Has the bank been a faithful agent of the Government? (3) Should the charter be renewed with modifications? (4) Should there be a new bank, and if so with what privileges? (5) What should be done with the Government revenues? Commenting on his own questions, Jackson said he was opposed to recharter and indicated that he favored removal of the deposits, but had not made up his mind whether they should be distributed among state banks or placed in a new national bank.[24]

Only two of the replies that reached the White House really mattered—those of the Attorney General and of the Secretary of the Treasury.

Taney's came first, leading off with a statement of "strong doubts whether the bank continued to be a safe depository for the public money." The Polk report, the Attorney General

thought, "exhibits a true and faithful picture of the . . . Bank."
Yet Taney did not commit himself to the proposition that the
bank was insolvent. It "may be perfectly able to meet its engagements and yet be a very unsuitable agent to be trusted with the
public money." "Gross and palpable violations of duty" were
pointed out: the business of the three per cents and other items
concealed from the Government directors "thus depriving the
government of that knowledge of its affairs which the charter
meant to secure"; the influence over the press and over the machinery of government.

Tellingly Taney demonstrated the significance of the twenty-
million-dollar increase in loans since 1830 at a time, when by
Biddle's own statement, the bank should have been contracting
unless a renewal of the charter seemed probable. Why this policy?
"Was it not to compel the people to continue . . . [the] monopoly
not on account of the benefits incurred by it, but to escape from
the sufferings which the corporation had the power to inflict?"
Yes. "A fiscal agent which has thus endeavored to fasten itself
upon the body politic, and to perpetuate its . . . exclusive privileges
by the lash . . . is no longer worthy of the confidence or employment of the government." The Government could properly "dismiss it at once" from its service. In that event Mr. Taney preferred
the distribution of revenue among "judiciously selected" state
institutions to the formation of another national bank.

The Attorney General knew the sort of an ending to put to
his effective letter. "I do not conceal from myself the fierce and
desperate struggle which the Bank will make to . . . procure a
restoration of the deposits"—already as good as removed! "Nor
am I insensible of its power. But I . . . [rely] on prompt, firm
and decisive measures on the part of the Executive, and for
support on the intelligence and patriotism of the people. And I
am Sir with highest respect yr. obt. st. R. B. Taney."[25]

The fighting heart of Old Hickory responded. "I long for
retirement & repose on the Hermitage. But until I can strangle
this hydra of corruption, the Bank, I will not shrink from my
duty or my part. I think a system can be arranged with the state
banks."[26]

Frank Blair and Amos Kendall beamed with joy. All winter long they had been plugging with Jackson for the removal of deposits and the use of state banks. Taney's vigorous adherence to their cause was the greatest stroke yet. The smoke that curled from the Attorney General's long black cigars mingled more frequently with that of the corn-cob pipe in the second-floor study. A new vein showed itself in the White House correspondence and new faces appeared in the capital as state banks, scenting the atmosphere, by post and by agent began to insinuate their excellence on the Executive. One such agent, a Philadelphia financier currently without a connection, wrote that sporting men were willing to wager that the deposits would be removed.[27]

Another White House visitor, more tastefully attired than Mr. Taney, whose clothes appeared as if he had slept in them, regarded these events with distrust. Vice President Van Buren's restful office afforded opportunity for observation. Having laboriously ascended to the rank of heir apparent, all he need do was to hold what was already gained until 1836, granting that General Jackson should retire no sooner. But to encompass this with the fewest ripples, awkward episodes like that of nullification should be avoided. Already Mr. Van Buren had given an opinion—and for once precipitously it seemed—on the subject of deposits. He had opposed their removal.[28] Still, the Vice President could console himself with the reflection that the memorandum of his friend, the Secretary of the Treasury, was not as yet in the President's hands.

Jackson was growing impatient when on May 20, 1833, seven weeks after Taney had reported, Mr. McLane's opinion, a volume of ninety-one manuscript pages, reached the President's writing table. Under no circumstances, said the Secretary of the Treasury, should the Bank of the United States be rechartered. But there he and Mr. Taney parted company. McLane would form a new national bank, free of the evils that afflicted Mr. Biddle's, to receive and disburse the public revenue. The deposits should not be removed from the old institution before the new was ready, however. In the first place the President had no power to remove them. Only the Secretary of the Treasury had the power—to be exercised in accordance with his sense of duty. No adequate reason existed for the removal. The Bank of the United States was solvent—and that was the ruling consideration. Even the debts of the western branches were "safe and wholesome." To deposit in the state banks would be calamitous for a staggering variety of reasons. These banks were unsafe. They would not support each other as could branches of the great bank in time of stress. They could not transfer funds satisfactorily, and such transfers as they could make would be attended by annoyance and expense. Terms of the Government's dealings with the present bank were fixed by law and usage. With state banks terms would be "a matter of bargain." State banks could not maintain a uniform currency. Did the President wish to return to the chaotic conditions of wartime and after? Moreover, the Bank of the United States would set upon the state banks, ruin them and cause a panic.

"To restore harmony throughout the country seems now all that is left to complete the President's patriotic labors. . . . The winding up of . . . [the bank's] concerns without embarrassment is under the most favorable circumstances rather to be hoped for than expected. It is not for the government to add to the inherent difficulties of the task, but rather to aid in obviating them; *not for the sake of the bank but that of the community*. I have the honor, to be, Sir, with the highest respect. . . . LOUIS McLANE."[29]

The President laid the last sheet on his table and penciled beneath the signature: "Some strong points in this view— all ably discussed."

Strong points there were indeed—points which had turned back foemen of the bank since 1829. But there were also points so weak that so imprecise a critic as Blair could expose them.[30] Mr. McLane did the cause of a national bank more than justice. He sought to prove too much. For better or for worse, Taney had made the more convincing presentation of his case for removal and for a trial of the state banks.

But before anything definite should be done, Jackson decided to refresh himself with a rest from official duties, and before he could do that he must make two Cabinet changes which had been agreed upon as far back as December. Accordingly on June 1, 1833, McLane stepped into Edward Livingston's shoes as Secretary of State and Livingston took the legation at Paris on which he had so long had an eye. William J. Duane, a Philadelphia lawyer and son of the celebrated editor of the Jeffersonian *Aurora*, became Secretary of the Treasury. Duane was McLane's nominee for the office, the arrangement having been made long before the emergence of the deposit question had elevated Taney to the actual post of premier.

1

The vacation opened with a junket to Fredericksburg, Virginia, to lay the cornerstone of a monument to Washington's mother. At Alexandria a well set-up young man boarded the steamer and approached the President as if to greet him. "Excuse my rising, sir," said General Jackson, whose chair was wedged between a berth and a table. The newcomer appeared to be taking off a glove. "Never mind your glove, sir," said the President extending his hand. The young man thrust his fist violently into Jackson's face as if to pull his nose.

"What, sir! What, sir!" Old Hickory's cry and the crash of the table as he kicked it away aroused the room.

McLane, Livingston and Washington Irving grappled the intruder who threw them off and darted through a door with Jackson after him, cane upraised. Friends blocked the President's path and closed the door. Pounding on the panel, Jackson commanded them to open up or he would break down the door.

Gaining the deck the President learned that his assailant had escaped down the landing stage surrounded by confederates posing as indignant passengers. He was recognized as Robert B. Randolph, a former lieutenant of the Navy dismissed for attempted theft of funds belonging to the late John B. Timberlake whom he had succeeded as purser of the frigate *Constitution*. A considerate Virginian offered to pursue and "kill Randolph in fifteen minutes." "No, sir," said the old soldier, "I want no man to stand between me and my assailants, and none to take revenge on my account."[30a]

The President later observed privately that, had he been on his feet and prepared for the attack, Randolph "never would have moved with life from the tracks he stood in."[31] That opportunity having been lost, Jackson declined to avail himself of the law to punish his assailant. Not until after Old Hickory had left the presidency was Randolph placed on trial. Jackson refused to give evidence for the prosecution, and asked that in event of conviction the sentence or fine be remitted. "I have to this old age complied with my mother's advice to indict no man for assault or sue him for slander."[32]

General Jackson returned from the outing "looking much better than when he left." "The [Randolph] affair seem'd to have put his blood in motion," said John Campbell of the Treasury.[33]

After this salutary beginning a large and important-looking presidential party set out on June 6 for the Chesapeake. "Met by a number of Citizens with the Steam Carrs [of the Baltimore & Ohio Railroad] 12 miles in advance of the City which took us into Baltimore in a few minutes," the General recorded.[34] The first ride of a President of the United States behind a locomotive was followed by three days of ear-splitting celebration which left the guest of honor with a headache.

Then he moved on to Philadelphia where the reception lasted four days and nights. Entering the city on a "white charger," the "savior of the Union" accepted the obeisances of the crowds for five hours and was badly sunburned. "How old, how very old he looks," seemed to be the common thought of those who filled streets, windows, roofs.[35] Though profoundly moved by the "feelings of the people, . . . I sincerely wish my trip was over," the President wrote his son. "Except to my Hermitage or to the watering places I think it is the last journey I shall undertake. Kiss my little Rachel."[36] Philip Syng Physick, America's most famous physician, examined the President. "Now, Doctor," he said, "I can do anything you think proper, except give up coffee and tobacco." So taken was he by the "gentleness, the peculiar and indescribable charm" of his patient that Doctor Physick could talk of little else for days.[37]

New York's welcome exceeded anything of the kind the

metropolis had ever known. "I have bowed to upwards of two hundred thousand people to day, . . . and I hope little Rachel will not forget me until I return."[38] As Jackson crossed the bridge from Castle Garden to the Battery, the overburdened structure gave way, precipitating Secretary Cass, Secretary Woodbury, Jack Donelson and a medley of attendant dignitaries into the water.

8

That night at the American House the President met Martin Van Buren for a long conversation on the bank question for which Amos Kendall had attempted to prepare the Vice President by letter.

"The President seems to have made up his mind that the public deposits must be withdrawn," Kendall informed Mr. Van Buren. "As to the manner and time he is not so well satisfied, and on those points, and perhaps upon the expediency of the whole measure, he will consult you."

There followed an outline for erecting a system of depositories comprised of state banks under definite regulation. To minimize the shock, fresh deposits only would go to the state banks. Existing deposits would remain in the Bank of the United States until withdrawn in the normal run of Government business. "As to the time of this movement, I am firmly of the opinion that it ought to be made soon enough to take the last dollar out of the U. S. Bank and present the new machine in complete operation before the next session of Congress [begins in December]. This cannot be done unless the deposits in the state banks commence as early as the first of August or at furthest the first of September." Kendall saw "the President's popularity" and the Government-supported state banks as the spearhead of a sudden assault to drive Biddle to the wall and end his power forever.

"I pray you to consider these points and . . . hope your great influence may be exerted to effect the desired object.[39]

The Vice President's great influence was not so exerted, thus affording no counterweight to the views of McLane, Cass and Woodbury, who were with the President constantly. On quitting the official party in New York, Mr. McLane left with his chief a lengthy memorandum urging that no action be taken until Congress should meet.[40]

Passing slowly through Connecticut amid continuous ovations, the General pondered this document whenever he could snatch a moment for himself. He had, indeed, determined to dispense with the Bank of the United States as the Government depository. He meant to do this before Congress met. But the fresh objections of McLane, with which the President knew the new Secretary of the Treasury, Duane, to be in agreement,[41] moved Jackson to restate his reasons more fully than he had originally expected would be necessary. A detailed and explicit communication to Duane was begun—with only Donelson to help and apparently nothing except a memorandum by Kendall for a guide. When Hartford was reached, the President's young private secretary confessed himself worn out and anxious to shorten the tour.[42]

Across Rhode Island cannon boomed from town to town as if all New England were a battle line. Receptions overlapped each other. Though Jackson drove himself and his nephew unflaggingly, the letter to Duane was unfinished when, early in the morning of June 20, the travelers stood on the western end of a bridge across the Blackstone River beyond which lay Massachusetts. At their backs artillery roared a farewell salute, breaking so many windows in Pawtucket that the State provided new glass for nearly every householder who asked for it. General Jackson shook hands with his Rhode Island escorts and advanced toward the middle of the span. From the Massachusetts shore a man in the uniform of a member of the Governor's staff approached to welcome the President of the United States. He was Josiah Quincy, junior, a connection of General Jackson's predecessor in office, and he could have wished for a more congenial duty.

9

Reflecting that it is part of a lawyer's calling to be "equally fluent on all sides of a question," Barrister Quincy spoke the felicitations required of hospitality, for the President was in

Massachusetts by express invitation of the State Legislature. This reverent body, which in 1815 had thanked the Almighty for the victory at New Orleans without mentioning General Jackson's name, appears to have felt it no longer necessary to ignore the existence of the man whose stand against nullification had won approval from "the God-like Daniel" Webster. After a ceremonial breakfast at Attleborough, the party inspected a factory. The manager produced a card of badges stamped with palmetto trees for the South Carolina "army." "You have been interfering with our business, Mr. President," he said with a smile, "and should feel honor bound to take these buttons off our hands."

As the afternoon wore on, Mr. Quincy began to thaw out, finding the President's conversation "interesting from its sincerity, decision and point." Before Boston was reached, the Governor's aide had caught the spirit of the occasion and sent ahead for a horse that the General might enter the city mounted. Pleased and grateful, Jackson left the barouche and swung his long legs into the saddle. At the city line, the Mayor awaited with a carriage in which a place was reserved for the guest of honor. Quincy argued that the President had been seated all day and preferred the saddle; but he argued in vain.

On the next day Old Hickory and the aide-de-camp were on excellent terms. A military review was scheduled to take place on the Common. Quincy had scoured Boston for handsome mounts for the President and his suite. As the visitors appeared in front of the troops, a salvo of artillery shook the earth. The borrowed horses reared and leaped. Controlling his mount perfectly, Jackson galloped along the line of troops, the Cabinet officers and miscellaneous notables following as best they could.

"Where is the Vice President?" exclaimed Old Hickory as he drew up his prancing horse to take the marching salute.

Riding alongside, Mr. Quincy answered him. "About as nearly on the fence as a gentleman of his positive political convictions can get."

Mr. Van Buren's bolting steed had brought up, tail first, against a fence and refused to budge.

General Jackson looked and laughed. "And you've matched

him with a horse even more non-committal than his rider."[43]

Boston rubbed its eyes, scarcely able to believe the evidence of its own deportment. "Here is Pres. Jackson," apologetically wrote Edward Warren to his son, "for whom a short time ago no epithet was too bad, received with all the show of honor which we paid to Lafayette."[44] Quincy was unable to discern any particular injustice to Lafayette. Noting his tenderness to children and the wordless understanding the weatherbeaten warrior could at once establish with them, the aide-de-camp saw something incongruous in the old New England custom of frightening young ones when they were naughty with the name of Andrew Jackson.

Only Beacon Street seems to have been able to make a decent show of curbing its emotions. When the presidential party passed through this residential holy of holies, Quincy confessed that the audience was "undemonstrative"—until a window flew up and an eager-faced child, a little girl, appeared waving a kerchief. Later Mr. Quincy learned the secret of the unexpected drama. Well back from his window, where he could see without being seen, Daniel P. Parker, merchant, was observing the procession. The carriage containing Jackson approached. A chill east wind tossed the Hero's white mane, but something less tangible bore the compelling magnetism of his presence into that parlor on Beacon Street. "Do someone come here," the merchant shouted, "and salute the old man!" Mr. Parker's little daughter did what her father could not bring himself to do.[45]

On his fourth day in Boston a severe cold and bleeding of the lungs[46] confined the President to his bed in the Tremont House. Physicians bled him. Quincy entertained the patient by reading from Seba Smith of the Portland (Maine) *Courier,* whose letters over the name of Major Jack Downing were the most widely reprinted and plagiarized newspaper humor of the day. The Major had long appeared in the rôle of an intimate counsellor of the President. In the present instance he assumed to be a member of the official touring party. His two most recent letters described incidents of the journey. At Philadelphia, when the President became exhausted by handshaking, the indispensable Major had stepped behind him and, thrusting his strong arm beneath Jack-

ONE OF THE WHITE HOUSE BABIES

Rachel Jackson Donelson, daughter of Andrew Jackson Donelson and Emily Donelson, born in the White House, April 19, 1834. From a portrait by Earl, owned by Mrs. Pauline Wilcox Burke of Washington.

son's weary one, finished off the greetings as the President's understudy, with no one a whit the wiser. When the bridge broke in New York it was Major Downing who fished the dripping statesmen from the water.[47]

Old Hickory chuckled. "The Vice President must have written that. Depend upon it Jack Downing is only Van Buren in masquerade."[48]

On the fifth day also Jackson kept to his hotel while Quincy circulated among the brahmin set, singing the praises of Old Hickory with all the zeal of a new convert. He failed to convince his distinguished kinsman, the ex-President, that Jackson was even sick. John Quincy Adams said he knew Andrew Jackson. The supposed illness was "four-fifths trickery," a mere bid for "sympathy."[49]

Young Mr. Quincy was more successful in communicating some of his enthusiasm to his father whom he assured that even General Jackson's ignorance of books had been exaggerated. This conversation had results that shook Boston to bed-rock. Though the president of Harvard College, Josiah Quincy, senior, was a lawyer and man of action rather than a cloistered scholar who believed that all the knowledge in the world reposed between the covers of books. Calling the Harvard overseers together on that very day for a hurried and, as strict constructionists have said, "irregular" meeting, President Quincy obtained approval of a resolution to confer upon Andrew Jackson a degree of Doctor of Laws. John Quincy Adams was aghast. Was there no way, he asked the elder Quincy, to prevent this outrage? "None," replied the educator. "As the people have twice decided that this man knows law enough to be their ruler it is not for Harvard College to maintain that they are mistaken."[50]

The presentation ceremony was announced for the following morning.

10

During the two-day interim of illness, Jackson finished and Donelson began to copy two communications to Secretary of the Treasury William J. Duane, on the subject of discontinuing the use of the Bank of the United States as the depository for Government funds. The first, a letter of instructions, was fairly brief. The other, giving in deference to Duane's contrary views Jackson's reasons for the step, would fill twenty pages of this volume.

The letter of instructions suggested that on September 15, 1833, "at furthest," deposits in the Bank of the United States be discontinued and the balance remaining there drawn on until exhausted in the course of the ordinary needs of the Government. On that date, or before, deposits should go to a group of state banks whose composition would be determined as follows. An agent of the Treasury should proceed at once to Baltimore, Philadelphia, New York and Boston and in those four cities designate five banks (two in New York) as "primary banks." Later other primary banks might be chosen in western and in southern cities. The primary banks would select, with the Treasury's approval, "secondary banks" to assist them in receiving the deposits and performing all the functions for the Government hitherto performed by the Bank of the United States. This was to be done without cost to the Government.

Weekly reports on the state of deposits and monthly reports on the state of the banks would be submitted to the Treasury. At any time the Treasury could, on proper notice, drop a bank from the system "or break up the whole arrangement." Promptness was recommended in getting the preliminary survey under way and Amos Kendall was suggested as the agent for this work. Jackson said he wished "to present the new system to Congress, in complete and successful operation, at the commencement of the session."

The letter setting forth the President's reasons for dispensing with the services of Mr. Biddle's bank was largely a recast of Taney's indictment of that institution. Moreover, it took notice of McLane's contrary opinion which held that the power to remove the deposits from the Bank of the United States rested not with the Executive but with the Secretary of the Treasury. Jackson's whole communication was an implied denial of this, which the last line made more specific by adding that the President took "upon himself the responsibility."[51]

II

The seamed countenance of the old soldier was pale but "the spirit resolute to conquer infirmity," as Mr. Quincy wrote, when he set out for Harvard Yard. A full retinue attended, including the shade of Major Jack Downing. An address in Latin preceded the presentation of the degree. On receiving the scroll, the President expressed his thanks in a sentence or two. "[At this point]," recorded Major Jack, "the Gineral was going to stop but I says in his ear, 'You must give 'em a little Latin, *Doctor!*' . . . 'E pluribus unum,' says he, 'my friends, sine qua non.'"[52] This remark, destined to become the most widely quoted of all Major Downing's writings, was said to have been repeated in erudite circles as the President's veritable utterance. John Quincy Adams would have liked to believe it. Declining an invitation to honor the occasion with his presence, the ex-President wrote in his diary: "An affectionate child of my Alma Mater, I . . . [could not bear to] witness her disgrace in conferring her highest literary honor upon a barbarian who could . . . hardly spell his own name."[53]

After the degree had been conferred, a reception was held at the residence of President Quincy. The entire undergraduate body filed past. General Jackson began shaking hands with each one. "I am happy to see you, gentlemen." "I wish you all happiness." "Gentlemen, I wish you success in life." Perceiving the President's strength beginning to wane, friends discontinued the handshaking. When the faculty walked past, Doctor Palfrey led his two little girls by the hands. Jackson lifted the children up and kissed them.

So began an eventful day. Leaving Cambridge the President was driven in an open carriage to Charlestown, where he climbed the unfinished Bunker Hill Monument and listened to an oration by Edward Everett. Then followed a devastating series of receptions at which young Quincy, the aide-de-camp, rebelled. He begged Jackson to withdraw and conserve his strength. "These people have made their arrangements to welcome me," the old gentleman replied, "and so long as I am not on my back I will gratify them." In the middle of the afternoon, he was on his back—resting at Lynn while his suite struggled through a dinner in his honor, their fourth that day.

On to Marblehead, one of Massachusetts' rare Democratic towns. Quincy took matters in hand. After a brief pause a banquet was left untasted and a vast outpouring of genuine Jacksonians grievously disappointed while the carriage sped toward Salem. "An anxious drive," recorded Quincy, "the President was becoming weaker every moment." Dusk was falling as they entered Salem. The aide-de-camp ordered the carriage driven to a hotel by the quickest route. Before the citizenry was aware, he had Jackson in bed and under a doctor's care. Informing the local notables of the Executive's condition, Quincy suggested the cancellation of their program of arrangements. "Impossible," said the men of Salem. A barouche for the President was at the door and the procession actually in motion. Unconsciously or otherwise, Mr. Quincy borrowed an idea from Major Jack Downing. It had grown quite dark. He and Martin Van Buren entered the carriage of honor, which moved to its place in the parade. The applause was deafening. The hospitalities ended with dinner number five.

That night Jackson suffered a severe hemorrhage of the lungs. Quincy was sure the tour would have to be called off. In the morning Old Hickory walked in on his staff at breakfast. "An immaterial something flashed in his eye," wrote the aide-de-camp, "and it was evident that the faltering body was again held in subjection." On the next day, June 27, 1833, Mr. Quincy left the President at the New Hampshire boundary. "Come and see me at the White House, or better still at the Hermitage," said Jackson, taking his hand.

The two never met again. The letters to William J. Duane which Jackson had posted from Boston started a train of events that ended any chance of Josiah Quincy, junior's, allegiance to the Jackson cause, though nothing dimmed his admiration for the man. "A knightly personage," the Bostonian wrote in his old age, "prejudiced, narrow, mistaken upon many points, but vigorously a gentleman in his sense of honor and in his natural straightforward courtesies which are easily to be distinguished from the veneer of policy."[54]

12

The tour ended at Concord, New Hampshire, where the President collapsed. Borne back to Washington by steamer he suffered a relapse. For forty-eight hours his life seemed in danger.[55] Tiptoeing from the White House, Cabinet officers clustered anxiously about the spruce figure of Martin Van Buren. But the tough old gladiator rallied, thereby changing much history.

His first act was to direct Secretary of the Treasury Duane to start the machinery calculated to transfer the Government deposits from the Bank of the United States. That officer demurred and interposed subtle tactics of delay. McLane and Cass supported him. Mr. Van Buren sought the cooler temperature of Saratoga Springs, New York. Alone, and with noteworthy patience, Jackson contended against the refractory head of the Treasury, obtaining at the end of two weeks a promise that when the matter came up for final action Duane would co-operate or resign.[56] So racked by pain that to hold a pen was torture, General Jackson then indited a grave and kindly acknowledgment of another of his New England conquests, respectfully declining a proposal purporting to be from a Connecticut spinster whose object was matrimony.[57]

Not until the closing days of July, 1833, was Amos Kendall free to depart on his mission to select the key banks for the great experiment. Duane's quibbling had consumed precious time, and the President reconciled himself to a fortnight's delay in the execution of his plan. This deferred the beginning until October 1. As nothing could be done until Kendall reported, Jackson, still ill and very weary, embarked for his sea-island summer resort, the Rip Raps, taking the White House family including all the children and five servants.

CHAPTER XVI

MR. BIDDLE'S BIGGEST GAMBLE

ANDREW JACKSON paid his hotel bill at the Rip Raps with a personal check for three hundred and ninety-five dollars and seventy-five cents on Mr. Biddle's bank, and on August 23, 1833, he was at his desk in the White House after an absence of twenty-seven days. The relaxation of ocean bathing and games on the beach with the children had greatly improved though not restored his health. Yet, considering the distractions which marred this vacation, the change for the good was remarkable.

Kendall had immediately run into difficulties which every few days he reported to his chief. The enthusiasm of the state banks for Government deposits had suddenly begun to cool. In Baltimore one first-class bank refused to have anything to do with the proposal, another left the emissary's inquiry unanswered. Of three others which expressed a "desire" for a share of the deposits, only one seemed prepared to make the strict guaranties which Jackson demanded. Prospects in Philadelphia and New York seemed a little brighter; and in Boston brighter still, so far as the willingness of some of the banks was concerned. Yet, on the whole, the survey was very disappointing. The reasons for this were two: the safeguards demanded of the banks by the Government, and fear of the retaliatory power of Nicholas Biddle, who was making ready to strike back in earnest. As a sample of what he could do, the screws were put on Boston the week Kendall was there. In the face of a need by local merchants for a million dollars to pay duties on cargoes then at the wharves, the Bank of the United States discontinued discounts and demanded the return of its balances in the state banks. This so greatly crippled the state banks to which the importers applied that Kendall said unless relief were forthcoming some of the mercantile houses would have to suspend.[1]

350

Mr. Kendall's work was not made lighter by Secretary of State McLane, who had followed him to Philadelphia and to New York, talking up a proposal to postpone the transfer until January 1. Momentarily Kendall weakened. If McLane and Duane were not merely trying to throw up a screen behind which to defeat the whole project, Kendall told Jackson he would acquiesce. But after witnessing Mr. Biddle's demonstration against Boston, the President's agent said the state banks must be helped quickly: *"immediate removal or no removal"* at all.[2]

Duane continued recalcitrant and Jackson appealed to Van Buren for assistance. He received in return many mellifluous words attesting loyalty and admiration. The General's health being the prime consideration, the Vice President begged that he prolong his vacation. "The first weeks in September as you know are the worst in Washington." In the meantime the status of our public lands was suggested as a matter worthy of the Executive's especial attention. At last Mr. Van Buren mentioned the bank question, declaring himself in favor of preparing arrangements for the transfer, but deferring the execution thereof until the first of the year. All this was well and effectively said.[3]

If Martin Van Buren could write a seductive letter, Roger B. Taney could write one that was more so. The Attorney General said he did not close his eyes to developments which had "greatly strengthened the Bank and increased the difficulties to be surmounted by the Executive." Nor did he overlook the fact that if virtue were to prevail and vice be overthrown, it would be at the hands of Andrew Jackson because no other President would have the courage to carry to the death a fight with Nicholas Biddle. Still, the Attorney General would not press the issue upon his chief. "I should feel deeply mortified if after so many splendid victories, civil and military, you should in the last term of your public life meet defeat." The safe thing would be not to risk it. Mr. Taney would not presume to advise the President as to which course to take. But, in case Jackson wished to continue the fight, and to transfer the deposits now, he could count on Taney to stand by him.[4]

Instead of prolonging, Old Hickory curtailed his holiday. "is it possible," he asked Martin Van Buren, "that your friends are overawed by the power of the Bank. it cannot overawe me."[5]

Armed with stronger evidence than ever of the bank's moral unfitness—more secret loans to congressmen, more editors (including James Gordon Bennett) "bought up," sixty thousand dollars to printers for propaganda, light on the Asbury Dickins deal[6]—Jackson summoned his Cabinet on September 10. Presenting a report from Kendall claiming sufficient state banks available for immediate needs, the President said that the Government would change depositories on October 1. The meeting ended in an apparently irreconcilable disagreement—Taney and Woodbury supporting Jackson; McLane, Duane and Cass opposed; Barry absent.

On September 14, Jackson suggested that Duane retire in keeping with his promise. He refused. On September 19, Jackson read the Cabinet a statement of his reasons for removal which Taney, sustained by black cigars, had sat up most of the night revising.[7] Even Duane admitted it a strong document;[8] but he refused to sign an order discontinuing deposits in the Bank of the United States and he refused to resign. Had Mr. Duane been an officer of the bank, it is difficult to see how he could have served Mr. Biddle better. An interesting fact is that the banker knew six weeks in advance almost precisely the exasperating line the Secretary of the Treasury intended to take with his chief.[9]

Nicholas Biddle turned the screws of credit tighter, not in Boston alone but throughout the East, the West and the South. Every day of delay strengthened his hands and weakened those of the President. Not even in his bed chamber could Jackson find refuge from the incessant pressure, W. B. Lewis accosting him there to palliate the behavior of Duane and urge a postponement until Congress should meet. "No, sir," the General flashed back. "If the bank . . . [keeps the deposits until then] no power can prevent it from obtaining a charter— it will have it if it has to buy up all Congress."[10]

To add to these tribulations McLane and Cass threatened to abandon their posts, which would wreck, as many thought, popular confidence in the Administration.[11] Debilitating headaches and a pain in the chest constantly threatened to bring Old Hickory to bed. "Quite unwell today," he wrote. "Nothing but the excitement keeps me up."[12]

Through it all the Executive's forbearance was as remarkable as his inflexibility. Quarreling with no one, he met Duane's whimpering insolence with dignity. Not until September 23 did he dismiss this subordinate and name Roger B. Taney in his stead. The new Secretary of the Treasury lost no time giving official notice that Government deposits would not be made in the Bank of the United States after the last day of the month.

2

Nicholas Biddle thought Jackson would not dare to go that far, but, foresightedly enough, the banker had long and carefully prepared for any eventuality. He had placed his bank in tip-top shape and slyly drawn state banks into its debt. These astute measures were counted on to break up the removal campaign in its early stages. "When we begin," he told the head of his New York branch, "we shall crush the Kitchen Cabinet at once."[13] The beginning, which Amos Kendall had witnessed in Boston, brought on great consternation but failed to achieve its end. So, on October 1 Mr. Biddle turned the screws again, and hardest in the West and the South. Discounts were further reduced, more balances against state banks called in, the receipt of the notes of state banks restricted, bills of exchange limited to sixty days, exchange rates raised and rigged in favor of the East to draw capital in that direction. Sixteen days later western offices were required to squeeze their communities tighter still.[14]

The bank claimed these harsh measures necessary to its security, and this false statement contained a deceptive element of truth. Some contraction was necessary, the exact extent of which probably no two persons could have agreed on. Under the cover of this necessity Biddle went far and away beyond anything required by conservative banking.[15] At the outset his bank was in an exceptionally strong position. On October 1, Government money in its vaults amounted to nine million eight hundred and sixty-eight thousand dollars, to be drawn out gradually over a period of several months. The banker's deliberate purpose was to make people suffer, to bring upon the Administration a storm of protest by the threat of panic and, if that did not suffice, by panic in fact. The blame, he felt, would fall on Jackson and ruin him. Had not the then Secretary of the Treasury, Mr. McLane, solemnly warned the President of this identical calamity six months before? So Mr. Biddle sowed the wind, topping off that achievement with a manifesto in his jauntiest style, representing Jackson as an angry ignoramus intent upon the demolition of an institution whose aim was to scatter seeds of benevolence among a prosperous, a happy and a virtuous people.

Biddle's object was measurably assisted by the lame start the "pet banks," to use the opposition's term, made at taking over the work of the "monster." Amos Kendall, who did much of the actual work of erecting the new system, was a keen man and a capable organizer. Four years as Fourth Auditor of the Treasury, a post beneath his talents, had taught him something of the mysteries of banking and finance; and his constant thought had been to supplant the Bank of the United States. McLane and Duane so retarded his efforts, however, that in September he had brought Jackson an instrument admittedly imperfect. Confronted by the alternatives of giving battle with half an army or retiring from the field, Old Hickory chose to fight.

Roger B. Taney, taking over the subordinate command, sought to arm a few of the state banks with the means of defense should Biddle suddenly call on them to redeem large quantities of their notes in specie. Accordingly he issued to each of the New York depositories and to one depository in Philadelphia a draft for five hundred thousand dollars on the Bank of the United States. A Baltimore depository got three drafts for a hundred thousand each. These transactions were unnoted in the reports of the Treasury to the Bank of the United States, the strict understanding being that the drafts should be presented only in event of aggression by Mr. Biddle.

Temptation overcame some of the recipients of this ammunition. Finding itself adversely involved in speculation, the Union

Bank of Baltimore cashed one of the one-hundred-thousand-dollar drafts. The situation was made worse by the fact that Thomas Ellicott, president of this institution, was a close friend of Taney, himself a small stockholder. Then, in defiance of renewed pledges, Ellicott cashed the other two. The Philadelphia bank followed with its five-hundred-thousand-dollar draft, as did one of the New York banks. Biddle met these demands on the spot but filled the air with entirely justified remonstrances because of the intentional omission of the drafts from the Treasury statements. For awhile it looked as if the Baltimore bank would fail and, all in all, Mr. Taney was in an ugly fix—as he deserved to be. But he pulled out, no more emergency drafts being presented. Gradually additions were made to the chain of depositories until the country was covered. By day-and-night industry, the Treasury chief began to co-ordinate their activities.

3

Nicholas Biddle was equally busy, and the results of his handiwork made the improvements in Mr. Taney's system difficult to appreciate. The repressive proceedings of the great bank were bearing fruit. Commerce slackened, industry drooped, prices of securities and of agricultural products slumped; hands were laid off; wages cut; gold and silver were hoarded, money rates climbed from eight to twenty-five per cent and business houses began to go to the wall. Nor could all the inconveniences be attributed directly to Mr. Biddle, though it was in his power to relieve them. As the Government's fiscal agent the great bank had provided a national currency that was fairly uniform. A bill on an Atlantic seaboard branch was honored on the Mississippi River for about ninety-eight cents on the dollar. Mr. Taney's thrown-together group was unable to duplicate this arrangement. Troops transferred from Virginia to Alabama found their money had depreciated twelve and a half per cent. Government employees and creditors in Missouri and Illinois, heretofore paid in notes of the great bank's St. Louis branch receivable locally at par, got the paper of the "pet" bank in Washington, D. C., which they found hard to dispose of at a five percent shaving. Such things discomfited a stratum of society where Jackson's supporters were most numerous.

Mr. Biddle beat the drums and let the people know. More manna for congressmen, editors and pamphleteers quickened the spread of his gospel. The waters of public discontent began to rise and some of Jackson's personal followers to fall away. Clayton of Georgia, House leader of the anti-bank forces in 'Thirty-one, accepted a loan and apologized for his error. The banker's hireling, Representative Watmough of Pennsylvania, in receipt of a fresh accommodation of sixteen hundred and fifty dollars, made overtures to Major Lewis. Though fearful of the future, Lewis remained loyal,[16] as did McLane; and Cass's opposition changed to timid acquiescence. As for Martin Van Buren, he kept away from Washington until nearly Christmas time, carefully explaining that this was from motives of delicate consideration for the fame of his great leader. Once the die was cast, the Vice President assured Jackson that he was with him through thick and thin. "[But]," added the self-effacing statesman, "it would not do to expose the great measure to prejudice by doing anything that would tend in the slightest degree to withdraw it from the protection of your name."[17] No evidence to the contrary appearing, it would seem that General Jackson read this with a perfectly straight countenance; and to the end of his official life he deprecated the injustice of calling such a guileless soul "the Magician."

With at least the show of a friendly Cabinet behind him, Jackson struck back with all the vigor of a still well-disciplined Administration machine. Blair and Kendall prodded the partizan press to onslaughts as fierce as anything Mr. Biddle's rival troupe of performers could deliver. Results, however, were unsatisfactory in consequence of the fact that the campaign was predicated on a stupendous miscarriage of prophecy. From the first the Jackson press had taken the line that no public distress existed— only scare-talk put out by the bank to disguise its own distress. In Amos Kendall's vivid metaphor, the Secretary of the Treasury had his heel on the bank viper's head and could crush it at will.

These statements were susceptible of the criticism of being untrue. The bank was strong and arrogant, and public distress was nearing the panic stage. Frightened hoarders virtually withdrew the stock of precious metals from circulation. Communities began to supply the shortage of small coins with scrip, derisively called "Jackson money."

For years opponents had nourished their self-esteem in defeat with the reflection that "General Jackson's popularity can stand anything." Now it seemed that Nicholas Biddle had found the heel of Achilles. From the apex of the nullification victory, the fabulous Jacksonian prestige was falling like a spent rocket. Along the route of the grand tour from Maryland to New Hampshire, banquet orators who had strewn the Hero's path with the flowers of rhetoric publicly proclaimed their apostasy. The people were invited to button their waist-bands tighter and survey the state of the nation. Six months ago mills humming, farm prices high. Now—all a ruin. Why? Because Andrew Jackson, carried away by delusions of grandeur, had chosen to disregard the implicit warnings of two secretaries of the treasury in favor of the schemes of a reckless crew of politico-financial adventurers.

Though few had the courage to resist the pack in full cry, one rather surprising exception was Robert Vaux who in Philadelphia bore a name almost as well-known as that of Nicholas Biddle. A man of wide culture, Mr. Vaux's patronage of the arts, his philanthropies and his works of prison reform had been copied throughout the United States and in Europe. On the bank question, he remained silent until his views were solicited. Then he expressed apprehension that "a Government Bank was perhaps a dangerous institution, as it might in the hands of unscrupulous men be used as a lever against popular liberty." Philadelphia rang with denunciations. "From mouth to mouth," recorded an eye-witness, "flew the exclamation, 'Robert Vaux is a Jackson man.' An edict of social extermination was registered against him. To the right and left he was shunned. A crusade was organized to eject him from all societies he had for the most part founded, and it was done."[18]

With the breaking storm's sharp growl assailing every ear, statesmen made their ways to Washington for the Twenty-third Congress which was to convene on December 2, 1833. Clay, Calhoun and Webster stood forth as the giants of an opposition whose prospects never had seemed brighter. Jackson's shaken ranks realized the supreme crisis of their leader's public life to be at hand, with the odds against him the heaviest ever faced. As never before his lieutenants needed a ringing battle cry to electrify the spirits of their followers. They needed to regain the initiative and carry a fight to the enemy.

Through it all Old Hickory himself remained detached and tranquil, singularly so. Though seldom without headaches and chest pains, he seemed on the whole to gain strength. Minutely he followed the multifarious details of managing the Hermitage establishment. A colt he had given to Sarah won a four-mile purse at Baltimore. When Andrew, junior, and the little family left for Tennessee a stream of letters followed them. "My dear Sarah, I dreaded the long travel for our sweet little pet, fearful that it might get sick & no doctor near. I have not rested well at night since you left me—every thing appeared silent & in gloom about the House, and when I walked into your room—found it without its occupants —everything changed, the cradle of my little pet without it, and its little waggon there—my feelings were overcome for the moment."[19] He would sit in his bedroom with Sarah's or Andrew's letters in his hand, gazing at a portrait of the grandchild as if to give reality to the parents' descriptions of her. "I wish I could see her walk, and hear her begin to prattle."[20] The long, unhurried missives contained no word of politics.

In his message, read to Congress on December 3, the Executive clung to the malapropos tactics of defense. "I am happy to know that through the good sense of our people the effort to get up a panic has hitherto failed. . . . No public distress has followed the exertions of the bank."[21] No battle cry to drown the clamors for bread welling up from a stricken land. Administration men shook their heads despairingly.

4

The bank struck first, respectfully memorializing Congress to direct the restoration of the deposits on the ground that their tranfer represented a breach of contract. Two days later Henry Clay, wearing the air of a man with grave purposes afoot, moved to call on the President to lay before the Senate the "paper" he was "alleged" to have read to the Cabinet on September 18 last. As this paper, giving reasons for his contemplated action on the deposits, had been printed in every newspaper in the country, Senator Clay's request for an official copy seemed to foreshadow some direfully legalistic procedure. Courtly John Forsyth of Georgia, Administration floor leader in the Upper House, asked the object of the unprecedented request. Was it, by any chance, for the purpose of impeaching the President of the United States? This unruffled anticipation left the quick-witted Kentuckian for once without a ready reply.

His resolution was adopted, however; Jackson refused to comply. "As well I might be required to detail to the Senate the free and private conversations I have held with those cabinet officers relating to their duties."[22] Under the spur of Clay and of Calhoun, the Senate refused to receive the President's reply, though this bit of ill-humor failed to alter the fact that Jackson had acted clearly within his constitutional rights. Mr. Clay countered with an equally constitutional victory for the bank, the Senate rejecting four of the President's five renominations of Government directors. These men had been a thorn in the flesh of Mr. Biddle and useful to Jackson in exposing the banker's autocratic irregularities. The House, too, aimed a charge of bird-shot at the Executive. Ignoring the well-heeled agents of the bank who overran the ante-rooms, a resolution was introduced to exclude the President's none-too-happy observer, Major Lewis. It failed of passage.

Picayunish preliminaries seemed at an end, though, when, on December 26 Mr. Clay began a tremendous speech, his first of sixty that session. It took three days to deliver, and is one of that statesman's finest philippics. Jackson's whole record as President came under review. Finally Mr. Clay moved a resolution of censure proclaiming that "in relation to the public revenue" Andrew Jackson had violated the Constitution and the laws. The speaker was rewarded with such demonstrations of approval that Vice President Van Buren, who had tardily taken up his gavel only a few days before, suffered a lapse of his traditional urbanity. He cleared the galleries.

While Mr. Clay's motion did bear on the bank issue, Mr. Biddle would have greatly preferred a direct demand for the restitution of deposits. But neither he nor Henry Clay had been honest with the other. In 1832 Biddle had sought to use Clay for the purposes of the bank. Now Clay was using the bank to promote his own fortunes with an eye to 1836. The fate of the bank was only incidental to the harassment of Jackson and Van Buren. The Clay speech started a tide of oratory, pro and con, which veered further and further from the specific object that was vital to Nicholas Biddle.

The banker moved to get his forces in hand and throw them behind a resolution for the return of the deposits. He thought it could be shoved through quickly,[23] and to this end Mr. Biddle adopted grim and practical means.

In January the panic struck, and some of Biddle's allies winced at the carnage. "I should be very well pleased to see the scarcity of money increased," wrote one, describing the scenes in New York, "if it were not ... [injuring] *your friends*."[24] It was perhaps natural for Editor James Watson Webb of the *Courier and Enquirer*, gambling on the fall of stocks, and for Congressman Watmough, who had not felt the pinch, to offer contrary advice:[25] "Do not alter your course the thousandth of a point."[26] Yet the plea of a woman who seems to have known Nicholas Biddle in happier days must have been difficult to resist. She asked for twenty dollars to buy a lottery ticket as a last cast to save her aged father from ruin.[27]

One may hope that Mr. Biddle lent her twenty dollars and that she held a lucky number, but, if the banker did that, it was about all he did to ameliorate distress except among congressmen susceptible of cultivation and other supposed molders of public opinion. On the contrary he turned the screws again, on January 23, 1834, directing his branch heads to squeeze three million three hundred thousand dollars more from a prostrate public in forty days. This would bring the contraction since August 1 to eighteen million three hundred thousand dollars, or more than one third of the total discounts of the bank. The contention that such excesses were necessary to protect the bank would be difficult to prove.[28] In private, Biddle's mask slipped. To the head of his Boston branch he wrote: "Nothing but the evidence of suffering abroad will produce any effect in Congress. . . . A steady course of firm restriction will ultimately lead to . . . the recharter of the bank."[29] Dropping all pretense that the retrenchment was anything but a lash applied to the backs of the voters, the realistic Webb told Biddle that his measures were not severe enough. "If you do not curtail, and largely too, you must & will lose . . . the approaching election in New York."[30]

To make out Jackson the culprit, Nicholas Biddle created an engine of propaganda the like of which no private person had set in motion before. Its fuel was cash. In his latest distribution of largess, Mr. Biddle had omitted Daniel Webster, possibly feeling that thirty-two thousand dollars in "loans" exclusive of outright fees should suffice the man from Massachusetts. If so he reckoned without a proper understanding of the facility with which the "God-like" one could run through money. The following reached the Greek temple in Chestnut Street: "I believe my retainer has not been renewed or *refreshed* as usual. If it be wished that my relation to the Bank should be continued it may be well to send me the usual retainers. yours with regard DanL WEBSTER."[31]

Mr. Clay, too, was advanced a paltry thousand dollars;[32] but, unlike Webster, he gave security for all his loans and paid them. The Kentuckian was not above recommending extraordinary favors for others, however. "Mr. Knower [a bankrupt] is, you know, the father in law of Gov Marcy and he belongs to that powerful interest in N. York. The desired accomodation would have the best effects."[33] While pressing honest merchants to the wall, Mr. Biddle could assure a North Carolina congressman of elastic convictions that "in paying off the whole or any part of the loan you will consult exclusively your own convenience."[34] In John Forsyth, the first man in the Senate to raise his voice for Andrew Jackson, the banker found a legislator of different stuff. Owing twenty thousand dollars he could not pay, the Georgian offered to deed over property in that amount.[35]

On the banker's roster of acquisitions from the profession of letters were such men of standing as Thomas Ritchie of the Richmond *Enquirer* and Thomas Cooper, president of South Carolina College,[36] as well as a personage entitled to standing of a different sort, Charles Hammond of the Cincinnati *Gazette*.[37] But, oddly enough, the most useful services in this field were performed by a talented amateur, Charles Augustus Davis, whose brilliant counterfeits of Major Jack Downing were to win the author a permanent place in the annals of American humor. Davis was a New York City-bred silk-stocking. Yet his imitations of the homely parable for which Major Downing was famous were often better than the originals of Downing's creator, Seba Smith, a Maine country editor. Many readers[38] confused Davis's Downing with Smith's, concluding that the true Major Jack, who might spoof General Jackson but was usually for him, had turned his coat. "Squire Biddle," the hero of the new Downing letters, was a democratic and kindly character whose droll and plausible philosophy of finance fascinated cross roads store audiences throughout the land: a vastly different individual from the terrible "Czar Nick" of the Jackson press. Davis's letters were more widely read than the speeches of Webster and of Clay combined. Appreciating their value and always the litterateur, Biddle flooded his author with guidance and rewarded him with a post on the board of directors on the New York branch.[39]

5

The banker was not always so fortunate in the matter of immediate dividends from his propaganda investments, however. When Henry Clay led the Senate astray with his self-seeking resolution of censure, Mr. Biddle asked Webster to bring it back to earth. "You *must make a speech*, one of your calm, firm, solid, stern works."[40] Despite a meticulous insistence on pay for his work Mr. Webster, like his Kentucky colleague, reserved to himself considerable latitude as to what that work should be. On the occasion in question he made no speech. Instead, this acute observer directed Mr. Biddle's attention to the results of a significant change in Administration tactics. For the Jackson press had abandoned its ostrich-like policy on the general distress. Distress was admitted and Biddle blamed for it. The effect was adverse to the bank, said Webster, who recommended that Biddle moderate his pressure.[41]

The banker refused, bluntly instructing one of his Washington lobbyists, the distinguished-looking Judge Joseph Hopkinson of the Federal bench: "The relief must come from Congress and Congress alone. . . . The bank feels no vocation to redress the wrongs inflicted by these miserable people. This worthy President thinks that because he has scalped Indians and imprisoned Judges he is to have his way with the Bank. He is mistaken."[42] And to a member of Congress: "All the other banks and all the merchants may break, but the Bank of the United States shall not break. . . . [Those who doubt this] must rely on Providence or Amos Kendall."[43]

The worthy President kept his counsel and let subordinates do the talking. The bank continued to attack, finding a spectacular weapon in the ancient right of petition. "Memorial from the city of Portsmouth, New Hampshire," noted the journal of the Senate, "complaining of great embarrassment and pecuniary distress . . . [owing] to the removal of deposites from the Bank of the United States." Memorial from New Orleans, Louisiana, praying that deposits be restored. Same from Bridgeport, Connecticut, Plymouth, North Carolina, Madison County, Kentucky; same from Philadelphia, signed by seven hundred "cabinet-makers, chairmakers, upholsterers &c." A meeting in Bucks County, Pennsylvania, offered "the deliberate opinion . . . that if Andrew Jackson . . . is sustained in his reckless usurpations . . . this country . . . will cease to be a republic."

Singly and by twos and threes and tens such documents showered upon Congress, each an occasion for a speech, and sometimes five or six. Administration tacticians answered with counter-petitions. Memorial of seven thousand citizens of Boston "explicitly approving the course of the President"; resolutions of the Ohio State Legislature endorsing the removal of deposits;[44] resolutions of the "freemen" of Schuylkill County, Pennsylvania, declaring "the United States Bank . . . corrupt and corrupting, and now, in its desperation a vampyre that would draw the last drop of blood from the honest yeomen of the country." The whole number of memorials from both sides mounted from the hundreds to the thousands, the speeches keeping pace: Clay, Calhoun, Webster, bell-wethers for the bank; Benton, Forsyth, James K. Polk, for Jackson—a Niagara of oratory seeking to drench a Vesuvius.

The bank people seemed to have the better of it. By the wide margin of one hundred and fifty-one thousand names to seventeen thousand, they presented the more numerously signed memorials. The histrionics of their orators were professionally superior. Calhoun, by no means the most vehement of the President's critics, pronounced the looting of the Roman exchequer by Caesar less reprehensible than the conduct of Jackson and the Kitchen Cabinet. "They have entered the Treasury, not sword in hand, as public plunderers, but with the false keys of sophistry, as pilferers, under the silence of midnight."

In private the President occasionally bridled up. "Oh, if I live to get these robes of office off me, I will bring that rascal to a dear account," he exclaimed of Henry Clay. The editor of the *Globe* exhibited what he described as notes for a speech by a member of the House which characterized the President's revolutionary exploits as electioneering fiction. "The damned, infernal scoundrel," roared the old man, pointing to the deep scar on his forehead. "Put your finger there, Mr. Blair."[45]

On the whole, however, the President seems to have betrayed less anxiety than Martin Van Buren, on whom devolved the unenviable duty of listening to hostile speeches day after day. Early in the session the Vice President enclosed to General Jackson a letter received from a friend. Old Hickory replied at once:

"I have read Col H.[46] with attention. he is in a *panic*. . . . I am not in any panic. were all the worshippers of the golden Calf to memorialize me and request a restoration of Deposits I would cut my right arm from my body before I would do such an act. . . . I am mortified at the . . . [timidity of] our friends."[47]

That spirit had won the Creek campaign. But Red Eagle had not at hand the resources of Nicholas Biddle.

6

In proof of this the technique of the hostile petition was immensely improved. Instead of sending their memorials by post, signers were instructed to choose delegations to bring them to the capital. These emissaries filled hotel lobbies with their bitter talk and lined the benches of House and Senate galleries. The bolder ones began to finish off their sojourns by calling on the President. The first were received with stately courtesy, the Executive saying little in reply to their remonstrances. At length the time came when the old fighter's battle-instinct told him the hour was at hand to turn to other uses the pit Nicholas Biddle had been digging for Andrew Jackson. Old Hickory took the offensive.[48]

A delegation from Philadelphia brought the largest petition of all, bearing ten thousand signatures. Jackson received the representatives courteously, but before the spokesman had uttered a dozen words he interrupted.

"Go home, gentlemen, and tell the Bank of the United States to relieve the country by increasing its business." The old man's voice was shrill. "Sooner than restore the deposits or recharter the bank I would undergo the torture of ten Spanish inquisitions. Sooner than live in a country where such a power prevails I would seek an asylum in the wilds of Arabia."[49]

At the allusion to Arabia, Nicholas Biddle smiled and said the General might "as well send at once and engage [his] lodgings."[50]

A committee of mechanics and artisans of New York presented itself. "Well, what do you want?" demanded Old Hickory. "I tell you I will never restore the deposits. I will never recharter the United States Bank. Here I am receiving one or two anonymous letters every day threatening me with assassination. Is Andrew Jackson to bow the knee to the golden calf? I tell you if you want relief go to Nicholas Biddle."[51]

That was it. The very cry. "Go to Nicholas Biddle!" The old warrior drove it home.

Members of Congress, Jackson members, were not so sure of their leader's strategy. A parcel of them brought to the White

House a rumor of a Baltimore "mob" which did not intend to be turned aside with words. It would lay siege to the Capitol until the deposits were restored. "Gentlemen," said the President, "I shall be glad to see this mob on Capitol Hill. The leaders I will hang as high as Haman to deter forever all attempts to control the congress by intimidation."[52]

No mob came from Baltimore to encamp on Capitol Hill, but a respectful deputation to present its memorial in the regular way, and to seek an audience with the President.

"General," said the chairman, "the committee has the honor to be delegated by the citizens of Baltimore, without regard to party, to come to you, sir, the fountain head, for relief . . ."

"Relief, sir!" the high-pitched tones cut like a knife. "Come not to me, sir! Go to the monster! It is folly, sir, to talk to Andrew Jackson."

"Sir, the currency of the country is in a dreadful situation."

"Sir, you keep one-sided company," retorted the President. "Andrew Jackson has fifty letters from persons of all parties daily on this subject. Sir, he has more and better information than you, sir, or any of you."

"The people, sir. . . ."

"The people! The people, sir, are with *me*."[53]

Lengthy accounts of these interviews in the Biddle press represented the President as a cantankerous old man about as amenable to reason as a bolt of lightning. More friendly reporters did not destroy this impression entirely;[54] and the Executive himself had the bad taste to let Blair publish some of the letters threatening assassination.[55]

The simulation of rage was an old Jackson trick, and effective. Young Henry A. Wise, who as a bridegroom had visited the Hermitage, was serving his first term with the Virginia delegation in Congress. He witnessed one of the President's harangues. When the petitioners had gone Jackson lighted his pipe. "They thought I was mad," he chuckled, and went on coolly to instruct his lieutenants "on the policy of never, never to compromise a vital issue."[56] One afternoon as Frank Blair reviewed the situation Jackson's eye lighted on the head-dress proffered by Black Hawk as a token of his surrender. Old Hickory put it on and shook his head until the quills rattled. "I don't think those fellows would like to meet me in this."[57] Thomas Hart Benton usually dropped in after the Senate had adjourned for the day. "We shall whip them yet," Old Hickory would tell the big Missourian. "The people will take it up after a while."[58]

When Andrew Jackson said, "Go to Nicholas Biddle!" it was not as if an ordinary man had said it.

people will take it up after a while.

When Andrew Jackson thought of Nicholas Biddle," it was

CHAPTER XVII

Doom of the Bank

I

In February of 1834 the bank fight reached the zenith of its
fury.

Flying the flag of no quarter, Nicholas Biddle threw his reserves
into the effort to bring the country to its knees, and with it Andrew
Jackson. The white-haired President, ill and rarely free from pain
for an hour, counter-attacked so savagely that it seemed to some
as if the gods were about their business of making mad one whom
they had marked for destruction. On the other side is the testimony of Congressman Wise that deliberate calculation prompted
Old Hickory's flailing exhortations to "Go to Nicholas Biddle."
The General's personal correspondence and the administration of
his private affairs during this critical period appear to bear out
Mr. Wise. Instead of a man beside himself with passion, they
reflect an example of extreme self-possession.

For instance, not until January, 1834, did the President select
another depository in the capital for his personal funds. This was
three months after he had discontinued the public deposits in the
Bank of the United States. An account was opened with the Bank
of the Metropolis, the "pet" institution in Washington, though the
President was in no haste to withdraw the balance remaining in
Mr. Biddle's vaults. On July 7 when he closed out the account it
amounted to eleven hundred and thirty-seven dollars.[1]

At the beginning of the year the General's private concerns
seemed to be flourishing. Andrew, junior, reported one hundred
and eighty to two hundred thousand pounds of cotton on the way
through the gin. Though the young man was a little late with
that operation, his father did not complain. The crop, as estimated,

stood to net at least fifty thousand pounds baled, which at fifteen cents, a low estimate, would gross seventy-five hundred dollars,[2] an excellent showing for a beginner. Typically the old frontiersman thought of branching out and creating a greater estate for his son. Hunter's Hill, which Andrew Jackson had been obliged to relinquish at forced sale in 1804, was said to be on the market. The place embraced five hundred and sixty-three acres adjoining the Hermitage. The two properties could be thrown together nicely and operated as a unit. Telling the boy to open negotiations with an inquiry as to the price expected,[3] the President turned to a subject nearer his heart. "I am truly delighted to hear our dear little Rachel has cut her jaw teeth. we have now a right to hope that she has passed the dangerous stage of teething."[4]

His running horses, too, were coming on, with three promising fillies in the White House stables—Emily, Lady Nashville and Bolivia. At the Hermitage two fillies and three young stallions engaged the old turfman's particular interest. As three of them were all that could be trained without hiring professional help, Jackson wrote his son to breed the fillies and train the studs, forwarding opinions "of the action of each."[5]

The first thing to divert the President's attention from the breaking in of the Hermitage colts was a small matter but "mortifying," as he expressed it. A Mr. George Hibb of Cumberland, Maryland, had presented a demand note for two hundred dollars signed by Andrew, junior. The instrument had been given in part payment for a negro girl whom the young man, already traveling with five servants, bought on his way to Tennessee the autumn previous. This was a violation of the General's instructions on the subject of debt. He paid the note, gently voicing the hope that the transaction had not impaired his son's credit.[6] The boy begged his father's pardon and wrote pridefully that sixty-three bales of cotton had been shipped to New Orleans, and that when the ginning should be finished he hoped for one hundred bales. The corn was not all gathered, Andrew said—writing on January 25—"but we are at it." General Jackson replied that the information concerning the cotton was of little value as the weight of the bales had been omitted, also the handling charges. Moreover, had the cotton been sold or merely shipped? And finally, no statement of the plantation's obligations at the beginning of the year had been received. Jackson had repeatedly directed his son to reckon up his debts on the first of each year, arrange for their payment out of the proceeds of the crops, and order his scale of living accordingly.

Nor was this all. The young man placidly announced the purchase of Hunter's Hill: price ten thousand dollars, "in one and two years payments," with a possible extension to three years. Other details were as meager as they had been about the cotton: "I could get it for no less. . . . What think you of it. I think the place worth it." Though General Jackson thought the place far from worth it, he merely requested his son to ask for no extension of time and to forward at once the weight of the cotton, the charges against it, and other outstanding bills. But the old man was worried. When four days elapsed and no copy of the agreement with Harry R. W. Hill, the seller of Hunter's Hill, arrived he wrote again. "I am anxious to receive your contract with Mr. Hill. he is a very keen man, and do nothing with him but what is reduced to writing."[7]

Two months later Jackson was still writing his son for the contract with Hill, the weight of the cotton and the amount of the Hermitage debts. Then came word from Maunsel White, the General's broker and honest friend, announcing the arrival in New Orleans of the first shipment. The cotton was of inferior quality, the shipping charges excessive and the shipping agreement negligently drawn from the standpoint of the owner of the cotton. White did not mention the weight of the cotton, doubtless assuming that Jackson knew it, and he mentioned only casually that he would pay the proceeds of the sale over to N. and J. Dick & Company, assuming that Jackson must have known of that arrangement also. This was disconcerting information. The Dicks were the New Orleans agents of Harry R. W. Hill. "Is it possible," Old Hickory asked his son, "[that] you have given Mr. Dick a power to receive the proceeds of our crop? . . . I am fearful you have been dealing too loosely with Mr. Hill . . . [who is] a keen mony making man. . . . I have had much writing on this subject, and uneasiness."[8]

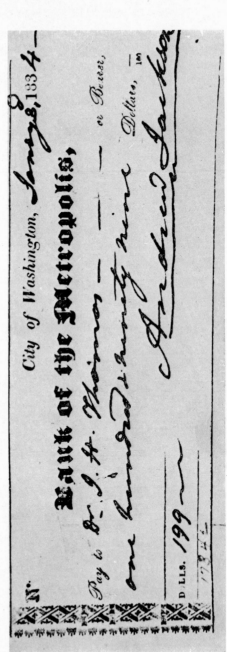

GENERAL JACKSON AND MR. BIDDLE SEVER BUSINESS RELATIONS

But not until they had been fighting each other officially for three years, and not until nine months after the President had transferred the Government deposits to other banks. Above is Jackson's last personal check on the Washington branch of the Bank of the United States, withdrawing his balance. Below is one of his first checks on an account he had started some months previously in Washington's "pet" bank. From the Jackson Papers, Library of Congress, Washington.

The apprehensions were justified. The Dicks were, indeed, empowered to collect at New Orleans the proceeds from the sale of the Hermitage cotton and to hand the money over to Harry R. W. Hill. This was a part of the agreement between Hill and Jackson, junior, a copy of which Jackson, senior, had been vainly trying to get hold of for ninety days. The reason the young man failed to send it seems to have been that he had no copy in his possession. Jackson, senior, directed him to obtain one at once "or you will have *trouble*." The arrangement with Dick also was most unfortunate, the father said. "He is unworthy of trust, my deadly enemy." Although under no delusions as to the advantage the sharp Hill had taken of his inexperienced son, Old Hickory meant to stand by and to liquidate as quickly as possible any bargain the boy had made. Quotations for cotton were up in Liverpool—fifteen to twenty cents. Maunsel White was a competent trader. At these prices fifty thousand pounds should easily bring five thousand dollars clear of all charges and plantation debts. By taking something out of his salary as President—twenty-five thousand dollars a year, payable monthly—Jackson hoped to be clear of Mr. Hill in short order.[9]

The next letter from the Hermitage brought tears of joy to the old man's eyes. Sarah was a mother again—this time of a "fine son" already named Andrew. "Present to my dear Sarah and the sweet little babe my blessings, and a kiss to each. Kiss my dear little Rachel and tell her [that] Granpa, if he is permitted to get to the Hermitage this summer, will bring her a pretty."[10]

Subsequent news was less pleasant. The whole of the cotton crop weighed thirty-seven thousand eight hundred pounds, not fifty thousand as anticipated. It had sold for eleven and a quarter cents, bringing a net sum of thirty-nine hundred and seventeen dollars, or about half the amount originally counted on. At the same time Jackson received the terms with Hill: five thousand dollars payable in May, 1834, and five thousand on January 1, 1835. By drawing on his own funds, Jackson placed in his son's hands enough to complete the first payment on time.

With this went tender letters patiently directing the young man's attention to several things. The price paid for Hunter's Hill was high out of reason; five thousand dollars would have been enough. No excuse existed for the overestimate of the weight of the cotton crop. An accurate "cotton book" kept day by day during the picking season would obviate that. Baling costs were too great. Jackson said he could bale fifty thousand pounds for what the boy had spent on thirty-seven. "My son these things are only brought to your view that you may profit by them hereafter." The young man must remember that he had another five thousand dollars to pay on the first of the year. Only by economy and prudent management could it be done. "And there is no certainty that I will live to aid you."[11]

Tardily the young man replied that seven late frosts—three in April and four in May—had killed much of the new cotton. A poor half-crop was about all they could hope to market in 1835. Still, he was cheerful and optimistic, qualities that never seemed to desert Andrew Jackson, junior.[12]

2

John R. Montgomery was a lawyer from the pleasant town of Lancaster, Pennsylvania, the home of James Buchanan. Coming to Washington on Supreme Court business, the attorney bore letters of introduction which brought an invitation to dine at the Executive Residence. After that experience, had he been permitted to read the admonitions of frugality which the President pressed on his son, Mr. Montgomery might have found the General's words inconsistent with his example. On February 20, 1834, the visitor wrote for his daughter Letitia a narrative of the evening's entertainment.

"About 5 o'clock I got to the White House, as the President's mansion is generally termed. The company had mostly assembled, for the party was small. There were three gentlemen from New York, a Tammany Committee, Judge Hopkinson [the bank lobbyist] of Philadelphia, Mr. Ham[m], our late charge to Chile, Mr. David of Baltimore, the Vice-President and his son, Major [Abraham] Van Buren, Mr. Rogers and myself. These constituted the party, with the President's own family and Mrs. Sherman from Baltimore and Miss [Elizabeth] Martin, a very pretty little girl from Tennessee." Miss Martin was a member of the Donelson clan, and a cousin, therefore, of Emily.

"About 1/2 after six o'clock we sat down to dinner. The table was very splendidly laid and illuminated. There was a large chandelier hanging over the middle of it with 32 candles besides those on the table, mantles and on the piers. The first course was soup in the french style; then beef bouille, next wild turkey boned and dressed with brains; after that fish; then chicken cold and dressed white, interlaided with slices of tongue and garnished with dressed salled; then canvass back ducks and celery; afterwards partridges with sweet breads and last pheasants and old Virginia ham. The dishes were placed in succession on the table, so as to give full effect to the appearance and then removed and carved on a side table by the servants. The first dessert was jelly and small tarts in the turkish style, then blanche mode and kisses with dryed fruits in them. Then preserves of various kinds, after them ice cream and lastly grapes and oranges.

"The wines on the table were Sherry and Port to drink with soups and the first course of meats. When the wild turkey and fish were served, Madeira was handed and while the wild fowl was eaten Champaigne was constantly poured out by the servants; after these were gone through with, Claret was substituted to be taken with the dessert and old Cherry was put on to drink with the fruits. As soon as all had taken what their appetites could possibly endure, we left the table and returned to the drawing room.

"I think I can hear Bud say, if father ate and drank all this he must have needed an 'Eoff pill.' But french servants know how to guard American appetites from the ill effects of too much indulgence and in helping to any one dish do it so sparingly as to leave room for another and yet another to follow. We were at table until nearly 9 o'clock and were eating and talking all the time. The President was very affable and his niece, Mrs. Donnelson, the lady of the house, near whom I sat, a very agreeable woman, so that the evening passed very pleasantly. Soon after our return to the drawing room, a cup of coffee was handed, then the ladies played the piano and sung and after this a glass of 'liquer' was sent around as the signal for adjournment and the party broke up about 1/2 past nine o'clock."[13]

This had been an informal affair, a degree removed from a family dinner. General Jackson's state entertainments were marked by a richness and a dignity devoid of stiffness unequaled since Washington's day. He brought to the Executive Mansion and all its concerns the tangy savor of the best that was in Tennessee. The stable, with its complement of colored jockeys, was as much a part of the White House establishment as the East Room, and as frequently honored by eminence and fashion.

On a spring day in 1834 the President rode out to the National Jockey Club to watch a trial of the White House horses. Jack Donelson, Congressman Balie Peyton of Tennessee and other devotees of the turf were in the party; also Martin Van Buren, who had bet more money on elections than on horse races. At the track were the fillies Emily and Lady Nashville, nominally owned by Donelson, Bolivia owned by Jackson, and a celebrated stallion, Busirus, owned by a friend of Jackson named Irvine.

The General admired Busirus and later acquired some of his progeny. He was an immense animal and two men were required to hold him so that Jesse, a jockey from the White House stable, could mount. When the holders let go, Jesse lost control of the horse which plunged against a fence. The crowd scattered. Jackson's high-pitched voice was heard above the commotion. "Get behind me, Mr. Van Buren! They will run over you, sir." The Vice President safe, Old Hickory turned his attention to the refractory stallion. "Hold him, Jesse! Don't let him break down that fence." He berated the horse's trainer. "Why don't you break him of those tricks? I could do it in an hour."

Behind his hand Balie Peyton observed that he would like to see any man break Busirus of those tricks in a week.

The remainder of the day's performances was satisfactory and Jackson left the course in fine humor. As he rode home, scenes from famous races of other days swam before the old sportsman: the Truxton-Greyhound match at the Hartsville course in 1805; the great contest between Newton Cannon's Expectation and Jackson's Doublehead in 1811 at Jackson's own Clover Bottom track. Doublehead had won and Jackson had collected a side bet of five thousand dollars from Colonel Cannon.

THE WHITE HOUSE

This popular name for the Executive Mansion received the accolade of polite usage during General Jackson's administrations. The portico was erected during his tenancy, and two pumps removed from the side yards. Unfortunately obscured by trees is the new stable, which Jackson filled with race horses and made as much a part of the presidential establishment as the East Room. From a print in the Library of Congress.

Expectation had been heavily backed by Cannon's friends. They took their losses to heart, which threatened serious consequences to Patton Anderson, a member of Jackson's racing set. "[After the race]," related the President, "I went to the stable to see the old horse cool off, and about dusk observed Patton Anderson approaching at a brisk walk, pursued by a crowd of excited men. . . . I was bound to take up common cause with Patton." Facing the mob across a stile, Jackson denounced their conduct as unmanly and promised that Anderson should meet any one of them at sunrise. And if Anderson did not Jackson would. The challenge gave Anderson an opportunity to escape into the tavern house that adjoined the stables.

The mob insisted on adjusting matters on the spot. "I saw there remained but one chance for us," Old Hickory continued. "Putting my hand behind me, into my coat pocket, I opened a tin tobacco box, my only weapon, and said, 'I will shoot dead the first man who attempts to cross that stile.' "

One man set his foot on the first step.

"I raised my arm and closed the box with a click very like the cocking of a pistol. It was so dark they could not distinguish what I had in my hand—and, sir, they scampered like a flock of deer!"

Jackson turned to the Vice President. "I knew there were men in that crowd who were not afraid to meet me or any other man. But, Mr. Van Buren, no man is willing to take a chance of being killed by an accidental shot in the dark."[14]

Fortunately the Vice President was never to find occasion to test the accuracy of General Jackson's conclusion. The phrase of the day destined to become most highly treasured in the fragrant memorabilia of the Jackson Era was Old Hickory's "Get behind me, Mr. Van Buren."

3

A saying that had a more immediate bearing on events, however, was "Go to Nicholas Biddle." The people were beginning to repeat it.

A politician wise in the ways of popular trends cautioned the banker as to the consequences. If the bank were to continue its policy of contraction without regard for public suffering the public would be persuaded that the institution was too powerful and deserved destruction. Mr. Biddle was advised to retreat. Hezekiah Niles of Baltimore, whose long-standing friendship for the bank was not dependent on subsidies, declared in his influential *Register* that the bank had shown too much ability to protect itself. Its power over the common welfare was too great; "which power," concluded the editor, *"I would not agree to continue."*[15] A New York adherent also sought to stay the hand of the banker. "Our friends complain, Our enemies exult." Sentiment was growing for "a new bank and a New Deal."[16]

Contemptuously Biddle scorned them all. He would yet force the nation to accept the old bank and the old deal and be thankful for them. "Rely upon it that the Bank has taken its final course and that it will not be frightened nor cajoled from its duty by any small drivelling about relief to the country."[17]

The bank's agents asked Governor George Wolf[18] of Pennsylvania, to address a strong pro-bank message to the Legislature.[19] So confident was Biddle of Wolf's continued friendship,[20] and so little did he do to retain it, that the State of Pennsylvania found it impossible to borrow three hundred thousand dollars. Incensed, Wolf denounced the bank for trying to bludgeon from Congress a charter and a return of deposits "by bringing indiscriminate ruin on an unoffending community."[21]

The effect was electrical. Unmindful of Mr. Biddle's hysterical threats, the Upper House of the Pennsylvania Legislature adopted resolutions declaring (1) "That the present bank of the United States *ought not to be rechartered by congress,*" and (2) "That the *government deposites . . . ought not to be restored.*" Forty-eight hours later the Governor of New York recommended the creation by the State of a stock issue of four or five million dollars to be loaned to state banks to ease the stringency. The Legislature authorized six million.[22]

While these momentous measures were in the making at Harrisburg and at Albany a committee of New York City merchants and bankers was formed under the chairmanship of James G. King.

The object was to obtain relief. Previously Mr. King had piloted a similar group to Washington to present the usual memorial to Congress and to call at the White House. "What do you come to me for?" rasped the President. "Go to Nicholas Biddle."[23] Shortly after, the *Globe* had announced that the Executive would see no more memorialists. They had served their purpose—or more correctly, Andrew Jackson's.

Mr. King took the advice. In the name of the merchants' committee he asked the banker to relax the pressure in New York. Endorsing the plea, aged Albert Gallatin, whose prestige in American finance was second only to that of Mr. Biddle, reminded the banker that it was within his power to afford the relief requested. Hitherto Mr. Gallatin had heartily espoused the cause of the bank. So ended a black week, beginning with the message of Governor Wolf. The drum-fire of disaster left its mark on the architect of the Greek temple in Chestnut Street. Nervously fingering the demands of King and the warning of Gallatin, Mr. Biddle was no longer a jaunty autocrat conscious of his power, but a cornered man.

He hesitated, he blundered. He told King that he would have eased the plight of New York ere this except for the action of the Governor of Pennsylvania.[24] So New York must continue to suffer because Pennsylvania abused the bank.

Fatal admission. The mask was off, revealing Mr. Biddle and his panic in their true colors. The bank party had said much of the one-man rule of Andrew Jackson. What now of the one-man rule of Nicholas Biddle?

What other modern prototype of robber baron has had the power to be so ruthless and so callous on so large a scale?

Mr. King coolly replied that the banker's reason for withholding relief "would not be deemed sufficient by our community."[25] When Albert Gallatin threatened to say the same thing publicly, Biddle struck his flag. It was no voluntary capitulation. "The Bank had to do something for the evil of such an announcement [from Gallatin] would have been enormous."[26] True; but Mr. Biddle's private apology for succoring New York overlooked the more important fact that the evil of his own conduct was beyond

repair entirely. New York accepted as a right too long denied
the relief wrung from reluctant hands—and not as a favor for
which it owed a debt of gratitude. The bank's goose was cooked.

General Jackson expressed his thanks to Governor Wolf of
Pennsylvania. "It was to have been hoped that our past experience
had sufficiently demonstrated the futility of all attempts, however
formidable in their character or source, to controul the popular
will: but there are unfortunately too many amongst us who are
not only destitute of knowledge of the people, but who seem
wholly incapable of acquiring it."[27]

This precise statement of the crowning weakness of Nicholas
Biddle's temperament contained nothing to indicate the part
Andrew Jackson's generalship had played in making that weak-
ness serve the people's ends.

4

In the ensuing weeks of March, 1834, the retreat of the bank's
forces in Congress became a rout. Mr. Biddle had met his Water-
loo, a Pennsylvania senator exclaimed, with only himself to blame.
The Pennsylvania delegation, led by the senators, deserted almost
in a body. Everywhere the lines gave way. Too late Calhoun and
Webster repudiated the self-centered leadership of Clay and introduced bills for recharter on a temporary basis. Perceiving the hope-
lessness of the cause, Webster tabled his own bill. Clay, too, knew
the bank was gone, but enough life remained to serve the purposes
of the Kentuckian's private feud with the Administration. This
remarkable parliamentarian brought up his almost-forgotten resolution of censure of the President. Marshaling apostate bank senators who had been none too cordially received in the camp of the
victorious Jacksonians, Mr. Clay obtained the passage of the resolution on March 28 by a vote of twenty-six to twenty. The President
replied that the Senate's act was unconstitutional and asked that
this protest be entered in the journal of that body. The Senate
declining to receive the reprimand, the censure alone remained in
the record.

This personal triumph for Clay, signifying nothing so far as the bank was concerned, precipitated a victory for Jackson in the House which impressed the seal of formality on the doom of Mr. Biddle's institution. Though not a spectacular legislator, James K. Polk, Chairman of the Committee on Ways and Means, was an exceedingly competent one. On April 4 he reported four sweeping resolutions.

1. "That . . . the bank of the United States ought not to be re-chartered."

It was carried by a vote of one hundred and thirty-four to eighty-two.

2. "That the public deposites ought not to be restored."

Ayes, one hundred and eighteen; noes, one hundred and three.

3. "That the state banks ought to be continued as the places of deposites."

Carried by the close vote of one hundred and seventeen to one hundred and five.

4. That a committee of the House investigate the bank's affairs and the reasons for the commercial crisis.

Carried by the vote of all but the bank die-hards, one hundred and seventy-five to forty-two.

"The history of this day," wrote one of Mr. Biddle's directors who observed the scene, "should be blotted from the annals of the Republic. . . . The Chief Magistrate of the United States seized the public Treasure, in violation of the law of the land; and the Representatives of the People have confirmed the deed!!!"[28]

Jackson's comment was briefer. "I have obtained a glorious triumph," he said in a letter otherwise dealing with a proposal to bring out a biography of General John Coffee.[29]

Disobeying a subpoena to produce the bank's books and defying arrest, Biddle defeated the attempted investigation. The net result was to confirm in the popular belief all the Administration charges. In June Henry Clay did what Mr. Biddle had hoped he would do in December and laid before the Senate a resolution asking for a restoration of deposits. Moreover, the resolution was adopted and went to the House. A desperate gambler's hope glowed in the breast of Nicholas Biddle. Casting ordinary precautions aside, he made the frankest offer of all to exchange the bank's money for political support, promising Louisiana two million dollars in relief loans in return for eleven votes which he thought were needed to pass the resolution in the House.[30] The banker was wasting his time. The House had spoken on April 4. It laid the Clay resolution on the table.

The Kentuckian had one more arrow in his quiver. He launched it when Jackson, waiting until within a week of the close of the session, presented to the Senate the name of Roger B. Taney for confirmation as Secretary of the Treasury. The nomination was rejected, and this time Jackson's white anger was real. Lost to the Cabinet was the one man who had not faltered an instant in the fight. It availed Mr. Biddle nothing. Like Wolfe on the plains of Abraham, Taney fell victorious, "the fate of the Bank," as Jackson observed, "sealed forever."[31]

5

Louisiana received her two million, and more, without paying any price whatsoever in votes. Boston was relieved, Pennsylvania relieved—relief everywhere, credit rushing like a stream long dammed to the farthest reaches of the country as the beaten Biddle cut the dikes with a stroke of the pen on July 11, 1834. By the end of the month, money was plentiful and commerce reviving so rapidly that one was apt in the bustle to pass by the stark débris of ruined careers and impoverished families. Taney's system of state depositories was working better. Though not all that its creator had hoped, the performance was superior to anything that the anti-removal people in the Administration had imagined possible. Many reflective men, and a multitude of others who had thought differently a year before, or had not thought at all, accepted the new order as an expedient preferable to perpetuating the authority of such a man as Nicholas Biddle had shown himself to be.

Jackson's popularity soared again. But Old Hickory found a deeper satisfaction in penning an affectionate letter to his former ward, Andrew Jackson Hutchings, who had married Mary Coffee. The young fellow was proving a far better planter than he had been a college student, his place showing a larger profit than the Hermitage. "You have not hinted whether a cradle will be necessary to compleat the furniture of your house. do inform me."[32]

6

On the evening of August 5, 1834, four very tired horses pulled a dust-stained coach past the brick gate-posts of the Hermitage. An old man in black alighted wearily. In his arms was a doll—the "pretty" he had promised Rachel. "I found . . . [her] as sprightly as a little fairy and as wild as a little partridge. . . . [The doll] was the only thing that induced her to come to me." The young lady's diffidence did not endure. She and her grandfather were soon inseparable.[33] Another measure to the patriarch's cup of happiness was the news that Mary Coffee Hutchings was going to have a baby. She being unable to journey to the Hermitage, the President replied that he would take a stage to Alabama and visit her. Only the sudden illness of Sarah deterred him.

In all it was the quietest visit the President had enjoyed in Tennessee. Yet there was a good deal to do. Andrew, junior, had run into debt again. Holtzclaw was let go and Edward Hobbs engaged as overseer. The cotton yield would be no more than half of normal, and exacting Harry Hill would expect satisfaction for young Jackson's five thousand dollar note. Not in twenty years had the Hermitage stood so in need of close and watchful handling.

Moreover, there was the self-perpetuating problem of what to do with the Eatons. Once had Hugh Lawson White and twice had the Tennessee Legislature politely defeated General Jackson's design to return the former Secretary of War to public life by way of the Senate. Eaton, himself, no longer cared a great deal. His library and his lands might have occupied him agreeably enough but for the inclinations of his wife. Margaret was bored by the provinces, though existence there was not so dull as it might have been without her. Tennessee had witnessed a pistol affray over Bellona's private life and the undoing of one of her active detractors—the wife of a former congressman of the blue blood and from the blue grass of the fastidious Gallatin district. In Washington this mighty lady had declined an introduction to Mrs. Eaton. She was now an exile in the remoter province of Missouri, disowned by her husband as a result of the disclosure of a liaison with one of his nephews.[34] Jackson offered Eaton the governorship of Florida. After sulking a while, presumably in the expectation of something better, he and Peggy departed for Tallahassee.

In September the President reluctantly entered his coach and started eastward, writing ahead to Major Lewis to have the White House rid of bed bugs.[35]

7

Thoughts on the future of the Hermitage and the Hermitage family kept General Jackson uneasy company on that journey. No letters overtook him en route, and none awaited in Washington though Andrew had promised faithfully to write. Two weeks more and no letter. "My son, Thirty one days has elapsed since we left sarah on a sick bed and the babe [Andrew] not recovered from its attack. I am wearied with anxiety and disappointment." The cotton, too, concerned him. Were the gin and the press working well? Much depended on these things if Hill were to be paid in January. Economy, economy: the old farmer dinned it in. Plant more potatoes and garden truck. That was one way to stop the leaks and make a place sustaining.[36]

Bring the hay and grazing fields back to where they were when Jackson was in charge, and cease buying feed for the stock. "The blue grass I want sowed in the two small lotts near the stud stable— The Timothy with a small portion of clover say one quart to the acre in the old timothy Lott, or mares lot, adjoining the north western field of cotton— the herds grass in the colts lott south of the timothy, and such other lots as you judge best for grazing and cutting. . . . The timothy lott ought to be prepared in the winter and sowed in the month of March— It ought to be thrown over by the large patent plow and four horses— after lying exposed to the frost until February it ought to be plowed with a small plow and when ready for sowing ought to be harrowed with the iron

"Sprightly as a Little Fairy"

General Jackson's characterization of his idolized first grandchild, Rachel, daughter of Andrew, junior, and Sarah Yorke Jackson, born at the Hermitage, November 1, 1832. From a portrait by Earl, owned by the Ladies' Hermitage Association, Nashville.

harrow, the seed sowed & harrowed in, and then rolled with a heavy logg drawn by two horses." Explicit directions followed for rigging the log.[37]

Pages of such instruction flowed from Jackson's pen. He sent to Philadelphia for seed. Andrew, junior, was cautioned to be careful with the clover. "It has cost me $83.75 besides the freightage."[38]

Forty-eight hours after the last of these letters had left his hands, Jackson heard from his son. The Hermitage had been swept by fire. The beloved house was a ruin.

Letters from neighbors who had rallied about the young man further enabled the President to reconstruct the calamity. On the afternoon of October 13, 1834, the roof had caught from a spark from the dining room flue. The family was absent. Hands from the Hermitage and from neighboring fields tried to mount the roof with buckets but could find no ladder. When Andrew and Sarah arrived, Sarah turned her attention to saving the furniture. Nearly all the downstairs and most of the upstairs things were carried out, some much damaged. The General's papers were saved. Rescued also was Rachel Jackson's wardrobe which had remained in her closet as it was on the day of her death. Considerable of the thick walls resisted the flames and, if protected from the weather, they could be used in rebuilding. To this end Robert Armstrong, the heroic artilleryman of Enotachopco who had eloped to the Hermitage with Josiah Nichol's daughter and married her there, undertook to "assist" Andrew the younger. Three whipsaws were started in the timber lot, and carpenters called from their work of building a house for Jack Donelson on the property adjoining. By the time the tidings of the disaster reached Washington the scaffolding was going up.[39]

The news was received with one of the few recorded expressions of submission to pass the lips of Andrew Jackson. "The Lords will be done. it was he that gave me the means to build ... my dwelling house and he has a right to destroy it. Tell Sarah [to] cease to mourn its loss. I will have it rebuilt."[40] On reflection the old man altered that brave declaration to say that the reconstruction would be in the hands of a "benevolent providence ... [who] will spare me long enough to have it rebuilt." And as a final token of humility he took his pen and after the word "enough" traced "I hope."[41]

Gratefully he approved the prompt procedure of Armstrong.[42] "was it not on the site selected by my dear departed wife I would build it higher up on the Hill. . . . Have it covered in before the hard frost and rain injures the walls. Have a tin roof put on it. . . . I write to . . . [Philadelphia] to send on by the Ship *Chandler Price* via New Orleans as much tin as will cover a House 80 feet by 44. This will enable you to borrow tin in Nashville from any one who has it."[43]

Other matters equally important remained. "In all your bustle my son have your cotton picked and Housed, gin'd, baled and sent to markett.[44] . . . My son, I regret to see that we are without seed wheat and that the negroes are without shoes in these heavy frosts. . . . [This] shows careless management." Nor were the sweet potatoes gathered. "They must be all tainted [by frost] and will rot before spring."[45] More detailed reports on the fire indicated that the early estimates of the loss of furniture were far too low.[46] "My son economy now upon all hands must be used . . . [if we are] to pay Hill for the land, meet my other engagements and rebuild my house. . . . Have the useless stock sold, the blooded stock well attended."[47]

8

Nicholas Biddle, too, could look adversity in the face, though not with the composure of Andrew Jackson. He knew this. Instinctively and from the first this singular man—poet, glass of fashion, philanthropist, in whom the quiet tastes of an esthete joined the reckless courage of a marauder—had felt Jackson the superior being. His whole conduct betrays it, and betrays more: a nervous anxiety to preserve "face," to o'ermaster Jackson as he had o'ermastered every other man who had stood in his way. In December, 1831, Mr. Biddle, himself, had made the decision that destroyed the bank when deliberately he chose to unite with Clay, whom he regarded as his inferior in ability, rather than with Jackson.

By autumn of 1834, the financier had sufficiently recovered from the débâcle of the spring preceding to try quietly to turn the fall elections in favor of the bank. He backed the Whigs. (Mr. Clay's party had dropped the name, National Republicans, and the Jacksonians frankly called themselves Democrats.)[48] But the Administration forces kept the initiative. The coinage of gold had been resumed that summer. "Jackson's yellow boys," they called the glittering pieces. Democratic stump-speakers were provided with long green purses to jingle before the huzzaing crowds as they flayed the bank. Riots startled the cities. Sending his wife and children to the country on election night, Mr. Biddle filled his residence and the Chestnut Street temple with armed men. He himself stood guard until dawn when he learned that the Democrats everywhere had been victorious.

"We bet largely," a field captain wrote in, "all the money you sent us, hoping by that means we might influence the election. but we have *not* succeeded. Almost all the anti-Bank members of Congress elected. . . . All hope is now in bribery! I think some of the members of Congress might be sounded successfully! You understand.——"[49]

Yes, Mr. Biddle understood—that the time had passed for that. Confessing final defeat, he good-naturedly turned to the task of selling the branches of the Bank of the United States, preparatory to winding up its affairs on the date of the expiration of the charter, March 3, 1836.

CHAPTER XVIII

THE ETIQUETTE OF COLLECTING TWENTY-FIVE MILLION FRANCS

I

ANDREW JACKSON PAGEOT, the capital's youngest subject of King Louis Philippe, had never seen the land of his paternal ancestors. He had never seen anything very far away from his birthplace, a large house in Washington which his proud maternal grandsire, Major William Berkeley Lewis, had strapped himself to provide. This infant's father, Alphonse Pageot, the attaché of the French Legation, had courted Mary Lewis in the White House. Their marriage had received the benediction of its venerated occupant and their son, his godchild, was christened in the Red Room.

These events were responsible for the cordial personal intercourse between the Executive Residence and the French Legation, a circumstance which added to the embarrassments of Louis Sérurier, the French minister and Monsieur Pageot's superior, when, on October 22, 1834, he donned his silk hat to pay the Secretary of State an official visit. Unfortunately the official relations between Monsieur Sérurier's government and that of the United States no longer could be defined as cordial.

When General Jackson took office, the United States for twenty years had been endeavoring to interest the government of France in sundry damage claims of our citizens arising from the depredations of Napoleon. Though they paid similar claims to other nations, the French refused to pay ours. Presidents came and went, so able a diplomat as John Quincy Adams getting nowhere against an almost intangible barrier of polite evasion and delay. With equal politeness Jackson adopted a firmer, stronger line than his predecessors, the result of which was rather surprising. In 1831 a treaty was signed and in 1832 ratified providing for the disbursement of twenty-five million francs in six annual installments, in consideration of which we should reduce the duty on French wines. Coming on the heels of the reopening of the British West Indian market to American trade, the French agreement was hailed as another triumph for the vigorous foreign policy of the soldier president.

We lowered the wine tariff. In 1833 the first installment of the French settlement was due and, though Louis Philippe's government had said nothing of any arrangement for meeting it, Jackson directed the Secretary of the Treasury to write out a draft for the amount. This was handed to the Bank of the United States for collection. The draft came back unpaid and the Treasury received a bill for one hundred and seventy-five thousand dollars in protest fees and the like. The French explanation was that the Chamber of Deputies had failed to make the necessary appropriation. The excuse did not rest well with Jackson who saw an effort to resume the old game of hide-and-seek. When the Chamber went further, defeating a bill to provide the funds, Old Hickory ordered the Navy ready for sea duty[1] and began to speak of laying the matter before the country in a "strong" message to Congress.[2]

This was the situation that brought Monsieur Sérurier to the State Department on October 22, 1834. The French diplomat had seen enough of Andrew Jackson's strong messages not to wish his country the subject of one. Our Secretary of State was courtly John Forsyth of Georgia, promoted for his part in the last battle against the bank. His greeting to the Frenchman was courteous but cool. When Sérurier expressed the hope that the United States would pursue a "discreet" course, Mr. Forsyth said that the President, "deeply mortified" by the behavior of France, was determined to inform Congress of the state of affairs. Sérurier continued his persuasions. Forsyth was unmoved. At length the French minister said:

"What do you wish, Monsieur, a collision between us or the execution of the treaty?"

Collision is one of diplomacy's less obscure synonyms for war. The usual urbanity of the Secretary of State did not desert him.

"The execution of the treaty," he replied adding, however, that the President deemed the people entitled to an explanation of the recent proceedings, and intended that they should have it.[3]

A month later the French minister repeated his request. Forsyth repeated his refusal and Sérurier wrote his government to expect "very painful" developments.[4]

2

To date General Jackson's conduct of our foreign affairs presented an almost unbroken pageant of successes: the West Indian agreement of 1830; claims against Denmark favorably settled the same year; claims against the Kingdom of Naples settled 1832; against Spain 1834; several commercial treaties conceding us most-favored-nation advantages. Only the effort to annex Texas presented a diplomatic spectacle about which the less said by Jackson partizans the better. And now this French question also approached a stage from which one party or the other would find it difficult to recede with dignity. The same, however, had been true of the situation with Naples when King Bomba found multiple excuses for not paying up. Whereupon Jackson sent a commissioner to receive the money, but he did not send him alone. Master Commandant Daniel T. Patterson and five men-of-war sailed into the Bay of Naples, with cannon firing—though merely the salutes required by international etiquette. They sailed out again—with the commissioner and the money. Would Jackson risk a similar line of tactics with France? Thinking he would, the captain of a Liverpool packet delayed the sailing of his vessel in order to be the first man to reach Europe with the President's message to Congress.[5]

One or two evenings later Frank Blair's partner in the printing business, John C. Rives, brought to the White House study a proof of the document, as revised by Forsyth. Donelson began to read it while Jackson patrolled the carpet with a pipe in his hand. Rives thought he heard the private secretary intentionally slur over a passage. Jackson paused in his walk. "Read that again, sir," he said. Donelson repeated the words more distinctly. "That, sir, is not my language," said the President taking up a pen. He scratched out the amended passage and wrote on the margin of the proof the robust words of the original draft.[6]

The packet-master's precautions were justified, the French minister's forebodings borne out. Without a trace of bluster, Jackson nevertheless had spoken of France as he had not spoken of another foreign power, going further than the energetic Edward Livingston, our minister at Paris, or most of the President's supporters at home, had expected to be asked to follow.

The time had come, he said, to "take redress into our own hands." "After the delay on the part of France of a quarter of a century in acknowledging the claims by treaty it is not to be tolerated that another quarter of a century be wasted in negotiation about the payments." Therefore, in view of France's continued "violation of pledges given through her minister here, . . . I recommend that a law be passed authorizing reprisals upon French property in case provisions shall not be made for the payment of the debt at the approaching session of the French Chambers." The next sentence disclaimed an intention to wound French honor. The law requested "ought not to be considered by France as a menace. Her pride and power are too well known to expect anything from her fears. . . . She ought to look upon it [only] as the evidence of an inflexible determination on the part of the United States to insist on their rights."[7]

Couriers spurred their horses, perspiring firemen piled wood beneath the boilers of locomotives and steamboats to speed the message to the country. The two hundred and twenty-five miles to New York were covered in thirteen hours and forty minutes. A flurry swept the seaboard's commercial marts. Marine insurance companies refused to assume risks resulting from a rupture with France. Pride swelled the breasts of common men: "Hurrah for Jackson!" Such a persistent heckler of the Administration as Philip Hone of New York privately characterized the message as "dignified, and its sentiment manly and patriotic."[8] A Massachusetts politician, grooming Webster for 1836, woefully admitted that in event of war the Whigs would have to support the President because he was right.[9] Despite a minor strain of criticism,

Old Hickory had the country with him. His touch had changed an obscure question, with which other presidents had fumbled in the dark, into a popular national issue.

3

Having rallied the country, Jackson restrained himself. He pursued the substance and not the shadow.

The French section of the message went to the Senate Committee on Foreign Relations, three of whose five members, Clay among them, were of the opposition. No three men in the French Chambers, sputtered the *Globe,* would take greater delight in "thwarting the measures of General Jackson's administration."[10] This statement, however, was not to be borne out by events. Though neither Congress nor the country showed a disposition to recede from the high ground the President had taken, a sentiment existed that we should do nothing further until the French Chambers had had a chance to act.[11] In a lengthy report the Senate Committee presented an exposition of the French issue not materially different from that of the President. It was suggested that Congress await the action of the French Chambers. Clay introduced a resolution to this effect which, with Jackson's silent consent,[12] was adopted by a unanimous vote. Some of the opposition senators, however, could not resist the temptation to make a wholesale distribution of the resolution as political propaganda against the President.

The atmosphere was growing tense a fortnight later when, on January 30, 1835, General Jackson visited the House chamber to attend funeral services for the late Representative Warren R. Davis of South Carolina. The burden of the chaplain's sermon was that life is uncertain, particularly for the aged. "There sat the gray-haired president," wrote an English visitor, Harriet Martineau, "looking scarcely able to go through this ceremonial."[13] The discourse finished, he filed past the casket and with the Cabinet descended to the rotunda of the Capitol.

A stranger of good appearance, his face covered by a thick black beard, was standing six feet away. No one noticed him draw the small, bright pistol he aimed at the Executive, but, as he pressed the trigger, the report rang through the stone chamber "like a rifle shot." Calmly the man produced another pistol. Jackson was one of the first to realize what was happening. Clubbing his cane he started for the man. *"Crack!"* went the second weapon. Old Hickory lunged at his assailant, but a young army officer reached the man first.[14]

The President was unharmed. Only the caps of the pistols had exploded, the charges failing to go off, although the weapons had been properly loaded "with fine glazed duelling powder and ball." Jack Donelson recapped one and squeezed the trigger. It fired perfectly. An expert on small arms calculated that the chance of two successive misfires was one in one hundred and twenty-five thousand. Rushing to the White House to congratulate the President on his narrowest escape from death, Martin Van Buren found him with the Donelson children in his lap, talking of something else to Major General Winfield Scott.[15]

The assailant said he was Richard Lawrence and that Jackson had killed his father. When it developed that Lawrence was an Englishman whose parents had never been in America, the prisoner described himself as the heir to the British crown. He said that he wanted to put General Jackson out of the way in order to strengthen his claims to the throne. When the prisoner was committed to a lunatic asylum, partizans on both sides objected to that undramatic disposition of the case, Frank Blair hinting that Lawrence was a tool of Jackson's enemies and Duff Green that the affair had been devised to create popular sympathy for the President.[16]

It did create sympathy for him, John C. Calhoun detaining the Senate with a denial of complicity, and John Quincy Adams proclaiming his allegiance on the floor of the House. These protestations were succeeded by the report of another explosion, set off by the arrival of the President's message in France. Gallic honor was officially outraged and Louis Sérurier appeared at the State Department to demand his passports. He received them and left with the Secretary a defense of his country's conduct:

"Les plaintes que porte M. le Président contre le prétendu non-

accomplissement des engagements pris par le Gouvernment du Roi . . . ne sont pas seulement étranges par l'entière inexactitude des allégations sur lesquelles elles reposent, mais aussi. . . ."[17]

The State Department's staff linguist rendered this as conveying the idea that General Jackson had made charges against the French government which he knew to be untrue. Edward Livingston was directed to inquire whether these were the sentiments of the French government, and if so to say that they would not be tolerated by the government of the United States.[18]

General Jackson asked Congress for heavy military expenditures, and the martial ardor of America matched that of the Parisian boulevards. As chargé d'affaires, Alphonse Pageot succeeded to the uncomfortable station of France's diplomatic agent in the United States. Beside himself with anxiety for his daughter and his grandson, poor Major Lewis trunneled to the White House letters which Mary Lewis Pageot had translated in the French Legation to show that not all her husband's countrymen were spoiling to fight us.[19]

So, for the time being, the matter sank into a state of uneasy repose.

4

Breaking the seal on a letter from George C. Childress, a kinsman of Mrs. James K. Polk, the President read that New Orleans had started public subscriptions to rebuild the Hermitage. To accommodate as many contributors as possible, no offering of more than fifty cents would be accepted. Mr. Childress desired to father such a movement in Tennessee.

General Jackson scribbled a notation at the foot of the page directing Donelson to thank Mr. Childress and the citizens of New Orleans and to give the money already raised to charity. "I am able to rebuild [my home]."[20] At the same time the proud old man wrote his son: "Draw on me for fifteen (1500) hundred dollars. This is as much as I can spare." If more were needed to pay the carpenters, borrow on the cotton crop.[21]

A new Hermitage was rising from the ruins of the old. Jackson's first impulse had been to reconstruct it brick for brick and timber for timber except for a fireproof roof. But as the abode his cherished Rachel knew had been altered almost out of recognition in 1831, the President consented to further extensive changes. The house was to be taller. The elaborate and rather vain front portico gave way to a simpler, statelier one supported by six great white pillars. This is the Hermitage that we know today.[22]

Andrew, junior's, family had found shelter in the remnant of the ancient blockhouse—the original Hermitage—which still stood on the place. Jackson professed to count this no hardship, recalling that he had spent some of the happiest days of his life in that log fort.[23] Nevertheless he asked Lewis, who was in Tennessee, to bring Sarah and the two children to Washington. They arrived shortly before midnight on November 26, 1834. "Grandpa, the great fire burnt my bonnet," little Rachel said. Sarah complained of fatigue. "I gave her a dose of medicine and she is quite lively this morning," the President related.[24]

She was lively enough to brave the rigors of a shopping tour, for the great fire had burned mamma's bonnet also. On Pennsylvania Avenue, she found others that struck her fancy—a "Blue Lame Toque," for ten dollars, a "Pink Silk Hat & flower $12" and a "Pink Bérét & feathers $13." Then the expedition was fairly under way: "14 yds Bleu Fig^d. Satin [$] 21, 14 yds Bro[wn] Fig^d. Silk 17.50, 14 yds Plain Silk 12.25, 1 Blond scarf 25., 3 Pr Worked Silk Hose, 9., 2 Pr. Plain Silk Hose 4, 2 Pr Long Gloves 9. . . ." General Jackson paid the bill—three hundred and forty-five dollars and eighty cents.[25] Nor was that the last of Sarah's shopping.

If compensatory economies marked the management of the White House, they were invisible to a boy from Ohio who, reporting for his first cruise as a second lieutenant of Marines, viewed everything in the capital with fresh, astonished eyes. A note from Mr. Van Buren had procured an invitation to partake of a family dinner at the Mansion, served at the proper Tennessee hour of four o'clock. One could judge the degree of formality of a White House dinner by the time the guests sat down. An affair for the diplomatic corps might be as late as seven thirty.

Walking very erectly in his new, high-collared uniform, Lieutenant Caldwell met the other guests in what he described as an "anti-chamber." After a little the President entered, greeted every one and chatted for fifteen minutes. Then a "porter" announced that the meal was served. "Led by the porter we passed through a spacious Hall and entered another finely furnished room which was darkened by the window curtains and blinds and contained two tables richly laden with fine plate and dishes and tall splendid lamps— around one table were chairs, so we were seated— What attracted my attention first was the very nicely folded napkin on each plate with a slice of good light bread in the middle of it." Light bread, made of wheat flour, was so designated to distinguish it from ordinary or corn bread. "Well, all being seated the Gen. asked the blessing, then the servants about the table, I believe one to every man, commenced—'Will you have some roast beef?— some corn beef?— some boiled beef?— some beef stake?'

"Well, the beef being through with away goes your plate and a clean one comes. 'Will you have this kind or that kind or the other kind of fish?' Fish being through, a new plate & then comes some other dish. Then a new plate comes and some other dish— then a new plate and the pies— then the desert— then & in the mean time the wines— sherry, madaira & champagne. . . . [We] drink one another's health— then after so long a time, all of which made very agreeable by miscellaneous conversation, we retire again to the Chamber whence we had come, where being seated in comes a servant with a dish of coffee for each of us. . . . Directly aside looking at my watch [and] find[ing] it almost 7 o'clock I conclude to retire. So I takes the Prest. by the hand and says Gen, I bid you good-night and it will always be my pride to do you honor.' "[26]

The Chief of State thus honored concealed the private worries that plagued his mind. "My son, I have waited with great anxiety to receive a Statement of the precise amount of our cotton that I might make a probable calculation . . . of the debt to Mr. Hill which becomes due the first of next month. . . . Surely these long nights you might write a few lines to your D'r sarah if you cannot write to me. Your own interest is involved."[27] Sarah exhibited less tolerance toward her husband's inattention and wrote that flirting proved a sovereign antidote for the shades of melancholy. Andrew, junior, replied that this was a fact he, too, knew very well, naming as the objects of his gallant addresses "the Beautiful *Mrs. Haggatt* . . . and the all accomplished and gentle *Mrs. Baldwin.* . . . So you see I am going ahead of you. . . . I will say no more except that you must try to enjoy yourself."[28]

Anxious to be useful in any particular, Major Lewis escorted Sarah to Baltimore and to Philadelphia to choose wall paper and furniture for the new Hermitage. In their absence General Jackson heard that his son was carrying on a game that went beyond innocent flirtation.

"I now address you with the fondness of a father's heart. how careful then ought you to be to shun all bad company, or to engage in any dissapation whatever and particularly intoxication. When I reflect on the fate of your cousin Savern, reduced to the contempt of all by his brutal intemperance I shudder when I see any appearance of it in any other branch of our connection. . . . [The happiness of] your charming little wife and sweet little ones depends on your upright course. this my son ought always to be before your eyes. . . .

"You must, *to get thro' life well,* practice industry with economy. . . . Nothing can be more disgraceful than the charge truly made that he has promised to pay money at a certain day, and violating that promise. Our real wants are but few, our imaginary wants many, which never ought to be gratified by creating a debt to supply them. These subjects [are] so essential to your happiness here and hereafter and that of your charming little family."[29]

Yet despite all young Jackson could do, or his father do for him, the five-thousand-dollar note held by Harry Hill which Andrew, junior, had promised to pay on January 1, 1835, was not met. It began to draw interest at six per cent.

5

More fortunate in the field of public finance, General Jackson was able seven days later, on January 8, to pay the final installment of the national debt. Owing no one and with a surplus in its Treasury, this Government enjoyed a fiscal standing unique in the history of the modern world. The favorable balance showed every indication of increasing, for in eight months the country had passed from a depression to a state of prosperity, with visions of overflowing abundance which French war clouds failed to dispel.

In the spring of 1835 the march of plenty crossed the line into the green pastures of speculation. The impetus came in part from a speculative wave in Europe, in part from the momentum of over rapid recovery from the Biddle panic, in part from the Treasury surplus creating an excess of loanable funds in the custody of the "pet" banks. The phenomena of inflation began to appear. New state banks were chartered by the score, most of them bidding for a share of the Government deposits, many of them getting it, and all printing their own money. Bad money drives out good. "Jackson's yellow boys," the gold pieces minted in 1834, vanished into the hiding places of the thrifty who knew that gold could be spent any day but were less certain of the current flood of paper. Bank notes flew from hand to hand in fantastic transactions of purchase and sale.

As prices rose the builders of the Hermitage were unable to keep within their estimates or to find carpenters or masons. "Hands cannot be got. I have written to Cincinnati, Louisville, Huntsville and Lexington."[30] Everywhere it was the same as artisans, shopkeepers, factory workers, farmers, judges, statesmen neglected their pursuits to take the easier road to fortune. City folk gambled in commodities, houses, rentals and stocks, making such terms as "bull" and "bear" and "corner" a part of the common speech. Everyone gambled in that illimitable American resource—land. A timber tract in Maine, bought for twenty-five cents an acre seven years before, was sold at an advance of thirty-six hundred per cent, profit two hundred and fifteen thousand dollars. The proprietor of an estate on the Hudson ten miles from New York subdivided it into a hundred parts, selling each for two thousand dollars. A farm near Louisville was turned over for two hundred and seventy-five thousand dollars. Secretary of War Cass exchanged a part of his farm adjoining the village of Detroit for one hundred thousand dollars. Lots in the swampy hamlet of Chicago sold for seven thousand dollars each. As a possible way out of his private involvements, the President sent his son to Mississippi to report on property the Chickasaw Indians were vacating for a site beyond the western line of Arkansas Territory.[31] Nothing came of the trip so far as Jackson was concerned, though Jack Donelson bought nine hundred and twenty acres.

The greatest stake in the speculative saturnalia was our almost incalculable public domain—an unpeopled stage of empire billowing from the westernmost settlements toward the sunset. This land was purchasable from the Government for a minimum of a dollar and twenty-five cents an acre. Speculating syndicates fell upon it and, elbowing aside genuine homesteaders, bought by the fifty-thousand-acre swoop, hoping for resale at ten and fifteen dollars an acre. In wilderness and prairie solitude, towns and cities were sketched in imagination and linked to the markets by imaginary railroads, canals and turnpikes. Public land sales rose in one year from four million to fourteen million dollars. The consideration therefor was the paper money of the deposit banks and of such other banks as the deposit banks would honor. As the banks could not hold this money idle in their vaults, they loaned it out to other speculators who purchased more land—a perpetual metamorphosis of paper dollars into paper towns and paper railroads emerging from a paper horn of plenty.

Another form of property, and the political ideas concerning the same, affected by this whirligig was the negro slave. As Jackson saw, slavery and not the tariff was the soil that nurtured the roots of disunion; eliminate the one and you eliminated the other. The early 'Thirties found Virginia, Kentucky, North Carolina and to some extent Tennessee debating proposals for gradual emancipation. The movement received a setback when Nat Turner's slave rebellion in Virginia took sixty white lives. Then the boom enhanced the prices of negroes. The Cotton Kingdom burst from the bud to a flower whose narcotic perfumes put to sleep emancipation schemes under the convenient delusion that, for better or for worse, the black race was a part of the South's heritage and could be controlled only in slavery. "The county court of Davidson,"

General Jackson was informed, "last week refused to emancipate the negroes of your [lately deceased] Uncle Alexander [Donelson] unless they would go to Liberia. They refuse to go. Their obstinacy will give you two or three negroes—a kind of property I suppose you but little care about."[32]

Fanatical William Lloyd Garrison launched his abolition crusade in Boston which, mistakenly it seems, was supposed to have been Nat Turner's inspiration. A storm swept the South, which southern members carried into Congress, for the exclusion of abolition literature from the mails. "On this great question," Jackson read in a letter from the New Orleans veteran, A. P. Hayne, "the South must stand or fall. *Man* loves *property* as he *does* his *life* and no government where the right of property is not secure can be looked upon as a good government."[33] So marched the South in these deceiving times, counter to the current of the world. With England liberating its blacks in the adjacent West Indies, our South sought to throw about itself a wall behind which to eternize a self-contained anachronism, Mr. Calhoun going so far as to proclaim slavery "a good—a positive good" for both races.

For the times it was not a bad life for the negro, as those of the late Alexander Donelson somehow realized when they preferred slavery in Tennessee to freedom in Africa. At the Hermitage was a black man named Sam whom Jackson had freed in 1816, but could not induce to leave the place. In retrospect it seems fairly clear that nowhere in the contemporary world did the negro find tutelage in the arts of civilization on the whole so beneficial to him as in the American slavery states. The overtone of Mr. Garrison's theme was the brutal treatment of the serfs. In the mill towns encircling Boston the average factory worker fared no better, if as well. A mill master could work his hands out of health without paying the doctor's bill. Deprived of civil status, property and family rights, the southern negro imperceptibly had acquired something greater—the power to mold the economic and social pattern of a people. Nearer the truth than Garrison, Hayne or Calhoun was General Jackson's Yankee friend, Washington Irving, when, taking a close-range view of slavery, he penciled in a pocket note-book: "In these establishments the world is turned upside down—the slave the master, the master the slave. The master has the idea of property, the latter the reality."[34]

And now began another phase as the enslaved race commenced to exercise its fatal influence on the political destinies of the free.

Andrew Jackson viewed the gilded panorama with apprehension. The perils of inflation were bad enough, as Old Hickory knew from dear experience. But the perils of slavery struck deeper, and would be the more difficult to meet.

6

Jackson did not direct his policy of rotation in office against political adversaries alone. Nowhere was it employed more freely than in the President's own official family.

In 1835 the General faced across his Cabinet table but one man who had held the same post a year before—Secretary of War Lewis Cass, and he was presently to go. The strong frontier face of the man from Michigan had lost its tan and grown a little soft under the blandishments of Washington living. With the French crisis on, Jackson complained of having to be his own Secretary of War. Old Hickory had no such fault to find with the man who sat at his right hand—the fourth occupant of the chair of the Secretary of State under Jackson. John Forsyth bore his responsibilities without troubling the President over details—and without neglecting the tailor who turned out the Georgian in splendid velvet-collared coats and black stocks reaching to the chin.

By trimming his sails to suit prevailing breezes, Levi Woodbury had ridden out the bank storm, making port as Jackson's fifth Secretary of the Treasury when the Senate refused to confirm Taney. Whereupon Mahlon Dickerson of New Jersey, a Jacksonian subaltern in the Senate, had received a handsome promotion as the third Secretary of the Navy. Martin Van Buren's law partner, Benjamin F. Butler,[35] with small black eyes and thin white fingers restlessly riffling the papers before him, was the third holder of the portfolio of Attorney General. At the foot of the table sat no stranger, but quiet, slender Amos Kendall, the only Kitchen Cabinet member to attain actual Cabinet rank. Jackson had lifted the unobtrusive Kentuckian from his insignificant closet in the Treasury to become his third Postmaster General barely in time to avert a scandal from Barry's amiable and innocent mismanagement.

Of all who had passed in and out of the Cabinet Jackson most sorely missed Roger B. Taney. Determined to reward the Marylander for his part in the bank war, the President nominated him for a place on the Supreme bench. But the opposition still controlled the Senate. On the last day of the session the clock in the Upper House was stopped at midnight, and Daniel Webster moved the indefinite postponement of action on the nomination. It was carried by three votes.

His Administration harried by a captious opposition, the country beset by fresh problems at home and abroad, Old Hickory was confronted by a revolt in his own party. It came about over the unbending insistence on Van Buren for Democratic standard-bearer in 1836. In 1832 Jackson had been able to quell but not extinguish opposition to the New Yorker. He was able to point to Van Buren's record of four years as the Executive's most useful lieutenant. He could point to no such record in 1835. In the nullification and the bank fights Benton, White, Taney, Forsyth and Polk, to name only those in the forefront, had served the cause of the embattled chieftain with greater fortitude and effectiveness. Yet Jackson clung to Van Buren, and would listen to no other word from anyone. The serious nature of the insurrection could no longer be disguised when the Tennessee delegation jumped the traces and, with only White, Grundy, Polk and one other absent, formally presented for the consideration of the forthcoming Democratic National Convention the name of Hugh Lawson White for president. Tacitly accepting the honor, Senator White's intercourse with the Executive Residence ceased.

Old Hickory refused to treat with the insurgents. Denouncing them as victims of a scheme of Henry Clay to "divide and conquer" the Administration, he toiled to tie up the convention for the Magician.[36] The revolt spread, gaining adherents in other states. Whereupon Jackson served notice that he would relieve the convention of the responsibility of selecting a vice-presidential candidate as well, his designee being Colonel Richard M. ("Tecumseh") Johnson of Kentucky.

This was an astonishing choice. Admitting the expediency of a western running-mate for Van Buren, Jackson could have found half a dozen men who were Johnson's superior in the qualities desirable in a candidate. Chief Justice John Catron of the Tennessee Supreme Court wrote the President a long and earnest letter. Mentioning only in passing the Kentuckian's want of capacity, Judge Catron rested his case on Johnson's open acknowledgment of a mulatto mistress, and the liberal education bestowed on two octoroon daughters who "rode in carriages and claimed equality." He suggested that to force the party to accept such a man would meet with a success in the South similar to that of Johnson's own efforts to introduce his daughters to society.[37]

7

Following the recall of Louis Sérurier, France strengthened its naval stations in the West Indies, which England took as a preparation to blockade our coast in event of war. At the same time, however, Louis Philippe laid before the Deputies a bill for the payment of the indemnity which, in May, 1835, we learned, had become a law—with an amendment to the effect that nothing should be paid until France received "satisfactory explanations" of the language of Jackson's message to Congress.

This time our national pride was touched. Jackson immediately recalled Livingston from Paris, leaving his son-in-law, Thomas P. Barton, behind as chargé. "France will get no apology," spread-eagled the Globe, "nothing bearing even a remote resemblance to one."[38] The President's bitterest foe dared not intimate anything else. Once more the country stood firm and ready behind old Jackson.

The spectacle was not lost on the statesmen in the Quai d'Orsay. In September when Secretary of State Forsyth returned from his summer holiday, he found young Monsieur Pageot awaiting an audience. By some means—Major Lewis is an obvious suspect[39]—the President had received notice of the object of the visit. The chargé asked leave to acquaint the Secretary with the contents of a letter from the Duc Achille de Broglie, the French Minister for Foreign Affairs. The communication occupied the twilight zone between official and unofficial papers wherein a minister who has something too delicate for state utterance may assume to step, with one foot, out of his official character and speak as a private person. Considering the saber-rattling that had gone on in France and the powdery amendment to the indemnity-payment law, Broglie's letter was astonishingly pacific. His Majesty's government would accept as meeting the requirements of the amendment a statement from our Government explaining "the true meaning and real purport" of Jackson's message in terms that would banish the idea that any affront to the French *amour propre* was intended. As Jackson had made this explicit statement in the message itself, all France asked was a formal repetition of the disclaimer.[40]

At the end of his visit, Pageot asked permission to leave with the Secretary a copy of Broglie's interesting letter. Mr. Forsyth knew what to say, for Jackson had told him. He could not receive the communication. To do so would be to admit the right of a foreign nation to concern itself in a purely domestic affair of the United States such as a President's communication to a co-ordinate branch of the Government. Such an admission would be degrading to the United States.[41]

On this display of French weakness Jackson acted at once. With his own hand he drafted instructions to Barton in Paris to say that the United States stood ready to receive the indemnity. If this note were not answered in three days, Barton was to ask when payment might be expected. If in five days this did not bring the payment or definite arrangements for the same, Barton was to close the legation and come home.[42]

Before Barton could be heard from, the time came to prepare the annual message of 1835 to Congress. Again Pageot attempted to press upon Forsyth the Broglie letter and again he was rebuffed.

"The honor of my country," wrote General Jackson in that message, "shall never be stained by an apology from me for the statement of truth or the performance of duty." This, however, was preceded by a statement that his message of the year before was not intended "to menace or insult the Government of France."[43]

Amid the almost universal acclaim this utterance evoked, the country learned that Barton had asked for his passports. Pageot immediately did the same. The first week of January, 1836, Andrew Jackson Pageot, attended by his anxious parents, began the long journey to the land of his paternal forbears, while his distinguished godfather plied the pen over a special message to Congress which Edward Livingston regarded as tantamount to a declaration of war.[44]

The united efforts of Livingston, Forsyth and Van Buren induced the old chieftain to tone down the document, but the version that went to Congress was no skimmed-milk affair. In view of the "peremptory refusal [of France] to execute the treaty except on [inadmissable] terms," the Executive requested "large and speedy appropriations for the increase of the Navy and the completion of our coast defenses." Nothing, said the President, would remain undone by him to "preserve the pecuniary interests of our citizens, the independence of our Government, and the honor of our country."[45]

At this juncture England stepped in to save the face of Louis Philippe with an offer of mediation. France immediately, and Jackson after just enough hesitation to avoid a look of precipitation, agreed to arbitrate. A sigh of relief was heard on two continents. "The war of etiquette," wrote Philip Hone, "is on a fair way now of being averted."[46]

8

France solemnly accepted General Jackson's message of 1835 as proof that nothing in the message of 1834 had been intended to wound her sensibilities. But before the British could congratulate themselves on the success of their pacific offices, the United States presented the note of ex-Minister Sérurier.

"Les plaintes que porte M. le Président contre le prétendu non-accomplissements des engagements. . . ."

Our translator had rendered this as follows:

"The complaints which the President brings against the pretended non-fulfillment of the engagements. . . ."

In fine, the issue of peace or of war between France and the United States ostensibly had been narrowed down to the meaning of one word. It was the word *"prétendu,"* which we translated as "pretended." In the text under review our linguist held that this conveyed the idea that Jackson had acted in bad faith. Against this rendering the British and the French foreign offices opposed their combined erudition. The whole trouble, the diplomats said in chorus, lay in our faulty translation. *"Prétendu"* meant "alleged," and nothing in the entire passage was susceptible of a construction implying that General Jackson was aught but the soul of truth and honor.[47]

This explanation was accepted as satisfactory to the government of the United States, and for the enlightenment of posterity and the advancement of the study of the French language in America a memorandum to that effect was filed in the archives of the State Department.

On May 10, 1836, the President made a gracious announcement of his complete victory. Four back installments of the twenty-five-million-franc indemnity had been paid with interest. Cordial relations were re-established with France.

To wipe the slate clean the two countries were to staff their respective legations with new personnel. Jackson arranged to send Lewis Cass to Paris and consented to receive as the French minister one Édouard Pontois. Imagine, then, his surprise when who should turn up to reopen the legation in Washington but Alphonse Pageot with his wife Mary Lewis and son Andrew Jackson. The tricky French again! Much as General Jackson loved Mary Lewis and his little godson, and much as he respected Pageot as a man, he was for packing the three of them back across the ocean.

So great was the presidential ire that a thoroughly alarmed Major Lewis came forward with explanations. The French were not villains in this affair, but the victims of a side-door intrigue between the good Major and the new minister to the court of Louis Philippe, Lewis Cass. Naturally, the Major wanted his

"QUI PAYE SES DETTES S'ENRICHIT"

A French jibe at their government for bowing to Jackson's terms in the debt settlement. The caption, "Who Pays His Debts Enriches Himself," accuses the government of wringing money from the country not only to satisfy the United States but to line its own pocket as well. From a contemporary cartoon in the collection of Emil Edward Hurja of New York City.

daughter back. So he had connived with Cass to get from Jackson, in private conversation, an expression of his personal friendship for the chargé. This Cass had transmitted to Paris in such a way that the French monarch had consented to restore Pageot to his old post as a private compliment to his esteemed fellow-ruler, the brave General Jackson. Still, as a rebuke to Cass, Jackson was for making a clean breast of it to Louis Philippe, and asking for Pageot's recall. At this point the British minister resumed his capacity as mediator and, with Major Lewis bringing to bear the weight of forty years of loyal friendship, Old Hickory relented and let the Pageot family stay.[48]

CHAPTER XIX

THE PRAIRIE ROSE

I

THE French question triumphantly disposed of, in the autumn of 1835 General Jackson turned to another problem in his foreign portfolio which, at the moment, seemed to be getting badly out of hand. For this the Executive himself was largely to blame.

Through the whole labyrinth of Jacksonian diplomacy, the topic of Texas had threaded a secretive and, as inhospitable critics were wont to imply, a sordid course. Two years before he became President, the General had received at the Hermitage a letter post-marked Jackson, Mississippi. "I have been into Texas," it read, "[and examined] the Soil, climate & local advantages of the coun-try— It must belong to the United States and I hope that it may be one of the Acts of your administration to obtain it."[1] The writer was Colonel Anthony Butler,[2] a bumptious South Caro-linian who had ranged the western border from the Lakes to the Gulf and fought at New Orleans. When this letter was written, in 1827, he was a member of the Mississippi Legislature and one of the increasingly numerous company of American speculators in Texas lands. They did much to keep alive the patriotic cry for a rectification of the international boundary which would bring their holdings under the stars and stripes.

In the summer of 1829 Colonel Butler joined another numerous company, that of General Jackson's super-serviceable friends gath-ered in Washington for the patriotic purpose of assisting the new Administration along the pathway of an illustrious destiny. Armed with maps and memoranda, he readily qualified as an expert on the Texas question with which John Quincy Adams had grappled for four years in vain. The grief-stricken Jackson listened to his oracular friend and instructed Secretary of State Van Buren to open negotiations for a boundary following the watershed between the Nueces River and the Rio Grande, with a cash inducement of five million dollars to enable the Mexican officials the better to appreciate the justice of our claim.[3] Adams had offered one million for about the same thing. Instructions for our minister at Mexico City, the competent Joel R. Poinsett, were quickly prepared. Owing to their confidential nature, these documents were not entrusted to the ordinary channels of communication. They were handed to Anthony Butler to deliver in person. Moreover, in the business at hand, Mr. Van Buren advised Poinsett to avail himself of the collaboration of the special courier.[4] Jackson himself added a personal note. "Col Butler . . . is entitled to your entire confidence."[5]

Four years' residence in mercurial Mexico had rendered Joel R. Poinsett somewhat immune to surprise. He has not illuminated the record with a description of his emotions when, a few days after the arrival of the Administration's breezy bearer of confidential dispatches, the newspapers of Mexico City announced that Colonel Butler had come with an offer to purchase Texas for five million dollars. The Government organ, *El Sol,* assured its readers that consideration of so degrading a proposal was unthinkable. Three weeks later Poinsett left for home. He resigned and Butler was named in his stead. The rise from obscure political adventurer to minister plenipotentiary with millions to dangle before Mexican statesmen was phenomenal even for the era of the "clean sweep."

Nor was this Colonel Butler's only remarkable achievement. For five years he held that post by the basically simple formula of redeeming one promise with another. At length, when the President's patience began to wear thin, Butler proposed military occupation of "that part of Texas which is ours. . . . [Place] me at the head of the country that is to be occupied [and] I will pledge my head that we shall have all we desire in six months." Jackson handed the letter to Donelson with the following endorsement: "A. Butler: What a scamp. The Secretary of State will . . . recall him."[6] Not until a year later, however—June, 1835—did the minister reach Washington. He did not come empty-handed. The new proposal was to cross the palm of one Father Hernandez, confessor of the sister of Antonio López de Santa Anna, the current president of Mexico, with five hundred thousand dollars as a stimulus to further negotiation. This suggestion had the advantage of being cheaper than others of a similar nature which Butler had laid before the Government.

Jackson replied: "Nothing will be countenanced by the Executive to bring the Government under the remotest imputation of being engaged in corruption." Our virtue thus made a matter of record, the Executive indicated no further readiness to interfere to an impractical degree with what Butler represented as a prevailing custom of Mexican statecraft.[7] Once the five million— no more—was paid over it would be no concern of ours as to the pockets the money might eventually reach. The President expressed himself more delicately, however: "The public functionaries of Mexico may apply it as they deem proper to extinguish *private claims* and give us the cession free of all encumbrance."[8]

Pleading for another chance and promising to work wonders, this man Butler was permitted to return to Mexico. He accomplished nothing and in December Jackson yanked him home for good. The diplomat expostulated against the ingratitude of republics. "Just at the period when a favorable moment presented itself to renew the work I am discharged from office."[9]

2

General Jackson did not despair. The Texas question was in the throes of another experiment, rendered the more exhilarating because it revolved about a personage whose history had run a course more bizarre than that of Colonel Butler—Sam Houston of Tennessee.

On the tearful January morning in 1829 when Andrew Jackson turned from his wife's grave to the road to Washington, he had paused to bestow his personal and political benedictions on Governor Houston. The occasion for the personal blessing was the announcement of Houston's prospective marriage into the influential Allen family of Gallatin. The Governor was thirty-five years old, six feet six inches tall, handsome, captivating, able. Marriage and a less roistering mode of life, his friends felt, were all that were necessary to complete his conquest of the heights. The occasion for the political blessing was the forthcoming contest in which Houston would be opposed for re-election by the powerful William Carroll, three times occupant of the State's executive chair. The weight of Jackson's influence, it was believed, would insure victory for Sam Houston, after which predictions as to his future ranged from the Cabinet to the White House itself.[10]

Twelve weeks after his marriage to Eliza Allen the glamorous Governor of Tennessee left his yellow-haired girl bride, resigned his office and under an assumed name boarded a steamboat for the western wilderness beyond the pale of civilization. The only explanation vouchsafed a stunned populace was that "private afflictions, deep, incurable," for which he alone was to blame had wrecked his happiness. Actually, Houston had accused his bride of infidelity, only to follow her to her father's house and on his knees withdraw the hot words and ask forgiveness. But it was then too late. A moment of wild accusation was paid for with a lifetime of regret.[11]

Twenty years before, Sam Houston, carrying a copy of the *Iliad* and a rifle, had run off from school to live with the Indians. That sojourn had lasted four years, a minor chief named Oo-loo-te-ka taking Sam into his family and naming him The Raven. In 1829 ex-Governor Houston again sought the wigwam of Oo-loo-te-ka, then principal chief of the Western Cherokees in what is now Oklahoma. He became again The Raven.

The first story Andrew Jackson received of the spectacular ruin of his protégé's fortunes included a report that he intended to rehabilitate himself by conquering Texas. Ordering a surveillance of Houston's movements, the President exacted from him a "pledge of honor" to respect the sovereignty of Mexico.[12] With little to lose and forgetfulness to gain, the exile turned to the whirlpool of internal Indian politics, momentarily giving Washington almost as much of a start as if he had gone to Texas. Under his leadership, border tribes united to oppose a resistance to white rapacity which gained a new respect for the rights of southwestern Indians. But on the whole he maintained good terms with Jackson, countenancing his policy of removal of the southern Indians as the best thing the red men could hope for. So passed three confusing years, during which The Raven stood forth, now an inspired leader of his adopted people, now a tribal vagabond known by another Cherokee name which casually translated means "Big Drunk."

Twice The Raven visited Washington, attractively clad in beaded buckskins and a blanket, to insist on the performance of Indian treaties. Jackson shocked the conservative wing of society by inviting him to the White House. On the second visit, in 1832, the President suggested a trip to a tailor and paid the bill. Never to be outdone in the matter of gifts was a part of Indian etiquette. From about his neck Sam Houston removed a small buckskin sack which for years had passed as a Cherokee witch charm. Opening the little bag, The Raven presented to Sarah Yorke Jackson Eliza Allen's engagement ring. Attired as a white man Sam Houston listened to his patron speak of Texas. Butler was getting nowhere, and Jackson desired dependable information from the Mexican province. Sam Houston left the capital with a War Department commission to hold parleys with nomadic Indians who pitched their camps at will on the Mexican and the American sides of the Red River. The instrument has the appearance of a subterfuge to cover a reconnaissance of Texas for the confidential use of General Jackson.[13]

3

The first activity of the unofficial envoy pleased Jackson no more than the diplomacy of Anthony Butler. Openly playing the game of the American land-speculating clique, hot for revolution, Houston aroused the suspicions of Mexico City so promptly that Jackson disavowed him.[14]

Houston changed his tune and sided with the conservatives who wished Texas under the stars and stripes rightly enough, but preferred the Jacksonian scheme of purchase to war. As prospects for a settlement by this means grew dimmer and Santa Anna's repressive measures harsher, Texas began to arm. General Jackson closed his eyes to an extraordinary emigration of American "settlers," lugging guns rather than ploughshares. The guns began popping in 1835 and, with Sam Houston one of their generals, the Americans in Texas drove the weak Mexican garrisons across the Rio Grande. The South and the West were alive with sentiment for the revolutionists, but Jackson preserved a stern show of official neutrality, sharply rebuking the Texan commissioner Stephen F. Austin when he requested the United States "openly" to take up the cause of the rebellious province.[15] Sam Swartwout incurred his chief's displeasure by presiding at a meeting in New York to raise funds for the friends of freedom in Texas.[16] Colonel Swartwout and other conspicuous New York Jacksonians were large shareholders in the great Galveston Bay and Texas Land Company, of which General Houston, in addition to his military duties, was the resident attorney.

Yet, despite the formal rectitude of Jackson the President, in his private character Old Hickory was unable to suppress a certain sympathy for the ardor of his southern and western countrymen, or an almost paternal interest in the fortunes of his old subaltern Sam Houston, now commander-in-chief of the scattered bands of adventurers grandiosely known as the Armies of the Texas Republic.

Early in 1836 came startling news. Santa Anna was north of the Rio Grande with seven thousand men. Houston ordered a general retreat and concentration. The leaders of the bands, remembering the easy victories of the year before, refused to obey. Santa Anna surrounded the Alamo and slew its defenders to a man. Then he wiped out a larger band at Goliad. Then another and another. With the government of the republic and the civil population in flight toward the United States border, Sam Houston managed to reach what remained of the "army," numbering three hundred and seventy-four men, and to get them out of Santa Anna's reach.

In the littered White House study Andrew Jackson pored over a map, trying to give reality to each meager, hysterical report from Texas. The one clear military fact seemed to be that Houston was making a zig-zag retreat, adding to his force while Santa Anna divided his in pursuit. The best that most observers hoped for was Houston's escape to American soil. Jackson disagreed. Sam Houston would turn and fight. Old Hickory's long forefinger crinkled the map at the western shore of Galveston Bay. He would fight *there,* the President said, or *there*—indicating a stream called Buffalo Bayou.[17]

In May came tidings too fantastic for belief: the Mexican army annihilated, Santa Anna a prisoner of war.

A few days later a travel-worn lieutenant of United States dragoons presented himself at the White House with dispatches from General Edmund P. Gaines, commanding our frontier troops— and from Sam Houston. Jackson fairly grasped the papers from the young man's hand. The old soldier's eyes lighted up as he read, exclaiming over and over, "Yes, that is his writing. I know it well. That is Sam Houston's writing. There can be no doubt about what he says."[18]

The fantastic tale was true. After a retreat of thirty-eight days, Houston had taken Santa Anna by surprise at the junction of Buffalo Bayou and San Jacinto River, obliterating the army under his immediate command and capturing the president of Mexico.

A note of congratulation went off to the conqueror. "I hope there may be no delay or discord in organizing a stable government to make the best use of the Independence you and your brave men have so bravely won. . . . Subscriptions are being made in Tennessee and elsewhere to aid you; to which I need not say I have contributed to the extent of my means."[19]

4

Before a week was out John C. Calhoun arose in his place in the Senate. He said there were "powerful reasons" not only for the recognition of the independence of Texas, but for her admission to the Union.

To add to the glory of Andrew Jackson was not among the ambitions of the statesman from South Carolina. He made this speech because Texas under the flag would open a vast field for the expansion of slavery and its peculiar political doctrines. So quickly did the dew begin to fall from the prairie rose and the thorns to appear. General Jackson could sympathize with many of the current complaints of the southern people. He had asked Congress for a law prohibiting the circulation of inflammatory abolition literature through the mails. Yet the Executive had no desire to risk the estrangement of conservative northern opinion by throwing Texas into the bubbling cauldron of slavery issues. Consequently a sharp line continued to divide the personal sentiments from the presidential behavior of Andrew Jackson as he strove to keep Texas from falling from the plane of national to that of sectional questions.

San Jacinto set the South and the West on fire. The Tennessee fund to which (in his personal capacity) General Jackson had contributed went to equip volunteers whose ambition was to conquer all Mexico. Troops swarmed into Texas until Houston had thrice as many as he could feed. Vainly he expostulated that the war was over and that Texas needed people to plant corn and not to perform military exercises. Even the ordinarily level-headed Gaines took leave of his senses. At a critical juncture of Santa Anna's invasion, Jackson had ordered this officer to march a small force a short distance across the international line ostensibly to avert border incidents. With Santa Anna a prisoner and the "On to Mexico" cry sweeping the West, Gaines called on the governors of five adjacent states for re-enforcements of militia. Jackson countermanded this at once, lecturing the Governor of Tennessee on "the obligations of our treaty with Mexico . . . to maintain a strict neutrality."[20]

5

Those not stricken by the Texas fever found ample excitement at home as the craze for land speculation reached new heights in 1836. One of the springs from which this speculation fed was the ever-mounting Federal surplus on deposit in the "pet" banks. In 1829 Jackson had pronounced in favor of distributing such a surplus among the states. Now he was less certain of the wisdom of this. But the people wanted it, not as a means of curbing speculation but as a means apparently of getting something for nothing. So a bill was passed for the distribution of the surplus, beginning in 1837, which in June, 1836, Jackson signed with misgivings.

Alarmed by the multiplication of banks and of paper money, the President perceived flaws in the "pet" bank deposit system,[21] which had begun to present evils as patent as those he had fought to extinguish in his long battle against the Bank of the United States. Deposit banks were lending Government funds on security of doubtful value, and were adding to the flood of paper currency far in excess of their power conveniently to redeem.

The best thing that could be said of the distribution of the surplus revenue was that it would force deposit banks to curtail their loans to the extent of thirty-odd millions. This might check, but it would not stop, the course of currency inflation so long as the land boom lasted. And land gambling would continue so long as the products of the other paper money mills were receivable at the Government land offices. Benton introduced a resolution providing that only gold and silver should be taken in payment for public lands. The grip of the speculative mania was too powerful, and it failed of passage. Jackson then took the responsibility on himself, directing the Secretary of the Treasury to issue the famous Specie Circular which appeared on July 11, 1836. Before the earth-shaking protests of the speculative fraternity, the President remained unmoved, and the land boom received a death blow. The fall of fictitious real estate prices carried down other prices. The inevitable inconveniences of this readjustment brought complaints from those who believed a paper prosperity could endure forever.

6

In still other details Old Hickory showed himself the master.

He gave his party as candidates not only Martin Van Buren but "Tecumseh" Johnson as well. Going through with his threat to secede, Hugh Lawson White accepted an independent nomination from the Tennessee Legislature. But as the Jackson party divided, so did the opposition. Massachusetts put forth Webster as an independent nominee. South Carolina played a lone hand, declining to affiliate with anyone. Under these circumstances the only chance to defeat Van Buren seemed to lie in throwing the election into the House, and Henry Clay showed little enthusiasm for that. Standing graciously aside, the Kentuckian permitted the apparently hopeless Whig nomination to go to William Henry Harrison of Ohio.

In the face of party revolt the old leader also achieved in 1836 a victory which did much to alter the controlling social philosophy of the United States Supreme Court.

John Marshall had died the year before. Jackson called him one of "the greatest men of his age, . . . [although] perhaps it is proper that I should say . . . [that I] dissent from some of his expositions of our constitutional law."[22] In a word, Marshall set property rights above human rights and Jackson did not, though in their differences over the Cherokee Indian cases this distinction does not hold. On the whole John Marshall had carried on the social philosophy of Hamilton while Jackson was revitalizing that of Jefferson.

Strange this was, because the two Democrats, the greatest of their century, disliked and distrusted each other. For all his service to Jeffersonian ideals, Jackson inconsistently regarded their author as a feathery doctrinaire; Jefferson looked on Jackson as a border ruffian. Actually the men were not well acquainted, neither having had an opportunity to see beneath the top layer of the other's personality. Twice only did they meet after Jefferson's retirement in 1809, once in 1815 and again in 1823. Neither meeting got beyond the scrupulous exchange of amenities. Earlier encounters seem to have been even more superficial. Yet, from these brief contacts were derived those hasty first impressions which crystallized into lifetime convictions—with which, however, neither man seems to have been wholly satisfied.

For Marshall's successor Jackson nominated Roger B. Taney. Perhaps personal reasons swayed him as much as any other. Perhaps partizan considerations, as much as any other, moved the Senate to confirm this nomination after having twice rejected Mr. Taney for lesser offices. Nevertheless, the accession of Chief Justice Roger B. Taney marked the beginning of an era in the history of the Supreme Court which was to remold its thought and carry into its decisions (excepting on the negro question) the liberal social spirit having as its goal the greater well-being of common men.[23] In Jackson's last days in office, Congress helped along the trend by increasing the number of justices from seven to nine. Of these Jackson, in his eight years, named six, or more than any previous President except George Washington. He could have named seven, for the court was passed on to his successor with one vacancy.

7

"Kiss your dear Sarah for me and my two sweet little ones," Andrew Jackson wrote to his son. "Tell the children grandpa is coming. . . . If convenient have the two year old filly out of the virginia mare broke by the time I get out."[24]

On July 10, 1836, the White House coach rolled across the bridge into Virginia behind four mettlesome horses, fresh for the long journey. The last thing the President had done before leaving was to borrow money to settle household bills, though the arrival of an unexpected draft for eighteen hundred dollars for work on the Hermitage obliged him to leave with some of the local items unpaid. Bad roads and bad weather met the travelers at the outset. Every few hours a horse would throw a shoe, and repairs to the coach cost as much as meals and lodging for its occupants. One day they were seven hours going ten miles, after which a single-tree and both fore-axles gave way. More drafts met the traveler en route. "My dear Andrew," he wrote ahead, "draw on me no more until I can get funds." On August 4 the coach creaked into the Hermitage drive. Notifying Frank Blair of his arrival, Jackson described the condition of the horses. Then he briefly accounted for himself. "The continued dampness gave me a bad cold and cough and I fear I will have to use the lancet soon."[25]

The handsome new Hermitage was finished. New curtains hung at the windows, new carpets covered the floors. Much new furniture appeared in the spacious rooms, with more to come replacing the eighteen crates from Philadelphia which had been lost when the steamboat *John Randolph* burned at Nashville. Moreover all was paid for, the bills footing up to more than ten thousand dollars, which was nearly four times the amount of the first estimates Jackson had received of the probable cost of repairing the damage wrought by the fire.[26] On top of this the five thousand dollar note in the hands of Harry Hill had been paid.

Drastic economies at the White House—fewer guests and less lavish fare—had made these things possible, for the 1835 cotton crop (for which Jackson normally would have been paid in April, 1836) represented the greatest failure in the history of the Hermitage.[27] This was the second failure in two years. Old Hickory anxiously looked forward to the time when he should be master of his own acres. "The eye of the owner maketh the ox fat."[28]

A source of trouble was the fact that Andrew, junior, shifted too many burdens to the shoulders of his overseer. The young man was frequently absent from the plantation. A letter from the harried superintendent reflects the diversity of the problems left behind.

"Your directions concerning the purchase of some mares shall be attended to. I shall also use my best exertions to sell your riding horses. I could have sold your grey horse long since had it not been for his eyes. As respects the tap for the screw [for the cotton press] I had the pattern made at home by Ned with the assistance of sharp 3 or 4 days to instruct him and it is now at the furnace ... [for] casting. ... I have the timbers all ready and so soon as I can get the Casting I will put up the press again. I have the shingles nearly ready for covering the gin house. ... We have a great many other Jobs to do, such as fixing our Corn houses, repairing lot fences and one or two of the negro houses wants new shingles. We have all our winter cloth for the negroes done. Our shues I have not yet began. I have been trying my best to get the leather. I shall finish gathering of fodder this week.

"Our neighbors are becoming a little alarmed about our cotton crop on account of verry cold rainy weather. I was at Mr. Pools a few days since and saw the colts gallop, they appear to be doing finely. Pool makes some considerable calculations on the black colt and Majr. Donelson's horse Mombrino he feels verry confident of taking the mile. . . . Some sickness Amongst us but nothing very serious. Aron the Blacksmith and Tom Franklin was both taken . . . [with] verry hot fever all night. I gave them a large dose of Calomel and Jalap this morning. Littleton is laid up with Gonerea, he got it from his wife."[29]

Such was the nature of the things with which the planter grappled on his last visit home before retirement from his country's service. Both Andrew, junior, and Overseer Hobbs came in for a strict talking to. The White House salary could not be depended on much longer to cover the losses of the farm. "My son, you must assume energy, and command our concerns. . . . We must make better crops and preserve our stock better or we will soon be in a state of *want* and *poverty*."[30] With increasing dismay the old man surveyed stables, stock lots and fields: not enough blue grass or herd's grass or wheat; more land in oats, hemp and millet than needed, and this "slovenly sowed." "We must plow better and cultivate less [acreage] and we will produce more."[31]

After six weeks of study General Jackson concluded, years in advance of his time, that the underlying defect in the Cumberland Valley's scheme of agriculture was an overdependence on cotton as a money crop. "We must change our culture in part to stock, hemp and perhaps tobacco." Preliminary arrangements were made accordingly,[32] and in September the President started for Washington for the last time, leaving Jack Donelson behind. Emily was very ill.

8

The desk in the second-floor study was nearly buried beneath a pile of papers which the winnowing of Donelson could have reduced to half. The President bent to the task encouraged by the thought that, after all, the end was in sight.

THE FOURTH HERMITAGE

Finished 1835 after its predecessor had been destroyed by fire, save for portions of the exterior walls which were used in rebuilding. In the background, right, is Tulip Grove, the residence of Andrew Jackson Donelson. From an engraving made in 1856 and owned by the Ladies' Hermitage Association.

Angrily Jackson conned the reports on the Seminole campaign in Florida, the second Indian "war" of his administrations. The Seminoles had declined to fulfill an agreement by which their pampered chiefs had consented to remove the tribe beyond the Mississippi. Jackson had sent Winfield Scott with an impressive body of Regulars and militia to teach the recalcitrants a thing or two about the sanctity of treaties—when broken by an Indian. Unfortunately the soldiers of General Scott's numerous army had simply got in each other's way, leaving the Indians in unenlightened possession of their swamps. Veterans of Jackson's celebrated Florida expedition filled the mails with derisive letters. The President recalled General Scott. Brigadier General Richard K. Call of the Florida militia, who in 1818 had followed Old Hickory as a captain, was given command. He promised to show the country an Indian campaign, Jackson style.

Another problem arose from an enthusiastic effort to quicken the work of destiny in Texas. That republic had elected Sam Houston president, voted overwhelmingly for annexation to the United States, and started a minister to Washington under the cordial assumption that everything would be as easy as falling off a log. Slavery extremists were in transports of joy, while Abolitionists uttered the most menacing threats yet. General Jackson thought the impulsive Texans, like the Seminoles, had something to learn.

In the midst of these difficulties it was a pleasure to consider the presidential campaign. Old Hickory could see nothing but a sweep for Van Buren.

9

Jack Donelson was on the way to Washington, making a journey which naught but a Jacksonian sense of duty could have impelled him to undertake. He had left his beautiful wife dying, as he believed, of "quick" consumption.

There being no appropriation for a private secretary to the President, Jackson had given his nephew a minor place in the Land Office. Ordinarily the duties were slight, but during the past summer forty thousand land patents had accumulated which only Donelson's signature could validate. It was imperative that they be signed. Fortunately, when Jack reached the capital, his wife was reported to be better. He fell to work night and day, and Jackson said he must start for home the instant the job was done.[33] By the time he had written his name forty thousand times, better news came of Emily. So strong was the hope for recovery that Donelson concluded to help with the annual message and return by way of Philadelphia to buy furniture for the new house he had built at Tulip Grove, his plantation which adjoined the Hermitage.

The message was begun—the last to bear the name of Andrew Jackson. As he worked the President was seized with coughing. Blood gushed from his mouth. Doctors cupped and blistered him. As if the hemorrhage had not taken enough, they drained his veins of sixty ounces of blood. For two days it was not known whether the President would live or die.[34]

Forty-eight hours later the incredible invalid was sitting up. They placed in his hands a letter which had come from Emily. It was a cheerful letter. Emily was able to leave her bed and to take a little exercise each day. A succeeding post, however, had brought tidings of a setback. Propped against pillows, Jackson began an answer to Emily. It does not appear that he was shown the letter bearing the bad news. He did not need to see it. Tuberculosis ran in the Donelson strain. Old Hickory had seen too many of the clan go to feel sanguine about Emily. At the time of their parting in Tennessee he had feared her doomed.

Yet the letter began in a hopeful vein. "I rejoice, my dear Emily, to find your spirits are good. This is necessary to your perfect recovery. . . . You are young——"

Yes, twenty-eight. In the eight years since General Jackson had brought her on to be the mistress of the White House, the bright, inexperienced country girl had matured into a notable hostess and lady of fashion. In the transformation nothing was lost of her youthful warmth and gaiety, her courage and integrity. She had matched that courage against the courage of her dear old uncle, preferring the public humiliation of exile to countenancing Mar-

garet Eaton. Incidentally General Jackson's once-flaming championship of Bellona was a thing he no longer spoke of. Not that
the old man had repudiated the obligations incurred in sponsoring
that mésalliance. Florida proving too undistinguished a theatre,
he had made Eaton the minister at Madrid. Tales that drifted
back were not pleasant to hear: Margaret smoking cigars with
her guests while her husband steeped himself in rum.[35]

The brave tone faded from General Jackson's missive. "We
know not when we may be called home. Then let us live so that
we can say with the sacred poet:

> " 'Deal gently, Lord, with those
> Whose faith and pious fear,
> Whose hope, and love, and every grace,
> Proclaim their hearts sincere. . . .'

"My blessing to you and the children. Emily farewell."[36]

Jackson begged Emily's husband to leave him. Concealing his
almost unbearable anxiety Jack Donelson remained until the message was finished. December 3 he started for Tennessee. On the
night of the sixteenth a dream of death alarmed the President.
Three weeks later he learned that on the day before that dream
Emily had suffered the relapse which took away hope. She asked
that her bed be moved so that she could look from a window commanding the road by which her husband would return. Telling
her children good-bye, she sought to save what remained of her
strength for the effort to keep alive until Jack should come. At
noon on December 20 Emily Donelson turned her head toward
the window and closed her brown eyes forever. Jack was then a
two days' ride away.[37]

10

In the course of these trials, General Jackson learned that Martin
Van Buren had been elected his successor, though not by the margin Old Hickory had anticipated. Tennessee, including the Her-

mitage polling district, had gone for Hugh Lawson White. This was hard to bear. "We live in a day of personal and political changes," the old man said—accurately enough before his emotions got the upper hand, "and I must add, of depraved morals."[38] Another example of depravity, in General Jackson's estimation, occurred when the Electoral College, for once exercising the independence intended by the framers of the Constitution, failed to supply the majority required to make "Tecumseh" Johnson Vice President. The Senate elected him, however.

Strangely, the Senate which convened in December was a body more than usually amenable to the Jacksonian will, due to changes during the recess brought about by deaths and by resignations. Old Hickory had always had trouble with the Upper House, the lair of Clay, Webster and Calhoun. The great victory over the bank was won in the teeth of a hostile Senate, which had retaliated with a resolution of censure against the President. At the time and on the spot Thomas Hart Benton had served notice that one day he would see this slur wiped from the official journal of the Senate.

The vow was kept. For nearly three years the Missourian waited and watched. Compromises were offered. Would the Senator consent to the "abrogation" or "rescinding" of the resolution? No, he would not. The resolution must be "expunged"—physically expunged from the journal. The annoyingly logical Webster asked how the Senate could be said to "keep" a record if it were to vote to destroy a part of it. To no purpose: Benton had his majority for expunging. On Saturday night, January 14, 1837, about a table laden with cold meats and wine, the expungers planned their course.

A resolution was introduced at the opening of Monday's session. At midnight the opposition surrendered. The Clerk of the Senate produced the thick ledger for 1834 and turned to the resolution of censure. In the presence of a gallery packed to the last inch and of such senators as cared to bear witness, he drew heavy lines around the offending act and wrote across its face, "Expunged by order of the Senate, this 16th day of January, 1837."

This tinsel, twilight triumph pleased the old man as much as if it had contributed something material to his fame. His eyes would kindle as he displayed the pen the Clerk had used—a gift from Benton.

II

On the twentieth of December, 1836, William H. Wharton, Envoy Extraordinary and Minister Plenipotentiary of the Republic of Texas, spread his credentials before Secretary of State Forsyth. At the moment of their preparation, the republic being without an official seal, Sam Houston had stamped the documents with the impress of one of his cuff links instead. The treasury of the republic being innocent of funds to defray the traveling expenses of its diplomatic staff, Mr. Wharton had used his own. He had used them with taste and propriety. No minister from the Court of Saint James's has presented a more confident façade in the interest of his country. This was needful. En route Mr. Wharton had read the President's message. To Texans as well as to our own southern and western expansionists, the passage on Texas was little short of dumfounding. As to annexation—not one word. As to recognition, mere acknowledgment that Texas was independent of Mexico—these lines:

"Recognition at this time . . . would scarcely be regarded as consistent with that prudent reserve with which we have heretofore held ourselves bound to treat all similar questions."

Mr. Forsyth told Mr. Wharton that the clamor for annexation had "embarrassed" the United States. In view of the ruction stirred up by the Abolitionists would it not be best if the matter were taken care of "under the administration of a Northern President?"

Mr. Wharton could see no point to giving Martin Van Buren more honors than he had already received at the hands of Andrew Jackson. Post haste he set out for the White House, intent that Old Hickory should not be "robbed" of "glory" rightly his.[39]

Wharton was a native Tennessean whom Jackson remembered

well. He received the envoy kindly—in his study, for since his illness in November the President no longer came downstairs. But Wharton's mention of glory awakened no spark. Recognition, the President said, was a matter for Congress. Congress, countered Wharton, would not act without a special message removing the impression of the previous one. Jackson declined to write a special message. This was another way of saying, "Leave it to Mr. Van Buren."

Again and again Wharton returned to the Executive Residence, each time to be rebuffed. He did not give up. "Night and day," the envoy assured Sam Houston, "I shall . . . [persevere in] every argument that can operate on his pride and his sense of justice."[40]

From these incessant interviews a better acquaintance grew between Sam Houston's energetic agent and the feeble old President. General Jackson laid aside his reserve. He had not relinquished, he said, his desire to bring Texas under the flag. But a more ardent desire was for the security of the Union. To annex Texas now, or to recognize its independence, would be fuel to the flames of sectionalism—too dear a price for any man to pay for the gratification of ambition. But Jackson said he saw a way whereby the acquisition of Texas could be made to bind together the Union instead of rending it apart. "Texas," he said, and his voice was thin and high-pitched, "Texas must claim the Californias. The fishing interest of the North and East wish a harbour on the Pacific." Offer it to them and they would forget their cry against the spreading of slavery through the southern reaches of Texas.[41]

General Jackson was too tired to say more—if more needed to be said. "A day of changes," in sooth. Who knew better than the man who had made it that the era of Florida conquests was over?

And the spacious "reign" was nearly so. Three weeks remained. The sick old soldier took his meals in bed. When unable to don an ancient dressing gown and hobble to his study, he worked on a couch strewn with official papers.

Three weeks seemed a long time.

CHAPTER XX

THE SCEPTER PASSES

I

BENEATH the mask of pre-inaugural gaieties, a feeling of sadness pervaded Washington. People crowded into the capital not so much to greet the new President as to tell the old good-bye. They brought parting gifts—pipes, canes, a light wagon made of hickory with the bark on, a splendid phaeton of timbers from the frigate *Constitution,* a cheese four feet in diameter and weighing fourteen hundred pounds, a hat from a hatmaker who begged leave to honor the man who had "bestowed the Blessings of Government upon the Poor as well as the Rich."[1] The services of Frank Blair were commandeered to help acknowledge the letters, resolutions and addresses which streamed in from the world over from all grades and degrees of men. As the editor's chirography was notorious, Jackson cautioned him to write "not in cypher but so it can be read."[2]

On Washington's birthday the cheese formed the *pièce de résistance* of President Jackson's last public levee. The people made this affair their own in a manner faintly reminiscent of the President's first "reception" in 1829. Draymen and milliners' girls touched elbows with Cabinet ladies and diplomats. Each sliced himself a piece of cheese and decorously departed. Leaning on the arms of his son and of Jack Donelson, who had come on to witness the closing scenes, the President descended the stairs and bowed to his guests for a while.

Upstairs packing boxes and trunks stood in the hallways. Rooms were being shorn of the eight-year accumulation of Jacksoniana, which included five gift busts of the General and twenty-eight pictures. Outside, the banter and soft, easy laughter of negroes no longer quickened life in the once populous stable. Gone were Marse Gen'l's corps of jockeys and hostlers and horse-wise hangers-on who had slept wherever they could spread a blanket and foraged victuals from the presidential kitchen. Sporting congressmen and major generals had used to seek them out as authorities on the points and performances of horses. Carefree, anomalous company of slaves—whose like no White House establishment had seen before or would see again—whose sojourn there drives into the core of the American saga: now on the winding, red road to Tennessee, convoying the racing, saddle and carriage stock. Only the four gray coach horses and their driver, the gigantic Charles, remained.

At the Mansion a caller announced himself with a speech which apparent practice had rendered letter-perfect: "Patrick Cunningham, sir; corporal Seventh Regulars, sir, at Pensacola and New Orleans; now for many years in Snyder's livery stable." Though Jackson rarely saw visitors except on official business, the Irishman's self-introduction so amused John Rives that he repeated it to the General. The President said to admit ex-Corporal Cunningham. The veteran counted out twelve dollars and handed them to his old commander. He had borrowed the money three years before.[3] Jackson could use it. The bill for crating and getting all his plunder home was two thousand dollars.

Money was scarcer everywhere, as the pendulum began its downward arc from the speculative zenith of 1836. In that desperate try which is always made to store up an artificial prosperity, the blame fell upon the Specie Circular. Placards appeared on the streets of New York:

> ### "BREAD! MEAT! RENT! FUEL!
> Their Prices Must Come Down!
> *The voice of the people shall be heard and will prevail . . ."*[4]

An apprehensive Senate voted to rescind the Specie Circular. The President's impulse was to veto the rescinding bill. He began to draft a message of rejection. Friends said a veto would be overridden, bringing upon the country a fresh flood of paper currency which could only postpone the day and aggravate the degree of retribution. Though he preferred to win his legislative battles in open fighting, Jackson "pocketed" this bill, and let it die.

William R. Wharton continued to press the claims of Texas for recognition. He was at the White House nearly every day, and the rest of the time on Capitol Hill. He wiggled into the diplomatic appropriations bill a line providing for the expenses of a minister to the "Independent Republic" of Texas. The line was stricken out. Another line was inserted providing funds for such a minister "whenever the President may receive satisfactory evidence that Texas is an independent power." This seemed harmless and was allowed to stay. When the bill was passed four days of Jackson's term remained.

Wharton flew to the White House. He repeated all his old arguments and invented new ones. On the afternoon of March 3, 1837, his last day in office, Old Hickory yielded, sending to the Senate the nomination of Alcée La Branche, of Louisiana, "to be chargé d'Affaires to the Texas Republic." One of the last acts of that body was to confirm this appointment. The hands of the White House clocks were converging upon midnight when Andrew Jackson and William R. Wharton, standing in the dismantled study, raised their glasses to Sam Houston's republic,[5] which Old Hickory had said should open the way to American dominion over the shore of the Pacific Ocean.

In his bedchamber General Jackson read a chapter from Rachel's Bible. He closed the Book and the mulatto George pinched out the candle. The "reign" was over.

2

The next day was bright and balmy. Andrew Jackson left the top floor of the White House for the fifth time since his illness in November. Seated beside Martin Van Buren, he rode toward the Capitol in the *Constitution* carriage drawn by the famous Jackson grays. Cheers stopped in the throats of the thousands who lined Pennsylvania Avenue. In reverential silence they removed their hats. "For once," wrote Thomas Hart Benton, "the rising was eclipsed by the setting sun."[6]

The multitude that filled the east lawn of the Capitol fell silent when the two men appeared on the portico. After Taney had administered the oath and Mr. Van Buren had delivered his inaugural address, the ex-President started slowly to descend the broad steps. The *Constitution* carriage, Charles and the grays waited at the bottom to bear the hero away. As in obedience to a signal a mighty shout burst from the throng. "[It was a cry]," recalled Benton, "[such] as power never commanded, nor man in power received. It was affection, gratitude and admiration, . . . the acclaim of posterity breaking from the bosoms of contemporaries. . . . I felt an emotion which had never passed through me before."[7]

Midway down the stone stairs General Jackson uncovered and bowed. A gentle wind stirred his silvery locks. The tumult died.

3

Why was it that the people loved him so?

In thronged Washington, where men slept in barbers' chairs, the question was debated that night as it was destined to be debated a hundred years to come.[8]

Mr. Justice Story, who thought that he instead of Taney should have had John Marshall's place, did not know the answer. "Though we live under the form of a republic we are in fact under the absolute rule of a single man."[9]

Senator Daniel Webster's opinion, as usual, had the merit of particularity. "General Jackson is an honest and upright man. He does what he thinks is right, and does it with all his might."[10]

A German nobleman recorded the views of an unnamed senator who assumed to speak without partizanship. "He called himself the people's friend and gave proofs of his sincerity. The people believed in General Jackson as the Turks in their prophet. With this species of popularity it is vain to contend; and it betrays little knowledge of the world and the springs of human action to believe that those who possess it [are] men of ordinary capacity. General Jackson understood the people of the United States better, perhaps, than any President before him, and developed as much energy in his administration as any American statesman. . . . Whether all his measures were beneficial to the people [is beside the point]; they were . . . in unison with his political doctrines and carried through with an iron [disregard of personal] consequence, notwithstanding the enormous opposition that wealth and talent could put in the way of their execution."[11]

William Cullen Bryant, a theoretical rather than a practical democrat, spoke further of this opposition, which he knew so well. "Faults he had, undoubtedly; such faults as often belong to an ardent, generous, sincere nature—the weeds that grow in rich soil. Notwithstanding this, he was precisely the man for the period in which he well and nobly discharged the duties demanded of him by the times. If he was brought into collision with the mercantile classes, it was more their fault than his own. No man, even the most discreet and prudent, could under the same circumstances have done his duty without exasperating them. The immediate and apparent interests, though not the permanent and true interests, of trade were involved in the controversy with the national bank. Artfully party leaders exaggerated the cause of the offense until they were almost entirely alienated. Had Zeno himself been President the result would have been the same."[12]

The trouble with Mr. Story's observation lies in the jurist's ignorance of the mass. At heart the people do not wish to govern themselves, all the catchwords of proletarianism notwithstanding. They wish to be governed. Their striving raises up two demagogues to one honest liberal of capacity; and a Jackson comes along about once in a century. Jackson knew this peculiarity of the people, knew it instinctively without conscious process of thought. In that way he knew many things. His early applications of this knowledge were not designed for the benefit of the common man. Jackson was born and reared in a frontier aristocracy—unpretentious, it is true, but all that an aristocracy could attain to in the Waxhaws of that day and time. Hacking his way upward in the Tennessee wilderness, he rose to the height of spokesman for one frontier class against another—nabobs versus leathershirts. Climbing higher, Jackson became a spokesman for the whole almost-autonomous West in the contests arising from the opposed interests of the settled, commercial seaboard. The things the West, even the nabob West, advocated then seemed alluring to the landless and the propertyless of the tidewater cities. This fermentation, shaped into a political movement during the hard times of 1818-22, found the underprivileged and the lackalls of the East one with the established currents of western thought.

Andrew Jackson brought to the presidency fewer personal ambitions than any man excepting Washington. The gradual alteration from border conservative to national liberal is noteworthy, but other eminent men have spanned a greater scale of change. John Adams and Patrick Henry storm into history not as liberals but as revolutionists shouting for bayonets and barricades. They rattle out not as conservatives merely, but as cantankerous reactionaries.

Emerging as a people's man, Jackson proffered no ordinary claims to that much-courted distinction. No mere arbiter between factions of followers, he strode forth to inspire, to lead, to govern. He not only reigned but ruled. He saw for the people what they could not see for themselves. The bank issue was as good as dead after the passing of the hard times of the Twenties. Jackson revived it, lashed up an apathetic public, lashed up apathetic lieutenants, silenced the unwilling; and drove on to victory. All this rested on the philosophy of majority rule. When a majority was at hand Jackson used it. When a majority was not at hand he endeavored to create it. When this could not be done in time, he went ahead anyhow. *He* was the majority *pro tem*. Unfailingly, at the next election, the people would return a vote of confidence, making his measures their own. This confidence was not misplaced. If not every day in the year providing a government *of* and *by* the people, Andrew Jackson did provide one *for* them.

He lived by valor. The people like that because it is exciting and because it clothes them in the mantle of Fortuna, with enormous power over the destiny of a public servant. Andrew Jack-

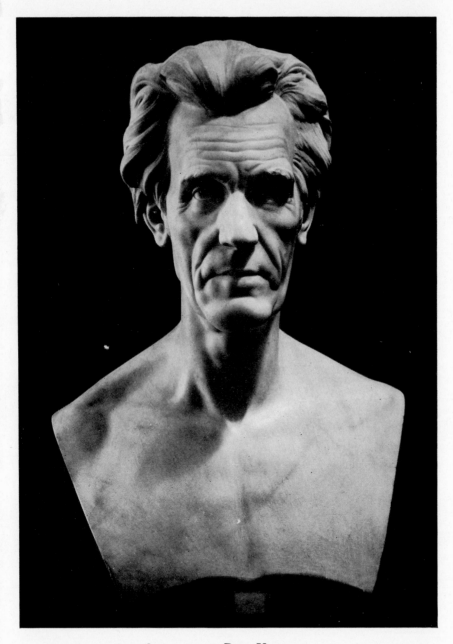

SCULPTOR AND DATE UNKNOWN

A bust of General Jackson, owned by Dr. Isaac M. Cline of New Orleans, and loaned by him
to the Louisiana State Museum.

son carried his political life in the hollow of his hand, ready to risk it for the cause of the hour whether that cause were great or small, good or bad—the Bank of the United States, the Spoils System, the French indemnity, Margaret Eaton. Time and again, heedlessly and needlessly, he exposed himself to destruction by the popular will. That the people did not destroy him bewildered the opposition. "Jackson's luck" became a Whig byword. Jackson's luck was the kind that gains respect for the proverb that fortune favors the brave.

Fortune also favors the competent. The opposition to Andrew Jackson has been mentioned. It was not composed of straw men. No other President has confronted a coalition of adversaries so able or so well furnished with the ordinary resources of political welfare. Henry Clay, Daniel Webster, John C. Calhoun, Nicholas Biddle: Old Hickory met these great captains and their legions separately and in alliance. He beat them to their knees.

Nor were the peculiar gifts Jackson brought to the presidency successful alone in the management of the domestic concerns of a democracy. His foreign policy raised the prestige of the young American nation to a height not before attained among the powers of the world. Genuine respect abroad for American rights dates from Jackson.

Through it all he had walked humbly. Departing for home one summer he directed that mail be forwarded to him, readdressed as follows:

> "Hermitage
> near the Fountain of Health
> Davidson County
> Tennessee"

The Fountain of Health was a healing spring of popular resort and, in the General's estimation, the most widely known place in the locality.

After eight years he laid down his burden, unsuspecting that on his times was an impress so characteristic and so deep that posterity would accord to Andrew Jackson an honor not as yet vouchsafed another American—that of marking out an Epoch in our national history and calling it by the name of one man.

4

The day after Mr. Van Buren's inauguration, and before the Jacksonian Epoch had been formally christened, the General conducted his own critique of the "reign." He had dropped in at Frank Blair's three-story house. The editor, Benton and young Senator-elect William Allen, a Jackson idolator from Ohio, were there. Old Hickory lighted his pipe and took his ease. The conversation ranged from the Carolina campaign of 1780 to the current moment.

His best piece of work as President, the General said, was getting rid of the Bank of the United States as the Government's fiscal servant. The problem was not solved, though. The state of the currency was alarming, and trying times doubtless were in store. But the people had been saved from the worse evil of placing themselves at the mercy of a monopoly for the enrichment of the few. If there must be paper money, let the issue be direct from the Treasury, based on the faith and the wealth in gold of the Government alone; no bank notes.

The tariff? A bad thing, a thing done only half right. Could the conflicting needs and wants and greeds ever be satisfactorily adjusted?

Texas? That would work itself out.

Oregon? Firmness and courage needed there, lest England "cheat our frank and candid statesmen." "Our motto should be, gentlemen, the words of our young friend Allen—'Fifty-four-Forty or Fight!'" Then England would yield. She would not go to war for the Northwest.

Regrets? General Jackson admitted two regrets. He had been unable to shoot Henry Clay or to hang John C. Calhoun.[13]

5

On the following morning, March 6, 1837, the *Constitution* carriage rolled from the White House drive. Mr. Van Buren had protested that Jackson was too tired to travel. This unavailing, he had directed Surgeon General Thomas Lawson to accompany the party. When Old Hickory undertook to alter this arrangement, Mr. Van Buren smilingly observed that the Surgeon General of the Army was under the orders of the President of the United States. The journey had been arranged with every consideration for the comfort of the distinguished traveler. The party would proceed by the steam cars to the western terminus of the Baltimore & Ohio railroad at Ellicott's Mills, Maryland, thence by coach to Wheeling, and by steamer to Nashville.

Almost as many people lined the thoroughfares as on inauguration day. They enveloped the railroad depot at Second Street and Pennsylvania Avenue, Northwest. They flowed onto the switch-tracks and the right-of-way. They took over every point from which one could see the waiting train. General Jackson stood on the rear platform, his hat off, his white mane flowing. No sound came from the multitude.

The conductor rang his bell. With a hiss of steam the cars began to move. General Jackson bowed. The crowd stood still. The train swung around a curve, its course described by a trailing plume of smoke. When this dissolved in the air the crowd began to melt away feeling, one has said, "as if a bright star had gone out of the sky."[14]

BOOK THREE

TWILIGHT OF A CHIEFTAIN

"I bequeath . . . my sword . . . with
the injunction that . . . [it be] used
when necessary in support and protection
of our glorious Union."

ANDREW JACKSON in his
last will and testament.

CHAPTER XXI

SHADOWS ON THE HERMITAGE

I

Ah, the Hermitage: memory-haunted garden; dark earth curling from the plow; blue hills standing in a blue haze on the river's yonder bank. Forty-nine years ago a raw, unsuspected heir to chieftainship first had beheld the Cumberland. So like the river had the course of his own life run—ever seeking, never finding tranquillity; until now, perhaps, at seventy.

"I am very thankful to a kind providence for sparing me to reach my home. I hope rest in due time may restore my health so as to be enabled to amuse myself in riding over my farm and visiting my neighbors."[1] So many concerns to catch up with. "I learn from Mrs. Donelson that your dear Mary is not well, [and] that Mrs. John Coffee [junior] was so much indisposed that she was obliged to wean her little infant. I hope that all this is not real."[2] On the journey home, he was never so honored as when his old soldiers brought their children to receive the chieftain's blessing. "I congratulate you and your dear Mary on the birth of a son. kiss the babe for me. Please say to Mary that she must constantly keep the croup sirup by her on the mantle piece. Sarah could not have raised Andrew . . . [without it]."[3]

The burdens of a patriarch supplanted those of a president. Had the old man surrendered a lock of his abundant white hair to everyone who requested it he would have resembled a moulting rooster. Had he complied with every request for a line from his pen, there would have been little time for anything else. To gratify every appeal for a loan would have swallowed his property. "An unknown youth," he scrawled on the back of a letter, "wants money to aid his education. I wish I had the means to supply his wants."[4]

This question of means was a serious one. When he took the presidency, General Jackson had carried five thousand dollars to Washington. He returned with ninety in his wallet. This he divided with Jack Donelson on overhearing his ex-secretary say he needed money to buy corn. Jackson's corn also was out, and oats and fodder, too. The stock was lean; the store of bacon low; the new tin roof of the mansion leaking; his son in debt for negroes bought to work Hunter's Hill. Yet Old Hickory fended without borrowing, though he did add his name to Andrew, junior's, notes for negroes. Virtually his only asset aside from the Davidson County farms was eight hundred and forty acres in West Tennessee. If need be he would sell that land to keep in the clear until the home places were paying again. To the restoration of the Hermitage the planter directed his immediate efforts. A field was carefully turned over and sowed in wheat with seed from Egypt.[5]

2

To stay free of debt in the spring of 1837 was a measure of elementary prudence, though a measure few could adopt because of involvements in the speculative craze, now on the brink of the abyss. On his way to Tennessee General Jackson had seen and heard alarming things: paper money falling in value everywhere; a blue-sky bank in Mississippi, chartered for fifteen million dollars, gone to the wall; planters "deeply indebted and paying 30 per cent for mony"; prime negroes down from eighteen hundred dollars to five hundred. "The speculators and borrowers in Mississippi and Alabama are broke," Jackson observed. "Their Bank paper at Neworleans and Nashvill, as I am informed, are at ten to 15 per cent below par and going down."[6]

The stories were true. Nashville was in a fever. During the two years past that keen real estate trader, Harry R. W. Hill, had bloomed forth as a capitalist of imposing stature with hundreds of trusting "investors" in his train. He was desperate. His fall would spread ruin like a holocaust. The banks of Nashville clubbed together to advance Hill three hundred and nineteen thousand dollars in one day when, as General Jackson dryly observed, an ordinarily solvent citizen could not discount a note for twenty-five hundred.[7]

Frenzied speculators, borrowers, bankers—all who found themselves in the path of the avalanche of tumbling paper—invoked the wrath of Heaven and of Martin Van Buren to strike down the iniquitous Specie Circular, or Treasury Order, as General Jackson always called it. Let the Government receive paper for public lands and confidence would return, and the American people regain their threatened Eden.

Old Hickory forgot his Egyptian wheat long enough to give the President a different view. "My dear sir, the Treasury order is popular with the people everywhere I have passed. But all the speculators, and those largely indebted, *want more paper*. the more it depreciates the easier they can pay their debts. . . . Check the paper mania *and the republic is safe and your administration must end in triumph*."[8] The storm grew fiercer. Nicholas Biddle joined the fray. Jackson expressed no surprise. "The gamblers and speculators, in and out of Congress, unite [against the Treasury Order]. . . . I thought it absolutely necessary at the time. . . . Its continuance [is] imperious now for the safety of the revenue. . . . I have done my duty to my country and my god, [and] have given [you] my opinion freely. . . . *I say, lay on, temporise not, it is always injurious*."[9]

The time was when Andrew Jackson thought the state banks safe custodians of the public revenue. He thought otherwise now. Caught up in the coils of speculation, going to the rescue of such men as Harry Hill, some of the depositories were falsifying their books to hide their peril. The Nashville banking house of Yeatman, Woods & Company suspended. Dark tales flew concerning the Government's local depositories, the Union and the Planters' banks. Old Hickory warned Van Buren to examine all deposit banks and get the Treasury funds in places of safety. The local anti-Jackson newspaper reprinted from the *National Intelligencer* of Washington a piece to the effect that General Jackson would be called on to redeem three hundred thousand dollars in notes bearing his endorsement held by the Yeatman bank, and that Jackson's draft for six thousand dollars had been protested in New York.[10]

These false stories made a small sensation in the East. The Old Chief hoisted on his own petard! New York merchants drafted a memorial to Nicholas Biddle to save them from the consequences of Jacksonian finance.

After a long silence Jackson heard from Martin Van Buren. The letter was dated April 24. "You cannot form an adequate idea of the dreadful state of the money market in New York. . . . My situation has been one of peculiar delicacy and difficulty. . . ."[11] Not a word as to the fate of the Specie Circular.

The same mail brought a letter, dated April 23, in the hierogly- phics of Frank Blair, which Old Hickory never learned to read easily. "Biddle was here yesterday and paid a complimentary visit to the President."[12]

By the Eternal!

3

Mr. Biddle's visit availed nothing. Martin Van Buren pre- served the Specie Circular. The banks of New York City sus- pended payments in coin. Others followed the country over. The United States Government could not get gold or silver for its funds. A panic was on which most articulate persons laid at the door of Andrew Jackson's financial policies, particularly the Specie Circular, the distribution of the Treasury surplus and the transfer of deposits from the Bank of the United States.

This incorrect view was destined for a long survival and is still widely held. Jackson's contribution to the boom had been a minor one. In view of efforts he made to arrest this inflation, his responsibility for the ensuing crash can be no greater than his participation in the original cause. Far from causing the crash, Jackson's measures rendered that inevitable catastrophe less severe than it would otherwise have been. The boom here was an ex- tension of one originating in Europe. When the inflation of land values on these shores got under way, foreign funds poured across the ocean to participate in the quick and rich rewards. Early in 1836 things began to tighten abroad, and European investors to withdraw their capital. The Specie Circular counteracted this movement, tending to keep coin at home and definitely checking the lavish use of paper here. But for that Circular, the disastrous reckoning might have been deferred at the expense of greater losses when it came; it could not have been avoided. The distribution of the surplus, depriving the deposit banks of additional loanable capital, certainly did not promote and it may have acted as another check on inflation.[13] Otherwise this act was bad, as Jackson realized at the time. He signed it reluctantly. Had he vetoed it the veto would have been overridden. The later cry against it sprang from wisdom after the fact.

As to the third point—the transfer of deposits from the Bank of the United States: in the bank fight, Jackson's primary aim had been to free the country of the shackles of a monopoly whose power he deemed too great, and whose public morals he believed too loose for the country's good. Stripping Nicholas Biddle naked, he had proved those indictments. As an experiment which he had believed would be successful, deposits were shifted to the state banks. Long before he left office, Old Hickory had begun to doubt the sagacity of this, and was examining plans by which the Treasury should care for its own funds and issue its own money based on the metal in its vaults.[14]

Swollen with public revenues, the "pet" banks were a factor in promoting the boom. How much more wisely Mr. Biddle might have handled those revenues is a matter of conjecture. One can draw inferences, however, from the manner in which he handled the funds of private depositors, for Mr. Biddle was still in the banking business. As the Federal charter was about to expire, Mr. Biddle had sent his agents to mingle with the members of the State Legislature at Harrisburg. The agents spent four hundred thousand dollars and obtained, by means corrupt on their face,[15] a charter to continue operations under the deceptive title of the United States Bank of Pennsylvania. Mr. Biddle's revamped bank plunged gaily into the waters of speculation and in May, 1837, ceased specie payments with the rest. But not from weakness, the glib wizard of finance was quick to explain. His bank had the means to go on; only a duty to his depositors, who might be forced to pay their debts in coin while others paid in paper, had induced him to suspend. "A great disaster has befallen the country. I shall strive to repair it."[16]

A drought was killing the Egyptian wheat, but Old Hickory had larger matters on his hands. "Mind not the clamour of . . . Biddle and Co," he wrote Martin Van Buren. "[Mind not] the demagogues, the Bankmen and gamblers. . . . Recollect the former panic and pressure; the present will soon blow over. . . . Be ye therefore steady, firm and unwavouring in your course and all is safe."[17]

Van Buren was steady. Calling Congress into special session in September he yielded nothing to the panic-stricken. He asked for a law rendering the Government independent of all banks, the revenues to be retained in the Treasury which would issue its own money—gold and silver for units under fifty dollars, notes for units over that. The plan was essentially Jackson's, forwarded from the Hermitage.[18]

On a raw October day in 1837 Amos Kendall, visiting at the Hermitage, found his host a quarter of a mile from the house without a coat, awaiting the mail coach with news of the Independent Treasury Bill. Jackson followed the progress of that measure—"Divorce Bill" in the vernacular—as keenly as he had followed any legislation in his days of power. His days of power— They were not done. With hearing failing, right eye nearly useless, and memory uncertain,[19] the white-haired warrior was still a chieftain—guiding, inspiring, strengthening faint hearts from his inexhaustible store of courage. Illness did not deter him, nor adverse election returns. Jackson's personal and political protégé Robert Armstrong was defeated for Governor of Tennessee. In the Hermitage countryside friends and family connections deserted the hickory standard. The chieftain heeded them not. Hold fast! he told Van Buren twenty times. Fight on!

Winter came and waned. Spring of 1838 brought word of the Divorce Bill's victory in the Senate, summer word of its defeat in the House.

Old Hickory cheered his successor. Never mind. "The eyes of the people are fast opening." Fight on![20]

4

Better success attended General Jackson in another battle. Conforming to his custom he paid his bills on January 1, beginning the year 1838 free of debts though it cost him his land in West Tennessee.[21] "I have no opinion of holding property when I need the money, and I will not borrow. . . . Since last spring we have paid upwards of seven thousand dollars." Most of this was to save Andrew, junior, from legal complications as a result of endorsing the notes of others, often as his father had told him to be no man's surety. "Andrew was inexperienced, and he happened to fall into the hands of men who pretended to be his friends."[22] The Hermitage was showing the results of the master's hand. Notwithstanding the drought, seventy-four bales of cotton went to New Orleans that spring. Jackson said the receipts would put him "in funds," and the eventual passage of the Divorce Bill restore prosperity to all.

But until that time should come the General meant to keep expenses within current means. He pressed those who owed him, placing claims in the hands of attorneys. When the cash was not available, he gave up a trip to one of Tennessee's many healing springs, relying on Matchless Sanative, a cough medicine which he said was making "a new man" of him. Frank Blair wrote that he hoped not, because "the old man" was good enough. Jackson recommended Matchless Sanative to ailing friends, with the advice to "carefully attend to . . . [the] directions [which] accompany each bottle."[23]

In July he joined the church, standing among the congregation in the little Presbyterian edifice he had helped to build for Rachel, and making a formal profession of faith. He would have done this much sooner, he said, but for the fear that this act might have been given a political interpretation. The hardest thing for Old Hickory to say was that he had forgiven his enemies; and he made it clear that only *his* enemies were absolved. Those who had slandered *her* remained for God to deal with.[24]

Banks were resuming specie payments. The outlook for the

Hermitage was so promising that General Jackson permitted his son to buy Halcyon Plantation, a property of more than eleven hundred acres on the Mississippi River in Coahoma County, Mississippi. The price was twenty-three thousand seven hundred dollars, payable in four installments, a year apart, beginning March 1, 1839.[25] This transaction completed without the use of a dollar of ready money, young Jackson stopped off at Nashville on his way home and bought a piano the same way.

In September Jackson suffered a great loss in the death of Ralph E. W. Earl. Seventeen years before a wandering portrait painter had turned up at the Hermitage—to find the only home he had ever known. Lovable, devoted, gently mocking at life—"Blair's the King's printer and I'm the King's painter"—[26] Earl had become almost as indispensable to the General's comfort as the mulatto George. "He was my constant companion when I travelled," the old man said. "Had I a wish to travel I have now no one to go with me."[27]

Autumn brought more adverse election news, and Samuel Swartwout, whom Jackson had made Collector of the Port of New York in the face of objections from Van Buren and from nearly everyone else, sailed for Europe. An examination of his accounts disclosed that Colonel Swartwout was entitled to the distinction of being the first American to steal a million dollars. This resounding blow to the prestige of the "reign" came at a moment when hard-pushed Mr. Van Buren was planning to sun himself in the Hero's renown. He had gone so far as to announce to friends a political fence-fixing junket in the South, to culminate in a reunion at the Hermitage. James K. Polk, who was running for Governor, suggested the omission of the reunion. The old man's feelings were hurt. "A visit to me surely could not be used to disadvantage the cause."[28]

Nevertheless, the tour was called off.

5

The year 1839 came in with cold weather. General Jackson put on a pair of woollen socks Mrs. Frank Blair had made, remarking that they would last him to the grave. This was intended as a compliment to Mrs. Blair's knitting, for the General was in a cheerful state of mind. He believed the end of hard times in sight. Though it took all he had, he paid his bills; and then turned his attention to an effort to solve the riddle of the death of Frank, the fiddler.

Frank was a colored man, lately the property of Stockley Donelson. The mulatto George and three other Hermitage negroes were in jail at Nashville charged with murder. General Jackson went to town and told his four "boys" to speak the truth. He heard the depositions of other negroes who had witnessed the killing, penciling notes on their testimony with his own hand. The trouble had taken place during a holiday spree and dance at which someone had asked Frank to stop his music until a fire could be built. This had started a fight in which about forty negroes joined. Frank was killed by a blow on the head with a rock.

Stockley Donelson had obtained the warrants for Jackson's four negroes. Stockley had gone over to the Whigs. He took his politics as seriously as did General Jackson, and for some time relations between them had been strained. Declaring his negroes innocent, Jackson denounced their arrest as spite work and engaged a lawyer to defend them. They were acquitted at a trial which cost the General a thousand dollars. He borrowed the money.[29]

The expectation of relief from the depression proved illusory. It was a hard year. Business continued at a standstill and money scarce. Negroes were almost the only article of commerce that could command cash. With notes of hand circulating with a freedom that recalled Jackson's trading post days at the beginning of the century, one had to be careful whose note he accepted or endorsed. In this situation Old Hickory not only kept the Hermitage on a paying basis, but he raised funds sufficient to meet the first installment of five thousand one hundred and seventy-six dollars on Andrew, junior's, Halcyon Plantation.

Meanwhile, louder were growing the cries against the financial policies of the Jackson régime, bolder the bids of the reviving

Biddle group for the restoration of their favorite to power, when suddenly the wheel of fortune turned. The hard year had been too much for Mr. Biddle. Financial wizardries were no longer equal to the task of sustaining the inverted pyramid of his speculations. His drafts were protested in Paris and the United States Bank of Pennsylvania closed its doors. So destructive to confidence was this failure that half of the specie-paying banks in the country again suspended. Nicholas Biddle buried himself on his country estate, his power seemingly gone forever. The greatest obstacle to the Independent Treasury Bill appeared to be removed.

Richard Rush whose last act as Secretary of the Treasury under John Quincy Adams had been to recommend the recharter of the Bank of the United States, wrote to Jackson: "[This] puts the seal to the foresight and wisdom of your course."[30]

At the next session of Congress, that of 1839-40, the Independent Treasury Bill became a law, taking the fiscal affairs of the nation out of the hands of the banks and completing the work commenced by Jackson in 1829. The mail coach waited beside the Hermitage gate while Old Hickory scribbled a note of congratulation to Mr. Van Buren.[31]

"Jackson's luck," said the Whigs of Mr. Biddle's misfortune. The old man's popularity revived so much that Martin Van Buren thought the sight of Old Hickory at a formal observance of the twenty-fifth anniversary of the Battle of New Orleans would be a good thing for the cause of Democracy. So an invitation reached the Hermitage. Amos Kendall felt it "cruel" to ask the old man to make the long mid-winter journey,[32] and the veteran himself perceived obstacles. "Again I am out of funds, and I cannot bear to borrow or travel as a pauper."[33]

As he wrote this, the General had before him a letter from Major Lewis asking for the satisfaction of a two-years-overdue note for five hundred and fifty dollars signed by Andrew Jackson, junior. The money had been used to purchase a carriage concerning which young Jackson had told his father a story contradicted by the evidence of the note. That must have pained the old man more than the debt. "I have exerted all my means," he informed the Major, "to clear . . . [my son] from his foolish as well as useless debts. . . . They are all exhausted, I can do no more." But on Andrew's return from Mississippi the father promised to "stimulate him to use every exertion to meet it."[34]

Never before had Andrew Jackson adopted such a tone toward a creditor of his adopted child.

6

General Jackson seems to have given up the idea of going to New Orleans in favor of a quiet Christmas season at his own fireside when the Nashville community was rocked by the financial collapse of Albert Ward, a son of the late Colonel Edward Ward, Jackson's long-time friend and one of the richest men in Middle Tennessee. Creditors pounced on Ward's properties, began to tear them to pieces and to pursue with judgments and with writs of attachment those who had gone security for the unfortunate man.

Chief on the list of these sureties was Andrew Jackson, junior.

The amount of his commitments no one seemed to be able to tell, both Ward and young Jackson being absent. But clearly this was no matter of the price of a carriage. Ward's liabilities would run high into the thousands of dollars. Moreover, the involvement brought to light other debts Andrew, junior, had contracted unknown to his father, as frightened creditors began to present their claims.[35]

Any resolution the humiliated father may have contemplated at the time of the discovery of the Lewis note was discarded.

First he made an arrangement with the Ward creditors to gain time.[36]

Next, he would go to New Orleans. If the trip should help the prospects of the Democrats well and good; the real object was to relieve his son.[37]

The time was short. On December 23 the General drove to Nashville and drew in advance on his cotton. After paying two notes for young Andrew and a few other bills only enough remained for traveling expenses to New Orleans. So he borrowed three thousand dollars which was placed to the credit of his son.

On the day before Christmas Andrew, junior, had not returned from Mississippi. Jackson could delay his departure no longer. Scratching directions to the boy to pay the Lewis note and other debts to the extent of three thousand dollars, Old Hickory was off for Louisiana to make his first public appearance in nearly three years.[38]

En route he wrote his son to sell Hunter's Hill, and to levy an execution on the negroes of a debtor named Cheatam. The negroes could be used to pay for the piano and other things. New Year's day of 1840 was spent aboard an Ohio River packet menaced by drifting ice. At Memphis Jackson obtained from Albert Ward pledges which he hoped would balance Andrew, junior's, obligations to the Ward creditors. Stopping briefly at Halcyon Plantation, Old Hickory was struck by its money-making possibilities. He obtained a modification of the terms under which his son had bought the place. In the most cheerful letter since his departure, he expressed the hope that two years hence would see all debts paid and Andrew, junior, assured of "ease and plenty."[39]

On January 4, the steamer *Vicksburg,* chartered by the State of Mississippi and loaded with notables, took the General aboard. What followed was a nightmare. Stricken with a hemorrhage which made every breath torture, the veteran drummed out the last reserves of his will-power "determined to go through [with the journey] or fall in the struggle." "I have long found that complaining never eased pain," he said.[40] The endless receptions, the speeches, the pageantry, the fireworks, the shouting, were somehow endured for ten days and nights. Leaning on his cane the chieftain slowly mounted the mouldering ridge that had been the rampart beside the Rodriquez Canal. Dim old eyes looked on a level field of cane stubble, . . . which memory may have peopled with pulsing platoons in red tunics latticed by white cross-belts, . . . hedges of bayonets receding into infinity. . . .

Alone in the cabin of a homeward bound steamer, the pain passed and a feeling of peace filled the heart of the soldier. He hoped he had done something to save Mr. Van Buren. In any event, he believed he had saved Andrew. "Recollect my son that I have taken this trip to endeavour to relieve you from present

AT NEW ORLEANS TWENTY-FIVE YEARS AFTER

So ill he could scarcely stand, General Jackson endured ten nights and days of festivity marking
the twenty-fifth anniversary of the Battle of New Orleans, in 1840. The object of the journey
was to raise money to pay his son's debts. This portrait, by Jacques J. Amans, was painted
during the visit. The original hangs in the Brown University Library, Providence, Rhode Island.

embarrassments, and if I live to realize it I will die contented in the hope that you will never again encumber yourself with debt that may result in the poverty of yourself and the little family I so much Love."[41]

7

The Whigs nominated William Henry Harrison for President and John Tyler, of Virginia, for the second place. Henry Clay swallowed a stiff drink of whisky. "I am," he said, "the most unfortunate man in the history of parties: always run by my friends when sure to be defeated, and now betrayed when I, or any one, would be sure of election."[42]

General Jackson, Mr. Van Buren and most other Democrats sympathized with Mr. Clay. They would have preferred him as an opponent. General Harrison exhibited too many possibilities reminiscent of the Jackson appeals of 1824 and 1828: a fine military record; a respectable if virtually forgotten civil record as a territorial governor and frontier congressman; and no record whatever on any current issue. Such a standard-bearer presented few points for attack.

Perceiving the necessity of a strong vice-presidential candidate, Old Hickory advised Van Buren to drop "Tecumseh" Johnson in favor of James K. Polk. The suggestion was wise. Stemming the Whig tide, Polk had reclaimed the governorship of Tennessee. Jackson declared that he would insure the victory of the national ticket in the West and the South.[43]

When Martin Van Buren took the oath in 1837, he had laid aside the magician's wand for the toga of a statesman. Courageously and high-mindedly he had fought for the right things, as he saw them, rather than for the politically expedient. Now for a moment he resumed his old trick of trying to please both sides. The Democratic Convention which renominated Mr. Van Buren for President left the choice of a vice-presidential candidate to the states. The idea was that Johnson should run in the North and the East where he was strong, and that Polk should run in the South and West. The scheme collapsed when Polk declined to co-operate, and Van Buren entered the campaign saddled with a running mate poorly equipped to woo votes in the slaveholding states.

Amos Kendall retired from the Cabinet to direct the Van Buren press, but surely he could not have been responsible for the squib by which the Baltimore *American* sought to belittle the pretensions of General Harrison:

"Give him a barrel of hard cider and settle a pension of two thousand a year on him and, my word for it, he will sit the remainder of his days in a log cabin."[44]

A genius among the Whigs agreed with the Democratic editor. Yes, the Hero of Tippecanoe could live comfortably on what Martin Van Buren spent on his wardrobe. A log cabin, a barrel of hard cider for his friends, plain folk like himself, and William Henry Harrison would be content.

Log cabins and barrels of cider began to blossom forth at Harrison rallies. In New York City a wealthy dabbler in politics enlivened a meeting with a song:

"What has caused this great commotion, motion,
    Our country through?
    It is the ball a-rolling on,
For Tippecanoe and Tyler too, Tippecanoe and Tyler too.
And with them we'll beat little Van, Van, Van;
    Van is a used-up man."

The song, the log cabins, the barrels of cider spread through the country. The West gave birth to another roundelay:

"Ole Tip he wears a homespun suit,
He has no ruffled shirt—*wirt—wirt;*
[*Wirt wirt* simulated by spitting through the teeth.]
But Mat he has the golden plate,
And he's a little squirt—*wirt—wirt.*"

Nicholas Biddle's bank was reopened (with another man as president), while the wizard himself came from retirement to raise funds to provide more log cabins and more cider. He also supplied advice for the candidate's managers. "Let him say not a single word about his principles or his creed—let him say nothing, promise nothing. Let the use of pen and ink be wholly forbidden."[45]

This course was followed. By mid-summer a greatly enlarged and improved edition of the Jackson campaign of 'Twenty-four was before the public: log cabins on wheels, transparencies showing Old Tip in a 'coonskin cap trapping the Red Fox; rivers of cider to loosen the vocal cords. "Tippecanoe and Tyler too!" . . . "Van, Van, is a used-up man!"

The initiative was with the Whigs. The best rebuttal the Democrats could offer in kind was a thin

> "Rumpsey, Dumpsey,
> Colonel Johnson killed Tecumsey. . . ."

8

In April General Jackson received two hundred and forty dollars in cash for three town lots in Florence, the last of his possessions in Alabama. The money came barely in time to save Andrew, junior, "from the sheriffs grasp."[46] Old Hickory regarded the revival of activity by his son's creditors as a reflex of the political campaign. "Every Whigg that he is indebted to has either sued or warranted him."

The hounded young man took to bed with "chills, shakes and fever," ailments common to the Mississippi country whence he had lately returned, though his father attributed the attack to visits by the bailiff. Jackson, senior, also was ill, but did not take to bed. He tried to get from his son an understandable statement of the sum of his debts and suretyships. From what Andrew said, the General judged these to be in the neighborhood of six thousand dollars.[47] On his journey to New Orleans General Jackson had established a line of credit, the particulars of which accessible records do not fully disclose.[48] In July the old man went to Nashville to settle once and for all Andrew, junior's, accounts.

He found them to total not six but twelve thousand dollars. He paid eleven thousand in cash, and promised the balance in a week. "My mind being relieved . . . of the great pressure of Andrews debts . . . I believe I will maintain better health." Andrew's health improved at once.[49]

The campaign pressed on, with Nashville an especial object of Whig attention—carrying the war into Africa. An Ohio delegation made a pilgrimage to present a canoe and a live 'coon to the Tippecanoe Club of Nashville. General Jackson's facile friend J. G. Harris, editor of the *Union,* wrote some amusing rhymes in the meter of *'Possum up de Gum Tree:*

> "Mum is the word, boys,
> Brag is the game,
> Cooney is the emblem
> Of Old Tip's fame."

Brag was a favorite card game of Henry Clay, and a forerunner of poker.

The Whigs incorporated the verses in their repertoire and the 'coon gained new authority as a Harrison emblem.

In August a rally at Nashville attained national proportions, with delegations and marching clubs from half the states of the Union. In a pageant with log cabins and 'coons galore, one banner took formal and respectful notice of General Jackson. It showed a fox following a lion. Henry Clay was the orator of the day. His effort also contained respectful allusions to "the illustrious captain in this neighborhood. . . . He was a great chieftain."[50]

Old Hickory did not relish the compliment. "The great gathering at Nashville to worship the coon and sour cider and desecrate the sabath had injured the Federal [Harrison] cause. . . . It is saying to . . . the people . . . that they can be led by hard cider, coons, Log cabins and demagogues. I have a higher opinion of the intelligence of the american people than this. I think Tennessee will give Mr. Van Buren a good majority." On the other hand Democratic rallies were models of deportment. After attending three, Jackson said he had "never seen more order or decorum in a church." Worldly campaigners among the General's friends were not so sure that this was a good sign. Unceremoniously turned out of the diplomatic corps, John Henry Eaton had hit the hard cider trail. In Florida Richard K. Call had done the same. "What apostacy! ... *O tempo, O Mores*," exclaimed Andrew Jackson.[51] Less affected by ethical considerations, a prominent Democratic editor sighed, "We have taught them how to conquer us!"[52]

No one had taught them how to conquer Andrew Jackson. Indignantly Old Hickory announced that he would take the stump for Van Buren—something he had never done for himself. When he was ready to start, it developed that not all of Andrew's obligations had been settled. Nevertheless, the old man set out, writing back: "Sell all [the beef] you can spare. . . . Sell the fillies if you can get five hundred dollars for the two *in cash*. If you can get as much for my riding mare as two hundred dollars let her go and pay Mr. Crutcher and Capt Dodson what you owe."[53] In the slightly conflicting capacities of public hero and electioneer, he traveled westward with James K. Polk as far as Jackson, Tennessee, blessing babies, giving autographs, shaking hands, and haranguing enormous crowds at highly respectable barbecues—not a drop of hard stuff, apparently, in sight. He thumped the banks and the speculators and the paper money people. He made light of Harrison's military achievements, a subject on which Major General Jackson had expressed a different view in 1814.[54] Back at the Hermitage, he was sure that Tennessee and the country were safe.

The first returns reversed the opinion about Tennessee where, it was said, there was not a sober Whig in the State on election day. The victors serenaded Editor Harris and presented him with a jug of corn whisky—a delicate gesture, for no Democrat would soil his lips with cider. Next, the country seemed in doubt. News that Pennsylvania and New York had gone for Harrison took the heart out of most western Democrats, though not Old Hickory. "I do not believe a word of it," he wrote the President. "Nor will I believe that you are not elected until I see *all* the official returns."[55] It was unnecessary to wait so long. Though the popular vote was close, Van Buren received the electoral votes of only seven states.

"Beaten by such a man as Harrison!" penned one western editor, slowly recovering the use of his senses. "Sung down, lied down, drunk down."[56] Hope seemed dead.

But not in the breast of the chieftain. *"Beaten but I trust not conquered,* . . . I do not yet despair of the Republick."[57] Reform the shattered battalions. Rally "round Mr. Van Buren and elect him by a triumphant Majority should he live to November 1844."[58]

"Should he live. . . ."

"Should I live" would have been a presumption on the good nature of Providence.

9

New Year's day, 1841.

In three months Andrew Jackson would be seventy-four. The exertions of the year closed had taken their toll. He was weaker and feebler. Only the inextinguishable spark of his spirit preserved him from all the marks of an old, old man; though the General himself gave the credit to the restorative powers of Matchless Sanative.

On this New Year's day the master of the Hermitage could scarcely reckon his debts, leave alone pay them, for every week seemed to add to the sum. The twelve thousand dollars laid out in August to clear his son of the Ward endorsements was not enough. In December the total had risen to fifteen thousand, ten thousand of which represented, in the General's view, "swindles" perpetrated on Andrew, junior.[59] The extra three thousand had no more than been found when word came that the negroes on Halcyon Plantation were shivering and starving—provisions out and no shoes; then notice of an action at law by the overseer for back wages.[60]

The Hermitage began to wear a look of neglect—the house out of repair and needing paint, the stable stripped of the master's saddle mare, the very beef from the smoke-house sold, the products of its soil indentured for years to come. Of all the children General Jackson and his wife had reared or cared for, the one he had adopted and given his name seemed the least equipped to make his own way through life. Not only had Andrew, junior, involved himself in this bottomless bog of debt, he had told his father untruths.[61] Andrew's falsehoods were not of the vicious kind; nor were they clever, for he was sure to be found out. They were the momentary refuge of the weak and immature. General Jackson was not legally liable for the debts of his son. He assumed them from a supersensitiveness to personal honor, and because of an affection for the boy which nothing had been able to destroy. Never, apparently, did it occur to Jackson to investigate the possibility of invoking the new bankruptcy law in behalf of his son. The General had opposed this statute as providing a means for dishonest debtors to bilk their creditors, and now he advocated its repeal.[62]

With characteristic faith in those he loved, old Jackson clung to the conviction that once Andrew was relieved, never would he be so gullible as to encumber himself again. He looked beyond Andrew to Andrew's children. These growing youngsters were ever by their grandfather's side. They invaded his disordered study, covering his papers with their scrawls. For their security he set himself to provide.

In all these private trials, the correspondent to whom Jackson most freely unburdened himself was his son's schoolmate, the once reckless Andrew Jackson Hutchings to whom Andy, junior, had been held up as a model. How differently young Hutchings had turned out, bravely and ably meeting life's adversities—hard times, the death of a baby boy, the death of his wife, lovely Mary Coffee. Now Hutchings himself battled against tuberculosis. A trip to Cuba having brought no relief, the young man had come home, as he knew, to die. Jackson set aside money to visit him in Alabama. Andrew, junior's, needs swept away the little nest-egg. Tied to the Hermitage, the old man could only write: "I urge your attention to the Matchless Sanative."[63]

10

It was a relief to turn from such things to the theatre of our public affairs, however unpromising from a Democratic standpoint it might appear to be. The General wrote to inquire, "Can Clay succeed in his attempt this session to have the independent treasury law repealed and a National Bank charter passed."[64] The answer came that the Whigs would try it. Their chances of success would depend on contingencies as yet difficult to foretell. But the General was told that he could take consolation from one thing: Nicholas Biddle's day was done. Even Clay was through with him.[65]

A month later General Jackson received confirmation of the opinion about Biddle. In a last gamble for power, the United States Bank of Pennsylvania had resumed specie payments. A run followed. The bank closed, its entire capital of thirty-five million dollars lost, thousands of stockholders and depositors ruined. Haggard and friendless, the man who had once disputed with Andrew Jackson for the control of the United States reached the end of his road at a prisoner's dock charged with fraud. A legal technicality saved Nicholas Biddle from the penitentiary.

With the ardor of an evangelist, the chieftain spent his failing strength to reanimate the drooping spirits of his party. To an admirer who wished a sentiment to preserve as a memento: "The Republic . . . may suffer under the present imbecile chief, but the sober second thought of the people will restore it at our next Presidential election."[66] To Amos Kendall: "The Mock Hero, the president elect, I see has reached Washington."[67]

General Harrison was, indeed, at Gadsby's Hotel, smothered by the most shameless swarm of fortune hunters the capital had seen since the coming of another Hero twelve years before. To afford the distressed man a sanctuary, Martin Van Buren offered to vacate the Executive Mansion in advance. Declining to avail himself of this distinguished courtesy, General Harrison was worn to distraction before inauguration day. A week thereafter a caller found the lower floor of the White House in the possession of patronage seekers. They filled every room and defied eviction. The President opened a door, expecting to meet his Cabinet. The spoilsmen crushed about him. Soon the Executive's pockets were filled with their petitions, then his hat, then his arms; and thus he staggered upstairs to revive himself with "stimulants."[68]

On his twentieth day as President, General Harrison took to bed. On the thirty-first day he died.

"A kind and overruling providence," said Andrew Jackson, "has interfered to prolong our glorious Union, ... for surely Tyler ... [will] stay the corruptions of this clique who has got into power by deluding the people by the grossest of slanders ... and hard cider."[69]

CHAPTER XXII

A Taper Burning Low

I

ON ONE of his trips down Chesapeake Bay to the Rip Raps, President Jackson was accompanied by George Washington Parke Custis, a rotund, fussy little gentleman with snuff on his lace who delighted in the appellation of "the child of Mount Vernon." He was a grandson of Martha Custis, and the adopted son of George Washington. The appearance of a storm arising, Mr. Custis had expressed a premonition of disaster. General Jackson smiled. "My good friend, you never traveled with me."

The President's companion was vexed. Next to his connection with the Father of His Country, Mr. Custis prided himself on an acquaintance with the classics. He confided to Blair that General Jackson had indifferently rendered the words of the Roman emperor to a pilot who hesitated to put out in a storm: "Why do you fear, you carry Caesar?"

The editor often recalled the incident with amusement.[1] Those who traveled with Old Hickory counted for security not on their chief's awareness of what another captain had said or done: they counted on that secret spring of certainty from which flowed Andrew Jackson's confidence in himself.

This still remained true.

Mr. Clay carried his bill for the re-creation of a national bank. Tyler vetoed it, as Jackson had predicted. For a second time in time Tyler vetoed it, and was sustained.

Democratic spirits rose. The letter of a grateful citizen of Baltimore expressed a prevailing sentiment.

"To providence and to you we give thanks—and some to Tyler. the same session Mr. Clay forced the bill through. For the second

458

It was you who gathered the Democrats together on this subject after they had been separated and scattered and deceived. . . . Every where, at every turn and every corner the expression may be heard—'It will do old Hickory's heart good when he hears of the Veto.' . . . 'Egad, he has found one of old Jackson's pens.' "[2]

2

Other prospects also were fair. On the way down the Mississippi the winter before, one swift view of Halcyon Plantation had revealed to General Jackson its advantages as a fueling station for steamers. Accordingly, a woodyard was established at the water's edge under management of Andrew, junior. It was immediately profitable. The land needed clearing to extend the cotton acreage, and good Democratic packet-masters made a special point of stopping at the Jackson woodyard. Transactions were cash, a dollar fifty a cord, and one hand could turn out two cords in a day.

"My son has become the man of business," Old Hickory proudly related. "Our plantation on the Mississippi, hitherto unproductive, this year [1841] will yield us some profit, and in two years will produce in cotton and wood at least a neat income of eight thousand dollars." With this statement of the family's prospects, Jackson authorized Major Lewis to contract a loan of six thousand dollars for six years. He wished to consolidate the obligations incurred in freeing his son "of some of the greatest scamps, sharpers and swindlers that honest and unsuspecting youth was ever surrounded with."[3]

Lewis submitted two proposals. From New Orleans came a volunteer proposal from Major Jean B. Plauché who, though he himself would have to borrow the money, asked the honor of assisting his old commander. Jackson agreed to accept the gallant old Creole's proposal, and proffered security—presumably a mortgage on the Hermitage, which was the security he had tendered to others. Plauché would not take it. The matter was settled by Jackson remitting a note signed by himself and his son, which Plauché accepted under protest rather than lose "the

only opportunity which has ever presented itself of being agreeable to you." Then he sent a letter of credit for seven thousand
dollars instead of the six.[4] Jackson declined to use the extra
thousand.

Whig newspapers reported the General's money troubles in a
way that would have impaired another man's credit. James C.
Pickett, the United States chargé d'affaires to Peru, wrote Blair
that a secret fund must be raised to discharge Jackson's debts.
Picket asked to be put down for a share. Frank Blair knew such
a proposal would meet a fate similar to that of the purse raised
long ago to pay the thousand-dollar fine Judge Hall had imposed
on General Jackson after the Battle of New Orleans, and of the
attempt to rebuild the Hermitage by public subscription. Yet
something should be done. Blair himself was closely run, the
Whigs having given the public printing to another man. However, the Government owed him twenty thousand dollars due
to be paid shortly. In the name of himself and his partner, John
C. Rives, Blair wrote that half of this sum was at Jackson's disposal.[5]

In Congress Jackson's friends introduced a bill to refund, with
interest, the New Orleans fine.

The veteran said he would accept a refund of the fine because
of the bearing such an act of Congress might have on the future
safety of the country. The time might come again when it would
be the duty of an army commander, ringed about with foes, to
take in his hands extraordinary powers. No threat of penalties
a civil authority might impose should be allowed to deter him.[6]

Acceptance of Blair's generous offer rested on another plane.
The cotton crop of 1841 at the Hermitage was a failure and
seven blooded horses had died, cutting off revenues by which
Jackson had expected to meet the installments due on Halcyon
Plantation. The loan would meet this unpaid balance and future
crops would meet the loan. Once more that vision of tranquillity
which Andrew Jackson had pursued through a long life seemed
an attainable reality. "This loan will place me at ease, and
secure to him [my son] and his dear little ones and charming
wife an ample fortune— therefore you see the obligation you

lay me under."[7] For the ten thousand dollar advance General Jackson devised, over Blair's protest, the following security: a mortgage on Halcyon Plantation; a bill of sale for "thirty-odd negroes now on said plantation"; a note jointly signed by Andrew, junior, and himself; a codicil to his will directing that all bequests under it be suspended until the debt should be paid.[8]

A sense of release and of accomplishment comforted the old man. "My son A.J. junr. seeing his way now clear begins to look up like a freeman. When I discovered his embarrassments, found out how he had been swindled and imposed upon, that he had been adopted and raised by my dear wife and myself, was the only representative to perpetuate my name, and when I viewed the goodness and amiability of his dear wife and little children I could not withstand stepping forward to extricate him."[9]

3

The Democrats also were beginning to lift up their heads in the manner of freemen. Mr. Tyler's veto of the bank bills, and other examples of independent behavior, tended to estrange him from the Whig leaders who saw themselves despoiled of the fruits of their hard cider victory. Dissension wracked the lately triumphant party and, in the elections of 1841 and 1842, the Democrats made striking gains—circumstances agreeable, indeed, to the two ex-Presidents who ruled over the destinies of that party, consulting each other occasionally by correspondence.

Martin Van Buren had retired not to his law practice in New York City, but to the neighborhood of his birth at Kinderhook, a village on the Hudson about twenty-five miles below Albany. He addressed General Jackson as one country squire to another touching, not too exhaustively, on the state of agriculture. "My health has never been better, nor my spirits either." Improvements on the residence at Lindenwald, as Mr. Van Buren had named his seat, were going forward. "How greatly would be its value increased if I could promise myself to see you at it. To come as near as practicable I have our friend Col Earles likeness of you well framed . . . [for] my dining room."[10]

It was a stately dining room that Earl's portrait looked upon, with places for many guests. Van Buren had bought the property during his presidency, thus reidentifying himself with a community which he had been glad to forsake as a boy. The Van Buurmalsens had come over as articled servants of the Van Rensselaers. One of their number simplified the name to Van Buren, needlessly it seems, for he could not write. Rising out of the indentured class, in a land and a time abounding with opportunities, they rose little higher during the next hundred years. Seven families of Van Burens residing in Kinderhook during the Revolution seem to have contributed to freedom's cause two militiamen of short-time service.

Into perhaps the most prosperous of these households was Martin Van Buren born in 1782, his father the neglectful proprietor of a small tavern. From this environment Martin escaped to perfect his knowledge of English (Dutch was the family tongue), to become a man of fashion, master politician, and, as he mentioned in his inaugural address, the first President of the United States not born a British subject. He returned a newly-made country gentleman, consciously treading the paths of his predecessors to the Executive Chair—saving the Adamses, townfolk whose careers, especially in their latter parts, Mr. Van Buren had no desire to emulate. The squire's sons made light of the struggle to select a right-sounding name for Lindenwald which, except for antecedent use by James Fenimore Cooper, would have become The Locusts.[11]

Unlike the master of Lindenwald, General Jackson was not enjoying good health. "I have been scarcely able to write— with pain in my ears, head and eyes it is quite an effort."[12] Yet, as Frank Blair observed, he had something better than strength of flesh. He had strength of spirit. "Your life is of the soul, more than the body."[13]

His finances readjusted, the General took a more active interest in public affairs, with two ambitions before him, the realization of which Old Hickory regarded as his final contributions to his country. He wished to insure James K. Polk second place on the ticket which in 1844 would achieve a restoration of the Jacksonian dynasty; and he wished to bring Texas into the Union.

After the defeat of 1840, the next vice-presidential nomination seemed Polk's for the asking. Mr. Van Buren saw the error of his strategy in the late disastrous campaign: with Polk instead of Johnson the Democrats might have polled a majority of the popular vote. Then came the encouraging returns of 1841, marred only by what seemed at a distance to be the incomprehensible defeat of Polk for re-election as Governor of Tennessee. Viewed at close range the defeat was susceptible of explanation: the Tennessee Whigs had discovered a *deus ex machina* in the person of "Slim Jimmy" Jones.

James Chamberlain Jones was born on a small farm almost within sight of the Hermitage. When General Jackson made his triumphal return from the Battle of New Orleans, Jimmy was six years old, fatherless and beginning to feel the weight of life's responsibilities. But care rode lightly on his sloping shoulders. Jimmy grew up to attain renown as a rustic buffoon and mimic. He moved away, married a wife who had a baby every year, and made a good country living. In 1840 his broad humor was ideal for the hard cider campaign, and in 1841 the Whigs nominated him for Governor. James K. Polk was a hard-working public servant with no frivolities and little humor. On the stump he did not thrill crowds; he sought to win their respect by earnest discussions of the issues. Slim Jimmy dogged Polk's steps throughout the State. When his adversary had concluded an address, Jones would draw a 'coonskin from his pocket and stroke it. "Did you ever see such fine fur?" In a few moments the voters would be splitting their sides over Jimmy's clownish misrepresentations of Polk's record.

Polk's defeat made party satraps uneasy and General Jackson very indignant indeed. To lose one's own state was not a good recommendation for vice-presidential honors.

The Texas question also presented perplexities. The taint of sectionalism would not wash off, and for this the indiscreet ardor of the slavery expansionists was largely responsible. During Van Buren's administration the republic had again offered itself for annexation. The President, fighting for his political life and not anxious to add to his troubles, had declined to act. Tyler's efforts to place the issue on nationalistic grounds by linking it to the Oregon question were unfruitful. Meanwhile, harassed by border raids and threatened with a determined attempt at reconquest by Mexico, Sam Houston's situation was critical. Turning to Europe for help, he found sympathetic ears in the chancelleries of England and of France. It would be to the interests of those countries to build up on the vulnerable southwestern flank of the United States a strong nation under European patronage.

Jackson had envisaged the acquisition of the Californias by a Texas which one day would become a part of the Union. The statesmen in London and in Paris did not overlook the possibilities of an identical conquest—by a Texas united to Europe by friendly ties.

These maneuvers were quickly noticed in the United States. Tyler was worried, and the southern extremists raised a great hullabaloo. New England Abolitionists replied in kind, John Quincy Adams scenting a "plot" on the part of the President and the "slavocrats" to encompass annexation.[14] On the other hand, the fear of foreign intervention revealed the germs of an influential northern sentiment for annexation arising from the old national policy of Jackson and from the fear of a loss of commercial advantage to our manufacturing states.

Already the question was beginning to disturb the serenity of political managers looking to 1844.

4

The extra places at Martin Van Buren's dinner table were filled by hopeful Democrats from the country over who beat a path to Lindenwald. As to 1844, they found their host receptive. When other aspirants—J. C. Calhoun, James Buchanan, Lewis Cass— began to appear, the squire of Lindenwald adopted less passive measures to impress his receptivity on the public mind. A pilgrimage to the Hermitage was announced, and in February, 1842, the pilgrim set out. The latter part of March he had progressed as far as South Carolina, when a letter from Henry Clay came to his hand.

His immediate aspirations confounded by Tyler, the Kentuckian also was bound for the shades of retirement, there to await the call of his party in 1844. Mr. Clay had given notice of his resignation from the Senate and soon would be at Ashland, which he cordially asked Mr. Van Buren to include in his all-embracing itinerary. The invitation was accepted. Six weeks thereafter the traveler reached the Cumberland. By contrast with refurbished Lindenwald the debt-plagued Hermitage looked seedy.

Though suffering from a chill, General Jackson bestirred himself to sponsor his guest to the community. Of private conversations neither principal has left a line for the enlightenment of posterity. Yet it is impossible to believe that Texas was not mentioned, or that Mr. Van Buren expressed any view on that subject which aroused a suspicion in Jackson's mind that he would interpose obstacles to annexation. The exertions of the visit left Old Hickory so weary that several days elapsed before he gave his friend Blair an account of the impression the candidate had made. "Instead of a dwarf dutchman, a little dandy who you might lift out of a bandbox, the people found him a man of middle size, plain and affable. W[h]iggery is done in Tennessee."[15]

The plain, affable traveler passed on to Kentucky. Some time went by before General Jackson heard from him. "The hospitable roof of our friend Col. ["Tecumseh"] Johnson affords me the first opportunity to drop you a line. . . . At Lexington the crowd was large and everything well conducted." Admirably so, it would appear. "Mr. Clay presented himself and remained some time surrounded by a dense mass of Democrats. He inquired respectfully and kindly about your health." For forty-eight hours the candidate remained in Lexington at the disposal of the Democratic reception committee. "After that I spent two or three days with Mr. Clay, and returned to the City for a day longer."[16]

Well as Martin Van Buren knew his patron's love of frankness, not one syllable did he utter concerning his visit to the home of the man in all probability to be the Whig nominee for President in 1844, and regarded by Andrew Jackson as "a pure unadulterated demagouge."[17] Was not "two or three days" a curiously vague phrase to use at a time when Van Buren's schedule was so closely packed that hours and minutes must be taken into account? He had tarried at the Hermitage less than three days.

On the poplar-shaded, secluded lawn at Ashland the two statesmen, too clever by far for their own good, had sat, their thoughts tending toward ambition. Neither has left the least record of that interesting rendezvous. It has remained for friendly biographers to offer the suggestion that they struck a bargain to omit Texas from the list of campaign issues.[18] Certainly the developments support this view.

Though political expediency had been the lodestar of each, Mr. Van Buren had shown disinterested statesmanship in dealing with the financial troubles dating from 1837 and Henry Clay had shown it on the looming menace of slavery. Their understanding, if they had one, is susceptible of an interpretation by no means unworthy. For one candidate to come out for annexation would be to gain votes in the South and the West, lose them in the East, and probably fan the fires of sectionalism. For both to come out, no political advantage would accrue, and a sectional issue be raised needlessly. If both remained aloof, the campaign might be waged around less combustible issues.

The detail this convenient formula left out of the reckoning was the peril arising from the possibility of European intervention in Texas. This complication had not been present in 1836 when Jackson retreated before the frowning visage of slavery. Believing the designs of England presented the greater danger, Old Hickory was determined to yield no more. Yet, should Andrew Jackson die before 1844, who would have the authority to revoke any gentleman's agreement Martin Van Buren and Henry Clay may have made?

5

The veteran's sands seemed to be running out. "I have been brought low with a severe attack of chills and fevers."[19] He could hardly see to write, and his discourse had an old man's way of rambling. Correspondence was neglected. Too poor to employ a secretary, he retained, however, the futile habit of jotting on the

JACKSON IN RETIREMENT

From a print of a drawing from life by William H. Brown, owned by Emil Edward Hurja of New York City.

covers of unanswered letters the gist of replies which, in other days, Jack Donelson would have made. They were the responses of a man finished with worldly vanities. On the letter of a portrait painter: "The last sitting I fully determined I would sit no more. I am now too old and infirm." On a communication from Clinton College, in New York: "I am too old to accept honorary titles that I do not merit." On the letter of a society wishing to confer a membership: "I am too old to be of any use."[20]

Too old? The bill to refund the New Orleans fine was altered to make the proposed restitution a gratuity to General Jackson rather than the rectification of a miscarriage of justice. Instantly new vigor fortified the flagging pen at the Hermitage. Andrew Jackson would scorn the benefits of such an act. "I would starve," he stormed in private, "before I would touch one cent of the money under that odious & insulting amended bill."[21] In long letters he elucidated his claim "on the basis of justice alone."[22]

When opponents of the original bill cited Martin's *History of Louisiana* in support of their contentions, Old Hickory indicated his familiarity with that work. Statement after statement he challenged, some on evidence difficult to controvert, though the summation—"a greater tissue of falsehoods never before eminated from a wicked head and corrupted heart"—hardly entitles General Jackson to recognition as a dispassionate critic of our historical literature.[23] The effort seemed to serve the more useful purpose of replenishing his energy. "I am like a taper. When nearly exhausted [it] will sometimes have the appearance of going out, but will blaze up again for a time."[24]

Now high, now low flared the taper, consuming its last inch. The continuance of gratifying election results proved a wonderful revitalizer. "[With] the overwhelming victory in Newyork, Pennsylvania, ohio and other states Clays fate is sealed. . . . I can scarcely hope to live to see the termination of the next Presidential election— should providence will it, and Van Buren [be] elected, and [I be] able to travel, I would cheerfully go on, take my constitution carriage and take him in it, to the capitol to be inaugurated, but my dear friend I have small hopes that I will be spared so long."[25]

To George Bancroft's request for reminiscences of the Revolution for inclusion in his history of the United States, the veteran replied: "From my weak and debilitated state I can only refer you to Major J. H. Eatons life of Jackson."[26] Amos Kendall applied for permission to write his patron's biography. The former Postmaster General was ill and in debt as a result of a judgment (subsequently reversed) obtained by avaricious mail contractors whose profits he had curtailed.

To help a friend old Jackson laboriously turned to his mountain of papers, the accumulation of half a century. Captivating fragments of the past drifted back: the titanic feud with John Sevier; the North Carolina land fraud; hoof beats at Clover Bottom. Alack, the task of assorting these documents proved quite beyond the old man. Kendall was under restriction of the court not to leave the District of Columbia. So a nephew of his, James A. McLaughlin, arrived at the Hermitage in December, 1842.

6

Intelligent, industrious, obliging, immediately this young man won the hearts of the General and of all his household. The quickening pulse of an alert and purposeful spirit infused with new life the shabby mansion and debt-burdened family, dependent in everything on the feeble chief of clan whose next step might be his last. Burrowing into the papers, McLaughlin soon had ready a boxful of material for his uncle. It went off with a note from the subject of the projected biography: "I hope ... [the] Book may relieve you from pecuniary embarrassments. . . . I am pressed to earth. I have not had one dollar in three years that I could call my own."[27]

Distinguished counsel on research came from the harassed Kendall who perceived what was scarcely visible to another writer of his day: the distinction between history and biography. "Your Biographies thus far," he wrote the General, "are destitute of incidents connected with your private life."[28] The public man is half the man, and sometimes less than half. With pencil and pad on his knee McLaughlin held long conversations with the General, leading him back and forth over the years in an effort to recapture those informal things which are the most elusive of the biographical ingredients. After a session the young man would put his notes in connected form.

"Narrative of a trip made in the winter of 1811 from *Nashville Tenn to Natchez Miss. T.*

"The road lead through the Chickasaw and Choctaw country. . . . The station of the U. S. agent for the Choctaw nation was on this road. The Genl. was going to Natchez for the purpose of getting some negroes. . . . On reaching the Agency he found some 7 or 8 families detained there. . . . They told him they were removing to Natchez but had been stopped by the Agent until one of their number should go down to Natchez and obtain a passport. In the meantime they were splitting rails for the Agent at 25 cents per 100 and buying corn from him at from $1.00 to $1.50 per bushel. The Genl. went with them to the Agent and . . . inquired how this happened. . . . The Agent with much severity inquired of the Genl. if *he* had a passport. 'Yes Sir,' he replied, 'I always carry it with me. I am a free born American and . . . [that is] sufficient passport to take me wherever my business leads me.' He then told the emigrants to gear up their wagons and start and if anyone attempted to stop them to shoot him."[29]

Soon Jackson's pen, too, was busy:

"Lord Rawden advanced in the fall of 1780 or 81 & encamped on Major Robt. Crawfords plantation at the crossing of the Waxhaw Creek— before Lord Rawdons advance Gen¹ Lasley or Col Lasly of the British army with Infantry & Tarleton with dragoons advanced, . . . passing our dwelling but we all *hid out*— Tarleton passed within a hundred yards of where I & a cousin crawford had concealed ourselves— I could have shot him."[30]

When Tarleton raided the Waxhaws Andy Jackson was thirteen years old. He wrote the above at seventy-six. That birthday anniversary—March 15, 1843—brought a flood of greetings, delaying work on the biography. "Wants my autograph," scribbled Jackson. "An entire stranger— having refused thousands I cannot from my debility & custom conform with this."[31] Some of the letters contained solicitations that were impossible to decline. "Dear General you will not I hope refuse even from a little girl eight years old the tribute of respect and affection on your birthday. Papa has taught us all to love you very much. . . . CAROLINE L. BUTLER."[32]

7

Another task of composition interrupted the labor of the memorialist.

"Hermitage, June 7, 1843.

"In the name of God Amen, I Andrew Jackson Senr. being of Sound mind memory and understanding, and impressed with the great uncertainty of life, and the certainty of death, and . . . whereas since executing my will of the 30th of September, 1833 my Estate has become greatly involved by my liabilities for the debts of my well beloved and adopted Son Andrew Jackson Jnr which makes it necessary to alter the same, Therefore I . . . do make, ordain publish and declare this my last Will and Testament, revoking all other wills by me heretofore made,

"I bequeath my body to the dust whence it comes . . . [to] be buried by the side of my dear departed wife in the garden of the Hermitage.

"To meet the debt [to] my good friends Genl. J B Plauché and Co of New Orleans for the sum of six thousand dollars with the interest accruing thereon . . . also a debt of ten thousand dollars borrowed of my friends Blair and Rives of the city of Washington District of Columbia with the Interest accruing thereon . . . I hereby bequeath all my Real and Personal estate.

"After these debts are fully paid thereby, I give and bequeath to my adopted son Andrew Jackson Junr, the tract of Land whereon I now live known by [as] the Hermitage . . . with all my negroes that I may die possessed of with the exceptions hereafter named, . . . all the Household furniture farming tools, Stock of all kind . . . to him and his heirs forever."

Jackson's language was clear. Yet to avoid any possibility of misconstruction he repeated:

"The true intent and meaning of this my last Will and Testament is that all my Estate real personal and mixed, are hereby first pledged for the payment of the above recited debts and Interest, and when they are fully paid, the residue of all my Estate, are hereby bequeathed to my adopted Son A Jackson Junr. with the exception[s] hereafter named."

Then followed a number of specific bequests of negroes to Sarah, who "has been more than a daughter to me," and to the grandchildren.

"I bequeath to my well beloved Nephew Andrew J Donelson, Son of Samuel Donelson deceased, the elegant sword presented to me by the state of Tennessee, with this injunction that he fail not to use it when necessary in support and protection of our glorious Union. . . . This from the great change in my worldly affairs of late is with my blessing all I can bequeath him, doing justice to those creditors to whom I am responsible.

"To my Grand Nephew Andrew Jackson Coffee I bequeath the elegant sword presented to me by the rifle company of New Orleans . . . with this injunction, that he wield it . . . against all invaders whether foreign foes, or intestine traitors.

"I bequeath to my beloved Grand son Andrew Jackson, son of A Jackson Junr. and Sarah his wife, the sword presented to me by the Citizens of Philadelphia, with this Injunction, that he will always use it in defence of our glorious Union.

"The pistols of Genl Lafayette I bequeath to George Washington Lafayette.

"The Gold box presented to me by the Corporation of the City of New York, the large Silver vase presented by the Ladies of Charleston, South Carolina, my native State, . . . I leave in trust to my Son A Jackson Junr with directions that should our happy country not be blessed with peace, he will at the close of the war present each of said articles to that patriot residing in the city or state from which they were presented, who shall be adjudged to have been the most valient in defence of his country. . . .

"As a memento of my high regard for Genl. Robert Armstrong . . . I give and bequeath to him, my case of pistols and sword, worn by me throughout my military career, well satisfied that in his hands they will never be drawn without occasion, nor sheathed but with honor,

"Lastly, I leave to my Beloved Son all my walking canes and other relics, to be distributed among my young relatives (name sakes)."

Though no sword was to go to Andrew, junior, General Jackson named him "my whole and sole Executor, .. and [I] direct that no security be required of him."[33]

A month later Sarah's fourth child was born. "Thinking as I was of Emuckfau heights, Enotochopco and Talladega we named him Robert Armstrong—remembering [that] when he [Armstrong] fell desperately wounded, he cryed out, .. ['] save the cannon ['].... If the child live he may perchance aid in saving our glorious Union."[34] Had the child lived it is probable that he would have followed his two brothers into the army of the Confederacy; but he did not live. Jackson saw the little lifeless form taken from the sobbing mother's breast. "It was the most distressing scene I ever witnessed."[35]

8

The pleasant young McLaughlin gathered up his notebooks and departed, planning to return as soon as his uncle should exhaust the material in hand. The Hermitage never saw him again. After *Harper's Magazine* had published seven installments, Amos Kendall's life of Andrew Jackson was abandoned following an estrangement between the author and Frank Blair. The widespread Democratic triumphs of 1843 had assured a majority in Congress sufficient to elect a public printer of the Jacksonian faith. By right of party service the place belonged to the firm of Blair & Rives. Harried by debts, Kendall entered the lists against his old friends, losing the favor of Andrew Jackson as well as failing to win the printership.[36]

Old Hickory mingled with his congratulations to Blair & Rives a painful request for the postponement of principal and interest due on his debt of ten thousand dollars. In an effort to obtain a better price, Jackson had shipped his 1842 cotton to Liverpool. He obtained no more than he could have had at New Orleans, and carrying charges virtually devoured the proceeds. The 1843 crop at Halcyon Plantation was ruined by a flood. On the heels of these events it transpired that Andrew, junior, had been endorsing notes again—"swindled," as Jackson put it, by his cousin Stockley Donelson. In anguish the old man wrote: "I have grappled with every debt Andrew ows and I trust I will be able to meet [these new ones]."[37] Governor Pierce Butler of South Carolina, was in Nashville looking for horses. Old Hickory asked Jack Donelson to offer three thoroughbred colts from the depleted Hermitage stable for a thousand dollars, then for nine hundred, then "as your judgment may direct. . . . I want mony. . . . The bay filly [alone] is worth $1000."

Andrew Jackson wanted money badly to throw away his horses for such prices. Butler took them.[38]

On January 1, 1844, for the fourth consecutive New Year's Day, the General was obliged to forego payments of his debts and to pray the indulgence of his creditors. Yet there were rifts in the clouds. With éclat the new Congress voted to wipe out the New Orleans fine. President Tyler himself enclosed to the master of the Hermitage a draft on the Treasury for two thousand seven hundred and thirty-two dollars and ninety cents (which included interest from 1815), accompanied by a most cordial letter. The event was celebrated from one corner of the country to the other. In New York City a transparency stretching across Broadway proclaimed:

JUSTICE TO THE BRAVE
Judge Hall's
Sentence on
GENL JACKSON
Repudiated by the
Nation
Feb. 14th 1844[39]

When the Treasury order arrived Jackson did not have a dollar. Ignorant of the exact terms of the refunding act, the old man asked Blair if he could "with honor" cash the draft.[40]

Blair extended for one year what was due on the ten thousand dollar loan. The veteran's gratitude was touching. This generous act, he said, and one good crop would rehabilitate the finances of the Hermitage. "To your unsolicited liberality and that of my friend Genl Plauché I ascribe the happy prospects of my dear adopted son and his precious little wife and sweet children. . . . . How long a kind providence may permit me to remain in the land of the living he only knows, . . . but when providence pleases to make the call I will go without any regrets . . . where the wicked cease to trouble and the weary are at rest."[41]

9

Eleven days after this was written a young man appeared at the Hermitage—William D. Miller, private secretary to the president of the Texas Republic. Beneath his careful courtesy was an air of settled resolution. Mr. Miller handed General Jackson a letter marked "Private" in the swelling script of Sam Houston.

It was a long letter. Feeble eyes strained over sheets held so closely they almost touched the hero's nose. They contained alarming news. Could it be true what Jackson had heard about Sam Houston's intrigues with England?[42]

Old Hickory reconsidered his hasty preparations for Paradise.

Texas must first be ours.

CHAPTER XXIII

LAST LEAVE

I

SAM HOUSTON had come a long way since the days of The Raven and of Big Drunk. When Andrew Jackson ordered Houston to a tailor for a suit of white man's clothes,[1] Old Hickory did not suspect that he was setting the stage for a drama in which one day Sam Houston should emerge as the dictator—and Jackson the one dictated to.

The constitution of the Texas Republic limited a president to two terms, and these not consecutive. Houston's first administration was a notable achievement in statecraft. Annexation unexpectedly refused by the United States, the executive confronted the task of molding into a nation, which could stand alone, a white population of thirty thousand distributed over an area as large as France. A high proportion of these prospective citizens were adventurers who preferred the rifle and the bowie knife as instruments of government. From these materials Sam Houston gave Texas the appearance of a sovereign state, its domestic concerns reasonably ordered and prosperous, its rights respected abroad.

His successor in the executive chair was Mirabeau Buonaparte Lamar, a gentleman afflicted with visions as soaring as his name. In three years the machinery of the republic virtually had ceased to function. Currency was worthless, Indians on the war path and Santa Anna gathering his forces for invasion. Another offer of annexation had been refused by the United States. Resuming the presidency in 1841, Sam Houston calmly looked into the face of chaos. Skillfully he inaugurated a foreign policy calculated to alarm the United States and to excite the cupidity of Europe.

Twice in the autumn of 1843, President Tyler offered to reopen negotiations for annexation. Unmindful of the desperate improvisations by which he kept his republic alive, Sam Houston replied with cold dignity. "[By] the interposition of foreign friendly governments ... an armistice has been established between Texas and Mexico. . . . Were Texas to agree to annexation [to the United States] the good offices of the powers would, it is believed, be withdrawn, and were the [annexation] Treaty to Fail of ratification by the Senate of the United States Texas would be ... without a friend."[2]

Tyler's reply was a mixture of persuasion, threat and entreaty. Immediate annexation was guaranteed. The Senate had been sounded and *"a clear constitutional majority of two-thirds are in favor of the measure."* The United States would not consent to see a rival power built up on her border, and would go to war to prevent it. What had Texas to gain from precipitating such a conflict?[3]

But Mr. Tyler was not so confident of his ability to cope with Sam Houston as he pretended to be. He sought the help of Jackson, currying favor by an espousal of the bill to remit the New Orleans fine. This was followed by a letter to the Hermitage from the President's confidant, Senator Robert J. Walker of Mississippi: "I think the annexation of Texas depends *on you.* May I request you to write by the first mail to President Houston?"[4]

Jackson wrote.

"You know my dear General that I have been & still am your friend. . . . Some of your enemies have been & are circulating at the City of Washington that you are endeavoring to athwart the wishes of an overwhelming majority in Texas to become annexed to the United States—that you are desirous to become closely allied to great Britain. . . . I have denied . . . the slanders, . . . [saying] that you never could become the dupe of England. . . . My strength is exhausted and I must close."[5]

More disconcerting reports from Mr. Tyler's confidants, and five days later the old man wrote again—a long letter scrawled amid such bodily and mental anguish that the wonder is the pen did not fall from the enfeebled fingers before the task was done:

"My dear Genl I tell you in all sincerity and friendship, if you will achieve this annexation your name & fame will become enrolled amongst the greatest chieftains. . . . Now is the time to act & that with promptness & secrecy & have a treaty of annexation laid before the United States Senate where I am assured it will be ratified. . . . It will be an unfailing laurel in your ploom. . . . I am scarcely able to write— The Theme alone inspires me with the strength. . . . Let me hear from you if only three lines. . . . your friend,

"ANDREW JACKSON."[6]

2

Instead of three lines, in which Sam Houston could have told Andrew Jackson all he wished to know and put his fears at rest, the Texas Talleyrand wrote three hundred lines. This was the communication Old Hickory received from the hand of Houston's private secretary, William D. Miller, on March 11, 1844.

It had not been an easy piece of composition. With relish Sam Houston could play off England, France, Mexico and the United States against each other in the cockpit of diplomacy. To play on the heart-strings of the frank and brave old patriot whom he truly loved was another order of business—but necessary to the game Houston had started. Old Hickory's painful letters contained nothing the Texan did not fully know from his alert chargé d'affaires in Washington. Far from being chagrined by the "slanders" connecting him with European intrigue, Houston had deliberately conducted that affair in a manner calculated to insure those tales a wide circulation. By stirring to action old Jackson, they had served one of their definite objects. Though the hand of death might be on his shoulder, Andrew Jackson could still do more than any other American to call to arms a national sentiment for annexation.

"Venerated Friend," began Sam Houston's long letter, "so far as I am [personally] concerned, I am determined upon immediate annexation to the United States." Houston could not consider the matter from a personal point of view, however. He must act as a chief of state, putting thoughts of self aside. "Our situation has been peculiar. . . . Surrounded with internal difficulties as well as external dangers, it was my duty as Executive to have an eye to every emergency that might arise." It was his duty to safeguard the future of Texas. He had done so. A friendly interposition of the powers having given the republic peace, "she has nothing to apprehend for years to come." With confident strokes Houston sketched the rise of a great nation, untroubled by the ominous question so determinedly dividing the United States into hostile camps, Texans being all of one mind on slavery. Indeed, "Texas with peace could exist without the U. States; but the U. States cannot, without great hazard, exist without Texas." As if old Jackson were not aware!

Notwithstanding previous humiliations at her hands, Texas was not without affection for the motherland. Houston was willing to offer once more to unite the destinies of the two nations. A "Secret Legation," with power to negotiate a treaty of annexation, was being formed in Washington, of which young Miller, the bearer of this letter, would be the secretary. The offer could not be made without reservation, however. The United States must guarantee Texas security from invasion "during the progress of negotiations." Moreover, there must be no delay. "An effort to postpone . . . [discussions] may be tried in the U. States, to subserve party purposes and to make a President; Let them beware! . . . [Texas] has been sought by the United States, and this is the third time she has consented. Were she now to be spurned, it would forever terminate expectation on her part; and . . . she would seek some other friend [among the nations of the world]."[7]

Jackson pondered these stipulations. To protect the integrity of Texas during the progress of negotiations was beyond the constitutional authority of a president of the United States. Did Houston mean to insist on impossible conditions?

England was permitted to gather that such was the case.[8] Old Hickory was more discerning. He ignored the unsatisfactory parts of Houston's letter and made use only of the satisfactory parts. He assured Houston's emissary, Miller, that the speedy action his chief insisted on could be had, reading confidential letters from Washington in support of this. Then he enclosed to Senator Walker ą copy of Houston's letter to be passed around as a spur to action. Then he wrote W. B. Lewis, who stood close to Tyler, to cultivate Miller's acquaintance and to press forward the negotiations. These letters were handed to Miller to deliver, and the young man departed after a sojourn of only a few hours. But he had tarried long enough to yield to the almost inescapable spell which the old leader could cast over men.[9]

Four days later, on his seventy-seventh birthday, Jackson replied to Sam Houston. Gone was the tone of entreaty which had marked (and how strangely) his earlier messages to the Texan. Old Hickory spoke as one who had gathered up the reins of authority once more. "My dear Sir, your much esteemed favor I [have] perused with much pleasure and satisfaction. . . . I sincerely congratulate you upon . . . [your statemanship as president of the republic.] You have a mixed population, heterogeneous and dificult to govern. I rejoice to find that you have triumphed." The chieftain rejoiced also in the bright future of Texas. "I have no doubt but that the Treaty will be ratified by the Senate." Confidential polls indicated "that 39 senators will vote for it," or four more than the two-thirds required.

General Jackson briefly noted his own endeavors to stimulate the energies of the senators, holding out to them the dire prospect of a Texas driven into the arms of England and lost to us "forever." That had been very well to tell the senators. Jackson himself did not mean that Texas should be lost "forever." Houston had emphasized his and his country's desire for peace, the implication being that English protection would afford it. Jackson painted a different picture. Granted that Great Britain should get "an ascendency over Texas," and then move on into Oregon forming, with her West Indies, "an iron hoop about the United States." This would bring Texas not peace but war. For the United States would "burst asunder" that iron hoop though "it cost oceans of blood & millions of money. . . . yr. friend

ANDREW JACKSON."[10]

Nowhere in this meaty letter was the least allusion to the audacious stipulations Houston had mentioned as a *sine qua non* to negotiation.

3

Yet, by the time his commissioners began their secret meetings with the commissioners of the United States, it appeared that Sam Houston had done his work almost incredibly well. The "impossible" demand for the protection of Texan integrity had been made, and a compromise wrung from Tyler. Moreover, dust had been thrown in England's eyes, and her guaranties, too, remained in force. Houston had maneuvered his country, two years before a disregarded mendicant among nations, into a position where it could scarcely lose, however the cards might fall.[11]

The deliberations of the negotiators were not altogether a secret from General Jackson whose spirits, though not his health, improved daily as he scanned the Washington mails. That a treaty would be signed was a foregone conclusion. Disconcerting news came from the ranks of the senators, however. Thirty-nine votes for ratification could no longer be counted on. Clay men spoke of laying the matter over until the next Congress. Even Van Buren men, emulating the silence of their chief, seemed to grow cool. "Much, very much, my dear General," wrote young Miller, "depends upon your continued efforts."[12]

Others thought the same. Partizans of Texas polished up an old letter of Jackson's urging annexation and, changing the date from 1843 to 1844, published it in the Richmond *Enquirer*.[13] Quickly the rejuvenated communication spread through the press. News of the secret sittings of the negotiators began to leak, and the country to bubble with the Texas question. The continued silence of the candidates after everyone else had begun to talk was placing followers at a loss. But not Jackson. Clay's silence pleased the veteran; Van Buren's did not disturb him. At the proper moment the man from Kinderhook would come out and ride high on the Texas tide. Old Hickory was certain of it.

On April 22, 1844, the treaty of annexation, signed by plenipotentiaries of the respective nations, was laid before the United States Senate.

Sentiment for Texas swept Tennessee like a cyclone. In Nashville a great mass meeting was planned for May 4. On the night before, the eastern mail brought copies of the *National Intelligencer* for April 27 which threw the Democrats into ecstasy and the Whigs into gloom. The newspaper contained a letter from Henry Clay against annexation.

"Clay [is] a dead political Duck," succinctly observed Andrew Jackson.[14]

Who could doubt it? The meeting was a thunderous affair, at which more than one Whig solemnly repudiated his leader. James K. Polk drove out to make his obeisances at the Hermitage. He found the master looking "years" younger. Now for a swinging pro-Texas pronunciamento from Mr. Van Buren and Polk was sure the election was safe.[15]

Stirring days these, at the Hermitage. As in bygone times, a stream of callers flowed to and fro. Democrats came to pledge allegiance, Whigs to confess their sins and beg absolution; and all to cut hickory canes. A hickory cane was the badge of a Jackson man, a hickory cane cut at the Hermitage the badge of a Jackson man who had been to Mecca. Had all the saplings that went into walking sticks been allowed to grow, they would have furnished enough stake and rail to fence the Hermitage's nine hundred and sixty acres.

At daybreak on May 6, General Jackson awakened to find Robert Armstrong and Willoughby Williams awaiting an audience. So brimming with Texas was the veteran that he began to talk the moment he caught sight of his friends. "I knew Clay would not be President. ... [I knew] he would commit some indiscretion. Gentlemen, mark what I tell you: no man can be President who opposes annexation."

"General," said Willoughby Williams, a forthright man, long the sheriff of Davidson County, "General, we came to submit other developments to you. The late mail brought a letter from Mr. Van Buren in which he takes the same ground that Mr. Clay has taken."

"It's a forgery," exclaimed Jackson. "Mr. Van Buren never wrote such a letter."

Williams placed in Old Hickory's hands a copy of the *Globe*.

Then the two visitors strolled over toward the spring house, leaving the General to read and reflect alone. The *Globe* bore the date April 27, as did the *Intelligencer* which contained Mr. Clay's letter. Being a morning newspaper, the *Intelligencer* had reached Nashville one tri-weekly mail ahead of its evening contemporary.

Van Buren's statement filled eight columns. After an hour Armstrong and Williams returned. The chieftain had accepted the fact. If it was in Frank Blair's paper it was so.

"Mr. Van Buren must write a second letter explaining himself," General Jackson said quietly.

Armstrong ventured that a second letter would do no good. The Tennessee delegation to the Democratic National Convention would be leaving for Baltimore in a few days. Whom should it support? Cass? Silas Wright? Calhoun?

Old Hickory shook his head. His eyes were wet.

Jack Donelson rode up. Presently there was quite a crowd. Jack was a delegate to the convention. After more earnest talk Donelson, Armstrong and a few others withdrew to summon James K. Polk to the Hermitage.[16]

4

On May 11 Old Hickory wrote to Frank Blair:

"I am quite sick really, and have been ever since I read V. B. letter. . . . Political matters out of the question, Texas [is] the key to our future safety. . . . We cannot bear that Great Britain have a Canedy on our west as she has on the north. . . . Some good democrat must be selected, with Polk [as vice president]. . . . can Wright be brought out and will he pledge himself, will Woodbury, or Buchanan."[17]

The chieftain wrote merely to relieve his harrowed feelings. By the time Blair's reply should be at hand the fate of the party, aye of the Union as Jackson believed, would be in the hands of the delegates at Baltimore. If anything were to be accomplished, Jackson must act now. Hours were too precious to waste on regrets.

In an Invalid's Chair

Mathew B. Brady of New York, the most celebrated American photographer of his day, transported his cumbersome daguerreotype equipment to the Hermitage and made this picture on April 15, 1845, when Jackson had less than two months to live. Three likenesses of Jackson by this process are known, of which Brady's is the best. When photographic plates came into use Brady made one from the original tin-type. This reproduction is from that plate, owned by Brady's successor, the L. C. Handy Studios, Washington.

As of old, Jackson prepared to appeal the question from the politicians to the people. He composed a letter to his friend Harris of the Nashville *Union*. The General began by saying that he had been asked whether Mr. Van Buren's statement had caused him to change his opinions on Texas. He had not changed them. The acquisition of Texas was not a party question. It was a question of national security. The theme was effectively developed. In conclusion a tactful paragraph gave the New Yorker a chance to retrace his steps.[18]

On May 13 Jack Donelson started to Nashville with this production. On the way he met Polk and Armstrong en route to the Hermitage. Polk had been in Nashville for a day and a night closeted with General Jackson's friends in preparation for the Hermitage interview. Martin Van Buren had never been popular in Nashville. Jack Donelson had declined a place in his Cabinet. On every street corner, men were drawing unpleasant inferences from the simultaneous announcements of Clay and of Van Buren on Texas; and "bargain" was a memorable word in the lexicon of Jacksonians. When Polk looked at the letter Donelson was taking to the *Union,* he knew that many true blue Nashville Democrats would regard it as dealing too gently with the squire of Lindenwald. Donelson knew this, too.

At the Hermitage Polk and Armstrong were patient, respectful, lucid. They emerged victorious, and James K. Polk headed for Nashville with high thoughts throbbing in his cool, intent and always practical brain. The chieftain had yielded up Martin Van Buren—reluctantly and with a heart of lead, but had yielded him up.

Mr. Polk had previously selected a field marshal to handle his vice-presidential ambitions at Baltimore—a needful precaution, for those aspirations had received a setback by reason of a second unfortunate encounter with Slim Jimmy Jones.[19] Upon this marshal, Congressman Cave Johnson of Tennessee, larger burdens now devolved. Back from the Hermitage Polk wrote Johnson a long letter.

"The Genl . . . speaks most affectionately of *Mr. Van Buren* but is compelled to separate from him. . . . [He says] the Convention must select another man," and he "hoped" that in the interest of harmony Van Buren would withdraw.

Who should take his place?

"Genl. J. says the candidate for the first office should be an annexation man."

As everyone knew, several such men were available—Cass, Buchanan, Calhoun, possibly Wright.

But General Jackson directed that he should be "from the Southwest, and that he and other friends should insist on that point."

Cass was from Michigan, Buchanan, Pennsylvania, Wright, New York; Calhoun—impossible on any ground. But Polk left nothing to inference. "I tell them, and it is true, that I have never aspired so high. . . . I aspire only to the 2nd office. . . . I am however in the hands of my friends and they can use my name in any way they think proper."[20]

Thus the picture contrived for Cave Johnson: the chieftain's word being law, what could Polk do but make the race?

This representation failed—or did it?—to take account of one thing: General Jackson's public appeal, due to appear in the next day's *Union,* containing no mention of Polk, but urging Van Buren to reverse himself on Texas, lead his party to victory and his country to peace. Its publication might seem to contradict Mr. Polk at vital points.

The General's letter did not appear in the next day's *Union,* however—and for an extraordinary reason, if one is to place implicit confidence in the prompt explanation of J. K. Polk. Editor Harris's paper was overset, as printers say, making it necessary to leave out a few items. The custom in such cases, naturally, is to omit the items of least public interest. Harris omitted Andrew Jackson's letter. And, before the type could be placed in the form for the succeeding issue, Old Hickory recalled the communication for "further consideration."[21]

Thus a little coterie of politicians in Nashville, who for years under the compelling eye of the master had pounded the tocsin for Martin Van Buren, edged a step nearer the goal so dear to their hearts. But Polk warned Johnson against over-optimism.

Old Hickory would probably "insist" on the publication of his letter after all. If so, it would be read in Baltimore before the opening of the convention, and would inspire the Van Buren people with hope.[22]

That same day, however, brought news from Washington that Van Buren appreciated the critical nature of his situation. Cave Johnson wrote that Senator Silas Wright had assured him that, in event of Van Buren's withdrawal, only James K. Polk could unite the northern Democrats.[23] Wright was Van Buren's friend and lieutenant.

Polk became a little bolder. Without revisiting the Hermitage for additional inspiration, he answered Johnson, quoting Jackson in stronger language than he had attributed to him the day before. Not only did Old Hickory agree with Senator Wright, he went further: Van Buren "has been misled and ruined" by his opposition to Texas; he "will and ought to withdraw," leaving Polk "the most available man." The convention must take Polk, with a running mate from the northern states. Thus the orders of the chieftain, as transmitted by James K. Polk with incidental expressions of surprise and modesty.

Though bold, Polk was not too bold. Let his friends speak at first not of Polk but of "saving the party" from the evils of internal strife. "I suggest a practical plan," continued the candidate. "[Prior to the convention] get one Delegate from each State in a room at Brown's Hotel and" talk to them about harmony—the particular brand of harmony of which J. K. Polk would be the corporeal embodiment. This should be done with delicacy, avoiding offense to the Van Buren people whose votes would be needed. Finally, Polk's friends must bear in mind that he was still a candidate for vice president—in case the first prize should be another's.[24] After this, the candidate drove back to his home in Columbia. He had done all any man in his situation could do.

Jack Donelson departed for Baltimore, leaving his uncle on the brink of mental confusion. Never before had the chieftain been so nearly at a loss for a handhold on the things he saw passing before his eyes; never so close the feeling that he had lost his grip on the ropes of destiny; never had his commands been so ambiguous and conflicting. Pressed by his vigorous young friends, one day the old man had consented to drop Van Buren and make the gamble for Polk. Next day he had muttered a prayer for a revelation from on High to reconvert Mr. Van Buren and return him the nominee on a Texas platform. Indeed, Jack Donelson carried with him a letter in which Old Hickory implored the New Yorker to reverse himself.[25] Two days after Donelson's stage had rolled away, the *Union* published Jackson's letter, the pro-Van Buren part of which the editor somewhat nullified with an out-and-out anti-Van Buren editorial.[26]

Sinking into a chair the sick chieftain awaited the Baltimore post.

After two days of balloting Van Buren and Cass were neck and neck, the party apparently irrevocably divided and the convention on the verge of dissolution, when a few cool heads brought about an adjournment. Most of the delegates were up all night. At dawn an agreement was reached. At nine o'clock the sleepy politicians tumbled into their seats. By acclamation they nominated James Knox Polk of Tennessee—"Young Hickory."

5

"Polk and Dallas!" rang the battle cry. "Oregon and Texas!"

George M. Dallas, of Pennsylvania, was Young Hickory's running mate.

The chieftain revived.

"Every letter brings us Joyfull news. You will get twenty states at least."[27] And to Mrs. Polk: "Daughter, I will put you in the White House if it costs me my life!"[28]

Not every pleasant letter pertained to the campaign.

"Dear Uncle

"I presented my husband with a fine Son which we have named Andrew Jackson. . . . Yr aff Niece

"SARAH K. SEVIER."[29]

Andrew Jackson Sevier, great-grandson of John Sevier: here

was something to tickle the ears of Nolichucky Jack should Old Hickory chance to meet him on the golden stairs.

Lines from one of the multitude of children Rachel had befriended:

"Derr Sir I have herd of your bad helth. . . . You have not now my good Freind Mrs Jackson [to nurse you]. I often Shed Teirs when I think of hur for I found her a kind Mother in a foren land. I have come through many troubles & trials since I left the Hermitage. I am now a widow living in the far west [Haw Creek, Missouri] with 8 children six sons & two dawters. It was my lot to get a triffling companion but blessed be god the best of children. I have not been able to given them any schooling only what I could myself teach. I begin to look old and feels old I am now close on to fifty & not a gray hair in my head but remains respectfuly Latitia Chambers."[30]

Seldom a week without something like this:

"Honored Genl
"I have long thought of Coming to See you but poverty forbids. I have not Seen you Since when the army was returning from st Marks—1817, but hope that you will write me a few Lines that I may have the handwriting of my Genl to Look upon. Respectfully Sir John Greere."[31]

Prospects for cotton and for feed crops were good, both at the Hermitage and "below," as the General spoke of Halcyon Plantation—until July when the Mississippi swept over Halcyon. The fences, most of the stock and sixty thousand pounds of cotton went with the yellow flood.[32] The loss was a small fortune. No debts could be paid that year or the next. Blair and Rives, who had bet twenty-two thousand dollars on Polk, would need their money in case the Whigs should win.

6

The campaign ran head-foremost into a serious complication. Since April the United States Senate had been tossing the annexation treaty about as if it were a hot potato. The Democratic platform provided a welcome solution: "Polk and Texas!" "Very well, Mr. Polk, you shall have the honor." So saying, the senators stood aside, rejecting the treaty by a smashing vote.

Haughtily Sam Houston turned to England's door. The latch-string was out. Jackson could not find it in his heart to blame him. "Houston has been most cruelly treated."[33] The olympian scorn of the chieftain was reserved for "those craven hearted Senators, Traitors to our country and to our Glorious Union. . . . [Must we now] go to war with England and France to gain Texas, offered to us on honorable terms [and] rejected for political effect?"[34]

Polk's election seemed the only alternative, and to elect him the rank and file of the Democratic Party would have to display greater unity and spunk than its leaders had done in the Senate. To this task the Old Chief gave his strength unsparingly. By August he could no longer ride—he who had spent a lifetime on horseback. By September he was too short of breath to walk the hundred and fifty steps to Rachel's grave without an arm to lean on. Propped before his writing table he labored on, sowing letters broadcast in an effort to arouse the country to a realization of its peril. Tyler was running on an independent ticket. He should withdraw, he must withdraw, the white-haired warrior said, and throw those votes to Polk. Jackson played his hand with the skill of a politician in the prime of his powers. Tyler withdrew.[35] He did more. To counteract European influence, the President diffused the atmosphere of the Hermitage about Sam Houston, appointing Andrew Jackson Donelson chargé d'affaires to the Texas Republic.

America began to respond, the tide for Texas to rise. Clay men strove to beat it down. "Slavery is the paramount issue," shouted an alarmed editor in Cincinnati, making common cause with Garrison's Liberator. But the current was setting the other way—even in New England where a young man had the effrontery to remind John Quincy Adams that Nature had given us Texas "and we must have it." The New Haven Register declared annexation a subject on which Democrats North and South should unite. Once more, and for the last time, the nation was taking its stride from Andrew Jackson.[36]

The warrior spurred his protégé to press the advantage, and never let up. "Lash Clay on Texas."[37] Young Hickory lashed him. The Whigs began to waver. Taking fright, Clay compromised, declaring he would be glad to receive Texas into the Union if it could be done without war and with the people's consent.

When the voters went to the polls in November, in one sense Old Hickory's success had been too sweeping. Clay as well as Polk had profited by Jackson's exploitation of the Texas issue. The General no longer claimed twenty states; he knew the result would be close. So did Polk. Glancing up from a page of tabulations in his own precise hand, the cool, objective contestant said that only fourteen states with one hundred and thirty-four electoral votes were sure, and that victory might turn on the votes of the doubtful states of New York and Tennessee.[38]

Slowly recovering from a hemorrhage and panting for breath, Jackson marked down the returns. It was a long ordeal. From Maine to Louisiana the candidates seemed to have run a dead heat. As votes were counted, it was found that Polk had carried exactly the fourteen states he had said would go to him. These were not enough to elect. Clay won Tennessee and its thirteen electoral votes by a popular majority of one hundred and thirteen. Now Polk must have New York to win. He got it by five thousand votes, making the count in the electoral college one hundred and seventy to one hundred and five. Polk's popular plurality was thirty-eight thousand out of two million six hundred thousand votes cast.[39]

The star of Henry Clay's ambition set in the ashes of his hopes. Finished was the long sequel to the drama of February 9, 1825, which the Kentuckian already recognized as the greatest error of judgment of his life.[40] Yet this engaging statesman's farewell to presidential aspirations was not a farewell to greatness. The finest days of Henry Clay's career were to come when he left Ashland for the last time to lead a courageous band of Southerners, mostly old Jackson men, in the hopeless fight against the trend toward secession.

7

At the Hermitage the architect of victory grew weaker, the last reserves of his strength seemingly gone. "I await with resignation the call of my god."[41]

But first he would see the fruits of his victory secure. While messages of congratulation piled up unacknowledged, Andrew Jackson wrote to his nephew in Texas. "Col Polk spent two nights with me. We had a full and free conversation upon all matters and things. . . . Congress will at an early day of her *now* session . . . [pass] a bill for the reannexation of Texas. . . . The voice of the people has pronounced upon the subject. . . . England wants Texas, next Cuba, and then Oregon." America must defeat this and save Texans from the fate of "Hewers of wood and drawers of water for the . . . [British] aristocracy. . . . My kind regards to Genl Houston. Bring those things which I have expressed to his view. . . . [He has] too much patriotism . . . [to make Texas] a Colony of England."[42]

Sam Houston begged Major Donelson to thank the Old Chief for his counsel. The words of Andrew Jackson would be prized as treasures.[43]

A fortnight later Houston finished his second term of office. "The attitude of Texas now," he said in his farewell address, "is one of peculiar interest. The United States have spurned her. Let her, therefore, work out her own political salvation," pushing her boundary to the Pacific. "If Texas goes begging again for admission to the United States she will only degrade herself." Suppose the United States should open her door? Ah, in that event the course of Texas would be a matter for Houston's successor to consider. Houston himself would be occupied with the more congenial task of farming and finished forever with public affairs.[44]

The new president of Texas was Anson Jones, a sort of orderly-clerk for Sam Houston. The imperialistic tone of the valedictory did not disturb Donelson. After a private talk with the retired executive, Jack assured his uncle that Houston's true goal was annexation. "He is devoted to you, considering that he owes his success at the battle of San Jacinto to the recollection of your plans of battle in your campaigns against the Creek Indians. . . . He says that his greatest ambition is to make a pilgrimage to the Hermitage and obtain your blessing on his boy. You may expect him this spring."[45]

Jackson pressed the Administration to strike while the iron was hot. Half a dozen resolutions, differing in detail, were plumped before Congress. The annexationists began to bicker and divide, the opposition to unite. His strength ebbing daily, Jackson took to an invalid's chair fitted with an attachment to write on. To indite a page made him "gasp" for breath.[46] Yet many pages were written, appealing for harmony. Polk sped to Washington to co-operate with Tyler. After anxious days an opposition senator exclaimed, "The pressure of two presidents and an ex-President is too much for us."[47] A resolution offering Texas a place as a state of the Union was adopted. Mr. Tyler signed it on March 1, 1845, three days before leaving office.

"I congratulate you, Dear General,"[48] exclaimed Frank Blair.

The man in the invalid's chair replied: "I congratulate my beloved country."[49]

8

Informed of the flood's damage to Halcyon Plantation, Blair and Rives again deferred all payments on account of their ten thousand dollar loan. "My Dear General, your convenience alone must be consulted."[50]

No sooner had this been arranged than a fresh revelation of the business practices of Andrew, junior, almost broke the old gentleman down. A note to Jack Donelson breathed despair. "Poverty stares us in the face."[51] Young Jackson had never thought highly of his father's idea of running a woodyard, and had neglected it for cotton. When the cotton was washed out, it transpired that Andrew had been duped by his overseer into closing the woodyard, his only source of ready money until another crop could be grown. Whereupon the overseer had leased land adjoining Halcyon and established his own fuel station which he palmed off on packet captains as belonging to Jackson. This was not all. Andrew had contracted debts amounting to six thousand dollars. At any rate that was what the General and Sarah computed them to be, confirmation being impossible due to Andrew's absence from home. Were creditors to learn of this state of affairs "the sheriff [would be] at our doors."[52]

The only thing, as Jackson saw it, was to sell Halcyon. "My son has not sufficient energy to conduct an establishment at a distance," the afflicted father wrote to W. B. Lewis in Washington. "You are in the thoroughfare of rich farmers." Here was "a certain fortune" for someone. "If there were ten thousand cords [of wood] on the Bank it would all be taken at a dollar and a half a cord by the middle of June." But all Jackson asked was enough money to pay his son's debts. He would let Halcyon, with all improvements, go for twelve dollars an acre. As virtually wild land it had cost twenty. "My dear Major aid me in getting a purchaser and I will die happy."[53]

Sarah was reading the General's mail to him when she crumpled something to her breast and burst into tears. It was a single sheet covered with Frank Blair's cabalistic scrawl. "Major Lewis has just shown me your letter about Andrew's affairs." General Jackson must not sacrifice his Mississippi property. The firm of Blair & Rives would advance the money needed. John Rives confirmed this. "Mr. Blair and myself are indebted to you for *all we are worth*."[54] Enclosed was the following:

"Washington, March 12, 1845

"General Andrew Jackson is authorized to draw upon us at one day's sight for any sum between one and one hundred thousand dollars and his draft shall be honored, . . . payable at Baltimore, Philadelphia or New York.

"BLAIR & RIVES."[55]

Before Sarah had finished, tears were trickling down the chieftain's cheeks. Again, the old man and his daughter-in-law pored over Andrew's muddled ledger. To be safe they decided to draw for seven thousand dollars. Andrew reached home in time to correct this estimate. So the General drew for eight thousand, raising to twenty-four thousand dollars the total of his indebtedness on his son's account. "Mr. A. Jackson junr will not create another debt of one dollar until he is clear of . . . [this]."[56] The hope that declined to die.

9

The thread of life can spin itself incredibly fine. Many who witnessed the unforgettable scene of General Jackson's departure from Washington in 1837 did not believe that he could survive to reach the Hermitage. Ever since that time Jackson men had journeyed thither with hastened steps, in the belief that the last chance to see the Old Chief alive was at hand. On March 4, 1845—Young Hickory's inaugural day—the cane of crippled Isaac Hill thumped the peeling planks of the Hermitage portico. He had come from New Hampshire to spend that day with Old Hickory.

"If he were another man I could scarcely suppose he would live a week. For the last four months he has not attempted to take his customary meals with the family. He sits through the day in a well constructed easy chair, with his writing materials, his miniature bible and hymn book before him. As soon as the mail arrives his first inquiry is for the daily Washington newspapers and the letters bearing the postmark of the capital. The absorbing topic with him is Texas. . . .

"His complaint is pulmonary: one lobe of the lungs he believes to be entirely consumed. His feet and ankles are swollen from continued sitting, and he finds a substitute for exercise in the bathing of his limbs every evening in those emolients calculated to produce a healthy reaction of the skin.—Weak as he is he shaves with his own hand and adjusts the ample gray hair which continues to add to the dignity of his appearance."[57]

On March 15 a group of old Jackson men gathered in Washington to celebrate the General's seventy-eighth birthday. It was a solemn company—until Auguste Davézac, of Louisiana campaign remembrance, raised his glass.

"There are craven hearts," the Creole said, "who would have re-

fused the boon of an empire lest the accepting of it should lead
to war: a war, they said, to be dreaded by a nation having no
army, no leader to match the great commanders of European nations. No leader! They forget that Jackson still lives. Even if
the hero were dead, go to the Hermitage, ye men of little faith;
Go! ask for that old *cocked hat;* it is still there; take it; raise it on
the top of a long hickory pole! One hundred thousand American
horsemen, rallying around that standard, will tread down Europe's
or Mexico's mercenaries like the grass of the Texan prairies."[58]

A naval officer brought from over the water the sarcophagus of
a Roman emperor which he offered to General Jackson. "With
the warmest sensations that can inspire a grateful heart I must
decline the honor intended," Old Hickory replied. "I have prepared an humble repository for my mortal body beside that
wherein lies my beloved wife."[59]

In April Justice John Catron reached the Hermitage. His appointment to the United States Supreme bench had been one of
the last that Jackson made. The General said he knew that he
would never leave his chair. "He then asked me to give him an
account of the start our friend President Polk had made. This I
did for an hour at which he laughed heartily, understanding to the
letter the office-seeking horde." General Jackson had not lessened
Mr. Polk's burden, his own recommendations for appointments
ranging from Cabinet officers to copying clerks.

After the visit Justice Catron fell to meditating on the qualities
that made Andrew Jackson great. He decided in favor of a natural gift of chieftainship, and the paralysing swiftness with which
he translated thought into action. "If he had fallen from the clouds
into a city on fire, he would have been at the head of the ex-
tinguishing hosts in an hour." Perhaps the Justice had heard of the
Jonesborough fire in 1803. "He would have blown up a palace
to stop the fire with as little misgiving as another would have
torn down a board shed. In a moment he would have willed it
proper and in ten minutes the thing would have been done. . . .
He cared not a rush for anything behind: he looked ahead."[60]

He looked ahead now—with one eye on eternity, the other on
Texas.

Disturbing reports came from Jack Donelson.

Anson Jones, Houston's successor as president, had declined to call the Texan congress to consider the ratification of the resolution of annexation. This was ominous, for Donelson knew Jones to be a pawn of Sam Houston. Old Hickory's nephew sought out the hero of San Jacinto. The interview was painful. The Texan dictator objected to the American terms on various far-fetched grounds.

A mighty struggle fevered the mind of Sam Houston. He had come to Texas an outcast. Now the first statesmen of two hemispheres addressed him in terms of equality. With his own hands and brain he had created a nation, which Sam Houston had no fear should become a British colony. Thrice had he offered this treasure to the United States. Thrice it had been rejected. Now that the United States, pricked in the tender flesh of self-interest, had deigned to change its mind, should Houston oblige: should he relinquish this personal possession of his, this republic which he had made strong; or should he keep it, snatch from Mexico the Pacific Coast and establish himself at the head of a nation which one day might rank with the powers of the world?

The acute Donelson had done more than communicate the American resolution of annexation to the Texan, however. He had placed in his hands a letter from Andrew Jackson, in which the Old Chief cordially chose to assume opposition to the American terms by Houston to be unthinkable. "I congratulate you, I congratulate Texas and the United States. Glorious result! in which you, General, have acted a noble part."[61]

Still, the Texan hesitated. Donelson warned his uncle: "Houston has disappointed me."[62]

The master of the Hermitage was sinking, the dropsical swelling taking possession of his whole body. Edward George Washington Butler, classmate of Jack Donelson at West Point and godson of General Jackson, arrived to take his last leave. With agony in his dying eyes, the right one blind, Old Hickory said:

"Edward, what will Houston do?"

In a vigorous letter Butler relayed the question to the Texan.[63] Donelson added to the pressure.

Surrendering his shimmering dream, Sam Houston signed to Jones to prepare to furl the flag of the lone star.

This decision was typical of the men who marched under the ensign of Andrew Jackson: a loyal breed. Long after the old leader was in the grave that power of his lived on. When the sections came to the parting of the ways, Frank Blair, junior, did much to save Missouri for the Union, Sam Houston tried to save Texas, and Andrew Johnson helped to reclaim Tennessee.[64]

On May 26 news of Houston's decision reached the Hermitage from Donelson. Nor was that all. The Texas titan himself was on the way to Tennessee to account in person to his chief.

Glorious tidings! Old Hickory traced a note to James K. Polk. "I knew British gold could not buy Sam Houston."

Fighting for breath, Jackson signed his name.[65] "My lamp is nearly burned out, and the last glimmer has come."[66]

Sam Houston, make haste.

II

The dying man could no longer lie down. His nights were spent propped up in bed, his days on the pillowed chair. The swelling extended to his face. The train of pilgrims grew in volume. On May 29 more than thirty persons, from every walk of life, made their brief farewells. A king's painter came—from Louis Philippe —to take a likeness for the royal gallery. The artist was George P. A. Healy, a young American residing in Paris. Painting the eyes, forehead and hair from life, he adapted the rest from a portrait by Earl.[67]

When Mr. Healy had finished, the General asked him "as a personal favor" to remain long enough to make a portrait of his "dear child," Sarah. Having already painted two portraits, not one, of Jackson, Healy had overstayed his time. The King had given him other American commissions to execute, among them a likeness of Henry Clay. Mr. Clay was at the moment passing through

THE DYING CHIEFTAIN

Painted in May, 1845, by George P. A. Healy who visited the Hermitage under commission of
Louis Philippe of France. A dropsical swelling having spread to Jackson's face, only the eyes,
the right one blind, the forehead and the hair were painted from life. The remainder was
adapted from a portrait by Earl. The majesty of the dying leader moved Healy to make two
portraits, one of which now hangs in the Louvre, the other in the Hermitage. This is a
reproduction of the latter, which is owned by the Ladies' Hermitage Association.

Nashville and Healy told the General he wished to join him there. The artist never forgot the look in Jackson's eyes at the mention of Henry Clay's name.

"Young man," Old Hickory said, "always do your duty."

Healy remained to paint Sarah. On the belated arrival at Ashland Mr. Clay observed to him:

"I see that you, like all who approached that man, were fascinated by him."[68]

On Sunday, June 1, the General asked the members of the family to cease their vigil and go to church. "This is the holy Sabbath, and apparently the last one I will be with you."[69] That night he slept little. The next day was one of great pain. He prayed to God to help him bear it. Opiates were given more freely. On Thursday he rallied, and listened to an account of plantation affairs from his son. Asking for pen and paper, he began a letter to Plauché in New Orleans:

"We want a supply of Pork & bacon at our Mississippi plantation— one thousand pounds of bacon, midlings, if to be had bottom shoulders, and five barrels of Miss[issippi] pork in all 2000#."

Alas, Andrew had mentioned a subject other than pork: money.

. . . ["May we] draw upon you a bill to mature the first of March next for not more than $2,000 before which maturity we shall have ample assets [the cotton crop] in your hands to cover. . . . You may rest assured that A. Jackson Jnr will never again draw unless covered by assets My health is bad. . . . I remain y^r. friend

"ANDREW JACKSON."[70]

Late that night after George had lifted his master into bed, it was Sarah's turn on watch. The beam of a candle cast restless shadows on the sufferer's face. The lips moved. Sarah bent nearer. She caught snatches of a prayer and the words of a hymn:

"When through the deep waters I call thee to go
The rivers of woe shall not then overflow."

At midnight Sarah asked her father how he felt. "Pretty comfortable," he said, "but I cannot be long with you all. I wish to be buried without display or pomp." And he added: "Or any superfluous expense."[71]

On awakening the next morning, which was Friday, the patient said he still felt "comfortable." About eleven o'clock he told his son he wished to write his friend Polk, and that this might be his last letter. Andrew suggested that it be put off until tomorrow.

"Tomorrow," the father said, "I may not be here."

"—*confidential*—

"Hermitage
"June 6th, 1845

"James K. Polk
  "president of the
  "United States—
    "My dear Sir,
      "Your letter of the 12th ultimo, (*confidential*) has been received— Be assured my friend that it is truly gratefull to learn from you that you have a united & harmonious Cabit——"

The dying man's hand was steady, the letters, though slowly formed, distinct and strong. His mind was clear. Looking back he missed the word "gratefull," written for "gratifying," but "Cabit" for "Cabinet" caught his eye and was corrected.

"... Sarah is truly grateful to learn from you that Mr. Taggart [a petitioner for office] will be provided for as you promised— We all salute you & M[rs]. Polk with the kindest good wishes.

"My dear Sir, I wish you to recollect the caution I gave you about the Treasury Department—." For a page and a half Old Hickory proceeded with the topic that was his object in writing. Mr. Polk had named Senator Robert J. Walker as Secretary of the Treasury—an appointment dictated by expediency, not choice. Walker was the head of a pro-Texas group which demanded recognition. Jackson had heard that he was also backed by speculators in depreciated script in the hope that a Treasury order would restore it to par. "I say put your veto on ... [this scheme] or you and your Secretary will be blown sky high. ... I can write no

— Confidential —

Hermitage
June 6th 1845

James K. Polk
President of the
United States

My dear Sir,

Your letter of the 12th ultimo, (Confidential) has been received. Be assured my friend that it is truly grateful to learn from you, that you have a united & harmonious Cabinett. May it so continue to exist thro your administration, is the prayer of your friend. Sarah is truly grateful to learn from you, that her friend Mrs Taggart is to be provided for as you promised. We all salute you & Mrs Polk with the kindest good wishes.

My dear Sir, I wish you to recollect the caution I gave you about the Treasury Department. Here you are to be assailed, and without great vigilence & energy in yourself, your administration wounded deeply, and in the strictest confidence as your real friend, I read your attention again to it. I was well advised, and by Mr Walkers friends, that Mr Walker would be sought for this office by all those who were interested in those chocktaw fraudulent claims, & by those deeply interested in them, and in their negotiation. There never was a greater fraud attempted & consummated than in these claims, and when these proposed investigated will throw shame and disgrace upon all concerned. The passed acts by Congress on this subject you cannot repeal, but look well to the future. Scrip has been issued upon those fraudulent claims to the amount of

$10,000 — this is now worth 50 cents in the dollar for entry land — The great aim of these Speculators are to get Walker as Secretary of the Treasury, by a circular, to place this scrip upon the same footing as the stocks, and at once to raise 100 pct, putting $750,000 in the pocketts of these fraudulent Speculators — Look to this my friend — let the scrip rest on its own basis if their Congress has placed it. Do you not believe that such an act in the Secretary of your Treasury would blow you & your administration sky high.

But again, I am informed thro a channel which I have a right to confide, and is a man of much truth himself — That the late accountant of the Treasury ——— for the short time he was at the head of it, made ninety thousand dollars, by arrangements with the two brokers Banks of Newyork where large Sums of the public money was deposited & other deposits Banks in N. York — Enquire cautiously amonghst the clerks in the city of Washington, by which you will find a key that may unlock the door to a proper enqy — But on enquiry by the whole you are prepared for you should Mr. Walker have the folly to have any thing to do with either of these horrible projects — I say to you put you rto upon them both, & you & your Secretary will be blown sky high. And & you know that the corrupt Speculators for yours, or his character if they can get hold of the cash — I can write no more, my strength has aroused me to make this attempt — yr friend

Andrew Jackson

more—friendship has aroused me to make this attempt— yr friend
"ANDREW JACKSON."[72]

The signature, free and fair, stretched two-thirds of the way
across the sheet.

At two o'clock Andrew returned.

"There is my letter to my friend Polk. Fold and back [address]
it for me, for I am too exhausted, my son, to do it."[73] A little
strength returning, his mind dwelt on the sunset rainbow of Sam
Houston's momentous decision. "All is safe at last!" His "old
friend and comrade in arms" had been true to his trust. British
gold could not buy Sam Houston. . . . That left Oregon. Polk
would attend to Oregon. Polk would be firm. Polk would get
Oregon—Jackson hoped without war. "If not," the soldier said,
"let war come."[74]

Sunday, June 8, dawned still and hot. In the forenoon General
Jackson swooned away. A cadenced cry from the servants spread
through the rooms.

"Oh, Lord! Oh, Lord! Old Massa's dead. Old Massa's dead."

Those outside the house caught up the wail, carrying it to the
outbuildings and the stables. Now close at hand it sounded, now
far away.

"Old Massa's dead. Oh, Lord! Old Massa's dead."[75]

A spoonful of brandy revived the General. He said farewell to
the household servants, kissed and blessed each member of the
family, his glance resting longest on the little granddaughter
whose name was Rachel Jackson. "My dear children, and friends,
and servants, I hope and trust to meet you all in Heaven, both
white and black—both white and black."

The yard had begun to fill with people: a mixed and sorrowing
company, some of them drawn, it would seem, by a force stronger
than volition. John Henry Eaton and Margaret were there. Eaton
had seen his Old Chief perhaps three times in five years, Margaret
not for nearly ten. In life they were not to see him again. Negroes
trooped from across the fields. Field hands at the Hermitage
enjoyed unusual privileges. Not segregated in "quarters," they
lived in individual cabins scattered all over the plantation. Form-

ing a group a little distance from the house, they began to chant and pray. Two large south windows of the master's first-floor bedroom gave upon the spacious gallery. The household servants collected on the porch before them, chanting softly.

William Berkeley Lewis came at noon. "Major," said the dying man, "you had like to have been too late." He gave his friend messages for Sam Houston, for Thomas Hart Benton and for Frank Blair.

Someone asked Hannah, in whose arms the first Rachel Jackson had died, to leave the room. "I was born on this place," the old negress said, "and my place is here."

At half past five Andrew, junior, leaned over the bed. "Father, do you know me?"

The voice was very weak. "Yes, I know you. I would know you all if I could see. Bring my specs."

The moans of the servants peering through the windows reached his ears.

"Oh, do not cry. Be good children, and we shall all meet in Heaven."

The chant on the porch sank to a whisper. The chieftain closed his eyes. At six o'clock his head fell forward. His heart stood still.[76]

12

At dusk a coach drawn by galloping horses careened into the Hermitage drive. A travel-stained, arresting figure dismounted, leading a very small boy by the hand. The newcomer towered half a head above the next tallest man present. Not everyone at first recognized Sam Houston.

The greatest of Old Hickory's expeditionary captains stood motionless before the candle-lit couch of death. Then he dropped to his knees, and sobbing, buried his face on his chieftain's breast.

The proprietor of the Texas Republic drew the boy to his side.

"My son, try to remember that you have looked on the face of Andrew Jackson."[77]

THE END

NOTES

CHAPTER I

[1]Planters in the Tennessee River Valley of Alabama sent their cotton over the Muscle Shoals with the rise of the waters in February, and thence to New Orleans via the Tennessee, Ohio and Mississippi Rivers. This long journey was easier of accomplishment than to haul the cotton overland to the head of navigation of the Alabama for shipment to Mobile.

[2]Nashville *Whig*, January 2, 1822.

[3]*Ibid.*, January 16, 1822.

[4]Bill of Thomas Barron & Company, dated April 23, 1822. Jackson Papers, Library of Congress, Washington.

[5]Philadelphia *Aurora*, January 23, 1822.

[6]Knoxville *Register*, February 26, 1822.

[7]Nashville *Whig*, March 20, 1822.

[8]Rachel Jackson to Mary Donelson, February, 1822, Augustus C. Buell, *A History of Andrew Jackson* (1904), II, 157.

[9]*Ibid.*, 155. Buell was acquainted with Campbell and doubtless had this anecdote from his lips. I have taken the liberty to correct Buell's text where he gives Jackson's age as fifty-four. See also Campbell to W. Jones, Philadelphia, April 1, 1822, private collection of Emil Edward Hurja, New York City.

[10]Nashville *Whig*, January 2, 1822.

[11]Jackson to Andrew Jackson Donelson, July 5, 1822, *Correspondence of Andrew Jackson*, edited by John Spencer Bassett (1926-1935), III, 167.

[12]Nashville *Whig*, May 15, 1822.

[13]*Ibid.*

[14]Jackson to J. C. Bronaugh, June 2, 1822, Jackson Papers.

[15]Jackson to R. K. Call, May 2, 1822, *Correspondence*, III, 162.

[16]Jackson to R. K. Call, May 20, 1822, Jackson Papers.

[17]Jackson to A. J. Donelson, April 22, 1822, Donelson Papers, Library of Congress.

[18]Jackson to Gadsden, May 2, 1822, *Correspondence*, III, 161. It is not known what became of Gadsden's ambition to write a book about Jackson, and if Jackson forwarded him the papers requested they were returned long before Jackson's death. In 1825 a *Civil and Military History of Andrew Jackson* was published under the authorship of "An American Officer." In *The Raven, a Biography of Sam Houston,* I intimate that Houston may have written this book. I am now inclined to believe that he did not write it. Possibly the author was Gadsden, but this is merely a guess.

[19]Jackson to A. J. Donelson, May 2, 1822, Donelson Papers.

[20]Jackson to A. J. Donelson, April 12, 1822, *ibid.*

[21]Jackson to A. J. Donelson, May 20, 1822, *Correspondence*, III, 162.

[22] John M. Lea was the son-in-law who burned the papers. The incident was related to the writer in 1933 by Lemuel R. Campbell of Nashville who had it from Mr. Lea. This evidence being destroyed, the reader may properly inquire as to the source of the author's statement that Judge Overton played a "masterful" part in the campaign. A few political papers escaped Mr. Lea and are in the Overton Papers, Tennessee Historical Society, Nashville. Others are in the Coffee Papers (Tennessee Historical Society), Jackson Papers (Library of Congress) and elsewhere. The correspondence of other members of the junto shows Overton's constant activity and a general deference to his views. In the matter of answering the slanders against Mrs. Jackson in 1827 Overton emerged for once. There his work was patently masterful. So greatly did he surpass in ability the other members of the junto that, to a person who has studied the whole situation, there can be no doubt as to the extent of his contribution to the eventual result.

[23] Jackson to James Gadsden, December 6, 1821, *Correspondence*, III, 140.

[24] Narrative of W. B. Lewis, written in 1858, James Parton, *Life of Andrew Jackson* (1859-60), III, 19-20.

[25] Jackson to James Gadsden, December 6, 1821, *Correspondence*, III, 140.

[26] Parton, III, 20.

[27] Nashville *Whig*, May 1, 1822.

[28] *Ibid.*, April 24, 1822.

[29] *Ibid.*, August 28, 1822.

[30] Jackson had acquired Melton's Bluff from John Melton who had grown wealthy by robbing the boats which passed along the Tennessee River. Melton had built a mansion for his Cherokee wife, but when the Creeks, displeased by his encroachments, began to make threats against his life, he disposed of his extensive property, which he had made famous by lavish expenditures and cruelties to his hands, and moved to the other side of the river. Anne Royall visited the plantation in 1818, and found Jackson's overseer living on the first floor of the Melton house and the second story bulging with stores of cotton. "No language can convey an idea of the beauties of Melton's Bluff," Mrs. Royall wrote. "I can sit in my room and see the whole plantation; the boats gliding down the river, . . . the ducks, geese, and swans, playing . . . on the bosom of the stream, with a full view of the many islands. . . . I took a walk with some ladies over the plantation. . . . We approached the mansion, by a broad street, running up the river bank east of the town. The street seems suspended between heaven and earth, as the whole premises for two miles, all in sight, appears to be elevated above the horizon. . . . We entered the courtyard, fronting the house, by a stile; and the first thing we met was a large scaffold overspread with cotton. Being damp from dew and often rain, it must be dried in this manner. The mansion was large, built with logs, shingled roof. . . . All the trade of East Tennessee passes by the Bluff, and halt here to take in their pilots." (Anne Royall, *Letters from Alabama* [1830], 59-62.)

[31]Jackson to Egbert Harris, April 13, 1822, *Correspondence*, III, 158.

[32]Jackson to A. J. Donelson, June 28, 1822, *ibid.*, 166.

[33]Jackson to A. J. Donelson, June 28, 1822, *ibid.*, 167.

[34]Felix Grundy to Jackson, June 27, 1822, *ibid.*, 163.

[35]Jackson to A. J. Donelson, August 6, 1822, *ibid.*, 173: "I have recd many letters from every quarter of the united states on this subject the presidency; I have answered none." This was written after the Grundy letter had been received.

Bassett (I, 328) states that Jackson did answer Grundy's letter, under date of July 18, and gives the summary of the answer, the original of which the author says is in the Library of Congress. Bassett apparently has mistaken a letter Jackson wrote to James Bronaugh on July 18 for an answer to Grundy. The summary he gives exactly fits the Bronaugh letter. In the Library of Congress collection of Jackson manuscripts or in no other collection to which Bassett had access, or in no collection to which I have had access, have I been able to discover a reply to the Grundy letter. The letter to Bronaugh is in the Library of Congress collection, as is also Grundy's letter to Jackson, bearing this endorsement in Jackson's hand "Mr. Grundy's confidential letter of the 27th of June 1822," but nothing to indicate that it was answered. Bassett included the Grundy letter and the Jackson letter to Bronaugh in the *Correspondence*, III, 163–170, but no answer to the former appears.

[36]The contemporary spelling of Murfreesborough, and of all other proper names, is used in this volume. The town is now Murfreesboro.

[37]Jackson to A. J. Donelson, July 16, 1822, Donelson Papers.

[38]Nashville *Clarion*, July 18, 1822.

[39]Jackson to J. C. Bronaugh, July 18, 1822, *Correspondence*, III, 170.

[40]Jackson to A. J. Donelson, August 6, 1822, *ibid.*, 173.

[41]John Spencer Bassett, *The Life of Andrew Jackson* (1911) I, 328.

[42]Jackson to Bronaugh, August 1, 1822, S. G. Heiskell, *Andrew Jackson and Early Tennessee History* (1921), III, 158.

[43]Sam Houston to Jackson, August 3, 1822, Jackson Papers.

[44]*Ibid.*

CHAPTER II

[1]New York *Evening Post*, August 22, 1822.

[2]Knoxville *Register*, January 29, 1822. The statement was also true of August of the same year.

[3]*Columbian Observer*, Philadelphia, June 23, 1822.

[4]*Western Carolinian*, Salisbury, August 20, 1822.

[5]Jackson to A. J. Donelson, August 6, 1822, *Correspondence*, III, 174.

[6]Jackson to A. J. Donelson, August 6, 1822, *ibid.*, 174.

[7]Jackson to A. J. Donelson, August 28, 1822, *ibid.*, 178.

[8]Jackson to A. J. Donelson, October 11, 1822, *ibid.*, 179.

[9]Parton, II, 585.

[10]J. H. Eaton to Jackson, January 11, 1823, Jackson Papers.

[11]*Ibid.*

[12]James Monroe to Jackson, January 30, 1823, private collection of Henry M. Flynt, New York City.

[13]Jackson to A. J. Donelson, January 8, 1823, Donelson Papers, Library of Congress.

[14]William Carroll to Henry Clay, February 1, 1823, Clay Papers, Library of Congress.

[15]Henry Shaw to Henry Clay, February 11, 1823, *ibid.*

[16]Benton, Jesse, *An Address to the People of the United States on the Presidential Election,* 1824, 8; "Curtius," *Torch Light,* . . . *an Examination of the* . . . *Opposition to the Administration* . . . 1826, 7.

[17]J. C. Calhoun to Virgil Maxcy, December 31, 1821, Maxcy Papers, Library of Congress.

[18]J. C. Calhoun to Jackson, January 20, 1823, *ibid.*

[19]J. H. Eaton to Jackson, January 11, 1823, Jackson Papers.

[20]Jackson to James Monroe, February 19, 1823, Monroe Papers, New York Public Library.

[21]Eaton to Jackson, March 23, 1823, Jackson Papers.

[22]J. H. Eaton to Jackson, January 11, 1823, *ibid.*

[23]Jackson to John Coffee, March 10, 1823, *Correspondence,* III, 192.

[24]*Ibid.*

[25]John M. Farland to Jackson, August 14, 1824, Jackson Papers.

[26]Edward Patchell to Jackson, August 7, 1824, *Correspondence,* III, 263.

[27]H. W. Peterson to Jackson, February 3, 1823, Jackson Papers.

[28]Jackson to H. W. Peterson, February 23, 1823, *Correspondence,* III, 189.

[29]J. M. Farland to Jackson, August 14, 1824, Jackson Papers.

[30]The only attempt at a biography of Crawford is J. E. D. Shipp's *Giant Days or the Life and Times of William H. Crawford* (1909), a brief and unsatisfactory work. *The Dictionary of American Biography,* IV, 529, contains a good sketch of Crawford's career by Ulrich B. Phillips. In a bibliographical note Professor Phillips adds: "His rivals for the presidency lived on to great prominence, attracting biographers each of whom wanted a foil for his hero. Crawford was made to serve, until the time of Carl Schurz (*Henry Clay,* I, 223) he was reduced to a reputation of a reputation." The biographer who can tell us in detail how it was that a figure now so obscure as Crawford rose among the men who then peopled the American stage to stand not once but twice on the threshold of the presidency will have made a distinct contribution to our political history.

[31]Worthington C. Ford, *Writings of John Quincy Adams,* VII, 272.

[32]C. Vandewater to Virgil Maxcy, July 10, 1823, Maxcy Papers.

[33]George McDuffie to an unnamed correspondent, January 18, 1823, Fisher Papers, State Historical Commission of North Carolina. This document is from "The Presidential Election of 1824 in North Carolina" (p. 237), an unpublished thesis by A. R. Newsome, head of the History Department of the University of North Carolina. Dr. Newsome kindly placed a copy at the disposal of the writer. Other copies are in the library of the University of Michigan.

[34]F. J. Wharton to Henry Clay, August 13, 1823, Clay Papers.

[35]John McKinley to Henry Clay, June 3, 1823, *ibid.*

[36]T. H. Benton to Henry Clay, July 7, 1823, *ibid.*

[37]A writer, whose signature is illegible, to Virgil Maxcy, July 24, 1823, Maxcy Papers.

[38]J. C. Calhoun to Virgil Maxcy, August 6, 1823, *ibid.*

[39]Dallas to Maxcy, March 8, 1823; Calhoun to Maxcy, March 12 and 13; Kent to Maxcy, March 2, 1823, Maxcy Papers; George McDuffie to Montfort Stokes, April 7, 1823, Fisher Papers, University of North Carolina, Chapel Hill.

[40]Jane Hays to Rachel Jackson, May 10, 1823, private collection of Andrew Jackson IV, Los Angeles.

[41]Robert Patterson to Rachel Jackson, March 20, 1823, New York *Evening Post*, July 31, 1823, reprinted from the *Franklin Gazette*, Philadelphia.

[42]Rachel Jackson to Robert Patterson, May 17, 1823, *ibid.*

[43]Robert Patterson to Jackson, March 20, 1823, *ibid.*

[44]Jackson to Robert Patterson, May 17, 1823, *ibid.*

[45]Was Jackson sincere in his first abrupt rejections of any suggestion that he stand for the presidency?

I think that he was. Whatever his shortcomings the General was truthful. Had he desired the presidency and assumed indifference to promote his cause, I do not think that he would have found it necessary to lie to Andrew Jackson Donelson whom he regarded with the affection of a father and before whom he desired to appear as a worthy criterion. Moreover Jackson loved his wife as he loved no other creature of earth. He appreciated his responsibility in the private considerations that had made her a fugitive from the white light of renown, and made an honest effort to order his life accordingly. There was little personal vanity of the meaner sort in Jackson's composition. His sense of self-esteem was considerable, but he knew that his place in history was secure. Leadership of men, however, was a birthright which Jackson was as powerless to alter as the color of his eyes.

The ardor of his spirit and an inherent love of combat, first directed against Crawford and Clay against whom he had valid grievances and later involved with the allurements of fame and switched to his own interests, I think, are the factors that swept him into the contest rather than any settled plan or disguised *a priori* ambition.

CHAPTER III

[1]The letter appears in *Correspondence*, II, 263. In later years, Lewis, an old man, liked to regard himself as the person responsible for Jackson's career in the White House, and talked a great deal on the subject. The series of letters to Monroe, of which this is one, attained a position of great importance in his mind. He imagined them almost wholly the product of his own intellect, and written with a view to future political use. These statements are not susceptible of proof. Parton accepted Lewis's story

without critical analysis, and his exaggerated account of Lewis's importance as Jackson's political monitor has colored most subsequent biographies and historical accounts. Bassett (*Jackson*, I, 339 *et. seq.*) gives the correct history of the correspondence.

[2]W. B. Lewis to Lewis Cass, a very lengthy letter which, though undated, is shown by internal evidence to have been written in 1844 or 1845. It appears in John Spencer Bassett, "Major Lewis on the Nomination of Andrew Jackson," *Proceedings* of the American Antiquarian Society, New Series, XXXIII, 20; also, with some textual changes in Parton, III *et. seq.* Manuscript copies are in the New York Public Library and the Henry E. Huntington Library, San Marino, California, in the later place under the date of 1850.

[3]George McDuffie to Charles Fisher, December 14, 1823, Polk Papers, University of North Carolina, Chapel Hill, Newsome thesis, 247.

[4]George McDuffie to an unnamed correspondent, probably Charles Fisher, December 12, 1823, Fisher Papers, University of North Carolina, Newsome thesis, 245.

[5]George McDuffie to an unnamed correspondent, probably Charles Fisher, November 21, 1823, *ibid.*, 244.

[6]J. C. Calhoun to Virgil Maxcy, August 27, 1823; L. Williams, Jr., to Maxcy, September, 1823, Maxcy Papers.

[7]George McDuffie to Charles Fisher, December 14, 1823, Polk Papers, University of North Carolina, Newsome thesis, 248.

[8]J. P. Kennedy to Virgil Maxcy, October 11, 1823, Maxcy Papers.

[9]B. B. Smith to Charles Fisher, January 24, 1824, Fisher Papers, University of North Carolina, Newsome thesis, 109.

[10]Shipp, 174.

[11]W. B. Lewis to Lewis Cass, *op. cit.*, 28.

[12]*Ibid.*, 29.

[13]Jackson to John Coffee, October 5, 1823, *Correspondence* III, 210.

[14]Nashville *Whig*, October 6, 1823.

[15]W. B. Lewis to Lewis Cass, *op. cit.*, 29.

[16]Jackson to John Coffee, October 5, 1823, *Correspondence* III, 210.

[17]Jackson to John Coffee, October 24, 1823, *ibid.*, 213.

[18]Jackson to his wife, November 28, 1823, Henry E. Huntington Library *Bulletin*, No. 3, 118.

[19]Jackson to his wife, November, 1823, *ibid.*, 119.

[20]Jackson to his wife, December 3, 1823, *ibid.*, 121.

[21]Jackson to his wife, December 7, 1823, *Correspondence* III, 216.

[22]J. H. Eaton to Rachel Jackson, December 18, 1823, *ibid.*, 217.

[23]Jackson to A. J. Donelson, December 5, 1823, Jackson Papers.

[24]J. R. Bedford to John Overton, December 11, 1824, Overton Papers, Tennessee Historical Society, Nashville.

[25]Hull & Townsend to Jackson, December 15, 1823; Jackson to Hull & Townsend, December 20, 1823, Jackson Papers.

[26]Notice of protest of draft, January 9, 1824; A. J. Donelson to Bedford & Macy, January 23, 1824, *ibid.*

[27]Wyoming, (pseud.) *Letters . . . to the People of the United States,*

(1824), 5. The contents of this pamphlet first appeared in the *Columbian Observer* of Philadelphia.

[28]Winfield Scott to Jackson, December 11, 1823; Jackson to Scott, same date, *Correspondence* III, 216-17.

[29]James L. Armstrong, *General Jackson's Juvenile Indiscretions* (1832), 8.

[30]Henry Clay, *Address to the Public,* (1827).

[31]J. H. Eaton to Rachel Jackson, December 18, 1823, *Correspondence* III, 217.

[32]Jackson to G. W. Martin, January 2, 1824, *ibid.,* 222.

[33]Daniel Webster to Ezekiel Webster, February 2, 1824, Fletcher Webster, editor, *Private Correspondence of Daniel Webster,* (1856), I, 346.

[34]Elijah H. Mills to his wife, January 22, 1824, [Elijah Hunt Mills] *Selections from Letters of the Hon. E. H. Mills* (1881), 21.

[35]Jackson to his wife, December 21, 1823, *Correspondence* III, 218.

[36]Jackson to John Coffee, December 31, 1823, *ibid.,* 220.

[37]Jackson to Francis Preston, January 27, 1824, Huntington Library *Bulletin,* No. 3, 124. See also Jackson to Samuel Swartwout, December 16, 1823, *Proceedings* of the American Antiquarian Society, New Series, XXXI, 74.

[38]Sam Houston to G. Mowry, December 13, 1823, Jackson Papers; see also D. W. White to J. J. Crittenden, February, 1824, Crittenden Papers, Library of Congress.

[39]Jackson to G. W. Martin, January 2, 1824, *Correspondence* III, 221.

[40]Jackson to A. J. Donelson, January 21, 1824, *ibid.,* 224.

[41]Jackson to A. J. Donelson, January 18, 1824, *ibid.,* 224.

[42]James Buchanan to Hugh Hamilton, December 14, 1823, private collection of Emil Edward Hurja, New York City.

[43]T. J. Green to William Polk, February 2, 1824, Newsome thesis, 120.

[44]Raleigh (North Carolina) *Register,* March 5, 1824.

[45]Phoebe Morris to Mrs. James Madison, January 19, 1825 (misdated 1824), Allen C. Clark, *Life and Letters of Dolly Madison* (1914), 217.

[46]Jackson to his wife, December 21, 1824, *Correspondence* III, 218.

[47]The statements concerning Miss O'Neale's early life and loves are derived from her memoirs, written in 1873 and published in 1932 under the title of *The Autobiography of Peggy Eaton.* This document, almost as remarkable for its admissions as for its omissions, was composed while the author was reflecting upon the consequences of the last amours of her eventful history. At the age of sixty she had captivated her granddaughter's dancing master, a youth of nineteen, named Buchignani, and married him. Whereupon Buchignani possessed himself of his wife's large fortune and eloped to Italy with the granddaughter. These events appear in a somewhat clearer perspective in Queena Pollack's *Peggy Eaton, Democracy's Mistress* (1931). A minor example of the literary license of which Mrs. Buchignani availed herself in her memoirs was to spell her maiden name O'Neil.

[48]Pollack, 59.

[49]Jackson to W. B. Lewis, September 10, 1829, *Correspondence* IV, 72.

[50]George McDuffie to Charles Fisher, December 14, 1823, *North Caro-lina Historical Review*, VII, 490; Henry Clay to James Erwin, December 29, 1823, private collection of Mrs. H. L. Bateman, Nashville, Tennessee.

[51]J. H. Eaton to John Overton, February 8, 1824, Overton Papers.

[52]Jackson to A. J. Donelson, January 21, 1823, *Correspondence* III, 225.

[53]*Niles Register*, XXV, 405.

[54]Daniel Webster to Ezekiel Webster, February 22, 1824, *Private Cor-respondence of Daniel Webster*, I, 346.

[55]"Pennsylvania is as firm as a rock," Calhoun wrote to J. G. Swift on January 25, 1824. See Thomas Robson Hay, "John C. Calhoun and the Presidential Campaign of 1824," *North Carolina Historical Review*, XII, 39.

[56]William C. Meigs, *Life of John C. Calhoun* (1917), 305-06; *Franklin Gazette* (Philadelphia) February 19, 1824.

[57]J. C. Calhoun to Virgil Maxcy, February 27, 1824, Maxcy Papers.

[58]Jackson to W. B. Lewis, March 31, 1824, Lewis Papers, New York Public Library.

[59]Jackson to his wife, January 21, 1824, Huntington Library *Bulletin* No. 3, 123.

[60]Jackson to A. J. Donelson, March 6 and 7, 1824, Donelson Papers.

[61]Jackson to his wife, March 16, 1824, Huntington Library *Bulletin* No. 3, 127.

[62]Charles Francis Adams (editor) *Memoirs of John Quincy Adams, Comprising Portions of His Diary* (1876), VI, 340.

[63]William Plumer Jr., to his father, December 3, 1823, Everett Somer-ville Brown (editor), *The Missouri Compromises and Presidential Politics, 1820-1825, from the Letters of William Plumer Jr.* (1926), 85; Adams, VI, 273.

[64]Adams, VI, 633.

[65]*Ibid.*, 333.

[66]*Ibid.*, 269, 274, 279, 285, 293.

[67]Harrisburg *Pennsylvanian*, May 4, 1824, from Herman Hailpern, "Pro-Jackson Sentiment in Pennsylvania," *Pennsylvania Magazine of His-tory and Biography*, L, 203.

[68]Mr. Clay's speech appears in *Annals of Congress*, 18th Congress, 1st Session, 1862 *et. seq.* Characterizations of it to which the present writer is indebted appear in Carl Schurz, *Henry Clay* (1899) I, 216.

[69]A. P. Hayne to Jackson, April 16, 1824, Jackson Papers.

[70]Jackson to L. H. Coleman April 26, 1824. The first publication of this letter was by the Raleigh (North Carolina) *Star*, May 28, 1824, after Coleman had obtained Jackson's leave to print. Parton (III, 35) was the first biographer to reproduce it, and in doing so he began the circulation of a curious error repeated in many other books. He printed what purports to be the letter from "L. H. Colman" that elicited Jackson's response. This is dated Warrenton, Virginia, and in it the writer is made to describe himself as a member of the Virginia Legislature. No Colman or Coleman was in the Virginia Assembly at the time. The author was a physician of Warrenton, North Carolina, and not a member of the Legislature of his

state. The importance of this letter has been overstated, and the missive itself strangely misinterpreted. For example Sumner (*Andrew Jackson* (1899), 95) called it an "ambiguous" bit of "electioneering, muddled . . . by contradictory suggestions." For the letter in full see Parton, III, 35, Bassett, I, 345 or Correspondence, III, 249.

[71] [Martin Van Buren] *Autobiography of Martin Van Buren* (1920), 240.

[72] P. M. Miller to Charles Fisher, January 3, 1824, Fisher Papers, University of North Carolina, Chapel Hill, Newsome thesis, 263.

[73] Jackson to his wife, April 23, 1824, *Correspondence* III, 249.

[74] Jackson to his wife, May 5, 1824, private collection of Andrew Jackson IV, Los Angeles, California.

[75] Jackson to A. J. Donelson, April 27, 1824, *Correspondence* III, 251.

[76] Alfred Balch to John Overton, May 4, 1824, Overton Papers, Tennessee Historical Society, Nashville.

[77] William Plumer Jr. to his father April 1, 1824, Brown, 108.

[78] Jackson to A. J. Donelson, April 23, 1824, Donelson Papers.

[79] Bassett, 1, 339 *et. seq.* gives a lengthy history of the Jackson-Monroe correspondence episode interesting to those whose ideas of the details of this affair have been derived from Parton.

[80] Alfred Balch to John Overton, May 4, 1824, Overton Papers.

[81] Daniel Webster to Ezekiel Webster, June 5, 1824, Claude H. Van Tine (editor), *Letters of Daniel Webster* (1902), 106.

[82] Jackson to John Coffee, July 1, 1824, *Correspondence* III, 258.

[83] Jackson to his wife, April 23, 1824, *ibid.*, 249.

CHAPTER IV

[1] A sidelight on the Clay campaign in Ohio concerns the grandfather of Woodrow Wilson, James Wilson, editor of the *Western Herald and Steubensville Gazette*. A violent free-soiler, Mr. Wilson originally opposed Clay as a friend of slavery and sponsor of the Missouri Compromise, but in the spring of 1824 he joined the Clay ranks and rendered useful service to the future standard-bearer of the Whig Party. Had Mr. Wilson worked as hard for Jackson it is not recklessness to assume that the Tennessean might have carried Ohio, without which it is almost impossible to see how Adams could have been elected.

[2] Pollack, 65.

[3] Farrell-Kirkman family papers, from the private collection of Mrs. Louis Farrell, Nashville, Tennessee. Mrs. Farrell is a great-great-granddaughter of Ellen Kirkman, mother of Mary Kirkman.

[4] Jackson to R. K. Call, November 15, 1821, *Correspondence* III, 130.

[5] Davidson County, Tennessee, records, Nashville. The ceremony was performed July 14, 1824.

[6] J. M. Glassell to Jackson, August 1, 1824, Jackson Papers.

[7] Farrell-Kirkman family papers, *op. cit.*

[8] Benton, Jesse, *An Address to the People* (1824).

[9] John Owen to Bartlett Yancy, July 21, 1824, Miscellaneous Papers,

Series One, II, 105, North Carolina Historical Society, Newsome thesis, 173.

[10]Jackson to Samuel Swartwout, March 4, 1824, *Proceedings* of the American Antiquarian Society, New Series, XXXI, 75.

[11]Parton, III.

[12]Joseph Gales, Jr., to Martin Van Buren, October 25, 1824, Van Buren Papers, Library of Congress.

[13]Daniel Webster to Ezekiel Webster, June 5, 1834, *Private Correspondence of Daniel Webster*, I, 346.

[14]A. S. H. Burges to William Polk, Polk Papers, Library of Congress, Newsome thesis, 127.

[15]Gales and Seaton to Martin Van Buren, September 15, 1824, Van Buren Papers. The letter is in the hand of Joseph Gales, junior.

[16]Jackson to Samuel Swartwout, September 27, 1824. *Proceedings* of the American Antiquarian Society, XXXI, 77.

[17][Smith, Margaret Bayard] *First Forty Years in American Society* (edited by Gaillard Hunt) (1906), 164.

[18]Washington *Gazette*, July 26, 1824. This item is from a manuscript thesis, "The Washington Press in the Jackson Period" (p. 31) by Culver H. Smith of the University of Chattanooga, a copy of which Dr. Smith kindly placed at the disposal of the writer. Additional copies are in the library of Duke University.

[19]Calhoun to Floride Colhoun, November 12, 1824, J. Franklin Jameson (editor), "Correspondence of John C. Calhoun," *Annual Report American Historical Association* for 1899, II, 227. Though Calhoun and his mother-in-law were blood kin, she spelled her name Colhoun.

[20]P. H. Mangum, Orange County, North Carolina, April 15, 1824, Mangum Papers, Library of Congress, Newsome thesis, 165.

[21]A Jackson broadside in North Carolina, *ibid.*, 65.

[22]Alexandria (D. C.) *Herald*, June 30, 1824. This item is from a manuscript thesis, "The National Election of 1824" (p. 72) by Curtis W. Garrison, librarian of the Pennsylvania State Library, Harrisburg, a copy of which Dr. Garrison kindly placed at the writer's disposal. Additional copies are in the library of Johns Hopkins University.

[23]A Jackson broadside, *ibid.*, 74.

[24]Davidson County, North Carolina, May, 1824, Newsome thesis, 165.

[25]Washington Irving to W. M. Blackford, October 27, 1833, collection of the late Thomas F. Madigan, New York City.

[26]Louisville *Public Advertiser*, October 9, 1824, Garrison thesis, 73.

[27]Robert Williamson to Bartlett Yancy, July 26, 1824, Newsome thesis, 176.

[28]Martin Van Buren to Benjamin Ruggles, August 26, 1824, Van Buren Papers.

[29]Gallatin to Van Buren, October 2, 1824, *ibid*.

[30]Joseph Gales, Jr., to Van Buren, October 17, 1824, *ibid*.

[31]Van Buren, 665.

[32]*National Gazette*, September 7, 1824.

[33]Raleigh *Register*, October 12, 1824, Newsome thesis, 170.

[34]*Ibid.*, November 5, 1824.

[35]Jackson to John Coffee, December 27, 1824, *Correspondence*, III, 270.

[36]Parton, III, 51.

[37]Jackson to John Coffee, October 24, 1823, *Correspondence*, III, 213.

[38]Testimony of John S. Hitt at an investigation conducted by the Kentucky Legislature, 1828, of the conduct of Henry Clay during the House election of 1825. Apparently the only surviving record of this proceeding appears in the *Argus of Western America* (Frankfort), February 25, 1828, from which it was copied by the *United States' Telegraph*, Extra No. 1, March 1, and Extra No. 12, May 10, 1828.

[39]New York *Evening Post*, November 24, 1824.

[40]*Ibid.*

[41]Testimony of Oliver Keene and Francis McAlear, Kentucky legislative investigation, *op. cit.* Clay later denied having sent and Jackson having received such an invitation.

[42]Testimony of Thomas D. Carneal, Kentucky legislative investigation, *op. cit.*

[43]Salem *Gazette* and Boston *Courier*, quoted by New York *Evening Post*, November 18, 1824.

[44]Jacob Barker to Martin Van Buren, November 7, 1824, Van Buren Papers, Library of Congress.

[45]Alexandria (D. C.) *Herald*, December 1, 1824.

[46]Richmond *Enquirer*, December 4, 1824.

[47]Jackson to Samuel Swartwout, December 14, 1824, *Correspondence*, III, 268.

[48]Charles Tutt to Jackson, *ibid.*

[49]Jackson to John Coffee, December 27, 1824, *ibid.*, 270. "Mr. Gadsbys tavern" was the Franklin House which had became renowned under the proprietorship of William O'Neale, father of the even more renowned Margaret Timberlake.

[50]Jackson to John Coffee, January 23, 1824, *ibid.*, 274.

CHAPTER V

[1]The *New-England Galaxy* (Boston), December 24, 1824, predicted that Jackson's administration would be satisfactory. See also Jabez Hammond, *History of the Political Parties in the State of New York* (1845), II, 188. Hammond was an Adams man.

[2]New York *Statesman*, December 17, 1824.

[3]Hay, 42.

[4]Benton, I, 48-49 does not state at what time he went over to the Jackson side but there could not have been much delay, despite John Scott's assertion (*An Address of Henry Clay to the Public Containing Certain Testimony in Refutation of the Charges Made By Gen. Andrew Jackson*, 1827, p. 49), which is probably correct, that the Missouri Senator's first impulse was to support Crawford. Several Clay men, including, it seems, the Speaker himself, appear to have flirted with this possibility.

[5]George Kremer of Pennsylvania to his constituents, Washington *Gazette*, February 28, 1825.

[6]Statement of T. P. Moore, Kentucky Representative in 1824, *United States' Telegraph* Extra No. 1, March 1, and Extra No. 12, May 10, 1828. Moore says Call exhibited as from Crittenden the letter in question and read the sentence quoted. No such letter to Call appears in the Library of Congress collection of Crittenden Papers. It was generally known, however, that Crittenden was at this time in favor of Jackson's election. (See Crittenden to Clay, September 3, 1827, *An Address of Henry Clay to the Public*, 50.) The quotation in the text, therefore, would have been a correct representation of Crittenden's views.

[7]A. L. Burnley to J. J. Crittenden, March 2, 1828, Crittenden Papers.

[8]Testimony of John S. Hitt, Kentucky legislative investigation, *op. cit.*

[9]George Kremer of Pennsylvania, quoting Johnson, in a letter to his constituents, Washington *Gazette*, February 28, 1825

[10]W. T. Barry to Henry Clay, January 10, 1825, Clay Papers.

[11]George Kremer to his constituents, *op. cit.*

[12]Duff Green to Ninian Edwards, July 14, 1828, Green Papers, Library of Congress.

[13]Statement of R. K. Call, *United States' Telegraph* Extra No. 12, May 10, 1828.

[14]Martin Van Buren to B. F. Butler, December 27, 1824, Van Buren Papers. In this letter Van Buren still puts Jackson first but remarks that the confidence of his supporters is waning. One gathers that before evidence of an Adams-Clay coalition began to accumulate the New Yorker considered Jackson's advantage very impressive.

[15]W. P. Mangum to Bartlett Yancey, December 25, 1824, *James Sprunt Historical Publications*, X, No. 2, 51.

[16]A. H. Everett to J. Blunt, November 28, 1824, private collection of Stanley Horn, Nashville.

[17]William Plumer, junior, to his father, December 16, 1824, Everett S. Brown (editor), *Missouri Compromises and Presidential Politics*, 123.

[18]Statements of R. K. Call and T. P. Moore, *United States' Telegraph* Extra No. 12, May 10, 1828; Kremer to his constituents, Washington *Gazette*, February 28, 1825. Call says that he arrived in Washington confident that Clay would vote for Jackson. I think that is putting it too strongly. Clay's *Address*, p. 57, contains a statement by John Braddock, a tavern-keeper of Rockville, Maryland, which relates that General Jackson's party, of which Call was a member, stopped at his house of entertainment en route from Tennessee to the capital. Discussing the presidential question, Braddock says Call "declared that the friends of Gen. Jackson did not expect Mr. Clay to vote for him, and if he did so, it would be an act of duplicity on his part." This seems the more reasonable statement of Call's attitude immediately upon his arrival in Washington. Very shortly, however, receipt of the Crittenden letter and other favorable straws in the wind doubtless changed Call's views until he entertained, if not the expectation, at least a strong hope that Clay would find himself in a position where he could hardly avoid supporting Jackson.

[19]Statement of R. K. Call, *United States' Telegraph* Extra No. 12, May 10, 1828. In his own account of this meeting Mr. Clay says: "I was very desirous that he [Jackson] should arrive [in Lexington] prior to my departure, . . . that I might offer him the hospitality of my house." However, Clay avers that he did not contemplate traveling with the General, having already made other arrangements. (*Address*, 28). Jackson's account of the meeting is similar to Call's. (Jackson to Thomas Hickey, September 25, 1827, Jackson Papers.)

[20]Henry Clay to an unnamed constituent, quoted in his "Address to Constituents" of March 26, 1825, Calvin Colton, *Works of Henry Clay* (1897), V, 302.

[21]Henry Clay to F. P. Blair, January 8, 1825, Clay Papers. In the original, misdated 1824.

[22]Statement of John Floyd, *United States' Telegraph* Extra No. 12, May 10, 1828.

[23]Statement of Thomas P. Moore, *ibid.*

[24]Statement of William Plumer, junior, *Supplement to an Address of Henry Clay*, 17. In this recital of the incident, written more than three years after its occurrence, Plumer shows that time had dimmed his memory of the actual event. In 1828 Plumer went so far as to say of Mr. Clay's reply to his felicitations, "I drew from it the obvious allusion that Mr. Clay intended to vote for Mr. Adams." Mr. Plumer's own letters, and his conversations with Adams as recorded by the latter in his diary, are proof that he drew no such inference at the time. The Plumer-Clay conversation took place December 10. Not until December 17 did the rapprochement between Clay and Adams begin. Plumer assumed from the outset that Clay was sounding out Adams to see what he could get in return for his support. Anxiously Plumer watched the development of this matter, and not until January, 1825, was he satisfied that Clay would vote for Adams. Plumer's letters are in Brown, *Missouri Compromises.*

[25]Statements of David Trimble, J. J. Crittenden and James Davidson, *An Address of Henry Clay*, 41, 50, 51.

[26]Statement of Alexander Robertson, *Supplement to an Address of Henry Clay*, 19.

[27]Benton, I, 48, who fixes the time of the conversation as prior to December 15.

[28]Statement of Thomas P. Moore, *United States' Telegraph* Extra No. 12, May 10, 1828.

[29]Martin Van Buren to B. F. Butler, December 27, 1824, Van Buren Papers.

[30]W. P. Mangum to Bartlett Yancey, December 25, 1824, *James Sprunt Historical Publications*, X, No. 2, 51.

[31]John Campbell to David Campbell, January 12, 1825, Campbell Papers, private collection of Lemuel R. Campbell, Nashville.

[32]For accounts of Webster's interview with Jefferson see George Tichnor Curtis, *Life of Daniel Webster* (1870), I, 222 and *The Writings and Speeches of Daniel Webster* (1903), XVII, 371; for proof that Webster repeated Jefferson's remarks on his return to Washington, William Plumer,

junior, to his father, December 24, 1824. In Brown, *Missouri Compromises*, 125.

[33]Benton, I, 48. Though the Benton interview places Jefferson in a better light as a prophet, it is impossible to say whether the Missourian or Webster gave the more accurate representation of the sentiments of the former President. A grandson of Jefferson later questioned the fidelity of Webster's quotation; see Henry S. Randall, *Life of Thomas Jefferson* (1858), III, 507.

[34]Statement of R. K. Call, *United States' Telegraph* Extra No. 12, May 10, 1828.

[35]Jackson to Samuel Swartwout, May 16, 1825, *Proceedings* of the American Antiquarian Society, New Series, XXXI, 87; George Kremer to Jackson, March 8, 1825, *Correspondence*, III, 281.

[36]According to Jackson's recollection, the Buchanan interview took place "early in January" 1825; according to Buchanan, December 30, 1824. This particular discrepancy is of no importance, and is noted here only that the reader may fix in his mind the approximate time. Two accounts of the meeting exist: Jackson's in a clear and vigorous letter to Carter Beverley, June 5, 1827, *Correspondence*, III, 355; and Buchanan's, in a letter to his constituents, August 18, 1827, which appears in John Bassett Moore (editor), *Works of James Buchanan* (1908), I, 263. Something of the history of these letters will appear in the next chapter. Suffice to say here that Buchanan's account is labored, incomplete and somewhat obscure, though on the whole a corroboration of Jackson's story of the interview. The most important point of difference is Buchanan's denial that in the matter he acted as an emissary of Clay. On March 8, 1825, (*Correspondence*, III, 281) shortly after the event George Kremer wrote Jackson an account of his conversations with Buchanan which strengthens Jackson's contention. Moreover the deletion by Buchanan from his own account of any mention of his meeting with Clay and Letcher, as subsequently will be related in the text on Clay's authority, is such a serious omission as to impair confidence in the Buchanan version. The direct quotations in the text are from Jackson's account. See also Note No. 40 *post*.

[37]George Kremer to Jackson, *op. cit.*

[38]James Buchanan to Thomas Elder, January 2, 1825, Moore, I, 120.

[39]Van Buren, 150.

[40]Calvin Colton, *Works of Henry Clay*, I, 441. This is Clay's own account of the interview, made public in 1844. Clay says he meant to include it in his *Address* of 1827, but refrained to do so on that and several subsequent occasions at the urgent request of Buchanan. It is no wonder that in 1827 Buchanan was disturbed by the thought of a public revelation of his visit to Clay, which he, Buchanan, had tactfully omitted from his own restrained version of the Jackson interview incident documented in Note No. 36 *ante*.

[41]Bennett Champ Clark, *John Quincy Adams, Old Man Eloquent* (1932), 186.

[42]Adams, VI, 444.

[43]*Ibid.*, VI, 447.

[44]*Ibid.*, VI., 452-53.

[45]William Plumer, junior, to his father, December 24, 1824, Brown, 124.

[46]Adams, VI, 457.

[47]Statement of Bouligny, *Address of Henry Clay*, 54. Bouligny fixed the date of his conversation with Clay as December 20.

[48]Statement of Lafayette who fixed the date "in the latter end of December," *ibid.*, 56.

[49]Nathaniel Macon to Charles Tait, January 7, 1825, Shipp, 179.

[50]Colton, *Works of Henry Clay*, I, 378.

[51]T. W. Cobb to a constituent, January 15 (?), 1825, Joseph B. Cobb, *Leisure Labors* (1858), 214. The contemporary evidence of alert politicians should be given at least equal weight with the statements of Clay's friends (see Notes No. 25, 26 and 47 *ante*). The former statements were written on the spot. They were designed neither to accuse nor defend Mr. Clay, but merely to indicate the prevailing impression of uncertainty as to his position as late as mid-January. The latter statements were made from memory two or three years after the event by friends of Clay anxious to deliver him from the difficulties in which his alliance with Adams had enmeshed him. I do not think it unfair to caution the reader that after this interim others besides Mr. Plumer may have been suffering from an impairment of memory as to precisely what happened in the autumn and winter of 1824.

[52]William Plumer, junior, to his father, January 4, 1825, Brown, 126.

[53]Henry Clay to F. P. Blair, January 8, 1825, Clay Papers.

[54]When Mr. Clay departed John Quincy Adams penned in his diary the entry which furnishes the only contemporary narrative of this meeting. Having attended church twice that day, Mr. Adams first gave the text of the sermons, and told how he had spent the time between services. Clay arrived at six. His opening speeches are given rather fully—how a Crawford man had approached him, and how friends of Mr. Adams, "always claiming to act on their own responsibility," had also come "urging considerations personal to himself." No mention is made of the Buchanan or any other visit in Jackson's interest. Next, Mr. Clay asked Adams "to satisfy him with regard to some principles of great public importance" which the diarist does not identify. Then the entry ends abruptly: "He had no hesitation in saying that his preference would be for me." The unsatisfactory feature of the account is that at no time does Adams report his part of the conversation. From Letcher and others Adams knew that the purpose of Clay's visit was to formulate a political working agreement. Clay's opening statement, as quoted by Adams, confirms this. Whatever Mr. Adams replied to this and other speeches of Clay, it was agreeable to the Speaker because from that day forth the two acted in concert. Clark, in his sympathetic biography (*John Quincy Adams*, 224), says this meeting marked the perfection of the Adams-Clay "alliance." In a conversation with the writer in 1933 Senator Clark said that from his knowledge of politics and of the circumstances of the Adams and Clay meeting he was sure that the terms of the alliance, as later carried out by

each party, were understood beforehand by both Adams and Clay; and that a political adversary was within his rights in calling this understanding a "bargain."

[55]Cobb, 214; Adams, VI, 467-69.

[56]Mr. Clay's defiance of the instructions of the Legislature involved a repudiation of his prior views on that subject. Notably in 1816 Clay had expressed a strong reverence for such instructions and denounced Congressmen who violated them. He did the same in 1839.

[57]J. J. Crittenden to David White, January 21, 1825, *United States' Telegraph* Extra No. 12, May 10, 1828. Crittenden also wrote to Francis Johnson (*ibid.*) and probably other Congressmen. None of these letters appears in the Library of Congress collection of his papers. In White's case this may be explained by the fact that Crittenden admitted, in the letter mentioned in the text, that he had so little stomach for his task that he was sending off the communication without reading it; apparently, therefore, he retained no copy. As time passed Crittenden overcame a measure of his distaste for Adams and supported Clay in his course more stoutly. This is established by the Crittenden Papers.

[58]F. P. Blair to David White, January 21, 1825, *ibid.*

[59]Testimony of J. Dudley, a member of the Legislature, Kentucky legislative investigation, *op. cit.*

[60]Statement of T. P. Moore, *United States' Telegraph* Extra No. 12, May 10, 1828.

[61][Margaret Bayard Smith], *The First Forty Years in Washington Society*, edited by Gaillard Hunt (1906), 172.

[62]Kremer to his constituents, February 25, 1825, Washington *Gazette*, February 28, 1825.

[63]John Campbell to his brother, probably David, January 25, 1825, Campbell Papers.

[64]John Campbell to James Campbell, February 1, 1825, *ibid.*

[65]R. Y. Hayne to S. V. Grimke, January 28, 1825, New York Historical Society.

[66]A. H. Tracy to Thurlow Weed, January 23, 1825, Thurlow Weed, *Autobiography* (1883), I, 175.

[67]William Plumer, junior, to his father, January 24, 1825, Brown, 136.

[68]Two or three days *after* the House election Jackson paid Crawford a brief call, externally a mere visit of courtesy. (Shipp, 191) This was their first meeting in several years and in view of the attitude of the Crawford following toward the election of Adams it is difficult to regard it as without political significance.

[69]Betty Coles to Andrew Stevenson, February 3, 1825, Stevenson Papers, Library of Congress.

[70]Statement of Representative Duncan McArthur of Ohio, *An Address of Henry Clay*, 32.

[71]Calvin Colton (editor), *Private Correspondence of Henry Clay* (1856), 489; Curtis, I, 574. Mr. Sloane delayed making this disclosure until 1844, a circumstance difficult to understand in view of Mr. Clay's need for and his efforts to obtain just such testimony to include in his

Address of 1827. The statement Sloane contributed to the *Address* contains only an indistinct allusion to the "importunity of some of his [Jackson's] Congressional friends." Why he should have waited until the General's public career was over to expand this vague phrase into a specific accusation against one of Jackson's intimates is a question no weigher of testimony can ignore.

[72]Adams, VI, 473; Senator Thomas W. Cobb of Georgia to a constituent, January 15 (?), 1825, Cobb, 214. This letter shows that the Crawford people also had been after Scott. Cobb, a Crawford leader, sums up a long analysis of the situation with the assertion that Jackson would probably be elected on the first ballot.

[73]Claude Moore Fuess, *Daniel Webster* (1930), I, 320-22.

[74]Adams, VI, 476.

[75]Jackson to John Coffee, December 27, 1824, *Correspondence*, III, 270.

[76]Jackson to John Coffee, January 5, 1825, *ibid.*, III, 273. So far as his known correspondence discloses, Jackson mentioned his suspicions only to Coffee, and to him he minimized the situation. Buchanan's visit was not specifically mentioned. As Coffee lived in Alabama, a three-weeks' journey distant, the letters could not have been designed to promote a backfire against Clay.

[77]Jackson to W. B. Lewis, January 29, 1825, Lewis Papers.

[78]Mrs. William Seaton, in Anne Hollingsworth Wharton, *Social Life in the Early Republic* (1902), 199.

[79]Mrs. Jackson to Eliza Kingsley, December 23, 1824, Parton, III, 52.

[80]Bassett, I, 355.

[81]Charles P. Tutt to Jackson, January 9, 1825, Jackson Papers. On the same subject Tutt wrote on January 4 and 6. These letters have not been found.

[82]Jackson to C. P. Tutt, January 6, 1825, *ibid.*

[83]This was accomplished rather obliquely on January 24 by the announcement that a majority of the Kentucky and Ohio delegations would vote for Adams. A few days later a letter from the Speaker to Francis Brooke (see note 88 *post.*), dated January 28, was published. In this the Speaker declared his personal intention to vote for Adams.

[84]Henry Clay to F. P. Blair, January 29, 1825, *Private Correspondence of Henry Clay*, 112.

[85]J. J. Crittenden to Henry Clay, February 15, 1825, Crittenden Papers.

[86]*Columbian Observer*, January 28, 1825.

[87]Henry Clay to a member of the Virginia Legislature, February 4, 1825, *Supplement to the Address of Henry Clay*, 22.

[88]Henry Clay to Francis Brooke, February 4, 1825, *ibid.*, 21.

[89]Henry Clay to James Brown, January 23, 1825, Clay Papers.

[90]Statement of T. P. Moore, *United States' Telegraph* Extra No. 12, May 10, 1828. In a weak and involved statement in *A Supplement to the Address of Henry Clay* (p. 20), White defended his course. "So far as I have been implicated, in connection with my late colleagues, in the alleged management, bargain, sale &c . . . I plead conscious innocence." Moreover he stated that as far as he knew the other Kentucky members

who supported Adams had done nothing "criminal." In 1828, when this was written, White, like several other congressmen, had lost his seat on acount of his vote for Adams and was knocking for admission to the Jackson party.

[91]Quoted from William O. Lynch, *Fifty Years of Party Warfare* (1931), 310.

[92]Statement of Representative William Brent of Louisiana, *Address of Henry Clay*, 59.

[93]Mr. Clay also expressed the "probability" that this was done with the knowledge and approval of Jackson (*ibid.*, 23-24), a supposition supported by no other evidence and opposed by much evidence. Kremer declared (*United States' Telegraph* Extra No. 12, May 10, 1828) that neither Jackson nor Eaton had knowledge of the letter until it was published. He said it was written on his own desk and, by implication, with his own hand. The letter itself, however, is good evidence that Kremer, a man of little schooling, did not write it.

[94]A. Levasseur, *Lafayette in America* (1829), II, 24.

[95]Lot Clark to Roger Skinner, February 28, 1825, Van Buren Papers. On January 24, Plumer of New Hampshire sent his father an optimistic prediction, indicating an Adams victory on the first ballot (Brown, 136). A day earlier, however, Clay had privately expressed himself as uncertain of the result (Clay to James Brown, Clay Papers).

[96]T. H. Benton to John Scott, February 8, 1825, Parton, III, 62.

[97]Van Buren, 152.

[98]Contemporary evidence that most of the broken Crawford following in Congress preferred Jackson to Adams is plentiful. On February 15, before he knew the result of the House balloting, Crittenden wrote Clay (Crittenden Papers) specifically mentioning New York and Virginia as reported to have gone over to Jackson. Georgia and North Carolina were certain to prefer him to Adams in a long contest. According to McLane's statement on January 24 (Brown, 136), Delaware intended to stand by Crawford to the end. After the election McLane went over to the Jackson camp speedily enough, however.

In his *History of the Political Parties in the State of New York* (II, 190), published 1845, Jabez Hammond reports that Van Buren contrived the tie with the expectation of throwing his support to Adams on a later ballot and appropriating some of the credit which otherwise would redound to Clay as a president maker. Nathan Sargent in his *Public Men and Events* (1875), 77-78, tells the same story, though the premise on which he bases his conclusions is faulty in one particular at least. (See Note 106 *post*.) Although such competent students of the period as Bassett (I, 364), and Lynch (313), are inclined to accept the Hammond-Sargent view, my reading of the evidence causes me to question it. [Since the foregoing was written I have discovered that Mr. Hammond experienced similar doubts, for in the fourth printing of his work in 1852 he inserted at the end of the volume (II, 540) a note correcting his text in that particular, and stating that Van Buren intended to support Crawford throughout the balloting.]

Mr. Van Buren's motives were seldom transparent and, with his fortunes at the low ebb that they were in 1825, there can be no doubt but that he had his own welfare in mind when charting his course in the House election.

If Van Buren really meant that Jackson should be beaten (and by his own statement after the first ballot the votes of two additional states would be required to elect Adams, owing to the defection of Maryland), he was very lenient toward his messmates, McLane and Cuthbert, both avowed anti-Adams men. Moreover the post-election wrath of Van Buren's intimates is significant. To say that it sprang not from the fact that Jackson was beaten but merely that Adams had been elected without Van Buren's having had time to get on the band-wagon, would be to say something I find hard to believe.

When the House balloting began time fought on the side of Jackson and in a long contest every vote the Crawford men kept from Adams would be half a vote for Jackson, a fact a politician of Van Buren's acumen could not have overlooked.

[99]Statement of Representative Kent of Maryland quoting Saunders of North Carolina, *Address of Henry Clay*, 60.

[100]Actually Van Buren's personal following numbered only fifteen men who were for Crawford, but the delegation contained two Jackson men who by their determination to vote against Adams were counted, for practical purposes, as part of the Van Buren strength. Indeed, without them the leader could not produce the tie that he hoped to produce on early ballots. One of the fifteen, Van Rensselaer, vacillated between Crawford and Jackson. It is significant that Van Buren should regard this with complacency, his only request being that the old man should *not* vote for Adams.

[101]Lot Clark to Roger Skinner, February 28, 1825, Van Buren Papers. Clark was apparently correct in his surmise, for after the election Clinton, not Webster, received the offer of the English mission. He declined it.

[102]Mrs. Smith, 185.

[103]Van Rensselaer's account of the interview as reported by Van Buren, 152. No other direct account exists, though Mrs. Margaret Bayard Smith's relation of McLane's meeting with Van Rensselaer directly afterward establishes that such an interview had taken place and gives McLane's version of its dire effect on the old man.

[104]Mrs. Smith, 191.

[105]Van Buren, 150; Mrs. Smith, 192.

[106]Van Buren, 152. Sargent (77) gives an entirely different story of how Rensselaer came to vote for Adams. He says the patroon was informed that Van Buren had purposely contrived the tie vote so as to throw his strength to Crawford on the second ballot, and thus snatch from Clay the credit for making a President. Therefore Van Rensselaer voted for Adams to defeat the scheme of Van Buren to whom he was "antagonistic." One trouble with this account is that Van Rensselaer and Van Buren were not antagonistic. Moreover, uncandid as Mr. Van Buren often was, it is difficult to believe that in his old age he deliberately invented a falsehood

to explain Van Rensselaer's vote. The weight of probability, therefore, seems on the side of his story and not Sargent's.

[107]*Niles' Register*, February 12, 1825.

[108]Mrs. Smith, 181; Shipp, 185.

[109]Mrs. Smith, 186.

[110]*Ibid.*, 186.

[111]*Ibid.*, 173; Shipp, 183.

[112]*Ibid.*, 186.

[113]Mrs. Smith, 181, 183.

[114]Samuel G. Goodrich, *Recollections of a Lifetime* (1866), II, 403.

[115]Parton, III, 65.

[116]Jackson to Samuel Swartwout and others, February 10, 1825, *Proceedings* of the American Antiquarian Society, New Series, XXXI, 80.

[117]Bill for food and drink, dated February 18, 1825, Jackson Papers.

[118]Jackson to W. B. Lewis, February 14, 1825, *Correspondence*, III, 276.

[119]Edward Patchell to Jackson, March 4, 1825, Jackson Papers.

[120]John Pemberton to Jackson, Philadelphia, February 15, 1825, *ibid.*

[121]Allegheny *Democrat*, quoted by *Columbian Observer* (Philadelphia), March 2, 1825.

[122]Pittsburg *Observer*, quoted by Columbian *Observer*, March 10, 1825.

[123]Lot Clark to Roger Skinner, February 28, 1825, Van Buren Papers.

[124]Testimony of John T. Johnson, brother of the Kentucky Senator, quoting Representative Metcalfe before Kentucky legislative investigation, *Argus of Western America*, February 25, 1825, and *United States' Telegraph* Extras Nos. 1 and 12, March 1 and May 10, 1828.

[125]Statements of John T. Johnson and O. B. Brown, *ibid.*, No. 12, May 10, 1828.

[126]Testimony of John Desha reporting a conversation with Metcalfe, Kentucky legislative investigation, *op. cit.* All during the winter this had been regarded as one of the remote possibilities. On December 12 James Hamilton, junior, of South Carolina wrote Van Buren: "Keep a sharp look out as to the Calhouns movement If I know the man and his friends he will endeavour to prevent a choice. look to it with all your eyes." (Van Buren Papers.) On February 18, the day Clay accepted Adam's offer of the secretaryship of state Calhoun wrote his political lieutenant in Maryland, Virgil Maxcy, somewhat enigmatically as follows: "Things have taken a strange turn. It would require a little volume to detail all of the occurrences of the last two months. . . . I wish to see you much so that you may clearly understand the present extraordinary . . . crisis. Form no opinion from what you see on the surface. Be here at least on the 4th of March." (Maxcy Papers) Mr. Desha's testimony was given under oath. Mr. Metcalfe's own account of his vote, which appears in Mr. Clay's *Address*, p. 45, does not mention Calhoun, and says that he voted for Adams because of "the *army*, the *anti-tariff and anti-internal improvements*" views of Jackson.

[127]Affidavit of John Griffith and others, *United States' Telegraph* Extra No. 12, May 10, 1828.

[128]Statement of A. Greer, *ibid.*

[129]Amos Kendall to Henry Clay, March 23, 1825, Clay Papers.

[130]I speak here of the reasons Mr. Clay advanced for his vote prior to the election, not after it, when, to his surprise, the storm of criticism grew in volume instead of dying away as he had expected. In an effort to pour oil on the troubled waters the Secretary, disregarding the advice of Kendall, issued a circular to his constituents, dated March 26, 1825. The immediate occurrence which seems to have called it forth was the publication of a letter from Jackson to Samuel Swartwout (February 22, 1825, *Correspondence*, III, 278), in which Old Hickory recapitulated his army services and said if that record made him a "military chieftain" he would not disown the title. Clearly, this letter was written for dissemination. In his reply Clay greatly toned down his military chieftain charge. Praising the General's career as a soldier, he said that only Jackson's lack of statesmanship had caused him to vote for Adams whose proved statesmanship made him the more intelligent choice. (Colton, *Works of Henry Clay*, V, 299.)

All very true, but these reasons, put forth in a defensive argument after the event, form no part of the picture with which we are here concerned: Clay, the political partner of Adams, toiling among the congressmen to encompass the defeat of his western rival. Note Clay's private letter to Blair dated January 8, 1825 (see Note No. 53 *ante*) which contained the barest indirect allusion to Mr. Adam's fitness and rested the weight of the case on the military chieftain charge. Note the letter to Francis Brooke, dated January 28, in which Clay publicly set forth his position: "I have interrogated my conscience as to what I ought to do, and that faithful guide tells me I ought to vote for Mr. Adams." This letter contained no reference to Adam's statesmanship or to Jackson's lack of it, and continued, "As a friend of liberty and to the permanence of our institutions I cannot consent by contributing to the election of a military chieftain to give the strongest guaranty that this Republic will march in the fatal road which has conducted every other Republic to ruin." (Colton, *Works of Henry Clay*, IV, 111.)

Taking the evidence as a whole, of which the foregoing are fair samples, it seems conclusive that by design Clay set out to defeat Jackson on the old militarism issue of 1819. Only when the repercussions became too great did the Secretary seek to shift his ground to Mr. Adam's superior qualifications as a civil servant. Nor is this the only particular in which Mr. Clay sought to alter the aspect of the past to support later contingencies. His *Address* of 1827 and the *Supplement* of 1828 seek to establish that, from October, 1824, he had not faltered in his resolution to support Adams. The object of this was to create the inference that if Mr. Clay had decided in October to vote for Adams, a bargain over that vote in December would have been impossible. What Mr. Clay omitted to make clear was that, so closely did he guard his secret, not only were Adams men in doubt as to his preference but also many of his own confidants, for example Crittenden and Blair who heard the news with surprise and dismay in January.

Kremer's letter to his constituents, probably written by Eaton, was published February 28, 1825, and may be taken as the earliest statement in detail of the Jacksonian point of view. This accepted the premise that before leaving Kentucky Clay laid the groundwork for his vote for Adams, but veiled his intentions until, step by step, he had worked into a position where he could carry with him a sufficient number of western congressmen to elect the New Englander. No evidence Mr. Clay and his partizans has brought to light seriously impairs this contention. Evidence from impartial sources tends to confirm it. Though, as Mr. Clay declared, the person cannot be found who ever heard him say he would vote for Jackson, it nevertheless remains that his cordial behavior toward the General led many Jackson people to hope and many Adams people to fear that he would do so. It is impossible to believe that a man of Clay's intuitions was unaware of this. By his cautious and indirect approach to Adams, Clay, at the outset, gave the impression of a man seeking a bargain. By the time Adams and his intimates learned that the support of Clay was a probability the bargain aspect of the arrangement was taken for granted by them.

To epitomize, this is my view: before coming to Washington, Clay hoped to be able to bring about a situation whereby he could benefit himself by supporting Adams; upon his arrival there he assumed an attitude of aloofness designed to put the Adams people on the anxious seat and bring them to his terms; after which Mr. Adams met the terms. The alternative is an assumption that Clay's support of Adams and Adams's appointment of Clay were merely a coincidence.

[131] Jackson to George Wilson, February 20, 1825, Tennessee Historical Society, Nashville.

[132] Colton, *Life of Henry Clay,* 319, quoting Benton's words to a constituent in 1827. Benton was not entirely consistent in his attitude toward the bargain charge, however. In 1854 in his final word on the subject (Benton, I, 48), the Missouri Senator said that the charge had been used "unjustly in prejudicing the public mind against Mr. Adams and Mr. Clay."

CHAPTER VI

[1] Statement of A. Wylie, *Supplement to the Address of Henry Clay,* 6.
[2] John Bach McMaster, *History of the People of the United States* (1883-1924), V, 489.
[3] J. T. Hitt to Jackson, April 22, 1825, Jackson Papers.
[4] Jackson to Samuel Swartwout, February 22, 1825, *Correspondence,* III, 278.
[5] See Note 130, Chapter V.
[6] Jackson to John Coffee, April 24, 1825, *Correspondence,* III, 283.
[7] Jackson to Samuel Swartwout, May 16, 1825, *ibid.,* 285.
[8] Marquis de Lafayette to Jackson, August 21, 1825, *ibid.,* 290.
[9] Una Pope-Hennessey, *Three English Women in America* (1929), 41.
[10] Bill of Josiah Nichols to Jackson, December 26, 1825, Jackson Papers.
[11] Jackson to John Coffee, October 20, 1825, *Correspondence,* III, 296.

[12]Robert Butler to Jackson, September 15, 1826, Jackson Papers.

[13]Jackson to John Coffee, May 19, July 23, 1825, *Correspondence*, III, 285 and 288.

[14]James Gadsden to Jackson, September 15, 1825, Jackson Papers.

[15]Jackson to the Tennessee Legislature, October 12, 1825, *Correspondence*, III, 293.

[16]Jackson to Henry Lee, October 7, 1825, *ibid.*, III, 291.

[17]Jackson to R. K. Call, March 9, 1829, Jackson Papers.

[18]John H. Marable to Jackson, April 3, 1826, *ibid.*

[19]Charles H. Peck, *The Jacksonian Epoch* (1899), 107.

[20]Blifil, a hypocritical rogue, and Black George, a candid rogue with some redeeming virtues, are characters in Henry Fielding's novel *Tom Jones*.

[21]Eaton to Jackson, May 5, 1826, Jackson Papers.

[22]Samuel R. Overton to Jackson, July 5, 1826, *ibid.;* Samuel R. Overton to John Overton, August 28, 1826, Overton Papers.

[23]Duff Green, *Facts and Suggestions, Biographical and Historical* (1866), 29.

[24]Jackson to James Loyd, July 14, 1826, Jackson Papers.

[25]Jackson to a Committee of the Davidson County Bible Society, September 30, 1826, *Correspondence*, III, 315.

[26]John Rowan to Jackson, August 20, 1826, Jackson Papers.

[27]Van Buren to C. C. Cambreleng, November 8, 1826, Van Buren Papers.

[28]Sam Houston to Jackson, January, 1827, *Correspondence*, III, 329.

[29]Jackson to Sam Houston, October 23, 1826, *ibid.*, VI, 485.

[30]Sam Houston to Jackson, December 13, 1826, *ibid.*, 486.

[31]Jackson to Sam Houston, January 5, 1827, *ibid.*, 488.

[32]Jackson to Secretary of Navy, January 5, 1827, *ibid.*, III, 329.

[33]Jackson to H. L. White, February 7, 1827, *ibid.*, 334.

[34]S. L. Southard to Jackson, February 9, 1827; Jackson to Southard, March 6, *ibid.*, 342 and 345.

[35]James Buchanan to Duff Green, October 16, 1826, Jackson Papers.

[36]Duff Green to Jackson, June 9, 1827, *Correspondence*, III, 361.

[37]Jackson to W. B. Lewis, May 5, 1827, *ibid.*, 355; to Amos Kendall, September 4, 1827, *ibid.*, 381.

[38]Jackson to Carter Beverley, June 5, 1827, *ibid.*, 356.

[39]Solomon Penn, junior, to Jackson, July 5, 1827, *ibid.*, 370.

[40]Parton, III, 125.

[41]Dated July 18, 1827. *United States' Telegraph*, August 9, 1827.

[42]Maunsel White to Jackson, August 4, 1827, Jackson Papers.

[43]Jackson to James Buchanan, July 15, 1827, *Correspondence*, III, 374.

[44]*United States' Telegraph*, August 9, 1827.

[45]*National Journal* (Washington), August 9, 1827.

[46]*United States' Telegraph*, August 13, 1827.

[47]See Note 40, Chapter V.

[48]John Campbell to his brother, probably James, August 23, 1827, Campbell Papers.

[49]Amos Kendall to Jackson, August 22, 1827, Tennessee State Library, Nashville.

[50]Amos Kendall to Jackson, August 27, 1827, *ibid.*

[51]Jackson to Kendall, September 4, 1827, *Correspondence*, III, 381.

[52]Martin Van Buren to Jackson, September 14, 1827, *ibid.*, 384.

[53]David Campbell to his brother, probably James, March 29, 1827, Campbell Papers.

[54]A communication signed "An Enquirer," which internal evidence shows to have been written in 1827, to John Overton. Private collection of J. M. Dickinson of Nashville, a great-great-grandson of Overton. Having been written in 1827 this could not have been the first evidence the Jackson people had of Day's activities or Clay's supposed knowledge of them, but the record indicates that the information they did have late in 1826 was almost precisely what this communication sets forth.

[55]Jackson to Sam Houston, December 15, 1826, *Correspondence*, III, 325.

[56]J. H. Eaton to Jackson, December 27, 1826, Jackson Papers.

[57]Charles Hammond to J. H. Eaton, January 3, 1827, *Truth's Advocate*, January, 1828; Eaton to Jackson, February 4, 1827, Jackson Papers.

[58]E. G. W. Butler to Jackson, Cincinnati, January 11, 1827, *ibid.*; Sam Houston to Jackson, January 5, 1828, *Correspondence*, III, 331; *United States' Telegraph*, March 8, 1827.

[59]Jackson to W. B. Lewis, December 12, 1826, private library of J. P. Morgan, New York City.

[60]J. H. Eaton to Jackson, January 27, 1827, Jackson Papers.

[61]This appeared in February, according to Arnold's second hand-bill, dated May 24, 1828, a copy of which is in the Tennessee State Library, Nashville. The writer has not seen a copy of the original. The quotation in the text is from the *National Journal's* reprint, March 26, 1827.

[62]*Liberty Hall & Cincinnati Gazette*, March 23, 1828. In this article Hammond does not mention Arnold but assumes to publish the story in reply to a "challenge" from the Cincinnati *Advertiser* which, taking notice of Hammond's whispering campaign, had called upon him to unmask himself in print.

[63]Nashville *Banner & Whig*, March 21, 1827.

[64]Surviving fragments of the private correspondence of John Overton indicate that the committee adopted a critical attitude toward evidence unusual under the circumstances. On May 27, 1827, Overton wrote to Jackson: "In the *defence* now in progress . . . it may be necessary to state explicitly that Hugh McGary . . . *never saw you and M*rs *Jackson together either before or since he came in company with you both Sept 1791* . . . with nearly 100 . . . [others] in the trip from *Natchez* to *Nashville*. Such I believe to be the fact and if so please communicate it. This letter nor your answer intended for publication but . . . your answer necessary to satisfy some of the Committee." (Jackson Papers.)

Jackson's reply cannot be found but apparently it deviated slightly from Overton's idea of the facts. In any event a slight deviation is found in the committee report, which seems to indicate the careful work of that body. On McGary's testimony the divorce was granted on ground of adultery in 1793. (See first volume of this work, pp. 74-78.) After mentioning the ex parte nature of that hearing the committee reflects on McGary's competence as a witness: "Hugh McGary . . . never saw Gen. and Mrs. Jackson together until the month of Sept. 1791, after their marriage at Natchez, when they were living together as married persons; in the most fair, honest and innocent belief that they were lawfully joined in wedlock. Hugh M'Gary came through the Indian country from Natchez to Nashville . . . in the same company in which General and Mrs. Jackson came, in Sept. 1791, and circumstances then occurred calculated to excite in M'Gary a strong feeling of dislike toward Gen. Jackson, which it is unnecessary to detail as they related solely to a meditated attack by the Indians."

While sparing no pains to blacken the characters of Jackson and his wife, the Adams papers portrayed Robards as a good husband, grievously wronged. Though evidence abounds that Robards was not a good husband, the Nashville committee was considerate of him. This testimony was not used: "I resided with the [Robards] family whilst they lived together [in Kentucky] & his conduct towards her was cruel, unmanly & unkind; . . . her deportment exhibited the exemplary & affectionate wife. . . . Lewis Robards was in the habit of leaving his wife's bed & spending the night with the negro women." The deponent said that Mrs. George Robards, a sister-in-law, would corroborate this. "She states that . . . the breach arose from Roberts's own improper conduct." (John Downing to J. H. Eaton, December 20, 1826, private collection of J. M. Dickinson, Nashville.)

Mr. Dickinson also has two letters to Overton from Henry Banks, a well-known figure of Frankfort, Kentucky, touching on Rachel's attachment to Peyton Short, which illuminate Robard's character and the length Rachel was prepared to go to escape from him. Had this material been available at the time, it would have been included in Chapter V of the preceding volume of this work. It is useful in the reconstruction of the background of experience which undoubtedly had its effect on Rachel's peace of mind in later life.

Under date of June 4, 1827, Banks wrote that not long before his death Short, whom Banks had known from youth, vowed "that so far as he knew or believed Mrs Jackson was as pure and virtuous as an Angel. . . . That in consequence of the politeness of his deportment to Mrs Robards Captain Robards became jealous of his wife, and therefore treated her in a rude and cruel manner. That the discontent appeared to be mutual. That they had agreed to part, and that she was about to go to Tennessee where her mother resided. That he (Short) was so much excited, both by his sympathy for Mrs Robards and his respect and affection for her, as induced him to form a determination to marry her after the intended separation should take place. That he was then about to go to Virginia with an intention of converting his patrimony into money or slaves—and if Mrs Robard would accept him as a husband to go with her to the Spanish Dominions on the Mississippi; and there to settle himself for life.

"With such views, and under such excitements, when on his way to Virginia he sent a letter to The Crab Orchard to Mrs Robards which was enclosed to a friend authorizing Mrs Robards to obtain what goods, etc. she might want, on his account. That Captain Robards obtained possession of this letter, and followed him to Virginia, uttering threats & vengeance against him. That being informed of what Robards had said he caused an enquiry to be made of him to know whether he sought blood or pecuniary atonement. That he was informed that Robard would be appeased by money. In consideration of which . . . Robards was paid and satisfied.

"Before Short returned to Kentucky Mrs Robards had gone to Natchez, and there married General Jackson."

In another letter, dated May 10, 1827, Banks gave his own testimony regarding the settlement between Short and Robards in Richmond. "Short . . . let him know that if blood was his object he should be ready to meet him, . . . but if a compromise could be made with money, it would be given." The two met at Gault's Tavern, and in Banks's presence "Short paid over about $1,000.00."

[65]*United States' Telegraph*, June 22, 1827. Later the material was issued as a pamphlet. Members of the committee who produced the document included John Overton, W. B. Lewis, John McNairy, G. W. Campbell, Alfred Balch, Edward Ward, Felix Robertson and John Catron. The restrained, judicial tone sounds like the work of Overton. The text refers to the final report of the committee, completed in June, 1827. A preliminary report was published in April to which Arnold's second production quoted in the text was a reply. In the interest of terseness the preliminary report is not mentioned in the text.

[66]Broadside by Arnold, May 24, 1824, Tennessee State Library, Nashville.

[67][Charles Hammond], *A View of Gen. Jackson's Domestic Relations* (1828). The material appeared originally in *Truth's Advocate* (Cincinnati), a campaign sheet edited by Hammond.

[68]Jackson to Coffee, June 2, 1828, *Correspondence*, III, 409; Coffee to Jackson, July 2, 1828, Jackson Papers.

[69]Rough draft of an undated letter, Jackson to Henry Clay, private collection of Andrew Jackson IV, Los Angeles. My opinion is that the letter was not sent. Otherwise some sort of sequel would hardly have been avoidable.

[70]*United States' Telegraph*, June 16, 1827.

[71]Duff Green to Jackson, July 8, 1827, *Correspondence*, III, 372.

[72]Jackson to Duff Green, August 13, 1827, Jackson Papers.

[73]Thomas Henderson to Jackson, July 28, 1827, *ibid.*

[74]Henry Clay to Charles Hammond, December 23, 1826, *Truth's Advocate*, January, 1828.

[75]Charles Hammond to Henry Clay, January 3, 1827, Clay Papers.

[76]The writer has consulted newspapers published in practically every state from 1822 to 1824. He believes that nearly any Adams, Crawford, Clay or Calhoun journal west or south of the Potomac that he examined will bear out the statement in the text.

[77]See page 275, Volume I of this work.

[78]Harriet Martineau, *Society in America* (1837), III, 166.

[79]Jackson to R. K. Call, August 16, 1828, *Correspondence*, III, 426; Holmes Alexander, *The American Talleyrand* (1935), 237.

[80]*United States' Telegraph*, April 10, 1828.

[81]Eaton to Jackson, August 21, 1828, *Correspondence*, III, 429.

[82]Jackson to Andrew Jackson, junior, November 27, 1827, Jackson Papers.

[83]Jackson to H. L. White, March 30, 1828, *Correspondence*, III, 396.

[84]Parton, III, 315 *et seq.*; J. C. Calhoun to Jackson, April 30, May 25, July 10, 1828, *Correspondence*, III, 400, 404, 413.

[85]Jackson to James K. Polk, December 27, 1826, Bassett, II, 396.

[86]J. H. Eaton to Jackson, March 28, 1828, Jackson Papers.

[87]Jackson to J. B. Ray, Governor of Indiana, February 23, 1828, private collection of Stanley Horn, Nashville; to G. W. Campbell, February 14, *Correspondence*, III, 390. On June 5, 1828 (Jackson Papers), R. Y. Hayne of South Carolina wrote Jackson a polite but strong warning that the South would expect him to meet its wishes on the tariff and improvements.

[88]L. Campbell to W. B. Lewis, October 30, 1828, Jackson Papers.

[89]Harvey Lee Ross, *Early Pioneers of Illinois* (1899), 153-54.

[90]Jackson to John Coffee, November 24, 1828, *Correspondence*, III, 447.

CHAPTER VII

[1]Rachel Jackson to Elizabeth Watson, July 18, 1828, *Correspondence*, III, 416.

[2]Moses Dawson to Mrs. Jackson, October 24, 1828, Jackson Papers.

[3]Parton, III, 153.

[4]A communication signed "L" in the Cincinnati *National Republican*, January 23, 1829.

[5]Henry A. Wise, *Seven Decades of the Union* (1872), 101.

[6]*Ibid.*, 98-99.

[7]Cincinnati *National Republican*, January 23, 1829.

[8]Alfred Balch to Van Buren, November 27, 1828, Van Buren Papers.

[9]John H. Eaton to Mrs. Jackson, December 7, 1828, *Correspondence*, III, 449.

[10]Columbus (Ohio) *Monitor*, reprinted in Lebanon (Tennessee) *Democrat*, January 17, 1829.

[11]Nashville *Banner*, December 26, 1828.

[12]Wise, 113.

[13]*Ibid.*; Bassett, II, 406, who had the newspaper-office detail from a daughter of Francis P. Blair.

[14]Dr. Henry Lee Heiskell in a letter to the Winchester *Virginian*, January, 1829; a bill for professional services, Doctor Heiskell to Jackson, October 22 to December 22, 1828, private collection of C. Norton Owen, Glencoe, Illinois; letter dated Nashville, December 23, 1828, Philadelphia *Mercury*, January 17, 1829; Parton III, 156.

[15]Buell, II, 210.

¹⁶Heiskell, *op. cit.*; Parton, III, 156.

¹⁷Scrapbook of Jacksoniana, Tennessee State Library, Nashville.

¹⁸A letter signed "L" in the Cincinnati *National Republican*, January 23, 1829.

¹⁹Louisville *Courier-Journal*, quoted in Ben Truman, *The Field of Honor* (1884), 283.

²⁰Will Alexander to Jackson, December 26, 1828, Jackson Papers.

²¹Buell, II, 204.

²²Jackson to John Coffee, January 17, 1829, *Correspondence*, IV, 2.

CHAPTER VIII

¹Mrs. Smith, 257.

²Quoted from Lynch, 357.

³John Chambers to J. J. Crittenden, January 29, 1829, Crittenden Papers.

⁴Frances M. Trollope, *Domestic Manners of the Americans* (Reprint of 1904), 125.

⁵Parton, III, 169.

⁶*Private Correspondence of Daniel Webster*, I, 473.

⁷Undated manuscript in Jackson's hand probably written in 1831, Jackson Papers, Item 242, Volume V, Second Series; see also Jackson to J. C. McLemore, December 25, 1830, Jackson Papers, New York Historical Society. This letter is catalogued as from Jackson to Calhoun. By a slip of the pen Jackson wrote "Mr. Jno. C. Calhoun" on the last page, but the content shows it to be one of a series of letters he wrote John C. McLemore on later developments in the imbroglio arising from Eaton's appointment.

⁸Mrs. Smith, 282.

⁹Undated manuscript in Jackson's hand, Item 242, Volume V, Second Series, Jackson Papers; Jackson to H. L. White, April 9, 1831, *Correspondence*, IV, 258. James A. Hamilton in his *Reminiscences* (1869), 91, speaks of the War Office being offered to L. W. Tazewell of Virginia, an assertion several biographers and historians repeat. Hamilton is sometimes unreliable in such details, and no other evidence of this offer appears to exist.

¹⁰On February 23, when Jackson understood Eaton to be firm in his refusal to accept an office, Eaton wrote to White plainly indicating his desire for a cabinet post, if it could be had without offending White. (Bassett, II, 414.)

¹¹William Wirt to William Pope, March 22, 1829, John P. Kennedy, *Life of William Wirt* (1849), II, 228. Mr. Wirt was quoting, without malice, a Jackson man.

¹²Caleb Atwater, *Remarks on a Tour to Prairie du Chien* (1831), 277.

¹³James Hamilton, junior, to Martin Van Buren, February 13, 1829, Van Buren Papers.

¹⁴Louis McLane to Martin Van Buren, February 19, 1829, Van Buren Papers.

¹⁵Jackson to J. W. Campbell, November 8, 1831, Jackson Papers.

[16] Mrs. Smith, 282; J. A. Hamilton to Van Buren, February 23, 1829, Van Buren Papers.

[17] W. B. Lewis to Lewis Cass, undated but written in 1844 or 1845, Bixby Collection, Henry E. Huntington Library, San Marino, California.

[18] Mrs. Smith, 284; Bassett, II, 422.

[19] James Hamilton, junior, to Martin Van Buren, March 5, 1829, Van Buren Papers.

[20] George R. Gilmer, *Sketches of Some of the Settlers of Upper Georgia* (Reprint of 1926), 244.

[21] James Hamilton, junior, to Martin Van Buren, March 5, 1829, Van Buren Papers.

[22] The quotations are from Gilmer, 245. See also Parton, III, 170; McMaster, V, 525; Bassett, II, 423; Claude G. Bowers, *Party Battles of the Jackson Period* (1922), 47.

[23] Jackson to John Coffee, March 22, 1829, *Correspondence*, IV, 15.

[24] *Ibid.*

[25] Henry B. Stanton, *Random Recollections* (1886), 32.

[26] Van Buren, 229-32.

[27] M. D. L. Sharp to Jackson, June 28, 1828; Jackson's reply, July 5, Jackson Papers.

[28] *New Hampshire Patriot & State Gazette*, November 24, 1828.

[29] *United States' Telegraph,* November 24, 1828.

[30] Ben: Perley Poore, *Perley's Reminiscences* (1866), I, 98.

[31] David Campbell to his wife, June 3, 1829, Campbell Papers.

[32] Dated February 23, 1829. Letter Book for 1829, Jackson Papers, Second Series.

[33] William Stickney (editor), *Autobiography of Amos Kendall* (1872), 308-16; Bassett, II, 488; Bowers, 75.

[34] James Schouler, *History of the United States* (1913 edition), III, 458; Jackson to J. C. McLemore, April, 1829, *Correspondence*, IV, 20.

[35] W. T. Simpson to John McLean, April 14 and 17, 1829, McLean Papers, Library of Congress.

[36] Martin Van Buren to Jackson, March 31; Thomas Ritchie to Van Buren, March 27, 1829, *Correspondence*, IV, 17.

[37] Jackson to Van Buren, March 31, 1829, *ibid.*, 19.

[38] W. T. Simpson to John McLean, April 14 and 17, 1829, McLean Papers.

[39] Amos Kendall to his wife, June 1, 1829, Stickney, 292.

[40] Jackson to John Coffee, March 22, 1829, *Correspondence*, IV, 14.

[41] Jackson to H. M. Cryer, May 16, 1829, *ibid.*, 33.

[42] John W. Forney, *Anecdotes of Public Men* (1873), 283.

[43] Buell, II, 213.

[44] *Harper's Magazine*, January, 1855.

[45] Martin Van Buren to Jackson, April 23, 1829, *Correspondence*, IV, 25; Bowers, 69.

[46] Van Buren, 251-60.

[47] Bassett, II, 448.

[48] Francis J. Grund (editor), *Aristocracy in America* (1839), II, 224.

[49] Jackson to John Coffee, March 22, 1829, *Correspondence*, IV, 14.

[50] J. J. Coddrington to Jesse Hoyt, March 29, 1829, Green Papers.

51Jackson to J. C. McLemore, April, 1829, *Correspondence*, IV, 21.

52J. C. McLemore to A. J. Donelson, April 3, 1829, Donelson Papers.

53Van Buren, 261.

CHAPTER IX

1Pollack, 74, 75. Though Timberlake's death was apparently due to tuberculosis, a few months before, he had attempted to end his life by cutting his throat. See Thomas Norman, a shipmate, to Margaret Eaton, April, 1829, New York Historical Society.

2J. H. Eaton to Jackson, Washington, December 7, 1828, private collection of Andrew Jackson IV, Los Angeles. In this letter Eaton, by way of recapitulation, repeats a conversation with Jackson that had taken place at the Hermitage some time before. For the sake of smoothness I have substituted the present for the past tense which Eaton used.

3This is Mrs. Eaton's version of the reply, given in her *Autobiography*, 80. Parton's version (III, 185), which he probably had from Lewis, is much like it. Eaton (*op. cit.*) covered Jackson's answer in these words: "It was a matter of infinite satisfaction to me to find that your advice and opinions accorded with my own; from that moment I was inspired with a new and fresh decision as to the course to be pursued."

4Eaton to Jackson, *op. cit.*

5*Ibid.*

6C. C. Cambreleng to Martin Van Buren, January 1, 1829, Van Buren Papers. The Congressman was attempting to quote Montaigne.

7Mrs. Smith, 252.

8David Campbell to his wife, May 24, 27 and June 3, 1829, Campbell Papers. The description of Mrs. Eaton is not Campbell's. It comes from many sources included in probably five hundred manuscripts the writer has read on the Eaton affair. Of numerous portraits of Mrs. Eaton that have been reproduced none made before her forty-fifth birthday is an authentic likeness.

9Pollack, 86; Mrs. Eaton, 80.

10Undated Memorandum in Jackson's hand, written after reorganization of the Cabinet in 1831. Posted in Jackson Papers, LXXIII, under date of September, 1829.

11Emily Donelson to Mary Coffee, March 27, 1829, private collection of Mrs. Andrew Jackson Martin, Memphis, Tennessee, a great-granddaughter of Mrs. Coffee.

12J. H. Eaton to Emily Donelson, April 8, 1829, *Correspondence*, IV, 29.

13Mary Eastin to Mrs. Stockley Donelson, April 9, 1829, private collection of Mrs. Mary Wharton Yeatman, Columbia, Tennessee; Emily Donelson to Mary Coffee, March 27, 1829, private collection of Mrs. Andrew Jackson Martin, Memphis; the attentions of Abraham Van Buren are a family tradition, communicated to the writer by Mrs. Lucius E. Burch, Nashville.

[14]David Campbell to his wife, May 28, 1829, Campbell Papers; R. G. Dunlap to Jackson, August 10, 1831, *Correspondence*, IV, 331.

[15]A. J. Donelson to J. C. McLemore, April 30, 1830, Donelson Papers.

[16]Fragment in Donelson's hand to Jackson, *ibid.*, for October, 1830.

[17]Emily Donelson to J. H. Eaton, April 10, 1829, private collection of Mrs. Pauline Wilcox Burke, Washington, D. C. Mrs. Burke is a great-great-granddaughter of Emily Donelson. Her copy of this letter is in the hand of A. J. Donelson.

[18]A. J. Donelson to J. H. Eaton, April 10, 1829, *Correspondence*, IV, 30.

[19]Jackson to J. C. McLemore, May 3, 1829, Jackson Papers, New York Historical Society.

[20]J. M. L. to Jackson, October 3, 1831, Jackson Papers.

[21]Stickney, 351. Though Stickney is not the most reliable of sources, the incident does no violence to Mrs. Eaton's established character.

[22]A. J. Donelson to Jackson, October 25, 1830, *Correspondence*, IV, 190.

[23]David Campbell to his wife, May 28 and June 3, 1829, Campbell Papers.

[24]E. S. Ely to Jackson, March 18, 1829, Parton, III, 186; Pollack, 90.

[25]Jackson to E. S. Ely, March 23, 1829, Parton, III, 187-92.

[26]Jackson to E. S. Ely, April 10, 1929, *ibid.*, 192-95.

[27]Undated memorandum in Jackson's hand, posted in Jackson Papers as Item 242, Volume V, Second Series.

[28]Jackson to R. K. Call, May 18, 1829, *Correspondence*, IV, 35.

[29]I have been unable to locate the letter in which Ely communicated the story of the miscarriage. That such a communication was made prior to the Reverend J. N. Campbell's visit to Jackson on September 1, 1829, appears from Jackson's letter of September 3 to Ely (*Correspondence*, IV, 67), and from Jackson's memorandum of Campbell's visit, also dated September 3. (Parton, III, 197.)

[30]Duff Green to David Henshaw, April 15, 1829, Green Papers.

[31]James Hamilton, junior, to Van Buren, July 16, 1829, Van Buren Papers.

[32]For Jackson's account of the two interviews see Parton, III, 197-202; for Donelson's account of the second interview, at which he was present, see *Correspondence*, IV, 68-72. Both are dated September 3, 1829. The direct quotation is from Donelson.

[33]The reactions of Jackson are taken from his account of the second interview, that of Towson and of Donelson from Donelson's account. (See note preceding.) The account which Towson himself left of the interview cannot be found.

[34]Lewis's account of the Cabinet meeting, Parton, III, 202-05; Van Buren's account, Van Buren to J. A. Hamilton, September 24, 1829, Hamilton, 146.

[35]Denis Tilden Lynch, *An Epoch and a Man: Martin Van Buren and His Times* (1929), 356.

[36]C. K. Gardner to John McLean, May 12, 1829, McLean Papers.

[37]P. Bradley to John McLean, May 6, 1829, *ibid.*

[38]Duff Green to Ninian Edwards, October 8, 1830, E. B. Washburne (editor), *The Edwards Papers* (1884), 548.

[39]Erik M. Eriksson, "The Federal Civil Service Under President Jackson," *Mississippi Valley Historical Review*, XIII, 524.

[40]*Ibid.*, 525.

[41]*Ibid.*, 529, quoting special reports of the heads of the departments named. These are to be found in *House Executive Documents*, Twenty-first Congress, First Session, Nos. 20, 27, 28, 97 and 105.

[42]T. L. Homer to John McLean, February 16, 1830, McLean Papers.

[43]James Kent to Daniel Webster, January 21, 1830, Kent Papers, Library of Congress.

[44]Various letters, 1829-32, McLean Papers.

[45]Parton, III, 276.

[46]Eriksson, 527. Thirty-eight of these nominations were not acted upon, a fact that has been held up as additional evidence of Jackson's spoils proclivities. Except in Professor Eriksson's undeservedly obscure study, I have never seen an allusion to the fact that forty of Adams' eleventh-hour nominations were confirmed after Jackson's inauguration.

[47]*Ibid.*, 527-28. Green's figures on removals from March, 1829, to September, 1830, given in the *Telegraph* for September 27, 1830, follow:

	Officers Removed	Total Number Office-holders
State Department	6	24
Treasury Department	22	174
War Department	3	20
Navy Department	5	23
General Post Office	5	61
Postmasters	543	8,356
Marshalls and attorneys	30	60
Territorial governments	4	12
Surveyors of public lands	7	21
Registrars of land offices	16	42
Receivers of public moneys	16	42
Indian agents and subagents	11	55
Collectors of customs	49	98
Appraisers	8	15
Naval Officers	6	14
Surveyors	14	68
Light house keepers	16	186
Subordinate customs officers	151	801
Consular and diplomatic service	7	21
Totals	919	10,093

I do not guarantee these figures, though on the whole they have not been overthrown by dependable evidence. In one respect Green did the cause of "reform" an injustice, for actually the total number of office holders was nearly 11,000. Therefore if his number of removals is correct the proportion is lower than he stated. On the other hand his figures for removals in the Washington offices are lower than those given by the various heads of departments whose evidence is certainly preferable to Green's. See note 41 *ante.*

[48] Eriksson, 529-30.

[49] Carl Russell Fish, *The Civil Service and Patronage* (1905), 51.

[50] James D. Richardson (editor), *Messages and Papers of the Presidents* (1899), II, 462; Jackson's uncompleted rough draft, *Correspondence,* IV, 97.

[51] Jackson's notes for the Maysville Road Veto appear in *Correspondence,* IV, 137. Van Buren (319-38) takes credit for suggesting and intimates that he wrote the veto message. Jackson's rough notes support the latter claim. The message as delivered differs in form and substance from Jackson's notes.

[52] The narrative of the Maysville veto is derived from Van Buren (312-38), and from Bassett (II, 374-96) who believed Van Buren reliable, but in his usual careful manner amplified the New Yorker's account with a study of other contemporary sources. In no communication that I can find did Jackson so much as mention the subject in his correspondence—one indication of the correctness of Van Buren's assertion that the matter was a secret between the President and himself.

[53] A. T. Burnley to J. J. Crittenden, June 13, 1830, Crittenden Papers.

[54] Jackson to John Donelson, June 7, 1829, *American Historical Magazine* (Nashville), IV, 232.

[55] Jackson to John Overton, December 31, 1829, with an explanatory note appended by W. B. Lewis, *Correspondence,* IV, 108.

CHAPTER X

[1] Parton, III, 282.

[2] Charles W. March, *Reminiscences of Congress* (1850), 151.

[3] Undated memorandum in Jackson's hand. Posted with papers for September, 1829, Volume LXXIII, Jackson Papers.

[4] Jackson to Samuel Swartwout, September 27, 1829, *Correspondence,* IV, 77.

[5] A. J. Donelson to John Coffee, August 27, 1829, Donelson Papers.

[6] Though another nine or ten months was to elapse before, in the summer of 1830, Jackson was in his private correspondence openly to accuse Calhoun of being the fomenter of the Eaton troubles, his course of action and his correspondence from autumn 1829 onward indicates that he suspected it and acted accordingly. (See Jackson to J. C. McLemore, November 24, 1829, Jackson Papers, New York Historical Society.) On October 24, 1830, he wrote Emily Donelson (*Correspondence,* IV, 187) that he had "long known" Calhoun to be "at the bottom of this" effort to strike him through Mrs. Eaton. The truth of the thing seems to be that it was all a struggle over the succession between Van Buren and Calhoun, in which Van Buren was ultimately successful as a result of excessive clev-

erness on his own part and some shady practices on the part of Lewis and of Eaton, his friends. At this stage Calhoun had done nothing in the Eaton affair calculated to discredit the Administration.

[7]Van Buren, 347-52; Parton, III, 290.

[8]Adams, VIII, 185.

[9]John Campbell to his brother David, December 27, 1829, Campbell Papers.

[10]Van Buren, 353.

[11]Memorandum by Jackson, *Correspondence*, IV, 123; Jackson to J. H. Eaton, July 19, 1830, *ibid.*, 163; to Martin Van Buren, August 8, 1831, *ibid.*, 328. After the dissolution of the Cabinet in 1831 Ingham, Branch and Berrien published statements which included their own versions of this interview (see Parton, III, 303-09). In the main I have followed Jackson's accounts, believing them the more reliable.

[12]A. J. Donelson to J. C. McLemore, April 30, 1830, Donelson Papers.

[13]Atwater, 269.

[14]Hayne's opening speech, delivered January 19, 1830, and Webster's reply, delivered January 20, appeared in the *United States' Telegraph* on February 3. Hayne's second speech, delivered January 21 and 25, appeared in the *Telegraph* on February 15 and 16. Webster's reply to this, delivered January 26 and 27, appeared in the *National Intelligencer*, February 23, 25 and 27. The *Telegraph* published it March 4 to 8.

[15]Fuess, I, 386.

[16]Jackson to R. Y. Hayne, April 26; to A. P. Hayne, April 27, 1830, *Correspondence*, IV, 135.

[17]Benton, I, 148.

[18]*United States' Telegraph*, January 28, 1830.

[19]*Ibid.*, January 30, 1830.

[20]*Ibid.*, February 2, 1830.

[21]*Ibid.*, January 29, 1830.

[22]*Ibid.*, February 3, 1830.

[23]Van Buren, 413.

[24]*Ibid.*, 414; Parton, III, 284.

[25]Quoted from Frederic Austin Ogg, *The Reign of Andrew Jackson* (1919), 165.

[26]Van Buren, 415.

[27]Ogg, 165.

[28]*United States' Telegraph*, April 17, 1830.

[29]Jackson's "reign" was a contemporary expression which in the early 'Thirties became common among the opposition.

[30]Atwater, 289.

[31]J. C. Calhoun to Christopher Van Deventer, May 12, 1830, *Calhoun Letters*, 272.

[32]Jackson to J. C. Calhoun, May 13, 1830, *Correspondence*, IV, 136.

[33]Jackson to J. A. Hamilton, May 29, 1830, *Correspondence*, IV, 140.

[34]H. Petrikin to Jackson, April 2; Jackson to Coffee, April 10, 1830, *ibid.*, 131 and 134.

[35]Lewis's narrative, Parton, III, 322-25.

[36]W. H. Crawford to John Forsyth, April 30, 1830, Richard K. Crallé (editor), *Works of John C. Calhoun* (1850-56), VI, 360.

[37]John Overton to Jackson, June 16, 1830, *Correspondence*, IV, 151.

[38]J. C. Calhoun to Jackson, May 29, 1830, Jackson Papers. The letter is also in Calhoun, *Works*, VI, 362.

[39]Jackson to J. C. Calhoun, May 30, 1830, *Correspondence*, IV, 141.

[40]Jackson to R. J. Chester, November 30, 1829, *ibid.*, 96.

[41]Charles J. Love to Jackson, enclosing "Memorandum of Stock Crops etc etc at the Hermitage," January 15, 1830, *ibid.*, 119.

[42]Jackson to his son, July 4, 1829, *ibid.*, 49.

[43]H. M. Cryer to Jackson, December 26, 1829; Jackson to Cryer, January 10 and February 28; Jackson to C. J. Love, February 28, 1830, *ibid.*, 106, 117, 126, 125.

[44]Jackson to R. J. Chester, November 7, 1830, Tennessee Historical Society, Nashville.

[45]Buell, I, 34.

[46]Jackson to his son, July 26, 1829, *Correspondence*, IV, 57.

[47]Jackson to his son, September 21, 1830, *ibid.*, 76. The only further clue to the identity of Flora given by this correspondence is that she was the orphaned daughter of a friend of Jackson's and the ward of Colonel Edward Ward, at whose home she lived near Nashville.

[48]Royall, 213.

[49]Jackson to Francis Smith, May 19, 1830, private collection of Andrew Jackson IV, Los Angeles; John Campbell to David Campbell, June 16, David Campbell to John Campbell, November 2, 1830, Campbell Papers.

[50]Royall, 213.

[51]Jackson to J. H. Eaton, July 20, 1830, *Correspondence*, IV, 164.

[52]Margaret Eaton to Jackson, June 9, 1830, *ibid.*, 145.

[53]Donelson's endorsement, dated June 10, 1830, on Mrs. Eaton's letter, *ante, ibid.*, 146; A. J. Donelson to Jackson, October 30, 1830, *ibid.*, 195.

[54]A. J. Donelson to J. C. McLemore, April 30, 1830, Donelson Papers; Jackson to John Coffee, July 9, 1830, *Correspondence*, IV, 160.

[55]On May 19, 1830, in his letter to Major Francis Smith, (See note No. 49 *ante*) Jackson mentioned that he would remain in Washington during the summer, though Mr. and Mrs. Donelson were going to Tennessee. On June 9 occurred the dinner which Mrs. Eaton would not attend, and apparently immediately thereafter (See Donelson's memorandum on her letter and his letter to Jackson, October 30, 1830, *Correspondence*, IV, 146, 195) the sentence of banishment was pronounced. On June 14, Jackson wrote John Overton (*ibid.*, 146) that he was leaving for home.

[56]The quotation is from Jackson to W. B. Lewis, June 21 and July [blank], 1830, *ibid.*, 156 and 159. See also Jackson to Lewis, June 26 and August 25, 1830, *ibid.*, 156 and 177.

[57]The Choctaw treaty of October 8, 1820.

[58]Seymour Dunbar, *A History of Travel in America* (1915), II, 484-587.

[59]Jackson to W. B. Lewis, August 25, 1830, *Correspondence*, IV, 176.

[60]Dunbar, II, 575.

[61]James Given to Jackson, October 16, 1830, Jackson Papers.

[62]Jackson to John Coffee, July 20, 1830, *Correspondence*, IV, 165; to W. B. Lewis, July 21 and 28, August 17, 1830, *ibid.*, 165, 167, 173; to J. H. Eaton, August 3, 1830, *ibid.*, 168.

[63]Jackson to W. B. Lewis, August 7, 15, 17 and 25, 1830, *ibid.*, 170, 173, 174, 178.

[64]For detailed expositions of the West Indian trade settlement see William MacDonald, *Jacksonian Democracy* (1906), 200-204; Bassett, II, 657-63; Van Buren, 521-27.

CHAPTER XI

[1]The account in the text of the abuse and danger of the branch draft system is taken from a manuscript account of Jackson's fight against the Bank of the United States, written by Roger B. Taney, and now in the Library of Congress. This manuscript is quoted extensively—and for the first time—in Carl Brent Swisher's *Roger B. Taney*, (1935), which the present writer will hereafter use in citing Taney's account. The criticism of the branch drafts appears on pp. 167-68. The difficulty in obtaining coin for drafts is also cited by Alfred Balch to Jackson, January 7, 1830, *Correspondence*, IV, 115.

[2]Thomas Cadwalader to Jackson, October 15; Jackson's answer, November 21, 1828, *Correspondence*, III, 438 and 445.

[3]This statement is true despite the fact that in Kentucky, for example, the bank's officers and supporters were almost solidly with Clay. This was a condition due to the vagaries of politics in Kentucky, where the banking question had long been an issue, rather than to any deliberate act of Biddle to pack the Louisville and Lexington branches with anti-Jackson men. In Nashville, of course, Biddle would have found it difficult to have erected a branch organization without including supporters of Jackson, as in New England it would have been difficult to have erected such a directorate politically favorable to Jackson. At the same time it seems plain that Cadwalader meant to demonstrate to Jackson that the bank had picked men favorable to his cause, and Cadwalader's ingratiating letter cited in the note foregoing is a clear bid to turn the Nashville branch over to Jackson organization. This was something new in the bank's affairs. For Biddle's customary position on mixing banking and political matters see Ralph C. H. Catterall, *The Second Bank of the United States*, (1903), 171, 243-51; also Biddle's letters in Reginald C. McGrane, *The Correspondence of Nicholas Biddle* (1919), 63, 68, 70, 72.

[4]Jackson to T. H. Benton, November 29, 1837, Jackson Papers. In this review of the situation Jackson says "the Aristocratic few at Nashville" wanted a branch of the bank in 1817, but omits to indicate that he was a member of that aristocratic group at the time. Indeed his failure to go along with the nabobs on the bank question is one of the few instances when Jackson, at that period of his life, opposed the majority of the frontier aristocrats.

[5]Bassett, II, 590.

[6]Jackson to T. H. Benton, *op. cit.*

[7]Jackson to A. J. Donelson, October 11, 1822, *Correspondence*, III, 179.

[8]Jackson to T. H. Benton, *op. cit.;* Catterall, 183; St. George L. Sioussat, "Tennessee Politics in the Jackson Period," *American Historical Review*, XIV, 62.

[9]Hamilton, 69; Bassett, II, 592.

[10]In 1833 Jackson's recollection was that two paragraphs on the bank included in an early draft of the address were stricken out after the President-elect's arrival in Washington. In none of the four drafts now among the Jackson Papers, Library of Congress, showing the address in process of evolution, do these paragraphs appear, however. See Bassett, II, 425-30.

[11]Sioussat, *op. cit.*, 64, 65.

[12]*Ibid.*, 65.

[13]In view of the Supreme Court's ruling in the case of McCulloch *versus* Maryland, upholding the bank, it is simple enough for modern commentators to dismiss Jackson's constitutional objections to the Bank of the United States as evidence of unenlightened thinking. The present day reader should bear in mind that the authority of Supreme Court decisions was not at that time generally established, except among lawyers. John Marshall's bold assumption of the court's right to be the final judge of the constitutionality of acts of Congress had in itself slender constitutional basis. To this day competent constitutional students challenge that right. In 1829 there was much doubt about it in the minds of the masses of the people, particularly in the West. Jackson's constitutional suggestions to the bank were a reflection of a widely spread western opinion. In the phrasing of J. A. Hamilton (*Correspondence*, IV, 113) they follow: "The present bank is unconstitutional: 1. Because it is a corporation which Congress had no constitutional power to establish. 2. Because it withdraws the business of Bank discounts and the property of private citizens from the operation of State laws and particularly from the taxing power of the states. . . . 3. Because it purchases . . . real estate within the States without their consent, under an authority purporting to be derived from Congress, when the General Government itself possesses no such constitutional power."

[14]The substance of Jackson's objections is derived from the memoranda Kendall and Hamilton submitted in response to the President's requests. The former, with a covering letter dated November 20, 1829, is in Jackson Papers, Ladies' Hermitage Association, Nashville; the latter, with covering letter dated January 4, 1830, in *Correspondence*, IV, 112. Grundy's reply, dated October 22, (*ibid.*, IV, 83), throws little light on the objections, confining itself to a rough and rather poorly stated plan for a substitute bank.

[15]Memoranda of Grundy, Kendall and Hamilton, *op. cit.*

[16]Grundy's letter, *op. cit.*

[17]Kendall's letter, *op. cit.*

[18]Hamilton's letter, *op. cit.*

[19]W. B. Lewis to Nicholas Biddle, June 28, 1829, Catterall, 186.

[20]Nicholas Biddle to Thomas Cadwalader, August 28, 1829, *Biddle Correspondence*, 75.

[21]The Biddle-Ingham correspondence is in *Reports of Committees*, First Session, Twenty-second Congress, IV, 437 *et seq.*

[22]Catterall, 182.

[23]*Ibid.*, 178, 254; Samuel Smith to Nicholas Biddle, September 22; Biddle to Asbury Dickins, September 16 and 30, 1829, *Biddle Correspondence*, 53, 75 and 77.

[24]Catterall, 187-88.

[25]*Ibid.*, 189, 246.

[26]W. B. Lewis to H. Toland, November 11, 1829, *ibid.*

[27]Bassett, II, 598-99; Catterall, 189-91; S. D. Ingham to Jackson (three letters), November 24, 1829, *Correspondence*, IV, 86-91.

[28]Biddle's memorandum of the conversation, *Biddle Correspondence*, 93. See also Nicholas Biddle to Alexander Hamilton, a brother of James A., November 28 and to Robert Lenox, December 4, 1829, Biddle Papers, Library of Congress.

[29]J. M. Berrien to Jackson, November 27, 1829, *Correspondence*, IV, 94.

[30]S. D. Ingham to Jackson, November 26 and 27, *ibid.*, IV, 92, 93.

[31]The passage appearing in the message apparently evolved from a draft by J. A. Hamilton, now preserved in the Jackson Papers, Library of Congress. In his *Reminiscences* (pp. 149-51) Hamilton implies that he wrote the entire message. An incomplete draft in Jackson's hand (*Correspondence*, IV, 97-104) and a later draft in Van Buren's (Jackson Papers), tallying closely with the message as submitted, casts doubt on the assertion of Hamilton.

[32]Jackson to J. A. Hamilton, December 19, 1829, Hamilton, 151.

[33]W. Catron to A. J. Donelson, December 31, 1829, Donelson Papers.

[34]Catterall, 198.

[35]Later Jackson got J. A. Hamilton to write a criticism of the report which the *Telegraph* was obliged to publish.

[36]Jackson to J. A. Hamilton, June 3, 1829, Hamilton, 167.

[37]Catterall, 198.

[38]Jackson to an unnamed correspondent, July 17, 1830, Bassett, II, 603.

[39]W. B. Lewis to Nicholas Biddle, May 25, 1830, Catterall, 200.

[40]J. A. Hamilton to Jackson, June 7, 1830, Hamilton, 168.

[41]Josiah Nichol to Nicholas Biddle, July 20, 1830, *Biddle Correspondence*, 106.

[42]Alfred Balch to Jackson, January 7, 1830, *Correspondence*, IV, 115.

[43]Benton, I, 187.

[44]Nicholas Biddle to Joseph Hemphill, January 15, 1831, Catterall, 207.

CHAPTER XII

[1]Parton, III, 277.

[2]Jackson to W. B. Lewis, June 26, 1830, *Correspondence*, 156.

[3]Catterall, 171.

[4]The description of Blair is by John C. Rives, quoted from Smith thesis, 252.

[5]Lewis's narrative, Parton, III, 336. See also William Ernest Smith, *The Francis Preston Blair Family in Politics* (1933), I, 62.

[6]Jackson to Samuel Hays, December 7, 1830, private collection of Samuel Jackson Hays, Memphis.

[7]J. C. Calhoun to J. H. Hammond, January 15, 1831, *Calhoun Letters*, 283.

[8]Van Buren, 377, 379.

[9]This is Van Buren's version (pp. 377-79), extraordinary for its frankness. Bassett (II, 517) bases his account on Duff Green's story, which is that he, Green, handed Eaton the manuscript to show to Jackson. Green says Eaton returned the production unchanged, from which Green concluded that Jackson had approved it. Eaton denied this, though admitting his interview with Grundy and his subsequent equivocal behavior in withholding the manuscript from Jackson. (Van Buren, *op. cit.*) As early as January 13, 1831, Lewis knew of the project to publish the correspondence (Lewis to John Overton, Overton Papers), and intimated that Jackson knew of it. On February 3, J. A. Hamilton, writing to Jackson, mentioned Calhoun's "plan to publish." (Hamilton, 195.) In view of this evidence one is surprised to find Jackson writing Donelson on March 24 that "I was thunderstruck when I saw the publication." (*Correspondence*, IV, 253.) The best that can be said for the General is that, although he had previously heard gossip about the intended publication, the actuality came to him as a surprise. By curious reasoning, in his letter to Donelson, he exculpates Eaton of questionable conduct, attributing everything to the "wickedness" of Green which is not evident to an impartial observer. Not even Van Buren, writing twenty-three years later, questions that Eaton's conduct deceived Calhoun into the belief that he was acting with Jackson's approval.

[10]Jackson to C. J. Love, March 7, 1831, *Correspondence*, IV, 245.

[11]Washington *Globe*, February 21, 1831.

[12]See Note No. 9 *ante*.

[13]John Campbell to his brother David, November 6, 1830, Campbell Papers.

[14]Jackson to Mary Eastin, October 24, 1830, *Correspondence*, IV, 186.

[15]Jackson to Emily Donelson, November 28, 1830, *ibid.*, 208.

[16]Jackson to Mary Eastin, October 24, 1830, *ibid.*, 187.

[17]Mrs. S. D. Ingham to Emily Donelson, November 28, 1830; Rebecca Branch to Emily Donelson, October [blank], 1830, private collection of Mrs. Pauline Wilcox Burke, Washington, D. C.

[18]Various notes between Jackson and A. J. Donelson dated from October 25 to October 30, 1830, *Correspondence*, IV, 189-97.

[19]A. J. Donelson's memorandum of a conversation with Jackson, dated November 10, 1830, *ibid.*, 202. I give the General's words in the present tense. Donelson used the past.

[20]A. J. Donelson to Jackson, October 25 and 27, 1830, *ibid.*, 189 and 192.

[21]Jackson to A. J. Donelson, October 30, 1830, *ibid.*, 194.

[22]John C. McLemore to A. J. Donelson, November 10, 1830, *ibid.*, 197.

[23]Emily Donelson to her husband, November 30, 1830, private collection of Mrs. Pauline Wilcox Burke, Washington, D. C.

[24]W. H. Overton to John Overton, December 21, 1830, Overton Papers.

[25]Samuel Bradford to W. B. Lewis, February 28, 1832, Jackson Papers.

[26]Van Buren, 402-07.

[27]Trollope, 286.

[28]Van Buren, 407.

[29]Pollack, 146.

[30]*Ibid.*, 152.

[31]*Ibid.*, 159; Jackson to A. J. Donelson, June 24; to J. C. McLemore, June 27, 1831, *Correspondence*, IV, 302, 304.

[32]Jackson to Coffee, May 26, *ibid.*, 285; to R. G. Dunlap, July 18, *American Historical Magazine*, IX, 85; to Van Buren, August 8, 1831, *Correspondence*, IV, 330.

[33]W. B. Lewis to Martin Van Buren, June 27, 1831, Bixby Collection, Henry E. Huntington Library, San Marino, California; W. T. Barry to John Overton, July 1, 1831, Overton Papers.

[34]F. P. Blair to J. J. Crittenden, June 10, 1831, Crittenden Papers.

[35]D. Morrison (the builder) to Jackson, December 6, 1831, Mary French Caldwell, *Andrew Jackson's Hermitage* (1933), 78-80.

[36]William W. Story, *Life and Letters of Joseph Story* (1851), II, 118.

[37]Jackson to Mrs. Mary Dunlap, October 13, 1831, *Correspondence*, IV, 359.

[38]Charles H. Hunt, *Life of Edward Livingston* (1864), 361.

[39]J. C. Calhoun to Virgil Maxcy, May 16, 1831, Maxcy Papers.

[40]Jackson was strongly urged to get rid of Lewis altogether. R. G. Dunlap, a plain-speaking friend of army days wrote: "It raises a suspicion of your fitness to rule, . . . when it is said Billy Lewis is your councillor." (June 30, 1831, Jackson Papers.)

[41]Harriet Martineau, *A Retrospect of Western Travel* (1838), I, 155.

[42]F. P. Blair to J. J. Crittenden, June 10, 1831, Crittenden Papers.

[43]Contemporary press quotations from Charles Warren, *The Supreme Court in United States History* (1922), II, 194-95.

[44]Jackson to a committee of citizens of Charleston, June 14, 1831, Parton, III, 370.

[45]Memorandum of J. H. Hammond, March 18, 1831, *American Historical Review*, VI, 742-45.

[46]Tomlinson Fort to J. C. Calhoun, July 15, 1831, private collection of George Fort Milton, Chattanooga, Tennessee. Mr. Milton is a great-grandson of Mr. Fort.

[47]James Hamilton, junior, to J. H. Hammond, June 11, 1831, *American Historical Review*, VI, 747.

[48]Excerpt from a legislative report, Frederick Bancroft, *Calhoun and the South Carolina Nullification Movement* (1928), 101.

[49]Jackson to J. A. Hamilton, November 12, 1831, Hamilton, 231.

CHAPTER XIII

[1]Biddle's memorandum of a conversation with McLane, October 19, 1831, *Biddle Correspondence*, 132.

[2]Louis McLane to Samuel Smith, August 24, 1831, Swisher, 174.

[3]Roswell L. Colt to Nicholas Biddle, October 3, 1831, Biddle Papers, Library of Congress. Colt was a gossip, and was not present at Carroll's. He said he had the story from a "Mr. Caton,"—presumably Carroll's son-in-law. The tale sounds likely enough, however.

[4]Worden Pope to Jackson, August 6, 1831, *Correspondence*, IV, 327. The cashier of the Lexington, Kentucky, branch had urged that loans be made to help pro-bank candidates there, saying that Clay thought it advisable. Biddle vetoed the idea. (Catterall, 251.)

[5]Biddle's memorandum of a conversation with Louis McLane, October 19, 1831, *Biddle Correspondence*, 131.

[6]*Ibid.*, 129; Catterall, 211, 212; Edward Shippen to Nicholas Biddle, December 6, 1831, *Biddle Correspondence*, 136.

[7]Biddle memorandum, *op. cit.*; for Livingston's view of the matter, Parton, III, 395.

[8]Catterall, 145.

[9]Biddle gave Dickins credit for inducing McLane to move for recharter. See Biddle's memorandum of a conversation with McLane, October 19, 1831, *Biddle Correspondence*, 128.

[10]*Ibid.*, 128-31. I have changed the remark—"I should be sorry," etc.—attributed to General Jackson from the third person, which Biddle used, to the first person.

[11]Mrs. Smith, 325.

[12]Henry Clay to Francis Brooke, December 9, 1831, Clay's *Works*, IV, 321.

[13]Biddle's memorandum of a conversation with McLane, October 19, 1831, *Biddle Correspondence*, 129, 130.

[14]Taney's manuscript account, Swisher, 175-78.

[15]Robert Gibbes to Nicholas Biddle, December 11, 1831, *Biddle Correspondence*, 179.

[16]Jackson to J. A. Hamilton, December 12, 1831, Hamilton, 234. Doctor Bassett (II, 616) thinks that up to this time and, indeed, until the collapse of the final efforts at compromise in February, 1832, Jackson "played a game, concealing his real purpose from the bank democrats and working for party harmony." This is possible, though I think Bassett overstresses the case. Clay was clearly the leading gamester in the picture. Jackson watched the progress of his effort to throw the bank issue into the campaign. If Jackson were playing a game I think it more of a counter-game to Clay's than anything else. Doctor Bassett supports his statement with the following evidence:

On December 19, John Randolph, a bitter anti-bank man, wrote that if Jackson made peace with the "Chestnut Street Monster," his, Randolph's, vote for the Jackson ticket would "be delivered with forceps." On December 22, Jackson replied that he was still opposed to the bank and that the McLane report committed him to nothing. On January 3, Randolph wrote again, and in reply Jackson said, "Never fear the triumph of the U. S. Bank while I am here." (Bassett, 612-13; *Correspondence*, IV, 386, 387, 395.)

In his rendering of the substance of Jackson's letter of December 22, Bassett merely says Jackson declared himself still opposed to the bank, whereas the President's exact language was "the bank as at present organized." True, Jackson's letters to Randolph were mollifying in tone and to that extent aimed at the preservation of party harmony. But his use of the qualifying phrase quoted reduces the depth of the "game," if any, which the President was playing. Moreover, this phrase has the effect of qualifying Jackson's assurance of January third in this sense: "Never fear the triumph of the U. S. Bank as at present organized," etc. The re-charter of the bank on modified terms such as Jackson would agree to could not have been regarded as a victory for that institution. I think that is what Jackson had in mind when he wrote Randolph, and I point to his letter of December 12 to Hamilton, another anti-bank man, as confirmation of this.

Of course, when Clay succeeded in his effort to induce Biddle to throw the question into the campaign, all Jackson's latent hostility to the bank sprang to life again. Compromise was no longer politically possible—but this had been Clay's doing, not Jackson's. As the fight reached its heated climax Jackson forgot his early efforts at compromise and made a number of strong and hasty statements which, detached from their antecedents, might seem to support the contention that he could never have seriously considered the idea of compromise. Yet he had entertained such an idea, as a wealth of evidence shows.

[17]For Cadwalader's and Biddle's exchanges of letters during the former's stay in Washington, December 20 to 26, 1831, see *Biddle Correspondence*, 146-61.

[18]Nicholas Biddle to Asbury Dickins, December 12, 1831, Catterall, 213.

[19]Nicholas Biddle to Samuel Smith, January 4, 1832, *Biddle Correspondence*, 163.

[20]Boston *Gazette*, January 21, 1832; Parton, III, 415.

[21]Buell, II, 268.

[22]Jackson to Andrew Jackson, junior, October 27, 1831, *Correspondence*, IV, 365.

[23]Reproduced facing page 144, first volume of this work.

[24]Amos Kendall, "Anecdotes of General Jackson," *Harpers Magazine*, September, 1842.

[25]Jackson to H. M. Cryer, June 17, 1832, *Correspondence*, IV, 448.

[26]Van Buren, 506.

[27]Jackson to Martin Van Buren, September 5 and December 6, 1831, *Correspondence*, IV, 348 and 379.

[28]Henry Wikoff, *Reminiscences of an Idler* (1880), 29-31.

[29]Benton, I, 215, 219.

[30]William Carroll to Jackson, February 20, 1832, Jackson Papers.

[31]John Campbell to his brother David, March 8, 1832, Campbell Papers.

[32]The Eastin-Polk nuptials took place April 10, 1832. On January 21, Jackson had written to Coffee that on February 4 next she would marry Captain W. B. Finch, *Correspondence*, IV, 401.

[33]Undated memorandum in Jackson's hand, filed with papers for 1832, Jackson Papers.

[34]Jackson to Sarah Yorke Jackson, April 30, 1832, *ibid*.

[35]Jackson to John Coffee, November 21, 1831, *Correspondence*, IV, 377.

[36]J. H. Eaton to Jackson, April 10, 1832, Jackson Papers.

[37]Jackson to Andrew Jackson, junior, April 30, 1832, private collection of Andrew Jackson IV, Los Angeles.

[38]Jackson to John Coffee, March 26, 1832, Coffee Papers.

[39]W. H. Sparks, *Memories of Fifty Years* (1870), 151.

[40]J. A. Hamilton quoting Jackson, March 14, 1832, Hamilton, 243.

[41]Nicholas Biddle to C. J. Ingersoll, February 13, 1832, *Biddle Correspondence*, 182.

[42]Jackson to Martin Van Buren, December 17, 1831, *Correspondence*, IV, 385.

[43]Benton, I, 238.

[44]Bassett, II, 625; Catterall, 258-64. James Watson Webb was the editor of the *Courier and Enquirer*.

[45]Sumner, 311-316.

[46]Taney's account, Swisher, 187-95; for the message see Richardson, II, 576-91.

[47]Van Buren, 625.

[48]Nicholas Biddle to Henry Clay, August 1, 1832, *Clay Correspondence*, 341.

[49]Swisher, 200; D. T. Lynch, 357.

CHAPTER XIV

[1]Horace Greeley, *The American Conflict* (1864), I, 106.

[2]Jackson to John Coffee, April 7, 1832, *Correspondence*, IV, 430.

[3]*National Journal*, April 7, 1832.

[4]David F. Houston, *A Critical Study of Nullification in South Carolina* (1896), 105.

[5]Buell, II, 245.

[6]Privately Green suggested the name Whigs in 1832, but not until the spring of 1833 did the Jackson opposition take up that name. See Duff Green to R. K. Crallé, March 12 and 28, 1832, Green Papers.

[7]Washington *Globe*, September 25, 1832, a reprint from the *New Hampshire Patriot*.

[8]Parton, III, 420.

[9]Jackson to A. J. Donelson, August 9, 1832, Donelson Papers; August 16, *Correspondence*, IV, 467.

[10]Bowers, 251.

[11]Louis McLane to Jackson, August 3, 1832, Jackson Papers.

[12]Jackson to Martin Van Buren, August 30, 1832, *Correspondence*, IV, 470.

[13]Jackson to Secretary of the Navy, September 11, 1832, *ibid.*, 474.

[14]Jackson to Sarah Yorke Jackson, October 5, 1832, Jackson Papers, Ladies' Hermitage Association, Nashville.

[15]Jackson to Sarah Yorke Jackson, October 21, 1832, Private collection of Andrew Jackson IV, Los Angeles.

[16]Jackson to Lewis Cass, October 29, 1832, *Correspondence*, IV, 483.

[17]Buell, II, 277.

[18]Henry S. Crabb to Jackson, November 6, 1832, Jackson Papers.

[19]Jackson to Andrew Jackson, junior, November 8, 1832, *ibid.*

[20]Washington *Globe*, November 24, 1832, quoting *Vermont Journal*.

[21]Statements of the popular vote cast in 1832 vary considerably, most historians giving Jackson in the neighborhood of 700,000 and Clay in the neighborhood of 350,000, excluding the votes he received on the fusion ticket in New York. I have used the figures of Samuel R. Gammon, junior, in his *The Presidential Campaign of 1832* (1922), 153, 170. Professor Gammon has, I believe, made the most careful study of the question from contemporary sources that we have to date. South Carolina cast its electoral vote for John Floyd of Virginia.

[22]Parton, III, 432; William Wirt to J. T. Lomax, November 15, 1832, Kennedy, II, 331.

[23]Jackson to Mary Eastin Polk, November 26, 1832, private collection of Lucius Polk Brown, Columbia, Tennessee.

[24]A remark to Blair and Kendall, Bowers, 253.

[25]J. R. Poinsett to Jackson, November 16, 1832, *Correspondence*, IV, 488.

[26]Jackson to J. R. Poinsett, December 2, 1832, *ibid.*, 493; Poinsett to Jackson, March 21, 1833, *ibid.*, V, 45.

[27]Jackson to Andrew Jackson, junior, November 12, 1832, private collection of Andrew Jackson IV, Los Angeles.

[28]J. F. H. Claiborne, *Life and Times of Gen. Sam Dale* (1860), 178.

[29]Bassett, II, 564.

[30]Jackson to J. R. Poinsett, December 2, 1832, *Correspondence*, IV, 494.

[31]Jackson to J. R. Poinsett, December 9, 1832, *ibid.*, 498.

[32]G. M. Dallas to Jackson, December 6, 1832, *ibid.*, 496.

[33]Adams, VIII, 503.

[34]John Randolph to Jackson, December 6, 1832, *Correspondence*, IV, 497.

[35]Jackson to Edward Livingston, December 4, 1832, *Correspondence*, IV, 495.

[36]Richardson, II, 640-656.

[37]J. H. Hammond to R. Y. Hayne, December 20, 1832, *American Historical Review*, VI, 751.

[38]R. Y. Hayne to F. W. Pickens, December 26, 1832, *ibid.*, 755.

[39]James O'Hanlon to Jackson, December 20, 1832, *Correspondence*, IV, 504.

[40]Jackson to Martin Van Buren, December 16, 1832, *ibid.*, 500.

[41]Jackson to Martin Van Buren, December 25, 1832, *ibid.*, 506.

[42]Jackson to Lewis Cass, December 17, 1832, *ibid.*, 502.

[43]Frances A. Kemble, *Journal* (1835), II, 120, 131, 132, 138.

[44]Martin Van Buren to Jackson, December 27, 1832, *Correspondence*, IV, 507.

[45]Jackson to Martin Van Buren, December 25, 1832, *ibid.*, 506.

[46]Martin Van Buren to Jackson, December 27, 1832, *ibid.*, 506. See also Van Buren, 445.

[47]Bassett, II, 573, 578, 580; D. T. Lynch, 366; Alexander, 301.

[48]J. R. Poinsett to Jackson, January 16, 1833, *Correspondence*, V, 6.

[49]Jackson to J. R. Poinsett, February 7, 1833, *ibid.*, 15.

[50]Jackson to H. M. Cryer, February 20, 1833, *ibid.*, 19.

[51]Jackson to Martin Van Buren, January 25, 1833, *ibid.*, 12; Van Buren, 553.

[52]John Coffee to G. W. Martin, February 25, 1833, private collection of Miss Estelle Lake, Memphis, Tennessee.

[53]Jackson to Martin Van Buren, January 13, 1833, *Correspondence*, V, 3.

[54]Silas Wright to Martin Van Buren, January 13, 1833, *ibid.*, 4.

[55]*Ibid.*

[56]Poore, 138; Benton, I, 143.

[57]Jackson to Van Buren, December 25, 1832, *Correspondence*, IV, 506.

[58]Jackson to J. R. Poinsett, January 24, 1833, *ibid.*, V, 11.

[59]Jackson to Martin Van Buren, January 25, 1833, *ibid.*, 13.

[60]A fragment in Jackson's hand, posted as Item 376, Jackson Papers, Second Series, Volume V.

[61]Van Buren, 544.

[62]This action was not taken by the nullifying convention, which had adjourned, but by a mass meeting at Charleston dominated by men who had been members of that convention. The action of this body was fully respected by the South Carolina authorities. It had all the effect of an action by the convention, with certain face-saving graces added.

[63]Jackson to J. R. Poinsett, February 17, 1833, *Correspondence*, V, 18.

[64]Jackson to Felix Grundy, February 13, 1833, *American Historical Magazine*, V, 17.

[65]Jackson to H. M. Cryer, April 7, 1833, *Correspondence*, V, 53.

[66]P. P. F. Degrand to Nicholas Biddle, July 4, 1833, Biddle Papers, reporting a remark by Jackson to the Mayor of Boston in June of that year. In transcribing the quotation I have substituted the first person for the third which Degrand used.

[67]Jackson to John Coffee, April 9, 1833, *Correspondence*, 56.

[68]Schurz, II, 21.

CHAPTER XV

[1]S. E. Burrows to Nicholas Biddle, March 2, 1833, Biddle Papers.

[2]J. G. Watmough to Nicholas Biddle, March 2 and 12, 1833, *ibid.*

[3]Jackson to A. J. Hutchings, April 18, 1833, *Correspondence*, V, 60.
[4]*Ibid.*

[5]Jackson to A. J. Hutchings, November 3, 1833, *ibid.*, 223.

[6]Jackson to John Coffee, April 9, 1833, *ibid.*, 56; Mary Coffee to Jackson, April 29, private collection of Andrew Jackson IV, Los Angeles.

[7]W. B. Lewis to Jackson, April 21, 1833, *Correspondence*, V, 61-65.

[8]Jackson to W. B. Lewis, May 4, 1833, *ibid.*, 73.

[9]Jackson to W. B. Lewis, April 29, 1833, *ibid.*, 66.

[10]Jackson to A. J. Hutchings, September 6, 1833, Jackson Papers, Tennessee Historical Society, Nashville.

[11]Jackson to Mary Coffee, September 15, 1833, *Correspondence*, V, 188; to J. D. Coffee, December 24, 1834, Coffee Papers.

[12]Jackson to H. L. White, March 24, 1833, *Correspondence*, V, 46.
[13]*Ibid.*

[14]Swisher, 208-13.

[15]For both reports see *House Reports* No. 121, Twenty-second Congress, Second Session.

[16]Henry Clay to Nicholas Biddle, March 4, 1833, Biddle Papers.

[17]Lewis Williams to Nicholas Biddle, March 2, 1833, *ibid.* Williams was a brother of Jackson's implacable enemy, Ex-Senator John Williams of Tennessee.

[18]J. G. Watmough to Nicholas Biddle, March 2 and 12, 1833, *ibid.*

[19]J. G. Watmough to Nicholas Biddle, April 25, 1833; Watmough's notes dated April 25 and May 1, *ibid.*

[20]S. Simpson to Nicholas Biddle, February 20, 1833; anonymous letters to Biddle, March 7, March 31, April 1 and 2, *ibid.*

[21]Jackson to H. L. White, March 24, 1833, *Correspondence*, V, 46.

[22]Parton, III, 498. Parton does not give his source or the quotation, though it appears to have been Blair who, in 1859 (October 10, Van Buren Papers), wrote Van Buren an account of a conversation with Jackson. Virtually the same words as Parton uses are attributed to the General. I am still disposed to question the accuracy of Blair's memory for nothing in Jackson's letters, official or private, which this writer has seen, expresses doubt as to the solvency of the bank. The fact that Jackson kept his money in Biddle's bank seems to be the best evidence that he believed it safe.

[23]The Nashville branch owed other offices $1,653,326 and had due it from other offices only $205,998, and adverse balance of $1,369,187. The specie in the branch was only $244,893. Some of the other western branches were in little better state. (Amos Kendall to Louis McLane, March 16, 1833, Jackson Papers.)

[24]Jackson to his Cabinet, March 19, 1833, *Correspondence*, V, 32.

[25]R. B. Taney to Jackson, April 3, 1833, *ibid.*, 33-41.

[26]Jackson to H. M. Cryer, *American Historical Magazine*, IV, 238.

[27]R. M. Whitney to Jackson, April 3, 1833, Jackson Papers.

[28]Parton, III, 504.

[29]Louis McLane to Jackson, May 20, 1833, *Correspondence*, V, 75-101.

[30]F. P. Blair to Jackson, a memorandum without date, *ibid.*, 102-104.

30aA. J. Donelson to John Coffee, May 19, Donelson Papers; Jackson to A. J. Hutchings, June 2, Jackson Papers, Tennessee Historical Society, Nashville; Parton, III, 487.

31Jackson to Martin Van Buren, May 12, *Correspondence*, V, 74.

32Jackson to Martin Van Buren, December 4, 1838, *ibid.*, 573.

33John Campbell to David Campbell, May 12, 1833, Campbell Papers.

34Jackson to Andrew Jackson, junior, June 6, 1833, *Correspondence*, V, 107.

35*United States Gazette* (Philadelphia), June 10, 1833.

36Jackson to Andrew Jackson, junior, June 10, 1833, *Correspondence*, V, 109.

37Parton, III, 489.

38Jackson to Andrew Jackson, junior, June 14, 1833, *Correspondence*, V, 109.

39Amos Kendall to Martin Van Buren, June 6, 1833, *ibid.*, 107.

40Van Buren, 602. The McLane memorandum which Van Buren gives the date June 4, 1833, was handed to the President on June 14, the day McLane left New York. I can find no account of the President's New York conference with Van Buren except the brief and vague mention the New Yorker makes in his autobiography. My statement that Van Buren did not oblige Kendall by exerting his influence in support of the removal plan is based on a study of Van Buren's behavior throughout the deposit transfer episode, some glimpses of which may be had in succeeding pages of the text.

41Duane had given Jackson his views before the President left Washington. See [William J. Duane], *Narrative and Correspondence Concerning the Removal of the Deposites* (1838), 9.

42Jackson to Andrew Jackson, junior, June 17, 1833, *Correspondence*, V, 110.

43Josiah Quincy, *Figures of the Past* (1883), 353-58.

44Edward Warren to J. M. Warren, July 4, 1833, J. S. Bassett, "Notes on Jackson's Visit to New England," *Proceedings* of the Massachusetts Historical Society, LVI, 245.

45Quincy, 361-63.

46Quincy does not mention the bleeding of the lungs which is established from other sources. Amos Kendall in "Anecdotes of General Jackson," *Democratic Review*, September, 1842, mentions it.

47[Seba Smith] *Life and Writings of Major Jack Downing* (1834), 214, 217.

48Quincy, 359.

49Adams, IX, 5.

50Quincy, 361.

51Jackson to W. J. Duane, two communications, June 26, 1833, *Correspondence*, V, 111-28.

52New York *Advertiser*, June 29, 1833. Inasmuch as Mr. Davis will appear in the main text of the succeeding chapter I have not interrupted the narrative at this point to mention the fact that this well-known quotation from Jack Downing was written not by Seba Smith, the creator of the character, but by Charles Augustus Davis, the most brilliant of Smith's many imitators. The comments of Smith's Downing on the Harvard degree are amusing, but not quite so good as those of Davis's Downing.

Smith, a Maine farmer boy who became editor of the Portland *Courier,* began the Downing letters in January, 1830. By 1833 they were being copied in newspapers throughout the Union. When the President appeared in New York in June of that year Davis, a city-bred silk-stocking and, like his friend Nicholas Biddle, a literary dilettante, began a second series of Downing letters in the New York *Advertiser.* These quickly attained a wide-spread popularity, so much so that most general historians and biographers seem to think Davis the originator and Smith the imitator. Davis, as we shall see, was in reality one of Mr. Biddle's controlled propagandists. Smith was a ruggedly independent commentator. The bank fight over, Davis ceased to write while Smith continued at intervals until after the commencement of the Civil War.

[53]Adams, VIII, 346.

[54]Quincy, 353, 367-74.

[55]Van Buren, 602.

[56]Jackson to Van Buren, *Correspondence,* V, 128-43.

[57]On July 2, 1833, Martin Van Buren received a letter signed Louisa C. Tuthill soliciting an introduction to the President in order to offer to marry him. Van Buren forwarded the letter to Jackson who replied through Van Buren under date of July 24. On receipt of the President's kindly refusal, Miss Tuthill wrote Van Buren (August 8) that the original letter to him signed by her name was a forgery, despite the remarkable similarity of the handwriting. The foregoing correspondence is in the Van Buren Papers.

CHAPTER XVI

[1]Amos Kendall to Jackson, August 2, 11, 14 and 25, 1833, *Correspondence,* V, 145, 150, 156, 169; see also Catterall, 293; Sumner, 351.

[2]Amos Kendall to Jackson, August 14 and 25, 1833, *Correspondence,* V, 156 and 170.

[3]Martin Van Buren to Jackson, August 19 and September 4, 1833, *ibid.,* 159, 179.

[4]R. B. Taney to Jackson, August 5, 1833, *ibid.,* 147.

[5]Jackson to Martin Van Buren, September 8, 1833, *ibid.,* 183.

[6]H. D. Gilpin and two other directors of the Bank of the United States to Jackson, August 19, 1833, *ibid.,* 160-665; manuscript in Jackson's hand entitled "Charges against the Bank", *ibid.,* 174-76; Jackson to Martin Van Buren, August 18 and September 8, *ibid.,* 168, 183.

[7]For the finished document commonly known as "The Paper Read to the Cabinet" see Richardson, III, 5-19; for Jackson's early draft, *Correspondence,* V, 192-203.

[8]Jackson to Martin Van Buren, September 19, 1833, *ibid.,* 203.

[9]Nicholas Biddle to John Potter, August 1, 1833, Biddle Papers.

[10]Parton, III, 506.

[11]F. P. Blair to Martin Van Buren, November 13, 1859, *Van Buren*, 608.

[12]Jackson to Martin Van Buren, September 29, 1833, *Correspondence*, V, 212.

[13]Nicholas Biddle to Robert Lenox, July 30, 1833, Biddle Papers.

[14]Catterall, 316-20.

[15]Catterall, 329, who makes the assertion without qualification and supports it with figures. I select this citation because Professor Catterall's book, once regarded as the standard work on the bank and still the most useful, has lost caste within recent years because it does that institution more than justice.

[16]John Watmough to Nicholas Biddle, November 6 and 28, December 18, 1833, Biddle Papers.

[17]Martin Van Buren to Jackson, October 2, 1833, *Correspondence*, V, 214.

[18]Wikoff, 65-66.

[19]Jackson to Sarah Yorke Jackson, October 6, 1833, Henry E. Huntington Library *Bulletin*, No. 3, p. 133.

[20]Jackson to Andrew Jackson, junior, November 13, 1833, January 5, 1834, *Correspondence*, V, 224 and 239.

[21]Richardson, III, 31.

[22]*Ibid.*, III, 36.

[23]Nicholas Biddle to Horace Binney, January 8, 1834, Biddle Papers.

[24]James Dunlap to Nicholas Biddle, December 14, 1833, *ibid.*

[25]J. W. Webb to Nicholas Biddle, February 4, 1834, *ibid.*

[26]John Watmough to Nicholas Biddle, December 18, 1833, *ibid.*

[27]L. Henry to Nicholas Biddle, January 15, 1834, *ibid.*

[28]Catterall, 319-21.

[29]Nicholas Biddle to William Appleton, January 27, 1834, *Biddle Correspondence*, 219.

[30]J. W. Webb to Nicholas Biddle, March 11, 1834, *ibid.*, 227.

[31]Daniel Webster to Nicholas Biddle, December 21, 1833, Biddle Papers.

[32]Henry Clay to Nicholas Biddle, January 17, 1834, *ibid.*

[33]Henry Clay to Nicholas Biddle, February 2, 1834, *ibid.*

[34]Nicholas Biddle to W. B. Shepherd, February 28, 1834, *ibid.*

[35]John Forsyth to Nicholas Biddle, December 25, 1833, *ibid.*

[36]Catterall, 256.

[37]Nicholas Biddle to Charles Hammond, March 11, 1834, *Biddle Correspondence*, 225.

[38]Many latter-day historians have followed their example.

[39]In the Biddle Papers from September, 1833, to October, 1834, are about twenty letters which passed between the banker and C. A. Davis. They have never been consulted by a writer on American humor of the period. Davis's writings are collected in [Charles Augustus Davis] *The Letters of J. Downing, Major* which ran through several editions between 1834 and 1836. See also Mary A. Wyman, *Two American Pioneers* (1924), 70-82 and Jeanette Tandy, *Crackerbox Philosophers* (1925), 32-38.

[40]Nicholas Biddle to Daniel Webster, January 8, 1834, Biddle Papers.

[41]Horace Binney to Nicholas Biddle, February 4, 1834, *Biddle Correspondence*, 220. Binney wrote at Webster's direction.

[42]Nicholas Biddle to Joseph Hopkinson, February 21, 1834, *ibid.*, 222.

[43]Nicholas Biddle to J. G. Watmough, February 8, 1834, *ibid.*, 221.

[44]Examples of these petitions may be found on almost any page of the *Congressional Globe* for the First Session of the Twenty-third Congress, from mid-January forward. Niles' *Register* is also filled with them.

[45]Parton, III, 542 and 554.

[46]James Alexander Hamilton of New York.

[47]Jackson to Martin Van Buren, January 3, 1834, *Correspondence*, V, 238.

[48]As early as January 3, 1834 (Jackson to Martin Van Buren, *ibid.*) Jackson had complained of the inaction of his followers in Congress and urged offensive measures, but it was not until more than a month later that he personally took the initiative and struck back at the delegations that flocked to the White House.

[49]*United States Gazette* (Philadelphia), February 24, 1834, McMaster, VI, 202.

[50]Nicholas Biddle to Joseph Hopkinson, February 21, 1834, *Biddle Correspondence*, 222.

[51]McMaster, VI, 202.

[52]F. P. Blair to George Bancroft, June 24, 1845, Bancroft Papers, New York Public Library.

[53]*United States Gazette* (Philadelphia), February 13, 1834; McMaster, VI, 203.

[54]Stickney, 412.

[55]Washington *Globe*, February 14, 1834.

[56]Wise, 107.

[57]F. P. Blair to Martin Van Buren, October 10, 1859, Van Buren Papers.

[58]Parton, III, 548; see also Van Buren, 353.

CHAPTER XVII

[1]Material regarding Jackson's personal bank accounts derived from canceled checks in the Jackson papers. These indicate that the Bank of Metropolis account was started early in January, 1834, and that the Bank of United States account was closed July 7 of that year. The amount of the balance remaining on July 7 raises a question whether actual deposits in the Bank of the United States ceased when the other account was opened. It appears that Jackson's Nashville funds were transferred to the Union Bank there in the fall of 1833.

[2]Jackson to Andrew Jackson, junior, November 25, 1833, May 4, 1834, *Correspondence*, V, 227 and 264.

[3]Jackson to Andrew Jackson, junior, November 25, 1833, *ibid.*, 227.

[4]Jackson to Sarah Yorke Jackson, January 5, 1834, *ibid.*, 239.

[5]Jackson to Andrew Jackson, junior, January 26, 1834, *ibid.*, 242.

[6]Jackson to Andrew Jackson, junior, February 16, 1834, *ibid.*, 248.

[7]Andrew Jackson, junior, to Jackson, January 25, 1834, *ibid.*, 240-41; Jackson to Andrew, junior, February 12 and 16, *ibid.*, 247 and 248.

[8]Jackson to Andrew Jackson, junior, March 16 and 26, *ibid.*, 255 and 256.

[9]Jackson to Andrew Jackson, junior, February 12, 1834, *ibid.*, 247; March 16, *ibid.*, 255; April 6, *ibid.*, 259.

[10]Jackson to Andrew Jackson, junior, April 15, 1834, *ibid.*, 261.

[11]Jackson to Andrew Jackson, junior, April 27, May 4 and May 5, 1834, *ibid.*, 263 and 264.

[12]Andrew Jackson, junior, to Jackson, May 25, 1834, private collection of Andrew Jackson IV, Los Angeles.

[13]J. R. Montgomery to his daughter Letitia, February 20, 1834, private collection of Emil E. Hurja, New York City.

[14]James Douglas Anderson, *Making of the American Thoroughbred* (1916), 241-47. This is Balie Peyton's account, written after he had read in Parton (I, 341) who relates the details of the tobacco-box incident somewhat differently.

[15]Catterall, 339.

[16]John Rathbone to Nicholas Biddle, January 18, 1834, Biddle Papers.

[17]Nicholas Biddle to Joseph Hopkinson, February 21, 1834, *Biddle Correspondence*, 222.

[18]This was his name though Catterall, usually accurate in such details, calls him Simon Wolf and others repeat the error.

[19]Senator William Wilkins of Pennsylvania to the Senate, April 29, 1834, Catterall, 340.

[20]*Niles' Register* (Baltimore), March 15, 1834.

[21]*Ibid.*, March 8, 1834.

[22]Catterall, 340-41.

[23]Parton, III, 549.

[24]Nicholas Biddle to J. G. King, February 28, 1834, Catterall, 343.

[25]J. G. King to Nicholas Biddle, March 11, 1834, *ibid.*, 343.

[26]Nicholas Biddle to J. G. Watmough, March 17, 1834, *ibid.*, 343.

[27]Jackson to George Wolf, February, 1834, *Correspondence*, V, 243.

[28]John Connell to Nicholas Biddle, April 4, 1834, Catterall, 342.

[29]Jackson to J. D. Coffee, April 6, 1834, *Correspondence*, V, 260.

[30]Nicholas Biddle to Senator Alexander Porter of Louisiana, June 14, 1834, Biddle Papers: "If such a vote were secured the Bank would feel no reluctance in giving one, or if necessary two, millions of loans to Louisiana as requested for her relief. This could be done because such a vote is peace and harmony & confidence between the Bank & the Congress. In truth I know of no way in which all the interests on the Western waters could be more immediately & substantially advanced than by such a vote. . . . I should think there were men enough in the House to do that good service even if it did cost them a frown from the palace."

[31]Jackson to Amos Kendall, July 8, 1834, private collection of Mrs. Arthur Chester of Rye, New York. Mrs. Chester is a great-granddaughter of Amos Kendall.

[32]Jackson to A. J. Hutchings, June 7, 1834, *Correspondence*, V, 269.

[33]Jackson to F. P. Blair, August 7 and 30, 1834, *ibid.*, 281 and 287.

[34]R. M. Barton to Jackson, February 13, 1833, Jackson Papers.

[35]Jackson to W. B. Lewis, September 14, 1834, *Correspondence*, V, 292.

[36]Jackson to Andrew Jackson, junior, October 11, 1834, *ibid.*, 293-94.

[37]Jackson to Andrew Jackson, junior, October 15, 1834, Jackson Papers.

[38]Jackson to Andrew Jackson, junior, October 21, 1834, *Correspondence*, V, 301.

[39]Robert Armstrong to Jackson, October 14, 1834; S. D. Donelson to Jackson, same date, *ibid.*, 295-97.

[40]Jackson to Andrew Jackson, junior, October 23, 1834, *ibid.*, 302.

[41]Jackson to Andrew Jackson, junior, October 25, 1834, Jackson Papers.

[42]Jackson's endorsement dated October 24, 1834, on Robert Armstrong's letter of October 14, *Correspondence*, V, 296.

[43]Jackson to Andrew Jackson, junior, October 23, 1834, *ibid.*, 302.

[44]*Ibid.*

[45]Jackson to Andrew Jackson, junior, October 30, 1834, *ibid.*, 303-04.

[46]Bills for new furniture for the Hermitage, *ibid.*, 382-83, 357-58. Some of Jackson's military papers also were lost.

[47]Jackson to Andrew, junior, October, 1834, *ibid.*, 304

[48]These changes of name had come about gradually. The Whig party represented more than a rechristening of the National Republicans. It took a large number of state rightists and some lesser elements. The Jackson party did not officially adopt the name of Democrats until the national campaign of 1844, though it was in almost universal popular use ten years earlier.

[49]David Gulliver to Nicholas Biddle, October 16, 1834, Biddle Papers.

CHAPTER XVIII

[1]Jackson to Secretary of the Navy, June 6, 1834, Jackson Papers.

[2]Jackson to Martin Van Buren, October 5, 1834, Van Buren Papers.

[3]Louis Sérurier to Count Henri de Rigny, French minister of Foreign Affairs, October 22, 1834, *British and Foreign State Papers, 1812-1922*, from Richard Aubrey McLemore, a manuscript thesis, "The French Spoliation Claims, 1816-1836" (1932), 162. This is the most thorough study that has been made of the diplomatic masterpiece of the Jackson administration. It establishes that Jackson personally deserves a larger share of the credit than historians generally have been disposed to give him. A twenty-one-page condensation of Dr. McLemore's study appears in the *Tennessee Historical Magazine*, Series II, Volume II, Number 4, and has been published as a pamphlet. Unfortunately, the complete manuscript of three hundred-odd pages is as yet unpublished. Dr. McLemore who is professor of history at Judson College, Marion, Alabama, kindly provided the author with a copy for which he is deeply indebted as subsequent documentation will show in part.

[4]Louis Sérurier to Count Henri de Rigny, November 29, 1834, *ibid.*, 164. Parton (III, 568) makes a statement concerning the President's de-

termination, subsequently carried out, to write a "strong" message on the French question, which a few later writers repeat. He says that Louis Philippe assured Livingston, our minister at Paris, of his embarrassment over the dilatory behavior of the French Chamber and suggested that a more "earnest" statement of the American case might remedy this. This information Livingston is said to have passed on to Jackson who acted on it. Parton apparently had the story from Thomas P. Barton, Livingston's son-in-law and a member of the Legation staff during the French crisis. Though nothing has been found in Livingston's or in Jackson's official or private correspondence to corroborate it, McLemore (*op. cit.*, 188) brings to light that the same report was afloat in Paris at the time. So there may be something to it. The matter is of little imporance, however. Jackson needed no suggestion from Louis Philippe to take a firm course with France. He had started that in June, 1834, when he ordered the Navy in readiness. As early as October 5, he had told Van Buren he meant to make strong representations in his annual message.

[5] [Hone, Philip] *The Diary of Philip Hone* (1889), I, 121, McLemore thesis, 164-65.

[6] Wise, 145-46.

[7] Richardson, III, 106-07.

[8] Hone, I, 122, McLemore thesis, 174.

[9] Taggard to Webster, December 17, 1834, Webster Papers, Library of Congress, McLemore thesis, 174.

[10] Washington *Globe*, December 17, 1834.

[11] Sir Charles Vaughn, British minister at Washington to Lord Palmerston, minister of foreign affairs, December 20, 1834, British Foreign Office Papers (copies), Volume 293, Library of Congress, McLemore thesis, 175.

[12] Obvious from the unanimous vote and from the changed tone of the *Globe* (January 15, 1835) which passed over the Senate's action without objection.

[13] Martineau, *Western Travel*, I, 161.

[14] Alexandria *Gazette*, February 2, 1835; John Tyler to Robert Tyler, January 31, 1835, Bixby Collection, Huntington Library, San Marino, California.

[15] *United States' Telegraph*, February 2, 1835; Van Buren, 353.

[16] Washington *Globe*, February 3; *United States' Telegraph*, February 2, 1835.

[17] Louis Sérurier to John Forsyth, February 23, 1835, State Department Manuscripts, McLemore thesis, 197.

[18] John Forsyth to Edward Livingston, March 5, 1835, State Department Manuscripts, *ibid.*, 198.

[19] W. B. Lewis to J. A. Hamilton, March 14, 1835, Hamilton, 284.

[20] G. C. Childress to Jackson, November 16, 1834, *Correspondence*, V, 310.

[21] Jackson to Andrew Jackson, junior, November 19, 1834, *ibid.*, 311.

[22] Jackson's agreement with the builders for reconstructing the Hermitage, dated January 1, 1835, is in *Correspondence*, V, 315. The stipulated

expenditure of thirty-nine hundred and sixty dollars was exceeded, however, the final bill being five thousand one hundred and twenty-five.

[23]*Continental Monthly*, September, 1862.

[24]Jackson to Andrew Jackson, junior, November 27, 1834, *Correspondence*, V, 313.

[25]Items 18,136, 18,137, and 19,145, Jackson Papers for December, 1834.

[26]Robert Caldwell to his father, December 29, 1834, *American Historical Review*, XXVII, 273.

[27]Jackson to Andrew Jackson, junior, December 9, 1834, *Correspondence*, V, 313.

[28]Andrew Jackson, junior, to Sarah Yorke Jackson, December 14, 1834, private collection of Andrew Jackson, IV, Los Angeles.

[29]Jackson to Andrew Jackson, junior, April 14, 1835, *Correspondence*, V, 335.

[30]Robert Armstrong to Jackson, August 13, 1835, *ibid.*, 362.

[31]Jackson to Andrew Jackson, junior, March 1, 1836, *ibid.*, 388.

[32]R. M. Burton to Jackson, February 1, 1835, Jackson Papers.

[33]A. P. Hayne to Jackson, November 11, 1835, *ibid.*

[34]Note-book No. 6, Washington Irving Papers, New York Public Library.

[35]Not the General Benjamin F. Butler of Civil War and Reconstruction notoriety.

[36]Jackson to Alfred Balch, February 16, 1835, *Correspondence*, V, 327.

[37]John Catron to Jackson, March 21, 1835, *ibid.*, 330-32.

[38]Washington *Globe*, May 29, 1835.

[39]Jackson to John Forsyth, September 6, 1835, *Correspondence*, V, 363, speaks of having received information on the French situation from the letter of one Harris. Levitt Harris, an American in Paris, was corresponding at the time with Major Lewis and Lewis was quoting him in a effort to show the pacific nature of French sentiment. See Lewis to J. A. Hamilton, March 14, 1835, Hamilton, 284.

[40]Duc Achille de Broglie to Alphonse Pageot, June 17, 1835, *National Intelligencer*, January 22, 1836, McLemore thesis, 211-14.

[41]Jackson to John Forsyth, September 6, 1835, *Correspondence*, V, 363. In this letter the Secretary of State was instructed to receive the document officially or not at all. Unofficially he was neither to "hear" nor to receive the document. It is apparent from what followed that while Forsyth may not have "heard" the document in a literal sense he received, orally from Pageot, a correct idea of its contents.

[42]"Instructions for Thomas P. Barton," September 14, 1835, *ibid.*, 364. Forsyth's formal letter to Barton conformed to this draft. See McLemore thesis, 215.

[43]Richardson, III, 158, 160.

[44]Edward Livingston to Jackson, January 11, 1836, Hunt, 428.

[45]Richardson, III, 192.

[46]Hone, I, 196.

[47]Lord Palmerston to H. S. Fox, British minister to the United States,

April 22, 1836, British Foreign Office Papers (copies), Volume 307, Library of Congress, McLemore thesis, 262-63.

⁴⁸Two memorandums in Jackson's hand, dated November 15, 1836, *Correspondence*, V, 436-38; McLemore thesis, 267-68.

CHAPTER XIX

¹Anthony Butler to Jackson, January 4, 1827, Jackson Papers.

²Anthony Butler, of Mexican problem distinction, and Jackson's one-time ward, Anthony Wayne Butler, were different persons.

³Jackson to Martin Van Buren, August 12, 1829; "Notes on Poinsett's Instructions," August 13; Jackson to Van Buren, August 14, *Correspondence*, IV, 57-61.

⁴Martin Van Buren to Joel R. Poinsett, October 16, 1829, George Lockhart Rives, *The United States and Mexico* (1913), II, 243.

⁵Jackson to J. R. Poinsett, August 17, 1829, *Correspondence*, IV, 66.

⁶Anthony Butler to Jackson, March 7, 1834, *ibid.*, 251-52.

⁷Anthony Butler to Jackson, February 6, 1834, *ibid.*, 245.

⁸Memorandum by Jackson dated June 22, 1835, Rives, II, 258.

⁹Anthony Butler to John Forsyth, January 15, 1836, *ibid.*, 260.

¹⁰Marquis James, *The Raven, a Biography of Sam Houston* (1929), 71-73, 76.

¹¹*Ibid.*, 78, 82, 139.

¹²Jackson's fragmentary journal, May 21, 1829, Jackson Papers; Jackson to Sam Houston, June 21, 1829, Henderson Yoakum, *History of Texas* (1856), I, 307.

¹³Buell, II, 351, states that Jackson loaned Houston five hundred dollars to help finance the trip to Texas. This may be corroborated by a statement of Jackson's in a letter written from the Hermitage on August 16, 1832, to A. J. Donelson in which he speaks of having lost a note "on Houston for money advanced to him whilst in the city." (Jackson Papers.) As to the real object of the journey see James, 192.

¹⁴Jackson to Anthony Butler, October 30, 1833, *Correspondence*, V, 221; James, 190-94.

¹⁵Jackson's endorsement on a letter of Austin dated at New York April 15, 1836, *ibid.*, V, 398.

¹⁶Samuel Swartwout to A. J. Donelson, May 6, 1836, Donelson Papers.

¹⁷Buell, II, 352; see also reminiscences of N. P. Trist, New York *Evening Post*, July, 1853, Parton, III, 605.

¹⁸Journal of Lieutenant Hitchcock, Clarence R. Wharton, *The Texas Republic* (1922), 165.

¹⁹Buell, II, 352.

²⁰Jackson to Newton Cannon, August 6, 1836, *Correspondence*, V, 417.

²¹Frederick Jackson Turner, *The United States 1830-1850* (1935), 257.

²²Jackson to J. R. Chandler, September 18, 1835, *Correspondence*, V, 366.

[23]James Truslow Adams, *The Living Jefferson* (1936), 298-301; Ernest Sutherland Bates, *The Story of the Supreme Court* (1936), 136-155; William Bennett Munro, *The Makers of the Unwritten Constitution* (1930), 53-113; Warren, II, 273-312; Swisher, 380-392.

[24]Jackson to Andrew Jackson, junior, July 4, 1836, Jackson Papers.

[25]Jackson to Andrew Jackson, junior, July 10 and 23, *ibid.;* to F. P. Blair, August 12, 1836, *Correspondence,* V, 418.

[26]Though conservative, this figure is in part an estimate, as the cost of the furniture lost on the *John Randolph* has not been ascertained exactly. The work on the house totaled five thousand one hundred and twenty-five dollars (itemized statement, *ibid.*, 414-15), against a first estimate of twenty-five hundred to three thousand dollars (Robert Armstrong to Jackson, November 4, 1834, *ibid.*, 305) and a formal contract for thirty-nine hundred dollars (*ibid.*, 315-16.). New furnishings exclusive of those burned on the *Randolph* cost thirty-seven hundred dollars (*ibid.*, 382-83, 457) exclusive of transportation costs.

[27]Robert Armstrong to Jackson, August 13, 1835, *ibid.*, 361; Jackson to Andrew Jackson, junior, October 25, 1835 and March 29, 1836, *ibid.*, 372 and 396.

[28]Jackson to E. Breathitt, March 30, 1835, Jackson Papers.

[29]Edward Hobbs to Andrew Jackson, junior, August 26, 1835, *Correspondence,* V, 361.

[30]Jackson to Andrew Jackson, junior, March 25, 1836, *ibid.*, 394.

[31]Jackson to Andrew Jackson, junior, August 23, 1836, *ibid.*, 423.

[32]Jackson to Andrew Jackson, junior, August 23 and September 22, 1836, *ibid.*, 423 and 426.

[33]Jackson to Emily Donelson, October 31, 1836, *ibid.*, 433.

[34]A. J. Donelson to Emily Donelson, November 20 and 21, 1836, Donelson Papers; Jackson to Emily Donelson, November 27, 1836, *Correspondence,* V, 439.

[35]C. P. Van Ness to Martin Van Buren, Madrid, February 10, 1837, Van Buren Papers.

[36]Jackson to Emily Donelson, November 27, 1836, *Correspondence,* V, 440.

[37]A. J. Donelson to Emily Donelson, November 20 and 21, 1836, Donelson Papers; A. J. Donelson to Jackson, December 23, *ibid.;* Jackson to Mary Eastin Polk, December 22, private collection of Mrs. Mary Wharton Yeatman, Columbia, Tennessee; Jackson to A. J. Donelson, December 17, *Correspondence,* V, 442.

[38]Jackson to H. M. Cryer, November 13, 1836, Cryer Papers, Tennessee Historical Society, Nashville.

[39]W. H. Wharton to Stephen F. Austin, Secretary of State, Texas Republic, December 22, 1836, and January 6, 1837, George P. Garrison (editor), *Diplomatic Correspondence of the Republic of Texas* (1908), I, 158, 169.

[40]W. H. Wharton to Sam Houston, February 2, 1837, *ibid.*, 179-80.

[41]W. H. Wharton to T. J. Rusk, Secretary of State, Texas Republic, undated, but about February 15, 1837, *ibid.*, 194-95.

CHAPTER XX

[1]W. Peck to Jackson, February 27, 1837, Jackson Papers.

[2]Jackson to F. P. Blair, February 25, 1837, *ibid.*

[3]Buell, II, 357.

[4]D. T. Lynch, 397.

[5]W. H. Wharton to J. P. Henderson, March 5, 1837, *Texas Diplomatic Correspondence*, I, 201.

[6]Benton, I, 735.

[7]*Ibid.*

[8]It is a coincidence that these lines were written on March 4, 1837.

[9]Story, II, 154.

[10]Buell, II, 297.

[11]Grund, II, 241-43.

[12]New York *Evening Post*, December 3, 1836.

[13]Buell, II, 364-66, from conversations, long afterward, with Blair and Allen.

[14]An unsigned article in *Harper's Magazine*, January, 1855.

CHAPTER XXI

[1]Jackson to Martin Van Buren, March 30, 1837, *Correspondence*, V, 466.

[2]Jackson to A. J. Hutchings, April 4, 1837, *ibid.*, 473.

[3]Jackson to A. J. Hutchings, April 4, 1838, *ibid.*, 547-48.

[4]An undated fragment, representative of many such, Jackson Papers.

[5]Jackson to A. D. Campbell, March 15, 1837, *Correspondence*, V, 465; to A. J. Donelson, April 22, *ibid.*, 477; to A. J. Hutchings, April 4, *ibid.*, 473; to F. P. Blair, May 11, *ibid.*, 481; to Martin Van Buren, August 7, *ibid.*, 504.

[6]Jackson to Martin Van Buren, March 22, March 30, 1837, *ibid.*, 465 and 467; to F. P. Blair, April 2, April 18, *ibid.*, 473 and 476.

[7]Jackson to F. P. Blair, April 18, 1837, *ibid.*, 476.

[8]Jackson to Martin Van Buren, March 30, 1837, *ibid.*, 467.

[9]Jackson to F. P. Blair, April 18, 1837, *ibid.*, 476.

[10]*National Intelligencer*, April 28, 1837; Nashville *Banner & Whig*, May 10, 1837; Jackson to F. P. Blair, May 11, 1837, *Correspondence*, V, 481.

[11]Martin Van Buren to Jackson, April 24, 1837, *ibid.*, 479.

[12]F. P. Blair to Jackson, April 23, 1837, *ibid.*, 477.

[13]The late Professor Edward Channing of Harvard cannot be regarded as a historian over-friendly to the political and economic ideals of General Jackson. From him, therefore, I quote: "The causes of the Panic of 1837 are by no means so simple of ascertainment as our historians have usually held. Jackson's financial misdeeds could not have had much effect in bringing on the crisis, because it was worldwide." These sentences summarize a treatment of the subject conforming to my own in the preceding

paragraphs of the text. (See his *History of the United States* (1923-1926), V, 453-56.

[14]Turner, 459.

[15]Sumner, 395-96.

[16]Nicholas Biddle to J. Q. Adams, May 13, 1837, Niles' *Register*, LI, 182.

[17]Jackson to Martin Van Buren, May 12, 1837, *Correspondence*, V, 483.

[18]Jackson to Martin Van Buren, June 6, 1837, *ibid.*, 489; to Amos Kendall, June 23, *ibid.*, 489-90; to F. P. Blair, July 23, *ibid.*, 500.

[19]Amos Kendall to Martin Van Buren, October 20 and November 6, 1838, Van Buren Papers.

[20]Jackson to Martin Van Buren, July 6, 1838, *Correspondence*, V, 555.

[21]Jackson to N. P. Trist, February 6, 1838, *ibid.*, 536.

[22]Jackson to A. J. Hutchings, April 9, 1838, *ibid.*, 549.

[23]Jackson to A. J. Hutchings, March 15, 1838, *ibid.*, 542; to same, December 3, 1839, *ibid.*, VI, 41; F. P. Blair to Jackson, May 20, 1839, *ibid.*, 15; S. C. McWhorter to Jackson, August 14, 1838, Jackson Papers.

[24]Nashville *Republican*, July 20, 1838; Jackson to W. P. Lawrence, August 24, *Correspondence*, V, 565; Parton, III, 644-49.

[25]Memorandum of agreement dated November 20, 1838, *Correspondence*, V, 571.

[26]F. P. Blair to Jackson, October 19, 1838, *ibid.*, 567.

[27]Jackson to A. J. Hutchings, September 20, 1838, *ibid.*, 566.

[28]J. K. Polk to Jackson, February 7, 1839, Jackson Papers, Tennessee Historical Society, Nashville; Jackson to Martin Van Buren, March 4, 1839, *Correspondence*, VI, 6.

[29]Jackson to J. A. Shute, January 3, 1839, *ibid.*, 1; to J. K. Polk, February 11, *ibid.*, 4; to A. J. Hutchings, May 20, *ibid.*, 14.

[30]Richard Rush to Jackson, October 22, 1839, Jackson Papers.

[31]Jackson to Martin Van Buren, July 13, 1840, Van Buren Papers.

[32]Amos Kendall to Jackson, March 4, 1840, Jackson Papers.

[33]Jackson to H. M. Cryer, December 10, 1839, *Correspondence*, VI, 41.

[34]Jackson to W. B. Lewis, November 11, 1839, *ibid.*, 40.

[35]Jackson to A. J. Hutchings, December 19, 1839, *ibid.*, 43.

[36]Jackson to Andrew Jackson, junior, December 31, 1839, *ibid.*, 46.

[37]*Ibid.*

[38]Jackson to Andrew Jackson, junior, December 24, 1839, *ibid.*, 44.

[39]Jackson to Andrew Jackson, junior, December 27 and 31, 1839, *ibid.*, 45-46; to Sarah Yorke Jackson, January 4, 1840, *ibid.*, 47.

[40]Jackson to Amos Kendall, April 16, 1840, *ibid.*, 58.

[41]Jackson to Andrew Jackson, junior, December 31, 1839, *ibid.*, 46. Though written on the journey to New Orleans the quotation expresses exactly Jackson's sentiments on his way home.

[42]Wise, 170.

[43]Jackson to F. P. Blair, February 15, 1840, *Correspondence*, VI, 49-51; to Martin Van Buren, April 3, Van Buren Papers; to Amos Kendall, April 16, *Correspondence*, VI, 58.

[44] Alexander, 370.

[45] *Ibid.*, 366.

[46] Jackson to A. J. Hutchings, May 1, 1840, *Correspondence*, VI, 60.

[47] On his return from New Orleans Jackson had borrowed on two notes of hand dated January 20, 1840, four thousand nine hundred and sixty-four dollars (Jackson Papers). The amount is hardly large enough to explain the source of the fifteen thousand dollars he raised during the year to apply on Andrew's debts, for the earnings of the Hermitage, including sales of stock, hardly could have made up the balance. On December 10, 1842, Hunter's Hill, which Jackson had had on the market since 1840, was sold to Mrs. Elizabeth E. Donelson for twelve thousand dollars (Transcribed Deed Book No. 9, Davidson County Records, Nashville). This money appears to have gone at once to satisfy old obligations, leaving Jackson still hard pressed.

[48] Jackson to A. J. Hutchings, August 3, September 7 and 11, 1840, *ibid.*, 69, 74, 77.

[49] Jackson to A. J. Hutchings, August 3 and 12, 1840, *ibid.*, 70.

[50] James Phelan, *History of Tennessee* (1888), 386-90; Parton, III, 637.

[51] Jackson to F. P. Blair, September 26, 1840, *Correspondence*, VI, 78.

[52] *Democratic Review*, June, 1840, p. 486.

[53] Jackson to Andrew Jackson, junior, September 28, 1840, *Correspondence*, VI, 79.

[54] Buell, II, 373-74.

[55] Jackson to Martin Van Buren, November 12, 1840, *Correspondence*, VI, 82.

[56] Wheeling (Virginia) *Times*, McMaster, VI, 590.

[57] Jackson to Martin Van Buren, November 24, 1840, *Correspondence*, VI, 83.

[58] Jackson to F. P. Blair, December 18, 1840, *ibid.*, 85.

[59] Jackson to W. B. Lewis, December 26, 1839, *ibid.*, 87.

[60] James Howerton to Andrew Jackson, junior, October 21, 1840, Jackson Papers; J. M. Parker to Jackson, February 21, 1841, *Correspondence*, VI, 91; James Howerton to Jackson, April 5, *ibid.*, 99-102.

[61] Jackson to W. B. Lewis, November 11, 1839, *ibid.*, 40; to A. J. Hutchings, September 11, 1840, *ibid.*, 77.

[62] Endorsement in Jackson hand on letter of L. Thompson to Jackson, June 26, 1842, Jackson Papers.

[63] Jackson to A. J. Hutchings, January 14, 1841, *Correspondence*, VI, 91.

[64] Jackson to Amos Kendall, January 2, 1841, *ibid.*, 89.

[65] John Catron to Jackson, January 3, 1841, *ibid.*, 89-90.

[66] Jackson to E. F. Purdy, March 16, 1841, private collection of Arthur G. Mitten, Goodland, Indiana.

[67] Jackson to Amos Kendall, February 17, 1841, Jackson Papers.

[68] F. P. Blair to Jackson, April 4, 1840, quoting General Alexander Hunter, *Correspondence*, VI, 97-98.

[69] Jackson to F. P. Blair, April 19, 1841, *ibid.*, 105.

CHAPTER XXII

[1] F. P. Blair to Jackson, November 13, 1842, *Correspondence*, VI, 175.
[2] D. S. Carr to Jackson, August 18, 1841, *ibid.*, 119.
[3] Jackson to W. B. Lewis, August 18, 1841, *ibid.*, 120.
[4] J. B. Plauché to Jackson, December 21, 1841, *ibid.*, 129.
[5] F. P. Blair to Jackson, January 18, 1842, *ibid.*, 136; Jackson to Blair, March 29, 1842, *ibid.*, 148, referring to a letter from Blair dated February 16 in which the offer of ten thousand dollars is made.
[6] Jackson to L. F. Linn, March 12, 1842, *ibid.*, 143-46.
[7] Jackson to F. P. Blair, February 24, 1842, *ibid.*, 140.
[8] Jackson to W. B. Lewis, February 28, 1842, *ibid.*, 141.
[9] Jackson to W. B. Lewis, March 26, 1842, *ibid.*, 147.
[10] Martin Van Buren to Jackson, May 15, 1841, *ibid.*, 112.
[11] Alexander, 14-16, 361.
[12] Jackson to F. P. Blair, April 23, 1842, *Correspondence*, VI, 150.
[13] F. P. Blair to Jackson, May 24, 1842, *ibid.*, 154.
[14] The southern "conspiracy" idea with reference to the annexation of Texas has been plentifully exploited by historians and biographers. Turner (p. 512) concludes that there is nothing in it, and cites good evidence.
[15] Jackson to F. P. Blair, May 23, 1842, *Correspondence*, VI, 152.
[16] Martin Van Buren to Jackson, May 27, 1842, *ibid.*, 155.
[17] Jackson to F. P. Blair, April 23, 1842, *ibid.*, 150.
[18] D. T. Lynch, 478; Edward M. Shepard, *Martin Van Buren* (1888), 343; Schurz, II, 244.
[19] Jackson to F. P. Blair, July 18, 1842, *Correspondence*, VI, 159.
[20] Miscellaneous endorsements without dates, *ibid.*, 416.
[21] Jackson to F. P. Blair, June 4, 1842, Jackson Papers.
[22] Jackson to L. F. Linn, June 2, 1842; to Amos Kendall, June 18; to F. P. Blair, July 14; to J. W. Breedlove, August 1, *Correspondence*, VI, 156-62.
[23] Jackson to J. W. Breedlove, October 3, 1842, *ibid.*, 172. See also Jackson to F. P. Blair, September 9, and October 3, *ibid.*, 165, 171.
[24] Jackson to Amos Kendall, *op. cit.*
[25] Jackson to F. P. Blair, November 25, 1842, *ibid.*, 178.
[26] Jackson to George Bancroft, December 9, 1841, *ibid.*, 128.
[27] Jackson to Amos Kendall, January 10, 1843, Tennessee State Library, Nashville.
[28] Amos Kendall to Jackson, November 29, 1842, Jackson Papers.
[29] J. A. McLaughlin to Amos Kendall, January 30, 1843, *Correspondence*, VI, 186.
[30] Fragment posted as item 23,655, Volume CVII, Jackson Papers.
[31] Fragment posted as Item 23,783, Volume CIX, Jackson Papers.
[32] C. L. Butler to Jackson, March 15, 1843, Jackson Papers.
[33] Jackson's Will, *Correspondence*, VI, 220-23.
[34] Jackson to F. P. Blair, July 14, 1843, *ibid.*, 224.
[35] Jackson to Amos Kendall, November 13, 1843, *ibid.*, 242.

³⁶F. P. Blair to Jackson, November 26, 1843; Jackson's reply, December 5; Blair to Jackson December 6, *ibid.*, 244-45, 247, 248. Before Jackson's death Kendall and Blair were reconciled and in the last weeks of his life Jackson solicited a federal appointment for Kendall from James K. Polk.

³⁷Jackson to F. P. Blair, November 22, 1843, *ibid.*, 243.

³⁸Jackson to A. J. Donelson, October 15, 1843, *ibid.*, 234; to Blair, *op. cit.* Accessible records do not give the prices Butler paid for the horses.

³⁹Henry Lieberman to Jackson, February 19, 1844, Jackson Papers.

⁴⁰Jackson to F. P. Blair, February 24 and 29, 1844, *Correspondence*, VI, 266, 267. Blair's reply to Jackson's specific request is not available, but the tenor of subsequent letters, and Jackson's disposition of the money, indicates its nature.

⁴¹Jackson to F. P. Blair, February 29, 1844, *ibid.*, 267-68.

⁴²The letter delivered by Miller, Sam Houston to Jackson, February 16, 1844, and Jackson's reply under date of March 15, appear in more detail in the next chapter. See notes 7 and 9 *post.*

CHAPTER XXIII

¹James, 167.

²Anson Jones, Secretary of State of Texas, to Isaac Van Zandt, Texan chargé d'affaires to the United States, December 13, 1843, *Texan Diplomatic Correspondence*, II, 232-33.

³A. P. Upshur, Secretary of State, to W. S. Murphy, American chargé to Texas, January 16, 1844, Justin H. Smith, *The Annexation of Texas* (1911), 158-59.

⁴R. J. Walker to Jackson, January 10, 1844, *Correspondence*, VI, 255.

⁵Jackson to Sam Houston, January 18, 1844, private collection of the late Houston Williams, Houston, Texas. Mr. Williams was a grandson of Sam Houston.

⁶Jackson to Sam Houston, January 23, 1844, *ibid.*

⁷Sam Houston to Jackson, February 16, 1844, *Correspondence*, VI, 260-64.

⁸J. H. Smith, 164.

⁹Jackson to Sam Houston, March 15, 1844, Houston (Texas) Public Library; to W. B. Lewis, March 11, *Correspondence*, VI, 272; W. D. Miller to Jackson, April 7, *ibid.*, 276.

¹⁰Jackson to Sam Houston, March 15, 1844, Houston (Texas) Public Library.

¹¹J. H. Smith, 166-76.

¹²W. D. Miller to Jackson, April 7, 1844, *Correspondence*, VI, 276; W. B. Lewis to Jackson, March 28, *ibid.*

¹³Jackson to A. V. Brown, February 12, 1844, Richmond *Enquirer*, March 22, 1844. In subsequent contemporary publications the date was changed to 1843, which was correct. A copy of the original letter, under date of February 9, 1843, appears in *Correspondence*, VI, 201-02, which shows that the language of the published copy was dressed up quite a bit.

[14]Jackson to F. P. Blair, May 7, 1844, *Correspondence*, VI, 283.

[15]James K. Polk to Cave Johnson, May 4, 1844, St. George L. Sioussat, "Letters of James K. Polk to Cave Johnson 1833-1848," *Tennessee Historical Magazine*, I, 238-39.

[16]Willoughby Williams to John Trimble, December 1, 1877, Jo. C. Guild, *Old Times in Tennessee* (1878), 163-64; J. K. Polk to Cave Johnson, May 13, 1844, Sioussat, *Polk Letters*, I, 242; Jackson to F. P. Blair, May 11, *Correspondence*, VI, 286: "I have shed tears of regret over [Van Buren's letter]."

[17]*Ibid.*

[18]Nashville *Union*, May 16, 1844. Jackson also sent to Van Buren a manuscript copy of the letter which is reproduced, from the Van Buren Papers, in *Correspondence*, VI, 289-91.

[19]In 1843 Jones had defeated Polk for Governor of Tennessee a second time.

[20]J. K. Polk to Cave Johnson, May 13, 1844, Sioussat, *Polk Letters*, I, 239-40.

[21]J. K. Polk to Cave Johnson, May 14, *ibid.*, 242.

[22]*Ibid.*

[23]Cave Johnson to J. K. Polk, May 8, 1844, Polk Papers, Library of Congress.

[24]J. K. Polk to Cave Johnson, May 14, 1844, Sioussat, *Polk Letters*, I, 242-43.

[25]Jackson to B. F. Butler, May 14, 1844, Jesse S. Reeves, "Letters of Gideon J. Pillow to James K. Polk, 1844," *American Historical Review*, XI, 833-34. Butler, the former Attorney General, was Van Buren's campaign manager. The letter was intended for Van Buren's eye. It is quite possible that it was designed to cover the further contingency of averting a break with Van Buren with a view to bringing more pressure to bear, should Van Buren be nominated on a platform silent on Texas.

[26]The letter appeared in the *Union* for May 16, 1844, the editorial in the succeeding issue, May 18.

[27]Jackson to J. K. Polk, June 29, 1844, *Correspondence*, VI, 299.

[28]Buell, II, 384.

[29]Sarah Knox Sevier to Jackson, February 3, 1844, Jackson Papers. The writer was one of the regiment of Rachel Jackson's grand-nieces. She was also related to James Knox Polk.

[30]Latetia Chambers to Jackson, January 15, 1844, *ibid.*

[31]John Greere to Jackson, November 20, 1844, *ibid.*

[32]J. M. Parker to Jackson, August 2, 1844; Jackson to W. B. Lewis, September 17, *Correspondence*, VI, 309 and 319.

[33]Jackson to F. P. Blair, August 15, 1844, *ibid.*, 313.

[34]Jackson to W. B. Lewis, July 12, 1844, *ibid.*, 302.

[35]Jackson to J. K. Polk, July 26, 1844; to J. Y. Mason, August 1; to W. B. Lewis, August 1, *ibid.*, 303-08; John Tyler to Jackson, August 18, *ibid.*, 315.

[36]J. H. Smith, 297-307.

[37]Jackson to J. K. Polk, July 23, 1844, Polk Papers.

[38]Jackson to F. P. Blair, September 19, 1844, *Correspondence*, VI, 322; J. K. Polk to Cave Johnson, October 30, Sioussat, *Polk Letters*, I, 253.

[39]The following tabulation (from Turner, 528) shows, in some measure, the extent to which Jackson had been able to popularize the cause of Texas in New England, where at the start of the campaign it was very weak, and the extent to which Clay was able to pick up pro-Texas votes in the West and South, where the Texas cause was overwhelmingly strong:

	Polk	Clay	Birney [Abolitionist]
New England	178,474	186,586	25,861
Middle Atlantic	442,618	432,003	19,081
South Atlantic	171,706	171,271	....
South Central	198,099	185,162	....
North Central	346,346	324,040	17,358
	1,337,243	1,299,062	62,300

It would not do, of course, to accept these figures as a reflection on Texas alone. The tariff, the currency question and other issues entered in. A high-tariff letter was credited as responsible for Polk's victory in Pennsylvania, for example. But Texas was the greatest single issue, and the foregoing figures can be considered with that in mind.

[40]A speech by Clay at Lexington, Kentucky, in 1842, in a collection of Clay's speeches in the library of the University of Chicago; see also Henry S. Foote, *Casket of Reminiscences* (1874), 27.

[41]Jackson to A. J. Donelson, November 18, 1844, *Correspondence*, VI, 330.

[42]Jackson to A. J. Donelson, December 2, 1844, *ibid.*, 334-36.

[43]A. J. Donelson to the Secretary of State, November 24, 1844, J. H. Smith, 370-71.

[44]*Ibid.*, 373.

[45]A. J. Donelson to Jackson, December 28, 1844, *Correspondence*, VI, 349-50.

[46]Jackson to F. P. Blair, January 21, 1844, *ibid.*, 367.

[47]James, 353.

[48]F. P. Blair to Jackson, February 28, 1844, *Correspondence*, VI, 375.

[49]Jackson to F. P. Blair, March 10, 1844, *ibid.*, 378.

[50]F. P. Blair to Jackson, December 22, 1844, *ibid.*, 348.

[51]Jackson to A. J. Donelson, without date but containing internal evidence of having been written in February, 1845, *ibid.*, 367.

[52]Jackson to W. B. Lewis, February 12, 1844; to F. P. Blair, March 3, *ibid.*, 368 and 376.

[53]Jackson to W. B. Lewis, February 12, 1844, *ibid.*, 368-69.

[54]F. P. Blair to Jackson, February 21, 1845, *ibid.*, 370; J. C. Rives to Jackson, March 12, *ibid.*, 380; W. B. Lewis to Jackson, March 13, Jackson Papers.

[55]Heiskell, II, 408.

[56]Jackson to F. P. Blair, March 3, 1844; to W. B. Lewis, March 22, *Correspondence*, VI, 376 and 386.

[57]Isaac Hill in an unsigned letter to the *New Hampshire Patriot* reprinted in *The Madisonian* (Washington), March 29, 1845.

[58]From a scrapbook of old newspaper clippings, Tennessee State Library, Nashville.

[59]Jackson to J. D. Elliott, March 27, 1845, *Correspondence*, VI, 391.

[60]John Catron to James Buchanan, June 11, 1845, The New York *Sun*, January 8, 1882. This item kindly furnished by Lindsey House, Tulsa, Oklahoma.

[61]Jackson to Sam Houston, March 12, 1845, Yoakum, II, 441.

[62]A. J. Donelson to Elizabeth Donelson, for Jackson's eye, April 16, 1845, Donelson Papers.

[63]E. G. W. Butler to W. C. Crane, April 9, 1881, William Carey Crane, *Life and Select Literary Remains of Sam Houston* (1885), 251.

[64]An example of the respect of humble citizens for the authority of Jackson's name occurred in Alabama in 1866 in a case involving a cloud on a land title. It appears that a patent originating during Jackson's administration exhibited some small irregularity. The holder was asked to surrender the same to have the technicality rectified. He responded as follows: "You think you are gon to git my paytent. I reckon not. I am not afeard of you. My paytent is signed A-N-D-R-E-W J-A-C-K-S-O-N. Now tech that if you dar." (Washington correspondence of the New York *Evening Post*, dated August 8, 1866.) This item kindly communicated by David Rankin Barbee, Washington, D. C.

[65]Jackson to J. K. Polk, May 26, 1845, *Correspondence*, VI, 412.

[66]Diary of William Tyack, May 29, 1845, Niles' *Register*, June 21, 1845; also in Parton, III, 673.

[67]John Catron to Sarah Yorke Jackson, May 19, 1845, *ibid.*, 409; Niles' *Register*, June 21, 1845.

[68]George P. A. Healy, *Reminiscences of a Portrait Painter* (1894), 144, 149.

[69]William Tyack's diary, *op. cit.*

[70]Jackson to J. B. Plauché, June 5, 1845, from an old clipping, apparently from a New Orleans newspaper. For an account of the writing of this letter see Andrew Jackson, junior, to J. K. Polk, October 10, 1845, Jackson Papers.

This draft for two thousand dollars raised the total of General Jackson's indebtedness, exclusive of household bills, to twenty-six thousand dollars at the time of his death. The principal creditors, Blair, Rives and Plauché, were specifically protected by the terms of Jackson's will. Blair and Rives did not avail themselves of this protection, making no claim against the estate. What Plauché did I do not know. In 1856 Andrew Jackson, junior's, debts had mounted to forty-eight thousand dollars. The State of Tennessee came to his relief, purchasing the Hermitage, and enabling Jackson to make a fresh start. In 1860 the State invited him to return to the Hermitage as a tenant at will. He died there in 1865. His widow, Sarah, died there in 1888.

The last of the Hermitage "family"—to use the term as General Jackson used it, meaning persons both white and black—to leave the old place was Alfred, an ex-slave. He died in 1901 at the age of 98, and was buried beside his master and mistress in the garden.

Long before his death Alfred became a personage of distinction, constantly pressed for reminiscences of General Jackson. The old darky did his best to accommodate, and in this way his name has become considerably involved with the local Jacksonian tradition. Alfred is usually referred to as the General's body servant. The remark attributed to him which I like best was one the late Judge John H. DeWitt, president of the Tennessee Historical Society, used to repeat. Someone asked the old negro if he thought General Jackson would get to Heaven on Judgment Day. Alfred replied: "If Gen'l Jackson takes it into his head to git to Heaven who's gwine to keep him out?"

Though a household negro, Alfred was not General Jackson's body servant. He was one of the four negroes tried in 1840 for the murder of Frank, the fiddler, and acquitted. Another of the defendants—George, the mulatto—was the General's body servant and constant attendant during the last twenty years of his life. During Jackson's last illness George's understudy and assistant appears to have been a negro named Dick. George married Manthis, the property of Albert Ward. In 1840 Ward offered to sell her to Jackson for one thousand dollars so that the couple might be together. At that time Jackson did not have the money to make the purchase, but later he made it for the two were at the Hermitage in 1845.

In 1858 they were separated again. Andrew Jackson, junior, sold George to Dr. John Donelson Martin. He sold Manthis to a Presbyterian minister named Carr who handed her over to Nathan Bedford Forrest, a slave dealer in Memphis, soon to achieve renown in another field. There Martin bought her in order to unite the couple at his place in Alabama where both died during the last year of the War Between the States. (For the history of George and Manthis after leaving the Hermitage I am indebted to Mrs. Mary Martin Frost of Florence, Alabama. The deeds of sale are in her family.)

[71]Andrew Jackson, junior, to A. O. P. Nicholson, June 17, 1845, Jackson Papers, New York Historical Society.

[72]Jackson to J. K. Polk, June 6, 1845, Jackson Papers, Library of Congress. Jackson signed his name once more after writing this letter when, on the following day, June 7, he franked a letter for Andrew, junior, to former Congressman Thomas F. Marshall of Kentucky. (Andrew Jackson, junior, to A. O. P. Nicholson, op. cit.) Emil Edward Hurja, who has studied the life of Walker from the sources, and who owns manuscript material concerning him, informs me that Jackson's misgivings concerning the influence of the Mississippi speculators were unfounded. Walker made a good Secretary of the Treasury, and financed the Mexican War without a bond issue.

[73]Andrew Jackson, junior, to J. K. Polk, October 10, 1845, ibid.

[74]Andrew Jackson, junior, to A. O. P. Nicholson, op. cit.; Parton, III, 676.

[75]Healy, 145.

[76]Statements of Dr. Esselman and W. B. Lewis, *ibid.*, 677-78; Andrew Jackson, junior, to A. O. P. Nicholson, *op. cit.*; statement of Hannah, the slave, *Correspondence*, VI, 415.

[77]Related to the writer in 1927 by the late Nettie Houston Bringhurst, of San Antonio, Texas, a daughter of Sam Houston; see also Sam Houston to J. K. Polk, midnight, June 8, 1845, *Correspondence*, VI, 415.

BIBLIOGRAPHY

BIBLIOGRAPHY

[No attempt is made here to give a full list of the sources, manuscript or printed, which have been read or examined. Only such manuscript collections are named as yielded something which is quoted in the text or cited in the Notes. The list of printed sources is confined to a recapitulation by full title of authorities referred to in the Notes, where short titles are used after the initial mention. Further remarks on sources appear under "Personal Acknowledgments."]

MANUSCRIPT SOURCES

PUBLIC COLLECTIONS

George Bancroft Papers, New York Public Library.
Nicholas Biddle Papers, Library of Congress, Washington.
Bixby Collection, miscellaneous manuscripts, Henry E. Huntington Library, San Marino, California.
Henry Clay Papers, Library of Congress.
John Coffee Papers, Tennessee Historical Society, Nashville.
John J. Crittenden Papers, Library of Congress.
Hardy M. Cryer Papers, Tennessee Historical Society.
Davidson County (Tennessee) Records, Nashville.
Andrew Jackson Donelson Papers, Library of Congress.
Charles Fisher Papers, University of North Carolina, Chapel Hill.
Duff Green Papers, Library of Congress.
Washington Irving Note Books, New York Public Library.
Andrew Jackson Papers, Ladies' Hermitage Association, Nashville.
Andrew Jackson Papers, Library of Congress. Manuscripts from this collection usually are designated in the Notes simply as "Jackson Papers." Manuscripts from other public collections of Jackson papers are identified by giving the location of the collection each time it is mentioned, for example, "Jackson Papers, Ladies' Hermitage Association, Nashville."
Andrew Jackson Papers, New York Historical Society, New York City.
Andrew Jackson Papers, Tennessee Historical Society.
James Kent Papers, Library of Congress.
William B. Lewis Papers, New York Public Library.
Virgil Maxcy Papers, Library of Congress.
John McLean Papers, Library of Congress.

Miscellaneous manuscripts, Houston (Texas) Public Library.
Miscellaneous manuscripts, New York Historical Society.
Miscellaneous manuscripts, Tennessee Historical Society.
Miscellaneous manuscripts, Tennessee State Library, Nashville.
James Monroe Papers, New York Public Library.
John Overton Papers, Tennessee Historical Society.
James K. Polk Papers, Library of Congress.
Andrew Stevenson Papers, Library of Congress.
Martin Van Buren Papers, Library of Congress.

PRIVATE COLLECTIONS

Oliver R. Barrett, Chicago.
Mrs. H. L. Bateman, Nashville.
Lucius Polk Brown, Columbia, Tennessee.
Mrs. Pauline Wilcox Burke, Washington.
Campbell Papers, Lemuel R. Campbell, Nashville.
Mrs. Arthur Chester, Rye, New York.
J. M. Dickinson, Nashville.
Mrs. Louis Farrell, Nashville.
Henry M. Flynt, New York City.
Mrs. Mary Martin Frost, Florence, Alabama.
Samuel Jackson Hays, Memphis.
S. P. Hessel, Woodmere, Long Island, New York.
Stanley Horn, Nashville.
Emil Edward Hurja, New York City.
Andrew Jackson IV, Los Angeles.
Miss Estelle Lake, Memphis, Tennessee.
The late Thomas F. Madigan, New York City.
Mrs. Andrew Jackson Martin, Memphis.
George Fort Milton, Chattanooga, Tennessee.
Arthur G. Mitten, Goodland, Indiana.
J. P. Morgan, New York City.
C. Norton Owen, Glencoe, Illinois.
The late Houston Williams, Houston, Texas.
Mrs. Mary Wharton Yeatman, Columbia, Tennessee.

UNPUBLISHED THESES

Curtis W. Garrison, "The National Election of 1824," manuscript copy
in the library of Johns Hopkins University, Baltimore.
Richard A. McLemore, "The French Spoliation Claims, 1816-1836,"
manuscript copy in the library of Vanderbilt University, Nashville.
Arthur R. Newsome, "The Presidential Election of 1824 in North Caro-

lina," manuscript copy in the library of the University of Michigan, Ann Arbor.

Culver H. Smith, "The Washington Press of the Jackson Period," manuscript copy in the library of Duke University, Durham, North Carolina.

PRINTED SOURCES

Charles Francis Adams (editor), *Memoirs of John Quincy Adams, Comprising Portions of His Diary* (1876).

James Truslow Adams, *The Living Jefferson* (1936).

Holmes Alexander, *The American Talleyrand, the Career and Contemporaries of Martin Van Buren* (1935).

Alexandria (D. C.) *Gazette*.

Alexandria (D. C.) *Herald*.

American Antiquarian Society *Proceedings*, New Series, XXXI.

American Historical Magazine.

James Douglas Anderson, *Making of the American Thoroughbred* (1916).

"An American Army Officer," *Civil and Military History of Andrew Jackson* (1825).

Annals of Congress.

Argus of Western America (Frankfort, Kentucky).

James L. Armstrong, *General Jackson's Juvenile Indiscretions* (1832).

Caleb Atwater, *Remarks on a Tour to Prairie du Chien* (1831).

Frederick Bancroft, *Calhoun and the South Carolina Nullification Movement* (1828).

John Spencer Bassett (editor), *Correspondence of Andrew Jackson* (1926-35).

——, "Major Lewis on the Nomination of Andrew Jackson," *Proceedings* of the American Antiquarian Society, New Series, XXXIII.

——, "Notes on Jackson's Visit to New England," *Proceedings* of the Massachusetts Historical Society, LVI.

——, *The Life of Andrew Jackson* (1911).

Ernest Sutherland Bates, *The Story of the Supreme Court* (1936).

Jesse Benton, *An Address to the People of the United States on the Presidential Election* (1824).

Thomas Hart Benton, *Thirty Years' View* (1854-56).

[Nicholas] *Biddle Correspondence*. See R. C. McGrane.

Boston *Gazette*.

Claude G. Bowers, *Party Battles of the Jackson Period* (1922).

Everett Somerville Brown (editor), *The Missouri Compromises and Presidential Politics 1820-1825, from the Letters of William Plumer, Jr.* (1926).

Margaret Eaton Puchignani. See Margaret Eaton.

Augustus C. Buell, *A History of Andrew Jackson* (1904).

Mary French Caldwell, *Andrew Jackson's Hermitage* (1933).

[John C.] *Calhoun Letters.* See J. F. Jameson.

[John C.] *Calhoun's Works.* See R. K. Crallé.

Ralph C. H. Catterall, *The Second Bank of the United States* (1903).

Edward Channing, *History of the United States* (1923-26).

J. F. H. Claiborne, *Life and Times of Sam Dale* (1860).

Allen C. Clark, *Life and Letters of Dolly Madison* (1914).

Bennett Champ Clark, *John Quincy Adams, Old Man Eloquent* (1932).

[Henry Clay], *Address of Henry Clay to the Public, Containing Certain Testimony in Refutation of the Charges Made by Gen. Andrew Jackson* (1827).

[——], *Supplement to an Address by Henry Clay* (1828).

[Henry] *Clay Correspondence.* See Calvin Colton.

[Henry] *Clay's Works.* See Calvin Colton.

Cincinnati *Advertiser.*

Cincinnati *Gazette.* Full title *Liberty Hall & Cincinnati Gazette.*

Cincinnati *National Republican.*

Joseph B. Cobb, *Leisure Labors* (1858).

Calvin Colton (editor), *Private Correspondence of Henry Clay* (1856).

—— and others (editors), *Works of Henry Clay* (1897).

Columbian Observer (Philadelphia).

Congressional Globe.

Continental Monthly.

Correspondence of Andrew Jackson. See J. S. Bassett.

Richard K. Crallé (editor), *Works of John C. Calhoun* (1850-56).

William Carey Crane, *Life and Select Literary Remains of Sam Houston* (1885).

George Tichnor Curtis, *Life of Daniel Webster* (1870).

"Curtius," *Torch Light,* . . . *an Examination of the Opposition to the Administration* (1826).

[Charles Augustus Davis], *The Letters of J. Downing, Major* (1834).

Democratic Review.

[William J. Duane], *Narrative of Correspondence Concerning the Removal of Deposites* (1838).

Seymour Dunbar, *A History of Travel in America* (1915).

[Margaret Eaton], *The Autobiography of Peggy Eaton* (1932).

Erik M. Eriksson, "The Civil Service Under President Jackson," *Mississippi Valley Historical Review,* XIII.

Carl Russel Fish, *The Civil Service and Patronage* (1905).

Worthington C. Ford, *Writings of John Quincy Adams* (1913-17).

John W. Forney, *Anecdotes of Public Men* (1873).

Franklin Gazette (Philadelphia).

Claude Moore Fuess, *Daniel Webster* (1930).

Samuel R. Gammon, junior, *The Presidential Campaign of 1832* (1922).

George P. Garrison (editor), *Diplomatic Correspondence of the Republic of Texas* (1908).

George R. Gilmer, *Sketches of Some of the Settlers of Upper Georgia* (Reprint of 1926).

Samuel G. Goodrich, *Recollections of a Lifetime* (1866).

Horace Greeley, *The American Conflict* (1864).

Duff Green, *Facts and Suggestions, Biographical and Historical* (1866).

Francis J. Grund (editor), *Aristocracy in America* (1839).

Jo. C. Guild, *Old Times in Tennessee* (1878).

Herman Hailpern, "Pro-Jackson Sentiment in Pennsylvania," *Pennsylvania Magazine of History and Biography*, L.

James A. Hamilton, *Reminiscences* (1869).

[Charles Hammond], *A View of Gen. Jackson's Domestic Relations* (1828).

Jabez Hammond, *History of the Political Parties in the State of New York* (1845).

Harper's Magazine.

Thomas Robson Hay, "John C. Calhoun and the Presidential Campaign of 1824," *North Carolina Historical Review*, XII.

George P. A. Healy, *Reminiscences of a Portrait Painter* (1894).

House Reports No. 121, Twenty-second Congress.

David F. Houston, *A Critical Study of Nullification in South Carolina* (1896).

Charles H. Hunt, *Life of Edward Livingston* (1864).

Henry E. Huntington Library *Bulletin* No. 3.

Marquis James, *The Raven, a Biography of Sam Houston* (1929).

J. Franklin Jameson (editor), "Correspondence of John C. Calhoun," *Annual Report of the American Historical Association* (1899).

Frances A. Kemble, *Journal* (1835).

Amos Kendall, "Anecdotes of General Jackson," *Harper's Magazine*, September, 1842.

John P. Kennedy, *Life of William Wirt* (1849).

Kentucky Legislature, investigation of Henry Clay's part in House Election of 1825, *United States' Telegraph* Extras No. 1 and No. 12.

Knoxville (Tennessee) *Register.*

Lebanon (Tennessee) *Democrat.*

A. Levasseur, *Lafayette in America* (1829).

Liberty Hall & Cincinnati Gazette.

Louisville (Kentucky) *Public Advertiser.*

Denis Tilden Lynch, *An Epoch and a Man: Martin Van Buren and His Times* (1929).

William O. Lynch, *Fifty Years of Party Warfare* (1931).

The Madisonian (Washington).

Charles W. March, *Reminiscences of Congress* (1850).

Harriet Martineau, *Society in America* (1837).

——, *A Retrospect of Western Travel* (1838).

William MacDonald, *Jacksonian Democracy* (1906).

Reginald C. McGrane, *The Correspondence of Nicholas Biddle* (1919).

John Bach McMaster, *A History of the People of the United States* (1883-1924).

William C. Meigs, *Life of John C. Calhoun* (1917).

[Elijah Hunt Mills], *Selections from the Letters of the Hon. E. H. Mills* (1881).

John Bassett Moore (editor), *Works of James Buchanan* (1908).

William Bennett Munro, *The Makers of the Unwritten Constitution* (1930).

Nashville *Banner.*

—— *Banner & Whig.*

—— *Clarion.*

—— *Republican.*

—— *Union.*

—— *Whig.*

National Gazette (Washington).

National Intelligencer (Washington).

New-England Galaxy (Boston).

New Hampshire Patriot & State Gazette.

New York *Advertiser.*

—— *Evening Post.*

—— *Statesman.*

Niles' *Register.*

North Carolina Historical Review.

Frederic Austin Ogg, *The Reign of Andrew Jackson* (1919).

James Parton, *Life of Andrew Jackson* (1859-60).

Charles H. Peck, *The Jacksonian Epoch* (1899).

James Phelan, *History of Tennessee* (1888).

Philadelphia *Aurora.*

—— *Mercury.*

Ulrich B. Phillips, "William H. Crawford," a sketch in the *Dictionary of American Biography*, IV.

Queena Pollack, *Peggy Eaton, Democracy's Mistress* (1831).

Una Pope-Hennessey, *Three English Women in America* (1929).

Ben: Perley Poore, *Perley's Reminiscences* (1866).

Josiah Quincy, *Figures of the Past* (1883).

Raleigh (North Carolina) *Register.*

—— *Star.*

Henry S. Randall, *Life of Thomas Jefferson* (1858).

Jesse S. Reeves, "Letters of Gideon J. Pillow to James K. Polk, 1844," *American Historical Review*, XI.

Reports of Committees, First Session, Twenty-third Congress, IV.

James D. Richardson (editor), *Messages and Papers of the Presidents* (1899).

Richmond (Virginia) *Enquirer*.

George Lockhart Rives, *The United States and Mexico 1821-1848* (1913).

Anne Royall, *Letters from Alabama* (1830).

Harvey Lee Ross, *Early Pioneers of Illinois* (1899).

Nathan Sargent, *Public Men and Events* (1875).

James Schouler, *History of the United States of America* (Edition of 1913).

Carl Schurz, *Henry Clay* (1899).

Edward M. Shepard, *Martin Van Buren* (1888).

J. E. D. Shipp, *Giant Days, or the Life and Times of William H. Crawford* (1909).

St. George L. Sioussat, "Letters of James K. Polk to Cave Johnson 1833-1848," *Tennessee Historical Magazine*, I and II.

——, "Tennessee Politics in the Jackson Period," *American Historical Review*, XIV.

Justin H. Smith, *The Annexation of Texas* (1911).

[Mrs. Margaret Bayard Smith], *The First Forty Years of Washington Society* (Gaillard Hunt, editor) (1906).

[Seba Smith], *Life and Writings of Major Jack Downing* (1834).

William Ernest Smith, *The Francis Preston Blair Family in Politics* (1933).

W. H. Sparks, *Memories of Fifty Years* (1870).

James Sprunt Historical Publications, X.

Henry B. Stanton, *Random Recollections* (1886).

William Stickney (editor), *Autobiography of Amos Kendall* (1872).

William W. Story, *Life and Letters of Joseph Story* (1851).

William G. Sumner, *Andrew Jackson* (Edition of 1899).

Carl Brent Swisher, *Roger B. Taney* (1935).

Jeanette Tandy, *Crackerbox Philosophers* (1925).

Texas [Republic] *Diplomatic Correspondence*. See G. P. Garrison.

Frances M. Trollope, *Domestic Manners of the Americans* (Reprint of 1904).

Ben Truman, *The Field of Honor* (1884).

Truth's Advocate (Cincinnati).

Frederick Jackson Turner, *The United States 1830-1850* (1935).

United States Gazette (Philadelphia).

United States' Telegraph (Washington).

[Martin Van Buren], *Autobiography of Martin Van Buren* (John C. Fitzpatrick, editor) (1920).

Claude H. Van Tine (editor), *Letters of Daniel Webster* (1902).

Charles Warren, *The Supreme Court in United States History* (1922).

E. B. Washburne (editor), *The* [Ninian] *Edwards Papers* (1884).

Washington *Globe*.

[Daniel Webster], *The Writings and Speeches of Daniel Webster* (1903).

[———], *Letters of Daniel Webster*. See C. H. Van Tine.

Fletcher Webster (editor), *Private Correspondence of Daniel Webster* (1856).

Thurlow Weed, *Autobiography* (1883).

Western Herald and Steubensville (Ohio) *Gazette*.

Western North Carolinian (Salisbury).

Anne Hollingsworth Wharton, *Social Life in the Early Republic* (1902).

Clarence R. Wharton, *The Texas Republic* (1922).

Mary Emily Donelson Wilcox, *Christmas Under Three Flags* (1900).

Winchester *Virginian*.

Henry A. Wise, *Seven Decades of the Union* (1872).

Henry Wycoff, *Reminiscences of an Idler* (1880).

Mary A. Wyman, *Two American Pioneers* (1924).

"Wyoming," *Letters . . . to the People of the United States* (1824).

Henderson Yoakum, *History of Texas* (1856).

PERSONAL ACKNOWLEDGMENTS

PERSONAL ACKNOWLEDGMENTS

Frederick Jackson Turner's *The United States 1830-1850* fills a volume about as thick as this one. The fruit of twenty years of work, it was published in 1935, posthumously and unfinished. In his preface Professor Avery Craven writes that the author "disliked to find his researches halted and his ideas crystallized by publication. There were new facts to be unearthed; new findings might alter old conclusions. Until all the evidence was in, the time had not come for the last word."

The evidence is never all in and the time for the last word remains a figure of speech. Only seven years have gone by, and how swiftly, since the present writer began his formal research for the undertaking which this book completes. One pleasant summer in the early days of that work, the base for my operations was a cabin in the Big Smoky Mountains of East Tennessee. One week-end two or three history professors turned up. One asked how many volumes my biography would be. With some emphasis I said, "One volume." Perhaps had I done my work as well as I then hoped it might be done one volume would have sufficed, though I am not sure. The one thing I am sure of is that I had trouble telling in two volumes the story of Andrew Jackson as he seems to me to be; and I may add, for the comfort it gives me, that I had professional encouragement to string it out beyond that length.

In the course of my preparation for this second volume I have examined in manuscript about forty thousand documents, exclusive of sources consulted more conveniently in print. Week by week and year by year the notes pile up, and there is born an insidious urge to justify or parade this labor by giving a place in the sun to too much of the resultant memoranda. Thus research may partake of the nature of vanity, and a book reflect a picture of the author's progressive grubbings in such strong light as to cast a shadow on the concerns of the other individual whose name appears on the title page. A biographer (I speak for myself only) must resist a temptation to compete with his subject for the reader's favorable notice. Oscar Wilde's observation that any fool can make history but that it takes a genius to write it should not be taken as a final judgment.

Usually worse than too much or too obvious research is too little. I am sorry that I feel bound to say "usually" and not "invariably": otherwise the task of those who would like to do something toward ameliorating the lowly estate biography occupies as a department of letters would not be so trying. The confusing truth is that biographies are available which, de-

581

spite an average of one error of fact per page, attain a sort of truth beyond the facts, giving a fairly faithful representation of the subject as a human being. There are biographies that approach factual perfection but leave the reader with a less adequate idea of the kind of *human being* the writer was trying to tell about than the average person could pick up in a fifteen-minute face-to-face conversation; and subjects of biography were human beings before they were soldiers or presidents or what not. Further disconcerting circumstances are that so many good writers who now and again dash showily into the biographical lists are careless, lazy and shallow about their research, whereas most of the honest and competent researchists can't write for sour apples. Though in the minority, the good writers, being easier to read, spread the greater number of submarginal ideas about the personnel of history. Yet one should not condemn them too roundly. Submarginal ideas may be better than none.

I have heard biographers imply that the public's preference for novels is a reflection on its taste. I am inclined to think it a reflection on the biographers. A sizable class of readers turn to novels for dependable representations of life and character, finding them in greater profusion than in the pages of biography. Though an inconsiderable reader of novels, in no biography that comes to mind offhand is there a character so real to me as Huckleberry Finn, Becky Sharp, Tom Jones or George Babbitt.

A biographer may argue that his task is technically the more difficult; and he is on solid ground there. He may point out that a novelist merely has to invent and create whereas a biographer is confined to a work of re-creation, and the re-creation of a particular person and not just any person. A palæontologist's is also a work of re-creation, but in a different way. He can take the shin bone of an extinct animal and reconstruct the complete skeleton, but this will not be the skeleton of the particular animal whose shin bone was found but of an average representative of the species. From the shin bone of an extinct person a biographer cannot reconstruct that particular person except by guesswork. The other bones must be found or accounted for.

Another thing a novelist can do more easily than a biographer is to give his story architectural symmetry. His supply of materials is limited only by his capacity for creation. A biographer's materials are limited, first by the question of their physical survival in the form of reliable record, and second, by the biographer's success, through the exercise of patience, intelligence, imagination and industry, in bringing that record to light. A biographer may be perfectly aware that he is not proportioning his narrative with proper regard for the art of story-telling, or even the balanced re-creation of personality, and be able to do nothing about it because he cannot find the materials to fill certain gaps. A good novelist is never in such a dilemma.

The second and some of the other early chapters of this book are badly balanced, being top-heavy with politics at a time when General Jackson's actual life was far from so. Politics was a great and threatening force playing about him but not touching him to the extent that my treatment would indicate, despite explicit disclaimers in the text which the reader may fail to notice because they are so weakly supported by corroborative evidence that actually Jackson had very much of anything else on his mind. I am sure that he had much else on his mind in the way of private and personal affairs, and in a general way I know what those things were. But specifically I could learn little.

To a novelist this would present no problem at all. On the other hand I had to choose between pruning the politics to balance my meager store of personal information and presenting an unbalanced picture. I pruned until to prune any more would have been to default an obligation to history. I had discovered a number of undisclosed facts concerning Jackson's emergence and progress as a candidate for the presidency, making, indeed, something of a new story of it. So I present this story; I present it ostensibly as biography of Andrew Jackson for that period of his life, and as such it lacks much. Dull and imperfect chapters in the fore part of a book are a bad thing. I feel pretty sure that some readers will chuck this book before they get to the more supportable parts of it.

There are professional historians who will not be impressed by the reverential mention of my obligation to history. In their opinion I give history short shrift nearly all through this book, compressing and generalizing too much. On the other hand many things which do not touch the main stream of history at all have been treated extensively. Though these things have little to do with history they had much to do with Jackson. History has concerned me only as it touched Jackson or as Jackson touched it. An excellent historian, to whose painstaking counsel I am truly indebted, notes on the margin of a page of the last chapter of the manuscript: "I am sorry that you have not mentioned Calhoun's period as Sec'y of State [under Tyler], and that he also did much to bring about the annexation of Texas. Every reviewer of your book will sharply criticize you for the writing of the history of annexation without mention of Calhoun."

If reviewers assume that I have attempted to write a history of the annexation of Texas their criticism will be justified. I have not attempted to do this, however. I have attempted to write a life of Andrew Jackson, giving such parts of the history of the annexation of Texas as seemed to me to bear thereon.

Before these maundering remarks become more involved I shall conclude with an attempt to justify their title, for without the good scholarship, the good companionship and the sound and serviceable help of many persons this book would be a poorer thing than it is. Of perhaps twenty authors of books about Jackson, I owe a basic debt to the biographers Parton, Sumner and Bassett. Though careless of the facts of history, and with little sense of its larger forces, Parton was one of the best of American biographers and *Jackson* is his best work. His treatment of the subject's early life, which is not covered in this volume, is, however, far superior to his treatment of the presidential years; yet he keeps by the side of his man as no other Jackson student does. Writing less than fifteen years after Old Hickory's death his work has almost a contemporary flavor.

Professor Sumner of Yale came along in the 'Eighties. Of Jackson the human being he tells us little but, considering the limited documentary evidence then readily available, Jackson the public figure is well-placed on the stage of history. Doctor Bassett's *Life* appeared in 1911. Here was the most indefatiguable Jackson student of his generation. He greatly improved on the work of Sumner, though to the casual reader the result is apt to appear a little cloudy; for Doctor Bassett had small insight into human values and next to no idea of what constitutes a literary pattern. Bassett's services to those who would study Jackson do not end with his biography. He tackled the mountain of manuscripts in the Library of Congress and in several other public depositories, in 1926 beginning the publication of selections therefrom under the title of *Correspondence of Andrew Jackson*. After Doctor Bassett's death Dr. J. Franklin Jameson, chief of the Manuscript Division of the Library of Congress, brought the work to a notable conclusion with the publication of the sixth volume in 1935.

To me research is the buoyant part of an adventure of this kind, filled with exhilarations of discovery that efface the memory of weeks of unexciting and sometimes poorly rewarded toil. In a moment I shall mention some of the persons met along the paths of research. Their names lie before me now as I jotted them down at different times, here, there and everywhere that part of the work called me. They bring back a flood of recollections, all pleasant and many light-hearted. Then there is a smaller list I have just made up of people who have been close to me during the last year and more which has been devoted exclusively to composition. Like most old hands from the city room I like to diffuse the impression that I write easily. I fancy I could bring evidence to support that premise, though this book would form no part of it. For in the main the going has been tough; and no one has borne the brunt of this to the extent that my wife has. Bessie has shared too much of the drudgery involved in this book and too little of the fun—a circumstance rendered inescapable by the fact that she is the best critic of composition I know.

Professor William O. Lynch of Indiana University generously read this book in primitive manuscript form. His advice and comments have been of great value. Further, I am indebted to Professor William MacDonald, late of Brown University and author of *Jacksonian Democracy*, and to Professor Thomas C. Cochran of New York University for reading it before publication and for their comments; likewise to Professor Allan

Nevins of Columbia for reading a part of it. I am indebted for enlightenment on the campaigns of 1824 and 1828 to assistance from Professor Arthur R. Newsome of the University of North Carolina, Dr. Culver H. Smith of the University of Chattanooga and Curtis W. Garrison, librarian of the Pennsylvania State Library, Harrisburg; also to Dr. Richard A. McLemore of Judson College, Marion, Alabama, on the subject of the French claims.

This acknowledgment, however, is not intended to imply that these gentlemen approve of everything I have written. David Laurance Chambers, a careful student of Americana and the president of the publishing house whose imprint this volume bears, should be mentioned for knightly conduct. He read the chapters as they were pulled from a typewriter and declined to be discouraged.

I am under especial obligation to Doctor Jameson of the Library of Congress and to his genial assistant, Dr. Thomas P. Martin; to Sylvester Vigilanti and to Miss Dorothy P. Miller of the American History Room of the New York Public Library; to Mrs. E. A. Lindsey, former regent, and to Mrs. Mary French Caldwell, of the Ladies' Hermitage Association, Nashville; to Clarence S. Brigham of the American Antiquarian Society, Worcester, Massachusetts; to Mrs. John Trotwood Moore, Nashville, librarian and archivist of the State of Tennessee; to the late Judge John H. DeWitt, president, Tennessee Historical Society; to Mrs. Evelyn H. Allen and staff of the Pleasantville (New York) Free Library; to the New York Historical Society, New York City; and to the New York State Library, Albany; and to the Troy (New York) Public Library.

The owners of private manuscript collections which I have kindly been permitted to examine are named under "Bibliography," but here I cannot forbear mentioning that Lemuel R. Campbell of Nashville shortened my labors by providing the services of his secretary to help go through the papers of his Campbell ancestors, fifteen hundred of which papers bear on the Jackson administrations.

For permission to reproduce pictures that appear in this volume I am, in addition to persons and institutions mentioned elsewhere, indebted to the Brown University Library, Providence; Mrs. Sarah Polk Burch, Nashville; Mrs. Pauline Wilcox Burke, Washington; Mrs. Arthur Chester, Rye, New York; Dr. Isaac Cline, New Orleans; Mrs. Betty Donelson, Nashville; Emil Edward Hurja, New York City; Mrs. Breckenridge Long, Laurel, Maryland; the North Carolina Historical Commission, Raleigh; Edward Asbury O'Neal III, Florence, Alabama.

For contributions to research, in addition to those mentioned elsewhere, I am indebted to David Rankin Barbee, Washington; Allen Churchill, New York City; Burton Craige, Winston-Salem, North Carolina; Dr. J. B. Cranfill, Dallas, Texas; Charles P. Everitt, New York City; Miss A. L. Frantz, Lancaster, Pennsylvania; Mrs. Mary Martin Frost, Florence, Alabama; Miss Estelle Lake, Memphis, Tennessee; Andrew Jackson Martin, Memphis; George Fort Milton, Chattanooga; J. F. Spainhaur, High Point, North Carolina; Mrs. Elsie Warren Stokes, Nashville; Miss Claude Wier, Dallas, Texas; Mrs. Mary Wharton Yeatman, Columbia, Tennessee; Mrs. Marshall Elise Janney, Montgomery, Alabama.

M. J.

Pleasantville, New York,
June 13, 1937.

INDEX

INDEX*

Aaron, slave, 418.

Abingdon, Va., 242, 243.

Abolition, 398, 413, 419, 423, 464.

Accomac County, Va., 167.

Adams, John, 430.

Adams, John Quincy, Cabinet officer, 17, 31; presidential candidate in 1824, 28, 33, 36, 38-41, 44, 47-49, 56-59, 66, 68, 72, 73, 75-77, 87-89, 91-93, 96-97, 100-127; diplomacy of, 37, 386, 406, 407; President-elect, 127-130; inaugural of, 131, 135; as President, 137, 141-143, 145, 147, 152, 159, 179, 184-186, 195, 200, 216, 220, 287, 307, 446, 511; presidential candidate in 1828, 151, 162-164, 191; connected with slanders, 157, 158, 175; 229; supporters of, 191, 194, 196, 241; in House of Representatives, 300, 312, 314, 391; 345, 347, 430, 464, 488, 527.

Adams, Mrs. J. Q., 68, 115, 157.

Africa, 398.

Alabama, 78, 249, 296, 310, 316, 355, 381, 451, 455, 567; Legislature of, 39; plantations, 15, 16, 29, 30, 31, 62, 139, 160; political sentiments in, 43, 52, 67, 72, 145, 255; military executions in, 159; Indians, 245, 318; Governor of, 320; speculators in, 438.

Alamo, the, 411.

Albany, N. Y., 97, 124, 125, 187, 196, 316, 376, 461.

Albany *Argus*, 143.

Alexander, Captain Will, 174.

Alexandria, D. C., 120, 182, 339.

Alexandria *Herald*, 98.

Alfred, household negro, 567.

Algiers, 215.

Alien and Sedition Laws, 233.

Allegheny Mountains, 278.

Allen, Eliza, 408-409, 410.

Allen, William, 432.

Ambrister, Lieutenant Robert C., 159.

America, 139, 293, 391, 392.
   see also United States.

American House, New York, 341.

American System, 162.
   see Tariff.

Anacostia River, 326.

Anderson, Patton, 375.

Andrews, Miss, of Philadelphia, 55.

Annapolis, Md., 58, 301, 302.

Anti-Masons, 306-307, 309.

Arabia, 365.

Arbitration of French claims, 403.

Arbuthnot, Alexander, 159.

Argus of Western America, 132, 151, 190, 266.

Arkansas Territory, 397.

Armstrong, Robert, 383, 384, 442, 471-472, 481-483.

Arnold, Thomas D., 155, 158.

Ashland, home of Henry Clay, 152, 287, 465, 466, 489, 497.

Assawaman Church, Virginia, 167.

Attleborough, Mass., 343.

Austin, Stephen F., 411.

* Index compiled by Pauline Peirce.

New York—*Continued*
378, 411, 467, 487; Governor of, 320.

New York City, 49, 69, 197, 232, 238, 268, 282, 283, 315, 340-341, 345, 360, 376, 389, 396, 426, 440, 450, 461, 471; Port of, 217, 444; Broadway, 307, 473; Battery, 341; Castle Garden, 341; banks, 346, 350-355, 362, 492.

New York *Courier and Enquirer*, 190, 300, 326, 360.

New York *Evening Post*, **35, 96,** 307, 332.

New York *Statesman*, 100.

New Yorkers, 109, 127, 167, 184, 189, 198, 214, 223, 258, 269, 273, 274, 279, 289, 293, 306, 316, 400, 483, 486.

Nichol, Josiah, 139, **253, 263;** daughter of, 383.

Niles, Hezekiah, 129, 376.

Niles's *Register*, 129, 376.

Noah, Mordecai, 190.

Norfolk, Va., 209, 212, 308.

North Carolina, 27, 28, 35, 49, 53, 57-59, 67, 68, 72, 74, 78, 86, 87, 90-91, 93, 101-103, 106, 124, 148, 168, 275, 320, 334, 361, 363, 397, 468.

Nourse, Mr., defaulting Treasury official, 192, 193.

Nueces River, 407.

Nullification, threatened by South Carolina, 218-219; Webster-Hayne debate, 224-226; Jackson's uncertain attitude toward, 232-233; Jackson's toast at Jefferson dinner, 235-238; nullification of Indian treaties, general, 244-245, by Georgia, 245-246; Cherokees fight treaty nullification, 246-247; Jackson

Nullification—*Continued*
averts issue by visit to Indian council, 244-248; Blair opposes nullifiers, 267; proposed reconciliation between Jackson and Calhoun fails, 269-270; issue of Indian treaties reopened in Georgia, 280-281; South Carolinians seek support of Georgians, 281; Calhoun and nullification, 281-283; Clay unwilling to champion, 287; Jackson confident of victory against, 294; Worcester-Butler case and aftermath, 304-305; activities of Hayne, Calhoun, *et al*, 305; Jackson's threat, 306; crisis in South Carolina, 308-321; South Carolina passes ordinance of nullification, 311; Proclamation on Nullification, 313-314; bill to lower tariff introduced in House, 318; Jackson asks Congress to authorize military force to collect customs, 320-321; South Carolina yields, 321; the "Force Bill" and Clay's tariff bill passed, 321-323; South Carolina rescinds ordinance of nullification, 323; Jackson predicts civil war, 324; Jackson's stand on nullification meets approval in Massachusetts, 343; Van Buren lukewarm opponent of, 337, 400; *see also* Andrew Jackson, Presidential Administrations, Nullification in South Carolina.

Nullification, Proclamation on, 313-314, 317-318.

Nullifiers, 281, 305-306, 308-309, 312, 318-321.

Ode to Bogle, 251.

Ohio, Legislature, 39, 363; politi-

Towson, Colonel Nathan, 211-213.
Transylvania University, 21, 24, 36.
Treason, 312, 316, 319.
Treasury.
    see United States Treasury Department.
Treasury Order.
    see Specie Circular.
Treaties.
    see United States, treaties of.
Tremont House, Boston, 344.
Trimble, David, 132, 143, 144.
Trollope, Frances, 180.
Truxton, race horse, 16, 17, 240, 241, 298.
Tulip Grove, home of A. J. Donelson, 420.
Tulip Hill Plantation, home of Virgil Maxcy, 58.
Turner, Nat, slave rebellion of, 397, 398.
Tyler, John, 321, 323, 324, 449-451, 457, 458, 461, 463, 464, 465, 473, 475-476, 479, 480, 488, 491.

Union Bank of Baltimore, 354-355, 439.
Union Party, in South Carolina nullification episode, 236, 281, 305, 310, 312.
United States, 37, 41, 73, 74, 90, 93, 97, 107, 127, 136, 138, 166, 173, 200, 234, 245 247, 251, 252, 264, 283, 306, 313, 315, 317, 340, 342, 357, 379, 386, 387, 389, 392, 402-404, 406, 411, 423, 429, 433, 440, 456, 464, 475-480, 490, 495; Bank of, *see under* Banks; boundaries of, 406-407, 432, 464; governmental departments of: navy, 70, 183, 185, 205, 216, 276,

United States—*Continued*
    278, 534; post office, 183, 184, 216; state, 183, 185, 198, 387, 392, 404, 534; treasury, 43, 80, 183, 185, 192, 193, 215-216, 220, 221, 230, 251-253, 258-260, 278, 284, 296, 332, 340, 346, 349, 354, 364, 387, 396, 400, 432, 441, 473, 498; war, 148, 183-185, 192, 216, 217, 278, 315, 410, 534; national debt, 218, 221, 222, 260, 285, 396; treaties of, 37, 218, 244-249, 280, 305, 386-389, 403, 410, 413, 419, 476-480, 488.
United States Bank of Pennsylvania, 441, 446, 456.
United States' Telegraph, 145, 146, 149, 150, 156, 157, 233, 266-268, 270, 307, 334, 534.
University of Pennsylvania, 250.
University of Virginia, 298.
Utica, N. Y., 102.

Van Buren, Abraham, 207, 273, 328, 372, 462.
Van Buren, John, 328, 462.
Van Buren, Martin, political influence in New York, 46-48, 67, 75, 87-88, 97, 124, 125, 194, 318; allied with Crawford, 46-47, 49, 73, 87-88, 91-93, 96; descriptions of, 101, 188; predicts Jackson victory, 103, 106, 107, 109, 116, 124, 126, 143, 145, 152, 203, 206, 221, 222, 234, 235, 244, 258, 267, 269, 278, 306, 307, 315, 320, 321, 327, 349, 391, 393, 423, 424; supporters of, 123, 161, 184, 196, 333, 399; election bets, 147, 374; anti-Calhoun efforts, 162, 167, 184, 194, 222, 223, 229, 236, 269, 272,

THE UNITED STATES
of the